W9-BRZ-133

BOOKS IN
THE WILLARD J. GRAHAM SERIES IN ACCOUNTING

CONSULTING EDITOR   ROBERT N. ANTHONY   *Harvard University*

THE

WILLARD J. GRAHAM SERIES

IN ACCOUNTING

Management Accounting
TEXT AND CASES

Management
Accounting

TEXT AND CASES

ROBERT N. ANTHONY, D.C.S.
Ross Graham Walker Professor of Management
Control
Graduate School of Business Administration
Harvard University

1970
Fourth Edition

Richard D. Irwin, Inc., Homewood, Illinois
Irwin-Dorsey Limited, Georgetown, Ontario

© RICHARD D. IRWIN, INC., 1956, 1960, 1964, and 1970

All rights reserved. No part of this publication may be reproduced, stored in a retrieval system, or transmitted, in any form or by any means, electronic, mechanical, photocopying, recording, or otherwise, without prior written permission of the copyright holder. The copyright on all cases in this book, unless otherwise noted, is held by the President and Fellows of Harvard College, and the cases are published herein by express permission.

Fourth Edition
First Printing, January, 1970
Second Printing, August, 1970
Third Printing, November, 1970
Fourth Printing, July, 1971

Case material of the Harvard Graduate School of Business Administration is made possible by the cooperation of business firms who may wish to remain anonymous by having names, quantities, and other identifying details disguised while maintaining basic relationships. Cases are prepared as the basis for class discussion rather than to illustrate either effective or ineffective handling of administrative situations.

Library of Congress Catalog Card No. 74–91789

Printed in the United States of America

LEARNING SYSTEMS COMPANY— a division of Richard D. Irwin, Inc. has developed a PROGRAMMED LEARNING AID to accompany texts in this subject area. Copies can be purchased through your bookstore or by writing PLAIDS, 1818 Ridge Road, Homewood, Illinois 60430

*To
My Son,
Bob*

PREFACE

The fourth edition is intended for the same types of courses as were the previous editions: (1) a full-year or half-year course for college students with no background in accounting; (2) a half-year follow-on course, building on an introductory course in accounting principles; and (3) a course in a management development program. Of these three types, I am most interested in the first. The beginning student, whether or not he is an accounting major, should, I believe, approach the subject with the point of view of the user of accounting information rather than that of the accountant who supplies the information. Such an approach makes the subject both more interesting and more intellectually challenging than does the alternative of focusing on mechanics. As in previous editions, the text is arranged so that the student can construct and use financial statements from the very beginning of the course.

Although designed for the beginner, the book does not contain enough "pencil-pushing" material for him. The beginning college student needs also the companion volume, *Accounting Problems and Cases.*[1] Many instructors assign my programmed text, *Essentials of Accounting*[2] either as a preliminary to study of the subject or as a review device. It corresponds to Part I of this book.

The conceptual underpinnings of accounting are gradually becoming clearer. In particular, since the third edition of this book was published, there has appeared Paul Grady's *Inventory of Generally Accepted Accounting Principles,*[3] which is a major effort by one of the most distinguished members of the profession to state principles and concepts

---

[1] John M. Sinclair and Robert N. Anthony, *Accounting Problems and Cases* (Homewood, Ill.: Richard D. Irwin, Inc., 1970).

[2] *Essentials of Accounting* (Reading, Mass.: Addison Wesley Publishing Co., Inc., 1965).

[3] American Institute of Certified Public Accountants, 1965.

of accounting in a logical framework. These developments make it increasingly feasible to make financial accounting texts less like "cookbooks"—recipes for handling individual transactions—and more in the nature of systematic descriptions of bodies of knowledge.

A similar movement is under way in management accounting, although this is a much younger subject, and the concepts are correspondingly less clearly perceived. Progress has been such, however, that a considerable recasting of Part III has been undertaken.

Much new material has been added reflecting recent developments in the field, including the 1966 *Statement* of the American Accounting Association and Opinions of the Accounting Principles Board through June 1969.

In Part I, the arrangement by chapters is substantially the same as in the third edition, but there has been considerable revision within each chapter. The exposition is built around 10 basic concepts, and an attempt is made to relate principles and techniques to these concepts. The arrangement of topics is governed more by pedagogical than by logical considerations; that is, the intent is to proceed gradually from the simple to the complicated, rather than to discuss all aspects of a topic at once. Thus, the basic idea of Cost of Goods Sold is introduced in Chapter 3, but the complications of the deduction method are deferred until Chapter 5, the process of calculating Cost of Goods Sold in a manufacturing company is described in Chapter 7, and the LIFO-FIFO issue is not mentioned until Chapter 9.

In Part II, the principal substantive change is in the approach used for Funds Flow analysis. I have dropped the approach of the third edition, and gone back to that used in the second edition, but with an attempt to clarify the presentation. Many professors prefer that approach.

Part III has been substantially rearranged and rewritten, with the aim of improving the pedagogy, expressing the essential unity of the subject, and incorporating new material. In particular, the chapter on budgeting has been greatly expanded.

In Part IV, there is a new chapter on automated data processing in which the operation of computers is described and the implications of computers on management accounting are discussed. The advanced management techniques which were previously grouped in a separate chapter are now discussed in the chapters to which the techniques relate.

Some of the cases are new or revised, but cases from the previous edition have been retained if they seem to be more useful than any other available cases.

As I wrote in the Preface to the first edition, the cases have been selected because of their interest and educational value as a basis for class discussion. They are not necessarily intended to illustrate either correct or incorrect handling of management problems. Skill in the management use of accounting information can be acquired, I believe, only through experience. Thinking about a case, and discussing it in the classroom and in informal discussion groups, can help to provide such experience. In preparing to discuss a case in class, the student is required to *do* something—to analyze a problem, to weigh various factors involved in it, to make some calculations, to take a position, and so on. In class, the student is required to explain his point of view, to defend it, to understand and appraise the arguments of his colleagues, and to decide what arguments are the strongest. Practice in doing these things helps to increase skill and understanding; in fact, many educators believe that the really important parts of a subject can be learned only by experience of some sort, as opposed to merely hearing or reading about them. Thus, although the case material comprises only about half the pages in this book, the discussion of these cases is by far the more important part of the educational process.

Although some professors suggested that each case should be accompanied by a set of detailed questions, others felt that such questions would tend to channel the preparation and discussion of the case too narrowly. I have decided to continue, for most of the cases, the practice of giving only a few broad questions, with the thought that those who prefer the other approach can easily supplement these when making assignments.

ACKNOWLEDGMENTS

Again, for myself and on behalf of the other authors of cases, I express our gratitude to the businessmen who were willing to give their time and the benefit of their experience in the development of cases. I wish also to acknowledge again my debt to Professors Ross G. Walker and Charles A. Bliss, who were largely responsible for creating and developing the Control course at the Harvard Business School, from which this book is descended.

As can be seen from the detailed list in the Index and Sources of Cases that follows, many people participated in the process of preparing the cases included herein. I appreciate the permission that both those at Harvard and those at other institutions have given me to use their cases in this book.

Many users of the book have been good enough to make suggestions for improving it. Of these, I want especially to thank Professors Donald D. Bourque, Syracuse University; Dean James S. Hekimian, Northeastern University; Robert Jaedicke, Stanford University; Rene P. Manes, Purdue University; Francis J. McGurr, John Carroll University; Leonard E. Morrissey, Dartmouth College; Dean John M. Sinclair, Bentley

College; W. Keith Weltmer, University of Kansas; Maj. Gen. Wendell E. Carter, Col. Joseph B. Warren, Donald L. McLagan, Lt. Joseph E. Kasputys, all of the Office of the Assistant Secretary of Defense (Comptroller); John M. Hamilton, President, Hamilton-Hastings Company, Ltd.; and my colleagues at the Harvard Business School: Brandt R. Allen, Charles J. Christenson, John Dearden, Robert Howell, F. Warren McFarlan, Richard F. Vancil, and William M. Zani.

Miss Jean McElroy was responsible for typing and other work connected with the production of the manuscript. Mr. Charles Roush and Mrs. Mary Wehle, CPA, assisted with the research. I am deeply grateful to them.

Boston, Massachusetts   ROBERT N. ANTHONY
December, 1969

TABLE OF CONTENTS

Financial Accounting and Management Accounting. Plan of the Book: *The Structure of Accounting. Uses of Accounting. Analyzing Financial Statements. Management Control. Decision Making.* Some General Considerations: *Figures for a Purpose. Different Figures for Different Purposes. Accounting Figures Are Approximations. Working with Incomplete Data. Figure Evidence is Only Partial Evidence. People, Not Figures, Get Things Done.* Summary.

Cases

PART I. The Accounting Structure

Accounting as a Language. Nature and Source of Principles: *Criteria. Source of Principles.* Basic Concepts: *1. The Money Measurement Concept. 2. The Business Entity Concept. 3. The Going-Concern Concept. 4. The Cost Concept. 5. The Dual-Aspect Concept. 6. Conservatism.* The Balance Sheet: *Account Categories. Assets. Current Assets. Fixed Assets. Other Assets. Liabilities. Current Liabilities. Other Liabilites. Owners' Equity.* Balance Sheet Changes. An Overall View of the Balance Sheet. Summary of Basic Concepts.

Cases

The Accounting Period. The Accrual Concept. Measurement of Expenses: *Expenses and Expenditures. Expenditures That Are Also*

Expenses. Assets That Become Expenses. Expenditures That Are Not Yet Expenses. Expenses Not Yet Paid. Asset or Expense? Measurement of Revenue. The Realization Concept: *Matching.* The Consistency Concept. The Materiality Concept. Other Changes in Owners' Equity: *Extraordinary Items.* Tax Accounting versus Business Accounting. The Income Statement: *Revenues. Cost of Goods Sold. Gross Profit. Expenses. Retained Earnings. The Report Package. A Reminder: The Dual-Aspect Concept.* Summary.

Cases

4. Accounting Records and Systems . . . .

Bookkeeping: *The Account. Debit and Credit. The Ledger. The Journal.* The Adjusting and Closing Process: *Adjusting Entries. Closing Entries. Ruling and Balancing Accounts. The Trial Balance. The Work Sheet. Reversing Entries. Summary of the Accounting Process.* Accounting Systems: *Special Journals. Control Accounts and Subsidiary Ledgers. Imprest Funds. Internal Control.* The Expert Accountant. Significant Bookkeeping Ideas. Appendix: *Locating Errors Revealed by the Trial Balance.*

Cases

5. Further Aspects of Income Measurement . . . .

Deducing Cost of Goods Sold: *Accounts. Adjusting and Closing. Limitation of the Deduction Process. Service Businesses.* Inventory Pricing: *Cost. Market.* Accounts Receivable and Bad Debts: *Accounting Recognition of Bad Debts. Write-Off of an Uncollectible Account. Collection of a Bad Debt Written Off. Summary.* Other Problems of Revenue Measurement: *Long-Term Contracts. Installment Sales. Cash Basis. Consignments.* Wages, Salaries, and Related Costs: *Pensions.* Income Tax Allocations. Losses. Conclusion.

Cases

6. Fixed Assets and Depreciation 146

Acquisition of Fixed Assets: *Betterments and Replacements versus Maintenance. Trade-Ins.* Depreciation: *Judgments Required. Service Life. Depreciation Methods. Choice of a Method. Accounting for Depreciation. Reporting in Financial Statements. The Investment Credit.* Disposal of Fixed Assets: *Debits to Accumulated Depreciation.* Group and Composite Depreciation. Significance of Depreciation: *Concluding Comment.* Other Aspects of Tangible Assets: *Depletion. Accretion and Appreciation.* Intangible Assets. Summary.

Cases

7. Income Measurement in Manufacturing Companies 175

Flow of Costs: *Elements of Cost. Product Costs and Period Costs. Inventory Accounts. The Account Flow Chart. Flow of Costs. Raw Materials Used. Cost of Goods Manufactured. Cost of Goods Sold. Condensed Closing Process. Alternative Income Statement Format. Entries with a Cost Accounting System.* Significance of the Process.

Cases

8. Long-Term Equities 196

Nature of Liabilities: *Contingent Liabilities. Distinction between Liabilities and Owners' Equity.* Bonds: *Recording the Issue. Balance Sheet Presentation. Bond Interest. Retirement of Bonds. Refunding a Bond Issue.* Shareholders' Equity: *Types of Capital Stock. Recording the Issue. Treasury Stock. Capital Surplus. Cash Dividends. Stock Dividends and Stock Split-Ups. Surplus Reserves. Earnings per Share. Significance of Shareholders' Equity. Balance Sheet Presentation.* Acquisitions and Mergers. Consolidated Financial Statements: *Basis for Consolidation. Consolidation Procedure. Asset Valuation. Minority Interest. Concluding Comment.* Unincorporated Businesses: *Single Proprietorships. Partnerships.* Summary.

Cases

The Lifo Method: *Arguments For and Against Lifo. Example. Basic Arguments. Dollar Value Method. Decreases in Inventory. Variations. Tax Considerations. Base Stock Method.* Depreciation on Replacement Cost: *Replacement Cost Proposal. Accelerated Depreciation. Investment Policy.* Price Level Adjustments: *The AICPA Studies. Holding Gains and Operating Gains.* Conclusion.

Cases

PART II. Using Information on Financial Statements

Criteria and Basic Concepts: *Conflict among Criteria. Concepts. Misconceptions about Concepts.* Limitations of Accounting: *Absence of a Complete Set of Principles. Lack of Agreement on Principles. Differences in the Application of Principles. Example: Nudoll Company. Implications of These Differences. Inherent Limitations. Attempts to Reduce Diversity.* Role of the Auditor. Significance of the Financial Statements: *The Balance Sheet. The Income Statement.* Conclusion.

Cases

Business Objectives: *Return on Investment. Sound Financial Position.* Some Common Ratios: *1. Tests of Profitability. 2. Tests of Liquidity. 3. Tests of Solvency. 4. Overall Measures.* Difficulties in Making Comparisons: *1. Deciding on the Proper Basis for Comparison. 2. Differences in the Situations Being Compared. 3. Changes in the Dollar Measuring Stick. 4. Differences in Definition. 5. Hidden Short-Run Changes. 6. The Past as an Indication of the Future.* Possible Bases for Comparison: *1. Experience. 2. Goals. 3. Historical Standards. 4. External Standards.* Use of Comparisons. Summary.

Cases

The Concept of Funds Flow: *Basic Relationships.* Constructing the Funds Flow Statement: *Comparative Balance Sheets. Adjustments. Illustration of the Procedure. Other Transactions. Hidden Transactions. Compound Transactions. Funds Provided by Operations. The Funds Flow Statement.* Cash Flow Statements. Uses of the Statement. Misuses of the Statement: *Misconceptions about Depreciation.* Summary.

Cases

PART III. Accounting in Management Control

Management Accounting and Financial Accounting: *Multiple Purposes. Not Governed by Generally Accepted Principles. Optional. Focus on Segments. Less Emphasis on Precision. A Part, Rather than an End in Itself. Similarities.* Systems for Cost Accumulation. Product Costing: *Cost Principle. Job Costing and Process Costing. Variations in Practice. Problems of Cost Accumulation. Direct Costs. Indirect Costs. Unabsorbed and Overabsorbed Overhead. Accuracy of Indirect Costs. Definition of Cost Center. Product Line Reporting. Selling and General Costs.* Standard Costs. Joint Products and By-Products. Direct Costing. Relation to Financial Accounting. Responsibility Accounting: *Responsibility Centers. Controllable Costs.* Summary.

Cases

Management Control: *Characteristics of Management Control Systems.* Motivation: *Principles of Motivation. Management Sponsorship. Participation and Understanding. Incentives. Individual Differences. Goal Congruence. An Example: Maintenance Costs.* The Management Control System: *Programming. Budgeting. Accounting. Reporting and Analysis. Need for Internal Consistency.* Responsibility Centers: *Expense Centers. Profit*

Centers. Investment Centers. Effectiveness and Efficiency. Function of the Controller: *Control of the Control System.* Summary.

Cases

15. Characteristics of Cost 451

Different Costs for Different Purposes. Relation of Costs to Volume: *Cost-Volume Diagrams. Behavior of Total Costs. Cost Assumptions. Formula for the Cost Line. Unit Costs. Estimating Cost-Volume Relationship. Measures of Volume. The Overhead Rate and Standard Volume.* The Profitgraph: *Construction of a Profitgraph. Interpretation of the Profitgraph. Improving Profit Performance. Limitations on Profitgraph Analysis.* Marginal Income Analysis Statement. Learning Curves. Controllable Costs: *Degree of Influence. Converting Noncontrollable Costs to Controllable Costs. Recording Noncontrollable Costs.* Engineered, Discretionary, and Committed Costs: *Engineered Costs. Discretionary Costs. Committed Costs. Spurious Relationships.* Summary. Appendix: *Fitting a Straight Line by Least Squares.*

Cases

16. Budgeting 491

Types of Budgets. The Operating Budget: *Relationships among the Budgets. The Budget Process. Choice of Time Periods. Organization for Preparation of Budgets. The Budget Timetable. Setting Guidelines. The Sales Estimate. Initial Budget Preparation. Negotiation. Coordination and Review. Final Approval. Variations in Practice. Revisions. Uses of the Budget.* The Cash Budget. The Capital Budget. Summary.

Cases

17. The Analysis of Performance   522

Structure of Analysis: *Inputs and Outputs. The Search for a Standard.* Difficulties in Performance Measurement: *Difficulty in Measuring Outputs. Long-Run versus Current Performance. The Special Problem of Investment Centers.* Performance Reports: *The Time Interval of Control. Content of Reports. Management by Exception. Feedback.* Formal Analytical Techniques: *Validity of the Standard.* Structure of Analysis: *Noncomparable Data. Price and Quantity of Inputs. Mix of Inputs. Quality of Output. Output Price and Volume. Volume and Overhead Costs. Measuring Stick Variance.* An Illustrative Analysis: *Marketing Variance. Manufacturing Variances.* Attacking an Appraisal Problem. Summary.

Cases

PART IV. Accounting in Business Decisions

18. Deciding among Alternative Courses of Action   579

Approach to Alternative Choice Problems: *Criteria. Outline of Approach. Definition of the Problem and of Alternative Solutions. Weighing and Measuring the Quantitative Factors. Evaluating and Weighing the Unmeasured Factors. Reaching a Decision.* Problems Involving Costs: *Future Costs. Differential Costs. Mechanics of the Calculation. The Margin of Error. Example: Operating an Automobile. Example: Economic Lot Size.* Pricing: *Theoretical Consideration. Full-Cost Pricing. Contribution Pricing.* Advanced Techniques: *Probability Theory. Mathematical Models. Linear Programming.* Nonprofit Organizations: *Cost-Benefit Analysis.* Some Practical Pointers. Summary.

Cases

19. Planning Capital Acquisitions 626

Framework of Analysis: *Essentials of a Business Investment. Concept of Return on Investment. Concept of Present Value. Present Value Method. Present Value of a Stream of Payments. Other Present Value Tables. Unadjusted Return on Investment.* Estimating the Variables: *Required Earnings Rate. Earnings. Economic Life. Investment. Summary of the Process.* Other Methods: *Time-Adjusted Return. MAPI Method. Comparison of Methods.* Preference Problems: *Profitability Index. Comparison of Preference Rules. Concluding Comment.* Summary.

Cases

20. Automated Data Processing 677

Description of Electronic Computers: *Input. Storage. Processing. Output. Processing Modes.* Computer Economics: *Conclusions.* Some Implications for Management Accounting: *Financial Accounting. Financial Analyses. Cost Accounting. Management Control. Alternative Choice Problems. Integrated Data Processing.* Summary.

Case

21. Review Cases 696

APPENDIX TABLES

INDEX

INDEX AND SOURCES OF CASES

The cases published in this book are listed below in alphabetical order, together with their authors and the institution with which they were associated when they wrote them. These institutions are the copyright owners. Cases without identification were written by the author of this book and are copyrighted by the President and Fellows of Harvard College. No case may be reproduced, in whole or in part, without the written permission of the copyright owner. Problems are not listed.

---

* Under the direction of R. N. Anthony.

---

* Under the direction of R. N. Anthony.

* Under the direction of R. N. Anthony.

CHAPTER 1

INTRODUCTION

Accounting is a system for collecting, summarizing, analyzing, and reporting, in monetary terms, information about an organization. The reader has already been exposed to a great deal of accounting information. The cash register receipt at the stores where he trades, the checks that he writes or (hopefully) that he receives, his bank statement, the bills which he is expected to pay, all these are parts of accounting systems. He reads in his newspaper about the profit of a company or of an industry, about dividends, about money being spent to build new buildings, and this information comes from accounting systems. Even before he begins a formal study of the subject, therefore, the reader has accumulated a number of ideas about accounting.

The trouble is that some of these ideas are likely to be incorrect. For example, it seems intuitively sensible that accounting should report what a business is "worth," but accounting does not in fact do this, or even attempt to do it. As another example, there is a general notion that the word "asset" refers to valuable things, good things to have; but the skill and ability of the chief executive of a company is not an asset in the accounting sense, even though it may be a principal determinant of the company's success.

Thus, as is the case with many other subjects, the student of accounting must be wary of his preconceptions. He will discover that accounting "like it really is" may be different in important respects from what he surmises it to be, or from what common sense tells him it should be. He will find that there are sound reasons for these differences, and it is important that he understand these reasons.

FINANCIAL ACCOUNTING AND MANAGEMENT ACCOUNTING

This book deals primarily with accounting in business organizations, although essentially similar concepts are used in government and other nonbusiness organizations, and even in national income accounting, which provides information about an entire nation. In studying a business accounting system, it is useful to consider it as consisting of two parts, labeled, respectively, financial accounting and management accounting. These two parts are not in fact neatly separable in practice, but the concepts and purpose related to each part are sufficiently different so that it is well to consider them separately.

Financial accounting has the primary objective of providing information to parties outside the business, that is, to shareholders, bankers and other creditors, government agencies, and the general public. Only in rare instances can these outside parties insist that a business furnish information that is tailor-made to their specifications. In most cases they must accept the information that the business chooses to supply. They could not conceivably understand this information without knowing the ground rules that governed its preparation. Since the typical outsider uses accounting information from many different businesses, there is a clear need for having the basic ground rules apply to all businesses, both so that the information from one business can be compared with that of another and also to obviate the necessity of learning a separate set of ground rules for each business. These ground rules are the subject matter of financial accounting.

When an outside party reads information that has been prepared in accordance with these ground rules, it is meaningful to him, provided, of course, that he understands what the ground rules are. Without such rules, clear communication between a business and the outside world would be practically impossible.

> EXAMPLE: When a person familiar with accounting sees on an accounting report the item "Inventory at Fifo Cost or Market, $1,435,655," he understands that this refers to a certain category of property, and that the amount of this property has been measured according to certain prescribed rules; and he can rely on this understanding even though he has had no personal contact with the accountant who reported this information.

The ground rules of financial accounting therefore facilitate communication between a business and outside parties who need information about that business.

The persons responsible for operating a business—that is, the management—also need monetary information to aid them in doing their jobs effectively. Although much of this information is the same as that contained in reports prepared for outsiders, management also needs a considerable amount of additional information. *Management Accounting*[1] is concerned with accounting information that is useful to management.

---

[1] Some persons prefer the phrase "managerial accounting." The choice turns on a fine point of grammar and is of no practical consequence.

The management of a business can establish whatever ground rules it wishes for the accounting information collected for internal use. Thus, although the rules of financial accounting are applicable to all businesses, the rules of management accounting are tailor-made to meet the needs of the management of a specific business.

There is nevertheless a similarity in the management accounting of most businesses, for two reasons. First, there are obvious economies in using financial accounting information wherever possible for management accounting purposes, rather than devising two completely different systems for the two purposes; thus the rules of financial accounting have a great influence on management accounting. Second, there are principles of management accounting that have wide applicability, and these tend to shape the management accounting practices of a great many companies.

This book is focused on management accounting. Because of the close relationship between financial accounting and management accounting, however, it starts with a description of financial accounting.

The terms "financial accounting" and "management accounting" are not precise descriptions of the activities they comprise. All accounting is *financial* in the sense that all accounting systems are in monetary terms, and *management* is responsible for the content of financial accounting reports. (This is the first of many problems in terminology that will be noted throughout this book. The reader is cautioned against drawing inferences from the labels alone; he must learn the concepts that the labels represent.)

PLAN OF THE BOOK

The Structure of Accounting

The structure of financial accounting underlies all accounting. This structure consists of a few basic principles and concepts, a set of relationships among the elements comprising the accounting system, a terminology, and a number of rules and guides for the application of the principles and concepts to specific situations. This underlying structure will be described in Part I.

The end product of financial accounting, the objective toward which the financial accounting system is directed, is a set of financial statements called the balance sheet and the income statement. We shall therefore emphasize the principles underlying the construction of these statements. Our objective, however, is not to discuss financial accounting per se; rather, it is to develop the concepts and terminology that underlie all accounting.

Furthermore, we do not describe in detail the techniques used to collect and summarize accounting information. Our point of view is that of the *user* of accounting information. The user needs to know something about these techniques in order to understand the nature and limitations of the information that they produce, but he does not need the detailed knowledge that the accountant must have.

The approach to accounting taken in Part I is something like that used by an airplane pilot in learning to use his instruments. The pilot needs to know the meaning of the message conveyed by each of his instruments; that is, he needs to know such things as the fact that a clockwise movement of a certain arrow probably means one thing and that a counterclockwise movement probably means another thing, that the flashing of a red light probably means that a certain component is not functioning, that a certain sound in his earphones probably means that he is on course, and so on. The word "probably" is used because, for one reason or another, an instrument may not always give the reading that it is supposed to give; the pilot must realize this, and he must also understand something of the likelihood of, and the reasons for, these abnormalities. On the other hand, the pilot does not need to know how to design airplane instruments, how to construct them, how to check them for accuracy, how to maintain them, or how to repair them. Specialists are available for these important functions.

Similarly a person who is to make intelligent use of accounting information must understand what a given accounting figure probably means, what its limitations are, and under what circumstances it may mean something different from the apparent "signal" that it gives. He does not, however, need to know how to design, construct, operate, or check on the accuracy of an accounting system. He can rely on accountants for these important functions. The discussion of accounting in Part I is limited, then, to matters which the *user* of accounting information needs to know about.

Uses of Accounting

Knowledge of the meaning of an instrument reading is by no means all, or even a very important part, of what the pilot needs to know in order to fly his plane. In addition, he must know how to use this knowledge to solve the problems that arise during flight, and he must know a great deal about the "art" of flying, which includes many matters that have little or nothing to do with the instruments. Parts II, III, and IV of this book deal with the use of accounting information. Just as there is much more to the art of piloting an airplane than the ability to read instruments, so there is much more to the art of management than the ability to use accounting information; this book is in no sense a book on the whole art of management.

Analyzing Financial Statements

Since the material in Part I focuses on the principles underlying the construction of financial statements, a good place to begin our examination of the use of accounting information is the use made of these statements. This is the subject matter of Part II.

The two principal financial statements are the balance sheet, which reports the financial position of a business at one moment in time, and the income statement, which summarizes its financial performance over period of time. We shall discuss how the businessman can obtain from these statements useful information both about his own business and about other businesses in which he may be interested. We shall at the same time point out the inherent limitations of financial statement information limitations which prevent these statements from providing the answer all, or even the most important, questions that are raised about business.

Management Control

An important process in which accounting information is used business is called *management control*. This is the process of assur resources are obtained and used effectively and efficiently in the plishment of the organization's objectives. In Part III, we discuss of accounting information in this process.

Management control has to do with the ongoing operati business. It consists of a more or less regularly recurring se interrelated activities. For convenience in exposition, these act be classified as either control activities or planning activities. N the whole process is a single, indivisible one, in which the t activities interact and merge into one another; the same p volved in both. Although pedagogical considerations make discuss these activities separately, we shall emphasize throug the relationship between them.

CONTROL. Control is the process by which managemer insofar as is feasible, that actions taken by the members of conform to management's plans and policies. Accountin useful in control as a means of communication, of mo appraisal.

As a means of *communication*, accounting reports ca ing the organization about management's plans and po eral, the types of action that management wishes t take.

Unless the business is a one-man enterprise, it is n

to do the work; that is, management does not personally manufacture and sell the product. Rather, it is the responsibility of management to see to it that the work gets done by others. This requires, first, that personnel be hired and formed into an organization and, second, that this organization be motivated in such a way that it will do what management wants it to do. Accounting information can help (and also, unless properly used, can hinder) this *motivation* process.

Periodically, management needs to evaluate how well the employees are doing their jobs. Such an *appraisal* of performance may result in a salary increase, promotion, reassignment, corrective action of various kinds, or, in extreme cases, dismissal. Accounting information can assist in this appraisal process, although an adequate basis for judging a man's performance cannot be obtained solely from information revealed by accounting records.

PLANNING.   Planning is the process of deciding what action should be taken in the future. The area covered by one plan may be a tiny segment of the enterprise, or it may be the whole enterprise. Thus, a decision as to whether the price of one product should be increased 10 cents is a plan, and so is a decision to merge or not to merge the company with another company.

The essential characteristic of a plan is that it involves a decision about action to be taken in the future. Planning is therefore to be distinguished from *forecasting*. A forecast is an estimate of what will happen in the future, but the forecaster makes no attempt to influence the future by his own decisions or action. People *forecast* the weather, but they do not— except in the few areas where cloud-seeding operations are carried on— attempt to *plan* the weather.

Some businesses have planning staffs whose full-time job is to assist in making plans. The planning function, however, is much broader than the work done by these staffs; it is performed at all levels in the organization and in all organizations, whether or not they have separate planning staffs. The foreman who decides to route a certain job through Machine A rather than through Machine B is planning in the same sense as, but on a smaller scale than, the president who decides how much the company will spend on research.

A systematic form of planning, called *budgeting*, occurs as part of the management control process. Budgeting is the process of planning the overall activity of the enterprise for a specified period of time, usually a year. An important objective of this process is to fit together the separate plans made for various segments of the enterprise so as to assure that these plans harmonize with one another and that the aggregate effect of all of them on the whole enterprise is satisfactory. For example, the budgeting process might reveal that the sales organization has planned a considerable increase in the sales of one product line but that the production organiza-

tion has not planned for the additional facilities and manpower necessary to turn out the increased volume; or an expansion of facilities might be planned without adequate consideration of where the funds required to build these facilities are to be obtained. In a very small business, top management may have a sufficient personal awareness of overall plans so that formal, written budgets are unnecessary, but a business of any considerable size is likely to be so complex that some systematic process of formulating and balancing the plans for the separate parts of the enterprise is essential.

Decision Making

Part IV describes how accounting information is used as an aid in making business decisions. Although in one sense all business activities involve decision making, our focus in Part IV is on the type of decision that relates to some specific segment of the business, rather than to operations as a whole. This might be a decision to buy a new machine, to enter a new market, to use a new type of raw material or a new method of manufacturing, to borrow money from a bank, or any of a host of other decisions.

All these decisions are arrived at by, essentially, recognizing that a problem exists, identifying the alternative ways of solving the problem, analyzing the consequences of each alternative, and comparing these consequences so as to decide which is best. Accounting information is useful especially in the analysis step.

SOME GENERAL CONSIDERATIONS

Before we plunge into detail, it may be well to consider briefly a few general matters that apply to all sorts of problems and to all types of figures, both accounting and nonaccounting. Although they are introduced here, it is not expected that these points will become entirely meaningful or concrete until the reader has had an opportunity to examine them and to think about their relevance in specific situations. It may therefore be desirable to refer back to these points from time to time.

Figures for a Purpose

Unlike mathematics, accounting is not an end in itself. As is indicated in the preceding section, accounting is done for some purpose—to convey information about what has happened in a business, to provide data that are of assistance in solving a business problem, to express future plans, and so on. The work of accountants is justified only insofar as it contributes to some activity that is external to accounting. Both the beginning student and also the person who has been long immersed in accounting have a tendency to think of accounting as being conducted for its own sake. This is regrettable, and we shall here try to avoid the creation of such an attitude by frequent references to the purposes for which accounting data are intended to be used.

Different Figures for Different Purposes

In mathematics, and in most of the physical sciences, there are definitions that are valid under a wide variety of circumstances. Such is not the case with most accounting definitions. Each of the purposes described in the preceding section requires a different kind of accounting figure. Since these different figures may superficially resemble one another and since they may even be called by the same name, a person who is not familiar with them may easily become confused or frustrated. The most common source of confusion is the word "cost." As will be seen in later chapters, there are historical costs, standard costs, original costs, net costs, residual costs, variable costs, differential costs, incremental costs, marginal costs, opportunity costs, direct costs, estimated costs, full costs and other kinds of costs. Some of these terms are synonymous; others are almost but not quite synonymous; still others, although not synonymous at all, are used by some as if they were.

Accounting figures should always be discussed in terms of the particular problem that they are intended to help solve, rather than in any abstract sense. A statement that "the cost of such-and-such is $100" literally has no meaning unless those who hear this statement understand clearly which of the several possible concepts of cost was intended. A useful procedure to follow in approaching a specific problem is to define, as carefully as possible, the purpose for which figures are to be used in that problem and then to consider how the figures should be assembled and used for that specific purpose.

Accounting Figures Are Approximations

Accounting is a system for recording and summarizing measurements of business facts, and, as is the case with any measurement, an accounting figure is an approximation rather than a precisely accurate statement. Most of the data used in the physical sciences are also measurements, and like scientists and engineers, the user of accounting information must acquire an understanding of the degree of approximation that is present in the data.

Consider, for example, the concept of temperature. With the proper instruments, the temperature of the human body is easily measured to a tenth of a degree and that of a room to a degree or so, but the temperature of the sun is measurable only with an accuracy of a hundred degrees or so. Although these measurements differ widely in their degree of accuracy, each is useful for a particular purpose. Similarly, some accounting figures, such as the amount of cash on hand, may be accurate within very narrow limits, while others are only rough approximations.

There are many reasons for the roughness of accounting figures. A few are mentioned here, and others will become apparent in later chapters. One of them is simply that a business is a complicated organism which includes vastly dissimilar elements—money, buildings, morale, machines, incentives, materials, policies, and so on. There can be no precise way of adding all these diverse elements together so as to form a completely accurate picture of the whole enterprise.

The problem of obtaining reasonably accurate measurements is further complicated by management's desire to obtain information quickly. A rough approximation that is available today is often more useful to management than a more accurate figure published a year from now. For instance, consider the cost of owning and operating an automobile. This cost includes the purchase price of the automobile, plus the cost of gasoline, repairs, and other operating items, less anything that is received when the automobile is sold or traded. The total cost cannot be known exactly until after the automobile has been sold or traded. Businessmen are unwilling to wait this long for information about what an automobile costs, however; they want information every year, every month, or even oftener. In order to provide this information, the accountant must work with estimates of how many years or months the automobile will be used in the future and how much will be received when it is eventually sold or traded. The accuracy of any interim figure on the cost of the automobile depends on the validity of these estimates.

For the same reason that automobile costs cannot be precisely determined until the automobile is sold, the profit of a whole company cannot be precisely determined accurately until the company goes out of business. Also, for reasons to be discussed subsequently, the profit of a division, a product, or other segment of a company usually cannot be measured with close accuracy. Nevertheless, management needs information on costs and profits for short periods of time, such as a month, and for individual divisions, products, or other segments of a business. Accounting will furnish such information, and it can be most helpful to management. (After all, one needs only a rough approximation of the outside temperature in order to decide whether to wear an overcoat.) Management must clearly understand, however, the approximations that are inherent in most accounting figures.

The degree of approximation is especially high in the case of the figures used for planning purposes. Such figures are always estimates of what will happen in the future. But businessmen are not clairvoyant; they do not *know* what will happen in the future, and the figures used for planning purposes can be no better than their estimates of what the future holds.

Working with Incomplete Data

No one could ask a person to solve a problem in mathematics without furnishing him all the information he needs. In a business problem, on the other hand, one almost never has exactly the information he would like to have. In nearly every practical situation, the person who is struggling with the problem can think of additional information that would be helpful if it were available. On the other hand, there are many business situations in which page after page of figures are available, but only a small fraction of them are at all relevant to the problem at hand, and perhaps none of them is quite what one needs to solve the problem.

It is a fact of life, however, that problems must be solved, business decisions must be made, and often the decision cannot be delayed until all the pertinent information is available. One does the best he can with what he has, and then moves on to the next problem. John W. Gardner writes:

Anyone who accomplishes anything of significance has more confidence than the facts would justify. It is something that outstanding executives have in common with gifted military commanders, brilliant political leaders, and great artists. It is true of societies as well as of individuals. Every great civilization has been characterized by confidence in itself.[2]

On the other hand, a decision should not be made if a vital, obtainable piece of evidence is missing. Deciding whether or not to act on the available evidence is one of the most difficult parts of the whole decision process. As the late Dean Wallace B. Donham has put it: "The art of business is the art of making irrevocable decisions on the basis of inadequate information."

Figure Evidence Is Only Partial Evidence

Few, if any, business problems can be solved solely by the collection and analysis of figures. Usually, there are important factors that cannot be, or have not been, reduced to numbers. For example, think of how you would judge the performance of a baseball player. Every time a baseball player comes to bat, and almost every time he handles the ball in the field, a statistic is generated. Detailed records are published on his times at bat, walks, hits, slugging, singles, two-base hits, three-base hits, home runs, strikeouts, putouts, sacrifices, fielding chances, assists, errors, earned run

---

[2] *Annual Report 1965*, Carnegie Corporation.

average, and so on. Nevertheless, when the manager of the team must decide whether A is a better ball player than B, he knows better than to rely completely on the numerical information. Such factors as how well a man gets along with his colleagues, his ability to hit in the pinches, and other unmeasurable characteristics must also be taken into account. If the question of a ball player's ability could be answered solely by an analysis of statistics, there would be no reason for the millions of man-hours of discussion by the "hot-stove league" during the winter months.

Most business organizations are much more complicated than baseball teams; the "game" of business goes on all day, every day, rather than 156 discrete times a year, and business results are not expressed by the number of games won and lost. Business measurements are therefore much more difficult and less precise than baseball measurements.

Some people act as if problems could be completely solved by numerical analysis. They have the erroneous idea that solely from a knowledge of loads, stresses, and material strengths the engineer can figure just how a bridge should look, disregarding the element of judgment completely. At the other extreme, there are those who believe that intuition is the sure guide to a sound decision, and who therefore pay no attention to the figures. Although the correct attitude is clearly somewhere between these extremes, there is no way of describing precisely where it is. The reader must reach his own conclusion on the relative importance of figure and nonfigure data in the solution of management problems.

People, Not Figures, Get Things Done

An obvious fact about business organizations is that they consist of human beings. Anything that the business accomplishes is the result of the actions of these people. Figures can assist the people in the organization in various ways, but the figures themselves are nothing more than marks on pieces of paper; by themselves they accomplish nothing. But figures don't talk back; they give the appearance of being definite and precise, and it is a comforting illusion to imagine that the construction of a set of figures is synonymous with acting on a real problem.

An accounting system may be beautifully designed and carefully operated, but the system is of no use to management unless it results in action by human beings. For instance, three companies may use exactly the same system—the same chart of accounts, the same set of records and reports, the same procedure for collecting and disseminating information—with entirely different results. In one company, the system may be *useless* because management never acts on the information collected, and the organization has become aware of this fact. In the second company, the system may be *helpful* because management uses the information as a general guide for planning and control and has educated the organization to use it in the same spirit. In the third company, the system may be *worse than useless* because management overemphasizes the importance of the figures and therefore takes unwise actions.

SUMMARY

In this book we shall discuss some powerful tools that can assist management in the tasks of operating a business. The invention and refinement of these tools have, in a significant way, made possible the creation and efficient operation of large enterprises, and it is scarcely conceivable that any business, except the smallest ones, could operate without them. At the same time we shall explore the limitations on the use of these tools. We shall see that in the real world, formulas or mechanical techniques rarely provide the complete solution to a problem. The essential reason for these limitations has been well summed up by G. K. Chesterton:

The real trouble with this world of ours is not that it is an unreasonable world, nor even that it is a reasonable one. The commonest kind of trouble is that it is nearly reasonable, but not quite. Life is not an illogicality; yet it is a trap for logicians. It looks just a little more mathematical and regular than it is; its exactitude is obvious, but its inexactitude is hidden; its wildness lies in wait.[3]

---

[3] *Orthodoxy* (London: Bodley Head, 1949 reprint), p. 131.

CASES

CASE 1–1. CONAN COMPANY

The Conan Company manufactured an inexpensive grade of men's clothing which it sold through house-to-house salesmen. A salesman took the measurements of the customer and entered them on the order blank, which the company used as a cutting order. Since the company found from experience that the measurements were usually of approximately regular sizes, it cut the garments from regular-sized patterns with only slight changes. The wool worsted goods used by the Conan Company cost approximately $3 per yard.

In order to insure very quick delivery the company made out cutting tickets for each garment as fast as orders were received and distributed them to the cutters together with a record of the standard yardage allowance for cutting that size of that style garment. It was expected that cutters would try to cut garments out of the least amount of cloth possible in order to keep down costs. They were, of course, also expected to cut as many garments as possible in a day. Each cutter earned $1.80 per hour and worked eight hours per day.

A careful record was kept of the garments cut each day. A transcript of the cutting record for one day is shown in Exhibit 1[4] given on page 14. Yardage figures are given to the hundredth of a yard for ease in computation.

---

[4] The sample used in this case is too small to be adequate. A small sample is used, however, to bring out certain points without requiring the reader to spend time on mere mechanical handling of a large number of figures. For purposes of class discussion, you may assume that this record is representative.

Exhibit 1

CUTTING RECORD

Cutting Ticket Number	Cutter	Style	Cloth	Color	Size	Yards Saved	Yards Lost
1	A	102	1073	Grey	37	...	0.10
2	B	101	1116	Blue	39	...	0.02
3	C	104	1178	Blue	37	...	0.10
4	D	103	1241	Brown	38	0.04	...
5	A	102	1073	Brown	40	...	0.14
6	B	101	1116	Brown	38	0.04	...
7	C	104	1178	Blue	38	...	0.06
8	A	103	1241	Brown	36	0.08	...
9	D	103	1241	Grey	35	0.10	...
10	B	104	1178	Grey	37	0.06	...
11	C	101	1116	Blue	36	...	0.06
12	A	101	1116	Grey	40	0.02	...
13	B	104	1178	Brown	37	0.00	0.00
14	D	104	1178	Blue	39	0.06	...
15	C	101	1116	Blue	36	...	0.08
16	A	103	1241	Brown	38	0.04	...
17	C	102	1073	Brown	40	...	0.18
18	D	103	1241	Blue	42	0.02	...
19	B	103	1241	Grey	36	...	0.04
20	A	102	1073	Brown	37	...	0.08
21	C	102	1073	Grey	37	...	0.16
22	B	102	1073	Brown	36	...	0.10
23	C	103	1241	Brown	38	0.02	...
24	A	104	1178	Grey	38	0.06	...
25	D	101	1116	Brown	36	0.04	...
26	B	104	1178	Brown	37	0.08	...
27	C	104	1178	Blue	39	0.02	...
28	A	101	1116	Grey	37	...	0.06
29	D	101	1116	Blue	42	0.08	...
30	B	104	1178	Grey	38	0.04	...
31	C	103	1241	Blue	37	...	0.12
32	A	103	1241	Grey	40	...	0.02
33	B	103	1241	Blue	38	0.02	...
34	C	101	1116	Blue	36	...	0.04
35	D	102	1073	Brown	39	...	0.06
36	B	101	1116	Grey	35	0.06	...
37	C	104	1178	Blue	44	...	0.06
38	A	102	1073	Grey	37	...	0.18
39	D	103	1241	Brown	40	0.02	...
40	C	103	1241	Brown	38	...	0.04

Questions

1. What conclusions can you draw from a cross-classification of yardage lost or saved according to cutters and styles? (By cross-classification is meant an orderly arrangement of the figures, grouped in column and row according to cutter, or style, or some other factor.) Who is apparently the fastest cutter? The most careful cutter? The best cutter?
2. Comment on the reliability and adequacy of the standards used to measure performance.
3. Should the most careful cutter specialize on the style for which losses are most frequent?
4. Before taking any action, what additional information would be needed?

CASE 1–2. CHARLES MAVIOLI

In the fall of 1966, Charles Mavioli, a general carpenter living in one of the suburbs of Boston, decided to invest a part of his savings in woodworking machinery and in a building which had formerly been used as a small garage. His plan for some time had been to prepare himself for contracting work of a modest sort, including small-home construction. He had always wanted to build low-priced dwellings "all on his own." Such an activity would be limited, he knew, by his ability to carry his share of the total investment load necessary for such an undertaking. So far in his career, Mavioli had been extraordinarily successful as a general carpenter, working at a wide variety of jobs throughout the communities of Greater Boston. At times he had been hired as "boss carpenter" on large and important constructions. For this kind of work he had received a very good salary, a large part of which he and his wife had been able to save against the time when he could have a business of his own.

By October 1966, Mavioli had his shop completely fitted and had hired two mill hands and a shop mechanic to help him in his new undertaking. As a "fill-in" between big jobs, it was his expectation to be able to provide fairly uniform employment for these people through making window frames, window screens, and similar construction parts both for stock and on order.

In that same month, in connection with a substantial order for window screens requiring six or eight weeks of shop activity, Mavioli talked with the credit officer of his bank about his need for some temporary financial assistance in the purchase of necessary materials and supplies. This assistance the bank was glad to extend to him. In granting the loan, however, the credit officer suggested that Mavioli would now need to spend more time and money on financial and operating records than had been necessary when his work was almost entirely a matter of personal services. "More paper work will be a painful necessity from now on," he said; "not only to make it easier for you to do a good job in managing your new business, but also in making your tax returns and in later dealings with this or other banks." The banker suggested that Mavioli talk with some qualified person about this problem. Mavioli said that he had a friend who was controller of a manufacturing business in Boston, and that he was sure this friend would give him some practical suggestions.

A week or so after the conference at the bank, Mavioli had a long and satisfactory talk with his friend about his need for additional records. At the outset he emphasized that up to this point he had gotten along pretty well with the stubs of his checkbook, plus some odds and ends of memoranda which he and his wife had been careful to keep for reference purposes. The controller agreed that it is easy to overdo "this business of keeping records," and said that in his opinion it would be best for them to make a small start and feel their way along for a few months before attempting anything that would call for much work.

He suggested that, as a starter, Mavioli and his wife might well spend an evening drawing up a list of the properties used in operating their shop and contracting business, and a corresponding list of the debts which had grown out of this business, together with the amounts of money that Mavioli had invested in it. The controller explained that the list of "properties used" should be confined to things having a money value in this particular business. "With these two lists," he said, "we can draw up a beginning financial statement of your assets and liabilities, which should be helpful in talking over your need for figures." To this he added: "Generally speaking, the problem of useful and understandable accounting information is built around this statement, and the job is to keep such a statement (or its supporting records) more or less continuously adjusted to what takes place in the affairs of the business it represents, with enough supplementary facts about resulting changes to help the owner be a better manager than would be possible without such tools to help him."

The controller assured Mavioli that he did not believe the cost of keeping the necessary records would be a very important consideration. He pointed out that he knew of experts in accounting procedures who specialized in making periodic visits to small concerns such as Mavioli's for the very purpose of relieving their clients of much of the clerical burden of keeping operating records. But he said it would nevertheless be necessary for Mavioli or his wife to keep a memorandum record or daybook of transactions practically as they occurred. The controller suggested that as time went on Mavioli might want to give some attention to the accepted ways of keeping accounting records; but he said there was no need for Mavioli to be apprehensive about the cost of supplying his simple requirements.

Questions

1. Why did Mavioli need any records? What did he need?
2. See what you can do to draw up a list of Mavioli's assets and liabilities, as the controller suggested, making any assumptions you consider useful. How should Mavioli go about putting a value on his assets?
3. Among the changes in the assets, liabilities, and proprietary claims of a business which the controller spoke of as the subject matter of accounting is an important variety growing out of "profit and loss" or "trading" operations. What would be the general construction of a profit and loss analysis for Mavioli's new business? How frequently would he wish to provide himself with such an analysis?
4. What other kinds of changes in assets, liabilities, and proprietary claims will need careful recording and reporting if Mavioli is to keep in control of his job as manager?

PART I

The Accounting Structure

CHAPTER 2

BASIC ACCOUNTING CONCEPTS: THE BALANCE SHEET

Suppose you were asked to keep track of what was going on in a business so as to provide useful information for management. One way of carrying out such an assignment would be to write down a narrative of important events in a diary or in a log similar to that kept by the captain of a ship. After some experience with your log or diary, you would gradually develop a set of rules to guide your efforts. For example, since it would be impossible to write down every action of every person in the business, you would frame rules to guide you in choosing between those events that were important enough to record and those that should be omitted. Thus, if your business was a retail automobile dealership, you certainly would want a record of each car sold, but you might well decide not to make a record of every person who came into the showroom.

You would also find that your diary would be more valuable if you standardized certain terminology. People who studied it would then have a clearer understanding of what you meant. Furthermore, if you standardized terms and definitions of these terms, you could turn the job of keeping the diary over to someone else and have some assurance that his report of events would convey the same information that you would have conveyed had you been keeping the diary personally.

In devising these rules of keeping a diary, you would necessarily be somewhat arbitrary. There might be several ways of describing a certain event, all equally good; but in order to have a common basis of understanding, you would select just one of these for use in your record-keeping system. Thus, since the products handled by your automobile dealership could be called "vehicles," "autos," "cars," or "trucks," some of

21

which are synonyms and others not, it would clearly be desirable to agree on a standard nomenclature.

All the foregoing considerations were actually involved in the development of the accounting process. Accounting has evolved over a period of several hundred years, and during this time certain rules and conventions have come to be accepted as useful. If you are to understand accounting reports—the end products of an accounting system—you must be familiar with the rules and conventions lying behind these reports. The purpose of this and the next eight chapters is to describe the more common of these rules and conventions.

Accounting as a Language

Accounting is often called "the language of business." In an important sense, this is an apt phrase, since accounting provides the principal formal means by which information about a business is communicated (although of course there are many other types of business communication). In any event, the task of learning accounting is essentially the same as the task of learning a new language.

This task is complicated by the fact that many of the words used in accounting mean almost, but not quite, the same thing as the identical words mean in everyday, nonaccounting usage. If you are an American learning French, you realize from the beginning that the words and the grammar in French are completely new to you and must therefore be learned carefully. The problem of learning accounting, however, is more like that of an American learning to speak English as it is spoken in Great Britain. Unless he is careful, the American will fail to recognize that words are used in Great Britain in a different sense from that used in America.

> EXAMPLE: The grain that Americans call "wheat" is called "corn" by the British, and the British use the word "maize" for the grain that Americans call "corn." To complicate the matter further, a grain grown in certain parts of America is called "maize," and it is almost, but not quite, like American corn. Unless they understand these differences in terminology, Americans and Englishmen will not communicate what they intend when talking with each other.

Perhaps the greatest difficulty that a beginning student of accounting encounters is that of distinguishing between the accounting meaning of certain terms and the meaning that he has attached to these terms in their nonaccounting, everyday usage.

> EXAMPLE: An amount labeled "net worth" appears on many accounting reports. The commonsense interpretation is that this amount refers to what something is "worth"—what its value is—but such an inteprertation is incorrect. For the correct meaning, see p. 42.

As is the case with language, accounting has many dialects. There are differences in terminology and practice among industries and among companies within industries. In this introductory treatment, we shall not attempt even to list all these differences, although the principal ones will be mentioned.

Accounting also resembles a language in that some of its rules are definite, whereas others are not; and there are differences of opinion among accountants as to how a given event should be recorded, just as there are differences of opinion among grammarians as to many matters of sentence structure, punctuation, and choice of words. Nevertheless, there are many practices that are clearly "poor English," and there are also many practices that are definitely "poor accounting." In these chapters, therefore, an attempt is made to describe the elements of "good accounting" and to indicate areas in which there are differences of opinion as to what constitutes good practice.

Finally, languages evolve and change in response to the changing needs of society, and so does accounting. The rules described here are currently in use, but some of them will probably be modified to meet the changing needs of business.

NATURE AND SOURCE OF PRINCIPLES

The rules and conventions of accounting are commonly referred to as "principles." The word "principle" is here used to mean "a general law or rule adopted or professed as a guide to action; a settled ground or basis of conduct or practice."[1] Note that this definition describes a principle as a *general* law or rule, that is, to be used as a *guide* to action. This means that accounting principles do not prescribe exactly how each detailed event occurring in a business should be recorded. Consequently, there are a great many matters in accounting practice that differ from one company to another. In part, these differences are inevitable, because a single detailed set of rules could not conceivably apply to every company. In part, the differences reflect the fact that the accountant has considerable latitude within the "generally accepted accounting principles" in which to express his own idea as to the best way of recording and reporting a specific event.

The reader should realize, therefore, that he cannot know the precise meaning of many of the items on an accounting report unless he knows which of several equally acceptable possibilities has been selected by the person who prepared the report. For example, as mentioned in Chapter 1, the simple word "cost" has many different meanings, and there is agreement on the definition of this word only in the broadest sense. The

---

[1] AICPA, *Accounting Terminology Bulletin No. 1*, p. 9.

meaning intended in a specific situation requires knowledge of the context.

Criteria

Accounting principles are man-made. Unlike the principles of physics, chemistry, and the other natural sciences, accounting principles were not deduced from basic axioms, nor is their validity verifiable by observation and experiment. Instead, they have evolved, and the process of evolution is essentially as follows: a problem is recognized; someone works out what he thinks is a good solution to this problem; if other people agree that this is a good solution, its use gradually becomes widespread, and then it becomes an accounting principle. Moreover, some hitherto accepted principles fall from favor with the passage of time. This evolutionary process is going on constantly; accounting principles are not "eternal verities."

The general acceptance of an accounting principle or practice usually depends on how well it meets three criteria: relevance, objectivity, and feasibility. A principle is *relevant* to the extent that it results in information that is meaningful and useful to those who need to know something about a certain business. A principle is *objective* to the extent that the information is not influenced by the personal bias or judgment of those who furnish it. Objectivity connotes reliability, trustworthiness. It also connotes verifiability, which means that there is some way of ascertaining the correctness of the information reported. A principle is *feasible* to the extent that it can be implemented without undue complexity or cost.

We shall illustrate and expand on the significance of these criteria in connection with the discussion of the principles themselves. At this point it is sufficient to point out that these criteria often conflict with one another. The most relevant solution is likely to be the least objective and the least feasible.

EXAMPLE: The development of a new product may have a significant effect on a company's real value—Xerography and Polaroid cameras being spectacular recent examples. Such information is most useful to the investor. It is indeed relevant. But the best estimate of the value of a new product is likely to be that made by management, and this is a highly subjective estimate; that is, some persons would make extremely optimistic estimates, whereas others would be equally extreme on the conservative side. Furthermore, many managements have a natural tendency to make the figures look as good as possible. Accounting therefore does not attempt to record such values. It sacrifices relevance in the interests of objectivity.

The measure of the value of the owners' interest in the Xerox Corporation obtained from the stock market quotations (i.e., multiplying the price per share of stock times the number of shares outstanding) is a much more accurate reflection of the true value than the amount at which this item appears in the corporation's accounting records. As of December 31, 1967, the marketplace gave this value as $6,657 million; the accounting records, $406 million. The difference does not indicate that there is an error in the accounting records. It merely underlines the fact that accounting does not, and does not attempt to, report market values.

In developing new principles, the essential problem is to strike the right balance between relevance on the one hand and objectivity and feasibility on the other. Failure to appreciate this problem often leads to unwarranted criticism of accounting principles. It is easy to criticize accounting on the grounds that accounting information is not as relevant as it might be; but the critic often overlooks the fact that proposals to increase relevance almost always involve a sacrifice of objectivity and feasibility. On balance, such a sacrifice may not be worthwhile.

Sources of Principles

Accounting principles are not codified in a single source that resembles, either in the amount of detail or in its authority, the codification of legal principles on which lawyers rely so heavily. Of the various sources, by far the most authoritative is the set of *Opinions of the Accounting Principles Board* of the American Institute of Certified Public Accountants (AICPA). As of 1968, there were a dozen of these opinions, each consisting of a paragraph, or a few paragraphs, describing the principle, together with several pages of explanatory material. In addition, the Accounting Principles Board has adopted certain of the opinions issued by its predecessor organization, the Committee on Accounting Procedures of the AICPA. These are published in Paul Grady's *Inventory of Generally Accepted Accounting Principles.*[2]

These statements are known as "generally accepted accounting principles." The AICPA emphasizes, however, that "generally accepted accounting principles" are those principles which have substantial authoritative support, and that although opinions of the Accounting Principles Board constitute "substantial authoritative support," "substantial authoritative support" can also exist for accounting principles that differ from opinions of the Accounting Principles Board.

The accounting reports of most companies of any substantial size are examined by certified public accountants, who are members of the AICPA. A company is not required to adhere to the set of principles stated by the Accounting Principles Board, but if the certified public accountant finds that the company has used a different principle, he

---

[2] Published by American Institute of Certified Public Accountants as its *Accounting Research Study No. 7,* 1965. References to these opinions will be cited herein as "Grady."

must call attention to this fact. The alternative principle is acceptable if the company can demonstrate that it has "substantial support." Such a demonstration can be made by showing that several reputable companies use the alternative principle.

As we shall see, the principles so far enunciated by the Accounting Principles Board do not encompass the whole of accounting, and in many cases they specifically permit alternative methods of treatment.

Another authoritative source of principles is publications of the U.S. Securities and Exchange Commission, particularly its *Regulation S–X* and its *Accounting Series Releases.* In general, these are consistent with the *Opinions of the Accounting Principles Board.* They amplify these opinions and describe their application to specific situations.

The American Accounting Association also publishes a statement of accounting principles, but these are to be regarded as normative rather than descriptive; that is, they state what accounting principles *should be,* rather than what they *are.* Thus, they are not necessarily a guide to current practice.

Various regulatory bodies also prescribe accounting rules for the companies they regulate. Among those subjected to such rules are banks and other financial institutions, insurance companies, railroads, airlines, pipelines, radio and television companies, and electric and gas companies. These rules are not necessarily consistent with those of the Accounting Principles Board.

> EXAMPLE: The Union Pacific Railroad company reported that in 1967 its net income, measured in accordance with generally accepted accounting principles, was $80.7 million. Measured in accordance with rules prescribed by the Interstate Commerce Commission, its net income was $102.1 million, or 26 percent greater.

The authority of these agencies exists, of course, only in the United States of America. Accounting principles in other countries differ in some respects from these, but there is a basic similarity throughout the world, including the USSR, but with the notable exception of the Chinese Peoples Republic, whose principles differ from these in some significant respects.

BASIC CONCEPTS

The principles of accounting are built on a foundation of a few basic concepts. They are so basic that most accountants do not consciously refer to them. Some of these concepts are currently undergoing a critical reexamination by the profession, but in this initial contact with them, the reader is asked to understand and accept them rather than to criticize them. As is the case with a language, one can criticize the way certain words are spelled (e.g., "bough," "cough," "doff"), but the fact remains that the words *are* spelled in a certain way. If a person is to use the language effectively, he must understand what the rules actually are.

Accountants differ as to how many basic concepts there are, and as to how they should be labeled and defined. Nevertheless, there probably is fairly general support for the following list:

1. Money measurement	2. Business entity
3. Going concern	4. Cost
5. Dual-aspect	6. Conservatism
7. Accrual	8. Realization
9. Consistency	10. Materiality

The first six of these are discussed below, and the remainder are discussed in Chapter 3.

1. The Money Measurement Concept

In accounting, a record is made only of those facts that can be expressed in monetary terms. The advantage of expressing facts in monetary terms is that money provides a common denominator by means of which heterogeneous facts about a business can be expressed in terms of numbers that can be added and subtracted.

> EXAMPLE: Although it may be a fact that a business owns $10,000 of cash, 6,000 pounds of raw material, six trucks, 10,000 square feet of building space, and so on, these amounts cannot be added together to produce a meaningful total of what the business owns. Expressing these items in monetary terms—$10,000 of cash, $5,000 of raw material, $20,000 of trucks, and $100,000 of buildings—makes such an addition possible.

This concept imposes a severe limitation on the scope of an accounting report. Accounting does not record the state of the president's health; it does not record the fact that the sales manager is not on speaking terms with the production manager; it does not report that a strike is beginning; and it does not reveal that a competitor has placed a better product on the market. Accounting therefore does not give a complete account of the happenings in a business or an accurate picture of the condition of the business. It follows, then, that the reader of an accounting report should not expect to find therein all, or perhaps even the most important, facts about a business.

Money is expressed in terms of its value at the time an event is recorded in the accounts. Subsequent changes in the purchasing power of money do not affect this amount. Thus material purchased in 1969 at $10,000 and land purchased in 1939 at $10,000 are each listed in the 1969 accounting records at $10,000, although the purchasing power of the dollar in 1969 was only 40 percent of what it was 30 years previously.

2. The Business Entity Concept

Accounts are kept for *business entities*, as distinguished from the *persons* who are associated with these entities. In recording facts in the accounts, the important question is, How do they affect the business? not, How do they affect the persons who own, operate, or otherwise are associated with the business? When the owner takes cash out of his business, for example, the accounting records show that the *business* has less cash than previously, even though the real effect of this event on the *owner* himself may have been negligible; he has taken cash from his business "pocket" and put it into his personal "pocket," but it remains his cash.

It is sometimes difficult to define the business entity for which a set of accounts is kept. Consider the case of a man and his wife who run a small unincorporated retail store. In *law* there is no distinction between the financial affairs of the store and those of the people who own it; a creditor of the store can sue and, if successful, collect from the owners' personal resources as well as from the resources of the business. In *accounting*, by contrast, a set of accounts is kept for the store as a separate business entity, and the events reflected in these accounts must be those of the store; the nonbusiness events that affect the couple must not be included in them. Clearly, this means that the family's expenses for food, clothing, shelter, and the like should be separated from the expenses of running the store. But suppose that the couple lives on the business premises. How much of the rent, the electric light bill, and the property taxes of these premises are properly part of the business and how much are personal expenses of the family? Because of questions like these, the distinction between the business entity and outside interests is a difficult one to make in practice.

In the case of a corporation, the distinction is often quite easily made. A corporation is a legal entity separate from the persons who own it, and the accounts of many corporations correspond exactly to the scope of the legal entity. There may be complications, however. In the case of a group of legally separate corporations that are related to one another by stockholdings, the whole group may be treated as a single business entity for certain purposes, giving rise to what are called "consolidated" accounting statements. Conversely, within a single corporation, a separate set of accounts may be maintained for each of the principal divisions of the corporation, especially when they are physically separated from the home office.

There follows from the distinction between the business entity and the outside world the idea that an important purpose of financial accounting is to provide the basis for reporting on *stewardship*. The managers of a business are entrusted with funds supplied by owners, banks, and others. Management is responsible for the wise use of these funds, and financial accounting reports are in part designed to show how well this responsibility, or stewardship, has been discharged.

3. The Going-Concern Concept

Unless there is good evidence to the contrary, accounting assumes that the business will continue to operate for an indefinitely long period in the future. The significance of this assumption can be indicated by contrasting it with a possible alternative, namely, that the business is about to be liquidated or sold. Under the latter assumption, accounting would attempt to measure at all times what the business *is currently worth* to a buyer; but under the going-concern assumption there is no need to do this, and it is in fact not done. Instead, a business is viewed as a mechanism for adding value to the resources it uses, and its success is measured by the difference between the value of its output (sales of goods and services) and the cost of the resources used in creating that output. Resources which have been acquired but not yet used in creating output are shown on the accounting records, not at their current value to an outside buyer, but rather at their cost. Their current resale value is irrelevant, since it is assumed that they will not be sold as such, but rather that they will be used in the creation of future output values.

4. The Cost Concept

Resources (i.e., rights in tangible and intangible property) owned by a business are called, in accounting language, *assets*. A fundamental concept of accounting, closely related to the going-concern concept described above, is that an asset is ordinarily entered on the accounting records at the price paid to acquire it—that is, at its cost—and that this cost is the basis for all subsequent accounting for the asset.

Since, for a variety of reasons, the real worth of an item may change with the passage of time, the accounting measurement of assets does not necessarily—indeed, does not ordinarily—reflect what assets are worth, except at the moment they are acquired. There is therefore a considerable difference between the accounting concept of cost and the everyday, nonaccounting concept of value, since in its ordinary usage "value" means what something is currently worth.

EXAMPLE: If a business buys a plot of land, paying $5,000 for it, this asset would be recorded in the accounts of the business at the amount of $5,000. Subsequent changes in the market value of this land would ordinarily not be reflected by changes in the accounts. If a year later the land could be sold for $10,000, or if it could be sold for only $2,000, no change would ordinarily be made in the accounting records to reflect this fact. (The word "ordinarily" is used since there are a few situations in which accounting records are changed to reflect changes in market value; these will be described subsequently.)

Thus, the amounts at which assets are listed in the accounts of a company do *not* indicate what the assets could be sold for. One of the most common mistakes made by uninformed persons reading accounting reports is that of believing that there is a close correspondence between the figure at which an asset appears on these reports and the actual value of the asset. Of course, there may well be a correspondence between accounting measurements and real market values in the case of certain assets. The asset "cash" is the best example. Readily marketable securities and inventories held by the company for only a short period of time may appear on the books at figures that are close to their actual worth. In general, it is safe to say that the longer an asset has been owned by a company, the less likely it is that the amount at which it appears on the accounting records corresponds to its current market value.

The cost concept does not mean that all assets remain on the accounting records at their original purchase price for as long as the company owns them. The figure for an asset that has a long, but nevertheless limited, life is systematically reduced over that life by the process called *depreciation*, as discussed in more detail in Chapter 6. The purpose of the depreciation process is systematically to remove the *cost* of the asset from the accounts and to show it as a cost of operations; depreciation has no necessary relationship to changes in market value or in the real worth of the asset to the company.

It follows from the cost concept that if the company pays *nothing* for an item it acquires, this item will usually *not* appear on the accounting records as an asset. Thus, the knowledge and skill that is built up as the business operates, the teamwork that grows up within the organization, a favorable location that becomes of increasing importance as time goes on, a good reputation with its customers—none of these appears as an asset in the accounts of the company.

On some accounting reports the term "goodwill" appears. Reasoning from everyday definition of this word, you may conclude that it represents the accountant's appraisal of what the company's name and reputation are worth. This is not so. Goodwill appears in the accounts of the company only when the company has *purchased* some intangible and valuable property right. A common case is when one company buys another company and pays more than the fair value of its tangible assets. The amount by which the purchase price exceeds the value of the tangible assets may be called goodwill, representing the value of the name, the reputation, the location, or other intangible possessions of the purchased company. Unless the business has actually purchased such intangibles, however, no item for "goodwill" is shown in the accounts. If the item does appear, it is shown initially at the purchase price, even though the management may believe that its real value is considerably higher.

It also follows from the cost concept that an event may affect the true value of a business without having any effect on the accounting records. To take an extreme case, suppose that several key executives are killed in a plane accident. To the extent that "an organization is but the lengthened shadow of a man," the real value of the company will change immediately, and this will be reflected in the market price of the company's stock, which reflects investors' appraisal of value. The accounting records, however, will not be affected by this event.

The cost concept provides an excellent illustration of the problem of applying the three basic criteria discussed in the preceding section: relevance, objectivity, and feasibility. If the *only* criterion were relevance, then the cost concept would not be defensible. Clearly, investors and others are more interested in what the business is actually worth today rather than what the assets cost originally.

But who knows what a business is worth today? The fact is that any estimate of current value is just that—an estimate—and informed people will disagree on what is the right estimate. (For illustrations, see the judgments about companies that are reported in the financial press. On the same day, some people will say that the stock of a given company is "overpriced" and others will say that it is "underpriced.") Furthermore, accounting reports are prepared by the management of a business, and if they contained estimates of what the business is actually worth, these would be management's estimates. It is quite possible that such estimates would be biased.

The cost concept, by contrast, provides a relatively objective foundation for accounting. It is not *purely* objective, for, as we shall see, judgments are necessary in applying it. It is much more objective, however, than the alternative of attempting to estimate current values. Essentially, the reader of an accounting report must recognize that it is based on the cost concept, and he must arrive at his own estimate of current value, partly by analyzing the information in the report and partly by using nonaccounting information.

Furthermore, a "market value" or "current worth" concept would be difficult to apply, because it would require that the accountant attempt to keep track of the ups and downs of market prices. The cost concept leads to a system that is much more feasible.

In summary, adherence to the cost concept indicates a willingness on the part of those who developed accounting principles to sacrifice some degree of relevance in exchange for greater objectivity and greater feasibility.

To emphasize the distinction between the accounting concept and the ordinary meaning of worth, the term "book value" is used for the amounts as shown in the accounting records and the term "market value" for the actual value of the asset as reflected in the marketplace.

5. The Dual-Aspect Concept

As stated above, the resources owned by a business are called "assets." The claims of various parties against these assets are called "equities." There are two types of equities: (1) *liabilities,* which are the claims of creditors, i.e., everyone other than the owners of the business; and (2) *owners' equity* (or "capital," or "proprietorship"), which is the claim of the owners of the business.[3] Since all of the assets of a business are claimed by someone (either by the owners or by some outside party) and since the total of these claims cannot exceed the amount of assets to be claimed, it follows that—

$$\text{Assets} = \text{Equities} .$$

Accounting systems are set up in such a way that a record is made of *two aspects* of each event that affects these records, and in essence these aspects are changes in assets and changes in equities.

Suppose that a man starts a business and that his first act is to open a bank account in which he deposits $10,000 of his own money. The dual aspect of this action is that the business now has an asset, cash, of $10,000, and the owner has a claim against this asset, also of $10,000, or—

$$\text{Assets (Cash), \$10,000} = \text{Equities (Owner's), \$10,000} .$$

If the business then borrowed $5,000 from a bank, the accounting records would show an increase in cash, making the amount $15,000, and a new claim against this cash by the bank in the amount of $5,000. At this point the accounting records of the business would show the following:

Cash.	$15,000	Owed to bank.	$ 5,000
		Owner's equity.	10,000
Total Assets.	$15,000	Total Equities.	$15,000

Every event that is recorded in the accounts affects at least two items; there is no conceivable way of making only a single change in the accounts. Accounting is therefore properly called a "double-entry" system.

An accounting system conceivably could be set up with some concept other than the one stated here. As a matter of fact, there is a system called "single-entry" accounting that records only one aspect of a transaction, very much like the record maintained in a ship's log or a diary. However,

---

[3] Some accountants use the word "liabilities" to include both the claims of creditors and the claims of owners; when so used it is synonymous with the word "equities" as used here. The narrower definition is used here for the sake of clarity.

as will become apparent in later chapters, there are many advantages, both mechanical and conceptual, in the dual-aspect concept, and this is so universally accepted that no further mention will be made of any other possibility.

6. Conservatism

The conservatism concept means that when the accountant has a reasonable choice, he ordinarily will show the lower of two asset amounts for a given item, or will record an event in such a way that owners' equity is lower than it otherwise would be. This concept is often stated as follows: "Anticipate no profit, and provide for all possible losses." It is especially important as a modifier of the cost concept. To illustrate, inventories (material held for sale, supplies, etc.) are ordinarily reported, not at their cost, which is what one would expect in accordance with the cost concept, but rather at the *lower* of their cost or their current replacement value.

The conservatism concept affects principally the category of assets called "current assets" (see page 38). It is ordinarily not applied to noncurrent assets.

The conservatism concept is applied much less strongly now than was the case a few decades ago when it was a common practice to report some assets at far less than either their cost or their current market value. Nevertheless, the concept still has an important influence on accounting. Many informed persons would say that this concept is illogical and that the accountant should attempt to report the figures either consistently on the basis of cost or consistently on the basis of market value rather than choosing the more conservative of these two possible approaches. Nevertheless, few would question the fact that the concept does exist and that it is important.

THE BALANCE SHEET

The balance sheet is the fundamental accounting report in the sense that every accounting transaction can be recorded in terms of its effect on the balance sheet. It shows the financial status of the business as of a given moment of time.[4]

A balance sheet for a hypothetical corporation is shown in Illustration 2–1. Let us examine this statement in terms of the basic concepts listed

---

[4] A balance sheet dated "December 31" is implicitly understood to mean "at the close of business on December 31." Sometimes the identical balance sheet may be dated "January 1," meaning "at the beginning of business on January 1," which is the same moment of time. Ordinarily, the "close of business" connotation is the correct one.

Illustration 2-1

GARSDEN CORPORATION

Balance Sheet as of December 31, 1968

ASSETS

Current Assets:

Cash.		$ 3,448,891
Marketable securities (market value, $248,420)		246,221
Accounts receivable		5,943,588
Inventories		12,623,412
Prepaid expenses and deferred charges		388,960
Total Current Assets.		$22,651,072

Fixed Assets:

Land, buildings, and equipment. . . .	$26,945,848	
Less: Accumulated depreciation. . . .	13,534,069	13,411,779

Other Assets:

Investments	$ 110,000	
Goodwill.	63,214	173,214
Total Assets.		$36,236,065

EQUITIES

Current Liabilities:

Accounts payable.		$ 6,601,442
Estimated tax liability		1,672,000
Accrued expenses payable.		640,407
Deferred income		205,240
Total Current Liabilities		$ 9,119,089

Other Liabilities:

Mortgage bonds payable.		3,000,000

Stockholders' Equity:

Common stock.	$15,000,000	
Retained earnings	9,116,976	24,116,976
Total Equities.		$36,236,065

above. The figures are *expressed in money* and reflect only those matters that can be measured in money amounts. The *business entity* involved is the Garsden Corporation, and the balance sheet pertains to that entity rather than to any of the individuals associated with the company. The statement assumes that the Garsden Corporation is a *going concern*. The asset amounts stated are governed by the *cost concept*. The *dual-aspect* concept is evident from the fact that the assets listed on one side of this balance sheet are equal in total to the equities, or claims against the assets, listed on the other side.

Incidentally, the practice of listing assets on the left-hand side and equities on the right-hand side of the balance sheet is common in the United States. An alternative practice of listing assets at the top of the page with equities underneath them is also common. The former format is called the *account* form, and the latter is called the *report* form of balance sheet. In certain other countries, assets are listed on the right-hand side and equities on the left-hand side. None of these differences have any real significance.[5]

It should be emphasized that the fact that the two sides add up to the same total necessarily follows from the dual-aspect concept; it does not tell anything about the company's financial condition. This equality of the two sides of the balance sheet is always found unless a clerical error has been made.

Since the term *balance* sheet may give the erroneous impression that there is something good or something significant about this balance or equality of the totals, the Accounting Principles Board recommends that this term be replaced by "statement of financial position" or "position statement." Many companies comply with this recommendation in their published reports, but the term "balance sheet" is still so widely used in ordinary business conversation that it is retained here.

Note also that the amounts are rounded to dollars. Pennies are eliminated in many published statements. In reports prepared for internal purposes, the amounts may be rounded even further, to thousands of dollars, or in large corporations to millions of dollars, so as to highlight the important figures.

Account Categories

Although each individual asset or equity—each building, each piece of equipment, each bank loan, etc.—could theoretically be listed separately

---

[5] Most of the balance sheets in this book are given in the report form for the simple reason that this fits better on a printed page. Most balance sheets typed on regular 8½ × 11 paper are in the report form for the same reason. In published annual reports, the balance sheet is often in the account form, since this makes an attractive two-page spread.

on the balance sheet, it is more practicable and more informative to summarize and group related items into categories or *account classifications*. There is no fixed pattern as to the number of such categories or the amount of detail reported; rather, the format is governed by the accountant's opinion as to the most informative way of presenting significant facts about the status of the business.

As in any classification scheme, the categories are defined in such a way that (1) the individual items included in a category resemble one another in some essential and significant respect, and (2) the items in one category are essentially different from those in all other categories. Although the items included in a category are similar to one another, they are not identical.

> EXAMPLE: The category labeled "Cash" usually includes money on deposit at savings banks as well as money on deposit in commercial banks. These two types of money are *similar* in that they both are in highly liquid form, but they are *not identical* because certain restrictions may apply to withdrawals from savings banks that do not apply to withdrawals from commercial banks. If an accountant thought this difference was important enough to report, he would set up two separate categories. This would, however, increase the amount of detail shown on the balance sheet.

The balance sheet in Illustration 2–1 gives a minimum amount of detail. The terms used on this balance sheet are common ones, and they are described briefly below.

Assets

We shall now supersede the short definition of "asset" given in the preceding section by the following more exact statement: *Assets are valuable resources owned by a business which were acquired at a measurable money cost.* The three key points in this definition are the following: (1) the resource must be valuable; (2) the resource must be owned; and (3) the resource must be acquired at a measurable money cost.

A resource is *valuable* either if it is cash or an item that probably will be converted into cash, or if it is expected to benefit the future operation of the business. In some cases the presumed benefit for the future is rather nebulous and debatable; for example, some accountants regard the cost of organizing a corporation as an asset on the grounds that the corporate form of organization is valuable to the business, but others do not.

> EXAMPLE: Amounts due from customers are assets, to the extent that customers are likely to pay their bills. The protection promised by an insurance policy is an asset, since the insurance provides a valuable protection against losses from future misfortunes. Merchandise that,

because of damage or obsolescence, cannot be sold is not an asset, even though it is owned by the business.

Ownership is a legal concept which is to be distinguished from possession or control. The accounting concept is close to, but not exactly the same as, the legal concept. Thus, when a business buys an automobile on the installment plan, the business may not own the car, in the legal sense, until the last installment has been paid; nevertheless, the automobile is regarded as substantially owned by the business and is shown as an asset. But possession or control, without substantial ownership, is not enough to qualify the item as an asset.

> EXAMPLE: A leased piece of equipment is not an asset of the lessee even though it is in his possession and he has complete control over its use. Goods on consignment are assets of the consignor who owns them, not of the consignee who has possession of them.

The *acquisition at a measurable money cost* test is usually clear-cut, but in some instances is difficult to apply. If the resource was purchased for cash or for the promise to pay cash, it is an asset. If the resource was manufactured by the business, then money was paid for the costs of manufacture, and it is an asset. If the resource was acquired by trading in some other asset or by issuing stock, then the item is an asset, although there may be problems in measuring its amount because of the difficulty in valuing the traded-in item or the stock. Ordinarily, the solution to this problem is to determine what the asset would have cost had cash been paid for it; but when no objective evidence of this amount can be found, the best possible estimate is made from whatever information is available. On the other hand, as already pointed out (p. 30), a valuable reputation or an efficient organization is not an asset if it arose gradually over a period of time, rather than being acquired at a specifically measurable cost.

> EXAMPLE: Both "Seagrams" and "Schenley" are valuable trade names. Nevertheless, the December 31, 1967, balance sheet for Joseph C. Seagrams and Sons shows a zero amount for this item, whereas the December 31, 1967, balance sheet for Schenley Industries shows $18,595,000 for "Brands, Trademarks, and Goodwill."

Assets are recorded at their total cost, not the company's "equity" in them.

> EXAMPLE: If a business buys land for $100,000, pays $30,000 cash, and gives a $70,000 mortgage, the asset is recorded at $100,000, not $30,000.

On most business balance sheets, assets are listed in order of their liquidity; that is, in order of the promptness with which they are expected to be converted into cash. On some balance sheets, notably those of public utilities, the order is reversed, and the least liquid assets are listed first.

Assets are customarily grouped into categories. Current assets are almost always reported in a separate category. All noncurrent assets may be grouped together, or various groupings may be used, such as "Fixed Assets" and "Other Assets" as shown on the Garsden Corporation balance sheet.

Current Assets

"The term *current assets* is used to designate cash and other assets or resources commonly identified as those which are reasonably expected to be realized in cash or sold or consumed during the normal operating cycle of the business."[6]

The distinction between current assets and noncurrent assets is important since much attention is given by lenders and others to the total of current assets. The essence of the distinction is *time*. Current assets are those that will be owned only for a short period of time, usually not more than a year from the balance sheet date, whereas noncurrent assets are those that are expected to be owned for a longer period of time.

Although the usual time limit is one year, exceptions occur in companies whose normal operating cycle is longer than one year. Tobacco companies and distilleries, for example, include their inventories as current assets even though tobacco and liquor remain in inventory for an aging process that lasts two years or more.

Cash consists of funds that are immediately available for disbursement without restriction. Usually, most of these funds are on deposit in checking accounts in banks, and the remainder are in cash registers or other temporary storage facilities on the company's premises.

Marketable securities are investments which are both readily marketable and which are expected to be converted into cash within a year. They are investments made so as to earn some return on cash that otherwise would be temporarily idle. According to generally accepted accounting principles, marketable securities are reported on the balance sheet at their cost or their current market value, whichever is lower, unless the decline in market value is believed to be only temporary. When reported at cost, a parenthetical note of the current market value is customarily given. Many insurance companies, banks, investment companies, and other financial institutions report marketable securities at market value.

Accounts receivable are amounts owed to the company, usually by its customers. Sometimes this item is broken down into *trade* accounts receivable and *other* accounts receivable; the former refers to amounts owed by customers, and the latter refers to amounts owed by employees and others.

---

[6] *Accounting Research Bulletin No. 43*, in Grady, *op. cit.*, p. 234.

Accounts receivable are reported on the balance sheet at the amount owed less an allowance for that portion which probably will not be collected. Methods of estimating this "allowance for doubtful accounts" are described on page 122.

If the amount owed is evidenced by a note or some other written acknowledgment of the obligation, it would ordinarily appear under the heading *notes receivable* rather than accounts receivable.

As defined by the Accounting Principles Board, the term *inventory* means "the aggregate of those items of tangible personal property which (1) are held for sale in the ordinary course of business, (2) are in process of production for such sales, or (3) are to be currently consumed in the production of goods or services to be available for sale."[7] Inventory is reported at the lower of its cost or its current market value.

The item *prepaid expenses and deferred charges* represents certain assets, usually of an intangible nature, whose usefulness will expire in the near future. An example is an insurance policy. A business pays for insurance protection in advance, often for a three-year or a five-year period. Its right to this protection is an asset—a valuable, owned resource —but this right will expire within a fairly short period of time.

Prepaid expenses and deferred charges are reported at the cost of the unexpired service. Thus, if a business has purchased insurance protection for a three-year period, paying $1,200, and one year has expired as of the balance sheet date, the asset is reported at two thirds of its cost, or $800, representing the cost of the protection for the next two years.

The distinction between "prepaid expenses" and "deferred charges" is not important. In some businesses, prepaid expenses and deferred charges are shown, not as current assets, but rather as "other assets" near the bottom of the balance sheet.

Fixed Assets

Fixed assets are tangible, relatively long-lived resources. The business has acquired these assets, ordinarily, in order to use them in the production of other goods and services. If the assets are held for resale they are classified as inventory, even though they are long-lived assets. In the balance sheet shown in Illustration 2–1 fixed assets are lumped together into the single item "land, buildings, and equipment," but in the balance sheets of many companies the figures for land, for buildings, and for various kinds of machinery and equipment are shown separately. In accordance with the cost concept, the figure $26,945,848 on the Garsden Corporation balance sheet represents the cost of these assets to the company at the time they were purchased. The next item, "accumulated

---

[7] *Ibid.*, p. 244.

depreciation," means that a portion of the original cost amounting to $13,534,069 has been already allocated as a cost of doing business, as will be described in Chapter 6.

Other Assets

Investments are securities of one company owned by another for reasons other than the temporary use of excess cash. They are therefore to be distinguished from "marketable securities," which is an item in the current asset section of the balance sheet. A company acquires such securities either to control another company or in the anticipation of earning a return from them. Investments are ordinarily reported at cost.

Intangible assets include goodwill (which was described briefly earlier in this chapter), patents, copyrights, leases, licenses, franchises, and similar valuable but nonphysical things owned by the business. They are distinguished from prepaid expenses, which are intangible current assets, in that they have a longer life-span than prepaid expenses.

Liabilities

Liabilities are the claims of outsiders against the business, or, to put it another way, the amounts that the business owes to persons other than the owners. Unless otherwise noted, all the liabilities shown on the balance sheet are claims against all the assets; ordinarily they are not claims against any *specific* asset or group of assets. Thus, although accounts payable typically arise through the purchase of material for inventory, accounts payable are claims against all the assets, not merely against inventories.

Even if a liability is a claim against a specific asset, it is shown separately on the right-hand side of the balance sheet, rather than as a deduction from the asset amount to which it relates.

> EXAMPLE: If land is purchased for $100,000, and a $70,000 mortgage is given, secured by the land, the balance sheet reports land at $100,000 on the asset side, and the mortgage payable of $70,000 on the equities side, *not*—

$$
\begin{array}{lr}
\text{Land} & \$100,000 \\
\text{Less: Mortgage} & 70,000 \\
\text{Net Amount} & \$\ 30,000 \\
\end{array}
$$

Liabilities are reported at the amount owed as of the balance sheet date, including interest accumulated to that date. Interest that will be owed subsequent to the balance sheet date is excluded. Note that it is the amount *owed* that governs, not the amount *payable* as of the balance sheet date. A loan is a liability even though it is not required to be repaid for another 10 years.

Current Liabilities

In brief, current liabilities are obligations which become due in the near future, usually within the next year, except for those obligations which are expected to be met by the incurrence of a noncurrent liability (as in the case of a maturing bond issue which is to be refunded). The Accounting Principles Board gives a more detailed definition, as follows:

The term *current liabilities* is used principally to designate obligations whose liquidation is reasonably expected to require the use of existing resources properly classifiable as current assets, or the creation of other current liabilities. As a balance-sheet category, the classification is intended to include obligations for items which have entered into the operating cycle, such as payables incurred in the acquisition of materials and supplies to be used in the production of goods or in providing services to be offered for sale; collections received in advance of the delivery of goods or performance of services; and debts which arise from operations directly related to the operating cycle, such as accruals for wages, salaries, commissions, rentals, royalties, and income and other taxes. Other liabilities whose regular and ordinary liquidation is expected to occur within a relatively short period of time, usually 12 months, are also intended for inclusion, such as short-term debts arising from the acquisition of capital assets, serial maturities of long-term obligations, amounts required to be expended within one year under sinking fund provisions, and agency obligations arising from the collection or acceptance of cash or other assets for the account of third persons.[8]

Accounts payable represent the claims of vendors and others. Usually these claims are unsecured. If the claim was evidenced by a note or some other written acknowledgment of debt, the item would be called *notes payable, bank drafts payable*, or some other term that describes the nature of the obligation.

Estimated tax liability is the amount owed the government for taxes. It is shown separately from other obligations both because of its size and because the amount owed is not precisely known as of the date of the balance sheet. Often, the liability for federal and state income taxes is shown separately from other tax liabilities.

Accrued expenses are the converse of prepaid expenses. They represent certain obligations which are indeed valid claims against the assets but which are "intangible" in the sense that they are not evidenced by an invoice or other document submitted by the person to whom the money is owed. An example is the wages and salaries owed to employees for work they have performed but for which they have not been reimbursed.

Deferred income represents the liability that arises because the com-

---

[8] *Ibid.,* p. 277.

pany has received advance payment for a service it has agreed to render in the future. An example is precollected rent, which represents rental payments received in advance for which the company agrees to permit the tenant to use a specified building (or other property) during some future period.

Other Liabilities

Other liabilities are claims of outsiders that do not fall due within one year. Evidently the mortgage bonds of the Garsden Corporation do not mature within the next year, nor do any fraction of them; otherwise all or part of this liability would appear as a current liability (unless, as stated above, it is planned to refund them).

Owners' Equity

The *owners' equity* section of the balance sheet shows the claims of the owners, in this case the shareholders. The terminology used in this section of the balance sheet varies with different forms of organization.

In a corporation, the claims of the owners are evidenced by documents called *stock certificates.* The first item in the shareholders' equity section of the Garsden Corporation balance sheet is the "stated value" of this stock. This may be the par value of the stock, or the price at which it was sold, or some other figure fixed by the board of directors. In the interest of consistency, once the basis of stating each share of stock has been determined, it is rarely changed.

The owners' equity increases through *earnings* (i.e., the results of profitable operations) and decreases when earnings are paid out in the form of dividends. The difference between the total earnings to date and the total amount of dividends to date is *retained earnings;* that is, that part of the total earnings which have been retained for use in the business.[9] If the difference is negative, the item is labeled *deficit.*

The term "surplus" was formerly used instead of "retained earnings," and is still used by some companies. The word "surplus" is apt to be misleading, since to the uninitiated "surplus" represents something tangible, something "left over." There is, in fact, nothing tangible about retained earnings. All the tangible things owned by the business appear on the assets side of the balance sheet. It is because of this misleading connotation that use of this word is no longer recommended. The word "surplus" is sometimes used with appropriate modifiers (capital surplus,

---

[9] Shareholders' equity is also affected by events other than the accumulation of earnings and the withdrawal of these earnings. Examples are the sale of stock at a premium or a discount, the revaluation of stock, and the creation of special reserves. Some of these events will be discussed in Chapter 8.

paid-in surplus, etc.) for certain special items that will be described in Chapter 8.

The term "net worth" is another obsolete term that should be noted. It was formerly used as a synonym for owners' equity, but is being abandoned because of the connotation that the amount states what the owners' interest is "worth," in the ordinary sense of this word. Such a connotation is completely erroneous.

In unincorporated businesses, different terminology is used in the owners' equity section. In a *proprietorship*, which is a business owned by one person, it is customary to show the owner's equity as a single figure, with a title such as "John Jones, capital," rather than making a distinction between the owner's initial investment and the accumulated earnings retained in the business.

In a *partnership*, which is an unincorporated business owned jointly by several persons, there is a capital account for each partner, thus:

```
James Smith, capital. . . . . . . . $15,432
John Smith, capital . . . . . . . .  15,432
       Total Partners' Equity. . . . . $30,864
```

In addition to these basic owners' equity items, a proprietorship or a partnership may, for convenience, use a temporary item called a *drawing account* in which amounts withdrawn from the business by the owner(s) are recorded. Periodically, the total accumulated in the drawing account is subtracted from the capital item, leaving the net equity of the owner(s). For example, a balance sheet might show the following:

```
John Jones, capital . . . . .  $25,000
   Less: Drawings. . . . . . .    2,400
     Net Proprietorship Equity          $22,600
```

After the two items have been combined, the balance sheet would read simply:

```
John Jones, capital . . . . .  $22,600
```

The reader may have heard of the terms "partnership accounting" and "corporation accounting," and from these he may have formed the impression that different accounting systems are used for different forms of business organization. As a matter of fact, the treatment of assets and liabilities is generally the same in all forms of organization; differences occur principally in the owners' equity section as noted above.

BALANCE SHEET CHANGES

At the moment a business starts, its financial status can be recorded on a balance sheet. From that time on, events occur that change the figures on this first balance sheet, and the accountant records these changes in accordance with the concepts given above. Full-fledged accounting systems provide a means of accumulating and summarizing these changes and of preparing new balance sheets at prescribed intervals.

In learning the accounting process, however, it is useful to consider the changes one by one. This makes it possible to study the effect of individual events without getting entangled with the mechanisms used in practice to record these events. The technical name given to an event that affects an accounting figure is *transaction*. An example of the effect of a few transactions on the balance sheet will now be given. For simplicity, they are assumed to occur on successive days.

Jan. 1. John Smith starts a business, called Glendale Market, by depositing $10,000 of his own funds in a bank account which he has opened in the name of the store. The balance sheet of Glendale Market will then be as follows:

GLENDALE MARKET

Balance Sheet as of January 1

ASSETS		EQUITIES	
Cash.	$10,000	John Smith, capital. . . .	$10,000

Jan. 2. The business borrows $5,000 from a bank giving a note therefor. This transaction increases the asset "cash," and the business incurs a liability to the bank. The balance sheet after this transaction will appear as follows:

GLENDALE MARKET

Balance Sheet as of January 2

ASSETS		EQUITIES	
Cash.	$15,000	Notes payable, bank. . . .	$ 5,000
		John Smith, capital. . . .	10,000
Total	$15,000	Total.	$15,000

Jan. 3. The business buys inventory in the amount of $2,000, paying cash. The balance sheet is as follows:

GLENDALE MARKET

Balance Sheet as of January 3

ASSETS		EQUITIES	
Cash.	$13,000	Notes payable, bank. . . .	$ 5,000
Inventory	2,000	John Smith, capital. . . .	10,000
Total	$15,000	Total.	$15,000

Jan. 4. The store sells, for $300 cash, merchandise that cost $200. The effect of this transaction is that inventory has been decreased by $200, cash has been increased by $300, and John Smith's own equity has been increased by the difference, or $100. The $100 is the profit on this sale. The balance sheet will then look like this:

GLENDALE MARKET

Balance Sheet as of January 4

ASSETS		EQUITIES	
Cash.	$13,300	Notes payable, bank. . . .	$ 5,000
Inventory	1,800	John Smith, capital. . . .	10,100
Total	$15,100	Total.	$15,100

These illustrations could be extended indefinitely. As we delve more deeply into the mechanics of accounting, it is worth remembering that every accounting transaction can be recorded in terms of its effect on the balance sheet.

AN OVERALL VIEW OF THE BALANCE SHEET

We have described the balance sheet as a list of assets and of claims against those assets. This is one useful way of thinking about it, especially when trying to decide how to record the effect of a specific transaction. In trying to understand the picture of a business that the balance sheet conveys, it is often useful to use a different, but equally correct, description, as given in the following paragraphs.

The right-hand side of the balance sheet may be viewed as a description of the sources from which the business has obtained the capital with which it currently operates, and the left-hand side as a description of the form in which that capital is invested on a specified date. On the right-hand side of the balance sheet, the several liability items describe how much capital was obtained from trade creditors (accounts payable), from banks (notes payable), from bondholders (bonds payable), and other outside parties. The owners' equity section shows the capital supplied by the shareholders. If the business is a corporation, the shareholders' contribution consists of two principal parts: capital directly supplied (capital stock) and capital which the shareholders provided by permitting earnings to remain in the business (retained earnings).

Capital obtained from various sources has been invested according to the management's best judgment of the optimum mix, or combination, of assets for the business. A certain fraction is invested in buildings, another fraction in inventory, another fraction is retained as cash for current needs of the business, and so on. The asset side of the balance sheet therefore shows the result of these management judgments as of the date of the balance sheet.

When the balance sheet is viewed in this way, some of the apparent inconsistencies in accounting principles and definitions described above may be resolved. Considering assets as items in which capital has been invested makes it reasonable to record assets at their cost rather than at market value, for the cost basis shows the amount of capital tied up in each asset category. Furthermore, a description of retained earnings as one source of capital—the accumulated earnings of past periods not paid out as dividends—is probably easier to understand than a description of retained earnings as someone's "claim" against the business; it is difficult to see how earnings can be a "claim" against anything.

In any event, either one of these approaches to the balance sheet is at best only a brief introduction to the balance sheet idea. Real comprehension comes through constructing and using balance sheets in practical business situations.

SUMMARY OF BASIC CONCEPTS

The basic concepts discussed in this chapter may be briefly summarized as follows:

1. Money Measurement. Accounting records only facts that can be expressed in monetary terms.

2. Business Entity. Accounts are kept for business entities as distinguished from the person(s) associated with those entities.

3. Going Concern. Accounting assumes that a business will continue indefinitely and that it is not about to be sold.

4. Cost. Assets are ordinarily entered on the accounting records at the price paid to acquire them, and this cost, rather than market value, is the basis for subsequent accounting for the asset.

5. Dual Aspect. The amount of assets equals the amount of equities.

6. Conservatism. An asset is recorded at the lower of two reasonably possible values, or an event is recorded in such a way that the owners' equity is lower than it otherwise would be.

SUGGESTIONS FOR FURTHER READING ON ACCOUNTING PRINCIPLES

(For Chapters 2–10)

There are several excellent textbooks, any of which may be useful either for additional information or to obtain a different viewpoint on topics discussed here.

Eric L. Kohler. *A Dictionary for Accountants.* 3d ed.; Englewood Cliffs, N.J.: Prentice-Hall, Inc., 1963. Much more than a dictionary, it contains a good discussion of many terms and concepts, and because of its dictionary format provides a quick way of locating desired information.

RUFUS WIXON (ed.). *Accountants' Handbook.* 4th ed.; New York: Ronald Press Co., 1966. A standard source for detailed information.

NORMAN J. LENHART and PHILIP L. DEFLIESE. *Montgomery's Auditing.* 8th ed.; New York: Ronald Press Co., 1957. Contains accounting principles arranged so they are easy to find.

Publications of the AICPA, AMERICAN ACCOUNTING ASSOCIATION, and U.S. SECURITIES AND EXCHANGE COMMISSION, referred to in the text, are important sources of the latest information on what constitutes "generally accepted accounting principles." *APB Accounting Principles,* published by Commerce Clearing House, Inc., contains all pronouncements of the Accounting Principles Board of the AICPA. In Volume 1, these are classified by topics, and in Volume 2 they are reproduced chronologically. *A Statement of Basic Accounting Theory,* American Accounting Association, 1966, gives the standards proposed by that organization. *Accounting Trends and Techniques,* published annually by the American Institute of Certified Public Accountants, gives detailed information on the accounting practices of 600 leading corporations as revealed in their annual reports.

CASES

CASE 2–1. PROBLEM IN BALANCE SHEET CONSTRUCTION

As of December 31, 1968, the accounts of the Fintley Corporation showed the following balances (000 omitted):

Accounts payable.................................$	131
Accounts receivable..............................	526
Accrued expenses................................	243
Accumulated depreciation on plant and equipment.....	840
Bank notes payable..............................	5
Bonds payable..................................	300
Capital stock...................................	438
Cash...	69
Deferred income (progress payments from customers)...	229
Dividends payable...............................	43
Estimated tax liability...........................	254
Inventories.....................................	610
Investments in other companies....................	157
Marketable securities............................	409
Other assets....................................	169
Other liabilities................................	131
Plant and equipment (at original cost)..............	1,553
Retained earnings...............................	879

Question

1. Prepare a balance sheet as of this date, in proper form.

CASE 2–2. PROBLEM IN BALANCE SHEET CHANGES

On a sheet of paper, set up in pencil the balance sheet of Glendale Market as it appears after the last transaction described in the text, page 44, leaving considerable space between each item. Record the effects, if any, of the following happenings on the balance sheet, either by revising existing figures (cross out, rather than erase) or by adding new items as necessary. At least one of these happenings does not affect the balance sheet. The basic equation, Assets = Equities, must be preserved at all

48

times. Errors will be minimized if you make a separate list of the balance sheet items affected by each transaction and the amount (+ or −) by which each is to be changed.

After you have finished recording these happenings, prepare a balance sheet in proper form.

1. The store purchased and received merchandise for $2,000, agreeing to pay within 30 days.
2. Merchandise costing $500 was sold for $800, which was received in cash.
3. Merchandise costing $600 was sold for $900, the customer agreeing to pay $900 within 30 days.
4. The store purchased a three-year fire insurance policy for $200, paying cash.
5. The store purchased two lots of land of equal size for a total of $10,000. It paid $2,000 in cash and gave a 10-year mortgage for $8,000.
6. The store sold one of the two lots of land for $5,000. It received $1,000 cash, and in addition, the buyer assumed $4,000 of the mortgage; that is, Glendale Market became no longer responsible for this half.
7. Smith received a bona fide offer of $15,000 for the business, and although his equity was then only $10,700, he rejected the offer. It was evident that the store had already acquired goodwill of $4,300.
8. Smith withdrew $500 cash from the store's bank account for his personal use.
9. Smith took merchandise costing $400 from the store's inventory for his personal use.
10. Smith learned that the man who purchased the land (No. 6 above) subsequently sold it for $8,000. The lot still owned by Glendale Market was identical in value with this other plot.
11. The store paid off $2,000 of its bank loan (disregard interest).
12. Glendale Market was changed to a corporation, Glendale Market, Inc. Smith received common stock with a par value of $9,800 in exchange for his equity in the store. (Disregard costs of organizing the corporation. Note that this event changes the title of the balance sheet.)
13. Smith sold one fourth of the stock he owned in Glendale Market, Inc., for $3,000 cash.

CASE 2–3. SMOKY VALLEY CAFE[10]

On August 12, 1946, three people who had previously been employed to wait on tables in one of the cafes in Baxter, Oregon, formed a partnership. The eldest of the three was Mrs. Bevan, a middle-aged widow. The other two were Mr. and Mrs. Elmer Maywood. The partnership lasted for slightly more than four months, and in connection with its dissolution the preparation of a balance sheet became necessary.

---

[10] Based on a case argued before the Supreme Court of the State of Oregon, March 28, 1950. See 216 P2d 1005.

Each of the partners contributed $2,000 cash, a total of $6,000. On August 12, the partnership purchased the Smoky Valley Cafe for $16,000. The purchase price included land valued at $2,500, improvements to land at $2,000, buildings at $10,500, and cafe equipment at $1,000. The partnership made a down payment of $4,500 (from its $6,000 cash) and signed a mortgage for the balance of the $16,000. The doors of the cafe were opened for business shortly after August 12.

One of the things that made this particular piece of property attractive to them was the fact that the building contained suitable living accommodations. One of these rooms was occupied by Mrs. Bevan, another by the Maywoods.

The Maywoods and Mrs. Bevan agreed that Mrs. Bevan would operate the kitchen, Mrs. Maywood would have charge of the dining room, and Mr. Maywood would attend the bar. Mrs. Bevan agreed to keep the accounting records. She was willing to perform this task because she was vitally interested in making the business a success. She had invested the proceeds from the sale of her modest home and from her husband's insurance policy in the venture. If it failed, the major part of her financial resources would be lost.

A beer license was granted by the state authorities. On August 15, the partnership sent a check for $35 to the distributor who supplied beer. This $35 constituted a deposit on bottles and kegs necessary for the operation of the bar and would be returned to the Smoky Valley Cafe after all bottles and kegs had been returned to the beer distributor.

In October, the partners decided that to continue to offer their patrons quality food, they would have to add to their equipment. This new equipment cost $415.95, and because the supplier of the equipment was unimpressed with the firm's credit rating, the equipment was paid for in cash.

The month of November did not improve the cash position of the business. In fact, the cash balance became so low that Mrs. Bevan contributed additional cash in the amount of $400 to the business. She had hopes, however, that the future would prove to be more profitable.

The Smoky Valley Cafe was located on a major highway, and a great deal of business was obtained from truck drivers. One of these truck driver patrons, Fred Mead, became a frequent customer. He soon gained the friendship of Mrs. Maywood. On the night of December 12, Fred Mead stopped in the cafe. Shortly after he left, Mrs. Maywood retired to her room. A few hours later, Mr. Maywood came in and asked for her, and after a brief search discovered that she had departed through a window. Her absence led him to the conclusion that she had departed with Fred Mead, and he thereupon set out in pursuit of the pair.

On December 16, Mrs. Bevan decided that the partnership was dissolved because she had not heard any word from either of the Maywoods.

(The courts subsequently affirmed that the partnership was dissolved as of December 16, 1946.) Although she had no intention of ceasing operations, she realized that an accounting would have to be made as of December 16. She called in Mr. Bailey, a local accountant, for this purpose.

Mrs. Bevan told Mr. Bailey that they had been able to pay $700 on the mortgage while the partnership was operating. Cash on hand amounted to $65.35, but the bank balance was only $9.78. Mr. Bailey found bills owed by the cafe totaling $92.01. Mrs. Bevan said that her best estimate was that there was $100 worth of food on hand.

Mr. Bailey estimated that a reasonable allowance for depreciation on the fixed assets was as follows:

Assets	*Depreciation Allowance*
Land improvements............	$ 44.45
Buildings.....................	233.45
Cafe equipment..............	44.19

Questions

1. Draw up a balance sheet for the Smoky Valley Cafe as of August 12, 1946, taking into account the events described in the first two paragraphs of the case.
2. Draw up a balance sheet as of December 16, 1946.
3. What were the equities of the Maywoods and Mrs. Bevan, respectively? (In partnership law, the partners share equally in profits and losses unless there is a specific provision to the contrary. Each partner in the Smoky Valley Cafe, therefore, would have an equity in one third of the profits, or his equity would be decreased by one third of the losses.)
4. Do you suppose that the partners received these amounts? Why?

CHAPTER 3

BASIC ACCOUNTING CONCEPTS: THE INCOME STATEMENT

Owners invest money in a business in the expectation of earning a return on that money. In the terminology of the preceding chapter, they expect that owners' equity will increase. The increase in owners' equity resulting from operation of the business over a specified period of time is called *income* or *profit*. Owners, and indeed all parties interested in the business, have a keen interest in how much profit has been earned and in an explanation of how it was earned. The accounting statement that conveys this information is called the *income statement*. The income statement and the concepts governing its preparation are discussed in this chapter.

In the course of this discussion, the last four of the ten basic concepts listed in Chapter 2 are explained, namely:

7. The accrual concept   8. The realization concept
9. The consistency concept   10. The materiality concept

THE ACCOUNTING PERIOD

It is relatively easy to measure income for the whole life of a business. This is simply the difference between the money that comes in and the money that goes out (excluding, of course, money invested by the owners or paid to the owners).

EXAMPLE: John Wainwright operated a boys' camp for one summer, renting all the necessary facilities and equipment. Before the camp opened, he invested $1,000 of his own money for food, the initial rental payment, and certain other costs. At the end of the summer, after all affairs were wound up, he had his $1,000 back and $2,179 additional. This $2,179 was the income of the camp business. It was the difference

52

between the fees he received from parents and the money he paid out for food, wages, and other costs. The income statement for the business would look like this:

Campers' fees............................		$21,400
Less costs:		
Food...............................	$6,252	
Wages..............................	8,645	
Rental..............................	2,500	
Other costs.........................	824	
Total costs............................		18,221
Income............................		$ 2,179

Over the whole life of any business, income is as simple to determine as it was for the summer camp; that is, it is the difference between the money the owners get out of the business and the money they put into it.

Relatively few business ventures have a life of only a few months, as was the case with John Wainwright's summer camp. Most of them operate for many years. For these businesses, management and other interested parties are unwilling to wait until the business has terminated before obtaining information on how much income has been earned. They need to know at frequent intervals "how things are going." Therefore, accountants choose some convenient segment of time and they measure the income for that period of time. The time interval chosen is called the *accounting period.*

For the purpose of reporting to outsiders, the year is the usual accounting period. Pacioli, the first author of an accounting text, wrote in 1494: "Books should be closed each year, especially in a partnership, because frequent accounting makes for long friendship."[1] Most corporate bylaws require an annual report to the shareholders, and income tax reporting is also on an annual basis.

Formerly, the accounting year, or *fiscal* year, corresponded to the calendar year, but an increasing number of businesses are finding that there are advantages in using the *natural business year* instead of the calendar year. For example, nearly all department stores end their fiscal year on January 31, after the Christmas rush and its repercussions in the form of returns and clearance sales.

Management invariably needs information oftener than once a year, and reports for management are therefore prepared more frequently. The most common period is a month, but the period may be as short as a week or even a day. These reports are called *interim* reports to distinguish them from the annual reports.

Businesses are living, continuing organisms. The act of chopping the stream of business events into time periods is therefore somewhat arbi-

---

[1] Lucas Pacioli, *Summa de Arithmetica Geometria Proportioni et Proportionalita,* from the translation by John B. Geijsbeck.

trary since business activities do not stop or change measurably as one accounting period ends and another begins. It is this fact that makes the problem of measuring income in an accounting period the most difficult problem in accounting.

> EXAMPLE: If, instead of a summer camp, John Wainwright operated a year-round hotel, his income for a year could not be measured as simply the difference between the money taken in and the money paid out. As of the end of the year, some of his guests would not have paid their bills, but these unpaid bills are an asset, accounts receivable, which surely increase the "well-offness" of the business, even though the cash has not yet been remitted. Conversely, some of the cash paid out may have been for the purchase of an asset, such as the hotel itself, and this asset still has value at the end of the accounting period; it would be incorrect to conclude that his income has been decreased by the amount of such payments.

In sorting out the transactions occurring during an accounting period so as to measure the income of that period, the basic guides are the accrual concept and the realization concept.

THE ACCRUAL CONCEPT

The essence of the accrual concept is that income is measured by operating transactions that affect owners' equity, and only by such transactions.

Let us refer back to the January 4 transaction of Glendale Market (p. 45). On that day, merchandise costing $200 was sold for $300 cash Looking first at the effect of this transaction on assets, we note that although inventory decreased by $200, cash increased by $300, so that the total assets increased by the difference, $100. From the dual-aspect concept, which states that the total of the assets must always equal the total of the equities, we know that the equities side of the balance sheet must also have increased by $100. Since no liabilities were affected, the increase must have occurred in the owner's equity item. In summary, because assets were sold for more than was paid for them, the owner's equity increased. Such increases in owner's equity are called income. In understanding how this income came about, it is useful to consider two aspects of this event separately: the $300 received from the sale, and the $200 decrease in inventory. If we look only at the $300, we see that it is an increase in cash, and a corresponding *increase* in the owner's equity. The $200, taken by itself, is a decrease in the asset, inventory, and a corresponding *decrease* in the owner's equity. These two aspects illustrate the only two ways in which business operations can affect owner's equity: they can increase it, or they can decrease it.

Any increase in owners' equity resulting from the operation of the business is called a *revenue*. Any decrease is called an *expense*. Income is therefore the excess of revenues over expenses. (If expenses exceed revenue, the difference is called a *loss*.) Restating the transactions described above in these terms, there was revenue of $300, expense of $200, and income of $100.

As an aside, it should be noted that the word *income* is often, but erroneously, used where *revenue* is intended. This is because the approved definitions are of relatively recent vintage and some companies have not kept up with the latest developments. For example, Western Electric Company, Incorporated, reported "gross income" in 1967 of $3,733,906,000; the term should have been "revenue." In this situation, the intended meaning was obvious, since no company has income of $3 billion; but in other situations, the misuse of the term "income" causes confusion. For example, if someone says Company X had an income of a million dollars, he gives a completely false impression of the size of the company if he actually meant that Company X had *revenues* of a million dollars.[2]

It is extremely important to recognize that income is associated with changes in owners' equity, and that it has no necessary relation to changes in cash. Income connotes "well-offness." Roughly speaking the bigger the income, the better off are the owners. An increase in cash, however, does not necessarily mean that the owners are any better off—that their equity has increased. The increase in cash may merely be offset by a decrease in some other asset or an increase in a liability, with no effect on owners' equity at all.

Again, reference to the transactions of Glendale Market may help clarify this point. When Glendale Market borrowed $5,000 from the bank on January 2 (p. 44), its cash was increased, but this was exactly matched by an increase in the liability to the bank. There was no change in owner's equity since Mr. Smith, the owner, had no greater claim on the assets. No income resulted from this transaction; the $5,000 was not revenue. Similarly, the purchase of inventory for $2,000 cash on January 3 (p. 44) resulted in a decrease in cash, but there was an exactly corresponding increase in another asset, inventory, and therefore owner's equity was not changed.

As we have already seen, the sale for $300 of inventory costing $200 did result in income, but it should be noted that the income was $100, whereas cash increased by $300, so even here the income is different from the amount by which the cash changed. In short, although the typical person measures his personal income by the amount of money he receives,

---

[2] The income tax Form 1040 still contains the phrases "dividend income," "interest income," and "pension and annuity income" for items that actually are *revenues*. The government is not always quick to change its ways.

he must be careful *not* to use a similar line of reasoning when thinking about the income of a business.

MEASUREMENT OF EXPENSES

The diagram in Illustration 3–1 shows a portion of the life of a business that has been divided into annual accounting periods. For each of these accounting periods an income statement is prepared, and for each point between periods (i.e., the close of business December 31) there is a balance sheet. In this section, the measurement of expenses in "this year" will be discussed.

Expenses are the costs incurred in connection with the earning of revenue. The term "expense" connotes "sacrifices made," "the cost of services or benefits received," or "resources consumed" during an accounting period. The term "cost" is not synonymous with "expense." As just explained, *expense* means a decrease in owners' equity that arises from

Illustration 3–1

the operation of a business during a specified accounting period, whereas *cost* means any monetary sacrifice, whether or not the sacrifice affects owners' equity during a given accounting period.

The American Accounting Association Committee gives the following definition:

Expense is the expired cost, directly or indirectly related to a given fiscal period, of the flow of goods or services into the market and of related operations. . . . Recognition of cost expiration is based either on a complete or partial decline in the usefulness of assets, or on the appearance of a liability without a corresponding increase in assets.[3]

Expenses and Expenditures

An *expenditure* takes place when an asset or service is acquired. The expenditure may be made by cash, by the exchange of another asset, or by

[3] "Accounting and Reporting Standards for Corporate Financial Statements," 1957 Revision, *Accounting Review,* October 1957, p. 541.

incurring a liability. Over the entire life of a business most expenditures made by a business become expenses, and there are no expenses that are not represented by an expenditure. In any time segment *shorter* than the life of a business, however, there is no necessary correspondence between expense and expenditure.

> EXAMPLE: In 1968, $1,000 of fuel oil was purchased for cash. This was an *expenditure* of $1,000, the exchange of one asset for another. If none of this fuel oil was consumed in 1968, there was no *expense* in 1968. If the fuel oil was consumed in 1969, there was an *expense* of $1,000 in 1969.

The American Accounting Association Committee describes the recognition of expenses as follows:

> Expense is given recognition in the period in which there is (*a*) a direct identification or association with the revenue of the period, as in the case of merchandise delivered to customers; (*b*) an indirect association with the revenue of the period, as in the case of office salaries or rent; or (*c*) a measurable expiration of asset costs even though not associated with the production of revenue for the current period, as in the case of losses from flood or fire.[4]

The expenses of "this year" therefore include the cost of the products *sold* during the year, even though these products were purchased or manufactured in a prior year; the wages and salaries *earned* by employees who sold these products, whether or not they were paid during the year; and the supplies, telephone, electricity, and other assets or services *consumed* or *used* during the year in connection with the production of this revenue, whether or not the bills for these items were paid.

Four types of events need to be considered in distinguishing between amounts that are properly considered as expenses of a given accounting period, and the expenditures or cash payments made in connection with these items. Focusing on "this year" in the diagram in Illustration 3–1, these are as follows:

1. Expenditures this year that are also expenses of this year.
2. Expenditures made prior to this year that become expenses during this year. These appeared as assets on the balance sheet at the beginning of this year.
3. Expenditures made this year that will become expenses in future years. These will appear as assets on the balance sheet at the end of this year.
4. Expenses of this year that will be paid for in a future year. On the balance sheet at the end of this year, these will appear as liabilities.

---

[4] *Ibid.*, p. 541.

Expenditures That Are Also Expenses

This is the simplest type of event, and the least troublesome to account for. If an item is acquired during the year, it is an expenditure; if it is consumed during the same year, it is also an expense of the year.

Assets That Become Expenses

On January 1, the balance sheet shows certain assets. During "this year" some of these assets are used up and hence are transformed into expenses. The three principal types of such assets are described below.

First, there are *inventories* of products; these become expenses when the products are sold.

Second, there are *prepaid expenses* and *deferred charges*. These represent services or other assets purchased prior to "this year" but not yet used up when the year begins. They become expenses in the year in which the services are used or the assets are consumed. *Insurance protection* is one such item; the premium on most types of insurance policies is paid in advance, and the insurance protection bought with this premium is an asset until the accounting period in which the insurance protection is received, at which time it becomes an expense. Prepaid rent follows the same pattern, with the expense being associated with the year in which the company receives the benefit of occupying the rented premises.

> EXAMPLE: A company purchased three-year insurance protection on December 31, 1967. The $900 appears as an asset on the balance sheet of December 31, 1967. In 1968, $300 becomes an expense and $600 remains as an asset on the balance sheet of December 31, 1968. In 1969, $300 more becomes an expense, and so on.

> EXAMPLE: A company paid $10,000 to its landlord on July 1, 1968, representing an advance payment of one year's rent. Of this amount $5,000 is rent expense of 1968. On the balance sheet of December 31, 1968, $5,000 appears as an asset, and this amount becomes an expense in 1969.

Another, and somewhat different, type of prepaid expense is *prepaid taxes*. Certain taxes are paid for in advance of the accounting period to which they apply, and although it is farfetched to say that this accounting period "benefits" from the taxes, it is reasonable to charge these taxes as an expense in the accounting period, or periods, for which the tax is levied.

The third category of assets that will become expenses is *long-lived* assets. Most fixed assets (with the exception of land) have a limited useful life; that is, they do not last forever. They are purchased with the expectation that they will be used in the operation of the business in future periods, and they will become expenses in these future periods.

The principle is exactly the same as that of the insurance policy previously mentioned, which also was purchased for the benefit of future periods. An important practical difference between a fixed asset, such as a building, and an insurance policy, however, is that the life of a building is usually difficult to estimate, whereas the life of an insurance policy is known precisely. It follows that estimating the portion of a building's cost that is an expense in a given accounting period is a more difficult task than that of determining the insurance expense of a period. The mechanism used to convert the cost of fixed assets to expense is called "depreciation" and is described in Chapter 6.

Expenditures That Are Not Yet Expenses

As the preceding examples show, some expenditures made to acquire assets "this year" are not expenses of "this year" because the assets have not yet been used up. These include not only the purchase of assets as such, but also expenditures incurred in connection with the *manufacture* of products that are to be sold in some future year. Thus, wages and salaries earned by production personnel and all other costs associated with manufacturing become part of the cost of the product manufactured and remain as part of the cost of an asset, inventory, until the product is sold. The distinction between manufacturing costs, which initially are added to inventory amounts, and other costs, which are expenses of the current period, will be discussed in more detail in Chapter 7.

Expenses Not Yet Paid

Some expenses which were incurred "this year" are not paid for by the end of the year. The parties who furnished these goods or services have a claim against the business for the amounts owed them, and these amounts are therefore liabilities of the company as of December 31. The liability for wages earned but not paid for is an example that has already been mentioned. Several other types of obligations have the same characteristic; namely, that although services were rendered in an accounting period prior to that for which the balance sheet is prepared, these services have not yet been paid for. The *incurrence* of these expenses reduces owners' equity; the subsequent *payment* of the obligation does not affect owners' equity.

For all obligations of this type, the transaction involved is essentially the same: the expense is shown in the period in which the services were used, and the obligation that results from these services is shown on the liability section of the balance sheet as of the end of the period.

EXAMPLE: In 1968 an employee earned $50 that was not paid him. This is an expense of $50 in 1968, and there is a corresponding liability of $50 (called accrued wages) on the balance sheet as of December 31, 1968. In 1969, when the employee is paid, the liability disappears, and there is a corresponding reduction in cash.

Note that in these examples, the basic equality, Assets = Equities, is always maintained. The earning of wages resulted in an expense of $50, which was a decrease in owners' equity, and there was an equal increase in the liability, accrued wages, so the total of the equities was unchanged. The payment of the $50 resulted in a decrease in cash and a decrease in the liability, accured wages; that is, both assets and equities were reduced by $50.

Another common item of this type is *interest*. Interest is the cost of borrowing money, and it is an expense of the period during which the money was borrowed. Interest rates are usually stated on an annual basis. The treatment is different depending on whether the interest is paid when the loan *matures* (i.e., falls due) or whether it is paid in advance. The latter practice is called *discounting* and is customary for short-term bank loans. An example of each will be given.

> EXAMPLE: On December 1, 1968, the company borrowed $1,000 for four months at 6 percent interest, the interest and principal to be paid on March 31, 1969. The loan itself results in an increase of cash, $1,000, and creates a liability, loans payable, of $1,000. The total interest cost is $1,000 × 4/12 × 0.06 = $20. One fourth of this interest, $5, is an expense of 1968. Since it has not been paid, $5 also appears as a liability item, interest payable, on the December 31, 1968, balance sheet. The remaining $15 interest is an expense of 1969. When the loan is repaid on March 31, cash is reduced by $1,020, and this is balanced by the decrease in loans payable of $1,000, the decrease in interest payable of $5, and the interest expense for 1969 of $15.

> EXAMPLE: On December 1, 1968, the company borrowed $1,000 for four months at 6 percent discounted. The company receives $980. Interest expense for 1968 is $5, as in the preceding example, but now there is an asset, prepaid interest, of $15 on the December 31, 1968, balance sheet, representing the interest cost that will not become an expense until 1969. Thus, the following items are affected by this transaction in 1968: cash has increased by $980; there is an asset, prepaid interest, of $15; owners' equity has decreased by the applicable $5 of interest expense; and there is a liability, notes payable, of $1,000. Note that, as always, the change in assets ($980 + $15) equals the change in equities ($1,000 − $5).

Asset or Expense?

When one part of a transaction results in a decrease in cash or an increase in a liability the accountant must often answer the question: Is the other part of the transaction an increase in an asset, or is it an expense?

If it is the former, income is unaffected; if the latter, income is decreased.

One useful way of approaching this problem is to consider whether, at the end of the accounting period, the business will own something that qualifies as an asset, as this word is defined in accounting. If not, the item must be "written off," as an expense.

There are many situations in which the answer is not clear-cut, and some of these can have a substantial effect on the income reported for a period.

> EXAMPLE: Consider expenditures for research and development. It can be argued, on the one hand, that such expenditures lead to new products or processes that will add to income in future periods and therefore that such expenditures, or at least part of them, create assets. It can also be argued, on the other hand, that the connection between an expenditure for research and development and the income from the new products or processes is so tenuous that no measurable asset value has been created. Often, there is no clear-cut right or wrong answer to such problems.

MEASUREMENT OF REVENUE

Revenues are also measured in accordance with the accrual concept; that is, revenues accrue in the accounting period in which they are earned, which is not necessarily the same as the period in which the cash is received.

As was the case with expenses and expenditures, a careful distinction must be made between revenues and cash receipts. Referring back to our diagram in Illustration 3–1, the balance sheet at the end of "last year" may show, as liabilities, some items that become revenues in "this year." On that balance sheet these are called *deferred revenues* or *precollected revenues*. They represent an advance payment which creates a liability to render a service in some future period. The building owner who receives rent in advance, the insurance company which receives insurance premiums in advance, and the magazine publisher who receives subscription revenue in advance will have such liabilities on their books.

Conversely, revenue may be earned "this year" even though payment is not received until "next year." In this case, the balance sheet as of the end of "this year" will show the asset *accounts receivable* representing amounts owed to the business on account of sales made "this year" for which payment has not yet been received. The year-end balance sheet may also show the asset, *accrued revenue* (or a more descriptive term such as accrued *interest* revenue), representing amounts due the business for services rendered during the accounting period that have not been actually invoiced to the recipient. For example, interest on funds loaned by the business is revenue for the period during which the loan is outstanding, and recognition of this revenue results in corresponding recognition of the amount of interest receivable from the borrower; the latter amount is an asset.

The difference between revenue and receipts is illustrated in the following tabulation that shows various types of sales transactions and classifies the effect of each on cash receipts and sales revenue for "this year":

		This Year	
	Amount	*Cash Receipts*	*Sales Revenue*
1. Cash sales made this year................	$200	$200	$200
2. Credit sales made last year;.............			
cash received this year..................	300	300	0
3. Credit sales made this year;.............			
cash received this year..................	400	400	400
4. Credit sales made this year;.............			
cash received next year.................	100	0	100
Total.............................		$900	$700

Note that in the above illustration the total cash receipts do not equal the total sales revenue for the period. The totals would be equal in a given accounting period only (1) if the company made all its sales for cash, or (2) if the amount of cash collected from credit customers in an accounting period happened to equal the amount of credit sales made during that period.

THE REALIZATION CONCEPT

We have referred to the "earning" of revenues. A basic accounting concept is that revenue is considered as being earned on the date at which it is *realized;* that is, on the date when goods or services are furnished to the customer in exchange for cash or some other valuable consideration. For services, revenue is recognized in the period in which the service is rendered. For tangible products, revenue is recognized not when a sales order is received, not when a contract is signed, not when the goods are manufactured, but rather when the product is shipped or delivered to the customer.

There are many fine points concerning the exact date on which legal title passes from one party to the other. In general, the accountant uses the date the product was shipped or the date shown on the invoice to the customer, whichever is later.

There is a difference here between accounting and economics. In economics (and in fact), the manufacturing process is regarded as creating value, and this value includes an allowance for profit, but in financial accounting only the *costs* of manufacture are recognized as adding to the value of the product during the manufacturing cycle; all the profit (i.e., the increase in owners' equity) is recorded at the time of sale.

This difference between accounting and economics is explained by the importance of the criterion of objectivity in accounting. There is no objective way of measuring how much profit is created during the manufacturing process. The outcome of the whole process is known with reasonable certainty only when the buyer and seller have agreed on a price and the goods have been delivered. Also, at this time there is usually an invoice, a cash register record, or some other tangible evidence as to the revenue arising from the transaction—evidence that permits the facts to be verified by some outside party. This "test of the marketplace," or "arm's-length agreement," as it is called, provides an objective measure of the revenue, and this is the essential reason for the realization concept.

In cases where revenue can be objectively measured earlier than the date of exchange between buyer and seller, it is often recognized on this earlier date. In gold mining, for example, revenue is recognized in the accounting period in which the gold is mined, rather than the period in which it is sold, because gold always has a specified value, and a market exchange is not necessary to establish this value.

Conversely, revenue may not be recognized in the period in which the goods are delivered if there is considerable doubt as to the amount of cash that is actually going to be received from the customer. In certain types of installment selling, for example, a sizable fraction of the customers default on their contracts; and in view of the uncertainty of realizing the full amount of the sale, the seller may decide to recognize revenue only as the installment payments are received.

The general rule that realization occurs on the date when goods are shipped or services rendered implies a reasonable certainty, but not an absolute certainty, that revenue has been earned on that date. The customer may not pay his bill, or he may return the goods, or he may, perhaps several months later, ask to have repairs made under the terms of a warranty agreement. These subsequent events, which make the actual income turn out less than it was originally thought to be, are recognized in the accounts if reasonable estimates can be made of their impact. The method of doing this is described in Chapter 5.

> EXAMPLE: A company manufactures a machine in March, ships and bills it to a customer in April, and receives payment in May. The machine carries a guarantee which provides for free repairs over the next five years. The revenue from this transaction is realized not in March, the month of manufacture, nor in May, the month in which cash is received, but in April, the month in which the exchange takes

place. The fact that there may be future costs associated with this transaction is recognized by setting up, also in April, a provision for the estimated future repair cost. This is an expense item in April.

Matching

The accrual concept is often described as the "matching" concept. It is important that the expenses recognized in an accounting period be *matched* with (i.e., be measured in a manner consistent with) the revenues recognized in that period. This means that under the usual practice of recognizing revenue at the time of shipment, the total cost of the products shipped is an expense of this same period. In other words, the "cost of products sold" item and the "sales" item on an income statement should refer to the same physical products.

Expenses incurred in producing revenue are also matched against the revenue produced. For example, if "this year" a salesman received an advance commission for selling a product that is to be shipped and recognized as revenue "next year," the commission is an expense of "next year" rather than of "this year." This distinction is not always easily made in practice.

Note that expenses are matched to revenues, not the other way around; that is, the first step is to determine what revenues are to be recognized in a given accounting period, and the second step is to determine the expenses that are associated with these revenues.

> EXAMPLE: If a company decides that revenues on- installment sales are to be recognized in the year in which the sale is made, then the cost of the products sold and any other costs associated with the sale are expenses of that year. If, on the other hand, revenues are recognized in the year in which the installment payments are received, then the costs are expenses in that same year.

If expenses cannot be traced to specific items of revenue, they are charged to the year in which they are incurred. Salary earned by a salesman whether or not he makes sales, as contrasted with a commission paid on a specific sale, is an example. Such salary is an expense of the period in which the salesman earned it.

THE CONSISTENCY CONCEPT

The eight concepts that have been described in this and the preceding chapters are so broad that there are in practice several different ways in which a given event may be recorded in the accounts. For example, when a company takes a cash discount in paying bills to its vendors, this discount may be treated as being revenue; it may be treated as a reduction in the purchase price of the goods purchased; or the cash discounts *not* taken may be treated as an expense. The consistency concept requires that once a company has decided on one of these methods, it will treat all subsequent events of the same character in the same fashion. If a company made frequent changes in the manner of handling a given class of events in the accounting records, comparison of its accounting figures for one period with those of another period would be difficult.

Because of this concept, changes in the method of keeping accounts are not made lightly. A company's auditors invariably include in their opinion (i.e., a letter summarizing the results of their annual examination of accounting records) the statement that the figures were prepared "in conformity with generally accepted accounting principles *applied on a basis consistent with that of the preceding year"*; or if there were changes in practice, these are spelled out in the opinion.

Note that consistency as used here has a narrow meaning. It refers only to consistency over time, not to *logical* consistency at a given moment of time. Some people argue that it is inconsistent to measure inventory at cost or market, whichever is lower, and to measure fixed assets at cost. Whatever the merits of this argument may be, it does not involve the accounting concept of consistency. This concept does not mean that the treatment of different categories of transactions must be consistent with one another, but only that transactions in a given category must be treated consistently from one accounting period to the next.

THE MATERIALITY CONCEPT

In law, there is a doctrine called *de minimis non curat lex,* which means that the court will not consider trivial matters. Similarly, the accountant does not attempt to record a great many events which are so insignificant that the work of recording them is not justified by the usefulness of the results. An example of these trivialities is the accounting treatment of pencils. A brand new pencil is an asset of the company. Every time someone writes with the pencil, part of this asset is used up, and the owners' equity decreases correspondingly. Theoretically, it would be possible to ascertain daily the number of partly used pencils that are owned by the company and to correct the records so as to show that fractional amount of the asset amount that remains, but the cost of such an effort would obviously be gigantic, and no accountant would attempt to do this. He would take the simpler, even though less exact, course of action and consider that the asset was used up at the time the pencils were purchased or at the time they were issued from inventory to the user.

There is no agreement as to the exact line separating material events from immaterial events. The decision depends on judgment and common sense. It is natural for the beginning student, who does not have an appreciation of the cost of collecting accounting information, to be more meticulous in recording events in the accounts than would the practicing accountant.

The *materiality* concept is important in the process of determining the expenses and revenue for a given accounting period. Many of the expense items that are recorded for a given accounting period are necessarily estimates, and in some cases they are not very close estimates. There is a point beyond which it is not worthwhile to attempt to refine these estimates. Telephone expense is a familiar example. Telephone bills, although rendered monthly, often do not coincide with a calendar month. It would be possible to analyze each bill and classify all the toll calls according to the month in which they were made. This would be following the accrual concept precisely. Few companies bother to do this, however. They simply consider the telephone bill as an expense of the month in which the bill is received, on the grounds that a system that would ascertain the real expense would not be justified by the accuracy gained. Since in many businesses the amount of the bill is likely to be relatively stable from one month to another, no significant error may be involved in this practice. Similarly, very few businesses attempt to match the expenses of making telephone calls to the specific revenues that might have been produced by those calls.

OTHER CHANGES IN OWNERS' EQUITY

If the logic of the accrual concept were considered narrowly, only those expenses that relate to operations of the current period would be shown on the income statement for that period. There are a number of events, however, that although not strictly conforming to this concept are nevertheless reported as expenses of the period in which they are recognized.

An example that happens frequently is the transaction required to correct an error made in a *prior* accounting period. Suppose that in 1969 a company receives a bill for services performed for it by a lawyer in 1968, but the cost of these services had been overlooked when the 1968 financial statements were prepared. This cost is not properly an expense of 1969, and the logical procedure, therefore, would be to make the deduction in owners' equity directly rather than to report it on the income statement for 1969 as an expense of that year. Until recently, such a procedure was followed by many companies, but the Accounting Principles Board has now adopted the doctrine of the *all-inclusive income statement*, which is that almost all changes in owners' equity, other than dividend payments and changes in capital structure, should be reported on the current year's income statement. Adjustments for prior periods are limited to those which:

1. Can be specifically identified with and directly related to the business activities of prior periods.

2. Are not attributable to economic events occurring subsequent to the date of the financial statements for the prior period.
3. Depend primarily on determinations by persons other than management.
4. Were not susceptible of reasonable estimation prior to such determination.[5]

Adjustments that meet these criteria are relatively rare.

Extraordinary Items

Transactions which affect owners' equity but which do not arise in the normal course of business operations appear on the income statement as a separate item. The Accounting Principles Board describes these extraordinary items as follows:

The segregation in the income statement of the effects of events and transactions which have occurred during the current period, which are of an extraordinary nature and whose effects are material requires the exercise of judgment. . . . Such events and transactions are identified primarily by the nature of the underlying occurrence. They will be of a character significantly different from the typical or customary business activities of the entity. Accordingly, they will be events and transactions of material effect which would not be expected to recur frequently and which would not be considered as recurring factors in any evaluation of the ordinary operating processes of the business. Examples of extraordinary items, assuming that each case qualifies under the criteria outlined above, include material gains or losses (or provisions for losses) from (*a*) the sale or abandonment of a plant or a significant segment of the business, (*b*) the sale of an investment not acquired for resale, (*c*) the write-off of goodwill due to unusual events or developments within the period, (*d*) the condemnation or expropriation of properties, and (*e*) a major devaluation of a foreign currency. . . .

Certain gains or losses (or provisions for losses), regardless of size, do not constitute extraordinary items (or prior period adjustments) because they are of a character typical of the customary business activities of the entity. Examples include (*a*) write-downs of receivables, inventories and research and development costs, (*b*) adjustments of accrued contract prices, and (*c*) gains or losses from fluctuations of foreign exchange. The effects of items of this nature should be reflected in the determination of income before extraordinary items.[6]

TAX ACCOUNTING VERSUS BUSINESS ACCOUNTING

In figuring its income tax, a business must determine its net taxable income. The amounts of revenue and expense used to determine federal taxable income are usually similar to, but not identical with, amounts measured in accordance with the principles of financial accounting. The

---

[5] AICPA *Opinions of the Accounting Principles Board No. 9*, Par. 23.

[6] *Ibid.*, pars. 21 and 22.

differences are such that it is unwise to rely on income tax regulations as a basis for solving business accounting problems.

Unless tax rates applicable to the business are expected to increase in the future, a business usually reports the minimum possible amount of taxable income in the current year, thus postponing tax payments as much as possible to future years. It does this generally by recognizing expenses as soon as legally possible, but postponing recognition of revenue for as long as possible. Note that this is a process of shifting revenue and expense from one period to another; over the long run in most businesses, there is little difference between the total expenses and revenues computed for tax purposes and the total expenses and revenues computed for financial accounting. The objective of minimizing current taxes is, as the Supreme Court has pointed out, a perfectly legal and ethical one, provided it is done in accordance with the tax regulations. It is also legal and proper under most circumstances to figure income one way for tax purposes and another way for accounting purposes.

The objective of minimizing current taxes is not by any means the same as the objective of financial accounting, which is to inform management and others as to the income earned. Therefore, the two measurements of income may well be different. For example, in order to encourage research, the tax regulations permit most research costs to be counted as expenses in the year in which the research is done; whereas if the research results in products that will produce revenue in future years, these costs can be spread over the years in which the revenue from the new products is earned.

As a practical matter, many businesses choose to pattern their accounting practices after the tax regulations. This policy is convenient in that it reduces somewhat the number of separate records that must be maintained. However, if it is carried to the point of complete subservience to the tax regulations, serious distortions in accounting reports can result. In constructing a business income statement, the accountant should not use the authority of a tax regulation as a substitute for careful thinking about the best way of measuring income in accordance with accounting principles.

Although tax regulations are not described in detail in this book, references are made to accounting practices which are or are not consistent with them. The businessman learns early the importance of becoming thoroughly familiar with the principal tax rules that affect his operations and also the importance of consulting an expert when unusual situations arise.

THE INCOME STATEMENT

The accounting report that summarizes the revenue items, the expense items, and the difference between them (net income) for an accounting period is called the *income statement* (or the "profit and loss statement," "statement of earnings," or "statement of operations"). In a technical sense the income statement is subordinate to the balance sheet in that it shows in some detail the items that together account for the change during an accounting period in one balance sheet category, owners' equity, and more specifically in one item in that category, retained earnings. Nevertheless, the information on the income statement is usually much more important than information on the balance sheet, since the income statement reports the results of operations and indicates reasons for the business's profitability or lack thereof. The importance of the income statement is illustrated by the fact that in situations where accountants in recording an event must choose between a procedure which distorts the balance sheet or one which distorts the income statement (a choice which is unfortunately necessary on occasions), they usually choose the former.

There is in practice considerable variation among companies in the format used for the income statement. The Accounting Principles Board has suggested a format along the lines shown in Illustration 3–2, but makes it clear that this is not mandatory.

The income statement in Illustration 3–2 gives information for the prior year, as well as for the current year, to provide a basis for compari-

Illustration 3–2

STATEMENT OF INCOME AND RETAINED EARNINGS

Years Ended December 31, 1967, and December 31, 1966

	1967	*1966*
Net sales	$84,580,000	$75,650,000
Other revenue	80,000	100,000
	$84,660,000	$75,750,000
Cost and expenses:		
Cost of goods sold	$60,000,000	$55,600,000
Selling, general, and administrative expenses	5,000,000	4,600,000
Interest expense	100,000	100,000
Other deductions	80,000	90,000
Income tax	9,350,000	7,370,000
	$74,530,000	$67,760,000
Income before extraordinary items	$10,130,000	$ 7,990,000
Extraordinary items	(2,040,000)	(1,280,000)
Net Income	$ 8,090,000	$ 6,710,000
Retained earnings at beginning plus Net Income	$33,770,000	$30,060,000
Cash dividends on common stock—$0.75 per share	4,380,000	4,380,000
Retained Earnings at End of Year	$29,390,000	$25,680,000
Per share of common stock:		
Income before extraordinary items	$1.73	$1.37
Extraordinary items	(0.34)	(0.22)
Net Income	$1.39	$1.15

Source: Slightly modified from Exhibit A of *Opinions of the Accounting Principles Board No. 9.*

son. The Accounting Principles Board recommends such a practice, both for the income statement and for the balance sheet.

Comments about the items listed on this income statement and variations often found in practice are given in the following paragraphs.

Revenues

An income statement often shows several separate items in the revenue section, the net of which is the *net sales* figure. For example:

Gross sales..........................		$15,400
Less: Returns and allowances...........	$450	
Sales discounts...................	350	800
Net sales............................		$14,600

Gross sales is the total invoice price of the goods shipped (or services rendered) plus the cash sales made during the period. It does not ordinarily include *sales taxes* or *excise taxes* that may be charged the customer. Such taxes are not revenues, but rather represent collections which the business makes on behalf of the government. They are a liability to the government until paid. Similarly, postage, freight, or other items billed to the customer at cost are not revenues; they appear not in the sales figure but as an offset to the costs the company incurs for these items. Exceptions are made to these rules when it is not feasible to disentangle the revenue and nonrevenue portions of the transaction.

Sales returns and allowances represent the sales value of goods that were returned by the customer or on which he was given a credit because they were not as specified or for some other reason. The amount could have been subtracted from the sales figure directly, without showing it as a separate item on the income statement, but it is often considered as being important enough information to management to warrant reporting.

Sales discounts are the amount of *cash* discounts taken by customers for prompt payment. For example, if the business sells merchandise for $1,000 on terms 2/10, n/30 (2 percent off if payment is made in 10 days, and the net, or total, amount due in 30 days), and the customer takes advantage of the discount by paying within 10 days, the business receives only $980 cash and records the other $20 as a sales discount. On some income statements, sales discounts are listed as an operating expense rather than as a deduction from sales; but showing them as an adjustment to the billed price, as above, is probably more common and is more indicative of their character. *Trade discounts,* which are formulas used in figuring the actual selling price from published catalogues or price lists (e.g., "list less 40 percent"), do not appear in the accounting records at all.

Cost of Goods Sold

At the identical moment that income is increased by the sales value of a product sold, it is also decreased by the cost of that product. Indeed, were it not for the fact that the separate figures for sales revenue and the cost of products sold are useful to management, a record could be made only of the net increase in owners' equity that results from a sale.

Some businesses, especially those that sell high unit value merchandise in small quantities (such as automobile dealers), keep a record of the cost of each individual item sold. In these businesses, the total cost of the goods sold in an accounting period can be determined simply by adding up the costs recorded for the individual transactions. This same cost is also subtracted from the asset, inventory, so that at all times the asset item shows the cost of merchandise still on hand. This method is referred to as the *perpetual inventory* method.

If the business does not have such a direct method for ascertaining the cost of the products sold during an accounting period, it must deduce the cost by indirect means. The procedure for doing this is described in Chapter 5. The measurement of cost of sales in a manufacturing business involves special problems that are discussed in Chapter 7.

Gross Profit

The difference between sales revenue and cost of goods sold is the *gross profit* or *gross margin*. On many income statements this amount appears as a separate item.

Conversely, some companies do not show cost of goods sold on their income statement, but instead list expenses by *object*, such as salaries and wages, purchases of goods and services, interest. In such an income statement it is impossible to calculate the gross profit.

Expenses

The classifications given on Illustration 3–2 are a minimum. In many income statements, especially those prepared for internal use, the "selling, general, and administrative expense" category is broken down so as to show separately the principal items of which it is comprised.

In Illustration 3–2, income tax is listed with the other expenses. In many income statements, the item "income before income tax" is given and income tax expense is then subtracted.

Retained Earnings

Strictly speaking, the income statement ends with the item "Net Income." Illustration 3–2 goes beyond this to show the other changes, other

Illustration 3-3

A "PACKAGE" OF ACCOUNTING REPORTS

Balance Sheet
As of December 31, 1967

ASSETS

Current assets.	$23,839,904
Fixed assets.	14,255,720
Other assets.	180,535
Total Assets. . . .	$38,276,159

EQUITIES

Current liabilities . .	$12,891,570
Other liabilities . . .	3,000,000
Common stock.	15,000,000
Retained earnings . . .	7,384,589
Total Equities. . .	$38,276,159

Income Statement
For the Year 1968

Net sales.	$75,478,221
Less: Cost of sales. . .	52,227,004
Gross profit	$23,251,217
Less: Expenses	10,784,830
Income before taxes. . .	$12,466,387
Provision for income taxes	6,344,000
Net income	$ 6,122,387
Retained earnings, beginning.	7,384,589
	$13,506,976
Less: Dividends. . . .	4,390,000
Retained Earnings, Ending	$ 9,116,976

Balance Sheet
As of December 31, 1968

ASSETS

Current assets.	$22,651,072
Fixed assets.	13,411,779
Other assets.	173,214
Total Assets. . . .	$36,236,065

EQUITIES

Current liabilities . .	$ 9,119,089
Other liabilities . . .	3,000,000
Common stock.	15,000,000
Retained earnings . . .	9,116,976
Total Equities. . .	$36,236,065

than net income, that have occurred during the period. This final section links the income statement to the retained earnings item on the balance sheet.

The Report Package

A moment's reflection will show that the two types of accounting reports, the balance sheet and the income statement, can be combined into a package that discloses important information about the events of an accounting period. Such a package would consist of (1) a balance sheet as of the beginning of the period, (2) an income statement for the period, and (3) a balance sheet as of the end of the period. A much condensed version of such a package, presented so as to show the relationships among the various components, is shown in Illustration 3–3. (The same December 31, 1968, balance sheet is shown in more detail in Illustration 2–1.)

A Reminder: The Dual-Aspect Concept

Each of the statements and examples given in the foregoing discussion is consistent with the dual-aspect concept. Going back to the fuel oil example on page 57, the purchase of fuel oil for cash is reflected on the balance sheet by a decrease in the asset, cash, and a corresponding increase in the asset, fuel oil inventory; the consumption of fuel oil is represented by a decrease in the asset, fuel oil inventory, and an equal decrease in owners' equity. The recognition of revenue, which increases owners' equity, is accompanied by an equal increase in cash or some other asset. Every other event described in this chapter can be analyzed in terms of its dual effect on balance sheet items, so that at all times the basic equation, Assets = Equities, is preserved. Expense and revenue items represent no more than decreases and increases in owners' equity during an accounting period. For purposes of management analysis, it is important to collect and report these items in some detail, but insofar as their effect on the balance sheet goes, they can all be expressed directly in terms of their effect on owners' equity.

SUMMARY

Management is especially interested in how the operations of the business change the owners' equity, that is, in revenues and expenses and the difference between them, net income. In measuring net income, the continuing life stream of the business is divided into accounting periods, and an income statement is prepared for each period. The basic concepts governing this measurement are those already discussed in Chapter 2, plus the following:

7. *The Accrual Concept.* Income is measured as the difference between revenues and expenses rather than as the difference between cash receipts and disbursements.

8. *The Realization Concept.* Revenue is recognized at the time it is realized.

9. *The Consistency Concept.* Events of the same character are treated in the same fashion from one period to another.

10. *The Materiality Concept.* Events that do not have a significant effect on the accounts are not recorded.

CASES

CASE 3–1. ELMER KUPPER

In 1960, Elmer Kupper opened his own retail store. At the end of 1961, his first full year of operation, he thought he had done moderately well, and he was therefore somewhat chagrined when the trade association to which he belonged sent him figures which indicated that he had operated at a loss.

Mr. Kupper had been employed as manager of the local unit of a chain store for several years. In 1960 he had received an inheritance, and this, together with his savings, provided him with enough funds to buy a small store building on the main street of his town for $30,000.

He joined the trade association to which several thousand independent retailers in the same line of business belonged. One of the services furnished by this association was the annual compilation of typical operating figures of member firms. These figures were prepared by Hartje & Mees, a large public accounting firm. Early in 1962, Hartje & Mees sent Mr. Kupper a standard form and requested that he report his revenue and expenses on this form and return it so that his figures could be averaged in with those of other member stores. Exhibit 1 shows the figures which, with some difficulty, Mr. Kupper entered on this form.

Subsequently, he received a request from Hartje & Mees for information on his salary and on the rental value of his building. Mr. Kupper answered substantially as follows:

I own my own business, so there is no point in my charging myself a salary. I drew $6,000 from the business in 1961 for my personal use. My annual salary as manager of a Mogell store in recent years was $5,000, although I don't see what bearing this has on the figures for my own store.

I thought I made it clear in my original submission that I own my own building. It would cost me $3,500 a year to rent a similar building, and you can see from the figures that I save a considerable amount of money by not being forced to rent.

On the basis of the information in this letter, Hartje & Mees revised Mr. Kupper's figures and sent him the income statement shown in Exhibit 2. Mr. Kupper was considerably upset by this revised statement.

Exhibit 1

INCOME STATEMENT FOR 1961, AS PREPARED BY MR. KUPPER

Gross sales..		$65,927
Less: Returns and allowances to customers..............		2,426
Net sales...		$63,501
Cost of merchandise sold................................		43,086
Gross margin..		$20,415
Expenses:		
Salaries and wages....................................	$7,232	
Advertising...	1,182	
Supplies and postage.................................	793	
Taxes, insurance, repairs, and depreciation on building......	1,347	
Heat, light, and power..............................	426	
Business and social security taxes......................	992	
Insurance...	472	
Depreciation on equipment...........................	375	
Interest expense.....................................	240	
Miscellaneous expense................................	1,827	
Income taxes..	1,220	16,106
Net Profit...		$ 4,309

Exhibit 2

INCOME STATEMENT FOR 1961, AS REVISED BY HARTJE & MEES

Gross sales..		$65,927
Less: Returns and allowances to customers..............		2,426
Net sales...		$63,501
Cost of merchandise sold................................		43,086
Gross margin..		$20,415
Expenses:		
Salaries and wages....................................	$12,232	
Advertising...	1,182	
Supplies and postage.................................	793	
Rent...	3,500	
Heat, light, and power..............................	426	
Business and social security taxes......................	992	
Insurance...	472	
Depreciation on equipment...........................	375	
Interest expense.....................................	240	
Miscellaneous expense................................	1,827	22,039
Net Loss..		$ 1,624

He showed it to a friend and said:

These fancy accountants have gotten my figures all mixed up. I want to know the profit I have made by operating my own business rather than by working for somebody else. They have turned my profit into a loss by calling part of it salary and part of it rent. This is merely shifting money from one pocket to another. On the other hand, they won't even let me show my income tax as an expense. I realize that the tax is levied on me as an individual rather than on the business as such, but my only source of income is my store, and I therefore think the tax is a legitimate expense of my store.

Questions

1. How much profit did Mr. Kupper's store earn in 1961? How do you explain the difference between the profit shown on Exhibit 1 and the loss shown on Exhibit 2? What, if any, accounting principles are violated in either statement?
2. Should Mr. Kupper continue to operate his own store? Has he been successful?
3. Does the income statement that would be most useful to Mr. Kupper differ from the income statement that would be most useful in compiling average figures for use by the trade association membership?

CASE 3–2. VITAR ELECTRONICS, INC.

After six months of operation, Victor Peterson and Harold Corning met to decide what to do next with their "baby," Vitar Electronics, Inc. The company seemed to be off to a profitable start, and they were intrigued by the possibility of changing it from a part-time to a full-time venture.

Mr. Peterson, 29, was a production engineer for the Davis Machine Company, a large manufacturer; Mr. Corning, 32, was on the sales promotion staff of the same company. Each earned a salary of $7,000 per year. They were neighbors and close friends. Mr. Peterson had an inventive bent, and among his ideas was a new type of stepping switch. A stepping switch is a device which activates a number of electrical circuits in sequence automatically, one after the other. One of its uses is in product inspection and testing.[7] On his own time, Mr. Peterson developed a working model and applied for a patent. He interested the Davis quality control department in his stepping switch, and after tests and negotiation, the Davis Company, on May 1, 1959, agreed to purchase 20 units at $375 each.

Messrs. Peterson and Corning thereupon formed Vitar Electronics, Inc. Each took 200 shares of stock in exchange for $2,000 cash, a sizable fraction of their savings. Mr. Peterson also assigned his rights in the

---

[7] A more complete description is: The Vitar Stepping Switch M–1 consists of 20 single-pole switching positions and can be wired through a plug board to perform any programming of switching forward, backward, or in any preselected pattern, up to 200 impulses per second. It can be wired to advance one position on each successive impulse fed into it or can be timed to complete the entire switching cycle automatically. There are no moving parts except for vacuum-sealed mercury whetted magnet-operated relays—each guaranteed to perform 4 million times. The controlling circuit is transistor powered and can operate at a speed of 7,000 impulses per second.

invention to the corporation in exchange for a noninterest-bearing 10-year note in the amount of $5,000.

The manufacture of the stepping switch involved principally assembly and wiring. The two men did this themselves in Mr. Corning's basement, working evenings and weekends. The 20 units were completed, and payment received, by September 1959.

Meanwhile, Mr. Corning wrote and placed free "product announcements" and a small amount of paid advertising in trade publications. These resulted in inquiries that led to orders for additional units from other companies. The owners were thereby encouraged to seek sales more vigorously, so in September they placed larger advertisements costing a total of approximately $1,000. In order to be able to fill promptly the orders expected to result from this advertising, they continued to assemble stepping switches in September and October, and by the end of

Exhibit 1

VITAR ELECTRONICS, INC.

Financial Statements as of October 31, 1959

Balance Sheet

ASSETS

Current Assets:		
Cash	$ 288.76	
Accounts receivable	750.00	
Inventory of parts and components	2,361.90	
Completed stepping switches	1,187.62	
Total Current Assets		$ 4,588.28
Equipment (at cost)	$2,879.42	
Patent rights	5,000.00	7,879.42
Total Assets		$12,467.70

EQUITIES

Liabilities:		
Accounts payable		$ 987.22
Notes payable		5,000.00
Total Liabilities		$ 5,987.22
Capital:		
Capital stock	$4,000.00	
Retained earnings	2,480.48	
Total Capital		6,480.48
Total Equities		$12,467.70

Income Statement for Six Months

Sales		$ 9,375.00
Cost of sales		4,862.21
Gross profit		$ 4,512.79
Advertising	$1,462.10	
Other expenses	570.21	2,032.31
Net Profit		$ 2,480.48

October had six completed units on hand. They also had on hand a supply of printed circuits and other component parts, most of which were made to Vitar's specifications by outside companies.

During the entire six-month period from May 1 to October 31, Messrs. Peterson and Corning each worked about 10 hours a week making stepping switches, plus some additional time in preparing promotional material, answering inquiries, talking with prospective customers, and handling other Vitar problems. During this time they had paid themselves no salary, since Vitar's available cash was needed to buy components and to pay for equipment, most of which was built to their design in a local machine shop. They decided that the time had come to think about devoting full time to Vitar. As part of their appraisal of where they stood, Mr. Corning prepared the financial statements shown in Exhibit 1. In addition to the component parts shown on the balance sheet, Vitar had also ordered $1,820.70 of printed circuits and other components, with delivery expected some time in November.

Mr. Peterson, upon seeing these statements, remarked: "Not bad for a starter. Even with our organization costs and advertising expenses deducted, we show an excellent profit, and a very gratifying return on our investment."

Questions

1. Comment on the performance of Vitar Electronics, Inc., and its status on October 31.
2. What additional information, if any, would you need before recommending a course of action for Messrs. Peterson and Corning?

CASE 3–3. JOHN BARTLETT

John Bartlett was the inventor of a hose-clamp for automobile hose connections. Having confidence in its commercial value, but possessing no excess funds of his own, he sought among his friends and acquaintances for the necessary capital to put the hose-clamp on the market. The proposition which he placed before possible associates was that a corporation, Bartlett Manufacturing Company, should be formed with capital stock of $25,000 par value.

The project looked attractive to a number of the individuals to whom the inventor presented it, but the most promising among them—a retired manufacturer—said he would be unwilling to invest his capital without knowing what uses were intended for the cash to be received from the proposed sale of stock. He suggested that the inventor determine the probable costs of experimentation and of special machinery, and prepare for him a statement of the estimated assets and liabilities of the proposed company when ready to begin actual operation. He also asked for a statement of the estimated transactions for the first year of operations, to be based on studies the inventor had made of probable markets and costs of labor and materials. This information Mr. Bartlett consented to supply to the best of his ability.

After consulting the engineer who had aided him in constructing his patent models, Mr. Bartlett drew up the following list of data relating to the transactions of the proposed corporation during its period of organization and development:

1. The retired manufacturer would pay the corporation $10,000 cash for which he would receive stock with a par value of $10,000. The remaining stock (par value, $15,000) would be given to Mr. Bartlett in exchange for the patent on the hose-clamp.
2. Probable cost of incorporation and organization, including estimated officers' salaries during developmental period, $825.
3. Probable cost of developing special machinery, $5,000. This sum includes the cost of expert services, materials, rent of a small shop, and the cost of power, light, and miscellaneous expenditures.
4. Probable cost of raw materials: $500, of which $300 is to be used in experimental production.

On the basis of the above information, Mr. Bartlett prepared the estimated balance sheet shown in Exhibit 1.

Exhibit 1

BARTLETT MANUFACTURING COMPANY

Estimated Balance Sheet as of Date Company Begins Operations

ASSETS		EQUITIES	
Cash	$ 3,675	Shareholders' equity	$25,000
Inventory	200		
Machinery	5,000		
Organization costs	825		
Experimental costs	300		
Patent	15,000		
Total Assets	$25,000	Total Equities	$25,000

Mr. Bartlett then set down the following estimates as a beginning step in furnishing the rest of the information desired:

1. Expected sales, all to be received in cash by the end of the first year of operation, $28,000.
2. Expected additional purchases of raw materials and supplies during the course of this operating year, all paid for in cash by end of year, $9,000.
3. Expected borrowing from the bank during year but loans to be repaid before close of year, $2,000. Interest on these loans, $50.
4. Expected payroll and other cash expenses and manufacturing costs for the

operating year: $11,000 of manufacturing costs plus $3,000 for selling and administrative expenses, a total of $14,000.

5. New machinery and equipment to be purchased for cash, $1,000.
6. Expected inventory of raw materials and supplies at close of period, at cost, $1,800.
7. No inventory of unsold hose-clamps expected as of the end of the period. All products to be manufactured on the basis of firm orders received; none to be produced for inventory.
8. All experimental and organization costs, previously capitalized, to be charged against income of the operating year.
9. Estimated depreciation of machinery, $600.
10. Dividends paid in cash, $3,000.

It should be noted that the transactions summarized above would not necessarily take place in the sequence indicated. In practice, a considerable number of separate events, or transactions, would occur throughout the year, and many of them were dependent on one another. For example, operations were begun with an initial cash balance and inventory of raw materials, products were manufactured, and sales of these products provided funds for financing subsequent operations. Then, in turn, sales of the product subsequently manufactured yielded more funds.

Questions

1. Trace the effect on the balance sheet of each of the projected events appearing in Mr. Bartlett's list. Thus, Item 1, taken alone, would mean that cash would be increased by $28,000 and that (subject to reductions for various costs covered in later items) shareholders' equity would be increased by $28,000. Notice that in this question you are asked to consider all items in terms of their effect on the balance sheet.

2. Prepare an income statement covering the first year of planned operations and a balance sheet as of the end of that year.

3. *Assume* that the retired manufacturer received capital stock with a par value of $8,000 for the $10,000 cash he paid to the corporation, John Bartlett still receiving stock with a par value of $15,000 in exchange for his patent. Under these circumstances, how would the balance sheet in Exhibit 1 appear?

4. *Assume* that the management is interested in what the results would be if no products were sold during the first year, even though production continued at the level indicated in the original plans. The following changes would be made in the 10 items listed above: Items 1, 6, 7, and 10 are to be disregarded. Instead of Item 3, assume that a loan of $29,000 is obtained, that the loan is not repaid, but that interest thereon of $1,050 is paid during the year. Prepare an income statement for the year and a balance sheet as of the end of the year. Contrast these financial statements with those prepared in Question 2.

CASE 3–4. JAMES STANTON

James Stanton took his savings, some money his mother had left him, some material he found in his father's garage, and started business for himself. It wasn't a large business, but it did give him the pleasure of being his own boss, and combined the inside work of manufacturing with the outside work of selling. His product was a painted wooden toy tank that was priced at retail at $14.50 each. It was a realistic toy, well designed and intended for boys aged 6 to 10 years. Stanton was an energetic person and he soon had output rolling. This had been accomplished despite difficulties, chiefly with paint, but at last Mr. Stanton had found a supplier who promised to provide him with the necessary quality.

At the end of the first six months' experience, James Stanton took pride in his first profit and loss statement. He hoped it would be the forerunner of a long series of reports showing operations "in the black."

Income Statement for Six Months Ending December 31, 1968

Net sales...............................			$8,300.35
Beginning inventory, July 1, 1968.........		$ 150.00	
Purchases of material....................	$5,005.00		
Labor................................	8,105.45		
Rent of machines and space.............	2,090.10	15,200.55	
		$15,350.55	
Less: Inventory at end of period,			
December 31, 1968....................		11,490.50	
Cost of goods sold......................			3,860.05
Gross profit...........................		$ 4,440.30	
Advertising and other selling expenses.....	$1,510.23		
Interest...............................	52.50	1,562.73	
Net Profit............................			$ 2,877.57

Mr. Stanton's "balance sheet" as of December 31, 1968, appeared as follows:

Assets:

Cash..	$ 305.90	
Inventory, at cost.............................	11,490.50	$11,796.40
Less: Liabilities:		
Note payable, L. K. Stanton....................	$ 3,000.00	
Accounts payable..............................	2,739.50	5,739.50
Leaving James Stanton's Net Worth as..............		$ 6,056.90

Question

Comment on Mr. Stanton's performance to date and on his prospects for the future.

CHAPTER 4

ACCOUNTING RECORDS
AND SYSTEMS

Up to this point, the effect on the financial statements of each individual transaction has been described separately. Thus, starting with a balance sheet that contained the item "Cash, $10,000," a transaction involving an increase in cash of $5,000 would be recorded by, in effect, erasing the $10,000 and putting in the new figure, $15,000. This procedure was appropriate as an explanatory device in view of the small number of transactions with which we have been dealing. Clearly, however, such a technique is not a practical way of handling the large volume of transactions that occur in actual business operations. This chapter describes some of the bookkeeping procedures that are used in practice. It should be emphasized that *no new accounting concepts are introduced;* the devices described here are no more than the mechanical means of increasing the facility with which transactions can be recorded and summarized.

Some of the considerations that are important in designing and operating accounting systems are also described.

BOOKKEEPING

We are not concerned with bookkeeping procedures per se, that is, for the purpose of training bookkeepers. Some knowledge of accounting mechanics is useful, however, for at least two reasons. First, as is the case with many subjects, accounting is something that is best learned by doing —by the actual solution of problems—and although any accounting problem can theoretically be solved without the aid of the tools discussed in this chapter, their use will often speed up considerably the problem-solving process. Secondly, the debit-and-credit mechanism, which is the principal technique discussed here, provides a framework for analysis that has much the same purpose, and the same advantages, as the symbols and equations that are studied in elementary algebra. This mechanism can often be used to reduce an apparently complex, perhaps almost incomprehensible, statement of facts to a simple, specific set of relationships. Thus, the debit-and-credit mechanism provides a useful way of thinking about many types of business problems—not only strictly accounting problems but also problems of other types.

The Account

Consider again a balance sheet on which the item "Cash, $10,000" appears. Subsequent cash transactions can affect this amount in only one of two ways: they can increase it, or they can decrease it. Instead of increasing or decreasing the item by erasing the old amount and entering the new amount for each transaction, considerable effort could be saved by collecting all the increases together and all the decreases together and then periodically figuring, in a single arithmetic operation, the net change resulting from all of them. This could be done by adding the sum of the increases to the amount of cash shown at the beginning and then subtracting the sum of the decreases. The difference would be the new cash *balance*, reflecting the net effect of all the separate increases and decreases.

In accounting, the device called an *account* is used for just this purpose. The simplest form of account, called a *T account*, looks like this:

Cash

(Increases)		(Decreases)
Beginning balance	10,000	2,000
	5,000	600
	4,000	400
	100	1,000
	2,700	
	800	
	22,600	4,000
New balance	18,600	

All increases are listed on one side, and all decreases are listed on the other. The saving in effort can be seen even from this brief illustration. If the balance were changed for each of the nine transactions listed, five additions and four subtractions would be required. By using the account device, the new balance is obtained by only two additions (to find the 22,600 and 4,000) and one subtraction (22,600 − 4,000).

Note that the dollar sign ($) is omitted; this is the usual practice in most accounting procedures.

In actual accounting systems, the account form is set up so that other useful information, in addition to the amount of each increase or decrease, can be recorded. A common arrangement of the columns is the following:

CASH

Date	Explanation	(R)	Amount	Date	Explanation	(R)	Amount

The above headings are self-explanatory except that of *"R"* (standing for "reference") under which is entered a simple code showing the source of the information recorded. This is useful if it is necessary to check back to the source of the entry at some future time.

Debit and Credit

The left-hand side of any account is arbitrarily called the *debit* side, and the right-hand side is called the *credit* side. Amounts entered on the left-hand side are called debits, and amounts on the right-hand side, credits. The verb "to debit" means "to make an entry in the left-hand side of an account,"[1] and the verb "to credit" means "to make an entry in the right-hand side of an account." *The words debit and credit have no other meaning in accounting.* The preceding sentence is emphasized because in ordinary usage these words do have other meanings. Credit has a favorable connotation (such as, "he is a credit to his country") and debit has an unfavorable connotation (such as "Chalk up a debit against him."). In accounting, these words do not imply any sort of value judgment; they mean simply "left" and "right." Debit and credit are usually abbreviated to Dr. and Cr.

If an account were considered by itself, without regard to its relationship with other accounts, it would make no difference whether increases were recorded on the debit side or on the credit side. In the 15th century a Franciscan monk, Lucas Pacioli, described a method of arranging accounts in such a way that the dual aspect that is present in every accounting transaction would be expressed by a debit amount and an equal and offsetting credit amount. This made possible the rule, *to which there is absolutely no exception,* that for each transaction the debit amount (or the sum of all the debit amounts, if there are more than one) must equal the credit amount (or the sum of all the credit amounts). This is

---

[1] The verb "to charge" is often used as a synonym for "to debit."

why accounting is called *double-entry* accounting. It follows that the recording of a transaction in which debits do not equal credits is incorrect. It also follows that, for all the accounts combined, the sum of the debit balances must equal the sum of the credit balances; otherwise, something has been done incorrectly. Thus the debit and credit arrangement used in accounting provides a useful means of checking the accuracy with which the work has been done.

The reader could reason out such an arrangement for himself from the simple equation: Assets = Liabilities + Owners' Equity, taking into account also the fact that expenses and revenue accounts are subdivisions of owners' equity, since the rules of debit and credit are merely an expansion of the algebraic relationships that follow from this equation. He may find it easier, however, to memorize the following five rules:

1. Increases in *assets* are debits; decreases are credits.
2. Increases in *liabilities* are credits; decreases are debits.
3. Increases in *owners' equity* are credits; decreases are debits.
4. Increases in *expense* are debits; decreases are credits.
5. Increases in *revenue* are credits; decreases are debits.

Rule No. 4 follows from the fact that expense items represent decreases in owners' equity, and Rule No. 5 follows from the fact that revenue items represent increases in owners' equity.

Note that assets, which are "good" things, and expenses, which are "bad" things, both increase on the debit side, and that liability and revenue accounts both increase on the credit side. This is another illustration of the fact that "debit" and "credit" are neutral terms; they do not connote value judgments.

These rules are illustrated in the diagram shown in Illustration 4–1.

Debits and credits to certain special accounts are not covered by these rules, but they can be deduced from them. As an example, consider the account, Sales Discount, which is a deduction from sales revenue. We know that Sales is a revenue account and that increases are therefore recorded on the credit side. Since Sales Discount is a deduction from Sales, it must be treated in the opposite way from Sales. Sales Discount, therefore, increases on the debit side.

The Ledger

A ledger is a group of accounts. The reader has probably seen a bound book with the word "ledger" printed on the cover. All the accounts of a small business could be maintained in such a book. Or, the business might have an "Accounts Receivable Ledger," an "Accounts Payable Ledger," and a "General Ledger," each containing the group of accounts suggested by the title. The ledger is not necessarily a bound book; it may consist of

Illustration 4–1

RULES OF DEBIT AND CREDIT

ASSETS	=	EQUITIES
Asset Accounts		*Liability Accounts*
(Example: Cash)		*(Example: Accounts Payable)*

Dr.	Cr.		Dr.	Cr.
Increases (+)	Decreases (−)		Decreases (−)	Increases (+)

Owners' Equity Accounts
(Example: Retained Earnings)

Dr.	Cr.
Decreases (−)	Increases (+)

TEMPORARY SUBDIVISIONS OF RETAINED EARNINGS

Expense Accounts		*Revenue Accounts*
(Example: Wage Expense)		*(Example: Sales)*

Dr.	Cr.		Dr.	Cr.
Increases (+)	Decreases (−)		Decreases (−)	Increases (+)

a set of loose-leaf pages, a set of punched cards, or, with the advent of electronic computers, a set of impulses on a reel of magnetic tape. No matter what its form may be, the essential character of the account and the rules for making entries to it remain exactly as stated above.

The ledger will contain at least as many separate accounts as there are items on the balance sheet and income statement. Usually there are many more accounts than this minimum number so that detailed information useful to management can be collected. The number of accounts is governed by management's need for information. For example, although the single item "accounts receivable" ordinarily appears on the balance sheet, a separate account for each customer is often maintained in a ledger so as to show how much is owed by each.

There is no limit, other than the cost of record keeping, to the proliferation of accounts that may be found in practice. Take, for example, transactions concerned with the inflow and outflow of merchandise in a store. In the simplest set of books, all such transactions could be recorded as debits or credits to a Merchandise Inventory account. Or, additional information could be obtained by setting up a Purchases account, in which all purchases of merchandise during the accounting period are recorded, or there could be several Purchases accounts, one for each type of merchandise. Carrying the detail further, the Purchases account (or accounts) could be further subdivided so as to record in separate accounts (1) the invoice cost of merchandise purchased, (2) inward freight, (3) discounts allowed on purchases, and (4) merchandise returned to vendors (i.e., purchase returns). The inward freight item could be subdivided according to the several means of transportation used, or into an account for the freight bills themselves and another account for transportation taxes, and so on.

The Journal

A journal is a chronological record of accounting transactions showing the names of accounts that are to be debited or credited, the amounts of the debits and credits, and any useful supplementary information about the transaction. A simple form of the journal is shown in Illustration 4–2.

Illustration 4–2

JOURNAL

1969		Transactions	LF	Debit	Credit
Jan.	2	Cash.	*1*	120.50	
		Sales	*41*		120.50
	2	Accounts Receivable	*2*	676.32	
		Sales	*41*		650.00
		Sales Tax Liability	*15*		19.50
		Postage	*32*		6.82
	2	Cash.	*1*	196.00	
		Sales Discount.	*43*	4.00	
		Accounts Receivable	*2*		200.00
	3	Sales Returns and Allowances.		47.00	
		Accounts Receivable			47.00

The entries shown relate to the sales transactions described on page 70. It helps in understanding these transactions if the reader reasons out for himself the events that gave rise to each of them.

With respect to format, note that the debit entry is listed first, that the debit amounts appear in the first of the two money columns, that the account to be credited appears below the debit entry and is indented, and that credit amounts appear in the second money column. "LF" is an abbreviation for "ledger folio," that is, the page reference to the ledger account where the entry is to be made; these references are inserted at the time the entry is recorded in the account, and their presence indicates that the entry has been recorded. (In the illustration, the first nine items have been recorded in the accounts, and the remaining two have not yet been recorded.) In some businesses, a brief explanation of each entry is written beneath it.

The journal contains explicit instructions as to the changes that are to be made to the balances in the accounts. The process of making these changes is called *posting*. No account balance is ever changed except on the basis of a journal entry. (The balance in the account is periodically computed and recorded, as explained on page 84, but this process does not in any way *change* the balance in the account.)

Thus, the ledger is a device for *reclassifying* and *summarizing*, by accounts, information originally listed in chronological order in the journal.

THE ADJUSTING AND CLOSING PROCESS

Adjusting Entries

Most of the entries that are to be made in accounts come to the accountant's attention easily and obviously. When checks are drawn against the company's bank account, it is obvious that an entry must be made crediting cash and debiting some other account. When invoices are sent out, a credit to Sales and a debit to Accounts Receivable is obviously generated. Entries of this type are called *original entries* or *spot entries*. They constitute the bulk of the entries made in the typical business.

Some events that affect the accounts are not evidenced by such obvious documents. The effects of these events are recorded at the end of the accounting period by means of what are called *adjusting entries*. The purpose of the adjusting entries is to modify account balances so that they will reflect fairly the situation as of the end of the period.

Continuous Transactions. Most adjusting entries are made in connection with events that are, in effect, continuous transactions. Consider a tank of fuel oil purchased for $1,000. On the day of delivery, the $1,000 of fuel oil was an asset, but each day thereafter some fuel oil was consumed in the furnace, whereupon part of the $1,000 became an expense. Rather than record this consumption daily, a single adjusting entry is made at the end of the accounting period to show how much of the fuel oil is still an asset at that time and how much has become expense during the period. There are two ways of handling these events, both of which come out to the same result. Under one method, the fuel oil is originally recorded as an asset, and at the end of the accounting period the asset account is adjusted by subtracting the cost of fuel oil consumed, thus:

```
*dr. Fuel Expense. . . . . . . . . . . . . . . . . . . . . . . 600
    cr.   Fuel Oil Inventory. . . . . . . . . . . . . . . . .          600
```

*As a reminder to the reader, the notations *dr.* and *cr.* are used in Chapters 4 and 5 to designate the debit and credit portions of each journal entry. These notations are not used in practice since the accountant understands from the order and indentation of the accounts what is meant.

Under the other method, the $1,000 expenditure for fuel oil is originally recorded in an expense account, and the fuel oil remaining at the end of the period is subtracted and shown as an asset, thus:

```
dr.   Fuel Oil Inventory. . . . . . . . . . . . . . . . . . . 400
    cr.   Fuel Expense. . . . . . . . . . . . . . . . . . . . .          400
```

Although neither method reflects the correct facts *within* the period (with the trivial exception that the first method does reflect the facts on the first day), both reflect a correct statement of the facts as of the *end* of the accounting period, namely, that the fuel oil inventory is $400 and that fuel oil expense for the period was $600. Since accounting focuses on deriving the proper amounts for the statements that are prepared at the end of the accounting period, and since both methods result in the correct final amounts, the choice between these methods depends solely on which is more convenient.

Several other types of events that require adjusting entries were described in the sections of Chapter 3 that dealt with the distinction between expense and expenditure (pp. 56–60) and between revenue and receipts (pp. 61–64). The following list gives the form of the adjusting entries for such transactions:

1. For insurance protection, originally recorded as Prepaid Insurance (an asset), $300 of which becomes an expense in the current period:

```
dr.   Insurance Expense . . . . . . . . . . . . . . . . . . . 300
    cr.   Prepaid Insurance . . . . . . . . . . . . . . . . .          300
```

2. For a rent paid in advance and originally recorded as an expense, $5,000 of which is an asset at the end of the period since it covers rental for the next period:

```
dr.   Prepaid Rent. . . . . . . . . . . . . . . . . . . . . . 5,000
    cr.   Rent Expense. . . . . . . . . . . . . . . . . . . .          5,000
```

3. For $200 of supplies consumed in the period:

```
dr.   Supplies Expense. . . . . . . . . . . . . . . . . . . .  200
    cr.   Supplies Inventory. . . . . . . . . . . . . . . . .          200
```

4. For $50 of wages earned by an employee during the period but not yet paid to him:

```
dr.  Wages Expense . . . . . . . . . . . . . . . . . .    50
     cr.   Accrued Wages Payable . . . . . . . . . . . .         50
```

5. For interest expense of $5 which has not yet been paid:

```
dr.  Interest Expense. . . . . . . . . . . . . . . . .     5
     cr.   Accrued Interest Payable. . . . . . . . . . .          5
```

6. For interest (i.e., discount) deducted from a loan in advance and originally recorded as Prepaid Interest (an asset), $5 of which becomes an expense of the current period:

```
dr.  Interest Expense. . . . . . . . . . . . . . . . .     5
     cr.   Prepaid Interest. . . . . . . . . . . . . . .          5
```

7. For $20 of interest earned by the business during the period, but not yet received:

```
dr.  Accrued Interest Receivable . . . . . . . . . . . .    20
     cr.   Interest Revenue. . . . . . . . . . . . . . .          20
```

DEPRECIATION. Most fixed assets are continuously being converted to an expense, just like fuel oil, prepaid insurance, and supplies. This expense is called depreciation. Instead of subtracting the amount of expense for the period directly from the asset amount, however, a separate account, *Accumulated Depreciation,* is used. This account shows the total of such subtractions to date and is subtracted from the cost of fixed assets on the balance sheet, thus:

```
Equipment (at cost). . . . . . . . . . . . . $1,000
    Less: Accumulated depreciation . . . . .    400
        Net Book Value . . . . . . . . . . .          $600
```

The adjusting entry to record the depreciation expense for a period is therefore of the following form:

```
dr.  Depreciation Expense. . . . . . . . . . . . . . . .   200
     cr.   Accumulated Depreciation. . . . . . . . . . .         200
```

This process is described in more detail in Chapter 6.

OTHER ADJUSTMENTS. The accountant may make a variety of other adjusting entries in his attempt to make the accounts reflect fairly the results of operations and the status of the business. An example, discussed in more detail in Chapter 5, is that for *bad debt expense,* an adjustment made in order to recognize the likelihood that not all credit customers will pay their bills and that therefore the Accounts Receivable account may overstate the collectible amount of the company's claims against its customers. An adjusting entry that records the estimated amount of bad debts is as follows:

```
dr.  Bad Debt Expense. . . . . . . . . . . . . . . . . 300
   cr.   Allowance for Doubtful Accounts . . . . . . . .     300
```

On the balance sheet, Allowance for Doubtful Accounts is subtracted from Accounts Receivable, thus:

```
Accounts receivable (gross). . . . . . . . . . . . $1,000
   Less: Allowance for doubtful accounts. . . . . .     50
      Net Accounts Receivable. . . . . . . . . . .            $950
```

A CAUTION. When the student is given a problem involving the preparation of accounting statements, he must be told the precise nature of the original entries since he has no way of finding them out for himself. He will not necessarily be told about the adjusting entries, however; and he, like any accountant, is expected to be on the lookout for situations that require adjustment. For example, if the balance sheet at the beginning of a period shows the asset, prepaid insurance, the accountant knows that he must make an adjusting entry at the end of the period to show the expired cost, even though no routine document tells him to do so.

Closing Entries

Revenue accounts and expense accounts are called *temporary* (or "nominal") accounts, as distinguished from asset, liability, and owners' equity accounts, which are called *permanent* (or "real") accounts. The temporary accounts are actually subdivisions of owners' equity. They are a means of classifying the various revenue and expense transactions that occur during an accounting period so as to provide the information needed to prepare the income statement for the period. The temporary accounts are periodically *closed* to owners' equity in order to determine the net effect (i.e., the profit or the loss) of all the revenue and expense transactions.

Closing procedures differ from company to company. Under all closing methods, however, revenue and expense accounts are ultimately closed to an account called *Profit and Loss* or *Loss and Gain* or *Expense and Revenue Summary,* which reflects the net income or loss for a given accounting period. Loss and Gain is a temporary account which in turn is closed to some owners' equity account, such as Retained Earnings, to complete the closing process. In many businesses, the revenue and expense accounts are not closed directly to Loss and Gain. Instead, one or more additional temporary or *clearing* accounts are set up, such as Cost of Goods Sold, and Trading (an account which shows the gross profit for the period), and successive closings are made to these accounts. The purpose of these intermediate clearing accounts is to show separately some or all of the elements comprising Loss and Gain (e.g., cost of goods sold and gross profit). The ultimate effect, however, is the same as direct closing to Loss and Gain.

The closing process consists of transferring the balance of each temporary account to the same side of a clearing account. This is done by making a journal entry debiting the account to be closed if it has a credit balance (or crediting it if it has a debit balance) in an amount equal to the balance. This has the effect of reducing the balance in the account to zero, thereby closing it. Note that each entry is made on the opposite side from the side with the balance. The other half of this entry is made to Loss and Gain or to one of the intermediate clearing accounts.

EXAMPLE: If the credit balance in the Sales account at the end of an accounting period is $174,000, the account is closed by the following entry:

```
dr.  Sales. . . . . . . . . . . . . . . . . . . . .  174,000
    cr.    Loss and Gain. . . . . . . . . . . . . . . .            174,000
```

EXAMPLE: If the Salaries and Wages expense account has a debit balance of $21,000, it is closed by the following entry:

```
dr.  Loss and Gain. . . . . . . . . . . . . . . . .   21,000
    cr.    Salaries and Wages . . . . . . . . . . . . .             21,000
```

At the completion of the closing process, all temporary accounts have zero balances; the only accounts remaining open are the permanent accounts—the asset, liability, and owners' equity accounts.

Ruling and Balancing Accounts

At the end of the accounting period, each account is ruled and balanced so that it is in a convenient form for the preparation of financial statements and ready to begin accumulating entries for the coming period. A frequently followed procedure is as follows: First, a balancing amount is written in the appropriate column so as to make equal totals in both columns. The totals are then shown and double-ruled to indicate the end of the accounting period sequence. Finally, the new balance is "brought down" on the opposite side from that in which it was first written, as the initial figure for the new period.

The Trial Balance

The trial balance is simply a list of the account names and the balances in each account as of a given moment of time, with debit balances in one column and credit balances in another column. The preparation of the trial balance serves two principal purposes (1) it shows whether the equality of debits and credits has been maintained, and (2) it provides a convenient transcript of the ledger record as a basis for making adjusting and closing entries or in the preparation of financial statements.

To maintain the relationship "Total Assets = Total Liabilities + Owners' Equity," debits and credits must be kept in balance. Although the fact that totals on a trial balance are equal does indicate that the integrity of the accounting equation has been maintained, it does not prove that errors have not been made. Entries may have been omitted entirely; they may have been posted to the wrong account; counterbalancing errors may have been made; or the transaction may have been analyzed incorrectly. For example, when a debit for the purchase of a truck is made incorrectly to an expense account rather than correctly to a fixed asset account, the totals of the trial balance are not affected. Nevertheless, errors that result in unequal debits and credits are common, and the fact that such errors exist is evident when a trial balance does not balance; that is, when the debit column does not add to the same total as the credit column.

A trial balance may be prepared at any time. A *preadjustment* trial balance is one prepared after the original entries for the period have been posted, but prior to the adjusting and closing process. A *postclosing* trial balance is prepared after the closing process.

The Work Sheet

The work sheet is a preliminary compilation of figures that facilitates recording or analysis. A work sheet is often used as a preliminary to the formal journalizing and posting of the adjusting and closing process. Its use permits the accountant to make a "dry run" of the whole process. Since a pencil is ordinarily used, any errors detected on the work sheet can be easily corrected, whereas alterations to the formal records are to be avoided wherever possible. The work sheet also classifies account balances according to the financial statements in which they are to be used.

The form of the adjusting-and-closing work sheet varies depending upon the procedure followed in closing the books, the form of the statements to be prepared, and the preference of the accountant. The work sheet consists of several pairs of columns. In each pair, the first column is used for debits and the second column for credits. On most adjusting-and-closing work sheets the first pair of columns contains the preadjustment trial balance. The next pair of columns is used for the adjustments for the period. These are followed by a pair of columns for the income statement items, and another pair for the balance sheet items. In some cases there are additional pairs of columns for principal subdivisions of the income statement, such as the cost of goods sold section.

A work sheet is often used *in lieu of*, rather than as a preliminary to, the process of adjusting and closing the accounts. Many companies close their books only once a year, but nevertheless prepare monthly financial statements. These interim statements are prepared from a work sheet on which are listed the account balances at the end of the month together with the adjustments necessary to reflect revenue and expense in that month. Statements are prepared from the adjusted account balances that are developed on this work sheet. The income statement figures on such a work sheet would be cumulative for the year to date. An income statement for the current month can be derived from the cumulative figures simply by subtracting the corresponding figures on the work sheet for the preceding month.

A sample work sheet for a merchandising company is shown in Illustration 4–3. The five adjustments shown thereon reflect:

a) Cost of merchandise sold, $121,300 (dr. Cost of Goods Sold, cr. Inventory). During the period all purchases of merchandise had been debited to inventory, but no entries had been made to show the movement of merchandise out of inventory.

b) Expired insurance of $300 (dr. Insurance Expense, cr. Prepaid Insurance).

c) Accrued interest expense of $100 (dr. Interest Expense, cr. Accrued Interest Payable).

d) Accrued wages of $1,000 (dr. Salaries and Wages, cr. Wages Payable).

e) Accrued employer's tax on wages of $30 (dr. Social Security Tax Expense, cr. Withholding and Social Security Taxes Payable).

f) Estimated income tax for the year of $5,400 (dr. Income Tax Expense, cr. Income Tax Liability).

Note that additional accounts are added as needed at the bottom of the work sheet.

The last item on this work sheet, $13,100, is the net income for the period. It is found by subtracting the sum of the other debits to "Income Statement" from the sum of the credits to "Income Statement." Showing the same amount in the credit column of "Balance Sheet" has the effect of closing the net income to retained earnings. After this amount is entered,

Illustration 4-3

ILLUSTRATIVE WORK SHEET

(in round numbers)

	Trial Balance December 31 Dr.	Trial Balance December 31 Cr.	Adjustments Dr.	Adjustments Cr.	Income Statement Dr.	Income Statement Cr.	Balance Sheet Dr.	Balance Sheet Cr.
Cash	18,600						18,600	
Inventory	156,300			121,300 (a)			35,000	
Prepaid insurance	900			300 (b)			600	
Accounts payable		8,700						8,700
Employee taxes payable		570		30 (e)				600
Notes payable		4,000						4,000
Capital stock		20,000						20,000
Retained earnings		1,300						1,300
Sales		174,000				174,000		
Rental and other space costs	8,300				8,300			
Salaries and wages	20,000		1,000 (d)		21,000			
Social security tax expense	670		30 (e)		700			
Advertising expense	2,100				2,100			
Miscellaneous expense	1,900				1,900			
Nonoperating revenue		400				400		
Interest expense	200		100 (c)		300			
	208,970	208,970						
Cost of goods sold			121,300 (a)		121,300			
Insurance expense			300 (b)		300			
Accrued interest payable				100 (c)				100
Wages payable				1,000 (d)				1,000
Income tax expense			5,400 (f)		5,400			
Income tax liability				5,400 (f)				5,400
Net income to Retained Earnings					13,100			13,100
			128,130	128,130	174,400	174,400	54,200	54,200

each column of a pair should add to the same total, which is a check on the arithmetic accuracy of the whole closing process.

So that the connection between the adjusting and closing process and the financial statements will be clear, financial statements prepared from Illustration 4–3 are shown in Illustration 4–4. All figures used are con-

Illustration 4–4

FINANCIAL STATEMENTS PREPARED FROM DATA SHOWN
IN ILLUSTRATION 4–3

Balance Sheet as of December 31

ASSETS		EQUITIES	
Cash.	$18,600	Accounts payable.	$ 8,700
Inventory	35,000	Employee taxes payable. . . .	600
Prepaid insurance . .	600	Wages payable	1,000
		Notes payable	4,000
		Accrued interest payable. . .	100
		Income tax lability	5,400
		Total Liabilities	$19,800
		Capital stock	20,000
		Retained earnings	14,400
Total Assets. . .	$54,200	Total Equities.	$54,200

Income Statement for the Year

Sales.		$174,000
Less: Cost of goods sold		121,300
Gross profit		$ 52,700
Expenses:		
Rental and other space costs	$ 8,300	
Salaries and wages	21,000	
Social security tax expense.	700	
Advertising expense.	2,100	
Insurance expense.	300	
Miscellaneous expense.	1,900	
Interest expense	300	34,600
		$ 18,100
Other revenue.		400
Profit before income taxes		$ 18,500
Provision for income taxes		5,400
Net Income		$ 13,100

densed and rounded in order to make the process easier to follow. These statements therefore do not indicate the amount of detailed work that is involved in an actual business situation.

Reversing Entries

Under some conditions, it is desirable to *reverse* the adjusting entries made to record accruals. This is done by making an entry, subsequent to the closing entries, which is the reverse of the adjusting entry. Consider the adjustment that recognizes $5 of interest expense accrued on transactions related to borrowing $1,000 for four months, one month of which is in one accounting period and the other three in the next period, the total interest cost of $20 to be paid when the loan is repaid (see p. 60). The adjusting entry at the end of the first period, which recognizes the interest expense of that period, is as follows:

```
dr. Interest Expense. . . . . . . . . . . . . . . . . .     5
    cr.  Accrued Interest Payable. . . . . . . . . . . .           5
```

Now what happens in the next period when the loan and interest thereon is paid? A natural entry to make is the following:

```
dr. Notes Payable . . . . . . . . . . . . . . . . . . . 1,000
dr. Interest Expense. . . . . . . . . . . . . . . . . .    20
    cr.  Cash. . . . . . . . . . . . . . . . . . . . . .        1,020
```

But this overstates interest expense for the next period, which is in fact only $15, and also leaves the liability, accrued interest payable, outstanding on the books even though it no longer exists. Such an error is avoided if the adjusting entry is reversed before the accounting for the next period starts, thus:

```
dr. Accrued Interest Payable. . . . . . . . . . . . . .     5
    cr.  Interest Expense. . . . . . . . . . . . . . . .           5
```

The credit to Interest Expense is made to offset a part of the debit entry that will be made in the normal course of bookkeeping in the next period. After this entry has been made, as above, the accounts will show the correct amount of interest expense for the period ($20 − $5 = $15). The following T account summarizes these entries for the two periods:

Interest Expense			
Dec. 31 (Adjusting)	5	Dec. 31 (Closing)	5
Mar. 31 (Payment)	20	Jan. 1 (Reversing)	5
		Dec. 31 (Closing)	15
	20		20

The same result can be attained by omitting the reversing entry and recording the repayment of the loan as follows:

```
dr.  Notes Payable . . . . . . . . . . . . . . . . . . 1,000
dr.  Interest Expense. . . . . . . . . . . . . . . . .     15
dr.  Accrued Interest Payable. . . . . . . . . . . . .      5
     cr.  Cash. . . . . . . . . . . . . . . . . . . .          1,020
```

This entry requires, however, that the bookkeeper remember the fact that part of the interest was an expense of the prior period.

Summary of the Accounting Process

1. The first, and by far the most important, part of the accounting process is the *analysis of transactions,* that is, the process of deciding which account or accounts should be debited, which should be credited, and in what amounts, in order to reflect events in the accounting records. This requires judgment.

2. Next comes the purely mechanical step of *journalizing original entries,* that is, recording the result of the analysis.

3. *Posting* is the process of recording changes in the ledger accounts, exactly as specified by the journal entry. This is another purely mechanical step.

4. At the ending of the accounting period, judgment is involved in deciding on the *adjusting entries,* and these are journalized and posted in the same way as are original entries.

5. The *closing entries* are journalized and posted. *Reversing entries,* if any, are also journalized and posted. These are purely mechanical steps.

6. *Financial statements* are prepared. This requires judgment as to the best arrangement and terminology, but the figures that are used result from the judgments made in Steps No. 1 and No. 4.

ACCOUNTING SYSTEMS

The simple journals, ledgers, and work sheets, together with the rules for using them, described in the preceding pages, constitute *an* accounting system, but such a system would not usually be the *best* system for an actual business. The best system is that which best achieves the following objectives:

1. To process the information efficiently, that is, at low cost.
2. To obtain reports quickly.
3. To insure a high degree of accuracy.
4. To minimize the possibility of theft, fraud, or misrepresentation.

Designing a good accounting system is a specialized job requiring a high degree of skill. Only a few of the principles and techniques are noted here.

Special Journals

The journal form illustrated on page 88 is called a *general journal*. This form requires that the title of each account affected by each entry be written down. If there are a large number of entries made to a single account, time can be saved, both in journalizing and in posting, by using a *special journal* or *register*. In the special journal there are several columns, each headed with the name of an account that is to be debited or credited plus, usually, a "miscellaneous" column in which entries to other accounts may be recorded. Entries to the accounts indicated by column headings are made simply by entering the proper amount in these columns. At the end of the accounting period, all the amounts in each column are added, and the total is posted as one figure to the appropriate account. Entries in the "miscellaneous" column are posted individually. Illustration 4–5 is an

Illustration 4–5

CHECK REGISTER

Date	To Whom Drawn	Cash Cr.	Accounts Payable Dr.	Miscellaneous Dr.	
				Account	*Amount*

example of a check register, which is a special journal used to record credits to Cash and debits to various accounts. Columns are provided for the accounts in which entries are likely to be made frequently (here, Cash and Accounts Payable), and a miscellaneous column is provided for other debits.

The special-journal device illustrates one of the important considerations in systems design: to keep to a minimum the amount of *manual copying* of information from one document to another. Copying not only requires effort, and hence costs money, but it also increases the likelihood of making errors. In the simple check register shown, the amount of copying required is reduced, as compared with the general journal, in that all the credits to Cash and all the debits to Accounts Payable are posted to the ledger as single totals. The special journal also reduces the amount of writing effort, since the name of the account at the head of the column does not have to be written for each entry.

The same idea can be extended further by the use of bookkeeping machines. In recording sales on credit, for example, the use of a machine makes it possible to make the journal entry and post the debit to the customer's ledger account in the same operation: the operator positions the journal form and the ledger account form properly in the machine, and the amounts are entered on both forms simultaneously by the use of carbon paper. Carrying the anticopying idea one step further, once information has been recorded on punched cards, magnetic tape, or in some other form that can be handled by automatic machines, it can be manipulated and recorded thereafter without any human intervention whatsoever.

Control Accounts and Subsidiary Ledgers

Most businesses use one or more *subsidiary ledgers*, which are groups of related accounts taken out of the general ledger. For example, all the separate accounts for individual customers may be kept in an accounts receivable ledger. One advantage of this practice is that several bookkeepers can be working on the ledger accounts simultaneously. Moreover, it facilitates the process of localizing errors, since each ledger can be made the responsibility of a specific individual. If there are three bookkeepers working on accounts receivable, for example, there can be three accounts receivable ledgers.

In order to keep the general ledger in balance, a *control account* takes the place of the individual accounts removed to the subsidiary ledgers. A control account shows in summary form debits and credits that are shown in detail in a subsidiary ledger. When subsidiary ledgers are used, each amount is, in effect, posted twice: it is posted, often daily, to the proper account in the subsidiary ledger, and it also becomes a part of the total which is posted at the end of the period to the control account in the general ledger. In a large business, most if not all of the general ledger accounts are control accounts.

The use of various *ledgerless bookkeeping* devices should also be noted. The accounts receivable "accounts," for example, may consist not of actual ledger records but rather of copies of the invoices themselves. Or, bills for vendors may be kept in an "accounts payable" file, with the accounting entry made when the bill is paid rather than when it is received. The total of bills in the file at the end of the accounting period constitutes the accounts payable liability for the balance sheet and is recorded by an adjusting entry, crediting Accounts Payable and debiting various expense and asset accounts. In the latter situation, work is saved, but the possibility of verifying the accounts against the invoices is sacrificed.

Imprest Funds

The imprest fund is another device for saving work. An imprest fund consists of cash advanced to a responsible person and periodically replenished by additional cash that equals the amounts expended by this person.

The operation of an imprest fund may be illustrated by its most common version, the *petty cash* fund. The fund is established by drawing a check on the regular bank account. The person responsible for the fund cashes the check and puts the money in a separate place, a petty cash box. This transaction is recorded by the following entry:

```
dr.  Petty Cash. . . . . . . . . . . . . . . . . . . . . .    50
   cr.   Cash. . . . . . . . . . . . . . . . . . . . . . . .         50
```

The petty cash is used to pay small bills until it is nearly exhausted. At that time, these bills are summarized, and a check is drawn for the amount they total. The journal entry for this check debits the various expense or asset accounts represented by the bills, for example:

```
dr.  Office Supplies . . . . . . . . . . . . . . . . . . .    21
dr.  Miscellaneous Expense . . . . . . . . . . . . . . .    25
   cr.   Cash. . . . . . . . . . . . . . . . . . . . . . . .         46
```

Note that the credit is to the regular Cash account. Once established, the Petty Cash account is not touched unless the size of the fund is changed.

This procedure saves the effort involved in drawing checks and making separate journal entries for small bills. It also provides a safeguard, since the petty cash box should at all times contain cash and receipted bills which together total the amount shown in the Petty Cash account.

The imprest device is by no means limited to petty cash. Many government disbursing agencies operate on the same principle, but in amounts that run into millions of dollars. These agencies are advanced funds from the central treasury, they disburse these funds to pay properly authorized bills, and they submit these bills to the treasury as a basis for replenishing the fund. The accounting entries are essentially the same as those given above for petty cash.

Internal Control

Two of the objectives of an accounting system stated above—accuracy and protection against theft, fraud, or misrepresentation—cannot be attained absolutely without conflicting with the other two—speed and economy. A system that "can't be beaten" would be prohibitively expensive and time consuming. A basic principle of internal control therefore is that the system should make it *as difficult as is practical* for people to be dishonest or careless. This is significantly different from making the system absolutely foolproof. Such a principle is based not on a cynical view of people in general but rather on the realistic assumption that a small fraction of people will be dishonest or careless if it is easy for them to do so.

Some of the devices used to insure reasonable accuracy have been touched on—the idea of verifying one set of figures against another, for example. The idea of divided responsibility is another important one. Whenever feasible, no one person should be responsible for recording all aspects of a transaction, nor should the *custodian* of assets (e.g., the storekeeper or the cashier) be permitted to do the *accounting* for the assets. Thus, one person's work is a check on another's, and although this does not eliminate the possibility that two people will steal through collusion, the likelihood of dishonesty is greatly reduced.

The *voucher system* is another commonly used internal control device. Under this system, every incoming bill is inserted in a voucher, or folder, which contains spaces in which authorized people write their initials to signify their approval of the appropriateness of the charge and the accounting entries made. Under this system, all bills, even those that are paid immediately in cash, are credited to Accounts Payable (or to Vouchers Payable) and debited to the appropriate asset or expense account. For cash payments, putting the bill through Accounts Payable involves additional work, but this is often warranted in the interest of having a single, uniform procedure through which all bills must pass and a prescribed set of approvals to assure that the business makes only proper payments.

These brief comments indicate only the nature of the problem of internal control, which is a big subject. Furthermore, a study that focuses on accounting principles, as this one does, leads to incorrect impressions of the complexities involved in operating accounting *systems*. Cash transactions, for example, are very easy to analyze, whereas *Montgomery's Auditing* contains a 16-page list of questions that should be considered in connection with the internal control of the single item, cash.

THE EXPERT ACCOUNTANT

Some of the knowledge that the expert accountant has acquired through study and experience, beyond the material in this introductory treatment, is listed below:

1. The expert accountant knows the procedures for recording accounting transactions quickly, efficiently, accurately, and in a way that minimizes the opportunity for fraud or theft. Only a few of the tech-

niques and mechanical or electronic aids for facilitating the bookkeeping process have been mentioned here.

2. The expert accountant knows techniques for summarizing, arranging, and presenting information so that it meets the needs of various types of users of the information.

3. The expert accountant knows the legal requirements that govern or influence certain types of transactions. These are especially important in transactions affecting owners' equity items.

4. The expert accountant knows, or knows how to find out about, tax laws and regulations. Although tax requirements should not govern financial accounting, tax considerations do play a major part in many business decisions.

5. The expert accountant knows, or can find by referring to accounting texts or handbooks, generally accepted ways of handling many specialized types of transactions. For example, whole books have been written on methods of valuing inventory, and even on the question, "What is a sale?"

6. The expert accountant has acquired knowledge about terminology and procedures that are customarily used by companies in the same industry as his company. Many industries tend to develop a more or less common pattern for handling certain types of transactions, and in some industries these common practices are set forth in industry accounting manuals.

7. The expert accountant knows a great deal about his own company, the type of information that management and others have found useful, the way in which recurring transactions have been handled—in short, all the matters that are connoted by the word "experience," for which no book or classroom is a satisfactory substitute.

SIGNIFICANT BOOKKEEPING IDEAS

At least two significant ideas should emerge from this description of the bookkeeping process.

The first is the idea of debit and credit equality—"every debit must have an equal credit." This idea is much more than a mechanical requirement of bookkeeping. It is a way of thinking that is extremely useful in analyzing what is going on in a business. There is a natural human tendency to think only about part of the consequences of a decision and to overlook some equally important part. For example, although a growing cash balance superficially looks good, this is only half of the story. It makes considerable difference whether the credits offsetting these debits to cash reflect income from profitable operations or whether they reflect emergency bank loans.

The second significant idea is that of *balancing*, the notion that one total should always equal some other total. Three balancing techniques have been described: (1) the fundamental debit-credit structure; (2) the control-subsidiary relationship, in which the total of the subsidiary items must always equal a control total; and (3) the imprest technique, in which the sum of cash and paid bills must always equal a predetermined total. As noted above, these devices provide a check on arithmetic accuracy, they lessen the risk of loss through dishonesty, and they lessen the chance that some part of a transaction will be overlooked.

These balancing techniques have a much wider applicability than in business accounting. In recent years economists have come to use the debit-credit idea to construct national income accounts which show, in balanced form, the impact of the main economic forces at work in a nation. Electronic computers are designed with built-in checks on accuracy which are derived from the control-subsidiary idea. Figures derived from a system that does *not* contain some balancing mechanism should be regarded skeptically; the likelihood of errors or omissions is great.

APPENDIX

Locating Errors Revealed by the Trial Balance

Following are four suggested aids in detecting errors revealed by differences in the totals of the trial balance:

1. If the difference between the totals is 1, 0.01, 1.00, 100, 1,000, etc., the error is probably in addition. Such an error is usually detected by re-adding the columns of the trial balance, or, if necessary, the columns in the ledger accounts.

2. When the discrepancy is an even number, the error may be the result of making a debit entry in a credit column, or vice versa. Divide the difference in totals by 2, and look, first, through the trial balance and, then, the ledger accounts for an amount corresponding to the quotient secured. The difference is divided by 2 because an item placed in the wrong column results in a difference of twice its amount.

3. If the difference is divisible by 9, the error is probably either a transposition or a transplacement, and the search can be narrowed down to numbers where these errors might have been made. A *transposition* occurs when 79 is written for 97, 318 for 813, and so on. A *transplacement* or *slide* occurs when the digits of the number are moved to the left or right, as when $6,328.00 is written as $632.80 or $63.28.

4. When the source of error is not readily discernible, it is advisable to check the trial balance against the ledger to determine whether all the account balances have been copied properly. This check may reveal that

certain accounts have been omitted. As a last resort, it may be necessary to check all of the figures in the ledger with the journal and to check all additions and subtractions in the several accounts.

Care in making the entries, such as writing legibly, double-checking additions and subtractions as journalizing and posting proceeds, and making sure all entries are entered properly, will save much time otherwise spent in hunting for errors.

SUGGESTIONS FOR FURTHER READING ON SYSTEMS AND AUDITING

HOLMES, ARTHUR W. *Auditing: Principles and Procedures.* 6th ed.; Homewood, Ill.: Richard D. Irwin, Inc., 1964.

LENHART, NORMAN J., and DEFLIESE, PHILIP L. *Montgomery's Auditing.* 8th ed.; New York: Ronald Press Co., 1957.

MOORE, FRANCIS E., and HOWARD F. STETTLER. *Accounting Systems for Management Control.* Homewood, Ill.: Richard D. Irwin, Inc., 1963.

NEUSCHEL, RICHARD F. *Management by System.* New York: McGraw-Hill Book Co., Inc., 1960.

CASES

CASE 4–1. SUMMA SHOP

The "Summa" was a small shop specializing in clothing and accessories for the high school and college age groups. It was opened by Elise Howard, a young woman who had previously been an art teacher.

Exhibit 1

GENERAL JOURNAL

Entry Number	Account	Amount Dr.	Amount Cr.
(1)	Cash.	9,000	
	Bank Loan Payable.		2,000
	Proprietor's Capital		7,000
(2)	Prepaid Rent.	300	
	Rent Expense.	300	
	Cash		600
(3)	Merchandise Inventory	4,200	
	Accounts Payable		4,200
(4)	Furniture and Fixtures.	1,800	
	Cash		1,800
(5)	Advertising Expense	200	
	Cash		200
(6)	Wages Expense	360	
	Cash		360
(7)	Office Supplies	259	
	Cash		259
(8)	Interest Expense.	8	
	Cash		8
(9)	Utilities Expense	37	
	Cash		37

Warned by her friends of the danger of trying to operate without adequate records, Miss Howard engaged Fred Cole, a local accountant, to set up her bookkeeping system.

Mr. Cole wrote up the earlier financial transactions in journal form to serve as an example, and then asked Miss Howard to write up the store's financial transactions for the remainder of September for his review.

Mr. Cole's journal for the early part of September appears in Exhibit 1.

At the end of September, Miss Howard had the following additional items to record:

```
10) Cash sales for September.................................$1,750
11) Credit sales for September.................................  590
12) Bills paid for merchandise................................. 2,700
13) Wages paid to assistant...................................   270
14) New merchandise received.................................. 1,455
15) Cash received from credit customers.......................   270
16) Wages earned but unpaid at the end of September...........    90
17) Petty cash fund established...............................    35
18) Rent paid for October....................................   300
19) Telephone bill paid......................................    38
20) Bills received but unpaid:
        Gas and light from utility company...................    47
        Weekly cleaning of store.............................    40
21) Miss Howard ascertained the cost of merchandise sold was..  1,125
22) Depreciation for September...............................    15
23) September interest paid..................................    10
```

Questions

1. Explain the events that probably gave rise to journal entries 1 through 9.
2. Set up a ledger account (in T account form) for each account named in the general journal. Post entries 1 through 9 to these accounts, using the entry numbers as a cross-reference.
3. Analyze the facts listed as 10 through 23, resolving them into their debit and credit elements. Prepare journal entries and post to the ledger accounts. (Do not prepare closing entries.)
4. Prepare an income statement for September and a balance sheet as of September 30.

CASE 4–2. LEGGATT COMPANY

The account balances in the ledger of the Leggatt Company on February 28 (the end of its fiscal year), before adjustments, were as follows:

Debit Balances		*Credit Balances*	
Cash	$ 30,970	Accumulated depreciation on	
		store equipment	$ 5,610
Accounts receivable	44,700	Notes payable	32,500
Merchandise inventory	352,300	Accounts payable	37,250
Store equipment	28,400	Common stock	50,000
Supplies inventory	6,750	Retained earnings	1,030
Prepaid insurance	4,800	Sales	375,000
Selling expense	4,200		
Sales salaries	18,200		
Miscellaneous general expense	7,310		
Sales discounts	1,290		
Interest expense	1,780		
Social security tax expense	690		
Total	$501,390	Total	$501,390

The data for the adjustments are:

1. Cost of merchandise sold, $224,700.
2. Depreciation on store equipment, $4,260.
3. Supplies inventory, February 28, $1,650. (Purchases of supplies during the year were debited to the Supplies Inventory account.)
4. Expired insurance, $2,500.
5. Interest accrued on notes payable, $150.
6. Sales salaries earned but not paid to employees, $750.
7. Interest earned on savings account, but not recorded, $35.

Questions

1. Set up T accounts with the balances given above.
2. Journalize and post adjusting entries, adding other T accounts as necessary.
3. Journalize and post closing entries.
4. Prepare an income statement and balance sheet.

CASE 4–3. BELMONT SPRINGS NEWS

Willard Green had just completed the first month of operation in his new location at the corner of Main and High Street in Belmont Springs, and looked forward to seeing whether the books confirmed his feeling that business was much better in his new store.

Mr. Green's store had previously been located on Cedar Street in an outlying area of Belmont Springs; this store he had rented to his former employee, Nick Caruso. He had also loaned Nick $2,000 for working capital.

Partly because of the loan he made to Nick, and partly to purchase new equipment for the Main Street location, Willard had applied for a $4,000 loan from Belmont National Bank. He had also arranged to rent part of the new store to James Jones, who would run the soda fountain. Mr. Jones had agreed to pay $150 each month plus 1 percent of sales over $1,000 each month.

Mr. Green's general ledger showed the following equity, revenue, and expense accounts for the month ended October 31. (Asset and liability accounts are not shown):

Willard Green, capital	$10,000	Insurance expense	$ 0
Willard Green, cash withdrawals	600	Supplies expense	0
Cost of goods sold	7,450	Rent received	450
Sales (of which $3,500 were charge sales)	15,000	Rent expense	250
		Purchase discounts	72
Salaries and wages	480	Bad debt expense	0
Payroll taxes paid	24	Interest income	0
Telephone	45	Interest expense	0
		Other expense	320

Adjusting entries based on the following information are required to determine October profit or loss:

1. James Jones had paid three months' rent in advance on October 1.
2. Nick Caruso's check for $10 representing one month's interest was received November 1.
3. The Belmont National Bank deposited $3,880 in the store's account on October 31, from the 120-day $4,000 loan Mr. Green had applied for earlier.
4. Past experience indicates bad debts run about 2 percent of charge sales.
5. The business has been billed $420 for a one-year comprehensive fire, theft, and public liability policy beginning October 1.
6. Although most of the soda fountain proceeds are collected by James Jones, occasionally customers pay at the news dealer's register. By agreement, Mr. Green collects the sales tickets for a month-end accounting. Mr. Jones reported that his soda fountain receipts for October were $1,160. Mr. Green had soda fountain sales tickets in his cash drawer worth $40.
7. At the month end, the following bills were unpaid:

   Belmont Springs Gas and Electricity $65
   Frank Halligan worked two Saturdays delivering
     complimentary papers at $10 a day (ignore payroll taxes) 20

8. Supplies (bags, string, adding machine paper) were inventoried at $75 less on October 31 than on October 1.

Questions

1. Set up T accounts with the balances given above.
2. Journalize and post adjusting entries.
3. Prepare an income statement for October.

CASE 4–4. SUNSET MOTEL

Mr. and Mrs. Ralph Clay had purchased the Sunset Motel in 1963 with their life savings, supplemented by a loan from a close personal friend. The motel consisted of 15 units (i.e., rentable rooms) in a favorable location near a sizable city. They had entered the motel business because Mr. Clay had long wanted to run a business of his own.

Both Mr. and Mrs. Clay felt that they had been successful. Each year saw a growth in revenue from room rentals. Furthermore, their bank balance had increased. They noted that many of their tourist and business customers returned year after year. This was attributed to their location and effort to provide consistently clean rooms and up-to-date furnishings. Fortunately, no significant competition had arisen along the route on which the Sunset Motel was situated.

Mr. Clay had no formal business training, but he felt his experience since acquiring the motel had alerted him to the management problems involved. Both Mr. and Mrs. Clay devoted their full time to operating the motel. In addition, they hired part-time help for cleaning and chambermaid work during peak seasons. They had no dining facilities, but had installed coffee, cigarette, and candy vending machines to supplement room rentals. The vending machines posed no inventory or maintenance problem as the vending machine company provided servicing and maintenance.

A frequent guest at Sunset Motel was Mr. George Austen, assistant controller of a large company. Mr. Austen visited a company branch plant in the nearby city several times a year. As he stayed at the motel during these trips, he became acquainted with the Clays.

In August 1968 Mr. Clay showed Mr. Austen the July issue of the *Tourist Court Journal*, a trade journal which contained operating percentages of motels for the calendar year 1967. Data were given for motels with 11 to 20 units. Mr. Clay commented: "These figures show a profit of 17 percent. Our profit last year was $13,910 on sales of $29,125, or 47 percent. We think 1967 was our best year to date, but we can't make our figures jibe with those in the magazine, and we wonder if we really are 30 percent ahead of the industry average. Can you help us?"

Mr. Austen was interested and willing to help. He told Mr. Clay to get the available figures for 1967 so that he could look them over that evening. The principal records Mr. Clay kept to reflect the motel's financial transactions were a record of receipts, taken from the cash register, and a checkbook describing cash paid out. In addition, certain rough notations of other expenses incurred were available.

That evening Mr. Clay showed Mr. Austen the cash summary for the year 1967 as given in Exhibit 2. Mr. Austen immediately noted that the difference between receipts and expenditures was $7,115, and asked Mr. Clay to explain why he had stated the profit was $13,910. Mr. Clay replied, "Oh, that's easy. Our drawings aren't expenses; after all, we are the owners. My wife and I have consistently taken only $8,100 a year out because we want the rest of the profits to accumulate in the business. As I said, our bank balance has steadily risen. Furthermore, I have a local accountant make out the annual income tax statements so I don't have to worry about them. That income tax business is so complicated that I avoid it."

Mr. Austen worked with the cash summary (Exhibit 2) and the *Tourist Court Journal* figures (Exhibit 1) that evening and quickly found he needed more information. He told Mr. Clay that he was returning to the home office the next morning but would be back in two weeks for another visit to the branch plant. Meanwhile, he wanted Mr. Clay to get together some additional information. Mr. Austen suggested to Mr. Clay that an important noncash expense was depreciation. Mr. Austen also wanted to know about expenses that had been incurred in 1966 but not paid until 1967. He told Mr. Clay to check up on wages and salaries, insurance, advertising, taxes, utilities, and any other items paid in 1967 but applicable to 1966.

In addition, Mr. Austen instructed Mr. Clay to try to find items of expense properly chargeable to 1967 but not paid by December 31, 1967. He told Mr. Austen the same types of expense were involved, that is, wages and salaries, insurance, advertising, taxes, etc. Also Mr. Austen inquired about income from room rentals. He asked if any of the cash receipts during 1967 related to rentals during 1966 and if there were any rentals during 1967 that had not been collected.

During the two weeks Mr. Austen was back at the home office, Mr. Clay checked his records and compiled the additional information requested by Mr. Austen. The evening Mr. Austen returned to the Sunset Motel, Mr. Clay gave him a summary of the information he had gathered (Exhibit 3). With all the additional information, Mr. Austen constructed an operating statement that matched in form the one appearing in the *Tourist Court Journal*. He calculated both the dollar amounts and percentage composition of each expense for more useful comparison with the *Journal* figures.

Exhibit 1

OPERATING DATA FOR TOURIST COURTS OF 11–20 UNITS, 1967 AND 1966*

(Expressed as Percentages of Total Income)

	1967	*1966*
Income:		
Room rentals	94.03	94.34
Other income	5.97	5.66
Total income	100.00	100.00
Operating expenses:		
Salaries and wages	9.41	10.46
Executive salaries	2.17	1.95
Laundry	3.90	3.04
Linen, chinaware, glassware	2.08	1.67
Advertising, printing, stationery	2.91	2.55
Payroll, taxes, insurance	0.96	0.78
Heat, light, and power	7.25	7.48
Repairs and maintenance	4.31	4.87
Cleaning and other supplies	3.22	3.67
Telephone and telegraph	2.21	1.70
Other operating expenses	3.66	4.26
Total operating expenses	42.08	42.43
Gross operating profit	57.92	57.57
Capital expenses:		
Real estate and property taxes	4.85	4.88
Insurance	2.07	2.11
Interest	7.81	10.07
Rent	1.41	0.47
Depreciation	24.63	17.51
Total capital expenses	40.77	35.04
Net Profit	17.15	22.53

* Copyright July 1968 issue of *Tourist Court Journal*, Temple, Texas. Further reproduction in part or in whole prohibited unless written permission obtained from the copyright owner.

Exhibit 2

CASH REGISTER AND CHECKBOOK SUMMARY DURING 1967

Receipts		*Checks Drawn*	
From rooms	$28,095	Owners' drawings	$ 8,100
From vending machines	1,030	Salaries and wages	1,737
		Paid to laundry	1,125
		Replacement of linen, glass, and china	519
		Advertising	341
		Payroll taxes and insurance	416
		Fuel for heating	1,018
		Repairs and maintenance	1,327
		Cleaning and other supplies	1,136
		Telephone and telegraph	515
		Light bill	934
		Real estate and property taxes	1,362
		Insurance	1,714
		Interest	1,766
Total	$29,125	Total	$22,010

Exhibit 3

ADDITIONAL INFORMATION ABOUT THE BUSINESS

Chargeable in 1966, but paid in January, 1967:

Wages and salaries	$205
Advertising	140
Fuel for heating	60
Telephone and telegraph	23
Light bill	84
Real estate and property taxes	234
Insurance	502
Interest	135
Payroll taxes and insurance	10

Chargeable in 1967, but not paid by December 31, 1967:

Wages and salaries	343
Advertising	232
Fuel for heating	147
Cleaning and other supplies	18
Telephone and telegraph	27
Light bill	180
Real estate and property taxes	315
Interest	100
Payroll taxes and insurance	24

Also depreciation charges of $4,850.

Also, 1967 cash receipts included a $275 payment from a company which had rented several units during December 1966 for a convention in the nearby city. There were no such uncollected rentals as of December 31, 1967.

Questions

1. Prepare an operating statement such as Mr. Austen prepared.

2. As Mr. Austen, what comments would you make to the Clays regarding their progress to date?

CHAPTER 5

FURTHER ASPECTS OF INCOME MEASUREMENT

In Chapters 2 and 3 the basic concepts governing the measurement of income were described, and some of the problems involved in applying these concepts were outlined. As noted there, this class of problems is by far the most difficult in accounting. Also, it is the area in which there is the greatest disagreement among accountants.

Additional aspects of the income measurement problem are discussed in Chapters 5 through 9. Those treated in Chapter 5 include the following: deducing cost of goods sold; inventory pricing; accounts receivable and bad debts; other problems of revenue measurement; wages, salaries, and related costs; income tax allocations; and losses. The techniques and conventions described are basically derived from the concepts already given; that is, they are an application of these concepts, rather than new concepts.

DEDUCING COST OF GOODS SOLD

When a company's accounting system contains a record of the cost of each item it sells, the amount to be recorded as cost of goods sold can be determined simply by adding up these costs for all items sold in the accounting period. In many businesses, notably in retail stores, it is not practicable to keep track of the cost of each individual item that is sold, however. One can easily visualize the delay, and indeed the embarrassment, that would result in a supermarket if the cashiers attempted to record the cost, as well as the sales value, of each item the customer brought to the check-out station. In such situations, the cost of goods sold during an accounting period is determined by the process of *deduction*.

This process requires that a physical inventory, or count, be taken of the merchandise on hand at the end of each accounting period. The dollar amount of this inventory appears as an asset on the balance sheet as of the end of the period. Having established the amount of inventory, the cost of goods sold during a period is determined by the following reasoning process: The total amount of inventory available for sale during a period is what was on hand at the beginning of the period plus what was added (through purchasing additional merchandise) during the period; the difference between the total amount available for sale and the amount remaining at the end of the period is assumed to have been sold. Thus:

Beginning inventory	$ 4,000
Plus: Purchases	7,400
Equals: Goods available for sale	$11,400
Less: Ending inventory	2,000
Cost of Goods Sold	$ 9,400

The amount of beginning inventory in the above calculation is, of course, the amount found by the physical inventory taken at the end of the *preceding* period.

Some companies show such a calculation in the cost of goods sold section of the income statement itself. Others, although deducing cost of goods sold by the method shown above, do not present the details.

The amount of detail shown can be carried even further. For example, the cost of a product includes not only its invoice price but also the cost of delivering it to the premises, and the amount of this "freight-in" might be shown separately. Also, a separate record might be kept of purchased items that were subsequently returned. A calculation giving this detail follows:

Beginning inventory		$ 4,000
Plus: Purchases, gross	$7,000	
Freight-in	600	
	$7,600	
Less: Purchase returns	200	
Net purchases		7,400
Goods available for sale		$11,400
Less: Ending inventory		2,000
Cost of Goods Sold		$ 9,400

Accounts

When the cost of goods sold is deduced by the method described above, a separate account is established for each element in the calculation. Thus, a Purchases account is established, and the invoice cost of merchandise purchased is debited to this account, rather than directly to Inventory. Accounts are also established for Freight-In, Purchase Returns, and any other items involved in the calculation.

Rules for debiting and crediting these accounts can be deduced from their relationship to other accounts. Since Purchases shows additions to the asset account, Inventory, it increases on the debit side. Purchase Returns is a reduction in Purchases and hence must have the opposite rule; it increases on the credit side. Freight-In adds to the cost of purchases and therefore increases on the debit side. (The rules can also be deduced by thinking of the offsetting part of the transaction. Whenever possible, it is simplest to assume that the other account is Cash. Thus, a cash purchase involves a decrease in Cash, which is a credit; therefore, the entry to Purchases must be a debit.)

Adjusting and Closing

The accounts described above are temporary accounts which must be closed at the end of each accounting period. Furthermore, when these accounts are used, no entries are made during the accounting period to the Inventory account; therefore the amount shown in Inventory when the adjusting process begins will be the amount of *beginning* inventory. The Inventory account must be adjusted to show the proper inventory amount as of the end of the period. These adjusting and closing entries are customarily made in a certain order, which is more in the nature of a ritual than something of fundamental significance. It is as follows:

(1) Transfer the beginning inventory to Cost of Goods Sold.
(2) Close Freight-In, Purchase Returns, and similar accounts to Purchases, thereby showing the amount of net purchases in the Purchases account.
(3) Close Purchases to Cost of Goods Sold.
(4) Enter the ending inventory by debiting Inventory and crediting Cost of Goods Sold.
(5) Close Cost of Goods Sold to Loss and Gain.

EXAMPLE: Using the figures given above, these entries would be as follows:

(1)

```
dr.  Cost of Goods Sold . . . . . . . . . . . . . . . 4,000
   cr.   Inventory. . . . . . . . . . . . . . . . . . .        4,000
```

(2)

```
dr. Purchases. . . . . . . . . . . . . . . . . . . . .    600
    cr.   Freight-In . . . . . . . . . . . . . . . . . . .        600

dr. Purchases Returns. . . . . . . . . . . . . . . .    200
    cr.   Purchases. . . . . . . . . . . . . . . . . . . .        200*
```

> * The entry is shown in this form for clarity. In practice, the two parts of this entry would be combined, thus saving some work, as follows:
> ```
> dr. Purchases...........................................................400
>     Purchase Returns....................................................200
>     cr.  Freight-In.....................................................       600
> ```

(3)

```
dr. Cost of Goods Sold . . . . . . . . . . . . . . . 7,400
    cr.   Purchases. . . . . . . . . . . . . . . . . . . .      7,400
```

(4)

```
dr. Inventory. . . . . . . . . . . . . . . . . . . . 2,000
    cr.   Cost of Goods Sold . . . . . . . . . . . . . .      2,000
```

(5)

```
dr. Loss and Gain. . . . . . . . . . . . . . . . . . 9,400
    cr.   Cost of Goods Sold . . . . . . . . . . . . . .      9,400
```

If a work sheet is used, there might be a separate pair of columns labeled Cost of Goods Sold, and amounts corresponding to the above would be entered in these columns.

Limitation of the Deduction Process

Note that the validity of the reasoning behind the calculation described above rests on the *assumption* that if the merchandise is not found to be on hand at the end of the period, it must have been sold. This assumption is not necessarily correct because some of the goods may have been lost, or stolen, or thrown away, or overlooked when the physical inventory was taken. Usually, but not always, safeguards are set up to detect or avoid most of the shrinkages resulting from these causes. Nevertheless, in this system the physical inventory count must be used to determine the cost of goods sold, whereas in the perpetual inventory system, an actual count of the goods on hand can be used as a check on the accuracy of the inventory records.

Service Businesses

The cost of the services from which a service business derives its revenue is not as easily identifiable as the cost of the physical products sold by a retail store. Many service businesses do not attempt to measure the cost of the services they sell and hence do not develop a gross profit figure, since gross profit is the difference between sales revenue and cost of sales. Others do calculate a cost of sales, counting wages and salaries and other direct costs as their "cost of services."

EXAMPLE: A plumbing business might show the wages of plumbers and the cost of pipes, fittings, and other material as its cost of sales, and list as operating expenses, below the gross profit figure, its management salaries, office costs, and other expenses.

INVENTORY PRICING

As is the case with other assets, the primary basis of accounting for inventories is cost, that is, the amount paid to acquire them. If, however, the goods are no longer worth as much as they cost, they are stated at what they are currently believed to be worth, that is, at their market value. Thus, the rule for pricing inventories is often stated as, "cost or market, whichever is lower."

Cost

As used in the above phrase, "cost" may or may not represent the actual cost of the specific items that are in the inventory. For one thing, the inventory of an item may consist of an intermingling of several lots purchased at different times and at different prices, in which case it may be literally impossible to determine the actual amount paid for the quantity remaining in inventory at the end of the period. In such cases, it is necessary to make some assumption about the flow of merchandise through inventory. Any of several assumptions is acceptable.

The most frequently used assumption is that the oldest items are used first, or "first-in, first-out." The opposite assumption, "last-in, first-out," is also acceptable; the reasons why some companies adopt this assumption, despite the undeniable fact that the oldest goods tend to be sold first, are given in Chapter 9. Use of an *average* cost is another acceptable practice.

EXAMPLE: Assume 50 units priced at $1 each are in inventory at the beginning of the year; that during the year 100 units are purchased at $1.20 each and another 100 units at $1.40 each; and that 50 units remain in inventory at the end of the year. What is the amount of the ending inventory and the cost of the 200 units that were sold?

Under *first-in, first-out,* the 50 units in inventory at the end of the year are priced at $1.40 each or $70, and cost of goods sold is $(50 \times \$1) + (100 \times \$1.20) + (50 \times \$1.40) = \$240$.

Under *last-in, first-out,* the 50 units in inventory at the end of the year are priced at $1 each, or $50, and cost of goods sold is $(100 \times \$1.20) + (100 \times \$1.40) = \$260$.

Under *average cost*, the average cost of the 250 units available for sale is $(50 \times \$1) + (100 \times \$1.20) + (100 \times \$1.40) \div 250 = \$1.24$. The 50 units in inventory are priced at $1.24 each, or $62, and cost of goods sold is $200 \times \$1.24 = \$248$.

Even if the cost of the specific items sold is known, one of the above assumptions as to flow, rather than this specific cost, may be used in inventory pricing.

Market

In the ordinary situation, inventory is reported at its cost. It is reduced below cost (i.e., "written down") only when there is evidence that the value of the items, when sold or otherwise disposed of, will be less than cost. Such evidence may reflect physical deterioration, obsolescence, changes in price level, or other causes. When this evidence exists, inventory is stated at "market."

Since the goods in inventory have not in fact been sold, their true market value is not ordinarily known and must therefore be estimated. The Accounting Principles Board states that this estimate should be the current *replacement* cost of the item; that is, what it would cost currently to purchase or manufacture the item. The APB further sets upper and lower boundaries on "market":

1. It should not be higher than the estimated selling price of the item less the costs associated with selling it. This amount is called the *net realizable value.*

2. It should not be lower than the net realizable value less a normal profit margin.[1]

ACCOUNTS RECEIVABLE AND BAD DEBTS

The main source of revenue in many businesses is the sale of merchandise to customers for credit, that is, "on account." This type of transaction gives rise to the asset, accounts receivable, and to an increase in sales revenue and hence in owners' equity. Let us assume that the Essel Company began operations in 1967 and that during the year the company made sales of $262,250, all on credit. In the interest of simplicity, let us further assume that none of the customers had paid their bills by the end of 1967. The record made of these transactions would show accounts receivable in the amount of $262,250 and sales of $262,250. It would be

---

[1] Paul Grady, *Inventory of Generally Accepted Accounting Principles* (AICPA 1965) pp. 246–49.

correct to report $262,250 as an asset on the balance sheet as of the end of 1967 and $262,250 as sales on the income statement for 1967 if, *but only if,* it is believed that the customers eventually will pay their obligations to the Essel Company. The unfortunate fact is, however, that some of these customers may never pay their bills; that is, their accounts may become *bad debts.*

Consider the extreme case: the person who purchases merchandise with no intention of paying for it and who in fact does not pay for it. In this case, the company has not actually made a sale at all. Although the fact was not known at the time, no revenue was actually earned and nothing valuable was added to the asset, Accounts Receivable, as a result of this transaction. If this event is recorded as an increase in Sales and as an increase in Accounts Receivable, both these accounts will be overstated.

In the more usual bad debt situation, the customer fully intends to pay his bill, but for one reason or another he never actually does make payment. The effect is the same as that in the extreme case. Such a sale is also recorded initially by debiting Accounts Receivable and crediting Sales at the sales value of the merchandise. In these situations, a subsequent entry must be made to show that the amount debited to Accounts Receivable does not represent a valid asset and that owners' equity has not in fact increased by the amount of the sale.

Accounting Recognition of Bad Debts

When the company made the sale, the fact that the customer would never pay his bill was not known; otherwise the sale probably would not have been made. Even at the end of the accounting period, the company probably does not know which of the obligations carried as accounts receivable will never be collected. An estimate of the amount of bad debts can nevertheless be made, and it is customary to adjust the accounting records at the end of each accounting period to reflect this estimate.

One method of making this adjustment is by a *direct write-off.* Accounts that are believed to be uncollectible are simply eliminated from the records by subtracting the amount of the bad debt from Accounts Receivable and showing the same amount as an expense item on the income statement. The entry to accomplish this would be as follows:

```
dr.  Bad Debt Expense. . . . . . . . . . . . . . . . .    200
     cr.   Accounts Receivable . . . . . . . . . . . . .          200
```

The direct write-off method, however, requires that the specific uncollectible accounts be detected, whereas this usually is not possible. An alternative procedure, therefore, is to estimate the *total* amount of uncollectible accounts, and to show this estimated amount as a deduction from accounts receivable on the balance sheet, and as an expense on the income statement. Instead of reducing the accounts receivable figure directly, the estimate is often shown as a separate figure on the balance sheet, so that the reader can observe both the total amount owed by customers and that portion of the amount which the company believes will not be collected.

An account used to record deductions in the amount shown in some other account is called a *contra* account. The balance sheet contra account for accounts receivable is often labeled *allowance for doubtful accounts* or *allowance for uncollectible accounts*. It may also be labeled "reserve for bad debts," but this is likely to cause confusion since the word "reserve" connotes to many people that a sum of money has been set aside, and such is not the case. The allowance for doubtful accounts is in the nature of a suspended credit to accounts receivable for specific, but as yet unknown, customers.

The corresponding item on the income statement is called *bad debt expense* or *loss on bad debts*. Ordinarily, this item appears as one of the miscellaneous operating expenses listed below the gross profit, on the grounds that this is an item that is an almost inevitable cost in any business that extends credit to its customers. Some companies show it as a subtraction from gross sales, reflecting the belief that bad debts represent sales that never actually resulted in revenue; still others show it as a nonoperating expense. This possible difference in treatment should be kept in mind when comparing the income statements of two companies in which bad debts are a significant item, since the gross profit of one may reflect the recognition of bad debt expense, while that of the other may not.

METHODS OF MAKING THE ESTIMATE.   Any one of several methods may be used to estimate the amount of bad debt expense in an accounting period. One method is to examine each of the customer accounts and to set up an amount that is large enough to equal those accounts that seem to be uncollectible. In companies with hundreds, or thousands, of customer accounts, an analysis of each individual account may not be feasible. A common practice, therefore, is to rely on some overall formula developed on the basis of experience over a period of years. Some of the methods commonly used are as follows:

1. Estimate bad debts expense as a *percentage of total sales* for the period. This method can logically be used only when cash sales are either negligible or a constant proportion of total sales, for bad debt expense is not, of course, related to cash sales.
2. Estimate bad debt expense as a *percentage of credit sales*.
3. Adjust the Allowance for Doubtful Accounts so that it equals a prescribed *percentage of accounts receivable* outstanding at the end of the period.

The percentage used in each case depends in part on what the records show as to experience in the past and in part on management's judgment as to the extent to which past experience reflects the current situation.

AGING ACCOUNTS RECEIVABLE. Sometimes different percentages are applied to accounts outstanding for various lengths of time. This requires the preparation of an *aging schedule,* which is also a useful device for analyzing the quality of the asset, accounts receivable. An example is shown in Illustration 5–1.

Illustration 5–1

AGING SCHEDULE FOR ESTIMATING BAD DEBTS

Status	Amount Outstanding	Estimated % Uncollectible	Allowance for Doubtful Accounts
Current.	$207,605	1	$2,076
Overdue:			
Less than 1 month.	26,003	1	260
1 up to 2 months .	10,228	5	511
2 up to 3 months .	7,685	10	768
3 up to 4 months .	3,876	20	775
Over 4 months. . .	6,853	40	2,741
Total.	$262,250		$7,131

THE ADJUSTING ENTRY. Once the amount has been determined, it is recorded as one of the adjusting entries made at the end of the accounting period. If Essel Company management estimated the Allowance for Doubtful Accounts on the basis of the above aging schedule, the entry would be as shown below:

```
dr.  Bad Debt Expense. . . . . . . . . . . . . . . . . 7,131
   cr.   Allowance for Doubtful Accounts . . . . . . .        7,131
```

The accounts receivable section of the December 31, 1967, balance sheet would then appear as follows:

```
Accounts receivable. . . . . . . . . . . . . .  $262,250
   Less: Allowance for doubtful accounts. . . . .      7,131
      Accounts Receivable, Net . . . . . . . . .  $255,119
```

The income statement for 1967 would show bad debt expense in the amount of $7,131.

For reasons to be described, the Allowance for Doubtful Accounts usually will have a balance even before the adjusting entry is made. In these circumstances the amount reported as bad debt expense on the income statement will be different from the amount reported as allowance for doubtful accounts on the balance sheet. (In the Essel Company example just given, this did not occur because the company was organized in 1967, and the above entry was the first one made to Allowance for Doubtful Accounts.)

When the Allowance for Doubtful Accounts has a balance, care must be taken in applying the formulas listed above. Formulas No. 1 and No. 2, which are related to sales, give the amount of bad debt *expense* for the period; this same amount is credited to whatever balance existed in Allowance for Doubtful Accounts prior to the entry. Formula No. 3, which is related to accounts receivable, gives the amount that is to appear as the Allowance for Doubtful Accounts; the journal entry is made in an amount that brings the Allowance for Doubtful Accounts *up to* the desired balance.

> EXAMPLE: If at the end of 1968, in the Essel Company, Allowance for Doubtful Accounts had a credit balance of $1,000, and if it was decided that the allowance should be 2 percent of accounts receivable, which at that time amounted to $300,000, the balance must be increased *to* $6,000, which is an increase of $5,000. The journal entry would therefore be the following:

```
dr.  Bad Debt Expense. . . . . . . . . . . . . . . . .  5,000
   cr.   Allowance for Doubtful Accounts . . . . . . .          5,000
```

The balance sheet as of December 31, 1968, would then show:

```
Accounts receivable. . . . . . . . . . . . . . . . . $300,000
   Less: Allowance for doubtful accounts. . . . . . . .    6,000
      Accounts Receivable, Net . . . . . . . . . . . . $294,000
```

Write-Off of an Uncollectible Account

When the company decides that a specific customer is never going to pay his bill, Accounts Receivable is reduced by the amount he owes and a corresponding reduction is made in the Allowance for Doubtful Accounts. This entry is made whenever it is recognized that a specific account is bad, which may be either during the accounting period or at the end of the period. This event has *no* effect on Bad Debt Expense.

> EXAMPLE: If sometime in 1969 the Essel Company decided that John Jones was never going to pay his bill of $200, the following entry would be made:

```
dr.  Allowance for Doubtful Accounts . . . . . . . . .   200
   cr.  Accounts Receivable. . . . . . . . . . . . . .        200
```

A balance sheet prepared immediately after this transaction had been recorded (assuming no other changes since December 31) would appear as follows:

```
Accounts receivable. . . . . . . . . . . . . . . . .  $299,800
   Less: Allowance for doubtful accounts. . . . . . . .     5,800
      Accounts Receivable, Net . . . . . . . . . . . .  $294,000
```

Note that the *net* amount of accounts receivable is unchanged by this entry.

Collection of a Bad Debt Written Off

If, by some unexpected stroke of good fortune, John Jones should subsequently pay all or part of his bill, cash would be increased (i.e., debited) and a corresponding credit would be recorded to have one of the following effects:

1. Increase retained earnings on the balance sheet.
2. Add back the amount to allowance for doubtful accounts on the balance sheet.
3. Show as bad debts recovered, a separate item of revenue on the income statement.
4. Decrease bad debt expense on the income statement.

The first method ordinarily is not used since it violates the "all-inclusive income" principle. The second method has the effect of reversing the previous entry, and it is often used. The third method is rarely used because the amount involved is ordinarily too small to warrant reporting it as a separate item. The fourth method is not entirely logical but is often used in practice since it provides a convenient way of handling the transaction.

Still another common procedure is, first, to reverse the entry by which the account was written off (i.e., debit Accounts Receivable and credit Allowance for Doubtful Accounts) and, then, to treat the collection just like any other payment on account (i.e., debit Cash and credit Accounts Receivable). This has the advantage of showing a complete record of the transaction in the account for the customer.

The allowance for doubtful accounts should be sufficient at all times to absorb the accounts that prove to be uncollectible. Because business conditions fluctuate, the amount may well turn out to be too large in some periods and too small in others. In practice, because of the doctrine of conservatism, it is common to find that the allowance is too large rather than too small. On the other hand, there have been some cases where the allowance for doubtful accounts turned out to be woefully inadequate.

Summary

Let us summarize the handling of events described above by showing the effect of hypothetical transactions in 1969 on the Essel Company accounts:

1. *Write-off of $5,000 more of bad debts during the year:*

```
dr.  Allowance for Doubtful Accounts. . . . . . . . . .  5,000
     cr.   Accounts Receivable. . . . . . . . . . . . . .          5,000
           The balance in Allowance for Doubtful Accounts
           becomes $800.
```

2. *Recovery of $500 previously written off:*

```
dr.  Cash . . . . . . . . . . . . . . . . . . . . . .  500
     cr.   Allowance for Doubtful Accounts* . . . . . . .          500
           The balance in Allowance for Doubtful Accounts
           becomes $1,300.
```

* As mentioned, this is only one of several possible treatments.

3. *Adjustments at end of 1969* assuming allowance is to be maintained at 2 percent of accounts receivable, which are $400,000 as of December 31, 1969.

```
dr.  Bad Debts Expense. . . . . . . . . . . . . . . .  6,700
     cr.   Allowance for Doubtful Accounts. . . . . . . .          6,700
           This brings the allowance up to $8,000, which
           is 2 percent of accounts receivable.
```

OTHER PROBLEMS OF REVENUE MEASUREMENT

The rationale of the bad debt adjustment is that expense should be matched with revenue, regardless of the time of *discovery* that accounts are uncollectible. The same rationale applies to sales discounts, sales returns and allowances, and similar items. If the amounts involved are material, similar adjustments should be made for these items; for example, the amount of sales discounts that will be taken in future periods on sales counted as revenue in the current period should be estimated, and the sales discount expense adjusted accordingly. However, although the procedure of estimating bad debt expense on a reasonable basis is acceptable for income tax purposes, such a procedure is not acceptable with respect to sales discounts and similar items. For tax purposes, most types of sales discounts can be deducted only if the customer actually took the discount during the period in question.

For other reasons, the amount specified in the sales contract may not be the best estimate of the revenue that actually will be realized from the transaction. The possibility that the company might incur repair costs or make replacements in order to discharge its obligations under a warranty agreement, mentioned in Chapter 3, is an example. When such amounts are significant, the matching principle requires that these future costs be estimated and set up as deductions from the current period's revenue. The mechanics of doing this are similar to those described above for bad debts.

Long-Term Contracts

When, under a firm contract, a business works for several accounting periods on a single product, a portion of the revenue is often recognized in each of these periods rather than solely in the final period in which the product is completed and shipped. Shipbuilding and major construction projects are examples of situations in which this *percentage-of-completion* method is used. The revenue recognized for a period can easily be estimated when the product is constructed under a straight *cost-plus* contract, since the revenue is a specified percentage of the costs incurred in the period. In the case of fixed-price contracts or contracts with a fixed dollar amount of profit (i.e., cost-plus-fixed-fee contracts), the total amount of profit, and hence the amount applicable to each period, cannot be known exactly until the total costs have been determined at the completion of the job. In these situations, an estimated revenue may nevertheless be assigned to each of the accounting periods in the same proportion to the cost for the period that total revenue is expected to be of total cost, the proportion being estimated conservatively so as to avoid overstatement of interim profits.

In accordance with the matching principle, when revenue is measured by the percentage-of-completion basis, the expenses for the period are the costs associated with the revenue.

Installment Sales

Consumers who pay for their purchases on installments (so much a month or so much a week) are, as a class, not exceptionally good credit risks; a significant number of them do not complete their payments, and the seller accordingly repossesses, or tries to repossess, the merchandise. When this happens, the face amount of the installment contract overstates the amount of revenue that actually is earned on the transaction. One way of allowing for these defaults is to use the estimated bad debt mechanism already described. Another method used by many businesses is to recognize the revenue only as the installment payments are received, rather than when the sale is made; this is called the *installment method*. Either method is acceptable for income tax purposes, but the Accounting Principles Board states that sales revenue should "ordinarily" be accounted for when the sale is made, and that the installment method is acceptable only when "the circumstances are such that the collection of the sales price is not reasonably assured."[2] If the installment method is used in measuring revenue, the relevant expense is that fraction of the product's cost that corresponds to the fraction of installment payments received during the period.

Cash Basis

Despite the realization concept, a number of businesses, particularly small ones, recognize revenue only when cash is received. Many physicians and other professional people use this so-called *cash basis* rather than recording revenue as of the period when they render the service. This practice is conservative and is permitted under certain circumstances for income tax purposes, but it is not in accordance with generally accepted accounting principles. A business that uses the cash basis cannot measure its net income in the accounting sense of this term.

Consignments

Shipments on *consignment* are not sales.[3] The consignor, that is, the manufacturer, retains title to consignment merchandise, and the sale is not consummated until the consignee, who is usually a retailer, resells to the final customer. A consignment shipment therefore represents only the movement of the asset, inventory, from one place to another. In order to show the amount of merchandise out on consignment, it may be desirable to reflect this movement by a journal entry, at cost:

```
dr.  Inventory on Consignment . . . . . . . . . . . . .    100
    cr.   Merchandise Inventory. . . . . . . . . . . . .          100
```

In the period in which the goods are sold, the effect on the accounts would be as in the following entries (although these amounts would probably be recorded, in practice, as a part of other summary entries for revenues and expense):

---

[2] *Opinions of the Accounting Principles Board No. 10*, December, 1966.

[3] Nevertheless, some businesses treat consignment shipments as if they were sales on the grounds that they have learned through experience that the consigned merchandise ordinarily is not returned, and that the sale for all practical purposes is therefore consummated at the time of shipment.

```
dr.  Cost of Goods Sold. . . . . . . . . . . . . . . .  100
   cr.    Inventory on Consignment. . . . . . . . . . . .         100
        To record the cost of consigned goods sold.

dr.  Accounts Receivable . . . . . . . . . . . . . . .  150
   cr.    Sales . . . . . . . . . . . . . . . . . . . .         150
        To record the sales value.
```

WAGES, SALARIES, AND RELATED COSTS

As a matter of custom, the word "wages" usually refers to the compensation of employees who are on a piece-rate, hourly, daily, or weekly basis; while the word "salaries" usually refers to compensation expressed in monthly, or longer, terms. Alternatively, the word "wages" may be related to employees who must be paid overtime when they work more than 40 hours in a week, as required by the Fair Labor Standards Act, and the word "salaries" may be related to employees who are exempt from this provision. (The latter are called *exempt* employees.) The effect on the accounting records of earning and paying wages and salaries is more complicated than merely debiting expenses and crediting cash, for when wages and salaries are earned or paid, certain other transactions occur almost automatically.

An employee is rarely paid the gross amount of wages or salary he earns since from his gross earnings there must be deducted—

1. An amount representing his contribution under the Federal Insurance Contribution Act (F.I.C.A.), which currently (1969) is 4.8 percent of the first $7,800 of wages earned each year.
2. The withholding deduction, which is an amount withheld from gross earnings to apply toward his income tax.
3. Deductions for pension contributions, savings plans, health insurance, union dues, and a variety of other items.

None of these deductions represents an expense to the business. In the case of the tax deductions, the business is acting as a collection agent for the government; the withholding of these amounts and their subsequent transfer to the government does not affect owners' equity. Rather, the withholding creates a liability, and the subsequent transfer to the government pays off this liability. Similarly, the business is acting as a collection agent in the case of the other deductions. The employee is paid the net amount after these deductions have been taken.

When wages and salaries are earned, other expenses are automatically created. The employer must pay a tax equal in amount to the employee's F.I.C.A. tax, and the employer must also pay an additional percentage of the employee's pay (the rate varies in different states) for the *unemployment insurance tax*. Collectively, F.I.C.A. and unemployment insurance are called *social security taxes.* The *employer's* share of these taxes *is* an expense of the business.

Thus, if an employee with three dependents earns $100 for his work in a given week in 1969, there would be deducted from his pay $4.80 for his F.I.C.A. tax contribution and $8.50 for withholding tax, and he would receive the balance, $86.70. This is his "take-home pay." (Other possible deductions are omitted for purposes of simplification.) The *business* would incur an expense of $4.80 for F.I.C.A. tax and an additional expense of, say, $3.20 for the federal and state unemployment insurance taxes, or a total of $8.00 for the two social security taxes.

The journal entries for these transactions are as follows:

1. *When wages are earned; wages expense:*

```
dr.  Wages Expense . . . . . . . . . . . . . . . . . . .  100.00
    cr.   Wages Payable . . . . . . . . . . . . . . . . .            100.00
```

2. *When wages are earned; business tax expense.*[4]

```
dr.  Social Security Tax Expense . . . . . . . . . . .    8.00
    cr.   F.I.C.A. Taxes Payable. . . . . . . . . . . .              4.80
          Unemployment Taxes Payable. . . . . . . . . .              3.20
```

3. *When the employee is paid:*

```
dr.  Wages Payable . . . . . . . . . . . . . . . . . .  100.00
    cr.   Cash. . . . . . . . . . . . . . . . . . . . .             86.70
          F.I.C.A. Taxes Payable. . . . . . . . . . . .              4.80
          Withholding Taxes Payable . . . . . . . . . .              8.50
```

4. *When the government is paid:*

```
dr.  F.I.C.A. Taxes Payable. . . . . . . . . . . . . .    9.60
     Unemployment Taxes Payable. . . . . . . . . . . .    3.20
     Withholding Taxes Payable . . . . . . . . . . . .    8.50
    cr.   Cash. . . . . . . . . . . . . . . . . . . . .             21.30
```

In practice, the above entries would be made for all employees as a group rather than separately for each person. The government does require, however, that a record be kept for the amount of F.I.C.A. tax and withholding tax accumulated for each employee, and that he be furnished a copy of this record.

Pensions

The above transactions, although complicated, involve no new problem in the application of accounting principles. One matter related to wages

---

[4] This entry matches the tax expense with wages *earned* in the period, which is in principle the correct treatment. Some businesses compute the tax as of the period in which the wages are *paid,* on the grounds that this involves a much simpler calculation and that there is no material difference between the results of the two methods.

does involve a very difficult problem. This is the liability and related expense for pensions.

About 25 million Americans work for companies that agree to pay them pensions when they retire. All or part of the cost of these pensions is borne by the company; the remainder, if any, comes from contributions made by employees. Accounting for the company's cost for pensions is a particularly difficult matter because the expense is incurred during the years in which the employee works for the company, but the payments to him are made at some distant future time, and the total amount of the payment is uncertain, depending on how long he lives, on his final wage or salary, and possibly on other considerations.

The pension plans of many companies are *funded;* that is, an estimate is made of the amount that will be necessary to meet the future pension payments arising out of the employees' earnings in the current year, and this amount is either set aside in a trust fund or paid to an outside agency that guarantees to make the future pension payments. The amount paid into such a fund is a deductible expense for income tax purposes, provided certain other conditions are met, and is usually treated as an expense of the current year for accounting purposes. If the company retains the fund, the following entries are required each year:

```
dr. Pension Expense. . . . . . . . . . . . . . . . .  xxxx
    cr.   Pension Liability. . . . . . . . . . . . .          xxxx
            To establish the expense and related liability.
```

```
dr. Pension Fund (a noncurrent asset). . . . . . . .  xxxx
    cr.   Cash . . . . . . . . . . . . . . . . . . .          xxxx
            To transfer cash to the fund.
```

When the pension is paid to the retired employee, the entry is as follows:

```
dr. Pension Liability. . . . . . . . . . . . . . . .  xxxx
    cr.   Pension Fund . . . . . . . . . . . . . . .          xxxx
```

If the plan is not funded, only the amount actually paid to retired employees is deductible for income tax purposes. This is *not*, however, an acceptable basis for measuring pension expense in accordance with generally accepted accounting principles. The accrual concept requires that the amount of expense in a year be computed on the basis of the pension obligation that was created in the year, which is related to employee earnings in the year, not to the pensions paid in the year. The amount of pensions paid in a year is, of course, a function of employee earnings in prior years.

When a pension plan is first adopted, an especially difficult problem arises: What shall be done about the liability created for employees who are entitled to benefits because of the years they have worked for the company up to the time of adoption of the plan? Although this liability arises as a result of work done in prior years, for income tax purposes the estimated amount thereof may be treated as a tax deduction over the next 10 or 12 *future* years. The Accounting Principles Board also requires that these *past-service benefits* be spread over the income of future years, not more than 40 years, nor less than 10 years.[5]

Even a careful estimate of the future liability under a pension plan may turn out to be wrong, partly because such factors as whether the employee will stay with the company until retirement and his length of life after retirement are quite uncertain, and also because there is a tendency to liberalize benefits as time goes on. Consequently, the actual amount of expense attributable to the work done in a given year cannot be known for many years later.

INCOME TAX ALLOCATIONS

In accordance with the matching concept, the income tax reported as an expense for a year should be related to the income reported for the year; that is, if the company reports an income of $1 million before taxes, and the tax rate is approximately 48 percent, the income tax expense should be approximately $480,000. If companies figured their taxable income exactly the same way they figured their net income on the income statement, there would be no matching problem. Many companies use different rules for tax purposes than they use for financial accounting purposes, however, and the income tax calculated for a given year will therefore be based on a different amount of income from that reported on the income statement. Under these circumstances, the income tax as calculated will not match the reported income. When there is a difference between net income measured in accordance with accounting principles and net *taxable* income calculated in accordance with tax regulations, a problem arises.

> EXAMPLE: Assume that in 1968 a company spends $400,000 on research and development which results in a successful new product; that it decides for accounting purposes to charge this cost as an expense over the next five years, 1969–73, during which time the new product is expected to be producing revenue; but for tax purposes it deducts the $400,000 in the year of expenditure, thus postponing the payment of a corresponding amount of taxes. If its net income in 1968 prior to considering the research and development item is $1 million for both tax purposes and accounting purposes, its income subject to tax will be $600,000, and its income tax will be approximately 48 percent[6] of this, or $288,000. If the company regarded this $288,000 as its income tax

---

[5] *Opinions of the Accounting Principles Board No. 8*, November, 1966.

[6] In 1968, federal income taxes on ordinary corporations were 22 percent of the first $25,000 of taxable income and 48 percent of income in excess of $25,000 (exclusive of a temporary surtax). Many states also impose corporate income taxes.

expense for 1968, then its net income for accounting purposes would be $1,000,000 − $288,000 = $712,000. This, however, would be incorrect, because the $288,000 tax matches, or relates to, an income of $600,000, not of $1 million. The tax applicable to the $1 million is $480,000, and the net income should be reported as $1,000,000 − $480,000 = $520,000.

The opposite situation will arise in the next five years, for in each of them the company will charge $80,000 as research and development expense for accounting purposes, but it cannot deduct this amount again for tax purposes, so its accounting income will be lower than its taxable income. By the end of the fifth following year, 1973, the difference between taxable income and accounting income will have washed out.

When such differences between accounting income and taxable income in a year are material, the Accounting Principles Board states that the income tax actually calculated for the year should be adjusted so that it equals the income tax that would have been paid had the accounting income been taxable in that year.[7] The offsetting entry is made to a liability account, Deferred Income Tax Liability.

EXAMPLE: Carrying on the above illustration, the estimated amount of income tax actually payable for 1968 is recorded by this entry:

```
dr.  Income Tax Expense . . . . . . . . . . . . . . 288,000
    cr.   Income Tax Liability . . . . . . . . . . .        288,000
```

A second entry is then made to bring the income tax up to the amount applicable to the accounting income, which is $480,000.

```
dr.  Income Tax Expense . . . . . . . . . . . . . . 192,000
    cr.   Deferred Income Tax Liability. . . . . . . .        192,000
```

Deferred Income Tax Liability appears on the balance sheet and is written off in each of the next five years by this entry:

```
dr.  Deferred Income Tax Liability. . . . . . . . . . 38,400
    cr.   Income Tax Expense . . . . . . . . . . . . .        38,400
```

In this way, the income tax expense figure is made to match the income as measured by accounting principles.

The practice described above is highly controversial. Some of the largest accounting firms disagree with it, and some of the government regulatory agencies prohibit its use for purposes of the financial statements required of the companies they regulate. This is the reason why the Union Pacific Railroad Company reports two figures for net income, as described on page 26.

---

[7] *Opinions of the Accounting Principles Board No. 7*, December, 1967.

LOSSES

A distinction is often made between an *expense*, which is made to benefit the operations of a period, and a *loss*, which is an expenditure that does not benefit anything. The destruction of an uninsured building by fire, or the theft of some asset, results in a loss. Since both expenses and losses are ordinarily charged to the accounting period to which they relate, there is no great need to draw a fine line between them.

CONCLUSION

As additional problems are discussed, it should become increasingly apparent that the goal of matching revenue and expense in an accounting period can never be exactly attained. This fact could easily lead to a sense of frustration, were it not for the concept of materiality. In this concept we have the practical solution: one does the best he can with the information and in the time available, realizing that despite his best efforts, a perfect matching is not likely to result.

CASES

CASE 5–1. PALMER CORPORATION (A)

On December 31, 1967, before the yearly financial statements were prepared, the controller of the Palmer Corporation reviewed certain transactions that affected accounts receivable and the allowance for doubtful accounts. The controller first examined the December 31, 1966, balance sheet, Exhibit 1. His subsequent review of the year's transactions applicable to accounts receivable revealed the items listed below:

1. Sales on account during 1967 amounted to $5,267,412.
2. Payment received on accounts receivable during 1967 totaled $5,062,798.
3. During the year accounts receivable totaling $14,323 were deemed uncollectible and were written off.
4. Two accounts which had been written off as uncollectible in 1966 were collected in 1967. One account for $1,022 was paid in full. A partial payment of $750 was made by the King Company on another account which originally had amounted to $1,205. The Palmer Corporation was reasonably sure this account would be paid in full because reliable reports were circulating that the trustee in bankruptcy for the King Company would pay all obligations 100 cents on the dollar.
5. The allowance for bad debts was adjusted to equal 3 percent of the balance in accounts receivable at the end of the year.

Exhibit 1

PALMER CORPORATION

Balance Sheet as of December 31, 1966

Assets

Current Assets:		
Cash		$ 358,050
Accounts receivable	$ 527,071	
Less: Allowance for doubtful accounts	15,812	511,259
U.S. Treasury securities at cost		143,299
Inventories		925,013
Total Current Assets		$1,937,621
Investments		$ 219,892

135

Exhibit 1 (Continued)

Fixed Assets:

Land...		$ 98,836
Building.......................................	$1,282,805	
Less: Accumulated depreciation......................	353,802	929,003
Factory machinery.................................	$1,826,979	
Less: Accumulated depreciation......................	875,924	951,055
Furniture and fixtures...........................	$ 30,125	
Less: Accumulated depreciation......................	21,546	8,579
Automotive equipment...........................	$ 31,093	
Less: Accumulated depreciation......................	19,817	11,276
Office machines..................................	$ 22,690	
Less: Accumulated depreciation......................	14,936	7,754
Tools...		32,690
Patent..		30,000
Total Fixed Assets................................		$1,869,193
Prepaid expenses.....................................		$ 56,963
Total Assets.....................................		$4,083,669

Liabilities and Capital

Current Liabilities:

Accounts payable......................................	$ 270,001
Unpaid taxes...	380,323
Accrued salaries, wages, and interest....................	75,455
Long-term debt, due within one year.....................	36,960
Total Current Liabilities............................	$ 762,739

Fixed Liabilities:

Long-term debt......................................	$ 665,263

Capital:

Common stock.......................................	$1,335,082
Retained earnings.....................................	1,320,585
Total Capital..	$2,655,667
Total Liabilities and Capital........................	$4,083,669

Questions

1. Analyze the effect of each of these transactions in terms of their effect on accounts receivable, allowance for doubtful accounts, and any other account that may be involved, and prepare necessary journal entries.
2. Give the correct totals for accounts receivable and the allowance on doubtful accounts, as of December 31, 1967, after the transactions affecting them had been recorded.

CASE 5–2. SENECA MEMORIAL HOSPITAL

Roy Sanders, a senior accountant on the staff of Young and Mitchell, was in charge of the examination of the financial statements of the Seneca

Memorial Hospital for the year ended June 30, 1966. The most difficult part of his examination had to do with accounts receivable. In a supplementary report by his firm to the board of trustees made in connection with the 1965 examination, the following statement had been included:

> It is estimated that accounts receivable amounting to over $160,000 are more than one year old. This is the result of a failure to charge off old and uncollectible accounts, to an apparent lack of a standard, routine follow-up, and to many instances when patients are discharged without an effective attempt to realize a collection of the balance due. Procedures and form letters are in use for credit follow-up, but our observation was that they are applied on a selective, individual basis instead of in a regular routine.
>
> The accounts have never been completely aged to determine the status and trend of collections. As a result, we found no person who could accurately evaluate the status of the accounts.

Mr. Sanders also remembered a public statement made by Mr. Samuelson, the president of the board of trustees, following a recent board meeting: "An examination of the status of our accounts receivable indicates that there is need of more arduous efforts in collecting accounts from those who can afford to pay, should pay, but are willing to evade a just debt where possible. Those responsible for many of these accounts have ignored our request for payment, and your board of trustees is instituting for the next fiscal year a more stringent collection policy."

The continued operation of the hospital was dependent on the recovery of the major portion of the operating expenses from the hospital's patients; nevertheless, a "hard" attitude on rates and collections would be inconsistent with the continued need for gifts, which were secured largely on the strength of the beneficent activities of the hospital.

In discussing the current year's results with Mr. Frank Abbot, the credit manager, Mr. Sanders learned that about six months ago Mr. Abbot had requested permission to press for collections on a number of accounts of people in Seneca who were clearly able to pay, but that he had been dissuaded by the hospital director. The director had stated that his desire to refrain from taking action was based on repercussions that might result from one group of board members. As a result of this incident, Mr. Abbot had concluded that there was no point in pressing anyone for collection. Since then, his clerical assistants had practically discontinued the mailing of follow-up letters which had been used in an effort to obtain collection after two statements had been mailed to the responsible party.

Among the voluminous details in the working papers prepared by his staff, Mr. Sanders gave particular attention to the data in Exhibits 1 and 2 on pages 138–39. (Amounts in these exhibits have been rounded for ease in analysis.)

Exhibit 1

Preliminary Summary of Hospital Operations

Year Ended June 30, 1966

Earnings from patients—gross..	$1,420,000
Less: Provision for uncollectible accounts, charity allowances, loss on state aid, etc..	121,000
Net earnings...	$1,299,000
Operating expenses...	1,325,000
Excess of expenses over net earnings....................................	$ 26,000
Endowment income..	46,000
Net Income...	$ 20,000

Exhibit 2

Selected Balance Sheet and Operating Figures

	Amount at June 30, or for Year Ended June 30		
	1964	*1965*	*1966 (Prelim.)*
Gross earnings from patients.................	$1,174,000	$1,254,000	$1,420,000
Allowance for:			
Free treatment (Note 1)..................	80,000	101,000	66,000
Uncollectible accounts (Note 2)............	39,000	48,000	55,000
Accounts receivable (per general ledger).......	625,000	742,000	698,000
Uncollectible accounts charged off (Note 3)....	106,000	68,000	274,000
Balance, allowance for bad debts..............	273,000	354,000	201,000

Analysis of Accounts Receivable at June 30, 1966, Together with Hospital Estimate of Reserve Necessary to Provide for Uncollectible Accounts

	Amount Receivable	*Estimated Loss*
In-patient accounts, loss estimated by Mr. Abbot:		
New account cards (Note 4):		
Free treatment balances.............................	$104,000	$104,000
Regular accounts...................................	322,000	20,000
Total new account cards (4,281 accounts).............	$426,000	$124,000
Employee free treatment balances........................	17,000	17,000
Old account cards (1,038 accounts; should be able to collect 50% if turned over to collection agency, less 30% fee— per Mr. Abbot).....................................	91,000	59,000
Patients still in hospital or recently discharged.............	49,000	6,000
Due from Blue Cross or from state.......................	30,000	
Out-patient accounts (9,266 accounts; 40% loss estimate used last year deemed "not unrealistic" by Mr. Abbot)........	97,000	39,000
Total (Note 5)...............................	$710,000	$245,000

Notes to Exhibit 2

1. An account receivable is established for every person treated by the hospital, and all services rendered are charged to the account at the regularly established rates. Free treatment represents the estimated loss on state-aid cases, certain Blue Cross cases (low-income families), and services to hospital employees (for whom all charges are waived). The estimated loss is based on the accounts charged, less collections from the state and Blue Cross. The state increased the state-aid stipend to hospitals July 1, 1965, and as a result a total of $108,000 was received from the state during the current year, as against $87,000 in the preceding year. The state-aid stipend has been deducted in arriving at the amounts shown in Exhibit 2.

2. The hospital has regularly followed the policy of providing for uncollectible accounts on the basis of 4 percent of in-patient charges and 10 percent of out-patient charges (exclusive of charges on state aid or other welfare cases). Out-patient charges in the year ended June 30, 1966, amounted to $66,000.

3. Mr. Abbot prepared each year a list of all accounts which he judged to be uncollectible (including remaining balances on state aid and other welfare cases), which was presented to the board of trustees for their approval. His list for 1966 included the following:

1,206 state-aid account balances	$126,000
2,091 other in-patient accounts	129,000
2,642 out-patient accounts	19,000
Total	$274,000

Mr. Abbot was unable to write off all the out-patient accounts that he believed to be uncollectible, because the hospital director had stated that the trustees did not want more than $25,000 charged off in any one year.

4. A new bookkeeping machine was installed on July 1, 1965, and a new form of ledger card was used on all accounts receivables beginning on that date. In addition, new account cards were used for accounts which had been billed prior to July 1, 1965, but on which partial payments had been made.

5. The hospital made no effort to balance the detailed accounts receivable cards against the general ledger control account. The only listing of the ledger cards was made by the auditor as a part of his examination, and the total shown was derived from such a listing. The total of the ledger cards at June 30, 1965, was $751,000, including out-patient balances of $88,000. No effort had been made to locate the difference between this figure and the general ledger amount of $742,000.

A special "aging" study was made of the accounts receivable "new" ledger cards for patients A through Cz. The ledger cards involved represented $97,000 of the total of $426,000 on new ledger cards. Of these, 28 accounts had a balance of $600 or more, and these 28 cards totaled $31,000.

Balances were aged according to the date of discharge, and the amounts of these balances were distributed as follows:

Discharged—June, 1966	7.2%	November, 1965	3.8%
May, 1966	18.0	October, 1965	4.3
April, 1966	10.7	September, 1965	4.6
March, 1966	6.4	August, 1965	5.8
February, 1966	5.4	July, 1965	3.6
January, 1966	5.4	Prior to 7/1/65	19.4
December, 1965	5.4		
		Total	100.0%

Question

1. What amounts should be shown for gross accounts receivable and for provision for uncollectible accounts on the balance sheet as of June 30, 1966?

CASE 5–3. BRADFORD PRESS

In the 1930's, Bradford Press had acquired a tract of land on the outskirts of Craneville, a large city, with the intention eventually of constructing a branch warehouse thereon. Over the years, however, the company's marketing practices had changed, and by 1966 the management concluded that a warehouse would never be needed at Craneville. Consequently, the company sought to dispose of this land.

Bradford Press had paid $3,000 for the land and had made permanent improvements on it at a cost of $1,600, so that it was carried on the accounts of Bradford Press at $4,600. The best cash offer that could be found in 1966 was $105,000. Since an independent appraiser, hired by Bradford Press, had appraised the land at $132,000, the management was unwilling to accept this offer.

As it happened, the Craneville land was located adjacent to a warehouse owned by the Birch Paper Company, one of Bradford's four regular suppliers of paper. Birch expressed an interest in acquiring the property so that it could later expand its own facilities. Birch was unwilling to pay cash but offered instead to exchange 6,000 cwt. (hundredweight) of 70-pound machine-coated paper, to be delivered at the rate of 1,000 cwt. per month for six months. In addition, Bradford was to pay the freight on this paper, in accordance with usual practice. The going market price for this grade of paper was at that time $24 per cwt., plus freight.

Bradford Press typically used more than 1,000 cwt. of 70-pound machine-coated paper per month in the manufacture of booklets, brochures, and similar items, but Bradford Press ordinarily placed orders for delivery not more than two months in the future, unless it had firm contracts from its own customers that required such paper. It had no such contracts in the fall of 1966. After considerable discussion among Bradford executives as to the risk involved in the unusually large commitment for paper, the Bradford management finally decided to accept Birch's offer.

The contract was signed on September 21, 1966, and as of that date the following journal entry was made by Bradford's accountant, recording the paper at its market price, and showing the difference between this amount and the book value of the land as profit:

```
dr.  Inventory Due from Supplier. . . . . . . . . . 144,000
  cr.    Craneville Land. . . . . . . . . . . . .           4,600
         Profit on Sale of Land . . . . . . . . .         139,400
```

During the last three months of 1966, 3,000 cwt. of the paper was received from Birch as promised, and in the aggregate the entries made to record this receipt had the following effect:

```
dr.  Paper Inventory. . . . . . . . . . . . . . .  72,740
  cr.    Inventory Due from Supplier. . . . . . . .        72,000
         Cash (for freight charges) . . . . . . . .           740
```

When he was examining the accounts of Bradford Press for 1966, the company's auditor raised questions about this transaction. He pointed out that the net effect of the above entries was that the entire profit on the transaction was shown in 1966, despite the fact that only 3,000 cwt. of paper had actually been delivered, and of this only about 2,000 cwt. had actually been used in the manufacture of products. (The physical inventory as of December 31 showed 1,000 cwt. of this paper as still on hand.)

A suggested alternative treatment was to split the profit into two parts. One part, $100,400, was the difference between the book value of the land and the best cash offer; this was to be called "profit on price-level changes" and shown on the 1966 income statement. The remainder, $39,000, was to be called "profit on sale of land" and divided one third to 1966 and two thirds to 1967, representing the fraction of the total paper consumed in each year. The auditor stated that such a separation was not usually made, but neither was this an ordinary transaction.

Bradford Press management disliked the implication in the above treatment that they had not made the $139,000 profit in 1966, especially since the price of 70-pound machine-coated paper had risen to $25 per cwt. as of December 31, 1966.

Questions

1. How to you think this transaction should be handled?
2. How would you answer the arguments of those who think it should be handled differently?
3. Would your answer be different if the market price had decreased to $23 as of the end of 1966?

CASE 5–4.   PRENTISS DRESS SHOP

For over 20 years, Mr. Murray Prentiss had owned and operated a women's specialty shop in a suburban town. Early in 1967 Mr. Milton Wilcox, a representative of Dynamic Stores Inc., discussed with Mr. Prentiss the possibility of selling his business to Burroughs Stores, which owned 16 specialty shops in the same metropolitan area. Over the past several years, several other chains had approached Mr. Prentiss with similar propositions, but the Dynamic proposal was the first one that he seriously considered.

After a series of conversations, Mr. Prentiss told Mr. Wilcox that he would consider selling his business provided they could agree on a fair price and provided Dynamic would agree to employ him as store manager. Mr. Wilcox assured him that Dynamic would certainly be happy to have Mr. Prentiss continue as manager of the store, and the discussion then turned to the problem of deciding the selling price.

Mr. Wilcox asked what financial information was available, and Mr. Prentiss replied:

The only formal statements I have are balance sheets and my income tax returns, which I have a tax man prepare for me. I expect him to work up the returns for 1966 within the next month. I know what is going on in the business well enough so that I don't need other statements. Of course, I have a checkbook, a file of charge slips showing what customers owe me, and a file of unpaid invoices from suppliers. On New Year's day, or the preceding afternoon, I take a physical inventory and determine the purchase cost of goods on hand.

I have two women salespersons helping me, but I am at the store most of the time, and I try to keep a close tab on everything that takes place. There are two cash registers which everyone uses regardless of the kind of merchandise sold. None of us specializes in the sale of any particular kind of goods.

Mr. Wilcox replied that the lack of financial statements for 1966 probably would not prove to be any great obstacle to the conclusion of negotiations. All that was necessary was permission from Mr. Prentiss to examine whatever records were available, from which it was highly probable that Dynamic could ascertain all the operating facts about the business that were needed. Mr. Prentiss agreed with this arrangement.

Mr. Wilcox was able to gather the data presented in Exhibits 1 and 2. In going over this information with Mr. Prentiss, Mr. Wilcox commented: "If Dynamic takes over this store, even if you stay on as manager, we will need more figures than you have been gathering for yourself."

Exhibit 1

PRENTISS DRESS SHOP

Balance Sheet as of December 31, 1965

ASSETS			EQUITIES	
Current Assets:			*Current Liabilities:*	
Cash............................	$12,919		Salaries payable...........	$ 820
Notes receivable.................	2,000		Notes payable............	7,600
Accounts receivable..............	8,562		Accounts payable.........	4,188
Merchandise inventory............	22,601		Total Current Liabilities.	$12,608
Total Current Assets.........	$46,082			
			Owner's Equity:	
Fixed Assets:			M. W. Prentiss, prop.	16,500
Furniture and fixtures......$6,870			Retained earnings.........	19,931
Less: Accumulated				
depreciation.......... 3,913	2,957			
Office equipment.........$1,920				
Less: Accumulated				
depreciation.......... 1,920	0			
Total Assets..............	$49,039		Total Equities......	$49,039

Exhibit 2

INFORMATION COLLECTED BY MR. WILCOX

Cash Record for 1966

Receipts:		*Expenditures:*	
Cash sales..............	$ 69,762	Payroll..................	$ 26,489
Collection of accounts re-		Rent....................	4,300
ceivable..............	39,118	Advertising..............	2,432
Total receipts.......	$108,880	Taxes...................	1,741
		Supplies................	3,890
		Travel..................	810
		Telephone...............	912
		Repairs to building........	710
		Insurance................	450
		Miscellaneous expenses....	978
		Paid on accounts payable	
		for merchandise.........	74,291
		Total expenditures....	$117,003
Plus cash balance, Decem-		Plus cash balance, Decem-	
ber 31, 1965............	12,919	ber 31, 1966............	4,796
Total..............	$121,799	Total.............	$121,799

Other Information

The expenditure for payroll includes Mr. Prentiss' salary of $16,000. Social security and withholding taxes may be disregarded since the expense portion was included in the payroll figure and amounts due to the government were immediately

Exhibit 2 (Continued)

deposited in a separate bank account that does not appear on the financial statements.

Wages payable (including taxes thereon) as of December 31, 1966. . . . . $ 1,448

Accounts payable represented only invoices for merchandise purchased on
   credit. As of December 31, 1966, these unpaid invoices amounted to. 9,896

Amounts due from customers on December 31, 1966, totaled. 17,310

Merchandise inventory, December 31, 1966. 37,936

The note receivable carried a 6 percent rate of interest. The note payable
   carried a 5 percent rate of interest. The note receivable was not collected in
   1966, nor was the note payable paid in 1966.

Miscellaneous expenses included $600 paid to Ajax Truck Rental for a three-
   month lease on a delivery truck. The lease began on December 1, 1966.

Depreciation on furniture and fixtures was computed at 10 percent of cost.

Questions

1. From the information given in Exhibits 1 and 2, determine (*a*) sales, (*b*) the cost of merchandise sold, and (*c*) the expenses for the year.
2. Prepare an income statement for 1966 and a balance sheet as of December 31, 1966.
3. Why should more figures apparently be justifiable under chain responsibility than when the store was owned by Mr. Prentiss?
4. How should the parties proceed to decide on a fair selling price for the business?

CASE 5–5. MOTION PICTURES

The motion picture industry has a number of accounting problems which are in part basic to all manufacturing and sales activities and in part peculiar to this industry.

The major items of expense in the production and distribution of motion pictures are as follows:

1. Salaries of actors, directors, musicians, and crew.
2. Payments of royalties, or outright payments, for scripts, screen rights, and music.
3. Travel and other expenses while on location away from the studio, including rental of facilities.
4. Negative and positive films, wardrobes, props, and accessories.
5. Cost of sets, some of which may be used in the production of additional pictures at later dates.
6. Depreciation on studio buildings and equipment.
7. Promotional expenses.
8. Administrative expenses.

It often takes many months, sometimes more than a year, to produce a picture. Unlike an ordinary manufacturing business, where productive effort results in the creation of large stocks of goods, the finished product in the motion picture business is a few rolls of negative film from which many positive prints are made for rental to exhibitors.

The revenue received from these rentals parallels the receipt of admissions in the exhibiting theaters to the extent that the films are leased based on a percentage of the box office receipts. Therefore, although films remain physically intact, except for wear, in the producer's inventory, their earning capacity declines as the play-off progresses. It has been found from experience that the rate of play-off, and thus the flow of revenues, differs among the various classes of pictures. In general, for example, feature pictures have a much shorter life than westerns or short subjects. Now and then old pictures are rereleased, and many old films have been brought back to life on television.

Question

1. On the basis of the brief facts noted above, discuss, with examples, the problems of a motion picture company in accounting for costs and revenues in the production and distribution of motion pictures; and state, with reasons, how you would treat these problems.

CHAPTER 6

FIXED ASSETS AND DEPRECIATION

This chapter discusses principles and procedures involved in recording the acquisition of fixed assets and in the subsequent amortization of their cost as expenses of the periods benefited.

ACQUISITION OF FIXED ASSETS

When an expenditure is recorded in the accounts as a fixed asset (rather than as an expense or a current asset), it is said to be *capitalized*. In accordance with the cost concept, the amount that is to be capitalized as the value of a newly acquired asset is its cost. In principle, this amount is the sum of all costs incurred in acquiring the asset, installing it, and getting it ready for service.

In many cases this amount can be determined easily. For example, the cost of a truck purchased for cash is simply the amount of cash paid. In other cases, the problem is more complicated. The cost of a parcel of land includes the purchase price, broker's commission, legal fees, and the cost of grading or tearing down existing structures so as to make the land ready for its intended use; and some of these items may be difficult to ascertain. The cost of machinery includes the purchase price, transportation costs to where the machinery is to be used, and installation costs.

Despite the principle stated above, many companies do not capitalize the costs incurred to make the asset ready to provide service. Instead they capitalize only the purchase price. They do this both because it is simpler and in order to minimize property taxes.

When the company constructs a machine or a building with its own personnel, the amount to be capitalized includes all the costs incurred in

146

construction. If the actual cost of building a machine is unreasonably high (as would be the case if the machine was an experimental model and required a considerable amount of development work), the doctrine of conservatism dictates that the asset be "booked" (i.e., recorded in the accounts) at an amount not greater than the purchase price of a similar machine from an outside vendor or not greater than what the cost of building a duplicate machine would be if the "trial-and-error" cost involved in building the original machine could be avoided.

Occasionally a company acquires a fixed asset that turns out to be worth significantly more than the amount paid for it, as, for example, when valuable minerals are discovered on land that was acquired at low cost. These are called *fortunate acquisitions*. Under such circumstances, an exception is often made to the principle that assets are carried on the books at an amount not in excess of their cost, and the asset is recorded at its estimated current value. The difference between this recorded value and actual cost is credited directly to a special category of owners' equity called capital surplus.

Betterments and Replacements versus Maintenance

Repair and maintenance is work done to keep the asset in good operating condition or to bring it back to good operating condition if it has broken down. Repair and maintenance costs are ordinarily expenses of the accounting period in which the work is done; they are *not* added to the cost of the fixed asset.

A *betterment is* added to the cost of the asset. The distinction between maintenance expenses and betterments is simple to state: maintenance work keeps the machine in good condition, but in no better condition than when it was purchased; a betterment makes the machine better than it was when it was purchased. In practice, the line between the two is difficult to draw. A new accessory designed to make the machine operate more efficiently or perform new functions is a betterment; an overhaul during which worn-out parts are replaced with new ones is maintenance. In the interests of conservatism some work which strictly speaking should be considered as a betterment is charged as an expense of the current period.

Replacements may be either assets or expenses, depending on how the asset unit is defined. The replacement of an entire asset results in the writing off of the old asset and the booking of the new. The replacement of a component part of an asset is maintenance expense. Thus, if one company treats a complete airplane as a single asset unit and another company treats the airframe as one unit and the engine as another, then the replacement of an engine results in a maintenance charge in the first company and in a new asset in the second. In general, the broader the definition of the asset unit, the greater will be the amount of costs charged as "maintenance" and hence expensed in the year of acquisition.

Trade-Ins

When a new fixed asset is acquired in exchange for another, the old asset is part of the consideration given; therefore its trade-in value is part of the cost of the new asset. If the stated trade-in allowance differs from the actual value of the old asset, as is often the case with automobiles for example, then this artificial price should not be used in valuing the new asset; under these circumstances, the value is arrived at indirectly, often by estimating what the new asset would have cost if it had been purchased for cash.

> EXAMPLE: An automobile dealer offers to sell Company X a new automobile with a list price of $3,500 for $1,800 cash plus one of Company X's old automobiles for which the dealer says he will make a trade-in allowance of $1,700. Neither the fact that the list price is $3,500, nor the fact that the cash plus trade-in allowance totals $3,500 is conclusive evidence that the asset value of the new automobile is $3,500. Automobiles are customarily sold for less than their list price. Upon further inquiry, it may be discovered that the new automobile can actually be purchased for $3,300 cash; if so, its cost is $3,300.

DEPRECIATION

With the exception of land, most fixed assets have a limited useful life; that is, they will be of use to the company over a limited number of future accounting periods. A fraction of the cost of the asset is properly chargeable as an expense in each of the accounting periods in which the asset is used by the company. The accounting process for this gradual conversion of fixed assets into expense is called *depreciation*. It is described as follows by the Accounting Principles Board:

> The cost of a productive facility is one of the costs of the service it renders during its useful economic life. Generally accepted accounting principles require that this cost be spread over the expected useful life of the facility in such a way as to allocate it as equitably as possible to the periods during which services are obtained from the use of the facility. This procedure is known as depreciation accounting, a system of accounting which aims to distribute the cost or other basic value of tangible capital assets, less salvage (if any), over the estimated useful life of the unit . . . in a systematic and rational manner. It is a process of allocation, not of valuation.[1]

[1] Paul Grady, *Inventory of Generally Accepted Accounting Principles* (AICPA *Accounting Research Study No. 7*, 1965), p. 126.

The question is sometimes asked: Why is depreciation an expense? The answer is that *all* goods and services consumed by a business during an accounting period are expenses. The cost of insurance protection provided in a year is an expense of that year even though the insurance premium was paid two or three years previously. Depreciation expense is like insurance expense except that the fraction of total cost of a fixed asset that is an expense in a given year is difficult to estimate, whereas the fraction of the total cost of an insurance policy that is an expense in a given year can be easily calculated. This difference does not change the fundamental fact that both insurance policies and fixed assets provide service to the company over a *finite* number of accounting periods and must therefore be charged as expenses of each of these periods.

The useful life of an asset is limited for one of two reasons: *deterioration,* which is the physical process of wearing out; and *obsolescence,* which refers to loss of usefulness because of the development of improved equipment or processes, changes in style, or other causes not related to the physical condition of the asset. No distinction need be made between the two since depreciation relates to both of them.

The word "depreciation" is sometimes used as referring only to physical wear and tear; this usage is incorrect. In many cases, a machine becomes obsolete, and consequently is no longer useful, even though it is in good physical condition.

Judgments Required

In order to determine the depreciation expense for an accounting period, three judgments or estimates must be made for each fixed asset:

1. The *service life* of the asset; that is, over how many accounting periods will it be useful to the company?

2. *Salvage or resale value* at the end of its life. The net cost of the asset to the company is its original cost less any amount eventually recovered through sale or salvage, and it is this net cost that should be charged as an expense over the asset's life. In a great many situations, however, the estimated salvage or resale value is so small and uncertain that it is disregarded.

3. *The method of depreciation;* that is, the method that will be used to allocate a fraction of the net cost to each of the accounting periods in which the asset is expected to be used.

Businessmen, not being clairvoyant, cannot *know* in advance how long the asset will last or what its salvage value will be; and they usually have no scientific or strictly logical way of deciding the best depreciation method. The figure of depreciation expense that results from all these judgments is therefore an estimate, and often it is only a rough estimate.

Service Life

The most widely used basis for estimating the service life of assets is the *Depreciation Guidelines,* published by the Internal Revenue Service.[2] This publication contains estimates for the service lives of machinery and equipment used in all types of industries. Some examples are: petroleum drilling, 6 years; aerospace industry and electrical manufacturing industry, 8 years; shoe manufacturing and printing and publishing, 11 years; cement making, 20 years. The booklet also gives estimates for other assets without regard to industry. Examples are:

Office furniture, fixtures, machines, and equipment...................10 years
Automobiles.. 3 years
Light trucks... 4 years
Heavy trucks.. 6 years
Land improvements...20 years
Apartments, hotels, theatres.................................45 years
Dwellings, factories, garages, office buildings, machine shops.........40 years
Banks, loft buildings, stores................................50 years
Grain elevators, warehouses..................................60 years

It should be emphasized that these figures are only *guidelines.* If a company has reason to believe that some other estimate is better, it should by all means use the better estimate.

Depreciation Methods

Consider a machine purchased for $1,000 with an estimated life of 10 years and estimated salvage value of zero. The problem of depreciation accounting is to charge this $1,000 as an expense over the 10-year period. How much should be charged as an expense each year?

This question cannot be answered by observing the amount of asset value physically consumed in a given year, for physically the machine continues to be a machine; usually, there is no observable indication of its decline in usefulness. Nor can the question be answered in terms of changes in the machine's market value during the year, for accounting is concerned with the amortization of cost, not with changes in market values. An indirect approach must therefore be used. Three conceptual ways of looking at the depreciation process are described below, together with the methods that follow from each.

STRAIGHT-LINE METHOD.   One concept views a fixed asset as existing to provide service over its life, with its readiness to provide this service being equal in each year of life, just as a three-year insurance policy

---

[2] *Depreciation Guidelines and Rules,* Internal Revenue Service publication No. 456 (Washington, D.C.: U.S. Government Printing Office, 1962).

provides equal protection in each of the three years. This concept leads to the straight-line method, which is to charge an equal fraction of the cost each year. For a machine costing $1,000 with an estimated service life of 10 years, $\frac{1}{10}$ of $1,000 is the depreciation expense of the first year, another $\frac{1}{10}$ is the depreciation expense of the second year, and so on. Expressed another way, the machine is said to have a *depreciation rate* of 10 percent per year, the rate being the reciprocal of the estimated useful life.

ACCELERATED METHODS. A second concept takes what is perhaps a broader view of the asset since it relates to the *amount* of service provided each year. Many fixed assets are more valuable in their youth than in their old age—because their mechanical efficiency tends to decline with age, because maintenance costs tend to increase with age, and because of the increasing likelihood that better equipment will become available and make them obsolete. It is argued, therefore, that when an asset was purchased the probability that the earlier periods would benefit more than the later periods was taken into account, and that the depreciation method should reflect this. Such a line of reasoning leads to a method which charges a larger fraction of the cost as an expense of the early years than of the later years. This is called an *accelerated* method.[3]

Accelerated methods have been widely adopted since their use was permitted for income tax purposes beginning in 1954. A survey of the 1968 annual reports of 360 manufacturing companies indicated that 9 percent of the companies used the straight-line method for both financial statements and for income tax purposes, 37 percent used principally accelerated methods for both purposes, 42 percent used principally accelerated methods for tax purposes and straight-line methods for their financial statements, and 12 percent used a variety of methods or did not disclose the method that they used. There seems to be a continuing trend toward the use of accelerated methods for tax purposes and straight-line depreciation for financial statements. In 1968, as compared with 1967, 5 percent of the companies in the study changed from accelerated methods for both purposes to this practice.[4]

The two methods specifically mentioned in the 1954 tax law, the double declining-balance method and sum-of-years'-digits (or simply "years'-digits") method, are described below. The effect of either of these methods is to write off approximately two thirds of the cost in the first half of the asset's estimated life, as contrasted with the straight-line method under which, of course, half the cost is written off in each half of the asset's estimated life. Thus, if an accelerated method is used,

---

[3] An argument can also be made for an opposite approach, that is, charging a smaller fraction of the cost to the early years and a larger fraction to the later years. This leads to an *annuity method*. It is relatively uncommon.

[4] Unpublished study by Charles H. Roush, Harvard Business School.

depreciation expense is greater in the early years and less in the later years as compared with the straight-line method.

In the *double declining-balance method,* the depreciation for each year is found by applying a rate to the book value of the asset at the beginning of that year rather than to the original cost of the asset. <u>Book value is cost less total depreciation accumulated up to that time.</u> If the declining-balance method is used, the tax law permits the company to take *double* the rate allowed under the straight-line method, hence the name, double declining balance.

In the *years'-digits method,* the numbers 1, 2, 3 . . . *n* are added, where *n* is the estimated years of useful life. The depreciation rate each year is a fraction in which the denominator is the sum of these digits and the numerator is for the first year, *n;* for the second year, $n - 1$; for the third year $n - 2$; and so on. Assume, for example, a machine with an estimated life of 10 years. The sum of the numbers 1, 2, 3 . . . 10 is 55. Depreciation in the first year would be $^{10}/_{55}$ of the cost; in the second year, $^{9}/_{55}$; in the third year, $^{8}/_{55}$; and so on.

Illustration 6–1 is an example of the way these three methods work out for a machine costing $1,000 with an estimated life of 10 years and no salvage value. Illustration 6–2 shows the same depreciation patterns graphically.

As an incentive to modernize, taxpayers are permitted to deduct in the

Illustration 6–1

Year	Straight-Line (10% Rate)		Declining-Balance (20% Rate)		Years'-Digits		
	Book Value, 12/31	Annual Depreciation	Book Value, 12/31	Annual Depreciation	Rate	Book Value, 12/31	Annual Depreciation
0..........	$1,000	$ ...	$1,000.00	$	....	$1,000.00	$ ....
First.......	900	100	800.00	200.00	10/55	818.18	181.82
Second.....	800	100	640.00	160.00	9/55	654.54	163.64
Third......	700	100	512.00	128.00	8/55	509.09	145.45
Fourth.....	600	100	409.60	102.40	7/55	381.82	127.27
Fifth.......	500	100	327.68	81.92	6/55	272.73	109.09
Sixth.......	400	100	262.14	65.54	5/55	181.82	90.91
Seventh....	300	100	209.71	52.43	4/55	109.09	72.73
Eighth.....	200	100	167.77	41.94	3/55	54.54	54.55
Ninth......	100	100	134.22	33.55	2/55	18.18	36.36
Tenth.....	0	100	107.38	26.84	1/55	0	18.18
Eleventh...	....	...	85.90	21.48	....	....	....
Twelfth....	....	...	68.72*	17.18	....	....	....
		$1,000		$931.28*			$1,000.00

* Under the strict declining-balance method, depreciation continues until the asset is disposed of or until the book value declines to salvage value. Many companies, however, switch from the declining-balance method to the straight-line method in the later years of life, and thus write off the entire cost in a specified number of years. This is permitted for tax purposes.

Illustration 6–2

PATTERNS OF ANNUAL DEPRECIATION

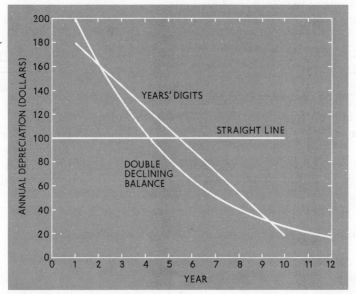

year of acquisition 20 percent of the cost of certain assets, in addition to regular depreciation for that year. This deduction is limited to a total of $2,000 per year. It is allowed only for tangible personal property (not buildings) with an estimated useful life of at least six years. It does not increase the total amount of depreciation that can be taken over the life of the asset; this remains equal to the net cost of the asset.

UNITS-OF-PRODUCTION METHOD. A third concept of depreciation views the asset as consisting of a bundle of service units, the cost of each unit being the total cost of the asset divided by the number of such units, and the depreciation charge for a period therefore being related to the number of units consumed in the period. This leads to the units-of-production method. If a truck has an estimated net cost of $12,000 and is expected to give service for 300,000 miles, depreciation would be charged at a rate of $0.04 per mile, the depreciation expense in a year in which the truck traveled 50,000 miles being $2,000.[5]

Choice of a Method

In deciding on the best depreciation method, tax considerations should be kept completely separate from financial accounting considerations. For

---

[5] An alternative method is to charge a decreasing rate as the number of miles increases, as in the accelerated methods.

tax purposes, the best method is that which minimizes the effect of taxes. Unless tax rates applicable to the business are expected to increase, this is usually one of the accelerated methods.

With respect to financial accounting, each of the concepts described above has its advocates. It should be emphasized that in a single business different methods can be used for different types of assets; for example, straight-line for buildings, accelerated for certain types of machinery and equipment, and units-of-production for other types. An essential requirement also is that there *be* a method. The former practice of charging "whatever the income statement can stand" is indefensible.

If a company uses one depreciation method for income tax purposes and a different method for financial accounting, its taxable income will not match the income as measured by financial accounting. Under these circumstances, it must adjust its reported income tax expense, as explained on page 132.

Accounting for Depreciation

Assume that the Trantor Company purchased, on December 31, 1957, for $90,000, a building with an estimated useful life of 45 years and zero salvage value and that it has decided to depreciate this building on a straight-line basis, that is, $2,000 per year. Let us now consider how to record this depreciation on the accounting records.

It would be possible to reduce the asset value by $2,000 a year and to show on the balance sheet only the remaining amount, which at the end of 1958 would be $88,000; but this is *not* ordinarily done. Instead, a separate contra account is shown on the balance sheet for the accumulated amount of depreciation. This item is usually called *accumulated depreciation*, or it may have some other name such as "allowance for depreciation," "reserve for depreciation," and so on. (The last term is another example of a misleading use of the word "reserve"; the depreciation process does not "reserve" money or anything else.) Both the original cost and the accumulated depreciation figures appear on the balance sheet. The figures as of December 31, 1958, would look like this:

```
Building. . . . . . . . . . . . . . . . . . . . . . .   $90,000
    Less: Accumulated depreciation. . . . . . . . . . .     2,000
       Net . . . . . . . . . . . . . . . . . . . . . .   $88,000
```

As of December 31, 1959, another year's depreciation would be added, and the balance sheet would then show:

```
Building. . . . . . . . . . . . . . . . . . . . . . .   $90,000
    Less: Accumulated depreciation. . . . . . . . . . .     4,000
       Net . . . . . . . . . . . . . . . . . . . . . .   $86,000
```

The foregoing figures can be interpreted as follows:

Original cost of the building...$90,000
That portion of the cost charged to operations for all periods to date.... 4,000
That portion of the cost remaining to be charged to operations of future
    periods...$86,000

On the income statement, the expense item is usually labeled *depreciation expense*. In the income statement for 1958, this item for the Trantor Company would be $2,000 (disregarding depreciation on assets other than the building we are considering), and $2,000 would also appear in the income statement for 1959, 1960, and following years until either the building was disposed of or it was fully depreciated. Usually, the depreciation expense account includes depreciation for all types of fixed assets, but there must be a separate accumulated depreciation account for each category of fixed assets (building, machinery, office equipment, etc.) shown separately on the balance sheet, except for the category, land, since land does not depreciate.

The annual journal entry, which is one of the adjusting entries, would therefore be as follows:

```
Depreciation Expense. . . . . . . . . . . . . . . . .   2,000
     Accumulated Depreciation, Building. . . . . . . .         2,000
```

If the Trantor Company should use its building for more than 45 years, depreciation would cease to be accumulated at the end of the 45th year, since by then the total cost of the building would have been charged to expense. (If the fact that its life will be longer than 45 years became apparent earlier, the depreciation rate should be decreased so as to spread the remaining book value over the longer period.) Until the asset is disposed of, it is customary to continue to show the asset on the balance sheet. Thus, from December 31, 2002, onward, the balance sheet would show the following:

```
Building. . . . . . . . . . . . . . . . . . . . . .   $90,000
     Less: Accumulated depreciation. . . . . . . . . .    90,000
     Net . . . . . . . . . . . . . . . . . . . . . .   $    0
```

Often, half a year's depreciation is recorded in the year of acquisition and half a year's depreciation in the year of disposal no matter what the actual date of acquisition or disposal is, on the grounds that depreciation is a rough estimate and there is no point in attempting to figure it to exact fractions of a year. This practice, if followed consistently, is permitted for tax purposes. Similarly, if accounts are kept on a monthly basis, half a month's depreciation may be recorded in the month of acquisition.

Reporting in Financial Statements

The Accounting Principles Board requires that the income statement show the amount of depreciation expense as a separate item, and that the

balance sheet show the balances of major depreciable assets by nature or
function, accumulated depreciation by classes or in total, and a general
description of the method(s) of computing depreciation for major classes
of depreciable assets.[6]

The Investment Credit

In order to encourage purchases of machinery and equipment, the
income tax statute (as of 1968) permits a credit against income tax of up
to 7 percent of the cost of such assets, provided they are long-lived and
meet certain other criteria. This is called the *investment credit*. The investment credit is a direct reduction in taxes; that is, if a company acquired $100,000 in equipment in 1968, it can deduct $7,000 from the income tax it would otherwise pay for 1968. Furthermore, the company
can depreciate the full cost of the asset (less salvage value) over its useful
life; it is not required to deduct the investment credit in calculating the
amount to be depreciated.

The Accounting Principles Board approves either of two methods of
handling the investment credit for accounting purposes. The first method,
called the *cost-reduction* method, is to spread the effect of the investment
credit over the useful life of the asset by making a reduction in the
depreciation expense of each year of the useful life. The second method,
called the *flow-through* method, reduces income tax expense, and hence
increases net income, in the year in which the credit is taken.[7]

The accounting entries involved in both methods are shown in the
following example:

> EXAMPLE: Assume that in December 1968 a company purchases
> $100,000 of machinery that qualifies for the investment credit, that the
> service life of these assets is 10 years and that (for simplicity) straight-
> line depreciation is to be used. The investment credit is $7,000, and this
> $7,000 is subtracted from the income tax liability in 1968.
>
> Under the cost-reduction method, the investment credit would be
> recorded, in effect, as:

```
Income Tax Liability. . . . . . . . . . . . . . . . . . .  7,000
     Machinery . . . . . . . . . . . . . . . . . . . . . .       7,000
```

Note that net income for 1968 is unaffected by this entry. In 1969
and subsequent years depreciation expense would be calculated on a net
cost of $93,000, rather than $100,000, and would therefore be $9,300 per
year. This has the effect of increasing net income $700 in each of the
next 10 years, as compared with what the net income would have been
had the depreciation expense been $10,000 per year.

---

[6] *Opinions of the Accounting Principles Board No. 12*, December, 1967.

[7] Grady, *op. cit.*, pp. 137–47.

Under the flow-through method, the investment credit would be recorded in 1968 as:

```
Income Tax Liability. . . . . . . . . . . . . . . .   7,000
    Income Tax Expense. . . . . . . . . . . . . . .         7,000
```

This has the effect of increasing 1968 income by $7,000.

DISPOSAL OF FIXED ASSETS

Suppose that at the end of 10 years the Trantor Company sells its building. At that time, $^{10}\!/_{45}$ of the original cost, or $20,000, will have been built up in the Accumulated Depreciation account, and the net book value of the building will be $70,000. If the building is sold for $70,000 cash, the accounts are changed, as follows: Cash is increased by $70,000; the Building account is decreased by $90,000, and Accumulated Depreciation is decreased by $20,000, which is the amount of depreciation accumulated up to that time. The entry is as follows:

```
Cash. . . . . . . . . . . . . . . . . . . . . . . .   70,000
Accumulated Depreciation. . . . . . . . . . . . . .   20,000
    Building. . . . . . . . . . . . . . . . . . . .          90,000
```

This has the effect of eliminating from the accounts both the original cost of the building and the accumulated depreciation thereon.

If the building were sold for less than $70,000, say $60,000, the transaction would be recorded as follows: Cash is increased by $60,000, the Building account is decreased by $90,000, Accumulated Depreciation is decreased by $20,000, and an account, Loss on the Sale of Fixed Assets, or some similar title, is set up, as in the following entry:

```
Cash. . . . . . . . . . . . . . . . . . . . . . . .   60,000
Accumulated Depreciation. . . . . . . . . . . . . .   20,000
Loss on Sale of Fixed Assets. . . . . . . . . . . .   10,000
    Building. . . . . . . . . . . . . . . . . . . .          90,000
```

Note that the effect on the Building and Accumulated Depreciation accounts is identical with that in the previous illustration: the amounts relating to this building disappear. The loss is a decrease in owners' equity, reflecting the fact that the total depreciation expense recorded for the preceding 10 years was less than what we now know to have been the actual net cost of the building over that period of time. The actual net cost turns out to have been $30,000, whereas the total depreciation expense charged has amounted to only $20,000.

Since the depreciation expense as originally recorded turns out to have been incorrect, the Retained Earnings account which reflects the net of all revenue and expenses is also incorrect, and there is therefore some logic in closing the Loss on Sale of Fixed Assets account directly to Retained Earnings, thus correcting the error contained therein. Nevertheless, the "all-inclusive income" principle requires that unless the loss is extraordinarily large, it be shown as an expense on the income statement of the current period.

If an asset is sold for more than its book value, the entries correspond to those described above. The account, Gain on the Sale of Fixed Assets, is usually classified as nonoperating revenue on the income statement.

A trade-in involves the disposal of an asset, and the asset traded in is treated in the accounting records exactly like the sale of the building described above; that is, both its cost and its accumulated depreciation are removed from the books. As mentioned in a preceding section, a problem may arise in determining the proper "sales" value to use in recording this transaction. For income tax purposes, however, a trade-in is treated quite differently. When one asset is exchanged for another of "like kind," no gain or loss is ordinarily recognized for tax purposes. The definition of "like kind" and the circumstances under which this principle is applicable are intricate, and expert tax advice is needed on all except the most routine fixed asset exchanges.

Debits to Accumulated Depreciation

If a machine is given an unusual major overhaul which makes it "as good as new," the cost of this overhaul is sometimes debited to Accumulated Depreciation rather than to Maintenance Expense on the ground that the overhaul has actually canceled or offset some of the accumulated depreciation. Or, it can be argued that the overhaul has extended the useful life of the machine, and that the depreciation accumulated up to the time of overhaul is therefore excessive. In theory, if the estimated useful life has changed, the depreciation rate should be recalculated and the accounts changed to reflect the new estimate of useful life; but in practice, charging the overhaul to Accumulated Depreciation may have approximately the same effect.

GROUP AND COMPOSITE DEPRECIATION

The procedure described above related to a single fixed asset, one building. To find the total depreciation expense for a whole category of assets, this procedure could be repeated for each single asset, and the total depreciation for all the assets in the category would then be recorded by one journal entry. This is the procedure used in many businesses.

An alternative procedure is to treat several assets together rather than making the calculation for each one separately. If similar assets with approximately the same useful life, such as all typewriters or all general-purpose lathes, are treated together, the process is called *group* depreciation. If dissimilar assets are treated together, the process is called *composite* depreciation.

The depreciation rate in composite depreciation is a weighted-average rate, the weights being the dollar amounts of assets in each of the useful-life categories. All the production equipment in a plant, for example, might be included in a single composite account, even though the useful lives of the various items of equipment were not the same. The *Depreciation Guidelines* referred to above give a single depreciation rate for all the machinery and equipment in most types of manufacturing plants (e.g., 11 years for the machinery and equipment in a chemical plant). These are composite rates.

The annual depreciation expense under group or composite depreciation is computed in a manner similar to that described above for an individual asset. If the straight-line method is used, for example, the depreciation rate is applied to the total cost of the whole group of assets.

The accumulation of depreciation does not stop when one item in the group reaches its estimated useful life, however, but continues indefinitely unless it becomes apparent that the accumulation is too large or too small for the whole group of assets. In this case, the depreciation rate is changed. For tax purposes, the Internal Revenue Service has established a set of maximum "reserve ratios" for various asset categories, and companies are penalized if they exceed these ratios. A reserve ratio is the ratio of accumulated depreciation to the cost of the assets in the group.

If a group or composite method is used, no gain or loss is recognized when an individual asset is sold or otherwise disposed of. The asset account is credited for the cost, and the difference between cost and the sales proceeds is simply debited to Accumulated Depreciation. This procedure assumes that gains on some sales are offset by losses on others.

SIGNIFICANCE OF DEPRECIATION

The amount shown as accumulated depreciation on the balance sheet does not represent the "accumulation" of any tangible thing; it is merely that portion of the assets' original cost that has been already charged off against income.

Occasionally a company does set aside money for the specific purpose of purchasing new assets, and this process is sometimes called "funding depreciation." This transaction is completely separate from the depreciation mechanism described above. If depreciation is funded, cash or securities are physically segregated; that is, they are set aside in such a way that they cannot be used in the regular operation of the business (for example, a special bank account may be created). This fact is reflected on the balance sheet by an asset titled "New Building Fund," or some similar name, the offsetting entry being a credit to Cash. This practice is not common and is mentioned here only to emphasize, by contrast, the point that the depreciation process itself is *not* a means of automatically creating a fund for the replacement of assets.

There is a widespread belief that, in some mysterious way, depreciation does represent money, specifically, money that can be used to purchase new assets. Depreciation is *not* money; the money that the business has is shown by the balance in its Cash account.

> EXAMPLE: This quotation is from a well-known publication: "Most large companies draw much of the cash flow they employ for expanding and modernizing their operations from their depreciation reserves." This statement is not true in anything remotely approaching a literal sense. Possibly the author intended some figurative, rather than literal, meaning, but it is difficult to imagine how the statement could be true in even a figurative sense.

There is also a widespread belief that the book value of assets is related to their real value, and this is equally erroneous.

> EXAMPLE: An auditor's report included the following statement: "Our inspection of insurance policies in force at the close of the year disclosed that the plant assets, on the basis of book values, were amply protected against fire." Such a statement has little if any significance. What the management wants to know is whether the insurance policies equal the *actual cash value* of the assets, and this is unlikely to correspond to their *book value*.

Concluding Comment

The key to a practical understanding of depreciation is a sentence from the AICPA statement quoted earlier: *Depreciation is a process of allocation, not of valuation.* Depreciation expense does *not* represent the shrinkage in real value during an accounting period; physically, the machine may be as useful and as valuable at the end of the period as it was at the beginning. Neither does the net book value represent the market value of the assets on hand. Depreciation expense is a write-off of a portion of the *cost* of the asset, and it follows that the net book value of fixed assets reported on the balance sheet represents only that portion of the original cost of the fixed asset which has *not yet* been charged to expense.

No one really knows how long an asset will last or what its residual value will be at the end of its life. Without this knowledge, the depreciation figure is necessarily an estimate.

OTHER ASPECTS OF TANGIBLE ASSETS

Depletion

Natural resources such as coal, oil, other minerals, and timber are called *wasting assets*. The process of writing off the cost of these fixed assets to expenses in the accounting periods benefited is called *depletion.* The objective is the the same as that for depreciation: to amortize the cost in some systematic manner over the asset's useful life. The unit-of-production method is ordinarily used. For example, if an oil property cost $500,000 and is estimated to contain 1 million barrels of oil, the depletion rate is 50 cents per barrel; the total depletion for a year in which 80,000 barrels of oil were produced would be $40,000.

For income tax purposes, however, the depletion allowance usually bears no relation to cost; rather, it is a percentage of revenue. The permitted percentage (as of 1969) varies from 5 percent on clay, gravel, and other common materials to 27½ percent on oil and gas. This is perhaps the most clear-cut example of an income tax provision that is inconsistent with generally accepted accounting principles. Advocates of this provision in the tax law claim that it stimulates exploration for and development of new supplies of natural resources and is therefore in the national interest.

Accretion and Appreciation

Accretion is the increase in value of timberland, cattle, and other agricultural products that arises through the natural process of growth. Since accretion does not represent realized revenue, it is ordinarily not recognized in the accounts, although the *costs* incurred in the growing process may be added to the asset value, just as is done in the case of costs incurred in the manufacture of products.

Appreciation is also an increase of value and is therefore *not* the opposite of depreciation, which is a write-off of *cost.* Appreciation of either fixed assets or inventory is recognized in the accounts only under highly unusual circumstances; for example, if a new owner took over a business and an appraisal disclosed that the current market value of fixed assets was substantially above their book value, it is conceivable that the asset values would be written up to their current value. Generally, however, increases in value are recognized in the accounts only when revenue is realized, whereas expiration of cost is recognized when it occurs.

INTANGIBLE ASSETS

Intangible long-lived assets, such as goodwill, organization cost (i.e., cost incurred to get a business started), trademarks, and patents are usually converted to expenses over a number of accounting periods. The periodic write-off is specifically called *amortization,* although the word "amortization" is also used in the broad sense of any write-off of a cost over a period of years. The amortization of intangible assets is essentially the same process as the depreciation of tangible assets. Amortization is ordinarily recorded as a credit directly to the asset account, not to a separate account analogous to Accumulated Depreciation.

The Accounting Principles Board suggests that these intangibles be classified into two categories:

(a) Those having a term of existence limited by law, regulation, or agreement, or by their nature (such as patents, copyrights, leases, licenses, franchises for a fixed term, and goodwill as to which there is evidence of limited duration);

(b) Those having no such limited term of existence and as to which there is, at the time of acquisition, no indication of limited life (such as goodwill generally, going value, trade names, secret processes, subscription lists, perpetual franchises, and organization costs.)[8]

The treatment recommended for each category is as follows:

The cost of the type (a) intangibles should be amortized by systematic charges in the income statement over the period benefited, as in the case of other assets having a limited period of usefulness. . . .

When it becomes reasonably evident that the term of existence of a type (b) intangible has become limited and that it has therefore become a type (a) intangible, its cost should be amortized by systematic charges in the income statement over the estimated remaining period of usefulness.[9]

Although the above statement does not sanction such a treatment, many companies *do* write off "type (b)" intangibles (those that do not have a definitely limited life) over one or more accounting periods. Organization cost is frequently handled in this manner, for although the "benefit" of organizing a company may be said, in a sense, to extend over the whole life of the company, it would be a considerable bother, with little offsetting advantage to anyone, to hold this cost as an asset on the balance sheet year after year. There is, by definition, no logical way of determining over how many periods such assets should be written off. In some cases, they are written off as an expense in the year of acquisition. Other companies choose to write them off over some fairly short period, such as 5 or 10 years, with the choice of the time period depending on the amount that safely can be charged without having a material effect on income.

These practices have been heavily influenced by the doctrine of conservatism, although custom has a great deal to do with them also. Customarily, for example, advertising expenditures are not capitalized even though it may be quite clear that these expenditures benefit future rather than current periods. Often, these practices are justified on the grounds that the future benefits are so uncertain that an attempt to estimate them is unwarranted. With respect to the argument for conservatism, it should

[8] Grady, *op. cit.,* p. 262.
[9] *Ibid.,* p. 263.

be pointed out that a practice that understates asset values and current income inevitably overstates future income.

Incidentally, some companies emphasize their conservatism by showing intangible assets at a nominal amount on the balance sheet, thus:

Goodwill, patents, and other intangibles..................$1.00

This practice stems from the pre-1930's when some companies *watered* their assets by capitalizing a wide variety of intangibles of dubious value and hiding these values in with other asset items. Companies that followed the more conservative practice of writing off intangibles as acquired have indicated this fact to the reader of the balance sheet by the above wording. Since current practice requires that intangibles be reported as a separate item if they are material in amount, the absence of any such item means that no material amount of intangibles is being carried as an asset, and the above method of presentation is not as necessary as formerly.

The *useful* life of a "type (a)" intangible may be shorter than its legal life; if so, the cost of the asset is written off over the shorter period. For example, although a patent is legally valid for 17 years, the company may decide that technological change or other forces may make it obsolete within a shorter period of time; if such is the case, the patent may be written off over 15 years, 10 years, or even less.

Leasehold improvements are the costs incurred by the lessee to improve leased property. Since, as a matter of law, any remaining value of these improvements reverts to the owner when the leased property is given up, the benefits to the lessee automatically end when he gives up the leased property, and the cost must therefore be written off over the time he expects to have the use of the property.

SUMMARY

Fixed assets are originally recorded at their acquisition cost, including costs involved in making them ready to provide service. This cost is charged off as depreciation expense in some systematic manner over the periods in which the asset is expected to be useful. The method selected may charge an equal amount each year, a larger amount in early years than in late years, or an amount that depends on usage. A corresponding reduction is made in the asset amount. Upon disposition, both the cost and the accumulated depreciation are removed from the accounts, and any gain or loss is reported separately, usually on the income statement.

Intangible assets are amortized by a similar process. Although the write-off of intangibles that have no limited life is not officially approved, many companies do amortize such assets on the grounds of conservatism.

CASES

CASE 6–1. PALMER CORPORATION (B)

After the controller of the Palmer Corporation had ascertained the changes in accounts receivable and the allowance for doubtful accounts in 1967, he made a similar analysis of fixed assets and accumulated depreciation. Again he examined the December 31, 1966, balance sheet [Exhibit 1 in Palmer Corporation (A), p. 136]. He also reviewed the following transactions which he found to be applicable to these accounts:

1. On January 2, 1967, one of the factory machines was sold for its book value, $1,964. This machine was recorded on the books at $15,865 with accumulated depreciation of $13,901.
2. Tools were carried on the books at cost, and at the end of each year a physical inventory was taken to determine what tools still remained. The account was written down to the extent of the decrease in tools as ascertained by the year-end inventory. At the end of 1967, it was determined that there had been a decrease in the tool inventory amounting to $3,988.
3. On March 1, 1967, the company sold for $831 cash an automobile which was recorded on the books at a cost of $2,970 and had an accumulated depreciation of $1,842 as of January 1, 1967. In this and other cases of sale of fixed assets during the year, the accumulated depreciation and depreciation expense items were both increased by an amount which reflected the depreciation chargeable for the months in 1967 in which the asset was held prior to the sale, at rates listed in Item 7 below.
4. The patent listed on the balance sheet had been purchased by the Palmer Corporation on December 31, 1960, for $50,000. This patent had been granted on December 31, 1958. The cost of the patent was to be written off as an expense over the remainder of its legal life. (The total life of a patent is 17 years from the date granted.)
5. On July 1, 1967, a typewriter which had cost $457 and had been fully depreciated on December 31, 1966, was sold for $35.

6. On October 1, the company sold a desk for $40. This piece of furniture was recorded on the books at a cost of $239 with an accumulated depreciation of $194 as of January 1, 1967.
7. Depreciation on fixed assets was figured as follows:

Buildings.. 2%
Factory machinery...10*
Furniture and fixtures...10
Automotive equipment...20
Office machines...10

   * Included in the factory machinery cost of $1,826,979 was a machine costing $41,602 which had been fully depreciated on December 31, 1966 and which was still in use.

Questions

1. Analyze the effect of each of these transactions upon the fixed asset accounts, accumulated depreciation, and any other accounts which may be involved in a manner similar to that used in Palmer Corporation (A), and prepare journal entries.
2. Give the correct totals for the fixed assets and the amount of accumulating depreciation as of December 31, 1967, after the transactions affecting them had been recorded.

CASE 6–2. PROBLEMS IN CAPITALIZATION

The brief descriptions presented below are representative of types of problems in which it is necessary to determine whether given expenditures should be accounted for as assets (i.e., be capitalized) or as expenses:

1. The Bruce Manufacturing Company used its own maintenance crew to build an additional wing on its existing factory building. Questions arose as to the proper accounting treatment of the following items:

a) Architects' fees.
b) The cost of snow removal during construction.
c) Cash discounts earned for prompt payment on materials purchased for construction.
d) The cost of building a combined construction office and tool shed which would be torn down once the factory wing had been completed.
e) Interest on money borrowed to finance construction.
f) Local real estate taxes for the period of construction on the portion of land to be occupied by the new wing.
g) The cost of mistakes made during construction.
h) The overhead costs of the maintenance department which include supervision; depreciation on buildings and equipment of maintenance department

shops; heat, light, and power for these shops; and allocations of cost for such items as the cafeteria, medical office, and personnel department.

i) The cost of insurance during construction, and the cost of damages or losses on any injuries or losses not covered by insurance.

2. The Archer Company bought a large piece of land, including the buildings thereon, with the intent of razing the buildings and constructing a combined hotel and office building in their place. The existing buildings consisted of a theater and several stores and small apartment buildings, all in active use at the time of the purchase.

a) What accounting treatment should be accorded that portion of the purchase price considered to be the amount paid for the buildings which were subsequently razed?

b) How should the costs of demolishing the old buildings be treated?

c) Suppose that a single company had owned this large piece of land, including the buildings thereon, and instead of selling to the Archer Company had decided to have the buildings razed and to have a combined hotel and office building constructed on the site for its own benefit. In what respects, if any, should the accounting treatment of the old buildings and the cost of demolishing them differ from your recommendations with respect to (*a*) and (*b*) above?

3. The Midland Manufacturing Company purchased a new machine. It is clear that the invoice price of the new machine should be capitalized and it also seems reasonable to capitalize the transportation cost to bring the machine to the Midland plant. Questions have arisen, however, on the following items:

a) The new machine is heavier than the old machine it replaced; consequently the foundation under the machine has had to be strengthened by the installation of additional steel beams. Should this cost be charged to the building, added to the cost of the machine, or be expensed?

b) The installation of the machine took longer and was more costly than anticipated. In addition to time spent by the regular maintenance crew on installation, it became necessary to hire an outside engineer to assist in the installation and in "working out the bugs" to get the machine running properly. His costs included not only his fee but also his transportation, hotel expense, and meals. Moreover, the foreman of the department and the plant superintendent both spent a considerable amount of time assisting the installation. Before the new machine was working properly a large amount of material had been spoiled during trial runs.

c) In addition to the invoice price and transportation, it was necessary to pay a state sales tax on purchasing the machine.

d) In connection with payment for the new machine the machine manufacturer was willing to accept the Midland Company's old machine as partial payment. The amount allowed as a trade-in was larger than the depreciated value at which the old machine was being carried in the books of the Midland Company. Should the difference have been treated as a reduction in the cost of the new machine or a gain on disposal of the old one?

CASE 6–3. MASSASOIT TRUST COMPANY

The Massasoit Trust Company conducted a commercial banking business in a city of approximately 100,000. The company did not own its banking quarters but operated under a lease which still had six years to run in 1968. While the lease contained no renewal provisions, the bank had occupied the building since 1905 under successive 10-year leases. Relations with the owner of the building, who was also the operator of a nearby department store, continued to be cordial. The lease provided, however, that the owner could cancel the lease on two years' notice if he required the property for his own business.

In the spring of 1968, the directors of the bank were considering a proposal to remodel and air condition the bank quarters. The bank had received firm bids from contractors on the work to be done, and these totaled approximately $63,000.

In the course of the discussion, a debate arose over the way in which the expenditure would be carried in the bank's books. One of the directors favored carrying the improvement as an asset and depreciating it over its physical life, which he estimated at about 25 years.

Several directors objected to this procedure. Under the so-called "rule of fixtures," which was a well-established legal principle, permanent improvements to leased property were generally considered to be the property of the owner of the real estate. Since the bank did not own the property, these directors did not think the improvements should be considered as an asset. They favored charging the entire cost of the improvements as an expense in the current year, which had been the procedure with minor renovation expenses in the past.

Other directors felt that capitalizing the expenditure would be acceptable, but they did not think it wise to adopt a depreciation period longer than the life of the lease. They also wondered what consideration should be given to the two-year cancellation provision.

The first director was not convinced by either of these approaches. He said he would not favor the remodeling project were he not convinced that the lease would be renewed as it had been in the past. He was also disturbed about the effect that a rapid write-off might have on the bank's earnings.

Section 178 (c) of the Internal Revenue Code provides that for income tax purposes, as a general rule, improvements made to leased assets should be amortized over either the remaining life of the lease or the life of the improvement, whichever is shorter. If, however, upon completion of the improvement, the remaining life of the lease is less than 60 percent of the useful life of the improvement, it is ordinarily presumed that the lease will be renewed, and this longer life will determine the amortization period.

Exhibit 1

MASSASOIT TRUST COMPANY

Statement of Condition, December 31, 1967
(Thousands of Dollars)

RESOURCES

Cash on hand and in banks	$ 2,464
U.S. government securities	6,886
Other securities	275
Loans and discounts	2,587
Other assets	42
	$12,254

LIABILITIES

Commercial deposits		$ 8,667
Savings deposits		2,402
Total deposits		$11,069
Reserve for taxes, etc.		61
Capital stock	$350	
Surplus	774	1,124
		$12,254

In 1967, the Massasoit Trust Company had a gross revenue of $285,000, including $205,000 in income from loans, discounts, and investments in securities. After operating expenses, but before income taxes, earnings were approximately $70,000. Federal income taxes amounted to about $20,000. The operating expenses were largely of a fixed nature.

The bank's statement of condition as of December 31, 1967, is given in Exhibit 1. According to the state banking law, trust companies could accept deposits of up to 10 times the amount of their capital and surplus. The law also required 15 percent of deposits to be maintained as a liquid reserve; the balance could be used for loans, discounts, and investments in United States government and other securities. The bank was not permitted to loan an amount greater than 20 percent of its capital stock and surplus to any one individual or firm.

Questions

1. Why should the directors be concerned about this problem?
2. What action do you recommend?

CASE 6–4. BRAZOS PRINTING COMPANY

The Brazos Printing Company was founded in 1940 as a one-man job printing firm in a small southwestern town. Shortly after its founding, the owner decided to concentrate on one specialty line of printing. Because of a high degree of technical proficiency, the company experienced a rapid growth.

Exhibit 1

BRAZOS PRINTING COMPANY

Condensed Balance Sheet as of March 31, 1962

ASSETS			EQUITIES	
Current Assets:			Current liabilities.....	$ 40,016
Cash.................		$102,612	Common stock.......	110,000
Other current assets.....		76,816	Retained earnings.....	88,933
Total Current Assets.		$179,428		
Fixed Assets:				
Land.................		7,000		
Buildings..............$72,000				
Less: Accumulated depreciation......... 41,000		31,000		
Equipment............$66,212				
Less: Accumulated depreciation......... 44,691		21,521		
Total Assets......		$238,949	Total Equities..$238,949	

However, the company suffered from a competitive disadvantage in that the major market for its specialized output was in a metropolitan area over 300 miles away from the company's plant. For this reason, the owner, in 1962, decided to move nearer his primary market. He also decided to expand and modernize his facilities at the time of the move. After some investigation, an attractive site was found in a suburb of his primary market, and the move was made.

A balance sheet prepared prior to the move is shown in Exhibit 1. The transactions that arose from this move are described in the following paragraphs:

1. The land at the old site together with the building thereon was sold for $36,000. The land had originally cost $7,000. The building appeared on the company's books at a cost of $72,000, and a depreciation allowance of $41,000 had been accumulated on it.

2. Certain equipment was sold for $5,000 cash. This equipment ap-

peared on the books at a cost of $18,200 less accumulated depreciation of $10,200.

3. A new printing press was purchased. The invoice cost of this equipment was $20,000. A 2 percent cash discount was taken by the Brazos Company, so that only $19,600 was actually paid to the seller. The Brazos Company also paid $80 to a trucker to have this equipment delivered. Installation of this equipment was made by Brazos workmen who worked a total of 60 hours. These men received $2.50 per hour in wages, but their time was ordinarily charged to printing jobs at $5 per hour, the difference representing an allowance for overhead ($2) and profit ($0.50).

4. The city to which the company moved furnished the land on which the new plant was built as a gift. The land had an appraised value of $25,000. The appraisal had been made recently by a qualified appraiser. The company would pay property taxes on its assessed value, which was $16,000.

5. The Brazos Company paid $3,800 to have an old building on the gift plot of land torn down. (The value of this building was not included in the appraised or assessed values named above.) In addition, the company paid $2,400 to have permanent drainage facilities installed on the new land.

6. A new strip caster with an invoice cost of $5,000 was purchased. The company paid $3,200 cash and received a trade-in allowance of $1,800 on a used strip caster. The used strip caster could have been sold outright for not more than $1,500. It had cost $3,000 new, and accumulated depreciation on it was $1,300.

7. The company erected a building at the new site for $100,000. Of this amount, $75,000 was borrowed on a mortgage.

8. After the equipment had been moved to the new plant, but before operations began there, extensive repairs and replacements of parts were made on a large paper cutter. The cost of this work was $1,000. Prior to this time, no more than $100 had been spent in any one year on the maintenance of this paper cutter.

9. Trucking and other costs associated with moving equipment to the new location and installing it were $1,500. In addition, Brazos Company employees worked an estimated 125 hours on that part of the move that related to equipment.

10. During the moving operation, a piece of equipment costing $2,500 was dropped and damaged; $500 was spent to repair it. The management believed, however, that the salvage value of this equipment had been reduced to $250. Up until that time, the equipment was being depreciated at $200 per year, representing a 10 percent rate after deduction of estimated salvage of $500. Accumulated depreciation was $800.

Question

1. Analyze the effect of these transactions on the items in the balance sheet and income statement. For transactions that affect owners' equity, distinguish between those that affect the net income of the current year and those that do not. In most cases, the results of your analysis can be set forth most clearly in the form of journal entries.

CASE 6–5. MILWAUKEE BRAVES, INC.

Milwaukee Braves, Inc. was incorporated under the laws of the State of Delaware on November 15, 1962, to operate the Milwaukee Braves baseball team of the National League. This case deals with the Milwaukee Braves' accounting for the costs of the player contracts acquired from a predecessor corporation and the subsequent costs incurred by the company for player development and acquisitions.

Players

The competitive success of a baseball club, which bears a strong relationship to its financial success, depends primarily upon the skill of players under contract to the club. In 1963, the policy of the Braves was to rely primarily upon players who were recruited and developed through the company's own player replacement program in the seven-club farm system it operated. During the period 1958–62, the National League Baseball Club of Milwaukee, Inc. spent about $6.6 million for the cost of scouting and team replacement, including the farm system, bonuses, schools, and tryouts. Occasionally, players' contracts were also acquired in major league trades or purchases. These costs were entirely written off as an expense in the respective years paid.

Forty-three players made up the Braves major league roster as of February 1, 1963. In 1963, Warren Spahn, with 327 major league wins, held the National League record for most games won by a left-handed pitcher and had two no-hit games. Also, he was a member of the National League All Star team 14 times. Frank Bolling led the league in fielding at his position in 1961 and 1962 and was a member of the National League All Star team in those years. Del Crandell led National League catchers in fielding in 1958, 1959, 1960, and 1962, and had been a member of the All Star squad eight times. Eddie Matthews had hit 399 home runs in his major league career and had played on the All Star team nine times. He ranked eighth on the all-time list of major league home run hitters. Hank Aaron led the league in total bases in 1956, 1957, 1959, 1960, and 1961, and was on the All Star team eight years. His lifetime major league batting average was .319, which was second highest among all active National League players in 1963.

The Braves controlled approximately 160 additional baseball player contracts. Player contracts were acquired through the services of 15 full-time scouts and 19 part-time scouts who covered the United States, Canada, and Latin America.

Player Acquisition

Young players often required at least three to five years' experience in the minor leagues before acquiring the skills needed to perform in the major leagues. In 1963, the Braves owned and operated two minor league clubs and in addition had working agreements with five other minor league clubs.

Once a player had signed a professional baseball contract with one of the clubs comprising the farm system of the Braves, his contract remained subject to the control of the Braves until such time as it was traded or sold to a club outside the Braves system, or until he was given an outright and unconditional release from his contract, or unless he was selected by another major league club in what was popularly called the baseball draft.

Most major league clubs often were interested in the same young baseball players. As a result of this tremendous competition, the practice developed on the part of many clubs to pay large bonuses to induce free-agent players to sign their first contract.

Player Acquisition and Development Costs

On November 16, 1962, the Milwaukee Braves entered into an agreement to purchase all of the outstanding capital stock of the National League Baseball Club of Milwaukee from Perini Corporation. On the closing date for this transaction, November 26, 1962, the National League Baseball Club of Milwaukee was liquidated and its assets and liabilities were transferred to the Milwaukee Braves.

The total cost of the acquisition, including broker's commission, was $6,218,480; the cost was allocated to player contracts ($6,168,480) and league membership ($50,000).

Prior to the acquisition, the predecessor company, the National League Baseball Club of Milwaukee, had expensed all costs in connection with the acquisition and development of players.

Starting with the 1963 season, for financial reporting purposes, the Milwaukee Braves intended to capitalize the total cost of developing players, including the net income or expense from purchase and sale of player contracts. The amounts so capitalized were to be amortized against operating income "over a period equivalent to the actual playing careers of major league players." The cost of player contracts acquired from the predecessor company were to be amortized against operating income "over a period estimated to reflect replacement through future player development expenditures."

For income tax purposes, the company intended to deduct future team replacement expenditures from income as incurred. The cost of player contracts acquired from the predecessor company were to be amortized over a 10-year period, which represented the major league experience of the players of the National League Baseball Club of Milwaukee.

Exhibit 1

MILWAUKEE BRAVES, INC.

Pro Forma Statement of Income from Baseball Operations
for the Year Ended October 31, 1962

	Statement of Income for the Year Ended October 31, 1962		
	Historical Statement	*Pro Forma Adjustments (Note A)*	*Pro Forma Statement*
Operating income.....................	$3,670,417		$3,670,417
Operating expenses:			
Team, park, games, and concessions......	$2,263,706	$ (60,032) (*a*)	$2,203,674
Team replacement, including net income or expense from purchase and sale of players.....................	599,433	(599,433) (*b*)	. . . . . .
Amortization of player costs...........	. . . . . .	691,777 (*c*)	691,777
Scouting salaries and expense..........	274,278		274,278
General and administrative............	336,718		336,718
Total operating expenses...........	$3,474,135		$3,506,447
Income from baseball operations.........	$ 196,282		$ 163,970
Interest expense.......................	3,567	150,000 (*d*)	153,567
Net income applicable to baseball operations before income taxes..............	$ 192,715		$ 10,403
Provision for income taxes, applicable to baseball operations (Note B)..........	104,000	(100,600) (*e*)	3,400
Net Income Applicable to Baseball Operations........................	$ 88,715		$ 7,003

NOTES:
(A) Explanation of pro forma adjustments:
    (*a*) Restatement of rental costs under terms of the new stadium lease.
    (*b*) Reduction in operating expenses for the amount of team replacement expenses to be capitalized and amortized over the estimated playing career of major league players.
    (*c*) Amortization of player contracts capitalized upon acquisition of the club and of amounts expended for team replacement subsequent to acquisition.
    (*d*) Annual interest charges estimated at 5% on the term note payable to bank.
    (*e*) Adjustment in the provision for income taxes to reflect the foregoing adjustments.
(B) On a pro forma basis, amortization of player contracts and future team replacement costs for tax purposes will exceed the amortization recorded in the income statement, and, consequently, there will be no income tax currently payable.

Exhibit 1 is an operating statement for 1962 prepared by the Milwaukee Braves. This statement shows the effect of certain adjustments to be made by the Milwaukee Braves. In the opinion of the company, these adjustments, when applied to the historical statements related to the baseball operations of the National League Club of Milwaukee, fairly presented the results of operation on a pro forma basis for the year ended October 31, 1962.

Questions

1. Do you agree with the decision to capitalize (*a*) the costs of the player contracts acquired from the National League Baseball Club of Milwaukee and (*b*) future player acquisition and development costs?

2. Do you approve of the company's policies covering the amortization of the costs referred to in Question 1? What accounting techniques do you recommend that the company adopt so as to achieve its goal of amortizing (*a*) the acquired player contract costs "over a period estimated to reflect replacement through future player development expenditures" and (*b*) the future player development and acquisition costs "over a period equivalent to the actual playing careers of major league players?"

3. Comment on the allocation of the purchase price ($6,218,480) between player contracts ($6,168,480) and league membership ($50,000).

CHAPTER 7

INCOME MEASUREMENT IN MANUFACTURING COMPANIES

Manufacturing companies perform different functions from those performed by merchandise trading companies (e.g., retail stores, wholesalers, distributors), and there is a corresponding difference between methods of accounting for the cost of goods sold in the two types of companies. This chapter describes the measurement of cost of goods sold in manufacturing companies. A manufacturing company has as a major function the conversion of raw materials into finished goods. In any company, cost of goods sold is the total of the purchase price plus conversion costs, if any, of the products that are sold. The manufacturer, therefore, includes in cost of goods sold the cost of raw material used, the cost of labor, and other costs incurred in the manufacture of the goods that are sold. The difference between accounting for the cost of goods sold in a merchandising company and in a manufacturing company arises because the merchandising company usually has no conversion costs; thus, its cost of goods sold is practically the same as the price that the company paid for the products that it sells.

The measurement of cost of goods sold is therefore more complicated in a manufacturing company than in a merchandising company. In a merchandising company, this cost is normally obtained directly from invoices. In a manufacturing company it must be obtained by collecting and aggregating the several elements of manufacturing cost.

Both manufacturing and merchandising companies usually have general and administrative expenses. Generally, the manufacturer is also a merchandiser and incurs selling expenses in disposing of his goods. These selling expenses, along with general and administrative and financial costs, appear on the income statement of a manufacturing company in the same manner as in a merchandising firm, that is, below the gross profit figure.

175

FLOW OF COSTS

Elements of Cost

Illustration 7–1 shows elements of cost that are frequently considered in determining the total cost of a manufactured product. These are described below.

Illustration 7–1

ELEMENTS OF COST

DIRECT MATERIALS.   Direct materials (sometimes called "stores") are materials which actually enter into and become part of the finished product. They are to be distinguished from *supplies*, which are materials used in the operation of the business but not directly in the product itself. Direct material costs include the cost of inward freight, and many companies also include storage and handling costs. Purchase discounts are often deducted from the invoice price of goods purchased.

DIRECT LABOR.   A second element of manufacturing cost is direct labor, which is labor applied to convert raw material into the finished product. Direct labor costs are those which can be specifically identified with a product or which vary so closely with the number of products produced that a direct relationship is presumed to be present. The wages and related costs of workers who assemble parts into a finished product, or who operate machines in the process of production, or who work on the product with tools would be considered as direct labor cost.

FACTORY INDIRECT. The third category of manufacturing costs is factory indirect, sometimes termed "burden," or, simply, "overhead." Factory indirect includes all manufacturing costs other than raw materials and direct labor. One such element is indirect labor, which represents wages and salaries earned by employees, such as foremen, truckmen, and janitors, who do not work directly on the product itself but whose services are related to the process of production. Factory indirect also includes such costs as heat, light, power, maintenance, supplies, and depreciation, taxes, and insurance on the assets used in the manufacturing process.

Selling costs or *distribution costs* or *marketing costs* are those incurred in an effort to makes sales and those costs incurred in storing the completed product and in transferring it to the customer. These costs incurred "beyond the factory door" include warehousing costs, billing costs, and transportation costs.

General and administrative costs is a catchall classification to cover items not included in the above categories. Such items are as follows: costs incurred in the general and executive offices; research, development, and engineering costs (which may be wholly or partly included in factory overhead); public relations costs (often included in selling); donations; and miscellaneous items.

Financial costs include interest and other costs incurred in connection with borrowed capital. Sometimes these costs are included in general and administrative costs, although they are often collected separately and treated as nonoperating expenses.

As Illustration 7–1 indicates, the cost figure which is used for inventory valuation and cost of goods sold is typically the factory cost, that is, the sum of direct material, direct labor, and factory indirect costs.

Product Costs and Period Costs

Elements of cost that are included in the cost of a product are called *product* costs; other elements of cost are called *period* costs. There is considerable disagreement among accountants as to where the line between these two types of costs should be drawn.

At one extreme there are those who view a business as performing only two functions, production and distribution. They therefore assign all costs to one of these functions, and thus assign a large fraction of general and administrative costs to product costs. Selling costs, however, are never included in product costs.

The great majority of companies define product costs as the sum of direct labor, direct material, and factory indirect, excluding general and administrative costs, as indicated in Illustration 7–1. Among these companies there are differences in the treatment of specific items. Some companies include the cost of such functions as manufacturing administration, personnel and industrial relations, plant protection, and accounting in factory indirect and hence in product costs; other companies include part of the cost of some or all of these functions; and still others exclude all of them.

At the other extreme are the advocates of "direct costing," a procedure in which all fixed indirect costs are excluded from product costs. Although a direct cost system may provide useful information for management, it is not an accepted procedure for financial accounting.[1]

The way in which a manufacturing company classifies its costs into period costs and product costs can have an important effect on its reported net income. Period costs are expenses in the accounting period in which they are incurred, whereas product costs add to the cost of the product and do not have an impact on net income until the product has been sold, which may well be a later accounting period than the period in which the costs were incurred. This point is discussed further in Chapter 13.

In view of these wide variations in practice, the reader of financial statements needs to know what types of cost a company has decided to include in its inventory if he is to understand what its statements mean.

Inventory Accounts

A manufacturing company typically has three types of inventory accounts: raw materials, goods in process, and finished goods. *Raw Materials Inventory* shows the cost of the raw materials on hand. *Goods in Process* (or *Work in Process*) *Inventory* shows the costs accumulated for those products on which production has been started but not yet completed as of the end of the accounting period. This includes the direct material, direct labor, and factory indirect costs assigned to such products. *Finished Goods Inventory* shows the cost of products that have been manufactured but not yet sold. This account is comparable to the Merchandise Inventory account in a trading company.

---

[1] AICPA *Accounting Research Bulletin No. 43* states: "As applied to inventories, cost means in principle the sum of the applicable expenditures and charges directly or indirectly incurred in bringing an article to its existing condition and location . . . the exclusion of all overheads from inventory costs does not constitute an accepted accounting procedure." Paul Grady, *Inventory of Generally Accepted Accounting Principles* (AICPA, 1965), pp. 245–46.

The Account Flow Chart

The flow of costs through the inventory accounts, ending with their appearance on the income statement as cost of goods sold, is described in the next section. As an aid in understanding this flow, the concept of the account flow chart is introduced. Such a flow chart consists of the accounts used in the system, shown in T account form, with lines indicating the flow of figures from one account to another.

Most of the accounts associated with the manufacturing process are either asset accounts (principally inventory accounts) or expense accounts. (For some purposes, the general term "cost account" is useful, but a cost account is always classifiable either as an asset, if the cost will benefit a future period, or as an expense, if the benefit has expired.) A characteristic of both asset and expense accounts is that increases are shown on the debit side and decreases are shown on the credit side. Since a line on a flow chart indicating a transfer "from" one account "to" another account signifies that the first account is being decreased and the second account is being increased, it follows that the typical line on a flow chart of the manufacturing process leads from the credit side of one account to the debit side of another. In addition to the lines designating "flow," other lines indicate debit and credit entries that are generated in the production process; an example is the entry for the acquisition of raw material, which is a debit to Raw Materials Inventory and a credit to Accounts Payable.

Flow of Costs

Illustration 7–2 illustrates the flow-chart concept and shows the essential cost flows in a manufacturing company. This flow chart contains a hypothetical set of figures for a month's operation in a small company manufacturing smoking pipes. The cycle of operations shown therein may be explained as follows:

1. During the month, $3,000 of raw material was purchased on open account, $4,200 of other assets were purchased, and $15,000 of accounts payable were paid.
2. During the month, raw material costing $4,000 (principally briar wood, hard rubber blanks for stems, and filters) was withdrawn from inventory and sent to the shop to be worked on. This decreased Raw Materials Inventory and increased Goods in Process.
3. During the month, men worked on this material and fashioned it into pipes. The amount which they earned, $2,500, was added to the value of the Goods in Process, and the resulting liability was credited to Wages Payable.

Illustration 7–2

FLOW CHART OF A PIPE COMPANY

NOTE: Circled numbers refer to events described in the text.

Bal. = Net income before taxes

4. The men were paid $2,700. This decreased the liability account, Wages Payable, and also decreased Cash. (The payment of wages also involved social security taxes, withholding taxes, and certain other complications; these matters have been omitted from this introductory diagram.)

5. Factory overhead costs were incurred during the month in the amount of $2,000. Of the total, $1,200 was ascertained from current invoices for such things as electricity and telephone bills, or current earnings of indirect labor and supervisors, so the offsetting credits were to Accounts Payable. The remaining $800 represented depreciation, the charge-off of prepaid expenses, and other credits to asset accounts or obligations credited to liabilities other than Accounts Payable. All of these items are here summed up in the general account, Overhead Costs, but in practice they are usually shown in separate overhead cost accounts, one for each type of cost.

6. Since the overhead cost is a part of the cost of the pipes that were worked on during the month, the total overhead incurred was transferred to Goods in Process.

7. Pipes whose total cost was $9,000 were completed during the month and were transferred to Finished Goods Inventory. This resulted in a decrease in Goods in Process and an increase in Finished Goods Inventory.

8. Pipes with a cost of $10,000 were sold during the month. Physically, these pipes were removed from inventory and shipped to the customer. On the accounting records, this was reflected by a credit to Finished Goods Inventory and a debit to Cost of Goods Sold.

9. At the same time, and for the same products, sales revenue of $18,000 was created, and this was shown on the books by a credit to Sales and a debit to Accounts Receivable. Later on, these receivables were paid, thus resulting in a debit to Cash and completing the accounting cycle. It should be particularly noted that the Sales transaction described here and the Cost of Goods Sold transaction described in Item 8 related to the same physical products, the same pipes. The difference between the balances in Sales and Cost of Goods Sold, $8,000, therefore represented the gross margin earned on products sold during the month.

10. During the month $3,200 selling and administrative expenses were incurred, $1,900 of which represented credits to Accounts Payable and $1,300 credits to various asset and liability accounts.

11. Since these were expenses applicable to the current period, Selling and Administrative Expense was closed to Loss and Gain.

12. The balances in Sales and Cost of Goods Sold were also closed to Loss and Gain, and Loss and Gain then showed the net profit for the period. (This is a somewhat oversimplified statement, for income taxes and certain nonoperating and financial items which would appear in many income statements have not been considered.)

A manufacturing company can find its cost of goods sold in either of two ways: (1) directly, or (2) by deduction.

In the direct method, the company keeps track of the costs that are accumulated on each product as it moves through the factory, and the total cost thus accumulated becomes the cost of goods sold in the accounting period in which the product is sold. The techniques for arriving at this cost are part of the branch of accounting that is called *cost accounting*. Since cost accounting data are also used for purposes other than the preparation of financial statements, a description of cost accounting is deferred to Chapter 13.

The process of deduction used to find the cost of goods sold in a manufacturing company is essentially similar to, but more complicated than, the corresponding process in a merchandising company that was described in Chapter 5. The increased complexity can readily be seen by comparing the income statement for a merchandising company in Illustration 7–3 with the income statement for a manufacturing company in Illustration 7–4.

Illustration 7–3

MALONE STORES, INCORPORATED

Income Statement, 1968

Net sales.			$666,720
Cost of goods sold:			
Beginning inventory, January 1		$184,350	
Merchandise purchases.	$454,920		
Freight and express.	30,210	485,130	
Cost of goods available for sale		$669,480	
Less: Ending inventory, December 31. . . .		193,710	
Cost of goods sold			475,770
Gross profit			$190,950
Selling, administrative, and general expenses:			
Salaries and wages		$ 88,170	
Employment taxes and benefits.		4,623	
Rent		24,390	
Light, heat, and power		8,840	
State and local taxes and licenses		5,130	
Depreciation		4,140	
Repairs.		2,110	
Other expenses		16,677	154,080
Profit from operations			$ 36,870
Other revenue.			5,810
Net income before taxes.			$ 42,680
Provision for income tax			15,120
Net Income			$ 27,560

In order to deduce cost of goods sold, the amounts for each inventory account as of the end of the period must be determined on the basis of a physical inventory. In the description that follows, these amounts are merely stated. In practice, however, the problem of assigning a reasonable value to the partially completed items in Goods in Process Inventory and to the completed items in Finished Goods Inventory without a cost accounting system can be formidable.

Illustration 7–4

ALFMAN MANUFACTURING COMPANY

Income Statement, 1968

Net sales.			$669,100
Cost of goods sold:			
Raw materials cost:			
Raw materials inventory, January 1		$154,300	
Purchases. $263,520			
Plus: Freight-in 9,400			
Total purchases.		272,920	
Total inventory and purchases.		$427,220	
Less: Raw materials inventory, December 31		163,120	
Cost of materials used		$264,100	
Direct labor cost.		150,650	
Manufacturing overhead cost:			
Indirect labor	$ 23,750		
Factory heat, light, and power	89,500		
Factory supplies used.	22,100		
Insurance and taxes.	8,100		
Depreciation--plant and equipment.	35,300		
Total manufacturing overhead cost. . . .		178,750	
Total manufacturing costs.		$593,500	
Add: Goods in process inventory, January 1 .		18,800	
Total.		$612,300	
Less: Goods in process inventory, December 31		42,600	
Cost of goods manufactured		$569,700	
Add: Finished goods inventory, January 1 . .		69,200	
Cost of goods available for sale		$638,900	
Less: Finished goods inventory, December 31.		66,400	
Cost of goods sold			572,500
Gross profit			$ 96,600
Selling and administrative expenses:			
Selling expense.		$ 38,500	
Depreciation--selling.		3,200	
Administrative expense		32,200	73,900
Net operating profit			$ 22,700
Other revenue.			15,300
Net income before taxes.			$ 38,000
Provision·for income tax			12,640
Net Income			$ 25,360

In order to find the cost of goods sold by the deduction process, two other costs must be deduced first—the cost of raw materials used and the cost of goods manufactured. A set of journal entries for finding these costs is given and explained below. They relate to the income statement in Illustration 7–4 and are diagrammed in a flow chart, Illustration 7–5.

Raw Materials Used

In determining the cost of raw materials used, the assumption is made that the amount of raw materials used is the difference between the materials available for use during the period (which is the total of the

Illustration 7-5

FLOW OF FIGURES THROUGH THE ACCOUNTS

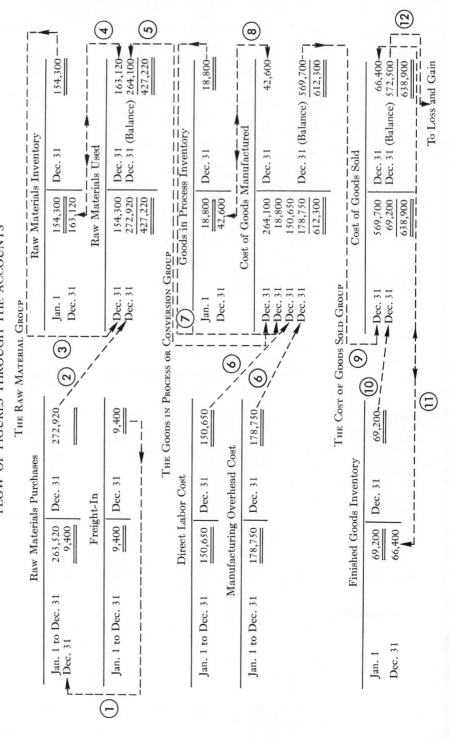

beginning inventory and the net purchases) and the ending inventory. This assumption does not take into account any waste or spoilage of material that might have occurred. In practice, waste and spoilage is either disregarded or is collected separately and removed from material costs by crediting Raw Materials Inventory and debiting a manufacturing cost account.

This calculation can be made in a temporary account, Raw Materials Used. The journal entries that bring the necessary data to this account are as follows:

(1)

```
Raw Materials Purchases . . . . . . . . . . . . . . . .      9,400
    Freight-In. . . . . . . . . . . . . . . . . . . .               9,400
  To find net purchases.
```

(2)

```
Raw Materials Used. . . . . . . . . . . . . . . . . 272,920
    Raw Materials Purchases . . . . . . . . . . . . .           272,920
  To transfer net purchases.
```

(3)

```
Raw Materials Used. . . . . . . . . . . . . . . . . 154,300
    Raw Materials Inventory . . . . . . . . . . . . .           154,300
  To add the beginning inventory.
```

(4)

```
Raw Materials Inventory . . . . . . . . . . . . . . 163,120
    Raw Materials Used. . . . . . . . . . . . . . . .           163,120
  To deduct ending inventory from raw material used
  and to set up this inventory as an asset.
```

These entries can be read as follows: (1) The net amount of purchases for the year is found by closing related accounts into the purchases account. (2) Net purchases is closed to Raw Materials Used. (3) The beginning inventory of raw material is added, thus giving the total amount of raw material available for use. (4) The amount of raw material on hand at the end of the period is subtracted, and the balance in Raw Material Used is assumed to have been used in the manufacturing process.

Cost of Goods Manufactured

The sum of raw materials used, direct labor, and manufacturing overhead, together comprise the total amount of cost added to Goods in Process Inventory during the period. Given the amount in Goods in Process Inventory at the beginning of the period and the amount remaining at the end of the period, the *cost of goods manufactured*, that is, the goods completed and transferred to Finished Goods Inventory, can be deduced. Again, the assumption is made that if the goods are no longer in

Goods in Process Inventory, they must have been completed and transferred to Finished Goods Inventory. To apply this line of reasoning, another temporary account, Cost of Goods Manufactured, is created, and the following journal entries are made:

(5)

```
Cost of Goods Manufactured. . . . . . . . . . . . . 264,100
    Raw Materials Used. . . . . . . . . . . . . . .         264,100
    To transfer raw materials used.
```

(6)

```
Cost of Goods Manufactured. . . . . . . . . . . . . 329,400
    Direct Labor Cost . . . . . . . . . . . . . . .         150,650
    Indirect Labor. . . . . . . . . . . . . . . . .          23,750
    Factory Heat, Light, and Power. . . . . . . . .          89,500
    Factory Supplies Used . . . . . . . . . . . . .          22,100
    Insurance and Taxes . . . . . . . . . . . . . .           8,100
    Depreciation--Plant and Equipment . . . . . . .          35,300
    To add direct labor and manufacturing overhead.
```

(7)

```
Cost of Goods Manufactured. . . . . . . . . . . . .  18,800
    Goods in Process Inventory. . . . . . . . . . .          18,800
    To add the beginning inventory.
```

(8)

```
Goods in Process Inventory. . . . . . . . . . . . .  42,600
    Cost of Goods Manufactured. . . . . . . . . . .          42,600
    To deduct the ending inventory from Cost of Goods
    Manufactured and to set up this inventory as an
    asset.
```

Cost of Goods Sold

Having determined the cost of goods manufactured, the cost of goods sold is found by adding this to the beginning Finished Goods Inventory so as to find the total amount available for sale, and then subtracting the ending Finished Goods Inventory. As with a merchandising company, the assumption is that if the merchandise is not in inventory, it has been sold. The following journal entries are made:

(9)

```
Cost of Goods Sold. . . . . . . . . . . . . . . . . 569,700
    Cost of Goods Manufactured. . . . . . . . . . .         569,700
    To transfer goods completed.
```

(10)

```
Cost of Goods Sold. . . . . . . . . . . . . . . . .  69,200
    Finished Goods Inventory. . . . . . . . . . . .          69,200
    To add the beginning inventory.
```

(11)

```
Finished Goods Inventory. . . . . . . . . . . . . . .    66,400
    Cost of Goods Sold. . . . . . . . . . . . . . . .              66,400
    To deduct the ending inventory from Cost of Goods
    Sold and to set up this inventory as an asset.
```

The balance in the Cost of Goods Sold account is the cost of goods sold during the year, and this is now closed to Loss and Gain:

(12)

```
Loss and Gain . . . . . . . . . . . . . . . . . . . . 572,500
    Cost of Goods Sold. . . . . . . . . . . . . . . .             572,500
```

Condensed Closing Process

The form of closing process that has just been described in detail was chosen so as to make it possible to relate the accounting entries to the actual events that occur in a manufacturing company: the acquisition of raw material, the conversion of this material into a manufactured product, the temporary storage of this finished product, and its eventual shipment to customers. The identical end result would be achieved if all the separate entries described were compressed into three entries which (1) closed all beginning inventory balances; (2) set up new inventory balances; and (3) closed purchases, direct labor, and manufacturing overhead accounts. The three entries would be as follows:

(1)

```
Cost of Goods Sold. . . . . . . . . . . . . . . . . . 242,300
    Raw Materials Inventory . . . . . . . . . . . . .             154,300
    Goods in Process Inventory. . . . . . . . . . . .              18,800
    Finished Goods Inventory. . . . . . . . . . . . .              69,200
    To close beginning inventories.
```

(2)

```
Raw Materials Inventory . . . . . . . . . . . . . . . 163,120
Goods in Process Inventory. . . . . . . . . . . . . .  42,600
Finished Goods Inventory. . . . . . . . . . . . . . .  66,400
    Cost of Goods Sold. . . . . . . . . . . . . . . .             272,120
    To enter ending inventories.
```

(3)

```
Cost of Goods Sold. . . . . . . . . . . . . . . . . . 602,320
    Purchases . . . . . . . . . . . . . . . . . . . .             263,520
    Freight-In. . . . . . . . . . . . . . . . . . . .               9,400
    Direct Labor. . . . . . . . . . . . . . . . . . .             150,650
    Indirect Labor. . . . . . . . . . . . . . . . . .              23,750
    Factory Heat, Light, and Power. . . . . . . . . .             89,500
    Factory Supplies Used . . . . . . . . . . . . . .             22,100
    Insurance and Taxes . . . . . . . . . . . . . . .              8,100
    Depreciation--Plant and Equipment . . . . . . . .             35,300
    To close costs.
```

The transfer of the Cost of Goods Sold to Loss and Gain would be made exactly as before:

```
Loss and Gain . . . . . . . . . . . . . . . . . . . . . 572,500
    Cost of Goods Sold. . . . . . . . . . . . . . . .          572,500
```

Alternative Income Statement Format

The income statement given in Illustration 7–4 is useful in showing the steps involved in calculating the cost of goods sold. It is, however, a cumbersome and complicated looking set of figures. Illustration 7–6 re-

Illustration 7–6

ALFMAN MANUFACTURING COMPANY

Income Statement, 1968
(Alternative Format)

Net sales			$669,100
Manufacturing costs:			
Raw material costs:			
Purchases	$272,920		
Increase in raw materials inventory	8,820		
Cost of materials used.		$264,100	
Direct labor cost		150,650	
Manufacturing overhead cost:			
Indirect labor.	$23,750		
Factory heat, light, and power. . .	89,500		
Factory supplies used	22,100		
Insurance and taxes	8,100		
Depreciation--plant and equipment .	35,300		
Total manufacturing overhead cost		178,750	
Total manufacturing cost. . . .		$593,500	
Changes in inventory:			
Increase in goods in process.	$23,800		
Decrease in finished goods.	2,800		
Net increase in inventory		21,000	
Cost of goods sold.			572,500
Gross profit.			$ 96,600
Selling and administrative expenses:			
Selling expense		$ 38,500	
Depreciation--selling		3,200	
Administrative expense.		32,200	73,900
Net operating profit.			$ 22,700
Other revenue			15,300
Net income before taxes			$ 38,000
Provision for income tax.			12,640
Net Income.			$ 25,360

casts this information in a form that is both shorter and better suited for analysis. Instead of showing separately the figures for beginning and ending inventories, this statement shows only the *changes* in inventory. These changes account for the difference between the costs incurred in manufacturing and the cost of goods sold. It is suggested that the reader think out for himself the reason why inventory increases are subtracted and why inventory decreases are added.

Entries with a Cost Accounting System

Since in a cost accounting system the cost of raw materials used, the cost of goods manufactured, and the cost of goods sold are found directly rather than by the roundabout process of deduction, the entries required under this system are even fewer than above. They would be:

(1)

```
Raw Materials Inventory . . . . . . . . . . . . . . 272,920
     Accounts Payable. . . . . . . . . . . . . . . .        272,920
     To record inventory purchased.
```

(2)

```
Goods in Process Inventory. . . . . . . . . . . . . 593,500
     Raw Materials Inventory . . . . . . . . . . . .        264,100
     Direct Labor. . . . . . . . . . . . . . . . . .        150,650
     Manufacturing Overhead. . . . . . . . . . . . .        178,750
     To show material, labor, and overhead costs put into
     process.
```

(3)

```
Finished Goods Inventory. . . . . . . . . . . . . . 569,700
     Goods in Process Inventory. . . . . . . . . . .        569,700
     To transfer completed products to finished goods
     inventory.
```

(4)

```
Cost of Goods Sold. . . . . . . . . . . . . . . . . 572,500
     Finished Goods Inventory. . . . . . . . . . . .        572,500
     To record cost of goods sold and reduce inventory.
```

SIGNIFICANCE OF THE PROCESS

For the objective of this book, there is no particular reason why the reader should memorize the details of the procedures described in this chapter; he can easily refer back to them as needed. He should, however, understand thoroughly the nature of the process, for without such an understanding, events that are reflected on the income statement of a manufacturing company can easily be misinterpreted.

A fundamental difference between a manufacturing company and a merchandising company is illustrated by the procedures described. In a merchandising company, costs of labor, supplies, depreciation, and so on affect net income *in the accounting period in which these costs are incurred.* In a manufacturing company, on the other hand, those labor and other costs that are associated with the manufacturing process affect, initially, the value of inventory; they affect net income only *in the accounting period in which the products containing these costs are sold.* This may be a later accounting period than that in which the product was manufactured. The larger the inventory in relation to sales, the longer the time interval that elapses between the incurrence of a cost and its impact on net income.

Consider, for example, a wage increase amounting to $50,000 per year. In a merchandising company, net income would be reduced $50,000 in the year in which the increase becomes effective, other things being equal. In a manufacturing company, however, that part of the increase paid to manufacturing employees would first go to increase the inventory value of the products they worked on, and net income would not receive the full impact of the increase until these products were sold. You may find it interesting to explore this phenomenon by tracing through the impact of a $50,000 increase in wages on the two companies whose statements are shown in Illustrations 7–3 and 7–4, assuming (so that the effect of the wage increase can be isolated) that selling prices are not changed.

CASES

CASE 7-1. PROBLEM IN INCOME STATEMENT PREPARATION

Listed below in alphabetical order are certain accounts of the Exco Manufacturing Company with balances for the year ended December 31. You are asked to prepare a detailed income statement on the basis of this information:

Administrative expense	$ 38,350
Customer returns and allowances	63,050
Depreciation—plant and equipment	41,600
Depreciation—selling	3,780
Direct labor cost	205,150
Dividends	13,000
Factory heat, light, and power	92,800
Factory supplies cost	26,500
Finished goods inventory, 1/1	78,650
Finished goods inventory, 12/31	82,130
Freight-in	8,580
Gain on disposal of machinery	13,600
Goods in process inventory, 1/1	30,970
Goods in process inventory, 12/31	31,920
Indirect labor	28,320
Insurance and taxes (factory)	13,860
Interest expenses	9,350
Provision for income tax	24,000
Purchases	303,050
Raw materials inventory, 1/1	186,210
Raw materials inventory, 12/31	163,100
Sales	913,250
Selling expense	45,600

CASE 7-2. MARRETT MANUFACTURING COMPANY (A)

The management of the Marrett Manufacturing Company prepared annually a budget of expected financial operations for the ensuing calendar year. The completed budget provided information on all aspects of the coming year's operations. It included an estimated balance sheet as of the end of the year and an estimated income statement.

The final preparation of statements was accomplished only after careful integration of detailed computations submitted by each department. This was done to insure that the operations of all departments were in balance with one another. For example, the finance department needed to base its schedules of loan operations and of collections and disbursements on figures that were dependent upon manufacturing, purchasing, and selling expectations. The level of production would be geared to the forecasts of the sales department, and purchasing would be geared to the proposed manufacturing schedule. In short, it was necessary to integrate the estimates of each department and to revise them in terms of the over-all effect on operations to arrive at a well-formulated and profitable plan of operations for the coming year. The budget statements ultimately derived from the adjusted estimated transactions would then serve the company as a reliable guide and measure of the coming year's operations.

At the time the 1969 budget was being prepared, in November of 1968, estimated 1968 financial statements were compiled for use as a comparison with the budgeted figures. These 1968 statements were based on nine months' actual and three months' estimated transactions. They appear as Exhibits 1, 2, and 3.

Exhibit 1

MARRETT MANUFACTURING COMPANY

Estimated Balance Sheet, December 31, 1968

ASSETS

Current Assets:

Cash...		$ 70,000
Accounts receivable (net of allowance for doubtful accounts).......................................		123,000
Inventories:		
Raw materials...............................	$119,000	
Goods in process.............................	47,000	
Finished goods...............................	15,000	
Supplies.....................................	33,000	214,000
Prepaid taxes and insurance.....................		9,000
Total Current Assets........................		$416,000
Fixed Assets:		
Manufacturing plant...........................	$620,000	
Less: Accumulated depreciation...................	210,000	410,000
Total Assets..............................		$826,000

LIABILITIES AND CAPITAL

Current Liabilities:

Notes payable................................	$ 64,000	
Accounts payable..............................	27,000	
Unpaid estimated federal income taxes...............	5,000	
Total Current Liabilities......................		$ 96,000
Capital:		
Capital stock.................................	$670,000	
Retained earnings.............................	60,000	730,000
Total Liabilities and Capital.................		$826,000

Exhibit 2

MARRETT MANUFACTURING COMPANY

Estimated Statement of Cost of Goods Sold, 1968

Finished goods inventory, 1/1/68.............			$167,000
Goods in process inventory, 1/1/68...........		$ 52,000	
Raw materials used........................		181,000	
Plus: Factory expenses:			
Direct manufacturing labor................		97,000	
Factory overhead:			
Indirect manufacturing labor.............$38,000			
Power, heat, and light.................. 27,000			
Depreciation of plant................... 29,000			
Social security taxes.................... 5,500			
Taxes and insurance, factory............ 5,000			
Supplies............................ 15,800		120,300	
		$450,300	
Less: Goods in process inventory, 12/31/68..		47,000	
Cost of goods manufactured (i.e., completed)...			403,300
			$570,300
Less: Finished goods inventory, 12/31/68....			15,000
Cost of Goods Sold.......................			$554,300

Exhibit 3

MARRETT MANUFACTURING COMPANY

Estimated Income Statement, 1968

Sales...		$728,600
Less: Sales returns and allowances....................$ 5,600		
Sales discounts allowed........................ 14,000		19,600
Net sales..		$709,000
Less: Cost of goods sold (per schedule)...............		554,300
Gross profit margin..................................		$154,700
Less: Sales and administrative expense................		120,200
Net operating profit.................................		$ 34,500
Less: Interest expense...............................		2,000
Net profit before federal income tax....................		$ 32,500
Less: Estimated income tax..........................		9,000
Net Profit after Federal Income Tax...................		$ 23,500

Below is the summary of expected operations for the budget year 1969 as finally accepted:

1. *Sales:* All on credit, $815,000; sales returns and allowances, $7,000; sales discounts taken by customers, $15,000. (The sales figure is net of expected bad debts.)

2. *Purchases of goods and services:*

a) New assets:

Purchased for cash: manufacturing plant and equipment, $31,000; prepaid manufacturing taxes and insurance, $12,000.

Purchased on accounts payable: raw materials, $227,000; supplies, $25,000.

b) Services used to convert raw materials into goods in process,[2] all purchased for cash: direct manufacturing labor, $152,000; indirect manufacturing labor, $56,000; social security taxes on labor, $9,400; power, heat, and light, $41,600. (Accrued payroll was ignored in these estimates.)

c) Sales and administrative service, purchased for cash: $234,000.

3. *Conversion of assets into goods in process:* This appears as an increase in the "value" of goods in process and a decrease in the appropriate asset accounts. Depreciation of building and equipment, $26,000; expiration of prepaid taxes and insurance, $8,000; supplies used in manufacturing, $29,000; raw materials put into process, $259,000.

4. *Transfer of goods in process into finished goods:* This appears as an increase in finished goods and a decrease in goods in process. Total cost accumulated on goods that have been completed and transferred to finished goods inventory, $549,000.

5. *Cost of finished goods sold to customers:* $499,000.

6. *Financial transactions:*

a) $180,000, borrowed on notes payable to bank.

b) Bank loans paid off (i.e., retired), $210,000.

c) Cash payment to bank of $3,000 for interest on loans.

7. *Cash receipts from customers on accounts receivable:* $807,000.

8. *Cash payments of liabilities:*

a) Payment of accounts payable, $249,000.

b) Payment of 1968 income tax, $5,000.

9. *Estimated federal income tax on 1969 income:* $28,000, of which $10,000 is estimated to be unpaid as of December 31, 1969.

10. *Dividends declared for year and paid in cash:* $11,000.

This summary presents the complete cycle of the Marrett Manufacturing Company's budgeted yearly operations from the purchase of goods and services through their various stages of conversion to completion of the finished product to the sale of this product. All costs and cash receipts and disbursements involved in this cycle are presented, including the provision for federal income tax and the payment of dividends.

---

[2] In a manufacturing company, inventory is assumed to increase in value by the amounts spent to convert raw material into salable products. These amounts include the items listed in 2(*b*) plus the items listed in 3 below.

Questions

1. Journalize each of the estimated transactions. Set up T accounts with balances as shown on the balance sheet for December 31, 1968, and post the journal entries to these accounts.
2. Prepare an estimated statement of cost of goods sold for 1969, an estimated income statement for 1969, and an estimated balance sheet as of December 31, 1969.
3. Describe the principal differences between the 1969 estimates and the 1968 figures as shown in Exhibits 1, 2, and 3. In what respects is 1969 performance expected to be better than 1968 performance, and in what respects is it expected to be poorer?

CHAPTER 8

LONG-TERM EQUITIES

The treasurer and other executives who are responsible for financial affairs in a company need a considerable store of technical knowledge regarding the various means of raising money, the legal and tax rules relating to financing, and so on. Other members of management should have some understanding of these matters, even though they scarcely can be expected to be conversant with all the details.

This chapter discusses the accounting aspects of these financial matters at a level that is intended to provide literacy to the nonfinancial manager. To cover the subject at the detailed level appropriate for the specialist would require a whole book, and a selection of such books is listed in the suggestions for further reading at the end of this chapter. The topics all relate to items listed on the equities side of the balance sheet: bonds and other long-term liabilities, the capital stock and surplus of corporations, and the owners' equity of unincorporated businesses. The principles underlying the preparation of consolidated financial statements are described briefly.

In the typical company, events of the type discussed in this chapter occur infrequently, but when they do occur they are likely to have a major impact on the financial statements. Thus, the nonfinancial manager can postpone acquiring a detailed knowledge of the accounting for these transactions until the need arises, but at that time he is well advised to acquire such a knowledge.

NATURE OF LIABILITIES

In Chapter 2, a liability was defined as a claim against assets by an outside party, as distinguished from a claim by the owners. This definition is approximately correct; however, not all legal obligations to outside parties are liabilities in the accounting meaning of this word, and not all liabilities are legally enforceable claims.

196

As an example of a claim that is not a liability, consider the case of an employee who has a written contract guaranteeing him employment at a stated salary for the next two years (e.g., professional athletes, coaches, executives). Such a contract is a legally enforceable claim against the business, but it is *not* a liability; in fact, this transaction is not recorded in the accounts at all until the man actually performs the work.

What distinguishes such a contract from those that do give rise to liabilities? Essentially, the distinction is determined by whether or not there is an asset or expense debit to offset the liability credit. When an employee works, the offsetting debit to the liability Accrued Wages Payable is Wages Expense. But when a contract is signed covering *future* employment, no expense account in the current period is affected, nor is an asset created. A liability is not created until the services have been performed.

For the same reason, a lease agreement, even though it may be just as binding and cover just as long a time period as a first-mortgage bond, is not a liability because the leased property is not owned by the lessee and hence is not an asset.[1] Similarly, the amount of interest on notes and bonds that is to accrue subsequent to the date of the balance sheet is not a liability.

An estimated allowance for future costs under a warranty agreement mentioned in Chapter 3 is an example of a liability that is not a definite obligation at the time it is set up. Liabilities of this type arise out of attempts to match revenue and costs. As explained in Chapter 3, revenue is ordinarily recognized when products are shipped; but when a warranty agreement applies, some of the costs associated with the transaction will not be incurred until later on when customers obtain repairs or replacement of products that turn out to be defective. The liability account is set up in the period in which the revenue is recognized, the offsetting debit being to an expense account of that period, such as Estimated Warranty Expense.

Contingent Liabilities

A *contingent liability* exists when a current situation may result in a liability upon the occurrence of some future event, but the amount, if any, of the liability cannot reasonably be predicted as of the balance sheet date. The situation must exist currently; hence, possible future losses from

---

[1] However, a long-term, noncancelable lease may create substantially the same equity in the property covered by the lease as if the property had been purchased on an installment basis. Such a lease should be capitalized; that is, both the asset and liability amounts should be shown on the financial statements. These amounts are calculated by discounting the stream of lease payments to which the company is committed. Also, other noncancelable leases, if material in amount, should be disclosed in a footnote to the balance sheet. (See *APB Opinion No. 5*, in Paul Grady, *Inventory of Generally Accepted Accounting Principles* [AICPA, 1965], pp. 171–80.)

fire, natural catastrophies, and war are not contingent liabilities. The amount must depend upon some future event, such as the settlement of a law suit; if the amount can be reasonably estimated now, it is not a contingent liability. Examples of contingent liabilities are possible penalties, fines, or damages from pending litigation; possible assessments of additional taxes; possible payments from default on debts which the company has guaranteed; possible refund resulting from renegotiation of contracts; and possible additional payments to employees for services they have already performed.

Contingent liabilities are not recorded in the financial statements themselves; however, they must be disclosed in a footnote if they are material in amount.[2] By contrast, an obligation whose amount can be reasonably estimated *is* a liability, and is so recorded, even though the precise amount is not now known.

Distinction between Liabilities and Owners' Equity

The exact dividing line between liabilities and owners' equities is a difficult one to draw. Although a distinction based on whether the claim is that of an owner or that of an outside creditor is satisfactory for most situations, in borderline cases fine-spun philosophical arguments can often be made for either treatment. A practical approach is to ask whether the claim involves a definite promise to pay; if so, the claim is a liability. If, on the other hand, the business does not incur a definite obligation to pay—definite in the sense that failure to make payment would be grounds for legal action—the item is part of owners' equity.

The problem of defining the dividing line has become acute in recent years because interest on a liability is a tax-deductible expense, whereas a dividend paid to owners is not; therefore companies have an incentive to make agreements that are sufficiently like liabilities to qualify for tax purposes but which impose as slight an obligation as possible.

BONDS

The most common form of long-term liability is a bond, which is a certificate, usually negotiable, promising to pay the holder a specified sum of money, usually $1,000, plus interest at a stated rate. Bonds may be sold to the general public through investment bankers, or they may be sold directly to an insurance company or other financial institution.

Recording the Issue

To illustrate the entries typically made to record the sale of an issue of bonds, assume the Mason Corporation sells an issue of 100 bonds, each

---

[2] See Grady, *op. cit.*, pp. 290–93.

with a face or *par* value of $1,000, with an interest rate of 5 percent, payable in 20 years, and secured by a first mortgage on certain Mason Corporation assets. (Such a bond would be called a "5 percent, 20-year, first mortgage bond.") If the corporation receives $1,000 each for the sale of these bonds, the following entry would be made:

```
Cash. . . . . . . . . . . . . . . . . . . . . . . 100,000
    Bonds Payable . . . . . . . . . . . . . . . . .       100,000
```

Frequently bonds are sold for less than their par value, that is, at a *discount*, or for more than their par value, that is, at a *premium*. This happens when the prevailing interest rate at the time of sale is different from the *nominal* interest rate, i.e., the rate printed on the bond.

> EXAMPLE: If the prevailing rate of interest in the bond market is 5.5 percent for bonds with a risk similar to those issued by the Mason Corporation, buyers will be unwilling to pay $1,000 for Mason Corporation 5 percent bonds. They would be willing to pay an amount such that the $50 annual interest on these bonds would be 5.5 percent of this amount. This amount (neglecting brokers' fees and other costs) works out to approximately $909. The bond would therefore be sold at a discount of $91.

The words "discount" and "premium" carry no connotation of "bad" or "good." They reflect simply a difference between the nominal interest rate for the issue and the going rate of interest at the time of issuance. The stated rate may be made intentionally different from the going market rate in the belief that this makes the bonds more attractive.

The sale of a bond issue is usually undertaken by an investment banking firm which charges a fee for this service. Determination of bond premium or discount is based on the net amount the corporation receives after this fee has been deducted, not on the price at which the bonds are sold to the public. In addition to this fee, the corporation also incurs printing, legal, and accounting costs in connection with a bond issue. These issue costs are usually taken into account when determining the net amount of discount or premium, but in some cases they are set up separately as an asset and amortized over the life of the issue.

If, because of a difference between the market rate and the nominal rate of interest, and taking into account the costs of issuance, the Mason Corporation received $88,000 from the issuance of $100,000 face amount of bonds, the following entry would be made:

```
Cash. . . . . . . . . . . . . . . . . . . . . . . 88,000
Bond Discount . . . . . . . . . . . . . . . . . . 12,000
    Bonds Payable . . . . . . . . . . . . . . . . .       100,000
```

If the corporation received more than the face amount, the corresponding entry would be:

```
Cash. . . . . . . . . . . . . . . . . . . . . . . . . . . 110,000
    Bond Premium. . . . . . . . . . . . . . . . . . . .          10,000
    Bond Payable. . . . . . . . . . . . . . . . . . . .         100,000
```

If bonds are sold after the bond contract date (i.e., the date on which interest starts to be earned), the purchaser pays both the price of the bond itself and the interest that has accrued up to the date of the transaction. This is done because the corporation, for reasons of convenience, will pay to all bondholders the interest earned for the full period (usually six months) beginning with the contract date, and the purchaser is clearly not entitled to interest for the period prior to the time he purchased the bonds.

> EXAMPLE: If the Luton Corporation sold a $1,000 6 percent bond three months after the contract date, at a price that netted par value to the corporation, the purchaser would pay one quarter of a year's interest, or $15.
>
> The following entry would be made:

```
Cash. . . . . . . . . . . . . . . . . . . . . . . . . .     1,015
    Bonds Payable . . . . . . . . . . . . . . . . . . . .          1,000
    Bond Interest Payable . . . . . . . . . . . . . . . .             15
```

In this case, when the semiannual interest payment is recorded, part of it will be debited to Bond Interest Payable, and the remainder to Bond Interest Expense; thus Bond Interest Expense will reflect the *net* interest expense of the period.

Balance Sheet Presentation

Bonds payable are shown in the long-term liabilities section of the balance sheet until one year before they mature, when ordinarily they become current liabilities. The description should give the principal facts about the issue, e.g., "5 percent first mortgage bonds due 1989." When a bond issue is to be refunded, however, it is not shown as a current liability in the year of maturity since it then will not require the use of current assets. If the bonds are to be retired in installments (as with *serial bonds*), that portion to be retired within a year is shown in the current liabilities section.

Bond discount is preferably shown on the balance sheet as a deduction from, and bond premium as an addition to, the face amount of bonds payable so as to reflect the net amount of the liability.

Bond Interest

An accounting entry is made to record the semiannual interest payments to bondholders and at the same time to amortize a portion of the bond premium or discount. The effect of this entry is that the *net* debit to

Interest Expense reflects, not the stated amount of interest actually paid to bondholders (unless the bonds are sold at par), but rather the effective rate of interest, which is larger or smaller than the stated rate, according to whether the bonds were sold at a discount or at a premium. The existence of bond discount in effect increases the interest expense, while the existence of bond premium decreases it.

Bond discount or premium may be amortized in one of two ways: by the straight-line method, in which the discount is debited (or the premium is credited) to Interest Expense in equal installments over the life of the issue; or by the compound interest method in which the discount or premium is written off in such a way that the net interest expense bears a constant ratio to the book value of the bonds over the whole life of the issue. This ratio is the effective interest cost of the borrowed funds.

The following entry records the semiannual bond interest payment and amortization of discount on a straight-line basis for the 5 percent Mason Corporation bonds that were assumed to have been sold at $880 each:

```
Interest Expense. . . . . . . . . . . . . . . . . . .    2,800
     Bond Discount . . . . . . . . . . . . . . . . . .             300
     Cash. . . . . . . . . . . . . . . . . . . . . . .           2,500
```

The cash that is paid out as interest is $2,500, which is 5 percent × $100,000 × ½ year. The $300 credit to Bond Discount is $\frac{1}{40}$ of the $12,000 that is to be amortized over 40 semiannual periods. The interest expense is the sum of these amounts.

If the interest payment date does not coincide with the closing of the company's books, an adjusting entry is made to record accrued interest expense and the amortization of discount or premium. Assuming that the Mason Corporation bonds are sold at $880 each on September 30, that the interest dates are September 30 and March 31, and that the fiscal year ends on December 31, the following entries would be made:

1. *Adjustment on December 31:*

```
Bond Interest Expense . . . . . . . . . . . . . . . .    1,400
     Bond Discount . . . . . . . . . . . . . . . . . .             150
     Accrued Interest Payable. . . . . . . . . . . . .           1,250
```

2. *Payment of semiannual interest on March 31:*

```
Bond Interest Expense . . . . . . . . . . . . . . . .    1,400
Accrued Interest Payable. . . . . . . . . . . . . . .    1,250
     Bond Discount . . . . . . . . . . . . . . . . . .             150
     Cash. . . . . . . . . . . . . . . . . . . . . . .           2,500
```

3. *Payment of semiannual interest on the following September 30:*

```
Bond Interest Expense . . . . . . . . . . . . . . . .    2,800
     Bond Discount . . . . . . . . . . . . . . . . . .             300
     Cash. . . . . . . . . . . . . . . . . . . . . . .           2,500
```

In the above examples, bond issuance costs were assumed to have been included in calculating the discount. If recorded separately, issuance costs would be amortized by debits to Interest Expense over the life of the issue, in the same manner as shown for bond discount.

Retirement of Bonds

Bonds may be retired in total, or they may be retired in installments over a period of years. In either case the retirement is recorded by a debit to Bonds Payable and a credit to Cash, or to a sinking fund which has been set up for this purpose. The bond discount or premium will have been completely amortized by the maturity date, so no additional entry is required for discount or premium at that time.

Bonds are sometimes retired at maturity out of a sinking fund which has been created in installments over the life of the issue. Bond sinking funds may be controlled by the originating corporation, or they may be controlled by a trustee under specified contractual arrangements. In either case, such funds usually appear in the investment section of the assets side of the balance sheet.

The company may decide to retire bonds earlier than the date originally specified. If such bonds were sold at a discount, an unamortized discount will exist as of the date of early retirement because the schedule of amortization was originally set up so as to charge off the discount over the specified life of the issue. Correspondingly, an unamortized premium will exist if the bonds were sold at a premium. Under the all-inclusive income concept, this unamortized balance is shown on the current income statement, as an item of extraordinary loss (if a discount) or gain (if a premium).

> EXAMPLE: If the Mason Corporation bonds are retired at the end of
> 10 years (i.e., half their scheduled life) by paying the face amount to
> each bondholder, half the bond discount would not have been amortized. The entry would be as follows:

```
Bonds Payable . . . . . . . . . . . . . . . . . . . . 100,000
Loss on Retirement of Bonds . . . . . . . . . . . .   6,000
    Cash. . . . . . . . . . . . . . . . . . . . . . .          100,000
    Bond Discount . . . . . . . . . . . . . . . . . .            6,000
```

Refunding a Bond Issue

The terms of some bond issues state that the bonds can be called, or retired before maturity, by paying for them at a premium, that is, by paying more than the par value. In this case, a schedule of *call prices* is included in the terms of the issue. In periods when interest rates have declined, a company may consider it advantageous to *refund* a bond issue, that is, to call the old issue and float a new one with a lower rate of interest. Problems then arise in accounting for the call premium (the difference between the call price and par value) and any unamortized issue costs and discount (or premium) on the old bonds.

The preferred treatment is to write off these costs over the remaining life of the issue being retired. Since for tax purposes these costs are a deductible expense in the year of refunding, thereby decreasing income taxes in that year, it is appropriate to report a fraction of the unamortized costs, equal to the income taxes saved, as an expense of the year of refunding and to spread only the remainder of the cost over the future years. This is consistent with the treatment of income taxes discussed in Chapter 5.

It is also in accordance with accounting principles to write off all the unamortized costs and the call premium in the year of refunding, as an extraordinary expense on the income statement.

The alternative of writing off the unamortized costs and call premium of the *old* issue over the life of the *new* bond issue is also permitted under certain circumstances (see Opinion No. 6).

Generally, if the alternative of amortizing over the remaining years of the old bond issue is chosen, the balances of all accounts which refer to the refunded issue, such as call premium, unamortized premium or discount, and issue costs, are closed into a single account, for example, "Unamortized Charges on 5 Percent Series A Mortgage Bonds." This single account is carried on the books and amortized over the remaining years of the old bond issue.

SHAREHOLDERS' EQUITY

The *shareholders' equity* (or *owners' equity*, or *stockholders' equity*) section of the balance sheet consists of two parts: (1) the amount contributed by the shareholders, and (2) retained earnings. The amount contributed by shareholders is called *contributed capital* or *invested capital*, and is further divided into (*a*) the par value or stated value of the stock, and (*b*) capital surplus. This section describes transactions related to these amounts.

Types of Capital Stock

Capital stock may be either *common* or *preferred*. Preferred stock has preference, or priority, over common as to the receipt of dividends, as to assets in the event of liquidation, or as to other specified matters. There is no substantial difference in the accounting treatment of these two types of stock, however, so no distinction is here made between them.

Stock may be either *par value* or *no-par value*. Par value stock appears in the accounts at a fixed amount per share (often $1, $10, or $100), which is specified in the corporation's charter or bylaws. Except by coincidence, the par value of the stock in a going concern has no relation either to the stock's market value or to its book value. *Market value* is what people will pay for the stock. *Book value* is the total shareholders' equity as reported on the balance sheet, that is, the sum of capital stock plus capital surplus plus retained earnings (or, stated another way, assets minus liabilities).

No-par value stock has a *stated value*, which is either specified in the corporation's charter or bylaws or fixed by the board of directors. The stated value governs the amounts to be entered in the Capital Stock account just as if it were a par value. The distinction between par value and no-par value stock is therefore of little practical significance.

Recording the Issue

To illustrate the issuance of stock, let us consider the Carroll Corporation, which received a charter from the state authorizing the issuance of 20,000 shares of $10 par value common stock. If 1,000 shares of this stock are issued at par ($10) and immediately paid for, the following entry would be made:

```
Cash. . . . . . . . . . . . . . . . . . . . . . . . . . 10,000
    Common Stock. . . . . . . . . . . . . . . . . . . .          10,000
```

Stock is often sold for more than its par or stated value; that is, it is sold at a *premium*. In such situations the Common Stock account still reflects the par or stated value, and the premium is shown separately, usually in the account, Paid-In Surplus (or Capital Surplus). If 1,000 shares of Carroll Corporation $10 common stock were sold at $12 a share, the following entry would be made:

```
Cash. . . . . . . . . . . . . . . . . . . . . . . . . . 12,000
    Common Stock. . . . . . . . . . . . . . . . . . . .          10,000
    Paid-In Surplus . . . . . . . . . . . . . . . . . .           2,000
```

Unlike bonds, stock is almost never sold at a discount. In most states and under most circumstances, this is illegal. Even where sale at a discount is permitted, individual shareholders would be required to contribute the amount of the discount in cash if the company should go bankrupt, and such a possibility makes discount stock unattractive to investors. Corporations therefore set the par value or stated value low enough so that the stock can be sold at a premium.

The sale of an issue of stock is often handled by an investment banking firm which receives a fee or "spread" for this service. Logically, the corporation should record only the net amount received from the investment banker, that is, the price paid by the public less the banker's spread, since this is the only amount that the corporate entity receives. Many companies, however, record the stock at the price paid by the public, and show the banker's spread as an expense. When this is done, the ultimate effect on shareholders' equity is the same as if only the net amount were recorded, since the expense item winds up as a decrease in shareholders' equity. The practice of recording the spread separately provides a useful piece of information, namely, the size of the spread, which is not revealed in the alternative treatment.

In connection with the issuance of stock, the corporation itself incurs issue costs over and above the banker's spread. These amounts may also be deducted from the amount received from the issue. The facts are perhaps more clearly shown, however, if these costs are recorded separately either as an expense of the current period or, if they are material, as an asset, such as organization cost.

EXAMPLE: The Dorith Corporation issued 10,000 shares of $10 par value common stock and the public bought these shares at $13. The investment banker's spread was $2 per share and the issue costs incurred by the Dorith Corporation were $4,000. The following entries would be made:

1. *Entry for issue costs:*

```
Stock Issue Costs . . . . . . . . . . . . . . . . . . .   4,000
     Cash (or Accounts Payable). . . . . . . . . . . .            4,000
```

2. *Entry when payment is received from investment bankers:*

```
Cash. . . . . . . . . . . . . . . . . . . . . . . . . 110,000
     Common Stock. . . . . . . . . . . . . . . . . . .          100,000
     Paid-In Surplus . . . . . . . . . . . . . . . . .           10,000
```

3. *Possible entry closing stock issue costs:*[3]

```
Paid-In Surplus . . . . . . . . . . . . . . . . . . .   4,000
     Stock Issue Costs . . . . . . . . . . . . . . . .            4,000
```

Note that the amount actually paid by the public does not appear in the company's accounts. Note also that these transactions are between the company and its shareholders. When one shareholder sells his stock to another shareholder, the amounts in the company's accounts are not affected in any way; the only change is in the secretary's detailed record of the identity of shareholders.

---

[3] This entry not made if stock issue costs are capitalized or charged to expense.

Treasury Stock

Treasury stock is a corporation's own stock that has been issued and subsequently reacquired by purchase or donation but not canceled. Although a few corporations show treasury stock as an asset on their balance sheet, this practice is not generally accepted since treasury stock is clearly not a "valuable thing or property right owned by the business"; a corporation can't own a claim against itself. The preferable practice is to treat treasury stock as a reduction in shareholders' equity, that is, as a reduction in the number and value of the shares outstanding, which is what it is.

In many companies, treasury stock purchased is debited to the Treasury Stock account at its cost, regardless of its par or stated value. It continues to be shown at cost until it is canceled or reissued, at which time adjustments are made in shareholders' equity to dispose of any differences between this cost, the paid-in value (i.e., the net proceeds at the time the stock was originally issued), and, in the event of reissuance, the amount then received.

Any excess of selling price above cost is credited to a surplus account (such as Capital Surplus from Treasury Stock Transactions), which may be shown as a separate item in the capital surplus section of the balance sheet. If treasury stock is sold at a price below cost, the loss may be deducted from the related surplus account if such an account already exists from prior transactions; otherwise the loss is debited to Retained Earnings.

If the capital stock was originally issued over a period of time at varying prices, there may be no way of determining the amount originally received from the issuance of the specific shares later reacquired as treasury stock. In this situation the "average paid-in value" becomes the base against which the costs of reacquisition are compared. The average paid-in value is determined by dividing the total number of shares outstanding at the time of the treasury stock transaction into total stated value less discounts or plus premiums.

None of these transactions enter into the determination of net income, nor are gains or losses from such transactions recognized for tax purposes.

Capital Surplus

As noted in Chapter 2, the Accounting Principles Board has recommended that the word "surplus" not be used in financial statements. The term "retained earnings" avoids the prohibited word for that part of shareholders' equity that results from the earning of net income, but the phrase suggested for another type of what was formerly labeled "surplus"

—"capital contributed in excess of the par or stated value of shares"—is cumbersome. Thus, although language that avoids the word "surplus" is used on many corporate balance sheets, the term "capital surplus" will be used here, simply as a matter of convenience.

The most common source of capital surplus is proceeds from the issuance of stock which exceed the par or stated value of the stock. This is the *paid-in surplus* described on page 204. Capital surplus also includes *donated surplus*, arising from gifts made to the corporation, and *appraisal surplus*, arising when the book value of assets is increased as a result of an appraisal. Appraisal surplus, however, is recorded only under highly unusual circumstances. As an example of its rarity, 1,800,000 acres of land owned by Kern County Land Company was carried on its books for some 70 years at its acquisition cost of less than $10 per acre, although its market value in 1967, when this company merged with Tenneco, was many tens of times this amount.

Cash Dividends

Dividends are ordinarily paid to shareholders in cash, but they sometimes are paid in other assets—the whiskey distributed by a distillery corporation to its shareholders being a noteworthy example.

Dividends are debited to retained earnings in the period in which they are declared, that is, voted, by the board of directors, even though payment is made at a later date. For example, if the Carroll Corporation declared a $5,000 dividend on December 15 to be paid on January 15, the entries would be as follows:

```
                          Dec. 15

Dividends (an owners' equity account). . . . . . . . .  5,000
    Dividends Payable (a liability account). . . . . .          5,000

                          Dec. 31

Retained Earnings. . . . . . . . . . . . . . . . . . .  5,000
    Dividends. . . . . . . . . . . . . . . . . . . . .          5,000
  A closing entry.

                          Jan. 15

Dividends Payable. . . . . . . . . . . . . . . . . . .  5,000
    Cash . . . . . . . . . . . . . . . . . . . . . . .          5,000
```

Stock Dividends and Stock Split-Ups

Some shareholders, in the mistaken belief that the amount reported as surplus is "their money," put pressure on the directors to authorize cash dividends equal to, or almost equal to, the amount of retained earnings. Clearly, retained earnings are not money at all, and for any of a number of reasons, cash may not be available for dividend payments even though the balance sheet shows a large amount of retained earnings. These same shareholders may be quite satisfied with a *stock dividend*, which actually does not change their equity in the corporation. As Mr. Justice Pitney said in *Eisner* v. *Macomber* (252 U.S. 189):

A stock dividend really takes nothing from the property of the corporation and adds nothing to the interests of the stockholders. Its property is not diminished and their interests are not increased . . . the proportional interest of each shareholder remains the same.

From an accounting standpoint, a stock dividend is recorded as a debit to retained earnings and as a credit to capital stock; the total owners' equity remains unchanged. The amount transferred from retained earnings to capital stock is usually calculated on the basis of the current market price of the stock.

EXAMPLE: The Bruce Corporation has 10,000 shares of common stock outstanding. Suppose that the directors voted a 5 percent stock dividend. Each shareholder would receive $\frac{1}{20}$ of a share of new stock for every share he then held. If the stock currently had a stated value of $12 a share, the common stock item on the balance sheet would increase by $6,000 (500 shares at $12 per share), and retained earnings would decrease by $6,000, but the *total* shareholders' equity would remain exactly as before.

As a matter of custom, a stock dividend is ordinarily not more than 25 percent of the number of shares issued, and usually it is 5 or 10 percent. Since a stock dividend reduces retained earnings, and since the amount of cash dividends that can be legally declared is related to the amount of retained earnings, the declaration of a stock dividend reduces the maximum amount of dividends that henceforth can be paid. By declaring a stock dividend, therefore, the directors signal their intention that this amount will be invested permanently in the company. The converse does not apply, however, for failure to declare a stock dividend is by no means an indication that the directors do plan to distribute all the retained earnings.

An advantage of a stock dividend is that a shareholder may realize cash by selling his dividend stock while preserving the number of his owned shares intact; but if he does this, he should recognize that he is in fact selling a fraction of his equity in the business.

A *stock split-up* merely increases the number of shares of stock outstanding, with no change in the total stated value of the stock and no change in surplus. As with a stock dividend, it has no effect on shareholders' equity; its effect is solely to repackage the evidence of ownership in smaller units. A stock split automatically reduces the market price of a share of stock. Often, however, the reduction is not quite proportional to the split since stock with a fairly low market price per share tends to be more attractive than stock with a high market price per share. Thus, if a stock selling at $150 is split "3-for-1," the new shares often will sell for somewhat more than $50 each.

The stock referred to in the preceding paragraphs is the company's own stock. If the company distributes to its shareholders the shares of some other corporation's stock which it owns, this distribution is similar to a regular cash dividend, and is recorded in the same manner except that the credit is to the Investments account rather than to Cash. Such a transaction is called a *spin-off*.

Surplus Reserves

In an attempt to explain to shareholders why they do not receive dividends that are equal to the amount shown as retained earnings plus other forms of surplus, a corporation may show on its balance sheet an appropriation, or reserve, as a separate item that is subtracted from surplus. Some of the terms used to describe the reasons for such an appropriation are as follows: *reserve for bond sinking fund*, which indicates a restriction on dividends in accordance with agreements made to bondholders; *reserve for contingencies*, indicating management's belief that funds may be required for an unusual purpose or to meet a possible obligation that does not yet have the status of a liability (such as settlement of a pending lawsuit, or a retroactive wage increase); *reserve for future inventory price decline*, indicating the possibility that inventory may be sold at a price less than the value reported on the balance sheet; and *reserve for expansion*, indicating an intention to use funds for the acquisition of new assets.

None of these reserves represents money, or anything tangible; the assets of a business are reported on the assets side of the balance sheet, not in the shareholders' equity section. The accounting entry creating the reserve involves a debit to Retained Earnings (or some other surplus account) and a credit to the reserve. This entry obviously does not affect any asset account, nor does the reserve represent anything more than a segregated portion of surplus.

Earnings per Share

In analyzing the financial statements of a corporation, investors pay particular attention to the ratio called "earnings per share." This is computed by dividing net income applicable to the common stock by the number of shares of common stock outstanding. The Accounting Principles Board requires that earnings per share be reported on the income statement, and in its *Opinion No. 9* (December, 1966) and *Opinion No. 15* (May 1969) provided detailed guidelines for making the calculation.

If the corporation has a simple capital structure, with only one class of stock, the net income used in this ratio is the same as the net income shown on the income statement.

> EXAMPLE: The 1968 income statement of McLean Corporation showed net income of $5 million. The corporation had one million shares of common stock outstanding in 1968. It therefore earned $5 per share.

The various classes of stock that a corporation might issue can be divided into one of two categories: (1) *senior securities, and* (2) *common stock* and its equivalent. Senior securities are those that have a claim on net income ahead of the claim of the common stockholders. The income figure used in the calculation of earnings per share is the amount that remains after the claims of the senior securities have been deducted from net income.

> EXAMPLE: The Nugent Corporation in 1968 had net income of $5 million. It had outstanding 100,000 shares of $6 preferred stock (which means that each share of preferred is entitled to an annual dividend of $6 before any dividends can be paid to common stockholders), and one million shares of common stock. Its earnings per share were therefore ($5,000,000 − $600,000) ÷ 1,000,000 shares = $4.40 per share.

If the number of shares of common stock outstanding fluctuates within a year, then a weighted average number of shares is computed.

> EXAMPLE: The Optel Corporation in 1968 had net income of $5 million. It had outstanding on January 1, one million shares of common stock, and on July 1 it issued an additional 500,000 shares, which were therefore outstanding for half of the year. Its average number of common shares outstanding was 1,000,000 + (500,000 × ½) = 1,250,000. Its earnings per share was $5,000,000 ÷ 1,250,000 = $4.

A *common stock equivalent* is a security which, although not in form a common stock, contains provisions that enable its holder to become a common stockholder and which, because of its terms and the circumstances under which it was issued, is in substance equivalent to a common stock. The value of a common stock equivalent is derived in large part from the value of the common stock to which it is related. One example is convertible bonds, which are bonds that can be exchanged for a prescribed amount of common stock if the bondholder elects to do so. Stock options and warrants, which permit their owners to buy common stock at a specified price, are other examples.

When a corporation has securities that are common stock equivalents, the Accounting Principles Board requires that the amount of such securities be taken into account in calculating earnings per share.

> EXAMPLE: Peter Corporation in 1968 had net income of $3,300,000. It had outstanding 1,000,000 shares of common stock and also convertible bonds which could be converted into 100,000 shares of common stock. When these bonds were issued, their market price was significantly higher than the price that would have reflected the going rate of interest, which indicates that they were common stock equivalents. Peter Corporation earnings per share was $3,300,000 ÷ (1,000,000 + 100,000) = $3.

The detailed criteria for deciding whether a security is a common stock equivalent and if so how the equivalent number of shares should be calculated are much too lengthy to be given here. APB *Opinion No. 15,* which states these criteria, is by far the longest opinion issued by the Accounting Principle Board.

APB *Opinion No. 15* also states that if a corporation has securities that *may*, under certain circumstances, have a claim on common earnings—even though these securities are not equivalent common shares—then the corporation should report two figures for earnings per share: (1) *primary earnings per share*, which is net income divided by the number of common and common equivalent shares, as above; and (2) *fully diluted earnings per share*, in which it is assumed that the maximum amount of potential conversion, exercise of warrants, and the like has taken place.

Significance of Shareholders' Equity

A study of the shareholders' equity section may provide some clues as to the methods used to obtain capital, as to transactions involving the purchase or sale of treasury stock, or as to the occurrence of unusual events not reflected in the income statement that result in changes in the shareholders' equity. An analysis of the growth in retained earnings in relation to net income may indicate the extent to which the company has obtained capital by "plowing back" its earnings.

In some states, dividend payments cannot exceed the amount shown as retained earnings, while other state laws allow dividend payments to equal retained earnings plus certain types of capital surplus. In still other states, however, dividend payments can be made if there are earnings in the current year, even though a deficit is shown from prior years. Banks or other lenders may impose other restrictions on the amounts that can be paid as dividends.

Whatever the legal restriction on dividend payments may be, factors other than the amount reported as retained earnings or surplus are likely to have a much more important bearing on dividend decisions in the ordinary situation. These factors include the amount of cash available, the funds required for expansion, the anticipated effect of dividends on stock prices and on the sale of new securities, the desire to maintain an unbroken record of dividend payments, a sense of fairness to shareholders, and so on.

Some accountants advocate that shareholders' equity be reported as a single figure rather than showing separate amounts for stock and for various types of surplus. Although this is not in accordance with generally accepted accounting principles, the suggestion does emphasize the difficulty of obtaining useful information from the separate figures that appear in the shareholders' equity section of the balance sheet.

Balance Sheet Presentation

In the shareholders' equity section of the balance sheet (or in a separate note, if presentation of all the detail would make the balance sheet itself too long), the following detail is presented:

1. For *each* class of stock, the par or stated value, the capital surplus attributed to that class, the number of shares authorized and issued and outstanding, rights and preferences as to dividends and as to amounts received in liquidation, and amount of treasury stock.

2. The amount of retained earnings, in total, and a note as to any portion of this amount that cannot be distributed as dividends (such as a restriction arising under the terms of a bank loan).

Thus, the basic distinction is maintained between (1) the capital contributed by shareholders, and (2) the equity resulting from net income that has been retained in the business.

The dollar amounts shown for each class of stock relate to the shares issued, not to the shares authorized.

In many balance sheets, the capital surplus is shown as one item, rather

Illustration 8–1

CARROLL CORPORATION

Owners' Equity Section of Balance Sheet

Shareholders' Equity:

Preferred stock, $0.60 dividend; par value $10, authorized and issued 2,900 shares	$ 29,000
Common stock, $10 par value; authorized 20,000 shares, issued 10,000 shares	100,000
Add: Paid-in surplus	4,000
	$133,000
Less: 100 common shares in treasury at cost	1,200
Contributed capital	$131,800
Retained earnings	10,000
Total Shareholders' Equity	$141,800

than being divided among the several classes of stock. In some balance sheets, the treasury stock item is listed below retained earnings, but this treatment is not preferred by the Accounting Principles Board.

The company must also report the details on all *options* to purchase capital stock. Such options are often granted to executives. They permit the holder to purchase stock at a stated price, and thus are valuable if the market price of the stock subsequently increases. The amount of stock options outstanding does not affect the balance sheet itself, so disclosure is by means of a separate note.

Illustration 8–1 shows the shareholders' equity section of a hypothetical corporation.

ACQUISITIONS AND MERGERS

In recent years there has been in the United States a surge in the urge to merge, a significant increase in the number of occasions on which two or more corporations join together to become one. These combinations take one or two forms; they are an *acquisition* or a *merger*.

In an acquisition, Corporation A buys either the assets or the stock of Corporation B, either by paying cash or other assets or by issuing bonds or preferred stock to Corporation B or to its shareholders. The shareholders of Corporation B therefore no longer have an interest in the activities heretofore carried on by that corporation, and in most cases Corporation B disappears.

In a merger, the shareholders of Corporation B exchange their stock for stock in Corporation A (or occasionally, the shareholders of both A and B receive stock in a newly organized Corporation C.) Corporation B usually disappears, and its business is henceforth conducted by Corporation A (or Corporation C, if such is organized). Occasionally Corporation B will continue in existence as a subsidiary of Corporation A.

Many difficult problems arise in accounting for a merger or acquisition. Basically, the transaction can be accounted as either a *purchase* or a *pooling of interests*.

If a purchase, the assets of Corporation B are recorded on the books of Corporation A at either their book value as shown on the books of Corporation B or at their current fair market value. The difference, if any, between this amount and the amount that Corporation A paid for Corporation B is recorded as goodwill. The fair market value may be difficult to estimate, and if the consideration for the purchase was other than cash, problems also arise in measuring the amount of goodwill. Acquisitions are always recorded as purchases, and so are mergers unless the merger meets certain criteria outlined below.

If the transaction is recorded as a *pooling of interests*, the book values of the assets and the retained earnings of Corporation B are simply added to those of Corporation A. No amount for goodwill is shown. Conceptually, a merger is treated as a pooling of interest when it resembles "two streams converging into a single river"; that is, when the relative rights of the shareholders of A and B are substantially the same in the merged entity as they were in the former separate entities. More specifically, there is a presumption that the transaction should be treated as a purchase, rather than as a pooling of interest, if the shareholders of Corporation B have significantly different voting rights or other rights in Corporation A than they formerly had; if a significant part of B's business is to be sold; if the shareholders of Corporation A clearly dominate the new entity; or if there is other evidence that the transaction was a disguised purchase.

The importance of the distinction between a purchase and a pooling of interest is that if the latter form is used improperly, the subsequent financial statements of the surviving corporation may not convey a realistic story of what has happened. One obvious possibility is that the comparisons with prior years may be distorted.

> EXAMPLE: The 1967 annual report of "Automatic" Sprinkler Corporation contains the statement, "Earnings after taxes rose from $4,425,000 reported in 1966 to $9,193,000 in 1967." The 1966 figure excludes the earnings of companies that were merged into "Automatic" Sprinkler in 1967. If the 1966 earnings of these companies had been included, the 1966 earnings would have been $10.8 million, and the 1967 earnings would then be less, rather than more, than 1966. (Reported in the *Wall Street Journal*, August 5, 1968, p. 1)

Such distortions can be avoided by restating the prior year balance sheet and income statements to include amounts for all the companies currently included in the corporation.

A more subtle problem arises when the assets of the acquired company are carried on the books at considerably less than their market value. In these circumstances the surviving corporation can add significantly to its income by selling some of these assets and reporting the gain as income.

CONSOLIDATED FINANCIAL STATEMENTS

A "company," as it is thought of by its management, its employees, its competitors, and the general public, may actually consist of a number of different corporations, created for various legal, tax, and financial reasons. The existence of a family of corporations is by no means peculiar to "big business." A fairly small enterprise may consist of one corporation that owns the real estate and buildings, another that primarily handles production, another for marketing activities, and over them all a *parent* corporation which is the locus of management and control. Each of these corporations is a legal entity, and each therefore has its own financial statements. The "company" itself may not be a separate legal entity, but it is an important *business* entity, and a set of financial statements for the whole business enterprise may be more useful than the statements of the separate corporations of which it consists.

Such statements are called *consolidated financial statements*. They are prepared by first adjusting and then combining the financial statements of the separate corporations; usually, no separate journals or ledgers are kept for the consolidated entity.

Basis for Consolidation

The legal tie that binds the other corporations, or *subsidiaries*, to the parent is the ownership of their stock. A subsidiary is not consolidated unless more than 50 percent of its common stock is owned by the parent; some companies use an even higher percentage as the criterion.

Even though it is 100 percent owned by the parent, a subsidiary may not be consolidated if its business is so different from that of the other companies in the family that including it in the consolidation would result in financial statements that do not well describe the family as a whole. General Motors Corporation does not consolidate the statements of General Motors Acceptance Corporation with those of its other corporations because GMAC is a huge financial corporation dealing principally in installment payments on automobiles, and its assets and liabilities are quite unlike those of an industrial company. Many companies do not consolidate their foreign subsidiaries.

If a subsidiary is not consolidated, the amount of the parent's investment in it appears as an asset on the consolidated balance sheet. *Opinion No. 10* of the Accounting Principles Board requires that for domestic subsidiaries the amount of the asset be the cost of the acquisition plus the parent's share of any retained earnings (or minus the amount of losses) that have been booked subsequent to the date of acquisition. Note that this is a departure from the basic concept that assets are reported at cost.

Consolidation Procedure

Illustration 8–2 shows the consolidation process in the simplest possible situation, consisting of the parent company and one subsidiary company, named "Parent" and "Subsidiary," respectively. Parent owns 100 percent of Subsidiary's stock; this is an asset which is shown on its balance sheet as Investment in Subsidiary. The investment is recorded at cost, and it is assumed here that Parent purchased Subsidiary's stock at its book value as of the time of acquisition.

In the illustration, the separate balance sheets of Parent and Subsidiary are given in the first two columns. The "combined" balance sheet in the third column is simply the sum of the figures in the first two columns

Illustration 8–2

CONSOLIDATION WORK SHEET

| | Separate Statements | | | Eliminations | | Consolidated Balance Sheet |
	Parent	Subsidiary	Combined	Dr.	Cr.	
Debit Balances						
Accounts receivable.....	40,000	11,000	51,000		(1) 5,000	46,000
Inventory............	30,000	15,000	45,000		(2) 1,000	44,000
Other current assets....	45,000	12,000	57,000			57,000
Fixed assets, gross......	405,000	65,000	470,000			470,000
Investment in Subsidiary	55,000	....	55,000		(3) 55,000	
	575,000	103,000	678,000			617,000
Credit Balances						
Accumulated deprecia-						
tion...............	160,000	20,000	180,000			180,000
Accounts payable.......	20,000	13,000	33,000	(1) 5,000		28,000
Other current liabilities..	25,000	9,000	34,000			34,000
Long-term liabilities....	100,000		100,000			100,000
Capital stock..........	100,000	40,000	140,000	(3) 40,000		100,000
Retained earnings.......	170,000	21,000	191,000	(2) 1,000 (3) 15,000		175,000
	575,000	103,000	678,000			617,000

This combined balance sheet contains some items which, so far as the consolidated entity is concerned, are counted twice, and the effect of this double counting is eliminated by the adjustments made in the next two columns and explained below. Essentially, these adjustments eliminate the effect of transactions that have occurred between the two corporations as separate legal entities. Since the consolidated financial statements should report only assets owned by the consolidated entity and the equities of parties *outside* the consolidated entity, these internal transactions must be eliminated. The consolidated balance sheet that results from these adjustments appears in the last column. The adjustments are as follows:

1. INTERCOMPANY FINANCIAL TRANSACTIONS. The consolidated balance sheet must show as accounts receivable and accounts payable only amounts owed by and owed to parties outside the consolidated business; therefore, amounts that the companies owe to one another must be eliminated. Assuming that Parent owes Subsidiary $5,000, this amount is eliminated from Accounts Payable and Accounts Receivable. The effect is as in the following journal entry (although it should be remembered that no journal entries actually are made in the books of either corporation):

```
Accounts Payable. . . . . . . . . . . . . . . . . .    5,000
    Accounts Receivable . . . . . . . . . . . . . . .         5,000
```

Interest on intercompany loans would also be eliminated in a similar manner.

The payment of dividends by the subsidiary to the parent is a financial transaction that has no effect on the consolidated entity. In the separate statements, this was recorded on Parent's books as a credit to Other Income (which was closed to Parent's Retained Earnings), and on Subsidiary's books as a debit to Dividends (which was closed to Subsidiary's Retained Earnings). Since this transaction affected only the two retained earnings accounts, adding to one the same amount that was subtracted from the other, the act of combining the two of them automatically eliminated its effect; therefore, no further adjustment is necessary.

2. INTERCOMPANY PROFIT.   In accordance with the realization principle, the consolidated company does not earn revenue until sales are made to the outside world. The revenue, the related costs, and the resulting profit for sales made between companies in the consolidated entity must therefore be eliminated from the consolidated accounts.

The sales and cost of sales on intercompany transactions are subtracted from the total sales and cost of sales figures on the consolidated income statement; if this were not done, the figures would overstate the volume of business done by the consolidated entity with the outside world. In order to do this, records must be kept that show both the sales revenue and the cost of sales of shipments made within the family.

On the balance sheet, these intercompany transactions may affect the Inventory account of the company receiving the goods and the Retained Earnings account of the company selling them, and adjustments to these accounts are required. Assume that during a year, Subsidiary shipped products with a sales value of $60,000 to Parent. During the year, Parent sold three fourths of these products to outside customers, and the other one fourth remains in Parent's inventory at the end of the year at its cost to Parent of $15,000. The products sold to the outside world present no problem, since they have disappeared from inventory and the revenue has been realized. If these products were sold by Parent for more than $45,000, the excess will wind up in Parent's Retained Earnings as profit. When Parent's Retained Earnings is added to Subsidiary's Retained Earnings, the total profit on this part of the transaction will be included, and properly so.

The $15,000 remaining in Parent's inventory, however, is regarded by Subsidiary as a sale, the profit on which appears in Subsidiary's Retained Earnings. This portion of the profit must be eliminated from the consolidated balance sheet. This is done by reducing Retained Earnings and Inventory by the amount of the profit, assumed to be $1,000, as in the following entry:

```
Retained Earnings . . . . . . . . . . . . . . . . . .   1,000
     Inventory . . . . . . . . . . . . . . . . . . . .          1,000
```

3. ELIMINATION OF THE INVESTMENT. The Parent company's investment in the Subsidiary's stock is strictly an intrafamily matter and must therefore be eliminated from the consolidated balance sheet. Since it is assumed here that the stock was purchased at book value, the $55,000 cost shown on Parent's books must have equaled Subsidiary's Capital Stock plus Retained Earnings at the time of purchase. We know that Capital Stock is $40,000, and the difference, $15,000, must therefore equal the balance of Retained Earnings at that time. The additional amount of retained earnings now shown on Subsidiary's books has been created subsequent to the acquisition by Parent. To eliminate the investment, therefore, the entry in effect is as follows:

```
Capital Stock . . . . . . . . . . . . . . . . . . . .   40,000
Retained Earnings . . . . . . . . . . . . . . . . . .   15,000
     Investment in Subsidiary. . . . . . . . . . . .           55,000
```

The necessary eliminations having been recorded, the figures for the consolidated balance sheet can now be obtained by carrying each line across the page.

In the preceding example, two of the most difficult problems in preparing consolidated statements did not arise because of simplifying assumptions that were made. These problems are described below.

Asset Valuation

In the example, it was assumed that Parent purchased Subsidiary's stock at its book value. Quite often, a subsidiary's stock is purchased at a figure other than its book value. Under these circumstances, the first step is to examine the value of Subsidiary's underlying assets; if their fair value differs from the amount at which they appear in Subsidiary's accounts, the accounts are adjusted to show the fair value, but not to exceed the purchase price. If after this revaluation, book value is still less than the price paid for the stock, the difference appears on the consolidated statement as Goodwill.[4] In the above illustration, if Parent had paid $65,000, rather than $55,000, for Subsidiary's stock, and if Subsidiary's assets were found to be recorded at their fair value, there would be goodwill of $10,000, and the adjustment marked (3) above would have been:

```
Goodwill. . . . . . . . . . . . . . . . . . . . . . .   10,000
Capital Stock . . . . . . . . . . . . . . . . . . . .   40,000
Retained Earnings . . . . . . . . . . . . . . . . . .   15,000
     Investment in Subsidiary. . . . . . . . . . . .           65,000
```

---

[4] As explained in the preceding section, if the merger were treated as a pooling of interest, no goodwill would arise.

Minority Interest

In the illustration above, it was assumed that Parent owned 100 percent of the stock of Subsidiary. If, instead, it owned less than 100 percent, the *minority interest*, which is the equity of the other owners in Subsidiary's assets, would appear as an equity item on the consolidated balance sheet. In measuring this equity, the matter of intercompany profits discussed in the second entry above raises a problem to which there is no completely satisfactory answer. From the standpoint of the minority shareholders of Subsidiary, products sold to Parent result in realized income, while from the standpoint of the consolidated entity these same products result in income only when they are sold to an outside party. This problem is often solved by eliminating the intercompany profit from the minority interest. In other words, the adjustment to inventory described in item (2) above would still be $1,000. Such a solution results in some understatement of the equity of the minority owners, but an attempt to show their equity correctly would inevitably result in an offsetting distortion of either the inventory or the retained earnings items on the consolidated balance sheet.

If in the above illustration, Parent purchased only 80 percent of Subsidiary's stock at book value of $44,000, adjustment (3) to eliminate the investment would be 80 percent of the figures given above, or:

```
Capital Stock . . . . . . . . . . . . . . . . . . . .  32,000
Retained Earnings . . . . . . . . . . . . . . . . . .  12,000
     Investment in Subsidiary. . . . . . . . . . . .           44,000
```

The remaining 20 percent of Subsidiary's Capital Stock plus 20 percent of Subsidiary's Retained Earnings after the elimination of intercompany profits would be set up as the equity of the minority interest on the consolidated statement, as follows:

```
Capital Stock . . . . . . . . . . . . . . . . . . . .   8,000
Retained Earnings . . . . . . . . . . . . . . . . . .   4,000
     Minority Interest . . . . . . . . . . . . . . .           12,000
```

Retained Earnings on the consolidated balance sheet would then be $174,000. The minority interest, $12,000, would appear just above the owners' equity section.

Concluding Comment

The preceding brief discussion of consolidated statements is by no means adequate as a basis for actually preparing consolidated financial statements. A great many problems in addition to those discussed above arise in practice. The illustration given does, however, indicate the main types of problems and the principles applied in solving them, and thus should help the user, as distinguished from the preparer, in understanding how the figures on a consolidated statement were derived.

UNINCORPORATED BUSINESSES

Single Proprietorships

Not much more need be said about the owner's equity accounts in a single proprietorship than the comments already made in Chapter 2. There may be a single account in which all entries affecting the owner's equity are recorded, or a separate *drawing account* may be set up to handle periodic withdrawals made by the owner. If a drawing account is used, it may either be closed into the capital account at the end of the accounting period, or it may be kept separate so as to show the owner's original contribution of capital separate from the effect on his equity of subsequent events. As far as the ultimate effect is concerned, it is immaterial whether the owner regards his withdrawals as salary or as a return of profit; but if he wishes to compare his income statement with that of a corporation, he will undoubtedly treat a certain part of his withdrawals as salary (although in a corporation that is managed by its owners, the distinction between salary and dividends may also be quite fuzzy in practice).

Partnerships

A partnership has the problem of showing in the accounts the equity of the individual partners, and this varies depending on the terms of the partnership agreement. The accounts are set up to facilitate the computation of each partner's equity, in accordance with whatever the agreement may be. In the absence of a specific agreement, the law assumes that net income is to be divided equally among the partners, and this is also common in written partnership agreements. If such is the case, in a three-man partnership the capital account, or the drawing account, of each partner is credited with one third of net income. It is debited with the actual amount of his withdrawals.

If the agreement is that profits are to be divided in proportion to the capital originally contributed by each partner, then the capital account is maintained to show the amount of that contribution, and other transactions affecting the partners' equity are debited or credited to separate drawings or personal accounts. If one of the partners made a temporary loan to the partnership, it would be shown in a liability account (but separate from loans made by outside parties) rather than in the partner's equity account.

Partnership agreements may also provide that the partners receive stated salaries and a stated share of residual profits after salaries, or a stated percentage of interest on the capital they invested and a stated share of residual profits, or a combination of salary and interest. The accounting required in connection with such arrangements depends on the specific terms of the agreement.

EXAMPLE: The partnership agreement of Paine and Webber provided that Paine (who worked half time) would receive a salary of $10,000 and Webber a salary of $20,000; that each would receive 6 percent interest on the capital they contributed; and that they would share equally in the remainder. In 1969 the average balance in Paine's capital account was $50,000 and in Webber's, $10,000. The partnership net income was $40,000.

The income of each partner would be computed as follows:

	Total	Paine	Webber
Salary	$30,000	$10,000	$20,000
Interest	3,600	3,000	600
Remainder	6,400	3,200	3,200
Total	$40,000	$16,200	$23,800

Whatever the partnership arrangement, the law does not regard salaries or interest payments to the partners as being different from any other type of withdrawal, since the partnership is not an entity legally separate from the individual partners. Neither does the partnership as such ordinarily pay a federal income tax; the income of the partnership, regardless of whether it has been withdrawn, is taxable income to the individual partners. A partnership can, however, elect to be taxed as if it were a corporation, and certain small corporations can elect to be taxed as partnerships; special rules apply in these cases.

SUMMARY

Long-term equities consist, in general, of bonds and of shareholders' equity.

The liability arising from the sale of bonds is shown at its face amount, and the difference between this amount and the net proceeds received is recorded as bond premium or discount. Premium or discount is amortized over the life of the issue. This amortization is combined with the periodic interest payments to give the effective interest expense of each period.

In a corporation, shareholders' equity consists of two parts which should always be reported separately: (1) the amount paid to the corporation by each class of shareholders, which may be further divided into (a) the par or stated value of stock, and (b) capital surplus; and (2) retained earnings, representing the cumulative amount of net income that has not yet been paid out as dividends. In unincorporated businesses, the distinction between the original contribution of capital and subsequent changes in shareholders' equity may or may not be set forth on the balance sheet.

A business may consist of more than one corporation. If so, consolidated financial statements are prepared for the whole enterprise as a single entity. This is done by eliminating the effect of intercompany transactions from the accounts of the separate corporations and then combining them.

SUGGESTIONS FOR FURTHER READING

BACKER, MORTON (ed.). *Modern Accounting Theory*. 2d ed.; New York: Prentice-Hall, Inc., 1968.

FINNEY, HARRY A. and MILLER, H. E. *Principles of Accounting, Intermediate*. 6th ed.; New York: Prentice-Hall, Inc., 1965.

WELSCH, GLENN A.; ZLATKOVICH, CHARLES T.; and WHITE, JOHN ARCH. *Intermediate Accounting*, chaps. xv and xvi. Homewood, Ill.: Richard D. Irwin, Inc., 1968.

WIXON, RUFUS (ed.). *Accountants' Handbook*. 4th ed.; New York: Ronald Press Co., 1966.

CASES

CASE 8-1.   RICHARD D. BREW AND COMPANY, INCORPORATED[5]

In order to retire funded debt and to provide funds for additional plant, equipment, working capital, and research, Richard D. Brew and Company, Incorporated, offered for sale 70,000 shares of $1 par value common stock in July 1959. The offering price to the public was $9 a share, from which an underwriting discount of $0.90 a share would be deducted, leaving $8.10 a share as proceeds to the company. Expenses in connection with the offering estimated at $16,900 also were to be borne by the company. Financial statements are shown in Exhibits 1 and 2.

The Brew Company started operations in 1946. It was engaged in research, design, development, and manufacture in the general area of applying advanced physics to military and civilian needs. Among its products were high-precision delay lines, used in missiles, in radar, and in electronic computers; and high-vacuum, ultra-high temperature electric furnaces used for processing certain rare metals used in missiles.

The balance sheet of May 31, 1959, reported 9,300 shares of no-par value common stock outstanding with a stated value of $112,664. Of this amount, $12,664 resulted from owners' equity transactions occurring prior to 1958. During the year 1958 the company transferred $100,000 from retained earnings to capital stock. In 1958 also, the company split the 310 shares of stock then outstanding on the basis of 30 for 1 and increased its authorized capital from 1,000 to 10,000 shares.

In 1959, concurrently with the sale of stock, the company again changed its capitalization. The common stock was changed from no-par to $1 par value, the number of authorized shares was increased to 500,000, and the number of shares outstanding (not counting the sale of additional stock) was increased from 9,300 to 310,000 by means of a 33⅓ for 1 split.

In its prospectus the company stated that it planned to use the proceeds of the stock issue as follows:

---

[5] Information in this case was obtained from the company's prospectus.

Of the net proceeds (estimated at approximately $550,000 after the deduction of expenses) from the sales by the Company of 70,000 shares of its Common Stock to the Underwriters, approximately $106,000 will be used to discharge the Company's outstanding short term Bank Notes, Second and Third Mortgage Notes and Land Mortgage. The borrowings evidenced by the Bank Notes were made to reimburse the Company's treasury for part of the funds spent for additions to the Company's plant facilities, substantially completed as of June 1, 1959, and for additional machinery and equipment related thereto, and to provide working capital.

It is presently contemplated that out of the balance of such proceeds ap-

Exhibit 1

RICHARD D. BREW AND COMPANY, INCORPORATED

Condensed Balance Sheet, May 31, 1959

ASSETS

Current Assets:		
Cash..		$ 24,580
Accounts receivable, net.........................		78,150
Inventories, at lower of cost or market:		
Raw materials and supplies.......................	$ 13,107	
Work in process...............................	289,168	302,275
Prepaid expenses................................		2,223
Total Current Assets...........................		$407,228
Property, plant, and equipment, at cost.................	$366,531	
Less: Accumulated depreciation......................	123,493	243,038
Other assets......................................		3,468
Total Assets................................		$653,734

LIABILITIES AND STOCKHOLDERS' EQUITY

Current Liabilities:		
Notes payable—banks............................		$ 66,000
Current maturities of long-term debt.................		5,994
Accounts payable................................		205,671
Accrued liabilities...............................		22,133
Federal income taxes............................		17,600
Total Current Liabilities........................		$317,398
Long-Term Debt:		
$4\frac{1}{2}\%$ first mortgage note, payable monthly to May 1974..	$100,000	
6% second mortgage note, payable monthly to December		
1969...	15,046	
6% third mortgage note, payable monthly to May 1974...	18,411	
5% land mortgage...............................	6,525	
	$139,982	
Less: Principal payments due within one year.........	5,994	133,988
Stockholders' Equity:		
Common stock, no-par value, authorized 10,000 shares,		
issued and outstanding 9,300 shares................	$112,664	
Retained earnings (exclusive of amounts transferred to		
capital).......................................	89,684	202,348
Total Liabilities and Stockholders' Equity.........		$653,734

proximately $25,000 will be expended for further equipment in connection with current expansion and of costs of rearrangement and moving of machinery and equipment.

It is likewise contemplated that an amount not yet definite (but currently estimated at not less than $75,000) will be applied to defray the cost of additional plant and equipment for expansion of the Company's Vacuum Furnace Division.

It is the intention of the Company to use $64,000 of the remainder to pay off the entire amount of short term bank borrowings made since June 15, 1959, for working capital requirements, approximately $36,000 of the re-

Exhibit 2

RICHARD D. BREW AND COMPANY, INCORPORATED

Summary of Earnings and Retained Earnings

	Year Ended December 31					Five Months Ended May 31	
	1954	1955	1956	1957	1958	1958	1959
Net sales.........	$375,697	$412,416	$443,538	$969,883	$1,178,897	$465,152	$367,900
Operating costs and expenses:							
Cost of sales....	$250,499	$282,095	$344,206	$658,931	$836,042	$289,299	$323,567
Selling, administrative, and general.....	46,115	65,755	116,426	181,351	221,387	90,876	106,474
Interest expense, principally on long-term debt.	1,802	4,025	5,506	7,362	5,900	2,122	3,455
Income (loss) before federal income taxes..	$ 77,281	$ 60,541	$(22,600)	$122,239	$ 115,568	$ 82,855	$(65,596)
Provision for federal income taxes.........	32,646	26,275	(11,476)	58,691	55,000	41,100	(34,100)
Net income (loss)..	$ 44,635	$ 34,266	$(11,124)	$ 63,548	$ 60,568	$ 41,755	$(31,496)
Retained earnings at beginning of period.....	29,287	73,922	108,188	97,064	160,612	160,612	121,180
	$ 73,922	$108,188	$ 97,064	$160,612	$ 221,180	$202,367	$ 89,684
Transferred to capital stock.....					100,000		
Retained Earnings at Close of Period.......	$ 73,922	$108,188	$ 97,064	$160,612	$ 121,180	$202,367	$ 89,684

mainder for current working capital requirements and the balance for an expanded program of research in delay lines, vacuum furnaces and related new products.

The additional common stock was offered to the public on July 28, 1959, and the issue was oversubscribed before that day was over.

Questions

1. Prepare journal entries to record the effect of the changes in capitalization made in 1958.
2. Prepare journal entries to record the effect of the change of capitalization and the sale of additional stock in 1959, including the entries (if any) for (*a*) the increase in the number of shares authorized, (*b*) the stock split, (*c*) the change in capitalization from no-par to $1 par value, (*d*) the incurrence of $16,900 expenses, (*e*) the sale of the additional stock, and (*f*) the disposition of the $16,900 expenses.
3. Assuming that the proceeds were utilized as described in the prospectus, prepare journal entries to reflect (*a*) the retirement of debt, and (*b*) the acquisition of equipment and plant. Explain, without making journal entries, how the use of the proceeds for "an expanded program of research" will affect the financial statements.
4. What do you suppose was the reasoning behind these changes in the company's capital structure?
5. Assuming that the entire amount of common stock prior to 1958 represented cash contributions of the original shareholders (which is in fact not the case), how much would an original shareholder have gained if, on July 28, 1959, he sold the equivalent of one of his original shares?

CASE 8-2.　KEMP FOODS CORPORATION

"Here's the entire mess," said Ed McCowan as papers of various sizes and colors fluttered from the large manila envelope and spread over the desk of Dan Conner, CPA. "I bought 40 shares of Kemp Foods common last year in May. Since then I've received proxy statements, notices of stock splits, stock certificates, quarterly financial statements and a few dividend checks. When this thick annual report came in yesterday's mail, I called you. I knew what to do with those little dividend checks, but to tell the truth I don't know what the rest of this means. I thought the annual report would explain things, but I don't see any relationship between my 40 shares and the big numbers and big words in the report."

"It appears that you saved everything, Ed," said Dan Conner. "Let's see if we can list things as they happened from the beginning." He made these notes on a desk pad as he selected papers from the assortment before him:

May	5, 1964—Bo't 40 common at 38 plus commission	$1,539.60
July	20	—Rec'd cash div.—40 at 25¢	10.00
Oct.	20	— " " " " " "	10.00
	25	—Rec'd 2 shares common stock div.	
Jan.	20, 1965—Rec'd cash div.—42 at 25¢	10.50
Mar.	15	—Rec'd 21 shares—3 for 2 stock split	
Apr.	20	—Rec'd cash div.—63 at 20¢	12.60

"Now, let's look at the quotations in today's *Wall Street Journal* and see how you've made out over the past year. Here it is on the Pacific Coast Exchange. The closing price yesterday was 28½. Now we'll look at the April 30, 1965, annual report together and see what it tells us."

This case concerns corporate financial reporting for changes in shareholders' equity and its meaning to the investor.

The Company

Kemp Foods Corporation was established in Illinois in 1927 to acquire and operate three small vegetable canning plants. Operations were expanded to include canning of fruits and frozen food processing. The growth of these newer activities in the late 1940's was responsible for transfer of company headquarters to California. In 1965 the company had 15 canning and processing plants throughout the Midwest and on the West Coast.

Kemp's operations had always been profitable. Earnings per share of common reached an historic high of $2.27 in the fiscal year ended April 30, 1965. Net income for the year was $1.3 million on sales of almost $59 million. Shareholders' equity at April 30, 1965, exceeded $13 million. The company's comparative balance sheets at the close of the two most recent years are shown in Exhibit 1. An analysis of common stock, paid-in surplus, and retained earnings is in Exhibit 2.

Most of the funds needed to finance the company's growth had been provided internally. Modest cash dividends had been paid quarterly without interruption since 1946, when the common stock was split 3 for 1. In 1952, after a public offering of preferred and common stock, a policy of supplementing the regular cash dividends with stock dividends to common stockholders was adopted. Five percent stock dividends were declared in each year thereafter except for 1955 and 1956 when stock dividends were 20 and 10 percent respectively. The 4 percent preferred stock was gradually being retired as it became available in the market at an attractive price. Some funds had been obtained by the use of long-term debt and future expansion was to be financed more extensively in this way.

The price of Kemp Foods' common stock had risen steadily since the early 1950's. For example, the price had ranged from a low of 12¾ to a

Exhibit 1

KEMP FOODS CORPORATION

Comparative Balance Sheet, April 30, 1965 and 1964

ASSETS	1965	1964
Current Assets:		
Cash	$ 996,020	$ 1,124,588
Receivables (net)	5,076,894	5,084,087
Inventories, at the lower of cost (first-in, first-out basis) or market	10,440,509	8,708,578
Total Current Assets	$16,513,423	$14,917,253
Prepaid expenses	$ 133,434	$ 230,002
Plant and Equipment:		
Land	$ 290,349	$ 346,319
Buildings and leasehold improvements	4,200,760	4,719,515
Machinery and equipment	3,916,508	4,275,927
Automotive equipment	601,393	586,030
Construction in progress	2,033,324	. . .
	$11,042,334	$ 9,927,791
Less: Accumulated depreciation and amortization	5,038,251	4,532,968
Net Plant and Equipment	$ 6,004,083	$ 5,394,823
Total Assets	$22,650,940	$20,542,078

LIABILITIES		
Current Liabilities:		
Bank loans	$ 2,192,500	$ 1,350,000
Current maturities of long-term debt	170,790	163,478
Accounts payable and accrued liabilities	2,187,440	1,770,026
Income taxes	1,014,527	936,889
Dividends payable	126,811	102,554
Total Current Liabilities	$ 5,692,068	$ 4,322,947
Long-term debt, noncurrent portion	$ 3,660,223	$ 3,831,013
Deferred income taxes and other expenses	$ 273,850	$ 174,225
Stockholders' Equity:		
Cumulative 4% preferred stock, par value $100; authorized 15,000 shares, issued 8,995 shares, less 198 shares in treasury	$ 879,700	
Common stock, par value $5; authorized 1,000,000 shares, issued 590,552 shares, (4,482 shares in treasury—see below)	2,952,760	
Paid-in surplus (Exhibit 2)	2,853,702	
Retained earnings (Exhibit 2):		
Reserve for plant expansion	1,466,676	
Unappropriated*	4,997,457	
	$13,150,295	
Less: Treasury stock, common (4,482 shares at cost)	125,496	
Total Stockholders' Equity	$13,024,799	$12,213,893
Total Liabilities	$22,650,940	$20,542,078

* Under terms of the long-term debt agreement $2,330,808 of retained earnings at April 30, 1965 is restricted against payment of cash dividends on or purchase of common stock.

Exhibit 2

KEMP FOODS CORPORATION

Common Stock, Paid-In Surplus, and Retained Earnings
For the Year Ended April 30, 1965

	Common Stock		Paid-In Surplus	Retained Earnings	
	Shares	Par Value		Reserve for Plant Exp.	Unappropriated
Balance at May 1, 1964......	375,130	$1,875,650	$3,197,277	$3,500,000	$2,742,831
Add:					
Net income for the year...					1,376,871
Gain on sale of 600 shares common treasury stock..			17,716		
Discount on 245 shares of preferred stock purchased.................			4,003		
Reduction in reserve for plant expansion........				(2,033,324)	2,033,324
Total...............	375,130	$1,875,650	$3,218,996	$1,466,676	$6,153,026
Transfer to common stock in connection with 3 for 2 stock split............	196,690	983,450	(983,450)		
Cash dividends:					
Preferred ($4.00 per share).............					(35,386)
Common ($0.95 per share)...............					(408,367)
5% stock dividend, recorded at fair market value of $38 per share...	18,732	93,660	618,156		(711,816)
Balance at April 30, 1965....	590,552	$2,952,760	$2,853,702	$1,466,676	$4,997,457

high of 18⅜ in the year 1959 and reached an all time high of 43½ early in 1964.

Questions

1. Evaluate Ed McCowan's investment at June 10, 1965.
2. Examine the stockholders' equity section of Kemp Foods' balance sheet to:
   (a) Determine how each item was originally created.
   (b) Explain changes during the year ended April 30, 1965.
3. Contrast Kemp's methods of reporting preferred treasury stock and common treasury stock.
4. What is the effect of Kemp's acquisition of treasury stock upon investor McCowan's holdings?
5. Suggest improvements Kemp might make in reporting stockholders' equity information on its balance sheet.

CHAPTER 9

THE PRICE LEVEL PROBLEM

The accountant measures the goods and services that enter into his calculation of net income essentially at their acquisition cost, that is, at the prices paid when these goods and services were originally acquired by the company. The economist, however, often measures cost not in terms of the price originally paid for the goods and services but rather in terms of "real prices"; that is, he adjusts acquisition prices to allow for changes in purchasing power or in the economic significance of the specific good or service. In periods when there are substantial changes in prices, such as the downward movement in the early 1930's or the inflationary movement which began in the 1940's, the difference between the accounting concept of income and the economist's concept of income can be substantial.

This difference arises because the purchasing power of the monetary unit of measurement is different at different times. Thus, the measuring stick used in accounting is unlike the yardstick used to make linear measurements; a yardstick is always 36 inches long. A balance sheet prepared at one moment of time contains some items, such as cash, that are stated at current purchasing power; other items, such as inventory, that may be stated in monetary units that reflect purchasing power of the recent past; and still other items, such as plant and equipment, stated at amounts that reflect purchasing power of several years previous to the current date.

Several proposals have been advanced for dealing with this problem, and three are described in this chapter. One of these, the Lifo method of inventory measurement, has become a generally accepted accounting principle and is also allowed for tax purposes. The second, depreciation on replacement cost, is not a generally accepted accounting principle in the United States. The third, price level adjustments, involves the preparation of supplementary financial statements rather than a change in the principles underlying the regular balance sheet and income statement. All

230

are important to know about, partly because they are widely discussed, and partly because they demonstrate, by contrast, some limitations of the figures developed under conventional principles.

THE LIFO METHOD

Lifo, which stands for "last-in, first-out," is a method of measuring inventory costs. In this method, inventory is costed *as if* the units most recently added to inventory (last-in) were the first units sold (first-out) *even though this is in fact not the case.* Ending inventory is therefore assumed to consist of the oldest units and is measured at the cost of these oldest units. If the number of physical units in inventory remains constant from period to period, the accounting measurement of the inventory will also remain constant, regardless of what happens to the market replacement price of the inventory items. It follows that under the Lifo method, cost of goods sold tends to reflect the cost of the items most recently purchased.

The Lifo inventory method normally does not correspond to the physical flow of material, nor do its advocates claim that it has any relation to physical flow. Physically, material moves out of inventory on approximately a Fifo, or first-in, first-out, basis; that is, the oldest stocks normally are used up first. Advocates of Lifo contend, however, that in certain industries Lifo does match the *economic* flow of values since, they claim, the profit margin that actually influences business pricing decisions is the margin between sales prices and *current* costs, not the margin between sales prices and cost levels that existed at the time the inventory was purchased.

If this contention is correct, the conventional Fifo system results in the reporting of false "inventory profits" during periods of rising cost prices. During these periods goods are sold at sales prices commensurate with current costs, while cost of goods sold reflects earlier, lower costs rather than current costs. (Lifo only *approximates* current costs since it shows the cost of *most recent* purchases, and this is not necessarily the same as current cost.)

Arguments For and Against Lifo

A frequently used example of what is meant by this economic flow is the following excerpt from the Report of the Special Committee on Inventories of the AICPA (1936), a report which had much to do with the adoption of Lifo as a generally accepted principle:

A wagon maker has a wagon in stock which cost him $50, the selling price of which is $65 to yield him his desired profit of $15 per wagon. Before he sells the wagon he learns from the concern supplying him with his material of a price increase, the result of which is to make the reproduction cost of his wagon $60. By reason of this knowledge the wagon maker "marks up" his wagon to $75, at which figure he sells it for cash and builds a new wagon costing him $60. The net change resulting from the whole transaction is that his till shows $15 more cash than he had before.

Now the advocate of "reproduction cost of sales" says to the wagon maker:

The profit you made is $15, and the proper inventory price for the present wagon you have in stock is $50. That is the number of dollars of your capital invested in your stock-in-trade; the only change that you have effectively realized in that investment is the substitution of one wagon for another exactly like it—the same wagon, in fact, except only as regards physical identity.

On the other hand, the advocate of "first-in, first-out" says to the wagon maker: Your profit is $25, although you may have only $15 more in cash to show for it. The other $10 is contained in the increased cost and value of the new wagon—$60 as against the old one at $50. You must not fail to recognize and to give effect to the price level change.

Considering the other side of the problem, let us assume that after the above transaction the price level reverted to its original status, thus consummating the economic cycle; accordingly the wagon at present in stock, which actually had cost $60 to build (but was inventoried at either $50 or $60, according to the procedure followed) is sold for $65 and replaced in stock by one which cost $50 to build. Now, under either procedure the latest wagon will be inventoried at $50. The profit on the second transaction, however, will have been $15 according to the "reproduction cost of sales" advocate, or $5 according to the "first-in, first-out" advocate. The aggregate profit on the two transactions, of course, will be the same in either case but the periodic distribution will differ.

One virtue of the Lifo method is its tendency to limit the amount of reported net income to an amount which might be made available to shareholders without imparing the scope and intensity of the operations of a going concern. Advocates also argue that such restrictions in reported income serve to conserve funds by reducing income taxes.

Opponents of Lifo, while agreeing that it is not good management policy to regard funds needed to maintain the level of operations as representing disposable income, attack the Lifo argument on the grounds that it confuses two distinct processes: (1) the measurement of income, and (2) the utilization of income. They argue that income may be realized and valid even though such income is to be subsequently invested in inventories or other assets. They also point out that the Lifo method falls short of achieving the underlying objective in that costs of only the most recent acquisitions are charged against revenue rather than the total cost of replacing all the items sold.

No one argues that Lifo is applicable to every company; rather it is recommended only when there is a definite relationship between selling price and *current* cost. For example, if a retailer sets his selling price by adding a fixed markup to the invoice cost of specific units of merchandise, and if he usually can sell the merchandise at this price, his profit is based not on replacement cost but rather on his invoice cost, and he should not use the Lifo system. If, on the other hand, he finds it necessary or possible to change his retail prices as soon as, or shortly after, a change in wholesale prices occurs, his cost may be considered to be the replacement or Lifo cost.

A close correspondence between changes in selling prices and changes in current costs may reflect a general change in the value of money in the economy. If this is the case, it is argued that it makes little sense to state the revenue component of profit at the current value of the dollar while stating the principal expense component, cost of goods sold, in terms of a different kind of dollar. On the other hand, if the facts are that in a particular company the profit margin has really changed, for reasons having nothing to do with fluctuations in price levels, the use of Lifo may conceal such changes.

In addition to companies whose selling prices are related to invoice costs rather than to current costs, Lifo is also not appropriate for companies which eliminate inventory profits or losses by the practice called "hedging," nor for companies which are in the business of speculating on price changes, as are certain companies that trade in grain and other commodities.

The relative importance of inventory profits varies among companies, and Lifo has a more important influence on profits when—

1. Material cost constitutes a relatively large part of total cost.
2. The inventory is relatively large.
3. The manufacturing process is relatively long (which is a variation of No. 2, because a long manufacturing process means a large work in process inventory).

Example

Illustration 9–1 illustrates the effect of the Lifo method on profit and on inventory valuation, as contrasted with the Fifo method. The situation illustrated is the simplest possible, namely, where—

1. Selling price is immediately and exactly adjusted for changes in material cost.
2. There is no change in inventory quantity, that is, as soon as a unit is sold, it is replaced in inventory by another unit.
3. Sales *volume* each year is constant (at 1,000 units).
4. One hundred percent of the product cost is material cost.
5. Inventory turnover is 1; that is, inventory consists of 1,000 units.

Illustration 9–1

GROSS PROFIT CALCULATION UNDER FIFO AND LIFO

	(1) Inventory, January 1	*(2)* Purchases	*(3)* Inventory, December 31	*(4)* Cost of Sales*	*(5)* Sales†	*(6)* Gross Profit
			UNDER FIFO			
19X1.........	1,000 at $1.00	1,000 at $1.00	1,000 at $1.00	$1,000	$2,000	$1,000
19X2.........	1,000 at 1.00	1,000 at 1.50	1,000 at 1.50	1,000	2,500	1,500
19X3.........	1,000 at 1.50	1,000 at 2.00	1,000 at 2.00	1,500	3,000	1,500
19X4.........	1,000 at 2.00	1,000 at 0.50	1,000 at 0.50	2,000	1,500	(500)
19X5.........	1,000 at 0.50	1,000 at 1.00	1,000 at 1.00	500	2,000	1,500
				Total Five-Year Profit........		$5,000
			UNDER LIFO			
19X1.........	1,000 at $1.00	1,000 at $1.00	1,000 at $1.00	$1,000	$2,000	$1,000
19X2.........	1,000 at 1.00	1,000 at 1.50	1,000 at 1.00	1,500	2,500	1,000
19X3.........	1,000 at 1.00	1,000 at 2.00	1,000 at 1.00	2,000	3,000	1,000
19X4.........	1,000 at 1.00	1,000 at 0.50	1,000 at 1.00	500	1,500	1,000
19X5.........	1,000 at 1.00	1,000 at 1.00	1,000 at 1.00	1,000	2,000	1,000
				Total Five-Year Profit........		$5,000

* Beginning inventory, plus purchases, less ending inventory, each being assumed in this example to be 1,000 units. With an inventory turnover of 1, cost of sales under Fifo will equal the value of the beginning inventory, since it is assumed that the units sold were the oldest units on hand and equal in units to purchases. Under Lifo, cost of sales will equal the value of purchases, since it is assumed that the units sold were the units most recently purchased.
† 1,000 units times sales price per unit, which is assumed to be the current purchase price +$1.

In the example, prices are assumed to go through a complete cycle; that is, they rise and then fall back to the starting point. The following points can be noted from these calculations:

1. There is no difference in total profits under Lifo and under Fifo over the complete cycle.
2. Under the conventional Fifo method profits are high in years of high prices and low in years of low prices, even though the quantity sold and the margin between selling price and current material cost remains constant; also inventory values fluctuate widely, and inventory is at its highest price at the very top of the cycle.
3. Under the Lifo method, profit and inventory values are the same in each year; in one year 19X4, inventory was valued at more than "market."

Basic Arguments

A more generalized argument in favor of Lifo goes beyond the limitation of exact agreement of cost and selling price, as was presumed in the example given above. The real issue, from this point of view, is whether or not the company has properly counted its current costs against its current revenue in figuring its net income. In periods of rising prices the company does have increased costs in maintaining its inventory position, and current sales should be charged with a cost of goods sold that reflects these current costs. To do otherwise, this argument runs, is to count a cost as a profit and to pay stiff taxes on the amounts so reported.

This broader view of Lifo looks on inventory as a necessary stock in trade, just as essential to operations as are plant or facilities. Accordingly, such an investment ought *not* to be revalued on the balance sheet with every cyclical swing of prices any more than plant is revalued. As Illustration 9–1 demonstrates, the Lifo method tends to stabilize both profits and the reported value of inventory as prices change.

Opponents of Lifo argue that one of management's primary responsibilities is effective utilization of the economic resources at its disposal. They admit that over sustained periods of price level changes, conventional accounting fails to reflect the economic values of such resources as plant and inventory, but they claim that Lifo confuses, rather than clarifies, the picture. Under Lifo, inventory is valued forever in terms of whatever the price level happened to be at the time Lifo was introduced. As time goes on and price levels change, the inventory figure under Lifo departs further and further from reality, becoming neither a reflection of actual purchase costs nor of current costs. Thus Lifo may make the inventory figure on the balance sheet of dubious usefulness to management or to others who attempt to appraise the financial status of the business.

Advocates of Lifo are thinking primarily of its effect on the income statement and are willing to accept the fact that the usefulness of the balance sheet inventory figure may be impaired. Opponents of Lifo emphasize its effect on the balance sheet; they admit that the conventional Fifo income statement may not reflect the flow of economic values, although they do not grant that this is necessarily bad.

Dollar Value Method

Originally, Lifo was used only by companies whose inventory consisted of fungible products, such as wheat, each unit of which is physically like every other unit. Other companies, however, argued that this was unfair to them, and Lifo may now be used for almost any kind of inventory. It is applied to an inventory of physically unlike items by the so-called *Lifo dollar value method.* In this method, items whose prices tend to move together are grouped into an *inventory pool.* A pool may consist of all the items in the hardware department of a department store, for example, or it may consist of a store's entire inventory. The dollar amount invested in such a pool is treated as a unit in figuring the Lifo inventory value and cost of goods sold, and changes in the value of the dollar during the accounting period are allowed for by the application of index numbers of price changes.

As an illustration, assume that the beginning inventory in a pool had an actual invoice cost of $780,000, and that the inventory at the end of the year had an actual invoice cost of $880,000. Without additional information, we do not know how much of the $100,000 increase in the amount of inventory represents an increase in the _physical size_ of the inventory and how much results from the same quantity being valued at a higher price because of inflation. By the use of an index number of price changes, the change associated with size can be separated from the change associated with price movements. Thus, if an appropriate price index increased from 100 at the beginning of the year to 110 at the end of the year, the year-end inventory can be _deflated_ to the beginning price level by multiplying it by the ratio of the index change, or $^{100}/_{110}$. The value of the ending inventory expressed in beginning prices is therefore $^{100}/_{110}$ of $880,000, or $800,000. Since $800,000 exceeds the beginning inventory of $780,000 by $20,000, we estimate that the physical size of the inventory has increased by $20,000 during the year. This $20,000 is expressed in beginning prices, however, and under the Lifo method it must be added to inventory at the most recent prices, so it is _reinflated_ by multiplying by the ratio $^{110}/_{100}$, to give $22,000. The ending inventory thus is valued at $802,000, which is the sum of the beginning inventory, $780,000, plus the increase in physical inventory, $22,000. Cost of goods sold is then found by the deduction formula—beginning inventory, plus purchases, less ending inventory— which results in a difference of $78,000 between the invoice cost and the Lifo cost of ending inventory going into cost of goods sold.

In applying the dollar value method, department stores use price indexes especially computed for this purpose by the government. Other companies compute their own index from the movement of prices of all, or a sample of, items in inventory.

Decreases in Inventory

When the physical size of the inventory increases, in a Lifo system the inventory account is increased by the current cost of the units added. During a period of growth, the inventory account will therefore consist of a number of _layers,_ a new layer being added each year. If subsequently the physical inventory should decrease in size, these layers in effect are stripped off, taking the most recently added layer first, in accordance with the basic Lifo rule. This process can have a peculiar effect on the income statement. If, for example, inventory is decreased even below its original size when the Lifo system started, inventory items will be moving into cost of goods sold at costs established several years previously; and if there has been constant inflation during the interim, such a shrinkage in inventory can result in a significant increase in reported income. Some people assert that in a recession some companies deliberately eat into their Lifo inventories in order to increase reported income in a lean year.

Variations

In applying the general idea of Lifo to a particular situation, several alternatives are possible:

1. Lifo may be applied to all inventories, or only to the raw materials inventory, or only to certain items in inventory.
2. Products may be run through the cost accounting mechanism at Lifo values, or the detailed cost records may show Fifo or specific invoice values, with an adjustment to Lifo being made only at the end of the accounting period.
3. Inventory changes may be calculated annually, or monthly, or even daily.

Usually the differences in results between the several methods of applying Lifo are small compared with the basic difference between Lifo and Fifo, but the fact that these differences in the application of Lifo exist is one reason why Lifo is criticized. It is difficult to compare the earnings of a company that uses Lifo with the earnings of a company that uses Fifo; variations within the general Lifo idea make "confusion worse confounded."

Tax Considerations

A company that wishes to use Lifo for income tax purposes must make application to do so, and once having been granted permission, it must continue to use Lifo thereafter unless it receives special permission to change again; such permission is not easily obtained.

If the company uses Lifo for tax purposes, it must also use Lifo in its annual financial statements (although not necessarily in monthly or quarterly statements). Incidentally, this is the only instance of a statutory requirement that the same method be used for financial accounting purposes as is used for tax purposes.

A company using Lifo cannot use the "lower of cost or market" rule for tax purposes; that is, it cannot write down its inventory to market if market values are below Lifo cost. On its financial statements, however, the company is permitted to show a write-down to market.

Although it is easy to calculate whether or not tax savings will result in the year in which Lifo is adopted, it is impossible to determine whether the net effect over a number of years will be a savings or not. The existence and amount of any future tax savings depends largely upon future price movements, fluctuations in tax rates applicable to the business, and variations in the amounts and kinds of physical inventories held at the end of each taxable year. Although over a period of years total income computed under either the Lifo or Fifo method may be the same, it does not follow that total income taxes will also be the same. Generally, total income taxes tend to be greater under Fifo than under Lifo if the following conditions exist: if income tax rates are progressive, if income tax rates are higher in years of rising prices than in years of falling prices, or if there is no provision for carry-back of losses. There is a permanent deferment of taxes, of course, if prices continue upward indefinitely; that is, if inflation is always with us. Although tax savings under Lifo are likely in periods of rising prices, they are by no means certain if prices are near their peak when the change to Lifo is made, for tax losses after prices begin to fall may be greater than the initial tax savings when prices were rising.

Base Stock Method

Another method of recognizing the impact of price changes on inventory, the *base stock method*, actually antedates Lifo in practice. It accomplishes approximately the same result as the Lifo method and indeed reflects current costs more closely than Lifo, but since its use is not permitted for tax purposes, it has not become widely adopted.

DEPRECIATION ON REPLACEMENT COST

Since the fixed assets of a company may have been purchased at various times extending many years into the past, price fluctuations cause the expense and asset amounts associated with these items to deviate even farther from current cost than is the case with inventory. The American Appraisal Company index of construction costs has more than quadrupled in the period from 1940 to 1968, and it doubled in the period from 1950 to 1968. This means that a dollar spent on construction in 1968 would buy only about half as many physical units of assets as a dollar spent in 1950, or that a 1968 dollar is a "50-cent dollar" in terms of its 1950 purchasing power.

Conventional accounting does not differentiate between 50-cent dollars and 100-cent dollars. If a company, for example, purchased an 80,000 square-foot factory building for $500,000 in 1950, this building, exclusive of accumulated depreciation, would appear on the balance sheet at $500,000; and if the building was replaced with a physically identical 80,000 square-foot factory building for $1 million in 1968, this would appear at $1 million. Although the balance sheet figure for the new building is double that of the old, the company actually has the same amount of factory space as it had before.

Moreover, the annual depreciation charge for fixed assets, being based on the actual cost of the asset, is not expressed in the same kind of dollars as the revenue item on the income statement. In periods of inflation, depreciation expressed in past dollars of relatively high purchasing power is matched against revenue expressed in current dollars of relatively low purchasing power.

Although the depreciation mechanism charges off the cost of the asset over its useful life, it does not, and is not designed to, provide for the replacement of the asset. Suppose, for example, that a company actually set aside a cash fund equal to its depreciation charge, paying out all its net income as dividends. Some might believe that a company could operate indefinitely on such a plan, using this fund to buy new assets as the old assets required replacement. If prices were steady this would be possible, but in periods of inflation the replacement fund could not purchase the same quantity of assets as those discarded, and the company would gradually shrink and eventually disappear.

The impact of income taxes increases the severity of the replacement problem. If the company recognizes the inadequacy of depreciation as a replacement medium and tries to earn additional income to add to its "replacement fund," it must, at a 50 percent rate, earn $2 of income before taxes for every $1 it wishes to put into a fund; the other $1 will be siphoned off in taxes.

Replacement Cost Proposal

In view of these problems, some people argue that depreciation should be calculated on the estimated replacement cost of an asset rather than on its original cost. The most famous attempt to do this is that of the United States Steel Corporation in the 1940's. This attempt did not succeed in obtaining either a change in accounting principles or a change in income tax regulations.

A change to a replacement cost basis of figuring depreciation would represent a fundamental modification in the concepts of accounting, since it would be a departure from the basic idea that balance sheet and expense amounts are based on monetary cost, and not on purchasing power or economic values. Even the Lifo inventory method uses monetary costs as obtained from actual transactions. The advantages of the cost basis of measurement—certainty, uniformity of interpretation, objectivity—have been discussed in earlier chapters. The question is whether an accounting system based on the attempt to measure the existence and flow of economic values has additional advantages that more than offset these.

A further question is whether assets should in fact be replaced by funds generated by current operations. Should selling prices be high enough so that net income will provide for both an adequate profit and the replacement of assets? Or should selling prices only provide for profits plus recovery of the costs actually incurred? Stated another way: Who should pay for the future machines, the current customers or the future customers who buy products made on the future machines? If operations do not generate enough funds for replacement, it is argued, the difference can and should be raised through borrowing or issuing new stock.

Accelerated Depreciation

Calculating depreciation on replacement cost is to be distinguished from *accelerated depreciation,* such as the double declining-balance or sum-of-years'-digits methods. Accelerated depreciation does mitigate somewhat the income tax problem discussed above since it permits depreciation to be written off faster than under the straight-line method, but accelerated depreciation is nevertheless restricted to actual cost. A replacement cost mechanism would, in periods of inflation, write off as expense *more than* the actual monetary cost of the asset.

Investment Policy

Although depreciation calculations in accounting are based on original cost rather than on replacement cost, the management of a company takes into account the effect of inflation in its decisions relating to the replacement of fixed assets. This is one reason why the Retained Earnings account tends to increase during an inflationary period. Management recognizes that the accounted amount of depreciation is likely to be inadequate as a measure of the amounts that must be provided to replace plant and equipment and that for this reason (as well as for other reasons) it is not prudent to declare dividends equal to the amount of net income reported on the income statement. The difference between recorded depreciation and the higher amounts that are likely to be required to replace assets may therefore be retained in the business.

This is a matter of management policy, not of accounting. There is no assurance that this policy is being followed in a given company, and even when it is followed, there is no way of estimating precisely what the actual cash needs for replacement will be since these needs depend partly on what the level of prices is at the time the assets are replaced and partly on changes in technology. Because of technological changes, new fixed assets are unlikely to cost the same as those they are replacing, even if there were no change in the general level of prices.

PRICE LEVEL ADJUSTMENTS

In studies sponsored by the AICPA, by the American Accounting Association, and by a few university groups, procedures have been devised for expressing each item on the balance sheet and the income statement in dollars that have the same purchasing power. Usually, these procedures are advocated as a supplement to, not a replacement of, the conventional procedures. In other words, the conventional statements would continue to be the "official" reports, and the adjusted statements would be given separately.

The process of making such adjustments is a fairly long and complicated one, and it requires information as to the approximate date on which each asset was acquired, which usually involves considerable searching of old records. Essentially, an index number of prices is selected and each item is converted to current prices by multiplying its original cost by the ratio of the current price index to the index value at date of acquisition. (The best index for this purpose is probably the "Gross National Product Implicit Price Deflator," prepared by the U.S. Department of Commerce.) Thus, if an asset were purchased when the index was 100, and currently the index is 200, the dollar amount of the asset value would be doubled. If this were a depreciable asset, depreciation would be recalculated on the basis of the doubled amount.

In a period of inflation, the effect of these adjustments is to increase the book value of the assets and to decrease the reported income for the year. The decrease in income results primarily from the increased depreciation charge but also from upward adjustments in other expense items.

The Reece Corporation is one of the few that reported net income on both a "historical dollars" basis and on a "uniform dollars" basis. In its 1957 annual report, management pointed out that although on the conventional basis net income for 1956 was the largest ever reported in the company's 76 years of existence, on a uniform dollars basis 1956 net income was actually less than that of 1955. Its 1961 annual report showed net income as 225 percent of that in 1943 when reported on a conventional basis, but only 130 percent of 1943 on a uniform dollar basis. Reece did not compute net income in 1962 on a "uniform dollars" basis, giving the severe illness of its office manager as the reason. It has not resumed the practice.

Advocates of the price level adjustment process point to this shrinkage of income as a measure of how much the company may be fooling itself by relying on conventional accounting as a measure of economic progress. Those who do not prepare these adjusted statements say that they are not in fact misled; they can recognize the approximate impact of price level changes without going through all the calculations.

Instead of adjusting all items, some accountants advocate that only depreciation expense be adjusted for changes in prices. Such a procedure would not give the same end result as the calculation of depreciation based on replacement costs since the underlying procedures are different. In both cases, however, the adjustment grows out of a desire to recognize the effect of inflationary forces on the accounts.

The AICPA Studies

In April, 1961, the Accounting Principles Board of AICPA took the action summarized in the following excerpt from its minutes:

. . . the Board . . . agreed that the assumption in accounting that fluctuations in the value of the dollar may be ignored is unrealistic, and that therefore the Director of Accounting Research should be instructed to set up a research project to study the problem and to prepare a report in which recommendations are made for the disclosure of the effect of price-level changes upon the financial statements. In this study, special attention should be paid to the use of supplementary statements as a means of disclosure.

The report on this research project, published in October, 1963, is an excellent presentation of all facets of the problem.[1] Some of the highlights of this study are quoted below:

1. [There is] clear evidence of the widespread concern of businessmen and accountants with the need for changes in financial reporting to reflect the effects of inflation and deflation.
2. The examples quoted from financial statements around the world are sufficient to demonstrate that recognition of price-level changes in financial statements is practical, and not misleading or dangerous to investors.
3. The study of the index number problem indicates that at least one index of the general price level is available in the United States and is reliable enough for use in financial statements.
4. The effects of price-level changes should be disclosed as a supplement to the conventional statements. This disclosure may take the form of physically separate statements, or of parallel columns in a combined statement, or of detailed supporting schedules (including charts and graphs), or some combination of these.
5. In the supplementary data, all elements of the financial statements (e.g., balance sheet, income statement, analysis of retained earnings) should be restated by means of a single index of the general price level as of the

---

[1] AICPA Accounting Research Division, *Reporting the Financial Effects of Price-Level Changes* (Accounting Research Study No. 6) (New York, 1963). For earlier studies, see Ralph C. Jones, *Price Level Changes and Financial Statements* (American Accounting Association, 1955); Perry Mason, *Price-Level Changes and Financial Statements* (American Accounting Association, 1956); and H. W. Sweeney, *Stabilized Accounting* (New York: Harper & Bros., 1936).

balance-sheet date so that all the financial data will be expressed in terms of dollars of the same purchasing power.

In June 1969, the Accounting Principles Board published a new statement on the subject.[2] The Board's position is that although financial statements adjusted for price-level changes provide useful information, these statements should be regarded as supplements to, rather than as substitutes for, the basic financial statements prepared in the conventional way. The Board gave detailed instructions for the preparation of such statements.

Holding Gains and Operating Gains

Some people propose that instead of recasting the financial statements to reflect price level changes, the income statement should be redesigned so that it distinguishes between (1) that part of net income which results from the physical process of manufacturing and selling products, and (2) that part which results from inflation. The former is called *operating gains*, and the latter *holding gains*, the word "holding" suggesting that the gain results from holding assets that were acquired at a cost that is lower than their current cost.

As an illustration, consider the second year (19X2) of the situation shown in Illustration 9–1. In that year, 1,000 units of goods that cost $1,000 were sold for $2,500, so the gross profit, measured on the Fifo basis, was $1,500. The current cost of these goods, however, was $1,500, and the gross profit on the Lifo basis was therefore $1,000 = ($2,500 − $1,500). Since the selling price in this situation was assumed to be set at $1 per unit above the current cost, it can be said that the *operating gain* was 1,000 units × $1, or $1,000, the same amount as measured on the Lifo basis. The difference between this amount and the $1,500 measured on the Fifo basis, i.e., $500, is a *holding gain;* it arises because goods bought at $1 were held until the selling price increased. Both the operating gain and the holding gain would be shown on the income statement, the latter as an extraordinary item appearing below the operating net income.

A similar separation can be made for depreciation on fixed assets. The operating gain would be calculated using depreciation based on replacement costs, and the holding gain would be the difference between this amount and the amount of depreciation based on historical costs.

This proposal is in accordance with generally accepted accounting principles, since it involves no change in the final figure for net income. Nevertheless, few companies follow it for their published financial statements, although some make this separation for purposes of internal analysis.

[2] Accounting Principles Board, *Financial Statements Restated for General Price-Level Changes,* Statement No. 3 (New York, 1969).

CONCLUSION

Of the techniques discussed in this chapter, only Lifo is currently (1969) in accordance with generally accepted accounting principles. In fact, *either* Lifo or Fifo is acceptable, although they are completely inconsistent with one another. Depreciation on replacement costs may become accepted either as in accordance with accounting principles, as a basis of income taxation, or both, although acceptance seems less likely now than was the case in the 1950's. The overall adjustment of all financial statement items to current prices is likely to remain as a supplementary report rather than as a substitute for figures based on historical cost.

CASES

CASE 9–1.   R. J. REYNOLDS TOBACCO COMPANY[3]

In 1957 the R. J. Reynolds Tobacco Company adopted the Lifo basis of inventory valuation, with results as indicated by the following quotation from its annual report:

During 1956 and prior years, inventories were valued on the average cost method. Effective for 1957, however, the Company adopted the last-in, first-out (LIFO) method of inventory valuation. By this method, the current costs of replacing materials used are more nearly reflected in determining earnings. In 1957, acquisitions of leaf tobacco were made at prices considerably higher than the average cost of tobacco in inventories at the beginning of the year. The effect of LIFO and related adjustments was to reduce earnings before income taxes by $26,897,049 and net earnings by $12,342,049. The resultant income tax saving for the year amounted to $14,555,000. Inventories at the year end were carried at $28,312,684 less than they would have been under the previous method.[4]

The reaction of investors to this change is indicated by the following quotation from the *Wall Street Journal* for February 3, 1958:

Last week saw a brief wave of selling in the hitherto strong tobacco shares. It apparently grew out of the change by R. J. Reynolds Tobacco Co. to the "last-in-first-out" method of valuing inventories. Although this reduced reported earnings below what they would have been under the old system of accounting, it did not in any way cut Reynolds' real earnings or the company's ability to pay dividends. On the contrary, the change saved the company $14 million, or $1.40 a share, in cash by cutting the Federal income tax that much. Because of increased prices, the tobacco bought by Reynolds in 1957 cost $28 million more than the average cost of its three-year inventory, such as every tobacco company must maintain. Under the LIFO system, that extra cost was

---

[3] This case is based on published information.

[4] Note the $26,897,049 was only 95 percent of the $28,312,684 reduction in inventories. This is because 5 percent of operating income in excess of a stated amount is set aside in a profit-sharing plan. The amount so set aside was reduced by $1,415,635 because of the reduction in operating income resulting from the shift to Lifo.

charged into the income account, reducing the pre-tax profit by that much. After taxes, it cut profit by $14 million, but it also cut the tax itself, at the 52% rate, by about the same amount. The LIFO system is expected to be put into force by the other tobacco companies. After the brief selling, the Street evidently saw it was unwarranted, because tobacco share prices recovered.

The 1958 Annual Report of Reynolds contains the following statement:

During the second year of the Company's use of the LIFO method of inventory valuation, first adopted in 1957, acquisitions of both flue-cured and Burley tobaccos were made at prices higher than were paid in the previous year. The resulting LIFO adjustment enabled the Company to effect a further saving in income taxes estimated at $8,500,000. Thus, during the two years under LIFO, the Company has been able to conserve about $23,000,000 that otherwise would have been required for taxes. Inventories at the close of the year were carried at $45,031,770 less than they would have been under the previously used average cost method of inventory valuation.

In its 1959 report, the company reported that inventories at the end of 1959 were carried at $64,399,895 less than they would have been under the average cost method used prior to 1957.

Financial statements of R. J. Reynolds Tobacco Company are given in Exhibit 1. Financial statements of two of its principal competitors are given in Exhibits 2 and 3; these companies continued to use average cost in valuing inventories. These statements have been condensed and rearranged from those presented in the annual reports. Of total operating costs, approximately 50 percent consists of excise taxes paid on finished products, approximately 25 percent is tobacco, and approximately 25 percent is all other manufacturing, selling, and administrative costs.

Inventory Values

Leaf tobacco is the most important element of cost in the manufacture of cigarettes and also the most volatile. Rising tobacco costs normally can be offset by higher prices, particularly since the average inventory method used results in only a gradual increase in tobacco costs charged to any one year's production.

Tobacco has to be aged before it is used in cigarettes, and the quality tends to vary from year to year. Hence, large inventories are needed.

The low point of the year's inventory cycle falls in June or July, when the companies have on hand supplies sufficient for 14 to 18 months' production. Tobacco markets open around the end of July in Georgia, followed by a succession of market openings moving north through the following February. Based on estimates made in June, when the inventory is low, the companies purchase according to plan their estimated needs for the succeeding 30 months. The peak of inventory holdings is reached in February.

As the tobacco is purchased at the auctions, the cost for each grade is esti-

Exhibit 1

R. J. REYNOLDS TOBACCO COMPANY

Financial Statements (000 Omitted)

Condensed Position Statements as of December 31

	1959	1958	1957	1956
ASSETS				
Current Assets:				
Cash........................	$ 27,109	$ 29,646	$ 26,142	$ 23,697
Accounts receivable, customers...	44,530	36,990	33,910	30,155
Inventories (Note A)..........	684,507	594,905	586,540	557,247
Total Current Assets..........	$756,147	$661,542	$646,593	$611,100
Fixed and other assets..........	97,205	81,791	66,505	48,294
Total Assets...............	$853,352	$743,333	$713,097	$659,394
EQUITIES				
Current Liabilities:				
Notes and accounts payable......	$179,656	$121,196	$106,460	$ 68,131
Federal and state taxes..........	87,619	75,002	63,744	71,202
Other current.................	10,470	9,984	9,780	8,231
Total Current Liabilities.......	$277,744	$206,182	$179,985	$147,564
Funded debt.....................	92,000	98,000	104,000	110,000
Capital stock....................	136,640	139,260	168,040	169,542
Retained earnings................	346,968	299,891	261,073	232,288
Total Equities..............	$853,352	$743,333	$713,097	$659,394

Statements of Earnings for Years Ended December 31

	1959	1958	1957	1956
Net sales.......................	$1,286,856	$1,146,559	$1,053,326	$957,367
Cost of sales and other expenses.....	1,082,700	969,712	907,914	815,323
Operating profit.................	$ 204,156	$ 176,847	$ 145,412	$142,044
Other income and deductions, net...	−6,386	−4,863	−6,805	−4,942
Income, before taxes..............	$ 197,770	$ 171,984	$ 138,607	$137,102
Taxes on income.................	107,412	93,658	74,446	75,190
Net earnings....................	$ 90,358	$ 78,326	$ 64,160	$ 61,913
Dividends*......................	43,280	39,248	35,375	33,470
Additions to Retained Earnings.....	$ 47,078	$ 39,078	$ 28,785	$ 28,443
Earnings per common share........	$4.45	$3.80	$3.08	$2.96

Note A: Inventories at average cost in 1956 and Lifo thereafter.
* Includes preferred dividends of $1,281,000 in 1959, $2,282,000 in 1958, $2,657,000 in 1957, and $2,763,000 in 1956.
Details may not add to totals because of rounding.
SOURCE: Annual reports.

Exhibit 2

THE AMERICAN TOBACCO COMPANY

Consolidated Financial Statements (000 Omitted)

Condensed Balance Sheets as of December 31

	1959	1958	1957	1956
ASSETS				
Current Assets:				
Cash...................	$ 17,740	$ 20,696	$ 22,972	$ 23,418
Accounts receivable, customers..	51,911	46,943	45,180	44,752
Leaf tobacco, at average cost....	586,605	578,305	612,315 ⎫	
Other inventories, at average			⎬	655,116
cost.....................	70,075	70,005	59,066 ⎭	
Other current assets..........	1,697	1,318	950	1,137
Total Current Assets........	$ 728,028	$ 717,268	$ 740,483	$ 724,423
Fixed and other assets...........	78,498	79,264	74,724	69,981
Total Assets.............	$ 806,526	$ 796,532	$ 815,207	$ 794,404
EQUITIES				
Current Liabilities:				
Notes and accounts payable.....	$ 71,760	$ 81,211	$105,779	$ 93,984
Accrued taxes...............	53,817	50,655	52,132	51,512
Other current...............	14,826	11,313	13,227	12,347
Total Current Liabilities.....	$140,403	$143,179	$171,138	$157,842
Funded debt...................	150,653	165,402	179,330	193,188
Capital stock..................	260,561	260,561	260,561	260,561
Retained earnings..............	254,908	227,390	204,178	182,813
Total Equities............	$806,526	$796,532	$815,207	$794,404

Income Statements for Years Ended December 31

	1959	1958	1957	1956
Net sales......................	$1,161,377	$1,105,176	$1,098,093	$1,091,206
Cost of sales and operating expenses.....................	1,019,129	971,132	969,805	971,168
Operating profit.................	$ 142,248	$ 134,044	$ 128,288	$ 120,039
Other income and deductions, net..	−6,177	−9,050	−9,683	−8,687
Income, before taxes............	$ 136,071	$ 124,994	$ 118,605	$ 111,352
Taxes on income...............	72,823	66,138	61,510	59,663
Net income....................	$ 63,248	$ 58,856	$ 57,095	$ 51,689
Dividends*....................	35,730	35,730	35,730	35,730
Additions to Retained Earnings....	$ 27,518	$ 23,126	$ 21,365	$ 15,959
Earnings per common share.......	$9.23	$8.55	$8.28	$7.45

* Includes preferred dividends of $3,167,000 each year.
Details may not add to totals because of rounding.
SOURCE: Annual reports.

Exhibit 3

LIGGETT & MYERS TOBACCO COMPANY

Consolidated Financial Statements (000 Omitted)

Condensed Balance Sheets as of December 31

	1959	1958	1957	1956
ASSETS				
Current Assets:				
Cash and government securities........	$ 12,321	$ 4,459	$ 12,263	$ 11,635
Accounts receivable, customers........	21,190	23,095	23,090	22,579
Leaf tobacco, at average cost..........	292,005	306,965	346,472	372,484
Other inventories, at average cost......	38,388	34,353	34,558	36,587
Other current assets.................	1,160	1,102	1,030	1,408
Total Current Assets..............	$365,064	$369,974	$417,412	$444,693
Fixed and other assets.................	39,327	39,128	39,028	36,978
Total Assets...................	$404,391	$409,103	$456,440	$481,671
EQUITIES				
Current: Liabilities:				
Notes and accounts payable..........	$ 3,296	$ 7,576	$ 57,119	$ 82,469
Accrued taxes......................	22,794	23,764	24,992	26,325
Other current liabilities..............	6,817	5,581	6,930	6,977
Total Current Liabilities..........	$ 32,907	$ 36,921	$ 89,041	$115,771
Funded debt........................	84,250	90,000	95,750	101,500
Capital stock.......................	138,066	138,453	138,111	138,111
Retained earnings....................	149,169	143,729	133,538	126,290
Total Equities.................	$404,391	$409,103	$456,440	$481,671

Income Statements for Years Ended December 31

	1959	1958	1957	1956
Net sales............................	$554,936	$556,046	$570,385	$564,966
Cost of sales and operating expenses......	488,216	485,935	506,027	503,923
Operating profit......................	$ 66,720	$ 70,111	$ 64,358	$ 61,043
Other income and deductions, net........	−1,645	−2,198	−2,463	−2,676
Income, before taxes..................	$ 65,075	$ 67,913	$ 61,895	$ 58,367
Income and franchise taxes.............	35,036	36,689	33,621	31,916
Net income..........................	$ 30,039	$ 31,223	$ 28,274	$ 26,451
Dividends*..........................	24,015	21,032	21,025	21,023
Additions to Retained Income..........	$ 6,024	$ 10,191	$ 7,249	$ 5,428
Earnings per common share............	$7.28	$7.60	$6.85	$6.39

* Includes preferred stock dividends of $1,430,000 in 1959, $1,461,000 in 1958, 1957, and 1956.
Details may not add to totals because of rounding.
SOURCE: Annual reports.

mated, adjusting for the loss of weight in drying, stemming, and regrading. The inventory cost for each grade is adjusted to average in new purchases as made. When all purchases for a crop year are completed, costs are reviewed in the light of experience in loss of weight and regrading, and average inventory costs are established for the season for each grade.

It will be seen that the costs of new purchases have an immediate effect on inventory costs of leaf used in manufacture. But it is to be noted that a large factor in that average is the previously established costs of the tobacco in inventory at the start of the buying season, which in turn had been determined by a process of averaging with costs established in former years. Hence, while changing prices of leaf are reflected quickly in costs, the changes in costs are not fully commensurate with the changes in prices paid. In fact, the process of averaging from year-to-year permits the prices in any one year to influence costs over a long period.[5]

Questions

1. Recast the R. J. Reynolds financial statements for 1957 and 1958 to show how they would have appeared if the company had not shifted to Lifo.
2. As well as you can, compare the performance of the three companies in 1957, 1958, and 1959.
3. Do you agree with R. J. Reynolds' decision to adopt Lifo? Do you think its competitors should also adopt Lifo?

CASE 9–2.   THE MILLION DOLLAR LATHE[6]

Thompson Products, for the 18th year, has continued its custom of furnishing its employees with a simple concise report of its financial operations, showing how much money the company took in and what happened to it. The income for 1956 totaled $306,508,120. Expenses, not including wages, salaries or dividends, were $175,535,061, leaving $130,973,059 to be divided among employees and shareholders. Of this, $117,960,454 went for payrolls, $4,183,904 was paid out in dividends, and $8,828,701 was plowed back into the business.

Why was it necessary to plow that much back into the business? The tale of the million-dollar turret lathe, included in the report, explains that. It seems that in 1942 the company bought a lathe for $12,000. Under federal tax laws, it was permitted to depreciate the cost of the lathe over a 14-year period. So, last year, when the lathe became obsolete, the company had $12,000 to buy a new one, plus $1,000, which was the resale

---

[5] Standard and Poor's Trade and Securities, *Tobacco*, Vol. CXXVII, No. 53, Sec. I (December 31, 1959), pp. 63–64.

[6] This case consists of a quotation taken from a report prepared by the management of a company for the information of its employees.

value of the old one. But the replacement cost in 1956 was $35,000 for a lathe that would perform the same functions as the old model, or $67,000 for a new one with attachments to meet today's more exacting needs.

The company had only $13,000 to do a $67,000 job. The difference of $54,000 had to come out of profits, and in order to get that amount in 1956 the company had to earn a profit of more than $112,500 before taxes, because $54,000 was all there was left after the government took its corporate profit tax of 52 percent. And to earn that amount of profit, the company had to sell more than a million and a quarter dollars' worth of products to customers. It took more than $1,250,000 of sales to buy just one machine!

Thus, while $112,500 sounds like a lot of profit, in this case, the shareholders got none of it. The government took more than half, and the rest went to replace a machine. This story is duplicated hundreds of times each year throughout the company in the case of machines, large and small. This is why only a relatively small amount of profit is paid to shareholders in dividends, and why a large portion must be retained to finance expansion and replacement so the company can continue to operate and employees can continue working.

Question

1. Comment on this statement. Is it the truth, the whole truth, and nothing but the truth?

CASE 9–3. UNITED STATES STEEL CORPORATION

United States Steel Corporation is the nation's largest steel producer. This case is concerned with U.S. Steel's depreciation accounting policies and treatment of the investment credit between 1946 and 1968.

The 1947 Change

For several years prior to 1947 the management of United States Steel Corporation had been concerned with the effects upon the company's capital replacement program of the steady rise in the general price level since the late 1930's. This concern, shared by a major segment of American business management, arose chiefly from the realization that the amounts being deducted from earnings to cover the depreciation and amortization of plant and equipment were not sufficient to provide for the replacement of such facilities when they were worn out or became obsolete.

As a step toward stating depreciation in an amount which would recover in current dollars of diminished buying power the same purchasing power represented by the original plant expenditure, the company deducted, in arriving at net income for 1947, an amount of $26.3 million over and above its regular depreciation charge (based on the straight-line method.) Although the federal tax authorities would not allow the extra depreciation as a deduction in arriving at taxable income for that year, the company's executives considered it essential that they recognize this element of cost in arriving at a measure of income to be used in other matters of company management.

In its 1947 annual report the management stated that "while awaiting accounting and tax acceptance, U.S. Steel believed that it was prudent for it to give some recognition to increased replacement costs rather than to sit idly by and witness the unwitting liquidation of its business should inadequate recording of costs result in insufficient resources to supply the tools required for sustained production."

In its opinion on the 1947 financial statements, the company's independent auditors stated that the corporation had included in costs additional depreciation of $26.3 million "in excess of the amount determined in accordance with the generally accepted accounting principle heretofore followed of making provision for depreciation on the original cost of facilities."

Carman G. Blough, director of research of the American Institute of Certified Public Accountants (at that time the American Institute of Accountants), commented on this practice as follows:

> There can be no argument but that a going concern must be able to replace its productive assets as they are used up if it is to continue to do business. It is also important for management to understand that the difference between cost and estimated replacement value may be significant in determining production and pricing policies. It does not follow, however, that the excess of the cost of replacement over the cost of existing assets should be accounted for as current charges to income. All who have dealt with appraisal values know how very difficult it is just to determine current replacement costs, but the most striking difficulty in this respect is the impossibility of predicting what will be the eventual cost of replacing a productive asset. How many men are prepared to state what the price level will be two years from today, to say nothing of trying to guess what it will be five or ten years hence when many of those assets are to be replaced.[7]

The AICPA Committee on Accounting Procedure issued, in late 1947, *Accounting Research Bulletin No. 33* (later restated as *ARB No. 43*, Chapter 9, Section A, paragraphs 4–9), in which it stated that it disapproved "immediate write-downs of plant cost by charges against current

---

[7] "Replacement and Excess Construction Costs," *Journal of Accountancy*, Vol. LXXIV (October, 1947), p. 335.

income in amounts believed to represent excessive or abnormal costs occasioned by current price levels."

The 1948 Retreat

In its annual report for 1948, U.S. Steel announced that it was abandoning the policy adopted in 1947 and was substituting in its place a method of charging "accelerated depreciation on cost," which was explained as follows in the annual report:

The accelerated depreciation is applicable to the cost of postwar facilities in the first few years of their lives when economic usefulness is greatest. The amount thereof is related to the excess of current operating rates over U.S. Steel's long-term peacetime average rate of 70% of capacity. The annual accelerated amount is 10% of the cost of facilities in the year in which the expenditures are made and 10% in the succeeding year, except that this amount is reduced ratably as the operating rate may drop, no acceleration being made at 70% or lower operations. The accelerated depreciation is an addition to the normal depreciation on such facilities, but the total depreciation over their expected lives will not exceed the cost of the facilities.

This method was made retroactive to January 1, 1947, and there was included, in the $55,335,444 deducted for accelerated wear and exhaustion of facilities for 1948, an amount of $2,675,094 to cover a deficiency in the $26,300,000 sum reported in 1947 as "depreciation added to cover replacement cost." In other words, the new method when applied to the 1947 situation resulted in a deduction that exceeded the figure actually reported in 1947. It was again pointed out at this time that the accelerated depreciation was not "presently deductible for federal income tax purposes."

The company's independent auditors stated in their report to the shareholders for 1948 that they "approved" the new policy.

The management's convictions on the change in policy were, however, clearly set forth by the chairman of the board of directors in the following quotation from the company's annual report for 1948:

U.S. Steel believes that the principle which it adopted in 1947 and continued in 1948 is a proper recording of the wear and exhaustion of its facilities in terms of current dollars as distinguished from the dollars which it originally expended for those facilities. However, in view of the disagreement existing among accountants, both public and private, and the stated position of the American Institute of Certified Public Accountants, which is supported by the Securities and Exchange Commission, that the only accepted accounting principle for determining depreciation is that which is related to the actual number of dollars spent for facilities, regardless of when or what buying power, U.S. Steel has adopted a method of accelerated depreciation based on cost instead of one based on purchasing power recovery.

The 1953 Change

United States Steel Corporation continued its policy of charging accelerated depreciation through 1952. Deductions for accelerated depreciation for 1947 through 1952 totaled slightly more than $201 million; none of this sum, however, had been allowed in computing taxable income during that period.

During and after the Korean War, U.S. Steel was granted Certificates of Necessity which permitted amortization of designated facilities over a 60-month period for tax purposes regardless of the facilities' probable economic life. Management decided to depreciate these facilities in the corporate accounts over the 60-month period.

In 1953, U. S. Steel changed its accelerated depreciation policy, as explained in this note to the 1953 financial statements:

Since 1946 U.S. Steel has followed the policy of reflecting accelerated depreciation on the cost of new facilities in the first few years of their lives when the economic usefulness is greatest. The amounts charged to income for accelerated depreciation have been related to U.S. Steel's rate of operations.

Under the Internal Revenue Code, that portion of the cost of facilities certified by the Defense Production Administration as essential to the defense effort is covered by a Certificate of Necessity and can be written off for tax purposes at the rate of 20% per year. The effect of amortization of these facilities is to charge to income a greater portion of their cost in the earlier years of life, and therefore, follows the principle of accelerated depreciation.

U.S. Steel has included in wear and exhaustion in 1953, as a measure of the accelerated depreciation for the year, $105,137,893, representing amortization on its facilities covered by Certificate of Necessity.

In commenting on the effect of accelerated amortization and the tax laws, management pointed out that it had to be regarded as a temporary expedient, since "for many companies the addition of amortization on new facilities to so-called regular depreciation on old facilities may approximate, temporarily, a truer total of wear and exhaustion on all facilities based on current dollar value. But it automatically guarantees something of a future crisis." As an example of this, management cited the recently constructed Fairless Works. A portion of this plant's cost was amortized over five years, thus partially offsetting "inadequate" depreciation charges for other facilities. It was stated that this situation would naturally change when the five-year amortization was completed.

Management noted in 1954 that the new methods of accelerated depreciation, first allowed for tax purposes in 1954, would ease the future crisis, but even these provisions, applicable to new assets only, would fall far short of providing adequate depreciation on the relatively more numerous and older existing facilities.

Exhibit 1

WEAR AND EXHAUSTION RECORDED VERSUS WEAR AND EXHAUSTION NEEDED

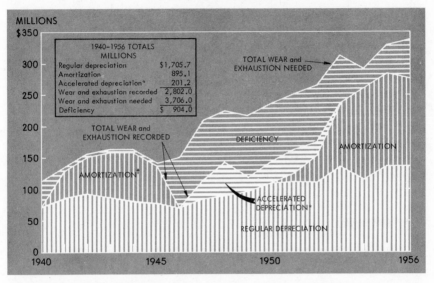

* Not deductible for tax purposes.
† Additional amortization due to ending of emergency period allocated to years 1941–1945.

Inflation in Cost of Facilities*

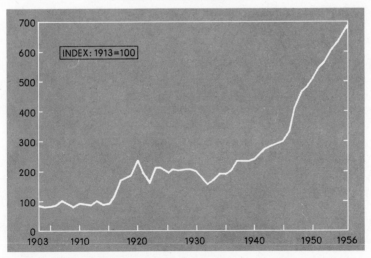

* From *Engineering News-Record* Construction Cost Index.

Source: *United States Steel Corporation Annual Report*, 1956. Used by permission.

1956

In its 1956 report, U.S. Steel included a chart (see Exhibit 1) comparing "wear and exhaustion recorded" with "wear and exhaustion needed." To calculate "total wear and exhaustion needed," as shown in the chart, the following statistical procedure was followed: Excluding the amount of nontax-deductible accelerated depreciation from 1947 through 1952 (see Exhibit 1), and including only regular depreciation on emergency facilities, the amount of wear and exhaustion previously recorded for *each year* included in the chart was subdivided according to the acquisition years of the assets being depreciated. Each yearly subdivision was then adjusted to reflect the change in the *Engineering News-Record*'s index of construction cost from the various earlier acquisition years to any given year included in the chart. The sum of that year's adjusted depreciation amounts gave the "total wear and exhaustion needed" for that year. The process was repeated for every year in the chart. Notice that each year's deficiency is in dollars of the buying power that prevailed in *that* year.

The 1959 Strike

In 1959, management noted the approaching exhaustion of emergency amortization:

This (depreciation) deficiency has been aggravated by the running out of 5-year amortization permitted on varying percentages of the total costs of certain defense and defense-supporting facilities covered by Certificates of Necessity. The need for revision of the tax laws as they relate to depreciation . . . continues to be most vital to the maintenance of existing and the addition of new productive capacity.

In the spring of 1959, the representatives of the United Steelworkers of America and the major steel companies met to negotiate a new wage contract to replace the contract expiring in June. The union requested sizable increases in wages and fringe benefits, contending that large steel profits would permit these increases without affecting the prices of finished steel. The steel industry spokesmen argued this was not possible; any *sizable* wage increase would have to be passed along in the form of higher prices. There was considerable government pressure for a settlement without the need for a price increase in order to avoid the threat of further inflation.

A full-page newspaper advertisement in May 1959, paid for by the union, read in part:

STEELWORKERS SHARE OF
STEEL INDUSTRY'S INCOME HAS
NOT INCREASED SINCE 1952

True, there have been wage increases, but because fewer men are making more steel, the total labor costs have remained the same.

Please examine these LABOR COSTS:

1952....................42.1¢ of each sales dollar
1958....................42.8¢ of each sales dollar

(notice they are about the same)

Now examine the NET PROFITS:

1952......................$143,678,740
1958...................... 301,558,231

(profits have DOUBLED)

A nationwide steel strike lasted from July until mid-November.

On December 8, 1959, J. S. Seidman, president of AICPA released to the press a statement explaining the issues in the steel strike:

The industry's contention was that under conventional accounting, depreciation is calculated based on the original dollar cost, and that this is inadequate because it fails to give effect to the tremendous change that has taken place in the purchasing power of the dollar, as a result of which it would cost many more dollars today to replace the plant than were originally spent. The industry maintains that realistic profits should be figured by reference to replacement figures. On that basis, the industry's profits are one half of what the financial statements show.

The labor officials contend that original cost is all that should be recovered, and that anything in excess of that is a profit. Furthermore, they say that the original cost should be spread over the expected period in which the plant will be used. However, the companies have been following the tax laws in the way they write off depreciation, and the tax laws have allowed a higher write-off to be bunched in early years and counterbalanced by a lower write-off in later years. The figures presented by the steel industry cover the earlier years where there is the higher write-off. The labor people say that the depreciation amounts should be reduced by this excess write-off in the early years. Reducing the depreciation would result in an increase in profits.

. . . All of this raises a question as to whether the conventional accounting use of historical dollars is meaningful in an inflationary period.

Investment Credit

By 1962, the inflationary pressures on the economy had diminished. Also in 1962, U.S. Steel benefited from two changes in the system of federal income taxation: adoption of the new guideline procedures for depreciation lives set forth in Revenue Ruling 62–21 added $44 million to the wear and exhaustion amounts previously determined; and the use of the investment tax credit resulted in a $8.2 million reduction in federal income taxes.

The investment tax credit provided by the Revenue Act of 1962 was intended to stimulate capital investment. It allowed a credit directly against the company's federal income tax liability of 7 percent of the cost of "qualified" depreciable property.

Shift to Straight-Line

During 1968, economic pressure increased on companies within the steel industry. The contract with the United Steelworkers was due to terminate and there was a widespread expectation that a strike would be called on August 1. As a result, steel users stockpiled inventories heavily. The high volume of orders during the first half of the year resulted in capacity operations by steel mills, including the use of less efficient, marginal production equipment. In addition, foreign imports of steel had increased substantially during the first half of 1968. To meet the stiff price competition, many domestic producers engaged in price "discounting" to customers despite general acceptance of standard prices by the industry.

The labor dispute was settled without a strike on July 30. Production fell sharply as customers reduced excess inventories. It was anticipated that the normal ordering pattern would not be resumed until January 1969.

Under these conditions (the high costs of cutting back production, the generally higher wage levels; and production pegged near the break-even point) third quarter earnings were sharply reduced. U.S. Steel's 1968 third quarter profits fell 70 percent below those of the corresponding quarter of 1967. Bethlehem Steel Corporation reported a decline of 0.6 percent, Republic Steel 31 percent, National 21 percent, Jones and Laughlin 86 percent, and Youngstown Sheet and Tube 57 percent. Only Armco Steel and Inland reported profit increases over the previous year.

The effect of the profit decline would have been more severe, except that many of the companies switched from accelerated to straight-line depreciation in the third quarter. The exact method of change varied among the steelmakers: some applied the change only to equipment purchased after 1967, others applied it to all depreciable property on hand. Several companies also switched from deferring to flowing through their investment tax credits.

Despite these changes, U.S. Steel continued to follow its policy of accelerated depreciation. It announced, however, that if it had changed to straight-line depreciation, profits would have increased $33 million, or $0.61 per share, for the third quarter, and $205.6 million, or $3.80 per share, for the first three quarters of the year.

One factor considered by some to have a bearing on the accounting changes of some steel companies was the takeover of Jones and Laughlin by Ling-Tempco-Vought. Many of the smaller steel manufacturers were also considered attractive acquisitions because of their high cash flows, understated assets, and low earnings per share and price earnings ratios.

As an admitted direct response to this potential problem, Armco Steel

Exhibit 2

U.S. STEEL CORPORATION

Selected Financial Statistics 1946–1967
(millions of dollars)

Year	Net Income	Depreciation	Capital Expenditures	Investment Tax Credit Taken	Amortization of Emergency Facilities
1967	$172.5	$354.7	$547.7	$33.4	...
1966	249.2	344.3	440.7	20.8	...
1965	275.5	324.5	353.6	13.7	...
1964	236.8	335.8	292.6	.6	...
1963	203.5	307.8	244.7	.6 (est.)	...
1962	163.7	265.9	200.6	.4 (est.)	...
1961	190.2	210.5	326.8	...	...
1960	304.2	208.4	492.4	...	13.7
1959	254.5	189.9	366.1	...	22.2
1958	301.5	204.9	448.1	...	57.2
1957	319.4	276.0	514.9	...	115.8
1956	348.1	277.6	311.8	...	140.2
1955	348.1	285.2	239.8	...	147.7
1954	195.4	261.8	227.4	...	142.8
1953	222.1	236.6	361.4	...	105.1
1952	143.6	176.9	469.2	...	46.2
1951	184.3	162.1	352.4	...	12.8
1950	215.5	143.9	179.3	...	...
1949	165.9	119.7	179.1	...	...
1948	129.6	146.0	275.2	...	...
1947	127.1	114.0	206.6	...	...
1946	88.6	68.7	201.0	...	...

had changed to straight-line depreciation methods in the first half of 1968. This change had added $0.46 to earning per share in the first two quarters of the year. By consolidation of European operations, an additional $0.19 per share had been obtained. As a result, earnings for the first half of 1968 ran 25 percent above the comparable period in 1967.

Financial statistics for the corporation are given in Exhibit 2.

Questions

1. Do you agree with U.S. Steel's handling of depreciation in its 1947 report? Should a company be prohibited from using such a method if in its own best judgment this is the best method?
2. Do you agree with the nature and timing of the subsequent changes in depreciation method?
3. Who was right in 1968: U.S. Steel; or the companies that shifted to straight-line depreciation; or were they all right?
4. Once having adopted an accounting practice, under what circumstances should a company be permitted to change it?

CASE 9–4. R. L. BOGGS

According to the terms of his grandfather's will, R. L. Boggs received a bequest of $50,000. At the time of his grandfather's death, the general index of prices was 100. It rose rapidly while the estate was being settled, however, and had reached 120 when Boggs actually received the money. Since he felt that the inflationary rise in prices was likely to continue, he borrowed $30,000 for one year at 6 percent, with the intention of keeping most of the $80,000 fund invested in common stocks. His transactions during the ensuing year were as follows:

1. He bought common stocks for $75,000 when the price index was 125.
2. Later when the index was 133⅓, he sold for $30,000 stocks which had originally cost $25,000.
3. While the index was 133⅓, he received dividends of $6,000.
4. He bought additional common stocks for $40,000 when the price index was 150.
5. Near the end of the year the price index rose to 180 and remained steady for several weeks. Strong antiinflationary measures were being prepared by the government, and some steps to curb the rapidly rising price level had already been taken. Because of this, Boggs sold his entire portfolio of common stocks for $100,000, paid off the $30,000 note with interest, and invested the entire fund (except the amount required to pay the income tax) in tax-exempt state bonds purchased to yield 3 percent per annum.

Questions

1. Mr. Boggs asks you to analyze the results of his financial and investment policies in order to determine the net gains and losses in terms of purchasing power during the settlement of the estate and during the full year between the receipt of the cash and the purchase of the state bonds. Assume, for simplicity, that Mr. Boggs is subject to a flat 25 percent tax on all income and capital gains. He is particularly anxious to learn where and why the real gains and losses occurred. It is suggested that the end-of-year dollar (price index 180) be taken as the basic unit of measurement.

2. Mr. Boggs also asks you to show how the results of a second year will compare with those of the first in terms of purchasing power if the price index falls to 150 within six months and remains there for the rest of the year. All this, of course, is entirely prospective, but he wants to know, nevertheless, how the book and real gains and losses on the state bonds under the assumed conditions would compare with the results obtained by investing in common stocks during the year just ended.

Using Information on Financial Statements

PART II

Using Information on
Financial Statements

CHAPTER 10

UNDERSTANDING FINANCIAL STATEMENTS

In the preceding chapters the basic concepts of accounting were discussed, accounting terms were defined, and conventions and procedures were described. This was done from the point of view of the user of accounting information, rather than that of the accountant. The user is primarily interested in the end products of the accounting process, which are the balance sheet and the income statement. This chapter discusses the uses and the limitations of these statements.

CRITERIA AND BASIC CONCEPTS

In Chapter 2 it was suggested that accounting concepts and principles gain acceptance according to how well they meet three criteria: relevance, objectivity, and feasibility. Others list these criteria somewhat differently. For example, an American Accounting Association publication, *A Statement of Basic Accounting Theory*, 1966, lists the two criteria of "verifiability" and "freedom from bias" rather than the single criterion of "objectivity."

Conflict among Criteria

Brief mention was also made in Chapter 2 of the inevitable conflict between the criterion of relevance on the one hand and the criteria of objectivity and feasibility on the other. Accounting principles in general use reflect a workable compromise between these opposing forces.

Of the many examples that have been discussed in the intervening chapters, perhaps the most clear-cut is that relating to the measurement of fixed assets. In general, the most relevant rule for stating fixed assets, the rule that would provide readers of financial statements with what they really want to know, would be: state fixed assets at their market value, what they are really worth. But such a rule would be neither objective nor feasible in most situations. The market value of assets in a going concern depends upon the future earnings that will be generated with these assets. In special circumstances, outside experts, i.e., appraisers, can be relied upon to make estimates of future earnings, but there are by no means enough appraisers in the country to make such estimates annually for all companies. Even if there were enough of them, the appraisers would be forced to rely heavily on the judgment of the management, which is in by far the best position to know about future earnings prospects. To rely on the opinions of management, however, would introduce a highly subjective element. Shareholders, prospective share-holders, banks, and others use financial statements, in part, to find out how well management has done. It would be highly unrealistic to expect that management would make unbiased estimates under these circumstances.

At the other extreme, the most objective and feasible rule for measuring fixed assets would be: state fixed assets at the price paid for them, i.e., at their cost, and hold them at cost until they are disposed of (or, alternatively, write them off the books immediately). In most cases such a rule would be perfectly simple to apply and would involve little, if any, judgment. But such a rule would prohibit accounting from reflecting on the income statement the expense called depreciation, which represents an estimate of the amount of asset cost that is properly charged to the operations of each accounting period. A net income figure that includes such an estimate of fixed asset expiration is much more useful for most purposes than one that omits depreciation altogether.

So accounting takes a middle ground. Assets are originally booked at cost, which is an objectively determined amount in most cases, and this cost is charged against income over the useful life of the asset. The annual depreciation charge is an estimate, and any of several ways of making this estimate are permitted, but the number of permitted alternatives is small, and freedom to tamper with the estimates is further restricted by the concept of consistency.

A similar conflict among objectives arises in the case of many other principles. As will be discussed further below, failure to appreciate this fact is behind the feeling of many of the uninitiated that "accounting doesn't make sense."

Currently (1969) the Securities and Exchange Commission is propos-ing that companies should report a breakdown of revenue and expenses for each of their major product lines. Unquestionably, the income by product lines is relevant information, especially in diversified or conglom-erate companies; investors would like very much to have this information. Some oppose this requirement, on the grounds that the principles governing the allocation of costs to product lines are so vague that the resulting data would not be meaningful. Thus, the conflict between relevance and objectivity/feasibility continues.

Concepts

Ten concepts that are basic to accounting were described in Chapters 2 and 3. Since no set of concepts has been adopted as such by any authoritative body, others would classify and describe them somewhat differently. For example, Paul Grady in his highly respected *Inventory of Generally Accepted Principles for Business Enterprises* lists 10 concepts, a majority of which are similar to, but not identical with, those given in this book. In the early 1960's the Accounting Principles Board gave some thought to approving a set of concepts, but it has not done so. Until it, or some other authoritative group, does so, the concepts must be deduced from practice.[1]

The many conventions and procedures described in Part I were amplifications to and applications of the basic concepts, rather than additions to them. As a matter of convention, for example, accumulated depreciation is shown in a separate account rather than being credited directly to the asset account, but the basic idea of depreciation accounting is nevertheless in accordance with the concepts that assets are recorded at cost and costs are matched against revenue in the period benefited.

Any conceivable transaction, provided that it is clearly described, can be analyzed in terms of its effect on the assets and equities of the business in accordance with the basic accounting concepts. For an extremely large fraction of the transactions in a typical business, the answer is simple and unequivocal: for a cash sale, debit Cash and credit Sales; for receipts from a credit customer, credit Accounts Receivable and debit Cash.

In a relatively small number of transactions, real analysis is required. For some of these, a correct answer can be found. For example, a number of transactions involve a credit to Cash or Accounts Payable for the purchase of something. The question is whether the offsetting debit is to an asset account or to an expense account, and the answer to this question depends on whether the business has, or has not, acquired a property right that has material value beyond the end of the accounting period. In still other cases, there is no unique "right" answer: accounting principles permit any of several treatments. In these cases, one simply uses his best judgment.

Many of these situations that require judgment do so because of inevitable uncertainties about the future. How long will the building

---

[1] The American Accounting Association publication, "A Statement of Basic Accounting Theory," is a statement of what accounting concepts *should be*, not what they *are*.

really last? Will this expenditure for research really result in future profits, and if so, how much? Is a decline in the market value of inventory only temporary, or should the inventory be written down? There are no unequivocal answers to such questions, and hence no way of arriving at a result with which everyone would agree.

Misconceptions about Concepts

Some of the basic concepts are intuitively sensible: for example, the idea that accounting data are expressed in monetary terms. Certain concepts, however, are rather different from the impression that the typical layman has about them. As Professor Walter F. Frese puts it:

. . . Generally, the character of accounting is not fully understood either by the people who use it as a means of communicating the results of operations for which they are responsible (business managers) or by people to whom such results are communicated (stockholders, investors, labor, general management and others). Those at both ends of this communication process often believe that somewhere in the middle the accountant, through application of mysterious specialized techniques, can translate the facts and judgments underlying business transactions into quantitative terms, predigest them, and come out at the end of the process with figures which precisely measure the results of business operations.[2]

Undoubtedly the greatest misconception on the part of laymen relates to the cost concept. To the layman, it seems only reasonable that the accountant should report the *value* of assets—what they are really worth —rather than merely to trace the flow of costs. The layman finds it difficult to believe that the balance sheet is not, even approximately, a statement showing what the business is worth, especially when he sees on many balance sheets an item labeled "net worth." And even if he eventually recognizes that the balance sheet does not in fact report values, he criticizes accounting and accountants for not being able to devise a way of doing this.

The root of the layman's difficulty is his failure to appreciate the importance of the criteria of objectivity and feasibility. A balance sheet that set forth the real value of the assets would of course be more relevant to the reader than a balance sheet based on cost. But there simply is no objective and feasible way of ascertaining true values under most circumstances. As noted above, a reasonable estimate of the value of the assets can be made only by the management, but the financial statements are supposed to be reports of management's stewardship. To base them on management's own estimates would be equivalent to letting the batter call his own balls and strikes.

---

[2] Walter F. Frese, in the Foreword to *Contemporary Accounting Problems* by Leonard Morrissey (Englewood Cliffs, N.J.: Prentice-Hall, Inc., 1963).

A related misconception is the layman's failure to appreciate the significance of the going-concern concept. If one accepts the idea that the productive assets are held not for sale but rather for their future usefulness, then one sees that there is no necessity for determining the current sales value of these assets.

The layman also finds the accrual concept—the matching of costs and revenues—a difficult one to comprehend. In his personal life, he knows that when he makes an expenditure to the grocer, to the service station, and so on, he is that much "out of pocket." He has difficulty in understanding the fact that many business expenditures are merely the exchange of one asset for another, with the business getting as much as it gives up. Expenses occur in the time period when costs expire—when they are used up—and this time period is not necessarily the same as the time period in which the expenditure is made.

Those who do understand the basic concepts do not necessarily agree with all of them. The accounting profession is constantly involved in debates over one or another of the currently accepted principles. Since they are not laws of nature, they are subject to change, and occasionally they are changed. At the same time, the *user* of accounting information must do the best he can with the situation as it exists. He may wish that the principles were different, but as he reads an accounting report he needs to know how it *was* prepared, not how it might have been prepared.

LIMITATIONS OF ACCOUNTING

Although the person who understands the basic concepts of accounting can make an acceptable record of any accounting transaction, this knowledge does not, unfortunately, equip him fully to understand the financial statements that have been prepared by others. The rules governing the preparation of financial statements vary considerably from one company to another, for at least three reasons: (1) there is no general agreement as to what the principles are; (2) not everyone applies even those principles that are generally agreed upon, and (3) principles are not applied uniformly.

Absence of a Complete Set of Principles

The most authoritative source of accounting principles is the Accounting Principles Board of the American Institute of Certified Public Accountants. Its pronouncements have been relied on heavily in the preceding chapters. (The Securities and Exchange Commission also makes authoritative pronouncements, but these usually follow, or are at least consistent with, those of the Accounting Principles Board.) These pronouncements, however, do not comprise a complete, consistent body of principles. Instead, they are statements on specific topics, usually topics about which a controversy arose at some time in the past.

Lack of Agreement on Principles

The pronouncements of the Accounting Principles Board are not binding, even on the members of the AICPA. Its members are required to so state when they have departed from the Board's pronouncements, but an auditor can, and does, in good conscience, state that a certain practice is "in accordance with generally accepted accounting principles" if he knows of a number of reputable companies that follow the practice, even though the practice is not consistent with pronouncements of the Accounting Principles Board. For example, in 1963 the APB recommended that the "investment credit" allowed under the 1962 Revenue Act be treated as affecting income in the years over which a fixed asset is depreciated, rather than the year in which the asset is acquired. Nevertheless, three of the eight largest accounting firms approved financial statements which followed the opposite practice. (As noted in Chapter 6, the APB now permits either practice.)

Moreover, certain groups of companies are required to adhere to principles that are not necessarily consistent with those recommended by AICPA. Railroads and other common carriers follow rules prescribed by the Interstate Commerce Commission; public utilities, by the Federal Power Commission; banks and insurance companies, by state regulatory agencies. Government agencies, colleges and universities, hospitals, and other not-for-profit organizations follow practices that in important respects are inconsistent with AICPA recommendations. In approving the financial statements of such bodies, the auditor does not state that the statements are prepared in accordance with "generally accepted principles"—rather, he says they are "consistent with practice followed in the industry," or words to that effect.

INCOME TAX PRINCIPLES. We should note at this point that the principles governing the calculation of income for federal income tax purposes are basically the same as the principles of financial accounting; that is, in general, taxable income is the difference between realized revenue and expired cost. There are, however, some important differences, which are as follows:

First, taxpayers may, if they wish, disregard the accrual concept and elect to be taxed on the difference between cash receipts and cash expenditures. Many small businesses do this.

Second, the depletion allowance computed for tax purposes bears no relation to the principles of financial accounting.

Third, in taxation, a distinction is made between ordinary income and capital gains, with the latter being taxed less heavily than the former. In financial accounting, the distinction, although present, is not so important since both ordinary income and capital gains usually enter into the measurement of net income.

Finally, as already pointed out, although the principles are basically the same, a company usually applies them differently in its tax accounting and its financial accounting, respectively. It does this primarily by changing the *timing*, rather than the *amount*, of revenues and expenses. Thus, for tax purposes, a company usually reports costs as early as it legitimately can and defers revenue until as late as it legitimately can. For accounting purposes, it tends to report costs in later time periods and revenues in earlier time periods.

Differences in the Application of Principles

In his *Inventory*,[3] Grady lists some 35 topics on which alternative treatments are permitted within generally accepted accounting principles, and gives from two to eight alternatives for each. These topics range in importance from cash discounts on sales which may be taken either at the time the sale is made or the time the receivable is collected, to the basic question of whether a merger is to be recorded as a purchase or a pooling of interest.

Andrew Barr, the Chief Accountant of the Securities and Exchange Commission, has listed the following areas of accounting where alternative practices could produce materially different results under generally accepted accounting principles: valuation of inventories, depreciation and depletion, income tax allocation, pensions, research and development costs, goodwill, time of recognizing income, "all-inclusive" versus "current operating performance" income statement, intercorporate investments, long-term leases, principles of consolidation, business combinations, income measurement in finance and small loan companies, and intangible costs in the oil and gas industries. Even this list is set forth as "illustrative" rather than complete. Note that the topics mentioned affect the income statement and practically every balance sheet asset item except cash.[4]

There is also considerable latitude in applying principles. Examples that have been mentioned in earlier chapters are as follows: inventory can be recorded at Lifo, at Fifo, or some parts of inventory may be handled one way and some the other; inventory cost may or may not include inward transportation, storage costs, handling costs, or cash discounts on pur-

[3] Paul Grady, *Inventory of Generally Accepted Accounting Principles* (AICPA *Accounting Research Study No. 7*, 1965), pp. 373–79.

[4] Testimony before the Subcommittee on Commerce and Finance of the Committee on Interstate and Foreign Commerce, House of Representatives, February 19, 1964.

chases; research and development costs, organization costs, goodwill, advertising costs, and the like may be charged to expense as incurred or they may be capitalized as an asset; if capitalized, they may or may not be written off over future periods; and if written off, the number of periods over which they are written off and the proportion written off each period may vary from company to company.

In part, these differences reflect differences in personal judgment as to what is or is not *material* and as to the importance that should be attached to the *conservatism* concept. In attempting to describe a complex situation, such differences are inevitable. In part, the differences reflect customs that have grown up in particular companies or industries.

Mr. Leonard Spacek, managing partner of Arthur Andersen and Company, illustrates this point with the following comparison between the reported earnings of two hypothetical companies, with the same revenue ($10 million) and the same physical operations.[5] Company A reports a net income of $480,000, and Company B reports a net income of $1,076,000. The difference of $596,000 is explained entirely by differences in accounting practices, as follows:

1. Company B uses Fifo in pricing inventory; Company A uses Lifo...........$192,000
2. Company B uses accelerated depreciation; Company A uses straight-line..... 48,000
3. Company B capitalizes research costs and amortizes over five years; Company A expenses on incurrence... 38,000
4. Company B charges the present value of pensions vested; Company A expenses actual current pension costs.................................... 72,000
5. Company B grants stock options to executives, which are not an expense; Company A pays a cash bonus... 96,000
6. Company B credits capital gains to income; Company A credits them directly to retained earnings... 150,000

Total...$596,000

Example: Nudoll Company

A company, here called the Nudoll Company, spent three years and some $90,000 developing a new product. By October, 1964, the product was ready for market and seemed to have a promising future. Of the funds used up to that point, $30,000 had been contributed by the management, in exchange for common stock, and $60,000 had been loaned by a friend of the principal owner, payable on demand. The balance sheet at that time, in round numbers, was as shown in Illustration 10–1. According to this balance sheet, current assets were about one ninth of current liabilities and the company had a substantial deficit.

The Nudoll Company needed additional capital, which the management planned to raise by selling stock. An advisor pointed out that the

---

[5] Quoted in Myles L. Mace and George G. Montgomery, Jr., *Management Problems of Corporate Acquisitions* (Boston: Division of Research, Harvard Business School, 1962), pp. 178–80.

Illustration 10–1

NUDOLL COMPANY

Balance Sheet as of October 31, 1964
(As Originally Prepared)

ASSETS		EQUITIES		
Cash...................	$1,000	Accounts payable.............		$ 2,000
Inventory................	6,000	Notes payable...............		60,000
Total Current Assets...	$7,000	Total Current Liabilities..		$62,000
		Capital stock................	$30,000	
		Less: Deficit..............	−85,000	−55,000
Total Assets.......	$7,000	Total Equities........		$ 7,000

balance sheet shown in Illustration 10–1 would look unattractive to prospective investors. Two steps were therefore taken: (1) the person who had loaned the $60,000 agreed to sign a five-year note, with the informal understanding that he would be repaid as soon as funds were available (this understanding was the same as his understanding when he made the loan, even though technically the original note was payable on demand); and (2) the expenditures to develop the new product were set up as an asset on the grounds that these costs were incurred in order to benefit future periods. These changes produced the balance sheet shown in Illustration 10–2. According to this revised balance sheet, current assets were 3.5 times current liabilities, total assets were 14 times as large as those shown on the first balance sheet, and the company had retained earnings (which had resulted from the profitable sale of trial lots of the new product).

Arguments can be made to support the view that both these balance sheets were prepared in accordance with generally accepted accounting principles. Each statement shows certain useful information: that the company has some cash and a little inventory, that it is probably going to have difficulty meeting its bills unless it obtains more cash quickly, and

Illustration 10–2

NUDOLL COMPANY

Balance Sheet as of October 31, 1964
(As Adjusted)

ASSETS		EQUITIES		
Cash......................	$ 1,000	Accounts payable............		$ 2,000
Inventory..................	6,000	Total Current Lia-		
Total Current Assets.....	$ 7,000	bilities...............		$ 2,000
Unamortized development		Long-term debt.............		60,000
costs...................	90,000	Capital stock..............	$30,000	
		Retained earnings............	5,000	35,000
Total Assets.........	$97,000	Total Equities........		$97,000

that it owes someone $60,000. Neither one describes the overall status of this company, for its status depends almost entirely on the excellence of the new product, and this will not be known until the product is marketed.

Implications of These Differences

No one can state reliably what the "general practice" is or how the majority of companies handle any specific problem. There are at least four million accounting entities in the United States, of which about one million are corporations. No report on the accounting practices of these companies exists. The best source, *Accounting Trends and Techniques,* an annual publication of the AICPA, reports the practices of approximately 600 of the largest corporations. A person who has a personal knowledge of the detailed procedures of as many as 100 companies has an unusually broad experience. Thus, generalizations about what "the majority of companies" do with respect to detailed accounting matters should not be taken too seriously.

It follows that a detailed comparison of the items reported in the financial statements of two companies is a difficult problem. Useful comparisons can often be made in terms of rough approximations, but precise statements are rarely possible.

The existence of diversity in accounting practice should not be considered as a reason for criticizing accountants or accounting. The fundamental fact is that a business is a complex organism. There is no conceivable way of prescribing a uniform set of rules by means of which the significant facts about that organism can be reduced to a few pages of figures, any more than there is any way of formulating a standard set of rules for biographers. Standard procedures for listing physical characteristics, birth dates, marital status, and certain other information about a person can easily be specified, but these details do not really describe the person completely. The accuracy and usefulness of the "picture" of a person that emerges from a biography depends on the author's skill and judgment in the collection, analysis, and presentation of information about his subject. So it is with financial statements.

Nor should the existence of diversity lead to frustration on the part of the user. The *consistency* concept prevents diversity from becoming chaos. Although Company A may follow practices that differ from those of other companies, Company A ordinarily follows the same practices year after year, or if it changes, the doctrine of consistency requires that it disclose the change. Thus its statements are likely to be comparable with one another from year to year. Also, although railroads use rules that are different from those used by industrial companies, railroad A is likely to use approximately the same rules as railroad B, and thus the two can be compared (with some notable exceptions).

Inherent Limitations

In addition to the points noted above, it is important to remember that accounting has inherent limitations. A business is such a complex organism that no one should expect that accounting, or any device, can record a complete and accurate picture of its activities. The two most important limitations—limitations which no foreseeable change in accounting can overcome—are (1) accounting reports are necessarily monetary, and (2) they are necessarily influenced by estimates of future events.

Accounting reports are limited to information that can be expressed in monetary terms. Nothing in the accounts explicitly describes personalities, the impact of outside forces, or other nondollar information that is vital to the complete understanding of a business.

Some accounting figures are influenced by future events which cannot conceivably be foreseen; these figures are necessarily estimates. The depreciation expense of the current period, for example, depends partly on how long the assets will be used in the future. The real significance of accounts receivable and the related item of sales revenue cannot be assessed until the number of credit customers who will not pay their bills is known. The actual value of inventory depends on what the merchandise can be sold for in the future. The possible impacts of contingent future events, such as the results of pending or threatened litigation, retroactive agreements on wage rates, and redetermination of profits on contracts, are not shown in the financial statements, although if material they should appear in a footnote. Incidentally, the very fact that footnotes, which may be numerous, are labeled as being an "integral part of the financial statements" is an indication of the limitation of the statements themselves.

Attempts to Reduce Diversity

The AICPA Accounting Principles Board is working vigorously to reduce the diversity in accounting practice, and it has made great progress since its establishment in 1959. It is discussing a number of proposals to resolve currently controversial accounting issues. If these efforts of the APB do not bear fruit, it is quite possible that the government will promulgate accounting principles, as is done in several European countries. The Securities and Exchange Commission has the statutory authority to do this under the Securities Act of 1933, the Securities Exchange Act of 1934, the Public Utility Holding Company Act of 1935, and the Investment Company Act of 1940, but to date the SEC has been most cautious about exercising this authority.

ROLE OF THE AUDITOR

All companies whose securities are listed on an organized stock exchange, nearly every company that sells its securities to the public, most other corporations, and a great many unincorporated businesses have their financial statements and the accounting records from which they are produced examined by independent, outside public accountants called auditors. Usually, these are certified public accountants (CPA's), who meet prescribed professional standards and who have received a certificate or license to practice from the state in which they do business.

When financial statements are examined by auditors, the results of this examination are reported in a letter that should be studied carefully by the reader of the statements. This letter ordinarily consists of two paragraphs. The first, or *scope,* paragraph reads as follows:

> We have examined the statement of financial position of . . . Company as of (date) and the related statements of income and retained income for the year then ended. Our examination was made in accordance with generally accepted auditing standards and accordingly included such tests of the accounting records and such auditing procedures as we considered necessary in the circumstances.

The key words in this paragraph are: *such tests . . . as we considered necessary.* They signify that the auditor, not the management, is responsible for deciding on how thorough a job is required. The management cannot ask the auditor, for example, to "make as much of an audit as you can for $10,000." If the auditor's freedom is abridged in any material way, he is required to indicate this fact by adding to the above paragraph, "except. . . ." Such exceptions are rare.

The second, or *opinion* paragraph reads as follows:

> In our opinion, the accompanying statements of financial position, of income, and of retained income present fairly the financial position of . . . Company at (date) and the results of its operations for the year then ended, in conformity with generally accepted accounting principles applied on a basis consistent with that of the preceding year.

There are three significant points in this opinion, indicated by the words: (1) *present fairly,* (2) *in conformity with generally accepted accounting principles,* and (3) *applied on a consistent basis.*

The word *fairly* should be contrasted with the word *accurately.* The auditor does not say that the reported net income is the only, or the most accurate, figure that could have been reported. He says, rather, that of the many alternative principles that could have been used, those actually selected by the management do give a fair picture in the circumstances relevant to the particular company. This contrast between "fairness" and "accuracy" is further emphasized by the fact that the auditor's report is called an "opinion" rather than a "certificate." The auditor does not certify the accuracy of the report; instead, he gives his professional opinion that it is fair.

The second phrase means that each of the accounting principles used in preparing the statements is "generally accepted." As noted in the preceding section, for many transactions there are several generally accepted principles, and the auditor's opinion merely states that the management has selected one of these.

If the Accounting Principles Board has issued an *Opinion* on a certain point, this, by definition, constitutes a generally accepted principle. However, an alternative principle is also regarded as being generally accepted if it has "substantial authoritative support." Evidences of such support are pronouncements of regulatory bodies or the practices of a number of other bodies. When a company uses a principle that is inconsistent with APB opinions, even though this principle has substantial authoritative support, the auditor is required to disclose this fact and to show, if practicable, the amount of decrease or increase in net income and retained earnings that would have resulted had the Accounting Principles Board *Opinion* been followed.

The third point, *consistency*, refers, it will be noted, to *the preceding year*. It does not mean *internal* consistency, that is, it does not mean that the principle used to measure fixed assets is consistent with that used to measure inventory, or even that each corporation in a consolidated enterprise follows practices that are consistent with those of other corporations in the same enterprise. The consistency doctrine is nevertheless of great significance because it does mean that the figures for one year are comparable with those of the preceding year, and assurance of such comparability is essential if meaningful comparisons are to be made to show the changes that have occurred in the company's financial position and earning performance.

The paragraphs quoted above constitute a *clean* opinion. If the auditor cannot make these statements, he adds in the appropriate place, "except that . . . ," and the opinion is then called a *qualified* opinion. Before making a qualified opinion, the auditor will of course discuss the situation with the management of the company, and in many cases the management is willing to change the financial statements rather than to have an exception reported.

Many people have the impression that the auditor is responsible for *preparing* the financial statements. This is not so. Preparation of the statements is the responsibility of the management, not of the auditor. When two or more alternative practices are permitted by generally accepted accounting principles, and either is "fair" (which is of course an ambiguous criterion), management, not the auditor, decides which one is to be used. In his opinion, the auditor does not state that management has necessarily made the *best* choice among alternative principles, but only that the choice made by management was an acceptable one.

It should also be noted that the auditor's opinion relates only to the financial statements, including the footnotes thereto, and not to other material that may appear in a company's annual report.

In making their examination, auditors no longer rely primarily on a detailed rechecking of the analysis, journalizing, and posting of each transaction; rather, they satisfy themselves that the accounting system is designed to ensure that the data are processed properly. This reliance on the internal control system is relatively new. As late as 1949, the U.S. General Accounting Office received a copy of every one of the millions of accounting documents generated annually in the federal government and, theoretically at least, checked each of them for propriety and accuracy. When the General Accounting Office changed its emphasis to a reliance on properly designed accounting systems, it not only was able to release several *thousand* employees but also was able to do a better auditing job by concentrating its efforts on checking the reliability of accounting systems and by examining the relatively few important or unusual transactions which previously had tended to be buried in the detail.

In addition to the examination of the adequacy of the accounting system, the auditors make test checks of how well it is working, they verify the existence of assets (for example, they usually are present at the taking of physical inventory, they ask a sample of customers to *confirm or verify the accuracy of the accounts receivable shown for each of them,* they check bank balances, and so on), and they make sure that especially important or nonroutine transactions are recorded in conformity with generally accepted accounting principles. The observation of inventories and the confirmation of receivables is regarded as being so important that the omission of either of these tests must be specifically mentioned in the "scope" paragraph of the opinion.

SIGNIFICANCE OF THE FINANCIAL STATEMENTS

The limitations mentioned above must be taken into account when one tries to understand a set of financial statements. The existence of these limitations should not, of course, lead to a complete rejection of accounting. After all, accounting does provide a way of summarizing numerous, complicated, and heterogeneous events into two brief documents, the balance sheet and the income statement. This is a remarkable achievement.

It is useful at this point to balance the limitations with the virtues, and attempt to describe their net effect in terms of the principal categories on the financial statements.

The Balance Sheet

It is not possible to define the whole balance sheet in anything other than vague terms. The AICPA definition of the balance sheet as a "list of balances in the asset, liability, or net worth accounts" is like the statement that "a rose is a rose"; it is accurate but not meaningful. A more meaningful statement is the following: the balance sheet shows the sources from which funds currently used to operate the business have been obtained (i.e., liabilities and owners' equity) and the types of property and property rights in which these funds are currently locked up (i.e., assets). This statement regards the balance sheet as essentially a report of management's *stewardship;* that is, what management has done with the funds entrusted to it.

In appraising the significance of individual balance sheet items, it is useful to make a distinction between *monetary items* and *nonmonetary items,* since items in the former category have a more clear-cut meaning than those in the latter.

Monetary items include not only cash itself, but also other assets that represent a specific monetary claim on some external party and liabilities that represent the specific monetary claim by some external party. Accounts Receivable is a monetary asset. The amount that each customer owes is definite, and it is usually possible to estimate the amount of uncollectible accounts within fairly close limits. Short-term investments held in lieu of cash also represent a definite claim, and although fluctuations in interest rates can affect the market value of these claims, such fluctuations are often not significant for the types of investments in this category.

Inventory, by contrast, is not a monetary asset. Its value depends ultimately on the result of a sales transaction that will occur at some future time, rather than on an agreement that already has been made.

On the liabilities side, accounts payable, notes payable, various accruals such as wages or interest payable, and bonds payable are all monetary items. They represent specific, measurable claims against the assets. Deferred liabilities, such as deferred income taxes, and the whole of the owners' equity section are in the nonmonetary category.

The analyst can use the amounts shown for the monetary items with reasonable assurance that they represent the current value of property rights in the case of assets, or the actual amount of claims against the business in the case of liabilities. He has much less confidence in the significance of the amounts shown for the nonmonetary items. He does know that the amounts for nonmonetary assets are based on cost, but he ordinarily has no way of relating these amounts to current market values.

In examining the balance sheet, the analyst usually makes a basic distinction between the working capital items and the other items. (Working capital equals the total current assets minus the total current liabilities.) Current assets are normally converted into cash within a year or a single operating cycle, and current liabilities are those that are payable within a year. Thus, items in the current section reflect reasonably recent transactions, and are more likely to reflect current market conditions than items in the other sections, which may reflect transactions that occurred many years previously.

Working capital items also tend to have more flexibility than other items; that is, management has more frequent opportunities to make decisions on the recommitment of funds in the case of current items than in the case of noncurrent items. Management can, for example, add an item to or delete an item from inventory on relatively short notice, but it cannot change the amount of investment in fixed assets as frequently or in as short a time after the decision to do so has been made. This flexibility relates to the individual items that make up the category more than it does to the total. Even though individual items flow through inventory rapidly, the inherent characteristics of the business may dictate that the total investment in inventory be relatively constant. In this sense, the amount of inventory may be as "fixed" as the amount of so-called fixed assets.

The *fixed asset* section of the balance sheet is a statement of unexpired costs; that is, it shows costs that have not yet been charged against operations. Ordinarily, the amounts listed bear no relation to market value, and no inference as to such value should be attempted solely on the basis of balance sheet information.

Interpretation of the *liabilities* section involves a subtle point. The items included there are indeed "claims against the assets," but they are only those claims which are recorded with an offsetting debit to an asset or another equity account, and these are not necessarily all the obligations which the company knows it must pay. For example, if an automobile is purchased on December 31 for $2,000 and if the business signs a note agreeing to pay the $2,000 at the rate of $50 per month for 40 months, the note appears as a liability (notes payable) on the December 31 balance sheet, and the automobile appears as an asset. On the other hand, if, instead, the business *rents* an automobile on December 31 and signs an agreement to pay $50 a month rent for 40 months, no record of this obligation appears as a liability (although it may be indicated in a footnote to the balance sheet).

One other important point about the liabilities section is that the amounts are usually definite, more so than the amounts in any other section. The amount shown as accounts payable *is* the amount owed to creditors; and the amounts shown as notes payable or bonds payable *are* the amounts owed to banks and to the bondholders. Even the tax liability and the other accruals, although estimated, are likely to be close estimates.

The *owners' equity* section gives some useful bits and pieces of information, such as the number of outstanding shares of stock of various types, clues as to dividend policy, and so on. Dividends may be limited to the amount shown as surplus, although considerations other than this accounting relationship are usually more important. In the event of liquidation or other crises, the amounts recorded as capital and surplus are important in determining the relative claims of the shareholders, and especially of each class of shareholders if there are several classes. In the usual situation, however, the amount shown as owners' equity in no way indicates the actual "worth" of the shareholders' equity, except in those rare instances where a company's assets consist entirely of cash or readily marketable assets.

The Income Statement

What is the meaning of "net income," the final item on an income statement? It is correct to say that net income is the difference between revenues and expenses, but this statement begs the question because there is no general agreement on the precise definitions of "revenue" and "expense" or on the method of measuring each of them. In the absence of such an agreement, there is room for considerable difference of opinion about the real meaning of net income.

How reliable is the estimate of the net income for an accounting period? Reliability depends primarily on (1) the length of the accounting period chosen, (2) the extent to which events relating to the current period are separated from events affecting prior or future periods, (3) the amount of long-lived assets owned by the company, and (4) the stability of prices.

Estimates of net income for a day or a month are likely to be much less reliable than estimates for a year, and estimates for a year less reliable than estimates covering a longer period.

Although the expenses assigned to a period are supposed to relate to the revenues realized in that period, it usually is not practicable to attempt a precise matching. For example, advertising is typically "bread cast upon the waters" in the hope of generating sales revenue in future periods, yet advertising is usually charged as an expense in the period in which the advertising is done rather than in the periods in which the revenues are earned. The difficulty of estimating the portion of the cost of a long-lived asset applicable to a given accounting period has already been described. The manner in which fluctuations in prices influence the income statement was discussed in Chapter 9.

For all these reasons, the net income reported on the income statement is unlikely to correspond exactly to the true increase in the owners' equity during an accounting period. The true *monetary* income of an enterprise can be known only after the enterprise has been completely terminated and its assets disposed of. The nonmonetary "income"—personal satisfaction, service rendered to society, and so on—are not determined from accounting reports even then. Any attempt to measure income for a shorter interval of time is necessarily inexact.

Nevertheless, certain of the individual items on an income statement may be highly reliable. The sales revenue figure is usually a close approximation to actual sales revenue, and the amounts for many expense items, such as wages, supplies, light, and power, are close approximations to actual expenses. Depreciation, on the other hand, is usually only a rough approximation, while some special adjustments reported as nonoperating expenses may be little more than informed guesses.

CONCLUSION

Perhaps the best way to summarize the intent of the discussion in this chapter is to point out that in accounting, one refers to the *measurement* of income rather than to the *determination* of income. To determine is "to fix conclusively and authoritatively"; accounting cannot do this. A measurement, on the other hand, is an approximation, according to some agreed-upon measuring stick, and this is what accounting sets out to do.

A person can and should find out about the particular rules that govern the accounting for the company in which he works. He usually cannot do this for other companies, and when he is using financial statements prepared in these companies, he must recognize, even though he cannot allow precisely for, the probable existence of differences in the preparation of these statements.

SUGGESTIONS FOR FURTHER READING

EDWARDS, EDGAR O., and PHILIP W. BELL. *The Theory and Measurement of Business Income.* Los Angeles: University of California Press, 1961.

MOONITZ, MAURICE. *The Basic Postulates of Accounting.* AICPA Accounting Research Study No. 1, 1961.

MORRISSEY, LEONARD E. *Contemporary Accounting Problems.* Englewood Cliffs, N.J.: Prentice-Hall, Inc., 1967. This text focuses on a number of current problems faced by the accounting profession, the need for generally accepted accounting principles, and the difficulty encountered in defining and applying such principles.

SPROUSE, ROBERT T., and MAURICE MOONITZ. *A Tentative Set of Broad Accounting Principles for Business Enterprises.* AICPA Accounting Research Study No. 3, 1962.

CASES

CASE 10–1. CIRCLE LUNCH

Early in 1959, Mr. and Mrs. Elmer Symington decided to go into the restaurant business. Mr. Symington was dissatisfied with his job as cook in a restaurant, where he earned $2 an hour.

During July, 1959, the Symingtons found a business which seemed to be what they wanted. This was the Circle Lunch, a lunch counter located in the Acme Department Store, in a working-class section of Jersey City. The Circle Lunch was operated under a lease with the department store; only the equipment was actually the property of the operator of the lunchroom. The equipment was old, but Mr. Symington thought that it was in fairly good condition.

The couple opened negotiations with the operator and quickly reached an agreement to take over the lease and equipment on September 1, and to pay the operator a price of $2,000. Of this price, Mr. Symington estimated that $900 represented the fair value of the equipment. The lease expired on August 31, 1960, and was renewable for three years if Acme consented. Under the terms of the lease, Acme furnished space, heat, light, and water, and the operators (i.e., the Symingtons) paid Acme 15 percent of gross receipts as rent.

The Symingtons paid the $2,000 from their personal savings account and also transferred $1,000 to a checking account which they opened in the name of Circle Lunch.

Shortly after they started operations, the cooking range broke down. The Symingtons thereupon sold the range for $80 (which was approximately its estimated value, as a part of the $900) and purchased a new range for $800. It was installed immediately, and they paid $120 for its installation.

The coffee urn also broke down, but Mr. Symington was able to repair it himself by working 16 hours one Sunday.

Early in 1960, the Symingtons called in a firm which specialized in making out reports for small businesses, and requested financial statements for Circle Lunch for the period ended December 31, 1959. From their cash register and checkbook, they had the following figures:

Cash Receipts:

Cash receipts from customers	$6,420
Sale of cooking range	80
Total Cash Receipts	$6,500

Cash Disbursements:

Food and supplies	$2,763
City restaurant license, valid September 1, 1959, to September 1, 1960	45
15 percent rent paid to Acme for September, October, and November	670
New cooking range	800
Installation of cooking range	120
Other operating expenses	18
Withdrawals for personal use	750
Total Cash Disbursements	$5,166

Before going home on December 31, the Symingtons had estimated the value of food and supplies then on hand to be about $146 at cost.

Early in January, they paid two bills, the December meat bill of $173 and the bill for the December rent of $293.

The Symingtons also explained to the accountant that the cash receipts of $6,420 included $620 received from the sale of 124 "coupon books" at $5 each. Each book contained coupons with a face value of $5.50, which could be used to pay for meals. As of December 31, coupons with a face value of $430 had been used to pay for meals; therefore coupons with a face value of $252 were still outstanding.

Questions

1. Prepare a balance sheet as of December 31, 1959, and an income statement for the four-month period ending December 31, 1959. Explain briefly your treatment of the coupon books and of anything else you believe needs comment.

2. Comment briefly on the significant information revealed by your financial statements.

CASE 10–2. PRESTONBURG COUNTRY CLUB

When the aging golf professional of the Prestonburg Country Club retired in 1962, there was a great deal of discussion among the members as to who his successor should be. Several of the senior members contacted other clubs, to see if their assistant professionals could fill the job, but without success. Mr. Augustus Burgoyne, a senior member and former president of the club, eventually came upon a man, who he believed to be "exactly the sort of fellow we need." He brought the man, Mr. Alastair McIntyre, in for an interview, and the committee agreed that he would be ideal. His qualifications and experience were excellent, and they believed that his reputation in competitions would enhance the prestige of the club.

When Mr. McIntyre saw the conditions that were attached to the position, however, he felt unable to accept it. He noted that he was expected to finance the pro shop himself, and to pay a rent of $120 a month for the use of the space. In addition, he noted that he would have to pay the retiring professional $2,000 on consideration for the goodwill that had developed during his tenure. Since he only had $600 in capital, he did not feel that he could manage to meet these obligations.

Mr. Burgoyne was not willing to allow this detail to interfere, however, and promised a loan to finance the operations and establishment of the shop in the early stages. After a few moments' thought, Mr. McIntyre agreed that this would be a satisfactory arrangement, and he accepted the position effective January 1, 1963.

Later on, Mr. Burgoyne took Mr. McIntyre aside, and said he would lend him $10,000, which was to be repaid by annual installments which would be computed at 60 percent of all his profits before taxes in excess of $5,000 each year. Interest, which was to be computed on the balance of the loan outstanding at the beginning of the year, was to be 3 percent for the first three years, and 6 percent after this, and would be paid annually in addition to the installments on the principal.

Mr. McIntyre agreed to take over the inventory of the retiring professional, and a figure of $3,500 was agreed on for the inventory of clubs, bags, balls, caddy carts, etc., in the shop. In addition, he agreed to take over for $650 the 65 caddy carts that were used for rental to members, and four electric golf carts at a valuation of $250 apiece. The 65 caddy carts had all been purchased at the same time, and were of identical design.

On December 31, 1962, Mr. Burgoyne gave Mr. McIntyre a check for the amount of the loan and, in turn, Mr. McIntyre paid for the stock, golf carts, and goodwill as indicated above. He deposited the residue, and his own $600, in a bank account which he had just opened for business use.

The year which followed was a very busy one for the new pro. He was socially successful, and was soon accepted by the members, and regarded as a great asset to the club. Even the elderly diehards, who had considered that "he could never be the same as old Tom," came to accept him as a really good man. His instruction was eagerly sought, and the better players in the club were all anxious to "have a round with Al."

In this busy round of activities, Mr. McIntyre was not able to keep very close track of financial matters. He decided that it would be best to keep an accurate record of cash transactions, and to worry about the rest at the end of the year.

On the 31st of December, 1963, faced with the problem of accounting, Mr. McIntyre began to examine his records.

An analysis of his cash records for the year showed the following:

Receipts:

Tuition	$ 4,665
Round fees	1,830
Cart hire	4,500
Club sales	5,283
Other sales	2,179
	$18,457

Payments:

Rental of pro shop	$1,440	
Two new electric carts	960	
15 new caddy carts	225	
Goods for resale	4,238	
Salary of shop assistant	4,500	
		11,363
Net cash taken in		$ 7,094
Personal withdrawals		5,300
		$ 1,794

While McIntyre was satisfied that the cash record was correct, he was not sure what to do next. He therefore went to Bill Simpson, a member of the club and a professional accountant, and asked him to help.

Simpson willingly agreed, and began by looking through the piles of invoices, scraps of paper, and used checkbooks which constituted the records. He found that two bills were outstanding. First, Mr. McIntyre had bought a total of three identical electric carts at $480 each during the year, two in January and the third just before the end of the year. Secondly, there had been a credit purchase of goods for resale of $197, which was in addition to the cash paid for such goods as shown above.

Included in the cash received for "other sales" was an amount for repairs to members' clubs. At the end of the year, there were clubs in the shop in various stages of repair. McIntyre estimated that these clubs would have cost the members about $780 when they were new, though they were worth only about $425 now.

Mr. McIntyre also estimated that he had spent about 18 hours working on the clubs now in the shop, and had used supplies in the work which he had taken over from his predecessor. He estimated that the cost of these supplies had been about $13.

Some of the clubs sold, amounting to about $650 in selling price, had been sold very recently. It was a custom of the trade in that region to permit a customer to return clubs for full credit within seven days if he was not satisfied with them. So far, no members had availed themselves of this guarantee in the current year.

The $4,500 received for caddy cart and electric cart hires included payment for 382 caddy cart rental tickets at $1 per round, which had been sold in books to members and had not yet been used.

Mr. Simpson also noted that six of the carts purchased during the year had been sold, two were in the shop awaiting sale, and the rest were in the group for hire. Nine of the older carts for hire had been broken during the year, six of them irreparably. The others had been repaired at no cost. It was thought that the carts would last about four years from January 1, 1963, on the average.

One of the old electric carts was not expected to last another year. It was thought that the three other old ones had at least two years' life left in them (as of December 1963), and that the three which had been bought during the year would be useful for a total of six years.

Mr. McIntyre said that he had spent a total of 422 hours tutoring in the year, for which he charged $15 an hour, and had played 55 rounds with members at $30 per round. He recalled that he had sometimes been given a bonus by the person with whom he was playing the round, and that three rounds had yet to be paid for. Mr. Simpson felt that social pressures would be more than adequate to ensure that all debts would be paid in full in due course.

With Mr. Simpson's help, Mr. McIntyre took a careful physical inventory, and decided that the cost to him of the goods in stock had been $3,260. In addition to this amount, Mr. McIntyre told Mr. Simpson that he had a supply of 500 of a new-type golf ball in the store, of which the wholesale price totaled $400. The supplying company did not ask for payment except for those balls which had been sold, and then allowed Mr. McIntyre a commission on the sales. As he had taken delivery very recently, he had only sold 20 of these balls, at a dollar each. The customer who had purchased these had yet to pay for them. There also were a few wooden-shafted clubs, part of the stock he had taken over, which he was sure would never be sold. No record was available as to their original cost, as Mr. McIntyre had bought the entire stock as a package. Mr. Simpson was not certain what cost to attribute to them.

Question

1. Prepare a balance sheet as of December 31, 1963 and an income statement for 1963.

CASE 10–3. FAIRMUIR INSTRUMENT CORPORATION

Fairmuir Instrument Corporation sold a line of high temperature measuring instruments called pyrometers. The principal users of the equipment were steel mills and various metal extraction companies, and Fairmuir's small sales force had concentrated almost exclusively on establishing good relations with these customers. Occasional inquiries and orders came from other sources, such as scientific laboratories, but the company had never actively solicited these markets.

The device in its present form had been developed and put into production in the early 1950's. Essentially it utilized principles which had been known for almost a hundred years, but until the present development the accuracy attainable had fallen short of the requirements of modern industry. The company had introduced no new products until the last quarter of 1964. Effectively, the company had not faced any serious competition in its market area until 1960 and had maintained a stable sales level of around $3 million until that time.

During 1960 a competing product had been introduced to the market.

Exhibit 1

FAIRMUIR INSTRUMENT CORPORATION

Financial Data as of December 31
(dollar figures in thousands)

	1960	1961	1962	1963	1964
Inventories related to pyrometers.......	$ 791	$ 806	$ 909	$ 805	$ 627
Working capital....................	933	1,021	1,165	1,155	819
Net assets........................	1,889	1,965	1,995	1,926	1,549
Net sales of pyrometers..............	2,881	2,475	2,025	996	583
Other sales (net)....................	...	...	...	...	115
Net income (loss)..................	108	77	67	(91)	(376)

Operating on completely different principles, this device performed substantially the same job as Fairmuir's product and gave similar levels of accuracy. The only major differences were in its useful life (five years) and its purchase price, each of which were about half of those of the Fairmuir product. The lower purchase price was an important sales advantage, and Fairmuir's sales had suffered accordingly. Exhibit 1 gives some of the financial data of Fairmuir Instrument Corporation from 1960 through 1964.

By 1961 the management of Fairmuir realized that without a new product to bolster its faltering sales volume, the company was facing a serious predicament. They therefore began a search for an additional product which would be suited to the capabilities of the company. In 1962 they approached an inventor who held patents for just such a product, with a view to buying the patents. After some negotiation a mutually satisfactory price was reached, and, as part of the agreement, the inventor agreed to join the company and lead the additional development work which was required before a commercial product was ready for marketing.

On top of the cost of the patents and the development expenses, the company was faced with substantial start-up costs and required an investment in inventories. The company's financial resources, already adversely affected by the lagging sales of pyrometers, were inadequate without an injection of fresh capital. The company's capital stock was closely held by members of top management and a few of their friends and family members. None of these people was willing to contribute any further capital.

Management believed that the recent poor operating results made it unwise to seek fresh equity capital at that time and they therefore decided that a bank loan was the only feasible recourse. It did not prove an easy matter to find a bank willing to make the required loan, but eventually this was done. In extending the loan the bank imposed several restrictions on the management of Fairmuir, one of these being that a minimum working capital[7] level of $800,000 should be maintained. By the end of 1964, with the sales of pyrometers still falling and the new product only just introduced to the market, the company was close to defaulting on the requirements of the working capital covenant.

In the 1964 audit, the public accountant was satisfied with all the accounts except for the valuation of the inventories related to pyrometers. Most of this inventory was in good condition, and had been carefully handled and stored. A few items of purchased parts had become obsolete and management had written them down. This represented an insignificant adjustment, however, and the bulk of the inventory was still reported on the company's books at cost. The auditor was not concerned about the physical condition of the inventory, but he had serious reservations as to the marketability of the product, and therefore the realization of the investment through profitable sales. In approaching management on this matter the auditor was aware that a large adjustment would throw the company into default on its loan covenant concerning working capital.

The auditor, Mr. Bill Adams, arranged a meeting with the president of Fairmuir Instrument Corporation, Mr. Tom Fairmuir, in order to discuss the 1964 financial statements. Part of the meeting is recorded below.

MR. ADAMS: Everything seems to be in fine order except for your valuation of inventories relating to pyrometers, Tom. Now we discussed this matter briefly a few days ago, and you expressed the opinion that there would be no material loss of value in the inventories and that you would in fact be able to sell it all in the normal course of business. Since then I have examined your record of sales orders. At present you have only $58,000 worth of open orders on your books, compared with $65,000 worth at the beginning of the year. Your billings by quarters for the past year were fairly stable: $149,000,

---

[7] Working capital was defined as the difference between current assets and current liabilities.

first quarter; $136,000, second quarter; $141,000, third quarter; and $157,000 in the final quarter.

I have also read several articles in trade publications, such as this one in *Steel Monthly*, which seem to indicate that your type of pyrometer is at a technical as well as an economic (in terms of purchase price) disadvantage.

Frankly, it appears to me that you are going to be left with a lot of inventory which will have to be marked down very significantly to sell it.

MR. FAIRMUIR: Now hold it, Bill, things are not so bleak as that. In fact, we have plans for our pyrometers which will return the sales volume to its previous level, or close to it. Look at these letters, Bill. These are inquiries concerning substantial orders, and we have been receiving such inquiries at a greatly increased rate recently. If this continues, and I have no doubt that it will, and if even half of them become firm orders, we shall be selling pyrometers in 1965 at twice the 1964 level.

You know we hired a new sales manager this year? Well, he has reorganized our sales force and is beginning to get results. At the same time we have gone over our production process and reduced the manufacturing cost of our lines by some 10 percent. No doubt you noticed that our cost of goods figures were lower for the past two or three months. We expect to improve on that further in 1965. Of course this gives us some price flexibility when we are faced with a competitive situation. So you see, I have good reason to predict better results in the future.

MR. ADAMS: What exactly has the new sales manager done?

MR. FAIRMUIR: He reorganized the sales territories and reassigned the salesmen, so that we should get greater market penetration. He released a couple of men who have clearly not been pulling their weight and hired a couple of bright young men to replace them. The main thing is that he has done wonders for the morale of the sales force. In addition he has identified new markets and is helping the men to break into these markets.

MR. ADAMS: Why don't we look at the prospects market by market, Tom. You had sales of only $62,000 to steel mills in 1964. It seems as if the steel mills market is almost defunct, wouldn't you agree?

MR. FAIRMUIR: It has certainly declined. However, some of our men have built up a good relationship with their customers in the steel industry and we expect this to produce a certain loyalty. We should keep a small part of the business, say, billings of about $50,000 a year.

In the other metal extraction industries we know that our product has some distinct competitive advantages, such as its ruggedness and lower maintenance costs. With the new emphasis on selling we expect that our customers will be well aware of these advantages, and the downward sales trend should be reversed this year. On this basis we expect 1965's sales to this market to be at least $400,000 and to increase further in the future.

MR. ADAMS: But look, Tom, that means an increase over this year's sales, bucking a strong downward trend. I can't base my opinion on your optimism, you know.

MR. FAIRMUIR: Well, look at this market, which we think has great potential—scientific laboratories. We are going to place advertisements in some of the engineering journals and pay direct sales calls to many of the labs in our market areas, those which do a lot of high temperature work. We anticipate a yearly volume of $200,000 to $300,000 in this market.

And, finally, we have set up a contract with a representative in Washington to handle our line in government sales. He has already gotten some orders for us and he seems certain that we can build up a stable volume of some $300,000 a year. Several government agencies are testing our product at the moment, including the Atomic Energy Commission. If we get our equipment specified for installation into government nuclear plants, we shall have a large continuing market.

Mr. Adams: So you expect sales of about $1 million this year, twice 1964's sales?

Mr. Fairmuir: No, not right away. But we are confident of substantially reversing the trend of recent years and eventually, say in two years or so, building our sales up to at least $1.5 million for pyrometers. For 1965 we predict sales of about $800,000.

Mr. Adams: Well, look at this from my point of view. I have a professional responsibility to give an opinion on your company's financial statements, and I cannot base my opinion on your predictions. I have to go on historic facts and reasonable expectations. The historic facts are that sales of pyrometers have been falling and you have only a small volume of open orders on your books.

You have a substantial inventory, the value of which can only be realized through the sale of pyrometers. Any other representation of these facts would mislead the reader of the statements.

Mr. Fairmuir: I agree with you on that, and in my opinion, we *will* realize the value of our inventory through normal sales. I could not contemplate a write-down in the value of the inventory. For one thing, it would not be right to do so since it would be misleading in valuing our assets. And for another, it could easily lead to a difficult situation with the bank and, at worst, lead to liquidation of the company. True, we have experienced a few bad years. But we are fighting back and I am confident we shall save our pyrometer line. And also our new line will start to contribute to profits this coming year.

The discussion continued for some time and became fairly heated. Finally, Mr. Adams terminated the discussion in order to consider the question further. He arranged a meeting with Mr. Fairmuir three days hence, at which time the two men agreed they would come to a decision as to whether or not the value of the inventory should be written down. Mr. Adams was concerned as to what opinion he should issue on Fairmuir's financial statements of 1964.

Questions

1. What further steps should Mr. Adams take in preparing for the coming meeting with Mr. Fairmuir?

2. Putting yourself in Mr. Fairmuir's position, what steps would you take in preparing for the meeting? If Mr. Adams insists that the value of the inventory be written down, what would you do?

3. Do you think that the value of the inventory should be written down? If so, how should the adjustment be made?

4. If it were not written down, how would you, as auditor, phrase your opinion?

CASE 10–4.   OTTOMAN CAR COMPANY

Fred Ottoman was a fire truck salesman for many years, while Bill, his brother, worked as a book salesman for a major publishing house. Although they had done fairly well financially they wanted to "be their own boss," so they decided to go into business together.

They agreed that selling cars would be a good line for them to go into as both had been interested in sports cars for many years. Also, the small town in Ohio where they lived did not have any automobile dealerships. The nearest dealer, a Ford dealer, was some 30 miles away.

After some searching they chose a suitable site for their proposed operation. It was situated on a popular shopping street. A dilapidated apartment building which had been condemned by the local authorities stood on the site.

The brothers decided to incorporate the business. The services of a lawyer were obtained to draw up the legal papers and to handle all aspects of the execution of the incorporation. The fee for this service was $200, and each of the brothers paid half of it.

Fred purchased 1,800 shares of the company's stock for $18,000 and Bill purchased 500 shares for $5,000. The above-mentioned payments for legal services were considered part of these investments. Further purchases of the company's shares could be made only at the prevailing book value per share at the time of the purchase, and only if both parties agreed to the transaction. If either brother wished at any time to sell his shares back to the company, this transaction would also be conducted at the prevailing book value of the shares. The brothers also agreed that they should each receive salaries of $6,000 per year at all times during which they were engaged on the company's business on a full-time basis.

On November 1, 1963, with the aid of a $10,000 bank loan and $8,000 of the company's money, Fred purchased the property which had been selected. The same day, he left his job to devote his full attention to the new enterprise.

First, Fred arranged to have the old building demolished. A cursory examination revealed there was nothing of any significance that could be salvaged, except for some building stone. Mr. Mahoney, the wrecker, agreed to clear the site for $3,500, provided he could have the stone. Otherwise, he would want $4,500. Fred was convinced he could get a better price for the stone, so he instructed Mr. Mahoney to clear the site and store the stone in a corner of it. This work was started immediately, and completed before Christmas. Mr. Mahoney agreed to defer collection of payment until May 31, 1964.

In the meantime Fred got in touch with a large automobile manufacturer, National Cars, Inc., who had previously indicated interest in the projected dealership. Fred asked National for financial help to construct the buildings needed to carry on the business. National agreed to provide all the finances needed for the building through a loan repayable in 10 equal annual installments, provided Ottoman Cars sell only National models. The loan earned an interest rate of 4 percent per year, payable from April 1, 1964. The first repayment, including interest, would fall due on March 31, 1965.

On December 31, National Cars sent a check for $10,000 to get Ottoman Cars started. Fred deposited the check in the business' bank account. The remainder of the loan would be forthcoming when the building was completed.

Next, Fred arranged through a consulting architect for several construction companies to bid for the job. The lowest bidder was the Birkett and Snell Company. They agreed to construct the specified building for $31,500. On the advice of his architect, however, Fred Ottoman decided to accept the Holmes Bros. Construction Company bid of $35,000; the architect knew Birkett and Snell Company was less reliable than Holmes in meeting promised completion dates.

The construction was started immediately, Holmes promising completion by the end of March 1964. Progress payments on certificates from the architects were to be made at the end of January, the end of February, and the date of completion, in amounts of $10,000, $10,000, and $15,000.

During the winter period, Fred tried to obtain some orders for the 1964 model cars, which he planned to deliver directly to customers from National's warehouse in Cleveland. Fred had some success with the model he had recently bought for himself. Between January 1 and March 30, Fred sold 17 of this model at an average cash cost to Ottoman Cars of $2,250. Nothing was paid to National for these cars during the period. These 17 sales realized $45,900, whereof $14,500 represented trade-in allowances, $28,000 was in cash, and the rest was outstanding at March 30. Fred sold all the trade-in cars for $13,700 cash before March 30. Bill and Fred agreed that the latter should receive $10 for every new car sale as compensation for using his private car as a display model.

At the end of March, the building was completed. However, there was an additional charge of $600 for materials, which Ottoman had to pay according to the provisions of the building contract. At the same time, the architect's bill for $650 arrived.

Fred sent the progress payments to the builder as previously arranged, making the January payment with $10,000 of the company's money and the February payment with the National loan. On March 31, the last $15,000 progress payment and the $600 materials surcharge were paid. The $10,000 bank loan plus interest of $300 was repaid by check on March 30.

On March 30, Bill quit his job with the publishing house and joined Ottoman Cars on a full-time basis. At Bill's request, it was agreed that financial statements would be prepared, to allow the two brothers to see where they stood as at the end of March. National Cars, Inc. asked that a portion of the amount the dealership owed the manufacturers for cars be regarded as the payment due to the dealership under the building contract, and Fred accepted this arrangement on behalf of Ottoman Cars. The two brothers agreed that they would invite Mr. William Hurley, an accountant who was a mutual friend of theirs, to prepare the accounts.

Questions

1. As Mr. Hurley, prepare journal entries to record the events that have taken place in the business up to March 31, 1964.
2. From these journal entries, prepare a balance sheet as at March 31, 1964, and an income statement for the period to that date.
3. Based on your financial statements, what is the value of each brother's equity in the company?
4. Suppose that the stone salvaged from the building was sold on February 1, 1965, for $1,880 cash. How would you record the effect of this transaction?

CHAPTER 11

FINANCIAL STATEMENT
ANALYSIS

The amount of time that an analyst spends on a set of financial statements depends on the nature of his interest in the company. At one extreme, the investor who wants to see what has happened in one of the several companies in which he owns stock may do little more than compare current earnings per share with last year's earnings per share. At the other extreme, the banker who has made, or who is considering making, a sizable loan will use every scrap of information that he can find. This chapter describes the more common, but by no means all, of the devices that are used in financial statement analysis.

All analyses of accounting data involve comparisons. An absolute statement, such as "X Company earned $1 million profit" is, by itself, not useful. It becomes useful only when the $1 million is compared with something else. The comparison may be quite imprecise and intuitive. For example, if we know that X Company is an industrial giant with tens of thousands of employees, we know intuitively that $1 million profit is a poor showing because we have built up in our minds the impression that such companies should earn much more than that. Or, the comparison may be much more formal, explicit, and precise, as is the case when the $1 million profit this year is compared with last year's profit. In either case, it is the process of comparison that makes the figure meaningful.

In general terms, the process of analysis can be described as one of comparing what actually happened with a *standard. A standard is a measure of what should have happened under the circumstances prevailing.*

BUSINESS OBJECTIVES

In order to decide the types of comparisons that are useful, we need first to consider what business is all about—what its objectives are—for the comparisons are essentially intended to shed light on how well business is achieving its objectives. As a generalization, it may be said that *insofar as it can be measured quantitatively, the overall objective of a business is to earn a satisfactory return on the funds invested in it, consistent with maintaining a sound financial position.*[1] It should be noted that this statement is limited to facts that can be expressed numerically. Personal satisfaction, public responsibility, ethical considerations, and other nonmeasurable objectives may be important and must be taken into account wherever relevant in appraising the overall success of the enterprise.

The foregoing statement of objectives has two aspects: (1) earning a satisfactory return on its investment, and (2) maintaining a sound financial position. Each aspect is discussed briefly below.

Return on Investment

The fact that return on investment is the broadest measure of overall performance can be seen from Illustration 11–1, which shows how return on investment is calculated and relates it to the main categories of items appearing on the balance sheet and income statement. The assets side of a balance sheet shows the categories to which investors' funds are committed. A portion of the current assets is offset by current liabilities, and investors must furnish only the remainder, which is called *working capital.*[2] They must also furnish the funds for noncurrent assets.

The return-on-investment measure is used in two senses: (1) the return on shareholders' investment, in which "investment" means assets less all liabilities; and (2) the return on total investment, in which "investment" includes both the stockholders' investment and that of bondholders and other long-term creditors. Illustration 11–1 is based on the latter meaning.

Investors who commit their funds to an enterprise do so because they expect to earn a return on these funds. The diagram shows how a change in any single category affects this return. Thus, an increase in gross profit, or a decrease in expenses, or a decrease in income taxes, increases net income and hence increases return on investment IF these changes are not accompanied by an offsetting change in some other category. On the other hand, if an increase in gross profit is accompanied by a correspond-

---

[1] This statement is not consistent with the *profit maximization* assumption often made in economics. The techniques in this chapter are equally applicable under a profit maximization assumption, however, so there is no point in arguing here whether the profit maximization assumption is valid and useful. Discussion of this point is deferred to Chapter 18.

[2] Occasionally, "working capital" is taken to mean total current assets. This is of course confusing and is unnecessary since "total current assets" is a perfectly good term. In order to avoid any possibility of confusion, the term "net working capital" is sometimes used for the difference between current assets and current liabilities.

ing increase in working capital (as can happen, for example, when a growth in sales volume is accompanied by a corresponding increase in inventories and accounts receivable), there will be no change in the overall percent return. It is therefore important that the relationships among the various categories be studied; this is done by the use of ratios as described in the next section. Illustration 11–2 shows the average return on owners' equity for various industry classes. Note the great differences among industries.

Illustration 11–1

FACTORS AFFECTING RETURN

ON INVESTMENT

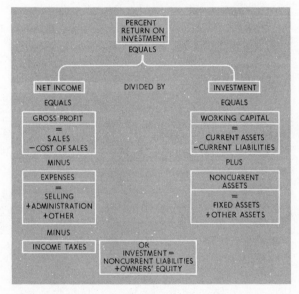

Sound Financial Position

In addition to desiring a satisfactory return, the investor expects that his capital will be protected from more than a normal amount of risk. The return on the *shareholders'* investment could be increased if a larger proportion of the investment came from low-cost, long-term liabilities and net income remained unchanged. This move, however, would increase the shareholders' risk of losing their investment, since the interest charges and principal repayments on the long-term liabilities are fixed obligations, and failure to make these payments when due could throw the company into bankruptcy. The degree of risk in a situation can be measured in part by the relative amounts of various types of liabilities

Illustration 11–2

RETURNS OF LEADING CORPORATIONS

	% Return on Equity		% Return on Sales	
	1967	*1968*	*1967*	*1968*
Dairy products	11.8	11.4	3.2	3.0
Meat packing	9.2	8.2	1.0	1.0
Other food products	12.3	12.5	4.0	4.1
Soft drinks	23.3	23.2	7.6	7.4
Distilling	10.5	9.5	4.7	4.3
Tobacco products	14.8	14.3	5.8	5.4
Textile products	8.8	9.6	3.6	3.7
Clothing and apparel	13.6	15.3	3.7	3.9
Shoes, leather, etc.	13.6	14.7	3.6	3.8
Rubber and allied products	10.8	12.7	4.1	4.7
Lumber and wood products	9.4	13.1	4.8	6.1
Paper and allied products	9.5	10.0	5.2	5.1
Printing and publishing	15.4	14.6	6.4	6.2
Chemical products	11.5	11.4	6.5	6.3
Drugs and medicines	20.3	20.0	9.8	9.5
Soap, cosmetics	19.4	18.7	6.7	6.6
Petroleum prod. and refining	12.8	12.9	9.1	9.0
Glass products	11.1	11.6	6.1	6.1
Other stone and clay products	7.3	8.7	4.8	5.3
Iron and steel	7.4	8.3	5.0	5.2
Nonferrous metals	11.4	11.0	7.2	6.6
Other metal products	13.8	13.3	5.1	4.9
Farm, constr, mat-hdlg, equip.	10.9	8.9	4.8	4.0
Office and computing equip.	17.8	19.1	8.3	8.5
Other machinery	14.7	13.4	5.5	5.2
Electr. equip. & electronics	15.4	14.2	4.5	4.3
Household appliances	14.7	15.0	4.6	4.7
Autos and trucks	12.0	16.6	4.9	5.8
Automotive parts	11.4	12.7	4.4	4.7
Aircraft and space	13.4	13.9	2.7	2.8
Instruments, photo goods, etc.	20.3	18.9	9.0	8.7
TOTAL MANUFACTURING	12.6	13.1	5.6	5.7
TOTAL MINING	16.2	15.1	12.6	12.6
TOTAL TRADE	13.2	13.5	2.5	2.5
Class I railroads	3.0	3.3	5.3	5.5
Common carrier trucking	15.7	19.1	3.2	3.6
Air transport	18.5	9.3	6.3	3.6
TOTAL TRANSPORTATION	5.4	4.9	5.6	4.8
TOTAL PUBLIC UTILITIES	11.0	10.5	13.9	13.0
TOTAL SERVICES	15.9	16.4	5.1	5.4
TOTAL FINANCE	6.0	5.6	..	..
GRAND TOTAL	10.6	10.6	5.9	5.8

Equity is stockholders' equity, i.e., the excess of total assets over total liabilities.

SOURCE: Adapted and condensed from First National City Bank *Monthly Economic Letter*, April 1969. Data are for 3,928 companies.

and of the funds available to discharge them, and this also involves the use of ratios.

SOME COMMON RATIOS

A *ratio* is simply one number expressed in terms of another. It is found by dividing one number, the base, into the other. A *percentage* is one kind of ratio, in which the base is taken as equaling 100 and the quotient is expressed as "per hundred" of the base.

Dozens of ratios can be computed from a single set of financial statements, but usually only a few are helpful in a given situation. Thus, although many frequently used ratios are described below, the best analytical procedure is not to compute all of them mechanically but rather to decide first which ratios might be relevant in the particular type of investigation being made and then to compute these, and only these, ratios.

Financial ratios can be grouped loosely into four categories: (1) tests of profitability, (2) tests of liquidity, (3) tests of solvency, and (4) overall ratios. The ratios listed under each category are illustrated by figures drawn from Illustrations 11–3 and 11–4, which show a simplified balance sheet and income statement for a hypothetical company.

Since the balance sheet figures refer to one instant of time while the income statement figures refer to events over a period of time, care must be taken in calculating ratios that use amounts from both statements. For many purposes, the income statement figure is best compared to the *average* of the balance sheet figures. In the examples below, such an average is necessarily computed as one half the sum of the amounts on the beginning and ending balance sheets. When other information is available, a more representative average is often preferable, such as the average of the 12 monthly balance sheet figures.

1. Tests of Profitability

Illustration 11–4 shows each of the items on the income statement expressed as a percentage of sales, which is a commonly used method of examining them. Usually, net sales is taken as 100 percent, as in the illustration. Of the percentages shown, gross profit (40 percent), the operating profit (14 percent), and net income, either before taxes (13.3 percent) or after taxes (6.7 percent), are perhaps the most important.

The *gross profit percentage* indicates the average mark-on or margin obtained on products sold. Since it is an average, it does not necessarily represent the mark-on on individual products, and these may differ widely from the average.

Illustration 11–3

ARLEN COMPANY

Balance Sheets
(in thousands of dollars)

	December 31	
ASSETS	1968	1967
Current Assets:		
Cash..	30	30
Accounts receivable............................	42	32
Less: Allowance for bad debts...................	2	2
Accounts receivable, net........................	40	30
Merchandise inventory..........................	60	50
Prepaid expenses..............................	10	10
Total Current Assets........................	140	120
Fixed Assets:		
Land...	30	30
Buildings and equipment........................	120	120
Less: Accumulated depreciation.................	70	60
Net buildings and equipment....................	50	60
Total Fixed Assets.........................	80	90
Other Assets:		
Goodwill and patents...........................	10	0
Total Assets...............................	230	210
EQUITIES		
Current Liabilities:		
Accounts payable..............................	30	25
Accrued wages and taxes.......................	10	10
Estimated income taxes payable.................	20	15
Total Current Liabilities....................	60	50
Fixed Liabilities:		
Mortgage bonds, 5 percent......................	40	40
Total Liabilities...........................	100	90
Shareholders' Equity:		
Common stock (5,000 shares outstanding).........	60	60
Retained earnings.............................	70	60
Total Shareholders' Equity...................	130	120
Total Equities.............................	230	210

Gross margin percentages vary widely among industries, but within an industry the percentages for individual companies tend to be similar.

The *net income percentage* is a measure of overall profitability. This measure is also referred to as the *return on sales* or the *profit percentage*. Some people, particularly critics of a given industry or company, treat this measure as if it were the most important single measure of performance. This is erroneous, because net income, considered by itself, does not take into account the assets employed to produce that income. The steel

Illustration 11–4

ARLEN COMPANY

Condensed Income Statement, 1968
(in thousands of dollars)

	Dollars	Percentage
Gross sales	303	101.0
Less: Returns and allowances	3	1.0
Net sales	300	100.0
Less: Cost of sales	180	60.0
Gross profit	120	40.0
Operating expenses	78	26.0
Operating profit	42	14.0
Interest	2	0.7
Income before taxes	40	13.3
Provision for income taxes	20	6.7
Net Income	20	6.7

industry, which is a favorite whipping boy, has a relatively high return on sales, but its investment is also high. The following example illustrates this point.

EXAMPLE: Company A operates a supermarket, and Company B operates a department store. Operating results of each are summarized below:

	A Super-market	B Department Store
Sales	$10,000,000	$10,000,000
Net income	200,000	1,000,000
Total investment	1,000,000	5,000,000
Return on sales	2%	10%
Return on investment	20%	20%

Supermarkets typically operate on a low gross margin, and therefore have a small profit on each dollar of sales, but they also have a much smaller investment per dollar of sales than do department stores. Thus an investor in Company A earns just as high a return on each dollar of his investment as an investor in Company B, even though Company A has a much smaller profit per dollar of sales.

2. Tests of Liquidity

Liquidity refers to the company's ability to meet its current obligations. The liquidity ratios therefore have to do with the size and relationships of current liabilities, which are the obligations soon coming due, and current assets, which presumably provide the source from which these obligations will be met. A company's financial position is not sound unless it has adequate liquidity. The ratios listed below help to answer the question: "Will the business probably be able to meet its obligations when they become due?"

CURRENT RATIO.

$$\frac{\text{Current Assets}}{\text{Current Liabilities}} = \frac{\$140,000}{\$60,000} = 2.3 \text{ Times, or } 2.3 \text{ to } 1.$$

In other words, current assets are 2.3 times current liabilities.

The current ratio is the most commonly used of all balance sheet ratios. It is not only a measure of the company's liquidity but also is a measure of the margin of safety that management maintains in order to allow for the inevitable unevenness in the flow of funds through the current asset and liability accounts. If this flow were absolutely smooth and uniform each day (so that, for example, money coming in from customers exactly equaled maturing obligations), the requirements for such a safety margin would be small. Since a company rarely can count on such an even flow, it needs a supply of liquid funds to be assured of being able to pay its bills when they come due. The current ratio indicates the size of this buffer.

In interpreting the current ratio, consideration of the proportion of various types of current assets is important. A company with a high percentage of its current assets in the form of cash is more liquid than one with a high percentage in inventory, even though the companies have the same current ratio.

ACID-TEST RATIO.

$$\frac{\text{Quick Assets}}{\text{Current Liabilities}} = \frac{\$70,000}{\$60,000} = 1.2 \text{ Times, or } 1.2 \text{ to } 1.$$

Quick assets include cash, temporary investments held in lieu of cash, and current accounts and notes receivable. Presumably, these items can be converted into cash quickly and at approximately their stated amounts, unlike inventory which is the principal current asset excluded. The acid-test ratio, or *quick ratio,* is therefore a measure of the extent to which liquid resources are immediately available to meet current obligations.

RECEIVABLES TO SALES.

$$\frac{\text{Receivables (Net)}}{\text{Net Sales}} = \frac{\$40,000}{\$300,000} = 13.3 \text{ Percent.}$$

If available, the base should be net *credit* sales, which is of course more closely related to accounts receivable than is total sales. Sometimes *average* accounts receivable ($35,000) is used as the numerator, but attention is more properly focused on the year-end figure. Receivables include trade accounts receivable plus trade notes receivable.

COLLECTION PERIOD.   This is derived from the preceding ratio:

Receivables to Sales × Days in the Period = Collection Period.
13.3%   ×   365   =   49 Days.

The collection period can be related roughly to the credit terms offered by the company. A rule of thumb is that the collection period should not exceed $1\frac{1}{3}$ times the regular payment period; that is, if the company's typical terms call for payment in 30 days, it is said that the average collection period should not exceed 40 days. Like all rules of thumb, this one has a great many exceptions. Changes in the ratio indicate changes in the company's credit policy or changes in its ability to collect its receivables.

INVENTORY TURNOVER.

$$\frac{\text{Cost of Sales}}{\text{Average Inventory}} = \frac{\$180,000}{\$55,000} = 3.3 \text{ Times.}$$

Inventory turnover is an indication of the velocity with which merchandise moves through the business. An increase in the absolute size of inventory, for example, may represent the additional stocks required by an expanding business, or it may represent an accumulation of merchandise because sales volume has recently declined. In the latter case, the inventory turnover will decrease. A decrease in the inventory turnover ratio may therefore be a significant danger signal.

If the cost of sales figure is not available, a turnover ratio may be computed using the sales figure instead. Such a ratio does not then show literally how many times the inventory turned over during the year because the numerator contains the profit margin while the denominator does not, and the two numbers therefore are not precisely comparable. Nevertheless, if profit margins remain roughly constant, a comparison of this ratio for several years may be useful.

3. Tests of Solvency

As liquidity refers to current obligations, *solvency* refers to a company's ability to meet the interest costs and repayment schedules associated with its long-term obligations.

EQUITY RATIOS. The division of equities among current liabilities, long-term liabilities, and owners' equity has an important bearing on solvency. These relationships are shown in the following condensed 1968 data of Arlen Company, derived from Illustration 11–3.

EQUITIES

	Percent
Current liabilities	26
Long-term liabilities	17
Equity capital	57
Total Equities	100

Of the ratios apparent in the above tabulation, the most important are those showing the relationship between *debt capital* and *equity capital*.

Debt capital is another name for liabilities. From the point of view of the company, debt capital is risky because if bondholders and other creditors are not paid promptly, they can take legal action to obtain payment which can, in extreme cases, force the company into bankruptcy. Equity capital is much less risky to the company because stockholders receive dividends only at the discretion of the directors.[3] Because the stockholders have less certainty of receiving dividends than the bondholders have of receiving interest, stockholders usually are unwilling to invest in a company unless they see a reasonable expectation of making a higher return than they could obtain as bondholders; that is, they would be unwilling to give up the relatively certain prospect of receiving 5 percent or 6 percent interest on bonds, unless the probable, but less certain, return on an equity investment were considerably higher, say 10 percent or more.

From the company's standpoint, the greater the proportion of its capital that is obtained from stockholders, the less worry the company has in meeting its fixed obligations; but in return for this lessened worry, the company must expect to pay a higher overall cost of obtaining its capital. Conversely, the more funds that are obtained from bonds, the more the company can *trade on the equity;* that is, it can use funds obtained at relatively low interest rates in the hopes of earning more on these funds for the stockholders. A company with a high proportion of bonds is said to be highly *leveraged.* The equity ratio shows the balance that the management of a particular company has struck between these forces.

Unfortunately, the equity ratio (often called the *equity/debt ratio* or the *capital/equity ratio* or simply the *debt ratio*) is defined in two quite different ways; the user must always be careful to ascertain which meaning is intended in a given situation. One definition includes the current liabilities, and the other excludes them. Including current liabilities, the equity/debt ratio for Arlen Company is 57 to 43, or 1.3 to 1. Excluding current liabilities, the corresponding figures are 57 to 17, or 3.4 to 1. This difference in meaning is confusing in general, but in particular situations it is less so, because a company or an industry usually settles on one meaning or the other, and those who use the ratios then have a common basis of understanding.

Times Interest Earned.

$$\frac{\text{Operating Profit}}{\text{Bond Interest}} = \frac{\$42,000}{\$2,000} = 21 \text{ Times.}$$

The numerator of this ratio is the amount of earnings available to meet the fixed obligation of bond interest. In the example, interest requirements

---

[3] Note that "risk" is here viewed from the standpoint of the company. From the standpoint of investors, the opposite view prevails. Thus bondholders have a relatively low risk of receiving their payments, and stockholders have a relatively high risk. From this latter standpoint, equity capital is called "risk capital."

are said to be *covered* 21 times. This ratio is a measure of the level to which income can decline without impairing the company's ability to meet interest payments on its fixed liabilities. Income is taken before income taxes because if income declined, income taxes would decline proportionately. The ratio implies that net income is equivalent to additional cash, which is not necessarily the case, of course.

If preferred stock is outstanding, a similar coverage ratio can be computed for the preferred stock dividends, but here the numerator is income after taxes and after interest charges ($20,000).

A company may have fixed obligations in addition to its interest payments, as, for example, when it has rental commitments on leased property. In such a case coverage is properly computed by adding these other obligations to the amount of interest. The ratio is then labeled "Times Fixed Charges Earned."

4. Overall Measures

RETURN ON INVESTMENT. This is the grand, overall measure described earlier in this chapter. It can be expressed in several ways. From the viewpoint of the shareholders, it is the *return on shareholders' investment:*

$$\frac{\text{Net Income}}{\text{Average Shareholders' Equity}} = \frac{\$20,000}{\$125,000} = 16 \text{ Percent.}$$

In computing the average shareholders' equity, a simple average of the beginning and ending figures should not be used if additional equity funds were obtained and put to use at other than the middle of the year. New funds obtained near the end of the year, for example, might well be excluded from the denominator of the fraction because the income in the numerator did not arise from the use of these funds.

A variation of the above, called the return on *tangible net worth*, eliminates intangible assets from the shareholders' equity, thus:

$$\frac{\text{Net Income}}{\text{Avg. Net Worth} - \text{Avg. Intangibles}} = \frac{\$20,000}{\$125,000 - \$5,000} = 16.7 \text{ Percent.}$$

Return on total investment looks at income in relation to the total of the permanent funds invested in the enterprise. These permanent funds consist of shareholders' equity plus noncurrent liabilities; or the same figure may be found by subtracting current liabilities from total assets. The earnings on these funds are usually taken as net income before income taxes, plus interest on noncurrent liabilities. The ratio is as follows:

$$\frac{\text{Operating Profit}}{\text{Average Equity} + \text{Average Fixed}} = \frac{\$42,000}{\$125,000 + \$40,000} = 25.5 \text{ Percent.}$$
$$\text{Capital} \qquad \text{Liabilities}$$

If the interest expense on the income statement included interest on current borrowings as well as bond interest, the interest on current liabilities would be subtracted from operating profit. Sometimes an after-tax figure is used.

The return-on-total-investment ratio is a measure of how well management has used all the permanent funds entrusted to the business. Or, put another way, this ratio is intended to measure the earning power of the net assets (net working capital plus other assets) of the business.

For many purposes, especially for comparing one division of a company with another division, return on investment is best figured on the basis of *gross assets*, which means working capital plus fixed assets at cost but with no deduction for accumulated depreciation.

Return on investment can be calculated in another manner which, although it is longer and gives the same result, is often more illuminating. Two subsidiary ratios, *investment turnover* and *operating profit on sales*, are calculated first. Investment turnover is as follows:

$$\frac{\text{Sales}}{\text{Equity Capital} + \text{Fixed Liabilities}} = \frac{\$300,000}{\$125,000 + \$40,000} = 1.82 \text{ Times.}$$

The operating profit ratio, 14.0 percent, is given on Illustration 11–4. Then:

$$\text{Investment Turnover} \times \text{Op. Profit Ratio} = \text{Return on Investment.}$$
$$1.82 \text{ Times} \quad \times \quad 14.0 \text{ Percent} = \quad 25.5 \text{ Percent.}$$

Many consider this to be the most useful way of looking at the overall performance of a business. It shows that performance can be improved either by generating more sales volume per dollar of capital employed or by increasing the profit margin on each sales dollar generated. It shows that a supermarket earning 2 percent on sales may be doing as good a job for its investors as a department store earning 10 percent on sales when the supermarket has an investment turnover of 10 and the department store a turnover of 2.

MARKET TESTS.   Persons who study the financial statements of companies as a basis for deciding where to invest their funds may use any of a number of other ratios in addition to those already listed. Some of these are mentioned below.

Earnings per share:

$$\frac{\text{Net Income}}{\text{Shares Outstanding}} = \frac{\$20,000}{5,000} = \$4 \text{ per Share.}$$

The calculation is more complicated when the company has preferred stock or convertible bonds, and these complications were discussed on page 210. Earnings per share is usually the most important single ratio for the investor. He watches changes in this ratio from year to year and also uses it, as explained below, to appraise the market price of the stock.

Price-earnings ratio:

The price-earnings ratio is based on the average market price of the stock. Assuming the market price for Arlen Company's stock is $36, the ratio is as follows:

$$\frac{\text{Market Price per Share}}{\text{Earnings per Share}} = \frac{\$36}{\$4} = 9 \text{ to } 1.$$

Turning this ratio upside down gives the *capitalization rate*, the rate at which the stock market is apparently capitalizing the value of current earnings:

$$\frac{\text{Earnings per Share}}{\text{Market Price per Share}} = \frac{\$4}{\$36} = 11 \text{ Percent.}$$

The price-earnings ratio is influenced heavily by how rapidly the company is growing and by its policy with respect to retained earnings, as well as, of course, the market's overall judgment as to the company's soundness. A P/E ratio as low as 10 to 1 is found for stable companies that pay out most of their income as dividends. The ratio can be as high as 25 to 1, and occasionally as high as 100 to 1, for "glamour" companies, those that are growing rapidly, that are expected to continue this growth, and that retain most of their net income.

The average price-earnings ratio of a selection of industrial stocks listed on the New York Stock Exchange was 15:1 in 1968, and it ranged from 14:1 to 21:1 in the period 1957 to 1968.

Yield:

The yield, or more properly the *dividend yield*, is based on dividends declared during the year. Assuming the Arlen Company declares a $2 dividend, the ratio is as follows:

$$\frac{\text{Dividends per Share}}{\text{Price per Share}} = \frac{\$2}{\$36} = 5.6 \text{ Percent.}$$

The yield on stocks is often compared with the yield, or interest, on bonds, but such a comparison is not valid. This is because the earnings of bondholders consist entirely of their interest, whereas the earnings of stockholders consist not only of their dividends, but also of retained earnings. Although stockholders have no guarantee that they will receive retained earnings, the fact that part of the net income has been retained in the business and presumably invested in income-producing assets should enhance the value of the stockholders' investment.

DIFFICULTIES IN MAKING COMPARISONS

Reasonably accurate reports of actual performance often can be obtained (although the problems involved in obtaining them may be by no means trivial). Finding an adequate standard against which these actuals can be measured, however, is often a perplexing and difficult matter.

Some of the problems are described below. Financial statement analysis is used as an example, but the same problems arise in analyzing other types of quantitative data. When a person says that performance is "good" or "poor," "better" or "worse," he is, either implicitly or explicitly, comparing actual performance to some standard that he believes is relevant.

1. Deciding on the Proper Basis for Comparison

Subject only to minor qualifications, a boy who runs a mile in six minutes (or, expressed as a rate, 10 miles per hour) is a better miler than a boy who runs a mile in seven minutes. In business, there are many situations in which one cannot tell whether a higher number represents better performance than a lower number, or whether it represents poorer performance.

A high current ratio is by no means necessarily better than a low current ratio. For example, the current ratio for the Arlen Company on December 31, 1968, was 2.3 to 1. Suppose that $40,000 of the current liabilities came due the very next day and that the company in fact paid these liabilities, using every dollar of its available cash and liquidating other current assets as well. A balance sheet prepared subsequent to this transaction would show $100,000 of current assets and $20,000 of current liabilities, and the current ratio would accordingly be 5 to 1, which is more than double the ratio of the previous day. Yet one could scarcely say that a company that had used up all its cash was in an improved financial condition. Or, conversely, consider what happens when a company expands, as illustrated by the Arlen Company balance sheet at the end of 1968 compared with its balance sheet for the end of 1967. Current assets have increased by $20,000, and current liabilities have increased by only $10,000; the current ratio has dropped from 2.4:1 to 2.3:1. The decrease may indicate no worsening of the company's liquid position at all; rather, it may reflect the result of a well-carried-out expansion program.

In some comparisons the direction of change that represents "good" or "better" is reasonably apparent. Generally, a high net profit percentage is better than a low one, and a high return on investment is better than a low one. Even these statements have many qualifications, however.

Many standards can usefully be thought of as a *quality range* rather than as a single number. When actual performance is within this range, it may be regarded as satisfactory. When it begins to go outside the range, *in either direction,* there is an indication of an unsatisfactory situation. For a certain company, the current ratio may be considered satisfactory if it is within the range 2:1 to 3:1. Below 2:1, there is the danger of being unable to meet maturing obligations. Above 3:1, there is an indication that funds are being left idle rather than being efficiently employed. As another example, a too-high profit ratio may indicate that the company is only "skimming the cream" off the market; a deeper penetration may increase sales and total return on investment even if the ratio of profit to sales is reduced.

2. Differences in the Situations Being Compared

No reasonable person would expect a 9-year-old boy to run as fast as a 19-year-old athlete; in judging the boy's performance, we attempt to compare his speed with that of other boys of the same age and with similar training. Differences in the factors that affect one company's performance this year as compared with those that affect the same company's performance last year, or the performance of another company, are complex and difficult to evaluate. Nevertheless, some attempt must be made to allow for these differences. In general, this task is least difficult when all the figures being compared pertain to the same company (although even here changes in size, in the functions performed by the company, in outside influences, and so on, may make comparisons of tenuous validity). The task is more difficult when attempting to compare one company with another, even if they are both of the same size and in the same industry, and it becomes exceedingly difficult if the two companies are in different industries or if they are of substantially different size.

3. Changes in the Dollar Measuring Stick

Accounting figures are expressed in historical dollars. A change in the value of a dollar, that is, a change in price levels, may therefore seriously lessen the validity of comparisons of ratios computed for different time periods. Also, a ratio whose numerator and denominator are expressed in different kinds of dollars may have no useful meaning.

The fact that asset amounts are stated as unexpired historical dollar costs causes particular difficulty in making comparisons of ratios calculated from such amounts. Two companies, for example, might have facilities that are physically identical in all respects except age, and they might operate exactly the same way and earn exactly the same net income. If, however, the buildings and equipment of one company had been purchased at a time when prices were low or if they had been almost fully depreciated, and if the buildings and equipment of the other company had been purchased at a time of higher prices or if they were relatively new, then the return-on-investment ratio for the company that carried its assets at a low book value would be much higher than the ratio for the other company.

4. Differences in Definition

The terms "one mile" and "six minutes" used to measure the runner are precisely defined and easily measured, but the individual elements making up such terms as "current assets" and "current liabilities" are by no means precisely defined, and there is considerable diversity in practice as to how they should be measured. Some of the many differences have been described in earlier chapters.

Similar differences affect the standards against which actual performance is compared. For example, the following are estimates of the "profits as a percent of sales of U.S. manufacturing companies in 1960" as reported by various agencies:[4]

	Percent
First National City Bank	5.5
Federal Trade Commission—SEC	4.5
Department of Commerce	3.3
Internal Revenue Service	2.7

The highest figure is twice as high as the lowest. The differences result both from differences in the way "profits" are defined and from differences in the data collected.

5. Hidden Short-Run Changes

A balance sheet may not reflect the average or typical situation. A balance sheet is prepared as of one moment of time, and it tells nothing about short-term fluctuations in assets and equities that have occurred within the period bounded by the two balance sheet dates. Many department stores, for example, end their fiscal year and publish annual balance sheets as of January 31. By that date, Christmas inventories have been sold out and many of the Christmas receivables have been paid, but Easter merchandise has not started to arrive and payables for this merchandise have not yet been generated. Current assets (other than cash) and current liabilities as reported on the January 31 balance sheet are therefore likely to be lower than at other times of the year; as a result, ratios such as merchandise turnover and the average collection period may be distorted, and other ratios may not be representative of the situation at other seasons. A company that is analyzing its own data can study the seasonal movements by using monthly, rather than annual, balance sheets, but these are ordinarily not available to the outsider.

The analyst should also recognize that companies have been known to

---

[4] Estimated from charts in *First National City Bank Letter*, January 1963, which gives some explanation of the differences.

take deliberate steps to "clean up" their balance sheets. They may, for example, pay off loans just before the end of the year, which usually increases the current ratio; they then borrow again early in the next year. Such transactions, which are called *window dressing*, may not be discernible on the balance sheet.

6. The Past as an Indication of the Future

Financial statements are historical documents, and financial ratios show relationships that have existed in the past. The analyst is, of course, interested in what is happening now and what is likely to happen in the future rather than what did happen in the past. Often the analyst has no choice but to rely on past data as an indication of the current situation, but he should not be misled into believing that the historical ratios necessarily reflect current conditions, and much less that they reflect future conditions.

POSSIBLE BASES FOR COMPARISON

There are four types of standards against which an actual figure can be compared: (1) experience; (2) a goal; (3) a historical figure; and (4) an external figure, that is, a figure for performance in another company, or other companies.

1. Experience

The analyst gradually builds up his own idea as to what constitutes "good" or "poor" performance. One of the important advantages that an experienced analyst has over inexperienced ones is that he possesses a feeling for what are "right" relationships in a given situation, developed on the basis of his knowledge about similar situations. (Of course, if he is not competent, his feeling may well be incorrect). These subjective standards of a competent analyst are more important than standards based on mechanical comparisons.

2. Goals

Many companies prepare *budgets*, which show *what performance is expected to be under the circumstances prevailing*. If actual performance corresponds with budgeted performance, there is a reasonable inference that the performance is good. There are two important qualifications that affect this inference, however. First, the budgeted figures may not have been set very carefully in the first instance, and the comparison can of course be no more valid than the goal figures themselves. Secondly, the goals were necessarily set on the basis of certain assumptions as to the conditions that would be prevailing during the period, and if these assumptions turn out to be incorrect, the goal figures are also incorrect as a measure of results "under the circumstances prevailing." If, because of a recession or other economic phenomenon outside the control of management, profits are lower than the amount budgeted, it cannot fairly be said that the difference between actual and budgeted profit indicates "poor" performance. Nevertheless, the budget is a type of standard that has fewer inherent difficulties than either the historical standards or the external standards.

3. Historical Standards

A comparison of current performance with past figures for the same company usually does not run into the problem of differences in accounting practice. If practices have changed, the change is presumably known to the analyst. Moreover, the analyst can also recollect, or find out from supplementary data, some of the circumstances that have changed between the two periods and thus allow for these changes in making his comparison. At best, however, a comparison between a current figure and a historical figure in the same company can show only that the current period is "better" or "worse" than the past. In many cases this does not provide a sound basis for judgment, for the historical figure may not have represented an acceptable standard. If a company increases its return on investment from 1 percent to 2 percent, it has improved, but it nevertheless is not doing very well.

4. External Standards

When one company is compared with another, the environmental and accounting differences affecting the two sets of figures may raise serious problems of comparability. If, however, the analyst is able to allow for these differences, even approximately, he obtains an outside check on performance that has the advantage, over a standard derived from internal sources, of being independently arrived at. Moreover, the two companies may well have been affected by the same set of economic conditions, so this important cause of noncomparability may not be operating.

Corporations whose stock is traded on organized security exchanges file annual reports with the U.S. Securities and Exchange Commission, and these "Form 10-K" reports are likely to be more useful for comparisons than the annual reports sent to shareholders, both because the SEC prescribes a uniform format and terminology and because the 10-K reports usually contain more detailed information than reports to shareholders.

Many sources contain *average ratios* for groups of companies in the same industry or of similar size. Perhaps the best known are those published by Dun & Bradstreet, Inc. For each of 125 industry groups, the following ratios are published (starred items have been described above; the derivation of the others should be apparent):

*Current ratio.
*Net profit as a percentage of net sales.
*Return on tangible net worth.
 Net profit as a percentage of net working capital.
*Net sales as a percentage of tangible net worth.
 Net sales as a percentage of net working capital.
*Collection period.
*Net sales to inventory.
 Fixed assets to tangible net worth.
 Current debt to tangible net worth.
*Equity ratio.
 Inventory to net working capital.
 Current liabilities to inventory.
 Funded debt to net working capital.

Ratios are also prepared by Robert Morris Associates for their members. A variety of ratios will also be found in *Moody's Manual of Investments, Standard and Poor's Corporation Records,* and other publications prepared for investors.

Standard and Poor's Corporation has available a COMPUSTAT service which consists of magnetic tapes containing pertinent financial and statistical information for 1,800 industrial, 100 utility, and 200 insurance companies in the United States, and 350 industrial companies in Canada. The information is available on an annual basis for the past 7 to 20 years, depending on the file being used. The financial information consists of 19 balance sheet items, 22 income statement items, 19 additional statistical items including stock prices, dividends, and a variety of ratios computed from the above, etc. All companies are grouped and coded by industry classifications.

Use of these industrywide ratios involves all the difficulties of using ratios derived from one other company plus the special problems that arise when the figures for several companies are thrown together into a single average. Nevertheless, they may give some worthwhile impressions about the average situation in an industry.

Many trade associations and other groups collect and publish figures for the companies in an industry. In some instances, the association prescribes in detail the accounting definitions and concepts to be used in reporting these figures, and the resulting figures are therefore much more comparable than those compiled by the sources mentioned above, which must use the basic data in whatever form the company chooses to report it.

USE OF COMPARISONS

The principal value of an analysis of financial statement information is that it suggests questions that need to be answered; such an analysis rarely provides the answers. An unfavorable difference between actual performance and whatever standard is used, if it is large, indicates that something *may be* wrong, and this leads to an investigation. Even when the analysis indicates strongly that something *is* wrong (as when one company's profits have declined while those of comparable companies have increased), the analysis rarely shows what the *cause* of the difficulty is. Nevertheless, the ability to pick from the thousands of questions that *might* be asked those few that are really worth asking is an important one.

It is well to keep in mind the basic relationships shown in Illustration 11–1, or some variation of these applicable to the situation being analyzed. The only number that encompasses all these relationships is a return-on-investment ratio. A change in any less inclusive ratio may be misleading as an indication of better or worse performance unless possible compensating changes in factors not covered by the ratio are taken into account. An increase in dollars of net income indicates improved performance only if there was no offsetting increase in the investment required. An increase in the net profit ratio indicates improved performance only if there was no offsetting decrease in sales volume or increase in investment. An increase in the gross profit percentage indicates improved performance only if there was no offsetting decrease in sales volume, increase in investment, or increase in expenses.

In short, the use of any ratio other than return on investment, taken by itself, implies that all other things are equal. This *ceteris paribus* condition ordinarily does not prevail, and the validity of comparisons is lessened to the extent that it does not. Yet the return-on-investment ratio is so broad that it does not give a clue as to which of the underlying factors may be responsible for changes in it. It is to find these factors, which if unfavorable indicate possible trouble areas, that the subsidiary ratios of profitability are used. Furthermore, the return-on-investment ratio tells nothing about the financial condition of the company; liquidity and solvency ratios are necessary for this purpose.

In addition to, or in place of, the simple ratio of one number to another, many businessmen develop a more complicated set of interrelationships that they find useful in isolating the key factors that affect good performance. An automobile dealer may say: "If the gross profit on service and parts sales is large enough to cover total general and administrative expenses, and if we break even on used car sales, then we will earn an adequate profit for the whole business from the gross margin less selling costs on new car sales." Usually, there is no way of demonstrating that these relationships are logically correct—there is no logical reason why gross profit on one part of the automobile dealer's business should just equal general and administrative costs for the whole business—but the fact is that they do work out.

SUMMARY

The figures on financial statements are usually most useful for analytical purposes when they are expressed in relative terms in the form of ratios and percentages. Although a great many ratios can be calculated, only a few are ordinarily necessary in connection with a given problem.

The essential task is to find a standard or norm with which actual performance can be compared. In general, there are four types of standards: (1) subjective standards derived from the analyst's experience; (2) goals, or budgets, set in advance of the period under review; (3) historical figures, showing performance of the same company in the past; and (4) the performance of other companies, as shown by their financial statements, or by averages compiled from the financial statements of a number of companies. None of these is perfect, but a rough allowance for the factors that cause noncomparability often can be made.

The comparison may then suggest important questions that need to be investigated; it rarely indicates answers to the questions.

SUGGESTIONS FOR FURTHER READING

FOULKE, ROY A. *Practical Financial Statement Analysis*. 6th ed.; New York: McGraw-Hill Book Co., Inc., 1968.

GRAHAM, BENJAMIN; DAVID L. DODD; and SIDNEY COTTLE. *Security Analysis: Principles and Technique*. 4th ed.; New York: McGraw-Hill Book Co., Inc., 1963.

KENNEDY, RALPH DALE, and STEWART YARDWOOD MCMULLEN. *Financial Statements: Form, Analysis, and Interpretation*. 4th ed.; Homewood, Ill.: Richard D. Irwin, Inc., 1962.

CASES

CASE 11-1. SWIFT AND COMPANY

Exhibits 1 and 2 show financial statements for Swift and Company. Exhibit 3 gives financial ratios for this company and three other meat packers.

Exhibit 1

SWIFT AND COMPANY

Income Statements

	October 28, 1967		October 28, 1966	
Sales and service revenues....	$2,839,790,701	100.00%	$2,974,280,034	100.00%
Cost of goods sold..........	2,606,920,996	91.80	2,764,496,597	92.95
Gross profit...............	$ 232,869,705	8.20%	$ 209,783,437	7.05%
Operating expenses:				
Selling and administration...	$ 177,887,014	6.26%	$ 170,770,256	5.74%
Loss on devaluation of foreign currency..........	896,426	0.03	......	
Total operating expenses.	$ 178,783,440	6.29%	$ 170,770,256	5.74%
Operating profit............	$ 54,086,265	1.91%	$ 39,013,181	1.31%
Interest charges............	$ 9,308,138	0.33%	$ 6,774,728	0.23%
Net income before taxes......	$ 44,778,127	1.58%	$ 32,238,453	1.08%
Taxes on income............	18,120,533	0.64	12,874,354	0.43
Special provision for cost of closing plant.............	......		15,000,000	0.50
Net Earnings after Tax and Special Provision..........	$ 26,657,594	0.94%	$ 4,364,099	0.15%

Additional Information for 1967

Average capital stock outstanding.............12,117,000 shares
Price range of stock.........................36⅝–23⅝
Dividends declared.........................$1.10

314

Exhibit 2

SWIFT AND COMPANY

Consolidated Balance Sheet

	Oct. 28, 1967		*Oct. 28, 1966*	
ASSETS				
Current Assets:				
Cash and marketable securities.	$ 19,557,999	2%	$ 28,953,583	4%
Accounts receivable..........	147,739,357	19	156,085,356	22
Inventories................	216,436,318	29	205,488,108	29
Prepaid items..............	4,705,405	1	4,099,986	1
Total Current Assets......	$388,439,079	51%	$394,627,033	56%
Investments and other assets....	$ 29,303,608	4%	$ 26,580,267	4%
Fixed Assets:				
Property, plant and equipment.	$633,733,167	83%	$576,377,307	81%
Less: Accumulated depreciation.................	(297,776,722)	(139)	(289,567,544)	(41)
Net Fixed Assets.........	$335,956,445	44%	$286,809,763	40%
Excess of investment over equity in net assets of business acquired (not being amortized)...	$ 4,098,234	1%	......	0%
Total Assets...........	$757,797,366	100%	$708,017,063	100%
LIABILITIES				
Current Liabilities:				
Notes payable.............	$ 49,268,179	7%	$ 44,864,539	6%
Accounts payable and accrued liabilities................	94,246,457	12	82,296,907	12
Income taxes..............	6,564,185	1	4,360,744	1
Provision for replacement of Lifo inventories..........	......		2,845,403	0
Current portion of long-term debt...................	8,292,616	1	8,119,940	1
Total Current Liabilities....	$158,371,437	21%	$142,487,533	20%
Long-term debt..............	$155,832,758	20%	$135,680,375	19%
Reserve for costs of closing plants.	$ 10,583,993	1%	$ 14,405,080	2%
Deferred income taxes........	$ 28,495,134	4%	$ 24,266,755	4%
Shareholders' Equities:				
Capital stock..............	$153,063,025	20%	$153,063,025	22%
Accumulated earnings........	253,848,981	34	240,534,508	34
Less: Treasury stock......	(2,397,962)	(0)	(2,420,218)	0
Total Shareholders' Equities.	$404,514,044	54%	$391,177,315	55%
Total Liabilities........	$757,797,366	100%	$708,017,063	100%

Exhibit 3

COMPARATIVE RATIOS IN THE MEAT-PACKING INDUSTRY

	1957	*1965*	*1966*	*1967*
Gross Profit as a Percent of Sales:				
Swift	8.2	8.2	7.1	...
Armour	8.8	11.0	11.2	11.8
Cudahy	5.7	3.9	3.6	4.7
Rath	2.2	0.04	7.7	9.6
Net Income as a Percent of Sales:				
Swift	0.53	0.60	0.15	...
Armour	0.73	0.89	0.09	1.02
Cudahy	0.61	(4.75)	0.21	0.90
Rath	0.45	(1.12)	(3.08)	(.90)
Current Ratio:				
Swift	2.63	3.54	2.75	...
Armour	3.30	3.72	3.50	3.29
Cudahy	2.05	1.21	1.24	1.50
Rath	2.58	1.66	1.06	1.16
Acid-Test Ratio:				
Swift	1.08	1.69	1.32	...
Armour	1.36	1.95	1.69	1.58
Cudahy	0.82	0.56	0.58	0.66
Rath	1.45	0.92	0.67	0.70
Receivables as a Percent of Sales:				
Swift	3.99	5.22	5.28	...
Armour	4.26	7.89	7.38	7.75
Cudahy	3.05	4.07	3.75	3.50
Rath	3.72	4.49	4.47	4.31
Average Collection Period in Days:				
Swift	14.6	19.1	19.3	...
Armour	15.6	28.7	26.9	28.2
Cudahy	11.2	14.8	13.7	12.8
Rath	13.6	16.4	16.3	15.8
Inventory Turnover (Based upon Sales):				
Swift	14.9	14.3	15.4	...
Armour	13.7	11.0	12.4	10.6
Cudahy	16.6	17.2	21.5	19.2
Rath	23.2	21.8	25.7	21.7
Equity as a Percent of Total Assets:				
Swift	69.0	65.6	55.3	...
Armour	47.0	55.1	49.4	50.0
Cudahy	55.2	32.8	41.0	48.9
Rath	56.2	50.6	26.0	24.0
Number of Times Interest Earned:				
Swift	5.3	6.6	5.7	...
Armour	1.4	6.0	5.0	4.1
Cudahy	3.2	def	1.5	3.0
Rath	2.8	def	def	def
Return on Investment:				
Swift	3.6	4.0	1.2	...
Armour	1.3	5.2	0.6	6.5
Cudahy	6.0	def	4.1	13.6
Rath	4.5	def	def	def

Exhibit 3 (*Continued*)

	1957	*1965*	*1966*	*1967*
Return on Total Assets:				
Swift..............................	2.5	2.6	0.6	...
Armour............................	0.8	3.5	0.3	3.2
Cudahy...........................	3.3	def	1.7	6.6
Rath..............................	2.5	def	def	def
Investment Turnover:				
Swift..............................	6.0	5.2	5.6	...
Armour............................	5.2	3.9	4.0	3.8
Cudahy...........................	7.6	19.9	18.5	13.6
Rath..............................	7.5	14.0	14.4	11.2
Earnings per Share:				
Swift..............................	2.26	2.71	1.60	...
Armour............................	0.72	2.86	0.08	2.61
Cudahy...........................	0.61	(9.45)	0.20	1.55
Rath..............................	1.29	(3.13)	(9.17)	(2.13)
*Price Earnings Ratio:**				
Swift..............................	15.2	20.1	14.7	...
Armour............................	18.8	15.4	467.0	14.5
Cudahy...........................	13.5	def	39.4	7.7
Rath..............................	17.1	def	def	def
*Capitalization Rate:**				
Swift..............................	6.5	5.0	3.3	...
Armour............................	5.3	6.4	0.2	7.2
Cudahy...........................	7.3	def	2.5	12.9
Rath..............................	5.8	Nil	Nil	Nil
*Dividend Yields:**				
Swift..............................	6.5	3.6	4.2	...
Armour............................	Nil	3.1	4.2	4.4
Cudahy...........................	Nil	Nil	Nil	Nil
Rath..............................	3.1	Nil	Nil	Nil

* In these ratios the market price was calculated on average of year's high and low.

Questions

1. Compute and fill in the 1967 ratios for Swift and Company.
2. What significant information about Swift can be learned from those data?

CASE 11–2. WESTERN PRINTERS LTD.

Western Printers Ltd. had operated a commercial printing business in Vancouver since 1926, when it was founded by Mr. P. R. Robson. Mr. Robson suffered a heart attack in July, 1961, and retired from active interest in the business, delegating complete responsibility to Phil Grange, who had joined the company in 1955. Mr. Robson died early in 1965. He willed the majority interest in the company to his son Barry, currently completing his final year of philosophy at a university. Barry has ap-

Exhibit 1

COMPARISON WESTERN PRINTERS LTD. TO INDUSTRY

Condensed Balance Sheets as of December 31

	Western Printers Ltd. (*in thousands*)		Total Industry (*in millions*)	
	1963	*1964*	*1963*	*1964*
ASSETS				
Current Assets:				
Cash...................................	$ 24	$ 30	$ 11	$ 7
Temporary investments (at market value).......	9	11	9	9
Accounts receivable.........................	30	34	40	36
Inventory.................................	20	26	24	29
Total Current Assets.....................	$ 83	$101	$ 84	$ 81
Land.......................................	3	3	5	4
Buildings and equipment......................	$109	$111	$122	$136
Less: Accumulated depreciation...............	56	64	66	74
	$ 53	$ 47	$ 56	$ 62
Total Assets...........................	$139	$151	$145	$147
EQUITIES				
Current Liabilities:				
Bank loan...............................	$ 18	$ 18	$ 11	$ 9
Accounts payable.........................	7	7	16	18
Due to finance companies..................	14	18	3	1
Taxes payable............................	4	4	5	5
Total Current Liabilities....................	$ 43	$ 47	$ 35	$ 33
Mortgages.................................	..	..	14	12
	$ 43	$ 47	$ 49	$ 45
Shareholders' Equity:				
Capital stock.............................	$ 30	$ 30	$ 32	$ 32
Retained earnings.........................	66	74	64	70
Total Shareholders' Equity.................	$ 96	$104	$ 96	$102
Total Equities...........................	$139	$151	$145	$147

Income Statement

	Western	Industry
Sales...	$212.2	$237.5
Cost of sales..	141.1	160.6
Gross profit...	$ 71.1	$ 76.9
Selling and administrative expenses............................	53.3	61.1
Operating income..	$ 17.8	$ 15.8
Interest paid..	$ 3.1	$ 1.5
Less: Interest and dividends received.........................	0.3	0.6
Net interest expenses..................................	$ 2.8	$ 0.9
Net income before income tax.............................	$ 15.0	$ 14.9
Income tax...	4.4	4.4
Net income...	$ 10.6	$ 10.5
Dividends..	2.7	4.4
Additions to Retained Earnings..............................	$ 7.9	$ 6.1

proached you to advise him whether Mr. Grange has been performing in a competent fashion and should be retained, or whether the company should look for a replacement.

Barry has condensed financial statements of the company for the past few years with him, and for the same period, comparative data for the printing industry. The financial statements for 1964 presented in Exhibit 1 are believed to be representative of the financial statements of both the company and the industry for the past few years.

Questions

1. From the information available, advise Barry whether he should keep the present manager of the company, look for a replacement, or take some other action.
2. List the most important additional bits of financial information that you feel are necessary to confirm these impressions.

CASE 11–3.   CONSOLIDATED CHEMICAL LTD.

The president of Consolidated Chemical Ltd., a Canadian subsidiary of an American company, was presented with the following report of the Nordstrand Division for the first quarter of 1965:

(thousands of dollars)

	1965		1964	
Cash	$ 151	14.8%	$ 153	12.4%
Accounts receivable	158	15.5	307	24.8
Inventories	189	18.5	258	20.8
	$ 498	48.8%	$ 718	58.0%
Plant and equipment cost	$ 922	90.5%	922	74.7%
Less: Accumulated depreciation	402	39.5	405	32.8
Net book value	$ 520	51.0%	$ 517	41.9%
	$1,018	100.0%*	$1,235	100.0%*
Sales	$ 975	100.0%	$1,020	100.0%
Cost of sales	$ 583	59.7%	$ 591	57.9%
Selling expenses	189	19.3	212	20.7
Delivery expenses	102	10.4	112	10.9
Admin. expenses	52	5.3	51	5.0
Total expenses	$ 926	94.7%	$ 966	94.7%
Contribution to Corporate Costs and Profit	$ 49	5.0%*	$ 54	5.3%
Depreciation included in the above	$ 73	7.4%	$ 76	7.5%

* Detail may not add to total because of rounding.

The Nordstrand Division manufactured synthetic fibres for sale to the textile and hosiery industries. There were eight major raw materials used in the processing of the fibres and a like number of standard fibres which were produced for inventory. This company had over 10,000 other items in the stores and materials inventory and 30 percent of its production was for custom-made fibres manufactured in accordance with the customer's specification.

During 1963 the American parent company had begun an investment in the European Common Market in conjunction with European manufacturers. The funds required for this project had not allowed the Canadian company to expand its production facilities. During the quarter under review no material additions to or disposals of plant and equipment were made by the Canadian division.

Question

1. You have recently been appointed as assistant to the president, and he has asked you to analyze the report and advise him of your impressions of what has gone wrong with the Nordstrand division during the first quarter. In addition he wants you to prepare a list of questions which he can ask the manager of the Nordstrand Division to confirm your impressions, and to insure that the division manager has recognized the problem, investigated it, and taken appropriate action. Finally he suggests that you present possible answers that the Nordstrand Division manager may give to your questions.

CHAPTER 12

FUNDS FLOW ANALYSIS

A *flow statement* explains the changes that occurred in an account or a group of accounts during an accounting period. The income statement is a flow statement; it explains the changes that occurred in retained earnings in connection with the operation of the business by summarizing the increases (i.e., revenues) and decreases (i.e., expenses) during the period. Another report, the *funds flow statement,* summarizes the events of the period from a different standpoint; it describes the sources from which additional funds were derived and the uses to which these funds were put. This statement is also called "statement of sources and applications of funds," "funds statements" and a variety of other names.

The funds flow statement is essentially derived from an analysis of changes that have occurred in asset and equities items between two balance sheet dates. It is *not* prepared directly from the accounts, as is the balance sheet itself.

THE CONCEPT OF FUNDS FLOW

Illustration 12–1 depicts the flow of financial resources in a typical business. As indicated by the "pipes" at the upper right, resources flow into the business from shareholders and from banks and other sources of borrowed capital. Some of these resources flow initially into the cash "reservoir," where they are held until needed; some of them flow directly to plant facilities and inventory. Valves on the pipes indicate the places where the flows can be turned off or on by management action. As resources are needed in operations, they are permitted to flow out of the cash reservoir, and these resources, together with material furnished by suppliers, are used in the manufacturing and selling process. At the end of this process, the cash reservoir is replenished by receipts from customers. The receivables reservoir indicates that cash is not replenished as soon as

321

Illustration 12–1

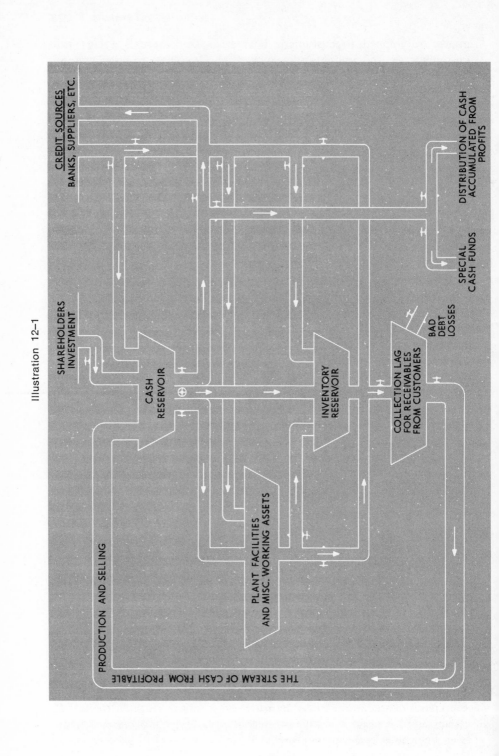

CREDIT SOURCES
BANKS, SUPPLIERS, ETC.

SHAREHOLDERS
INVESTMENT

CASH
RESERVOIR

PLANT FACILITIES
AND MISC. WORKING ASSETS

INVENTORY
RESERVOIR

COLLECTION LAG
FOR RECEIVABLES
FROM CUSTOMERS

BAD
DEBT
LOSSES

DISTRIBUTION OF CASH
ACCUMULATED FROM
PROFITS

SPECIAL
CASH FUNDS

PRODUCTION AND SELLING

THE STREAM OF CASH FROM PROFITABLE

goods are shipped to customers, but rather that there is a lag until customers pay the amounts they owe. Cash also flows to suppliers and others to reimburse them for the resources they have provided.

The funds flow statement describes these flows, but it does not describe all of them. The flows in the left-hand section of the diagram are the result of the constantly recurring process of manufacturing and selling goods and collecting receivables from customers. The funds flow statement does not show the details of this more or less continuous movement of resources. Instead, it focuses on more basic changes. These changes are associated with the *permanent capital* of the business.

Permanent capital consists of resources supplied by long-term creditors and by shareholders, including both their original investment and the resources they have supplied by permitting earnings to be retained in the business. On the balance sheet, the amount of such resources is the sum of noncurrent liabilities plus owners' equity; in other words, it is the total of the right-hand side of the balance sheet, less the current liabilities.

Part of the permanent capital is invested in buildings, equipment, and other noncurrent assets. The remainder is invested in current assets, but only a fraction of the current assets has to be financed from permanent capital, since vendors and short-term creditors provide the remainder. The amount that is financed from permanent capital is the difference between the total current assets and the total current liabilities. This difference, as we have already seen, is called working capital.

The funds flow statement shows changes in permanent capital and the assets in which this permanent capital is invested. Changes in the sources of permanent capital and the uses to which it is put are likely to be of more than ordinary interest both to management and to outsiders since these changes reflect the results of the important financial decisions that have significant long-run consequences. The funds flow statement shows these changes. In order to focus on this "big picture," the funds flow statement disregards the recurring circulation of resources among the individual current asset and current liability accounts. It does this by lumping all these accounts into a single item, working capital.

The funds flow statement therefore shows changes in the total amount of working capital, but not fluctuations in the individual items comprising working capital, much like national population statistics show births, deaths, immigration, and emigration for the country as a whole rather than complicating the picture by showing the continual movement of people from one house to another within the country.

It can be seen that the word "funds" in this context has a specialized meaning. It is not synonymous with "cash," for cash is only one of the items comprising working capital. Rather, it is associated with permanent capital, and the assets in which permanent capital is invested, one of these assets being working capital.

Basic Relationships

Illustration 12–2 summarizes the total flow of funds for American industrial and commercial companies for an average year in the 1950's. Collectively, American companies generated $34 billion of funds from operations (that is, from the excess of operating revenue over operating expenditures); they obtained $6.1 billion of new permanent capital from the sale of stocks and bonds to investors; and they obtained $2.2 billion from other long-term creditors, a total of $42.3 billion. They used this $42.3 billion to acquire $23.7 billion of new plant and equipment, to increase working capital by $10 billion, and to pay $8.6 billion in dividends.

Our present task is to construct a similar picture for an individual company. We can do this by working with the information shown on its balance sheets.

Illustration 12–2

FLOW OF FUNDS IN NONFINANCIAL BUSINESS FIRMS

Average Year in 1950's
(billions of dollars)

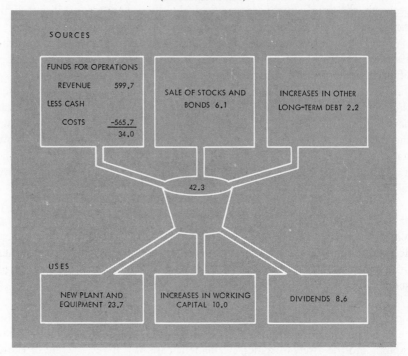

Source: Adapted from Claude Robinson, *Understanding Profits* (Princeton, N.J.: D. Van Nostrand Co., Inc., 1961), p. 137.

A balance sheet shows the net effect of all the funds transactions from the beginning of the business to the balance sheet date. The equities side shows the sources from which funds have been obtained, and the assets side shows the way in which these funds have been used. The balance sheet in Illustration 12–3 shows that as of the end of 1967, long-term creditors have furnished $145,000 of capital, and shareholders have furnished $394,000. Of the latter, $211,000 represents their original contribution and $183,000 represents earnings that they have permitted the company to retain in the business. The total amount of funds provided is therefore $539,000, of which $125,000 is used for working capital and $414,000 is in fixed assets.

If all earnings were paid out in dividends and if replacements of fixed assets exactly equaled the annual depreciation charge, the amounts shown on Illustration 12–3 could remain unchanged year after year. Although there would be numerous changes in the several current asset and current

Illustration 12–3

CONDENSED BALANCE SHEET

December 31, 1967

NET ASSETS		NET EQUITIES	
Current assets	$233,000	Long-term debt	$145,000
Less: Current liabilities	108,000	Capital stock	211,000
Working capital	$125,000	Retained earnings	183,000
Fixed assets	414,000		
Net Assets	$539,000	Net Equities	$539,000

liability accounts, these could offset one another so that the total working capital could remain constant. Under these circumstances, the business would not need additional financing. But of course the balance sheet items do change; additional funds are provided; and these are put to use.

From this simple balance sheet, we can see the possible ways in which the company can obtain additional funds. If it wished to buy a new plant, for example:

1. It could borrow, thus increasing long-term debt.
2. It could sell more stock, thus increasing the Capital Stock account.
3. It could forego dividends, which would show up as an increase in Retained Earnings.
4. It could use available cash, thus decreasing Working Capital.
5. It could sell some of its existing fixed assets, thus decreasing Fixed Assets.

The first, second, and third possibilities would be reflected on the balance sheet as an increase in equities; the fourth and fifth would show up as a decrease in assets. We can therefore generalize as follows: *sources of funds are indicated by increases in equities and decreases in assets.*

Looking at the other side of the coin, what uses could the company make of additional funds that it acquired? The possible uses are as follows:

1. It could add new fixed assets.
2. It could add to working capital.
3. It could pay off existing debt.
4. It could pay additional dividends to the shareholders, which decreases Retained Earnings.
5. It could repay capital to the shareholders.

The first two possibilities would show up as an increase in assets, and the last three as a decrease in equities. We can therefore generalize as follows: *uses of funds are indicated by increases in assets and decreases in equities.* (In describing both sources and uses, the reference is to *non-current* assets and equities since current items are lumped together in working capital.)

In accordance with the dual-aspect concept, total sources of funds must equal total uses of funds. The following relationships therefore exist:

1. Sources = Uses.
2. Increases in Equities + Decreases in Assets
$$= \text{Increases in Assets} + \text{Decreases in Equities.}$$

These same relationships can be explained in terms of debit and credit. Increases in equities and decreases in assets are both credits; increases in assets and decreases in equities are both debits. Thus, the above equation follows from the fact that changes in debits must equal changes in credits.

CONSTRUCTING THE FUNDS FLOW STATEMENT

The raw materials used for preparing a funds flow statement are the balances in asset and equities accounts, since these balances show the net effect of funds transactions. For example, if the company borrowed $26,000 from a long-term creditor, the following entry would be made:

```
Cash. . . . . . . . . . . . . . . . . . . . . . . . . .  26,000
     Long-Term Debt. . . . . . . . . . . . . . . . . . .          26,000
```

The increase in cash, which is an item of working capital, indicates that the business has obtained additional funds, and the credit part of the entry shows that the source of these funds was an increase in long-term debt.

Similarly, if the business purchased new fixed assets, the following entry would be made:

```
Fixed Assets. . . . . . . . . . . . . . . . . . . . . 61,000
     Cash (or a liability) . . . . . . . . . . . . . .            61,000
```

The decrease in working capital indicates that the business has used funds, and the debit part of the entry shows that these funds have been used to acquire additional fixed assets.

Not all transactions involve a flow of funds, however, and those that do not must be eliminated before the funds statement is prepared. The most common of these is the entry to record annual depreciation, for example:

```
Depreciation Expense. . . . . . . . . . . . . . . . . 29,000
     Accumulated Depreciation. . . . . . . . . . . . .            29,000
```

This entry, made in accordance with the accrual concept, records the write-off of a portion of the cost of fixed assets as a charge against current operations, but it did not involve a flow of funds. It involves neither the receipt of additional capital, nor the use of capital. Funds were used in the period in which the fixed assets were acquired, not the period in which they are written off.

In order to construct a funds flow statement, the effect of these nonfund transactions must be eliminated.

The account balances may lump together the effect of certain transactions which are individually important in understanding what has happened during the year. For example, the Retained Earnings account is typically (1) increased by net income earned in the year and (2) decreased by dividends declared. The balance in the account shows the net effect of these transactions, but it is desirable that the effect of each be shown separately. Adjustments are therefore necessary to show the separate effect of these transactions.

Following is a procedure for making these adjustments.

Comparative Balance Sheets

A first approximation of the flow of funds during a period is obtained by finding the changes in the balance sheet amounts between the beginning and end of the period. This is done in Illustration 12–4, where *comparative balance sheets* for the beginning and end of the year 1968 are given, and the differences between amounts on the two balance sheets are computed. Note that increases in asset accounts are debits, that decreases in asset accounts are credits, and that increases in equities are credits. (Although not shown, it is apparent that decreases in equities would be debits.) Note also that, in accordance with the basic accounting equation, the sum of the debit increases equals the sum of the credit increases.

If it were not for the fact that some accounting transactions do not involve a flow of funds, it could be said that during the year funds were obtained from an increase in long-term debt, $26,000, and in retained earnings, $20,000, and that these funds were used to finance additional fixed assets, $21,000, and working capital, $25,000. These changes are only first approximations of the flow of funds, however, for they do include the effect of nonfund transactions. Also, they mask certain important fund flows, by lumping together individual flows in a single account.

Illustration 12–4

BALANCE SHEET USED FOR FUNDS FLOW ANALYSIS

(in thousands of dollars)

	Balances as of Dec. 31		Change in 1968	
	1968	1967	Debit	Credit
Current Assets....................................	262	233		
Less: Current Liabilities.........................	112	108		
Working Capital.................................	150	125	25	
Plant and Equipment, Cost.........................	648	601	47	
Accumulated Depreciation.........................	(227)	(204)		23
Intangible Assets................................	14	17		3
Net Assets................................	585	539		
Long-Term Debt.................................	171	145		26
Capital Stock....................................	211	211		
Retained Earnings................................	203	183		20
Net Equities.............................	585	539		
Total Change.....................................			72	72

Adjustments

The balances must therefore be adjusted. The job of making these adjustments is difficult because it involves a clear understanding of the distinction between transactions that involve the flow of funds and those that do not. One approach is to think of the word "funds" as being synonymous with "working capital," since most individual funds transactions do involve an increase or decrease in some working capital item (i.e., a current asset or a current liability). The key questions then become: (1) Did this transaction, taken by itself, result in an increase in working capital? (If so, it was a source of funds.) (2) Did this transaction, taken by itself, result in a decrease in working capital? (If so, it was a use of funds.) (3) Did this transaction have no effect on working capital? (If so, it was neither a source nor a use of funds and must be eliminated.)

Of the several mechanical methods of keeping track of these adjustments, perhaps the most common is the work sheet, as shown in Illustration 12–5 and described below. The procedure is as follows:

1. Changes in balances in the balance sheet items are copied in the first two columns. (In the illustration, the changes are those derived from the comparative balance sheets shown in Illustration 12–4.)

2. Important funds flows that are concealed in the net balances are disentangled. This is done by making an entry in the account in which the amount was originally entered, so as to remove it from that account, and making a corresponding entry in a new account set up for that purpose. Since we want to remove the amount from the account in which it was originally recorded, the entry to this account must be the opposite of the entry originally made. Thus, if the original entry was a credit to the account, the adjusting entry would be a debit. The entry to the new account would be in this case a credit, because every entry must have debit-credit equality. These entries are made in the "adjustments" pair of columns.

3. Transactions that do not involve a flow of funds are discovered, and the balances are adjusted to remove the effect of these transactions. This is done by *reversing* the original transaction, that is, by making entries that are opposite to those that were made originally. These entries are also made in the "adjustments" pair of columns.

4. Each account balance is increased or decreased by the amount in the adjustment column opposite the item, and the adjusted amount is entered in the third pair of columns. The amounts in the debit column are uses of funds, and the amounts in the credit column are sources of funds.

Illustration 12–5

FUNDS FLOW WORK SHEET

(in thousands of dollars)

	Changes in Account Balances		Adjustments		Changes Affecting Funds	
	Debit	Credit	Debit	Credit	Debit (Uses)	Credit (Sources)
Working Capital............	25				25	
Plant and Equipment, Gross..	47		(e) 14		61	
Accumulated Depreciation....		23	(d) 29	(e) 6		
Intangible Assets...........		3	(c) 3			
Long-Term Debt...........		26				26
Capital Stock..............						
Retained Earnings..........		20	(b) 42	(a) 22		
Dividends................			(a) 22		22	
				(b) 42		
Funds from Operations......			(e) 2	(c) 3		72
				(d) 29		
Disposition of Fixed Assets				(e) 10		10
Total.................	72	72	112	112	108	108

Illustration of the Procedure

The adjustments shown in Illustration 12–5 are the most common type of adjustments that are made in constructing a funds flow statement. Each is described below. Information used as a basis for these adjustments can come from any of a number of sources. Most of them are derived from information shown on the income statement, and the income statement used for this purpose is shown in Illustration 12–6.

Illustration 12–6

INCOME STATEMENT, 1968

(in thousands of dollars)

Sales..........................		$1,080
Costs and expenses:		
Cost of goods sold..............$890		
Selling and administrative.........	68	
Depreciation....................	29	
Amortization of goodwill.........	3	
Interest.......................	7	997
Operating income................		$ 83
Gain on disposal of fixed assets......		2
Income before taxes..............		$ 85
Income taxes....................		43
Net income.....................		$ 42
Dividends......................		22
Added to Retained Earnings........		$ 20

DIVIDENDS.   From the income statement we learn that the net change in Retained Earnings, which was $20,000, was the result of two offsetting factors. There was an increase of $42,000, which was the net income of the year, and a decrease of $22,000 from the declaration of dividends. It would be useful to show these two elements separately, and this is done by reversing the entries originally made to Retained Earnings and setting up new accounts. In the case of dividends, the actual entry to Retained Earnings was a debit, so to reverse this, we credit Retained Earnings. The offsetting debit is to a new item set up on the work sheet below the balance sheet items. Thus, this adjustment is:

(*a*)

```
Dividends . . . . . . . . . . . . . . . . . . . . . . . . . .  22,000
      Retained Earnings . . . . . . . . . . . . . . . . .            22,000
```

FUNDS FROM OPERATIONS.   A corresponding adjustment is made for the other entry that affected Retained Earnings, the $42,000 net income for the period. Since the original entry was a credit to Retained Earnings, it is reversed by a debit. The offsetting credit is to another new item set up on the work sheet. Rather than labeling this item "Net Income," however, it is labeled "Funds from Operations" because when we finish making other adjustments to it, its balance will no longer be the net income for the year, but rather the new funds that have been provided from the operations of the business. The adjustment is:

(b)

```
Retained Earnings . . . . . . . . . . . . . . . . . .   42,000
    Funds from Operations . . . . . . . . . . . . .            42,000
```

These two adjustments were simply for the purpose of highlighting important funds flows. We shall now turn to the adjustments that are necessary in order to eliminate the transactions that did not involve a flow of funds at all.

AMORTIZATION OF INTANGIBLES. The income statement shows an expense labeled "amortization of goodwill" in the amount of $3,000, and the comparative balance sheet shows that Intangible Assets has decreased by the same amount. We can deduce that these items resulted from the write-off during 1968 of a portion of the intangible asset, Goodwill, by means of an entry debiting the expense item and crediting the asset.

This transaction did not involve a flow of funds in 1968. When the Goodwill was originally set up on the balance sheet in some previous year, a flow of funds was involved, but in 1968 the transaction reflects neither an inflow of resources to the business nor the use of resources. The entry was made in accordance with the accrual concept, which provides for a systematic write-off of such costs to the income of the periods benefited. To reverse it, the following adjustment is made:

(c)

```
Intangible Assets . . . . . . . . . . . . . . . . . .   3,000
    Funds from Operations . . . . . . . . . . . . .           3,000
```

The credit is made to Funds from Operations since the original debit was to an expense account, which had the effect of decreasing net income. The amount of net income now appears on the line "Funds from Operations," so the credit to reverse the transaction appears on the same line.

DEPRECIATION. The income statement shows that depreciation expense for the year was $29,000. We know that the credit part of such an entry is always to the Accumulated Depreciation account. As already noted, this entry did not represent a flow of funds. At the time the assets were purchased, funds were used, but the subsequent write-off of the asset cost by means of the depreciation mechanism involves neither a source nor a use of funds. The entry must therefore be reversed, and the adjustment to accomplish this is:

(d)

```
Accumulated Depreciation. . . . . . . . . . . . . . .   29,000
    Funds from Operations . . . . . . . . . . . . . . .       29,000
```

The credit is made to Funds from Operations for a reason similar to that given for the amortization of Goodwill, above.

DISPOSAL OF FIXED ASSETS. We note that the income statement contains an item, "gain on disposal of fixed assets, $2,000," and from this we know that fixed assets were sold for more than their book value. In order to find the facts about this transaction, we must go to the underlying accounting records (e.g., the general journal). Assume that these show that the gain on disposal arose in connection with the following transaction:

```
Cash. . . . . . . . . . . . . . . . . . . . . . . .  10,000
Accumulated Depreciation. . . . . . . . . . . . . .   6,000
    Plant and Equipment . . . . . . . . . . . . . .          14,000
    Gain on Disposal of Fixed Assets. . . . . . . .           2,000
```

This transaction means that the fixed assets being disposed of had a cost of $14,000 and accumulated depreciation of $6,000, so their net book value was $8,000. They were sold for $10,000, so there was a gain of $2,000.

The funds flow involved in this transaction was the $10,000 proceeds of the sale. The other items did not involve a flow of funds; they merely removed the asset and its accumulated depreciation from the books and recorded the gain. Note particularly that the amount of funds generated by this transaction was $10,000, not the $2,000 appearing on the income statement. An adjustment is therefore necessary, both to remove the nonfund items from the accounts and also to show the $10,000 as a source of funds. This adjustment is essentially the reverse of the original transaction. The reversal of the gain of $2,000 is made against Funds from Operations since that is where the net income, of which this item was a part, is now recorded. A new item, "Disposition of Fixed Assets," is set up on the work sheet. The adjustment is as follows:

(e)

```
Plant and Equipment . . . . . . . . . . . . . . . .  14,000
Funds from Operations . . . . . . . . . . . . . . .   2,000
    Accumulated Depreciation. . . . . . . . . . . .           6,000
    Disposition of Fixed Assets . . . . . . . . . .          10,000
```

ACQUISITION OF FIXED ASSETS. Refer again to the item on the work sheet labeled "Plant and Equipment, Gross." The comparative balance sheets showed an increase of $47,000 in the year, but to this, we have added $14,000 from adjustment (e) above, representing the write-off of plant that was sold. In order to show a net increase of $47,000, an entry must have been made during the year debiting Plant and Equipment for $14,000 more than this, or $61,000. Since the only debit entries to Plant and Equipment are those recording the acquisition of plant and equipment, we now know that fixed assets in the amount of $61,000 must have been acquired during the year, and this represented a use of funds.

PREPARATION OF THE STATEMENT. Having adjusted the amounts for all the nonfund transactions that we can discover, we are now in a position to compute the funds flows. This is done simply by extending the amounts on each line of the work sheet to the last pair of columns. The adjustments are added algebraically to the amounts in the first pair of columns. For example, for Accumulated Depreciation the calculation is $23 + 6 - 29 = 0$. Debit amounts in the last pair of columns now show uses of funds, and credit amounts show sources.

These amounts are used to prepare the funds flow statement, as shown in Illustration 12–7.

Illustration 12–7

FUNDS FLOW STATEMENT, 1968

Sources of Funds:

Funds provided by operations	$ 72,000
Proceeds from sale of fixed assets	10,000
Additional long-term debt	26,000
Total	$108,000

Uses of Funds:

New plant and equipment	$ 61,000
Dividends	22,000
Increase in working capital	25,000
Total	$108,000

Other Transactions

The nonfund transactions described above had to do with: (1) depreciation, (2) amortization of intangible assets, and (3) disposition of fixed assets. Other transactions that did not involve a flow of funds may occur, including: (4) amortization of bond discount or premium, (5) declaration of a stock dividend, and (6) creation of surplus reserves. When such transactions are found, the comparative balance sheet changes are adjusted in the same manner as described above, that is, by finding out what the original transaction was and then making an adjustment that is the reverse of it.

Hidden Transactions

The foregoing description assumed that the analyst had access to the company's accounting records, for the procedure required him to consult these records. An outside analyst may wish to construct a funds flow statement, even though he has only the information contained in the company's annual report, principally the balance sheet and income statement. (For example, he may be interested in a competitor's fund flow).

He often can do a reasonably good job of deducing what transactions *probably* caused the change in balance sheet items even without access to the underlying records.

In some cases, the exact nature of the transaction cannot be deduced, but an approximation can be derived that is better than nothing. The fixed asset transactions discussed above will be used as an example of what can be done.

After the depreciation adjustment (*d*) had been recorded, the "Accumulated Depreciation" line shows a debit balance of 6 $(29 - 23 = 6)$. Since the Accumulated Depreciation item never involves a flow of funds per se, some other nonfund transaction must have affected it. The most likely type of transaction is the removal of accumulated depreciation when fixed assets are disposed of. From the fact that "gain on disposal of fixed assets, $2,000" appears on the income statement, we know that there was such a transaction, and that proceeds exceeded book value by $2,000. We therefore can reconstruct part of the entry that must have been made:

```
Cash. . . . . . . . . . . . . . . . . . . . . . . . .      ?
Accumulated Depreciation. . . . . . . . . . . . . .   6,000
     Plant and Equipment . . . . . . . . . . . . . .            ?
     Gain on Disposal. . . . . . . . . . . . . . . .        2,000
```

We cannot complete the entry without more information, but we do know that the credit to Plant and Equipment must have been *at least* $6,000, since the accumulated depreciation on an asset never exceeds its cost. Accepting this minimum amount, the original entry becomes:

```
Cash. . . . . . . . . . . . . . . . . . . . . . . .   2,000
Accumulated Depreciation. . . . . . . . . . . . . .   6,000
     Plant and Equipment . . . . . . . . . . . . . .        6,000
     Gain on Disposal. . . . . . . . . . . . . . . .        2,000
```

If the indicated adjustment of $6,000 is made to Plant and Equipment on the work sheet, the total amount of this item becomes $47 + 6 = 53$. We can therefore deduce that funds were used to acquire plant and equipment costing *at least* $53,000. Reference back to the facts obtainable from the accounting records shows that this number understates the actual amount. Nevertheless, the deduction process brought us closer to the true facts than relying on the comparative balance sheet, which implies fixed asset additions of only $47,000.

Compound Transactions

A single transaction may involve the simultaneous source and use of funds. If so, it is usually more informative if the source is separated from the use. For example, if a $100,000 building was purchased and if $80,000 of this was financed with a mortgage loan, one could argue that the funds required for this transaction were only $20,000. Regardless of the theoretical merit of this argument, the reader of a funds flow statement undoubtedly wants to know about the two separate facts, the acquisition of the building and the incurrence of an additional liability. Such a transaction should therefore be shown on the funds flow statement as two separate items, a use of $100,000 for the building and a source of $80,000 from the mortgage loan.

Even in the case of a bond refunding, which involves only the exchange of one liability for another, with possibly no net change in the Bonds Payable account, it may be helpful to show separately the retirement of the old issue as a use of funds and the sale of the new issue as a source of funds.

Funds Provided by Operations

The $72,000 "funds from operations" that was developed from our analysis of funds flow differs considerably from the net income figure on the income statement, which was only $42,000. The work sheet shows that the $72,000 was arrived at by adding to net income the nonfund transactions involved in the net income calculation, principally the depreciation charge; that is,

Net income.	$42,000
Plus depreciation and other nonfund items.	30,000
Equals funds provided by operations.	$72,000

Many funds flow statements in fact show such a breakdown of "funds provided by operations," or, as it is often called, "internally generated funds."

Exactly the same result could have been obtained by subtracting expense items requiring the use of funds from revenue items that were a source of funds. The income statement (Illustration 12–6) shows these expense items as cost of goods sold, selling and administrative expense, interest expense, and income taxes. Each of these items is associated with either a decrease in a current asset (cash, inventory, prepaid expenses) or an increase in a current liability (accounts payable, taxes payable, accrued liabilities), both of which are decreases in working capital. The revenue item, Sales, is associated with an increase in cash or accounts receivable and hence with an increase in working capital. Operations generate funds to the extent that revenue which brings in funds exceeds expenses which require the use of funds, or—

Sales revenue.	$1,080,000
Less expenses using funds.	1,008,000
Equals funds provided by operations.	$ 72,000

This calculation shows more clearly how the funds were actually generated than the method of adding back depreciation and other nonfund items to net income. The "funds from operation" sections of some funds flow statements are prepared in this way.

The choice of methods is relatively unimportant; they give identical results. It is important, however, to appreciate the fact that *depreciation is not a source of funds.* In the first method, depreciation is added to net income to find the funds provided by operations, but it is operations, not depreciation, that provides the funds. Depreciation is neither a source nor a use of funds.

The Funds Flow Statement

There is no prescribed format for the funds flow statement. The items are arranged and described in whatever way seems most clearly to show the important financial events of the period. Minor items should be combined in order to emphasize the major changes.

Incidentally, reporting working capital as a source or use of funds may

Illustration 12–8

BOISE CASCADE CORPORATION

Sources and Application of Funds
(in thousands of dollars)

	Year Ended December 31 1968	1967
Sources:		
Net income...	$ 45,390	$ 29,544
Depreciation and depletion..........................	31,437	29,419
Total from Operations...........................	$ 76,827	$ 58,963
Borrowing under notes.............................	30,397	78,499
Sale of property and equipment.....................	17,196	8,293
Exchange of timber and operating properties..........	86,107	. . .
Increase in deferred income taxes...................	25,635	2,876
Exercise of stock options..........................	1,305	2,858
Issuances of common stock........................	22,817	. . .
Miscellaneous......................................	1,812	(1,911)
Total Sources..............................	$262,096	$149,578
Applications:		
Property and equipment...........................	$ 45,564	$ 52,093
Timber and timberlands...........................	17,365	40,977
Capital expenditures.........................	$ 62,929	$ 93,070
Investments in companies and realty.................	91,981	18,710
Increase in other noncurrent assets.................	3,520	23,327
Purchase of common stock for the treasury...........	. . .	3,061
Cash dividends declared...........................	8,606	7,525
Reduction of timberland rental obligations...........	30,779	
Reduction of long-term notes and other obligations.....	71,877	23,599
Total Applications...........................	$269,692	$169,292
Decrease in working capital......................	$ 7,596	$ 19,714

SOURCE: Condensed from 1968 annual report.

seem to involve a contradiction of terms. How can we regard uses of funds as "events that result in a decrease in working capital" and at the same time treat an increase in working capital itself as a use of funds? Actually, there is no contradiction if it is recalled that all transactions have two aspects. In a funds flow statement, increases in noncurrent assets and decreases in noncurrent equities are uses of funds, and the other aspect of each such change is a decrease in working capital; working capital *used* for the items stated is not available for other purposes. An increase in the working capital item itself represents management's decision to *use* this additional amount in the various working capital items rather than for some other purpose, such as paying it out as dividends.

In any event, the possible confusion can easily be avoided by treating the change in working capital as a residual item. This is done by arranging the funds flow statement in the following form:

Source — Uses = Working Capital Change.

The funds flow statements for Boise Cascade Corporation in Illustration 12–8 have such an arrangement. These statements show, for 1967, the financing of a major capital expenditure program (three times the annual depreciation charge) by funds generated from operations supplemented by long-term borrowing; and, for 1968, the financing of an even larger capital expenditure and investment program by funds generated from operations, from exchange of timber and operating properties, and from the issuance of common stock.

CASH FLOW STATEMENTS

Instead of lumping all current assets and current liabilities together as working capital, it may be desirable to consider changes in some or all of these items separately. A statement that has such a purpose is technically called a *cash flow statement*. Except that changes in individual current asset and liability items are treated separately, the procedures for analyzing transactions are the same as those described above. Increases in assets and decreases in equities indicate uses of cash; decreases in assets and increases in equities indicate sources of cash. Transactions that do not involve a flow of cash are eliminated.

Some people use the word "funds" as synonymous with "cash," as in statements such as, "We borrowed funds to increase our inventory," or, "We obtained funds by speeding up the collection of receivables." These people refer to the cash flow statement as a funds flow statement. This difference in terminology is unimportant, since the content of the statement will indicate which concept is used.

Illustration 12–9 shows a cash flow statement. This particular statement describes the effects of an expansion program, and since the expansion involved an increase in inventory and receivables as well as additional fixed assets, it was informative to show these current asset items on the statement rather than combining them into the single item, working capital. The unimportant changes, principally prepaid expenses and accrued liabilities, are lumped together as "miscellaneous changes."

Another cash flow statement, using a format suggested by Professor Almand R. Coleman of the University of Virginia, is shown in Illustration 12–10.

Illustration 12–9

BALDWIN MARKET COMPANY

Cash Flow Statement for the Year 1967

What We Did		*How We Financed It*		
Expanded:		Reduced cash		$ 2,453
Accounts receivable.	$ 67,477	Sold security holdings. .		100,000
Inventories.	61,586	Borrowed:		
Acquired new fixed assets.	255,861	Accounts payable. . . .		43,185
Paid dividends.	78,315	Bank loan.		26,000
Miscellaneous changes.	1,653	Mortgage.		175,000
		Obtained funds from operations:		
		Net income.	$95,679	
		Depreciation.	22,575	118,254
	$464,892			$464,892

Illustration 12–10

ALTERNATIVE FORM OF CASH FLOW STATEMENT

(in millions of dollars)

In 1963, sales revenue amounted to.		$150.6
Whereas cost of goods sold and operating "cash" expenses (exclusive of $7.2 depreciation) was.		128.8
So net income before noncash charges was.		$ 21.8
And there would have been a net inflow of cash of this amount from operations, except that—		
A. The company collected less from customers than it billed.	$(14.1)	
B. The company bought and manufactured more than the cost of goods it shipped.	(2.9)	
C. The company paid out less cash than the costs it incurred.	0.8	
The net effect of these items being.		(16.2)
So that operating activities resulted in an "internally generated" cash inflow of.		$ 5.6
There were inflows from—		
Sale of common stock.	$ 12.6	
Increase in short-term loans.	5.0	
Increase in long-term debt.	2.4	20.0
		$ 25.6
Outgo of cash was required for—		
Dividends.	$ 3.0	
Property, plant, and equipment acquired in excess of dispositions. . .	30.8	
Increase in investments and other assets.	2.0	35.8
So that the net decrease in cash during 1963 was.		$ (10.2)

Although not usually contained in published financial reports, a cash flow statement is essential to management in examining short-run financial movements. It is frequently prepared for monthly or weekly time intervals. The amount of cash required to finance peak seasonal needs is obscured in an annual statement.

USES OF THE STATEMENT

The funds flow and cash flow statements are used for two principal purposes: (1) as a means of analyzing what has happened in the past, and (2) as a means of planning what is going to happen in the future.

As a tool of historical analysis, the statements shed light on the financial policies that the company has pursued. Of particular interest is the policy with respect to the acquisition of new fixed assets. To what extent were new assets financed by internally generated funds, and to what extent by borrowing or other external sources? For financial resources obtained externally, what proportion was from debt and what from equity? Some companies deliberately limit their growth to an amount that can be financed from internally generated funds. Others do not hesitate to go to the capital market for funds. For these, the balance selected between risky, low-cost debt and less risky, higher cost equity is of considerable interest, as discussed in Chapter 11.

As a tool of planning, a projected funds flow statement is an essential device for planning the amount, timing, and character of new financing. Estimated uses of funds for new fixed assets, for working capital, for dividends, and for the repayment of debt are made for each of several future years, usually at least two or three years, but in some cases 10 years or more. Estimates are made of the funds to be provided by operations, and the difference, if it is positive, represents the funds that must be obtained by borrowing or the issuance of new equity securities. If the indicated amount of new funds required is greater than management thinks it is feasible to raise, then the plans for new fixed asset acquisitions and the dividend policies are reexamined so that the uses of funds can be brought into balance with anticipated sources of financing them.

For shorter term financial planning, a cash budget is essential. The cash budget is a cash flow statement, similar to those shown above except that amounts are estimates of the future rather than those recorded in the past. Projections are made for each of the next several months or several quarters. One way to prepare such a budget is to list all the estimated uses of cash and all the sources other than from additional financing. The difference between these totals is the amount that must be obtained by borrowing or selling additional stock if the planned program is to be carried out. If it is believed that this amount cannot be raised, the indication is that the estimated uses of cash must be cut back. In other respects, the technique is the same as that already described.

In making a cash budget, special attention is paid to the timing of the flows; that is, to the anticipated need for cash in each month or each quarter of the period covered. Particularly in businesses subject to seasonal fluctuations, there are likely to be heavy, but temporary, cash needs in months when inventories are being built up, and these needs may be concealed in a statement that is not broken into short intervals of time.

MISUSES OF THE STATEMENT

In recent years, the number of companies publishing funds flow or cash flow statements has increased rapidly. As is often the case with a newly popular idea, a great deal of misunderstanding, and hence misuse is prevalent. Basically, the misunderstanding results from a tendency to think that sources of funds are synonymous with increases in owners' equity. This is not so. For reasons examined in detail in Part I of this book, increases in owners' equity must be measured in accordance with the accrual concept; there is not necessarily a correspondence between the earning of net income and changes in working capital. The using up of fixed assets is a real cost, a real decrease in owners' equity, even though no change in funds flow is involved.

The Accounting Principles Board of the AICPA, alarmed at the misunderstandings, published a useful clarification, part of which is quoted below:[1]

In recent years a new concept (or more correctly, an old concept with a new name) has become increasingly important in the analysis of the flow of funds. The term "cash flow" has been used to refer to a variety of concepts, but its most common meaning in financial literature, and to a lesser extent in accounting literature, is the same as "funds derived from operations" in a statement of source and application of funds. . . . Synonyms which are sometimes used include "cash earnings," "cash income," and "cash throw-off."

Many of the comments made in connection with "cash flow" analysis leave the reader with the erroneous impression that "cash flow" or "cash earnings" is superior to net income as a measure of a company's real earning power. Calculations of the Price/Cash Flow ratio are sometimes made and presented as a substitute for or supplement to the Price/Earnings ratio in evaluating a company's stock. The amount of "cash flow" or the "cash flow per share" has often been presented in the president's letter, the financial review, or the statistical section of the annual report of a corporation apart from or in the absence of a complete statement of source and application of funds in the report. In other words, there has been a growing tendency on the part of

---

[1] Accounting Principles Board, AICPA, Opinion No. 3, *The Statement of Source and Application of Funds,* October 1963; cited in Paul Grady, *Inventory of Generally Accepted Accounting Principles* (AICPA *Accounting Research Study No. 7,* 1965), p. 314.

some people to single out one of the items on the statement of source and application of funds, thereby implying that this figure is more important than other information regarding the flow of funds and often carrying the implication that "net income plus depreciation" is the best measure of the company's profitability. There is a strong implication running through the comments in the literature, including those in the annual reports of some corporations, that the total "cash flow" can be considered available for the payment of dividends.

Misconceptions about Depreciation

Most of the difficulty referred to above stems from the misconception that depreciation is a source of funds; for example, the following quotations:[2]

Most people pay too little attention to depreciation reserves as a contributor to corporate health. In some years depreciation actually exceeds net profit.

Company X shifted to accelerated depreciation last year, thus increasing its depreciation charge and its cash flow earnings by $6 million.

Depreciation money is cash. In your bank account, depreciation dollars and profit dollars look alike.

The most charitable thing that can be said about such quotations is that they are half truths. Some are in no sense true; the statement that an increase in depreciation results in an increase in "cash flow earnings" overlooks the fact that such an increase in depreciation is exactly offset by a decrease in net income. As Gaa has put it: "Depreciation should be sued for nonsupport; it does *not* provide funds or any other assets for the replacement of property."[3] And Robert C. Tyson, chairman of the Finance Committee of U.S. Steel, puts it this way:[4]

. . . For the security analyst the sum of profits plus depreciation may provide a measure of management discretion to choose between paying dividends, paying off debt or spending money to replace depreciated facilities. But as a measure of corporate success it is just as fallacious to add these two items as it is to add back taxes to profits.

The misuse of this type of measurement may be partly attributable to the vocabulary quirks in which the financial fraternity indulges when speaking of depreciation as a source of funds. If those supposed to know of what they speak say that depreciation is a source of funds, then those less well-informed

---

[2] Adapted from quotations collected by William J. Vatter and reported by him in "Operating Confusion in Accounting," *Journal of Business*, University of Chicago, July 1963, pp. 290–301.

[3] Charles J. Gaa, "Depreciation—the Good Provider?", *Business Topics*, Michigan State University, Winter 1962.

[4] Speech before the Eastern Area Conference of the Financial Executives Institute, June 14, 1963.

can say, "The bigger the source, the better." So perhaps we had "better mind our language," as mothers used to admonish. The fact is, of course, that the only continuing source of cash that any firm has out of which to cover all its costs is its sales receipts from customers. Among those costs are the prepaid expenditures for facilities. It takes a long time to get them covered. Depreciation is the record of their cost slowly being covered. To hold that big depreciation cost in the guise of big cash flow is good for a company is the same as saying that the bigger its costs the better off it is. And that is plain nonsense! Here, then, is another area in which clarification of public understanding is necessary for establishment of prudent public policy.

Finally, from the opinion of the Accounting Principles Board of AICPA:[5]

The amount of funds derived from operations cannot be considered as a substitute for or an improvement upon properly determined net income as a measure of results of operations and the consequent effect on financial position. Misleading implications can result from isolated statistics in annual reports of "cash flow" which are not placed in proper perspective to net income figures and to a complete analysis of source and application of funds. "Cash flow" and related terms should not be used in annual reports in such a way that the significance of net income is impaired, and "cash earnings" or other terms with a similar connotation should be avoided. The Board regards computations of "cash flow per share" as misleading since they ignore the impact of cash expenditures for renewal and replacement of facilities and tend to downgrade the significant economic statistic of "earnings per share."

SUMMARY

A funds flow statement shows the sources from which funds were provided and the uses to which these funds were put during an accounting period. The term "funds" is equivalent to "working capital." The net effects of funds flows are indicated by changes in noncurrent asset and equities accounts between the beginning and ending balance sheets of the periods. Increases in noncurrent assets and decreases in noncurrent equities indicate uses of funds; decreases in noncurrent assets and increases in noncurrent equities indicate sources.

The actual flows are found by reconstructing the transactions that resulted in these changes. In this process, transactions which affected balance sheet items but which did not involve a flow of funds are eliminated. When the analyst has access to the company's accounting records, all transactions can easily be identified. Even when he has only the incomplete information obtainable in published statements, he often can make a good approximation of the funds flow by deducing what transactions probably caused the balance sheet changes.

---

[5] APB Opinion No. 3, *op. cit.*, paragraph 15.

The amount of funds provided by operations of the period is by no means the same as the reported net income of the period. In a sense, funds provided by operations is net income adjusted for depreciation and other nonfund expenses and revenues, but this adjustment should not lead to the inference that depreciation is itself a source of funds.

A cash flow statement is the same as a funds flow statement except that important current asset and current liability changes are identified separately rather than combined in the single item, working capital.

In recent years, there has been a widespread tendency to use "cash flow earnings" as an indicator of corporate health that is equal to or superior to the indication provided by the net income figure. This is erroneous.

SUGGESTIONS FOR FURTHER READING

SPROUSE, ROBERT T., and ROBERT K. JAEDICKE. *Income, Funds and Cash.* Englewood Cliffs, N.J.: Prentice-Hall, Inc., 1965.

CASES

CASE 12–1. THE ABC COMPANY[6]

Mr. Jones of the ABC Company started the year in fine shape. His company made widgets—just what the customer wanted. He made them for $0.75 each, sold them for $1. He kept an inventory equal to shipments of the past 30 days, paid his bills promptly, and billed his customers 30-days net. The sales manager predicted a steady increase of 500 widgets each month. It looked like his lucky year, and it began this way:

January 1. Cash, $875; receivables, $1,000; inventory, $750.

JANUARY

In January, he sold 1,000 widgets; shipped them at a cost of $750; collected his receivables—winding up with a tidy $250 profit and books like this:

February 1. Cash, $1,125; receivables, $1,000; inventory, $750.

FEBRUARY

This month's sales jumped, as predicted, to 1,500. With a corresponding step-up in production to maintain his 30-day inventory, he made 2,000 units at a cost of $1,500. All receivables from January sales were collected. Profit so far, $625. Now his books looked like this:

March 1. Cash, $625; receivables, $1,500; inventory, $1,125.

MARCH

March sales were even better: 2,000 units. Collections: On time. Production, to adhere to his inventory policy: 2,500 units. Operating results for the month, $500 profit. Profit to date: $1,125. His books:

April 1. Cash, $250; receivables, $2,000; inventory, $1,500.

APRIL

In April, sales jumped another 500 units to 2,500, and Jones patted his sales manager on the back. His customers were paying right on time. Production was pushed to

---

[6] Adapted from an article in *Business Week*.

344

3,000 units, and the month's business netted him $625 for a profit to date of $1,750. He took off for Florida before he saw the accountant's report. Suddenly he got a phone call from his treasurer: "Come home! We need money!" His books had caught up with him:

May 1.   Cash, $000; receivables, $2,500; inventory, $1,875.

Questions

1. Why did the ABC Company need money?
2. Assume that business keeps growing at 500 widgets per month. How much cash will the company need, month by month, through December?

CASE 12–2. MARRETT MANUFACTURING COMPANY (B)

Refer to the situation described in Marrett Manufacturing Company (A) (p. 191). Prepare an estimated funds flow statement for the year 1969.

CASE 12–3. GRETLIN CORPORATION

Balance sheets as of December 31, 1967, and December 31, 1968, for the Gretlin Corporation are shown in Exhibit 1.

Exhibit 1

GRETLIN CORPORATION

Comparative Balance Sheets

	Dec. 31, 1967		Dec. 31, 1968		Increase or Decrease*
ASSETS					
Cash.........................		$ 5,000		$ 6,000	$ 1,000
Accounts receivable (net)......		14,000		15,500	1,500
Inventory....................		22,000		8,000	14,000*
Prepaid insurance............		200		250	50
Prepaid rent.................		150		100	50*
Prepaid property taxes........		300		400	100
Land........................		4,000		8,000	4,000
Building and equipment........	$30,000		$48,000		
Less: Accumulated depr......	10,000	20,000	11,000	37,000	17,000
Total Assets.............		$65,650		$75,250	$ 9,600
EQUITIES					
Accounts payable............		$20,000		$19,500	$ 500*
Accrued expenses............		2,000		4,000	2,000
Income tax payable...........		1,000		1,100	100
Capital stock.................		30,000		37,000	7,000
Retained earnings............		12,650		13,650	1,000
Total Equities...........		$65,650		$75,250	$ 9,600

Sales for the year 1968 were $210,000. Net income after taxes was $7,000. In arriving at net profit, items deducted from sales included, among others: cost of goods sold, $165,000; depreciation, $5,000; wages and salaries, $20,000. There was a gain of $1,000 on the sale of a truck. The truck had cost $6,000, depreciation of $4,000 had been accumulated for it, and it was sold for $3,000. This was the only asset written off during the year. The company declared and paid $6,000 in dividends during the year.

Questions

1. Prepare a funds flow statement for the Gretlin Corporation for the year 1968.
2. Without redoing the detailed work, convert this to a cash flow statement.
3. Describe the most significant development revealed by this statement.

CASE 12–4. MANOMET ELECTRONICS, INC.

Balance sheets for Manomet Electronics, Inc., as of December 31, 1962, and December 31, 1963, are shown in Exhibit 1, and a statement of income and reconciliation of earnings for 1963 appears in Exhibit 2.

The only item in the Buildings and Equipment account sold during the year was a specialized machine that originally cost $15,000. The accumulated depreciation on this machine at the time of sale was $8,000. The machine was sold for $6,000, and full payment was received in cash.

Exhibit 1

MANOMET ELECTRONICS, INC.

Comparative Balance Sheets

	Dec. 31 1962	Dec. 31 1963	Increase or Decrease*
ASSETS			
Cash...................................	$ 74,000	$ 37,000	$ 37,000*
Accounts receivable......................	54,000	47,000	7,000*
Inventories.............................	312,000	277,000	35,000*
Prepaid expenses........................	6,000	4,000	2,000*
Land...................................	60,000	60,000	.....
Patents................................	55,000	65,000	10,000
Buildings and equipment..................	420,000	480,000	60,000
Less: Accumulated depreciation buildings and equipment.............	(105,000)	(120,000)	(15,000)
Total Assets......................	$876,000	$850,000	$ 26,000*

Exhibit 1 (*Continued*)

Comparative Balance Sheets

	Dec. 31 1962	Dec.31 1963	Increase or Decrease*
LIABILITIES AND CAPITAL			
Accounts payable..........................	$ 58,000	$ 94,000	$ 36,000
Notes payable............................	28,000	8,000	20,000*
Estimated real estate, excise and income tax...	86,000	12,000	74,000*
Social security taxes accrued...............	3,000	5,000	2,000
Bonds payable............................	220,000	60,000	160,000*
Capital stock.............................	250,000	460,000	210,000
Retained earnings.........................	231,000	211,000	20,000*
Total Liabilities and Capital...........	$876,000	$850,000	$ 26,000*

Exhibit 2

MANOMET ELECTRONICS, INC.

Statement of Income and Reconciliation of Earnings for 1963

Net sales...		$1,970,000
Less: Cost of goods sold................................		1,480,000
Gross profit...		$ 490,000
Less: Operating expenses (includes depreciation on buildings and equipment of $23,000; patent amortization of $6,000)		500,000
Net loss from operations...................................		$ 10,000
Less: Other revenue.......................................		7,000
Net loss...		$ 3,000
Add: Retained earnings, December 31, 1962...............		231,000
		$ 228,000
Less: Dividend paid......................................	$16,000	
Nonrecurring loss on sale of asset.....................	1,000	17,000
Retained Earnings, December 31, 1963......................		$ 211,000

Question

1. Prepare a funds flow statement.

PART III

Accounting in Management Control

CHAPTER 13

ESSENTIALS OF
COST ACCOUNTING

Up to this point, attention has been focused on financial accounting, that is, on the type of accounting whose purpose is to produce balance sheets and income statements for use by parties external to the business. We now turn to the subject of management accounting, that is, to the accounting whose purpose is to provide information useful to the management.

MANAGEMENT ACCOUNTING AND FINANCIAL ACCOUNTING

Whereas financial accounting has been written about for over 400 years, little was written about management accounting until well into the 20th century. The actual practice of management accounting goes back much further; many of the techniques to be described here were used by Josiah Wedgwood and Sons, Ltd., in the 18th century, for example. The need for a type of accounting that was not aimed primarily at the preparation of financial statements is set forth in this 1875 memorandum by Thomas Sutherland, a British business executive:[1]

The present system of bookkeeping in the Accountant's Department is admirably suited for the end it has in view, viz., that of ascertaining once a year or oftener the profits upon the company's transactions; but it is evident that in a business of this kind much detailed information is necessary regarding the working of the Company, and this information should be obtainable in such a practical form, as to enable the Directors to see readily and clearly the causes at work in favor of or against the success of the Company's operations.

[1] This memorandum was called to my attention by Professor Lyle E. Jacobsen, who saw it reprinted in the London *Economist* in 1960.

In contrast with financial accounting, management accounting:

1. Has more than one purpose.
2. Is not governed by generally accepted accounting principles.
3. Is optional.
4. Focuses on segments as well as on the whole of a business.
5. Has less emphasis on precision.
6. Is part of other processes, rather than an end in itself.

Multiple Purposes

The governing objective of financial accounting is to furnish information to outsiders in order to report on stewardship. A single set of principles and a single system is adequate to meet this single objective. The governing objective of management accounting is to furnish information that is useful to management. Management needs information for several different purposes, among which are: as an aid in planning, as an aid in measuring and appraising performance, as an aid in setting selling prices, and as an aid in analyzing alternative courses of action. The information that is relevant for one of these purposes is often not relevant for another, and management accounting information must therefore be put together in several different ways, according to the purpose for which it is to be used. The concept of "cost," for example, may mean one thing in connection with planning and quite a different thing in connection with performance measurement.

Not Governed by Generally Accepted Principles

Financial accounting information must be prepared in accordance with generally accepted accounting principles. Outsiders, who usually have no choice but to accept information just as the company provides it, need assurance that this information is prepared in accordance with a mutually understood set of ground rules. Otherwise, they could not make sense out of the figures. Management, by contrast, can make and enforce whatever rules and definitions it finds most useful for its own needs, without worrying about whether these conform to some outside standard. Thus, in management accounting there may well be information on sales orders received, even though these are not financial accounting transactions; fixed assets may be stated at appraisal values, overhead costs may be omitted from inventories, or profits may be recorded before revenue is realized, even though each of these concepts is inconsistent with generally accepted accounting principles. The basic question in management accounting is the pragmatic one: "Is the information useful?" rather than, "Does it conform to generally accepted principles?"

Optional

Financial accounting *must* be done. Enough effort must be expended to collect data in acceptable form and with an acceptable degree of accuracy, whether or not the accountant regards this information as useful. Management accounting, by contrast, is entirely optional. No outside agency specifies what must be done, or indeed that anything need be done. Being optional, there is no point in collecting a piece of information for management purposes unless its value is believed to exceed the cost of collecting it.

Focus on Segments

The balance sheet and income statement relate to the business as a whole. Most management accounting information relates to segments of the organization, that is, to departments or other organizational segments, to products, or to individual functions. As we shall see, the necessity for dividing the total costs of the business among these individual segments creates some problems in management accounting that do not exist in financial accounting.

Less Emphasis on Precision

Management needs information rapidly, and is often willing to sacrifice precision in order to gain speed in reporting. Thus, in management accounting, approximations are often as useful as, or even more useful than, figures that are worked out to the last penny.

A Part, Rather than an End in Itself

Financial accounting is a complete, self-contained entity. Management accounting information is usually only part of a larger system. The monetary data of accounting are often used in conjunction with non-monetary data (such as pounds of material, hours of labor, units of product), and the historical accounting data are used in relation to estimates of the future (such as budgets and forecasts).

Similarities

The criteria by which management accounting practices should be judged are essentially the same as those already discussed for financial accounting: relevance, objectivity, and feasibility. Application of these criteria may lead to different practices, however. For example, imputed costs, which are costs not evidenced by an exchange transaction, are not ordinarily included in financial accounting, but it is not uncommon to find such costs recorded in management accounting records.

> EXAMPLE: A trade association of retail hardware stores collecting records of expenses from its member firms may specify that the report include as rent expense an amount equivalent to what rental costs would have been even if the building were owned and no rent as such were actually paid. This would put the reports of members who owned buildings on a basis comparable with those who rented buildings, and thus increase the comparability of the data. Such a practice would not be permitted in financial accounting; in accordance with the cost concept, only the actual costs incurred in occupying the building could be shown.

The inclusion of imputed rent in the above example would increase the relevance of the report, would make it more useful. There would be a corresponding reduction in the objectivity of the information, but members of the trade association are not likely to introduce a deliberate bias into figures prepared for their mutual benefit, so on balance it probably is safe to relax the objectivity criterion in order to obtain more relevant data. By contrast, if financial accounting permitted the reporting of imputed rent, the possibility of manipulation would be increased.

Although differences do exist, most elements of financial accounting are also found in management accounting. There are two reasons for this. First, the same considerations that make these principles sensible for the purposes of financial accounting are likely to be present for purposes of management accounting. For example, management cannot base its reporting system on unverifiable, subjective estimates of profits submitted by lower echelons, which is the same reason that financial accounting adheres to the cost and realization concepts. Second, the internal accounting system must furnish the information used in preparing the financial statements. There is a presumption, therefore, that the basic data will be collected in accordance with generally accepted financial accounting principles, for to do otherwise would require two separate systems.

SYSTEMS FOR COST ACCUMULATION

Management accounting encompasses the same categories of data that have been described in Part I, namely, assets, liabilities, owners' equity, expenses, and revenues. In this chapter, the description will be limited to costs. Costs, it will be recalled, can be either expenses or assets, depending on whether the cost transaction does or does not decrease owners' equity in the current accounting period.

As already noted, management needs accounting information for several different purposes, and the type of information that is required varies with the purpose. Although there are many possible purposes, some of which (such as data for use in defense of an antitrust action) may not even be foreseeable when a system is being designed, most, if not all, of these purposes can be satisfied with two types of cost information: (1) costs accumulated in terms of products or programs, and (2) costs accumulated in terms of management responsibility. The first is called *product cost accounting*, and the second is called *responsibility accounting*.

In product costing, costs are accumulated for each product or groups of related products. If an organization performs services or carries out programs, rather than making a physical product, the procedure is called *program costing*. Product costs are used in determining the amounts to be reported as goods in process inventory, finished goods inventory, and cost of sales, and thus are a part of financial accounting. Many products or services are sold at a price that includes cost plus a predetermined allowance for profits. Such transactions range from the multibillion-dollar "cost-plus-fixed-fee" contracts for the development and production of complete weapons systems down to an order for printing 500 letterheads or repairing an automobile. Such transactions require the collection of costs by products or programs. Product costs are also used as an aid in setting selling prices, and in making other decisions related to products that will be discussed in Chapter 19.

In responsibility accounting, costs are accumulated by responsibility centers. A *responsibility center* is an organization unit headed by a responsible person. Since organizations function through the actions of human beings, it is important that costs be accumulated in such a way that they can be associated with the persons who manage each of the subdivisions into which the organization is divided. Responsibility accounting information is used as an aid in planning and controlling the activities of responsibility centers and in motivating the persons responsible for carrying out these activities.

In addition to these two main streams of cost information, some companies have a third type because they are required by an outside regulatory body to report costs in a certain way. These companies include gas companies, electric companies, water companies, trucking companies, railroads, airlines, bus companies, pipeline companies, telephone companies, broadcasting companies, banks, and investment trusts. Some government agencies that must report costs to legislative bodies require a separate stream of cost information for this purpose. Conceptually, the product or program cost information that a company collects for its own needs should also satisfy the needs of outside agencies, but the fact is that some regulatory bodies require reports that are of little or no use to company management. The essential reason for this discrepancy is that requirements of the regulatory bodies were promulgated many years ago, and they have not been modernized in accordance with more recent developments in cost accounting practice. These requirements differ with each regulatory body, and they will not be discussed further here.

Although a company has two, and sometimes three, streams of cost information, it has, or at least should have, only a single cost system; that is, product costs, responsibility costs, and regulatory costs can be viewed as end products that are produced by different ways of accumulating the same underlying data. Nevertheless, product costing and responsibility accounting are described separately here because this facilitates an understanding of each of them.

PRODUCT COSTING

The reader is asked to refer back to the flow chart in Illustration 7–2 (p. 180), which sketched the flow of costs as products (in this case, smoking pipes) moved through goods in process inventory to finished goods inventory, and then out to the customer. (It will be helpful, before going further, if the reader traces through each entry in Illustration 7–2 in order to refresh his memory.) Brief mention was made in Chapter 7 of the problem of assigning material, labor, and factory overhead costs[2] to the partially completed pipes in goods in process inventory, to the completed pipes in finished goods inventory, and to cost of goods sold when the pipes are shipped. This is the problem of product costing. Consider the transaction that recorded the transfer of pipes from Goods in Process Inventory to Finished Goods Inventory. (This was Transaction No. 7 in Illustration 7–2 in the amount of $9,000.) The number and types of physical units (pipes) involved in this transfer can be ascertained readily, but in order to assign dollar amounts corresponding to these physical units, a cost per unit must be established.

If the company manufactured only one style of pipe, it would be possible to divide the total amount of debits to Work in Process by the total number of units worked on to obtain an approximation of the cost per unit; this figure could then be used to calculate the amount to be transferred from Goods in Process Inventory to Finished Goods Inventory. If the factory made more than one kind of product, however, such a simple calculation would not give results that fitted the facts, since one product probably used more material, labor, or overhead—that is, it cost more—than another. If the entry transferring completed products from Goods in Process to Finished Goods Inventory is to reflect the facts of

---

[2] For the purpose of determining inventory amounts and cost of goods sold, it is not necessary to determine the selling, general, and administrative costs applicable to a particular unit of product; nevertheless, such a breakdown is useful for some pricing and other decisions relating to the product. Some cost accounting systems therefore do provide for the collection of these costs by units of product.

the situation, there must be some means of taking these differences into account.

Cost Principle

Basically, there is only one principle of product costing: the cost assigned to a product should be the sum of (1) the direct costs incurred in producing it, and (2) a fair share of the indirect costs. As will be seen, there are differences of opinion both as to what constitutes a direct cost and as to what is a fair or equitable share of the indirect costs. Thus, two companies making identical products with identical manufacturing techniques can come up with markedly different costs for these products simply because of differences in the way they interpret the basic principle.

The total costs to be assigned to the various products manufactured are measured in accordance with the principles of financial accounting, at least for those product costs that are used in measuring inventory and cost of sales on the published financial statements. Thus, the accrual concept, the distinction between costs that are to be capitalized and those that are to be expensed, the various methods of depreciation, and similar topics described in Part I, apply equally here. Product cost information is used for purposes other than the preparation of financial statements, however, and for these other purposes, the principles of financial accounting do not necessarily apply. For example, in accumulating costs as a basis for setting selling prices, a company may decide to figure depreciation on the replacement cost of fixed assets, rather than on original cost, or it may decide to omit depreciation altogether under certain circumstances.

Job Costing and Process Costing

There are two main methods of accumulating product costs, called, respectively, job costing and process costing. Each is described below.

Essentially, a job cost system collects costs for each physically identifiable job or batch of work as it moves through the plant, regardless of the accounting period in which the work is done, while a process cost system collects costs for all products worked on in an accounting period.

JOB COSTING. The "job" in a job cost system may consist of a single unit (e.g., a turbine or a house), or it may consist of all units of identical or similar products covered by a single production order (e.g., 1,000 printed books or 10 dozen white shirts).[3] Usually each job is given a number and costs are collected on a separate record that is set up for that number. This *job cost record* contains spaces to record the individual

---

[3] When the job consists of more than one unit of product, the system is often called "job-lot costing," or simply "lot costing."

elements of cost charged to that job, and these costs are recorded as the job moves through the various departments in the factory. Thus, when the job is completed, its costs can be readily totaled. The sum of all the costs charged to all the jobs worked on in the factory during an accounting period is the basis for the entries debiting Goods in Process and crediting Raw Materials Inventory, Wages, and Overhead accounts. When each job is completed, the total cost recorded on the job cost record is the basis for the entry transferring the product from Goods in Process to Finished Goods Inventory, and this same cost is the basis for the entry transferring the product from Finished Goods Inventory to Cost of Goods Sold when the product is sold. The total cost recorded on all job cost records for products still in the factory as of the end of an accounting period equals the total of the Goods in Process Inventory account at that time.

In summary:

1. A separate job cost record is established for each job or job lot.

2. Costs chargeable to the job are recorded on this sheet, and are also debited to Goods in Process Inventory.

3. When the job is completed and transferred out of the factory, the total cost accumulated on the job cost record is the amount used to debit Finished Goods Inventory and to credit Goods in Process Inventory (unless the job is immediately sold, in which case the debit is to Cost of Goods Sold.)

4. The balance in Work in Process Inventory at the end of the accounting period is therefore the sum of the costs accumulated on all jobs still in the factory.

PROCESS COSTING. In a *process cost system*, all the costs for a time period, such as a month, are collected, with no attempt to attach these costs to specific units of product. This system is used in a factory making only one product, such as cement, or in a factory where the difference between various types of products is not substantial, that is, where the products are relatively homogeneous. Essentially, in a process cost system the total cost incurred during the period and the total number of units of products worked on during the period are collected. By dividing total costs by total units, one derives the cost per unit; and this cost per unit is used as the basis of valuing the units transferred to Finished Goods Inventory and, later on, from Finished Goods Inventory to Cost of Goods Sold.

The units *worked on* in a period include the following: (1) units that were both started and completed during the period; plus (2) units that were started but not completed; plus (3) units that were started in prior periods and completed in this period. Since 100 percent of the costs of the first type were incurred in the current period, but only a portion of the costs of the second and third types, production activity for the period cannot be determined simply by adding up the number of units worked on. The three types of units must be converted to a common base, called *equivalent production*, that is, the equivalent of one completed unit. In order to convert the number of uncompleted products into their equivalence in terms of completed units, the assumption is often made that units still in process at the end of the period are 50 percent complete, and similarly that units in process at the beginning of the period were 50 percent complete at that time. Thus, in order to calculate the labor and overhead costs per unit worked on, each unit completed would be given a weight of one, each unit in process at the end of the period would be given a weight of one half, and each unit in process at the beginning of the period also would be given a weight of one half.[4]

EXAMPLE: If 200 units were completed, 50 units were in process at the end, and 10 were in process at the beginning, the number of equivalent production units worked on would be $200 + 50/2 - 10/2 = 220$. If total costs incurred were \$2,200, costs per equivalent unit would be \$10, and each of the 50 partially completed units in process at the end of the month would be costed at \$5.

Raw material would be costed according to its physical flow (unless the Lifo system was used). If material was added evenly throughout the production process, it could reasonably be costed by use of the 50 percent assumption described above. If, as is perhaps more common, all the raw material for a unit is issued at the beginning of the process, material cost per unit would be obtained by dividing the total cost of material used by the number of units *started* during the period.

In any event, some reasonable assumption has to be made. In a process cost system, there is no precise way of determining the amount of costs attributable to partially completed units.

In summary:

1. Costs incurred during the accounting period are accumulated as debits to Goods in Process Inventory.

2. Production is measured in terms of the number of equivalent units of production.

3. A cost per unit is found by dividing total costs by the number of equivalent units.

4. Finished Goods Inventory is debited and Goods in Process Inven-

---

[4] A more precise procedure would be to estimate the actual stage of completion, but this involves more effort. At the other extreme, some companies disregard the units in process and show no Goods in Process Inventory account. If the goods in process inventory is small, or if it remains relatively constant in size, no serious error is introduced. Another variation is to apply the 50 percent assumption separately to each department through which the product passes rather than to the factory as a whole.

tory credited by an amount equal to the number of units completed in the period multiplied by this cost per unit.

5. The balance in Goods in Process Inventory at the end of an accounting period is the material cost of the units still in the factory plus an appropriate share (say, 50 percent) of the labor and overhead cost of these units if they had been completed.

CHOICE OF A SYSTEM.   Since a process cost system requires less record keeping than a job order system, there is a tendency to use it even though the products manufactured are not strictly homogeneous. Thus, many shoe manufacturers use a process cost system, even though there are considerable differences in cost among the various sizes, styles, and colors of shoes manufactured; for pricing purposes, these companies measure the approximate effect on cost of these differences by calculations made outside the accounting system itself.

If there are important reasons for keeping track of the differences between one product and another, or between one production lot of the same type of product and another, then a job cost system is more appropriate. For example, a job cost system would invariably be used if the customer paid for the specific item or production order on the basis of its cost (as is often the case in so-called "job shop production"). Also, use of a job cost system makes it possible to examine actual costs on specific jobs, and this may help one to locate trouble spots; whereas in a process cost system costs cannot be traced to specific units in this fashion.

For our purposes, there is no need to study differences in the detailed records required for the two types of systems. Both systems are essentially devices for collecting information. Either furnishes the information required for the system shown in Illustration 7–2. In practice, there are many systems that have job costing in some departments or for some types of cost, and process costing in other departments or for other types of cost.

Variations in Practice

The accounting system outlined in Illustration 7–2 will probably never be precisely duplicated in actual practice since it is a schematic representation of underlying structures. Companies build on the basic structure by adding accounts that collect the data in more detail so as to meet their particular needs for information. A company may, for example, set up several raw material inventory accounts, each one covering a different type of material, instead of the single account shown in Illustration 7–2. Another common variation is to have several goods in process accounts, one for each main department or "cost center" in the factory. A system using several goods in process accounts is shown in Illustration 13–1. It will be noted that such a system is essentially like that shown in Illustration 7–2 except that work is transferred from one department to another. The finished goods of one department become, in effect, the raw material of the next department.

Problems of Cost Accumulation

Three problems must be solved in the accumulation of an equitable product cost:

1. *Assignment of costs to accounting periods.* This problem is one of measuring costs incurred, in accordance with the accrual concept. Since this problem was discussed at length in Part I, nothing additional needs to be said here.
2. *Measurement of direct costs.*
3. *Accumulation and allocation of indirect, or overhead, costs.*

The second and third problems will be discussed in the following sections.

Direct Costs

Direct costs are those that are specifically traceable to or caused by the manufacture of a product or the carrying out of a program. These costs are also called *separable* costs since they can be separately identified with individual products or programs, in contrast with *joint* costs which cannot be so traced. For a product, direct costs are usually classified as either direct material or direct labor. For a program, direct costs may also include other elements of cost that are specifically traceable to the program.

DIRECT LABOR.   Direct labor costs are the labor costs that can be specifically identified with a product or that vary so closely with the number of products produced that a direct relationship is presumed to exist. There are essentially two problems in the measurement of direct labor cost: (1) measuring the *quantity* of labor effort expended on the product (e.g., the time spent), and (2) ascertaining the *price* per unit of quantity.

Measuring the quantity of labor effort is relatively easy. In a job-cost system, there is often a time card, or comparable record, for each direct worker, and on it a record is made of the time he spends on each job. Or, if direct workers are paid a piece rate, the record shows the number of pieces completed. In a process cost system, all that is needed is the total of the time spent by all employees on activities directly related to production; these times appear on their time cards. (Actually, the matter is not quite this simple, for problems arise about the treatment of idle time,

Illustration 13–1

COST SYSTEM WITH DEPARTMENTAL ACCOUNTS

NOTE: Circled numbers refer to events described in Chapter 7 (pp. 179–81).

personal time, overtime, and so on. These are mostly beyond the scope of this introductory treatment.)

Deciding on the best way to price these labor quantities is conceptually more difficult. The great majority of companies have a simple solution, which is to price direct labor at the amounts actually earned by the employees concerned (so much an hour if employees are paid on a day-rate basis; so much a piece if they are paid on a piece-rate basis). There may be either a separate rate for each employee, or an average rate for all the employees in a section or department.

EXAMPLE: Assume that a certain job is worked on in four departments, and that the time worked in each department (as shown by time cards) and the labor rate is as indicated below. The direct labor cost of the job would be computed as follows:

Department	Hours on Job	Hourly Rate	Total
A	20	$3.00	$ 60.00
B	3	2.50	7.50
C	6	2.80	16.80
D	40	2.00	80.00
Total direct labor cost of job			$164.30

Some companies add *labor-related* costs to the basic wage rate. They reason that each hour of labor effort costs the company not only the wages paid to the employee but also the social security taxes, pension contributions, and other fringe benefits that are an inevitable part of the real cost of each employee. In some cases, they even add in a share of the costs of the personnel department and employee welfare programs. Using such a higher figure gives a more accurate picture of true labor costs. It also involves additional record keeping, however, and many companies do not believe the gain is worthwhile.

DIRECT MATERIAL. The measurement of direct material cost (or "raw materials cost") also has the two aspects of the quantity of material used and price per unit of quantity. The quantity is often determined from requisitions or similar documents that order material out of the storeroom and into production. The question of pricing this material is analogous to that already discussed under direct labor. It may be priced at solely its invoice cost, or there may be added some or all of the following *material-related* costs: inward freight, inspection costs, moving costs, purchasing department costs, and interest and space charges associated with holding material in inventory.

Indirect Costs

Indirect, or overhead, costs are those costs not associated directly with the products worked on; included are all manufacturing costs other than those classified as direct material and direct labor. Some costs are classified as indirect because it is *impossible* to associate them directly with products. Who can say how much of building depreciation or of a factory superintendent's salary actually belongs to each unit of product manufactured? Other costs are classified as indirect because it is *not convenient* to trace them directly to products, even though it would be possible to do so. Wage-related costs, as mentioned above, are one example.

Since, by definition, indirect costs are not associated directly with products, it is impossible to measure precisely how much indirect cost should be charged to a given product. Nevertheless, total indirect cost is properly part of the cost of the total products worked on, and some reasonable part of the total indirect costs incurred must therefore be charged to each unit of product. The procedure for doing this is called *allocation.*[5]

DISTINCTION BETWEEN DIRECT AND INDIRECT COSTS. Problems arise in attempting to define the precise line between costs that are "traceable to" or "caused by" a product and those that are not. For example, a cost may not be caused by a product even though it is incurred at the same time as the product is being manufactured.

> EXAMPLE: In a certain factory, Products A, B, and C were manufactured during regular working hours, and Product D was manufactured after regular hours. Overtime wages were paid to the men who worked on Product D. These overtime wages might, or might not, be a direct cost of Product D. If the factory worked overtime because of a general press of business, then the overtime was attributable to all the products worked on, and was an indirect cost. If, on the other hand, the overtime work on Product D was occasioned by a special request of the customer for Product D, then the overtime was a direct cost of Product D. It could also happen that the overtime was occasioned by a special need to make Product C quickly, and in order to meet this need, Product D was rescheduled from the regular work period to the overtime; in this case, the overtime was truly a direct cost of Product C, even though overtime was not in fact paid during the hours in which Product C was being manufactured.

Moreover, there are differences of opinion as to how close the causal relationship must be in order to classify a cost as direct. In many production operations, such as assembly lines of all types, refineries, and similar continuous process operations, a basic work force is required no matter what products are manufactured. Some would argue that the labor cost of this work force constitutes a cost that is required to operate the plant in general, much like depreciation on the machinery, and that it is therefore not properly considered as being direct to the specific products that are

---

[5] In Great Britain the name used for this procedure is *apportionment*, and the word "allocation" refers to the charging of *direct* costs to products. This is another example of semantic confusion.

manufactured. Nevertheless, most companies consider such costs as direct labor.

Steps in Indirect Cost Allocation.   The steps in the process are as follows:

1. Estimated indirect costs are accumulated in cost centers.
2. Costs accumulated in service cost centers are transferred to product cost centers.
3. The total cost accumulated in each product center is divided by a measure of activity, giving an overhead rate.
4. Indirect costs are allocated at this rate to each product passing through the cost center.

Usually, the first three steps leading to the determination of an overhead rate are carried out annually, prior to the beginning of the year, although the overhead rate may be changed more than once a year or even less than once a year, depending on the volatility of the underlying factors. The figures used, therefore, usually are estimates of what the costs will be, rather than historical records of what they actually were. These steps apply to both job and process costing, except that in process costing there is no need to calculate overhead rates for individual units of product.

These steps are described in the following paragraphs, using the pipe factory as an illustration.

Cost Centers. A *cost center* is merely an accounting unit for which costs are accumulated. It may be an organizational unit, such as a department, but, as will be seen, there is no necessary connection between cost centers and identifiable organization units.

One type of cost center is a *product center;* that is, a center through which the product passes. Often a product center corresponds to a production department, but a group of similar machines, such as a bank of screw machines, may be a product center, and so may a single machine, such as each printing press in a printing job shop.

A *service center,* another type of cost center, is a department or other unit that incurs costs, but that does not work directly on products, for example, the maintenance department and the general factory offices. If each machine in one department is a product center, then there is also a departmental service center in which the departmental costs not directly traceable to machines are collected.

As shown in Illustration 13–2, our pipe factory has three product centers—the Bowl department, the Stem department, and the Assembly department—and two service centers—Occupancy and General. The Occupancy center is used to accumulate building depreciation, building maintenance, heat, light, and other occupancy costs. The General center is used to accumulate the costs of factory supervision and miscellaneous general costs not traceable directly to other cost centers.

Cost Accumulation by Cost Centers. The first step in the allocation of indirect costs is to estimate the amounts that will be spent directly in each of the product centers and service centers. This procedure involves estimating the elements of cost that are traceable to each. Note that in this step, each cost component is recorded in one, and only one, cost center, so that the sum of the costs for all the cost centers exactly equals total

Illustration 13–2

CALCULATION OF OVERHEAD RATE

Cost Element	Product Centers				Service Centers	
	Total	*Bowl*	*Stem*	*As-sembly*	*Occu-pancy*	*General*
Indirect labor............	$ 9,700	$ 3,100	$ 2,700	$	$	$ 3,900
Indirect supplies.........	4,000	900	600	500	400	1,600
Other.................	12,000	3,900	1,200	700	4,300	1,900
Subtotals...........	$25,700	$ 7,900	$ 4,500	$1,200	$4,700	$ 7,400
	Allocation of Service Centers					
Occupancy.............		1,900	1,400	900	(4,700)	500
General..............		3,600	2,600	1,700		$(7,900)
Total Cost........	$25,700	$13,400	$ 8,500	$3,800	....	....
Direct labor cost........		$15,800	$10,600	$4,200		
Overhead rate per direct labor dollar..........		$0.85	$0.80	$0.90		

indirect costs. These estimates appear in the upper section of Illustration 13–2. Ordinarily, these estimates are based on past experience, adjusted for changes in wage rates, prices, or other factors that may be anticipated for the ensuing year.

Transfer of Service Center Costs. The second step is to transfer all service center costs to product centers, for this is the way in which they become a part of product costs. There are two general ways of doing this: (1) by a direct charge and (2) by allocation.

Some service center costs are charged directly to the product centers. Maintenance department costs may be charged to operating departments on the basis of the maintenance service actually performed, for example. The same possibility exists for other service activities, although beyond a certain point the rationale becomes so tenuous as not to be practicable. Theoretically, but not practically, the president's time could be charged directly to each of the cost centers he deals with.

Other service center costs are *allocated* to product centers on some basis that seems to have a reasonable relationship to "benefits received," or to a "fair share." The dozens of possible bases of allocations that are used in practice can be grouped into the following principal categories:

1. *Labor related.* Fringe benefits, personnel department costs, and other costs associated with employees may be allocated on the basis of the number of employees or total direct labor costs. Alternatively, as mentioned above, some or all of these costs may enter into the calculation of direct labor costs and hence not appear as overhead costs at all. If indirect costs are ultimately charged to products by means of a direct labor rate, the ultimate effect of collecting these labor-related costs in overhead is the same as that of charging them as part of direct labor costs.

2. *Material related.* This category, also discussed above, may be allocated on the basis of the volume or cost of material used in the product center, or, alternatively, it may be excluded from overhead and charged to products as part of direct material cost.

3. *Space related.* These are costs associated with the space that the cost center occupies, and are charged to cost centers on the basis of the relative areas or cubic content of the centers. Occupancy cost in Illustration 13–2 is an example. Assuming that the Bowl center has 40 percent of the total floor space, the Stem center 30 percent, the Assembly center 20 percent, and the General center 10 percent, the total occupancy cost of $4,700 is allocated to the other centers according to these percentages.

4. *Activity related.* Some costs are roughly related to the overall volume of activity, or size of the cost center; or at least there is a presumption that the larger the cost center, the more costs are properly chargeable to it. Electrical costs and steam costs, if not directly chargeable by meters, fall into this category, and so do a variety of other service center costs which, although not demonstrably a function of activity, are more fairly apportioned in this way than in any other. The measure of activity may be closely related to the item, as, for example, allocating electrical costs on the basis of the total horsepower of motors installed; or it may be an overall measure, such as total labor cost, total direct costs, or sales value of products processed. The General service center in Illustration 13–2 falls in this category. The total cost of $7,900 is allocated to the product centers on the basis of the relative direct material and labor costs of these centers, here assumed to be 46 percent for Bowl, 33 percent for Stem, and 21 percent for Assembly.

Step-Down Order. Note that in Illustration 13–2, part of occupancy cost is charged to the General service center. It may be that part of General's cost should be charged to Occupancy. When there are a number of service centers, the interrelationships among them could theoretically lead to a long series of redistributions and re-redistributions, but in practice this is avoided by distributing the service center costs in a prescribed order, which is called the *step-down order*. In the illustration, the order is Occupancy first, and General second. No additional cost is allocated to a service center after its costs have been distributed. Since the step-down order is adhered to in all calculations, the results are always consistent.

Overhead Rates. Having brought all the costs to product centers, we now seek some equitable means of loading them onto the products passing through the center, step three in the process of allocating indirect costs.

Essentially, the calculation of an overhead rate requires an answer to the question: Why should one unit of product bear more overhead than another? Possible answers are the following: (1) because more work has been done on it; (2) because the product is worth more and therefore is able to bear more overhead; (3) because it requires more labor, and overhead is largely associated with labor; and so on. These answers suggest some quantitative bases of making the charge, respectively: (1) the number of direct labor hours or machine hours required for the product; (2) total direct costs of the product; (3) direct labor cost; and so on. Of these, the machine hours basis is common for cost centers that consist primarily of one machine (such as a paper machine) or a group of related machines. The direct labor cost basis is perhaps most frequently used in other situations, since it is readily available on the job cost card. Direct labor hours are also often used if the number of hours worked on each job is readily available.

In our pipe factory, let us assume that a direct labor cost basis will be used in each product center. (Actually, the same basis of measurement is not necessarily used in all product centers.) All that remains, therefore, is to estimate the total direct labor cost for each product center in the ensuing year and divide this into the total indirect cost of the center. The result is the amount of indirect cost that is to be charged to pipes for each dollar of direct labor incurred. In the Bowl center, for example, the overhead rate is $0.85 per dollar of direct labor.

Allocation of Indirect Costs. The fourth step in the total process of accumulation and allocation of indirect cost is to apply the rate calculated above to the products passing through the product center. If for a given lot of pipes the direct labor cost in the Bowl center is $100 and the overhead rate is $0.85 per dollar of direct labor, the indirect cost of this lot of pipes is $85.

Because of the nature of the methods used, two observations should be made about the indirect cost: (1) The total amount transferred in this way may not coincide exactly with the total actual incurred costs for the period under consideration. If there are differences, then indirect cost is under- or overabsorbed, and various accounting techniques are used for handling such amounts. (2) The whole process, being based on subjective judgments of what is a "fair" distribution, cannot result in an *accurate* cost. These points are discussed in the following sections.

Unabsorbed and Overabsorbed Overhead

In any accounting period, the overhead costs charged to pipes worked on in the Bowl cost center will equal the total indirect costs charged to the cost center if, but only if, total indirect costs are exactly 85 percent of total direct labor costs. This is not likely to happen. If more overhead is charged to products than is actually incurred, overhead is said to be *overabsorbed*, and if less, it is *underabsorbed* (or more commonly, *unabsorbed*). For management purposes, the amount of unabsorbed or overabsorbed overhead is useful information, as will be discussed in Chapter 17.

For financial accounting purposes, this amount can be handled in one of three ways: (1) charge or credit it entirely to the income of the period on the income statement (often as an adjustment to cost of goods sold); (2) divide it between inventory and period expense in the proportion that inventory is to cost of goods sold; or (3) do nothing, in the expectation that unabsorbed overhead in one period will be offset by overabsorption in a succeeding period. An argument for the first alternative is that the difference between estimated and actual costs may reflect events occurring in the period and therefore should affect income of the period. An argument for the second alternative is that the difference may reflect an inability to make accurate estimates, and that the estimated costs in inventory and cost of goods sold should be corrected accordingly. The third alternative is not a generally accepted accounting practice for annual financial statements, but it is often used for monthly or other interim internal statements both as a matter of convenience and to avoid having income affected by short-term fluctuations in indirect cost absorption.

In the interests of simplicity, no account for overabsorbed or unabsorbed overhead was shown in Illustration 7–1 or 13–1. Such an account could be fitted into the system in either of two places, depending on whether the overhead charged to the cost center was the amount absorbed in the period or the amount incurred. If the cost center was debited for the amount of overhead *absorbed*, then the over- or underabsorbed account would take up the difference between this amount and the total overhead costs incurred as shown in the various overhead cost accounts (i.e., the $2,000 in Illustration 13–1). If the cost center was debited for the overhead cost *incurred*, then the balance in the cost center account would later be adjusted to remove the difference between cost incurred and cost absorbed onto products.

If there are seasonal variations either in costs (as in heating costs) or in the level of activity, the amount of overhead cost charged to the cost center each month is often a *normalized* amount rather than the actual amount of cost incurred. This normalized amount is set in such a way that the unit costs do not vary from month to month because of volume changes or seasonal factors. The difference between the normalized amount and actual costs incurred is held in an overabsorbed or underabsorbed account, with the expectation that over the course of a year, overabsorptions will be washed out by underabsorptions.

Accuracy of Indirect Costs

By definition, indirect costs are not traced directly to products; therefore the indirect cost charged to a product cannot be the "actual" indirect cost incurred in making the product in any literal sense of this word. Through the collection and allocation mechanism described above, we have indeed succeeded in adding a portion of building depreciation, for example, onto the cost of each unit of product, but judgments as to what is fair and reasonable were involved in each step of this process: in deciding on the costs applicable to the *period* (what really is the depreciation expense of this period?), in deciding how much of this cost is applicable to each *cost center*, and in deciding how much of the cost center's cost is applicable to each *product*. Two equally capable accountants can arrive at quite different amounts of indirect cost per unit, and there is no way of proving that one is right and the other wrong, that is, that one indirect cost figure is accurate and the other is inaccurate.

Definition of Cost Center

The amount of indirect cost charged to a product can also be significantly influenced by judgment as to how a cost center is defined. In some companies each important machine is a cost center. At the other extreme, the entire plant is a single cost center (giving rise to a *plantwide* overhead rate). There are a number of choices between these two extremes. In general, the more narrow the definition of a cost center, the more equitable is the resulting indirect cost of the product.

EXAMPLE: Assume a plant with two product departments. Department A does machining with expensive machine tools requiring much floor space, power, and supplies; and Department B does bench work and assembly with only inexpensive hand tools. Overhead rates are determined as follows:

Department	Estimated Annual Hours	Estimated Overhead Cost	Overhead Rate per Hour
A	20,000	$200,000	$10.00
B	40,000	100,000	2.50
Total plant	60,000	$300,000	$ 5.00

Assume a job that requires 20 hours in Department A and 100 hours in Department B. If the company used separate overhead rates for each department, the overhead cost for this job would be:

Dept. A...... 20 hours × $10.00 = $200
Dept. B......100 hours × $ 2.50 = 250
Total overhead cost...........$450

If the company used a plantwide overhead rate, the overhead cost of the same job would be:

120 hours × $5 = $600.

The overhead cost of $600 is less equitable than the $450 cost derived from the departmental rates because the plantwide rate costed each hour at $5, despite the fact that almost all the hours on this job were incurred in Department B, where the rate was only $2.50 per hour.

On the other hand, it is also true that the more narrow the definition of the cost centers, the more cost centers there will be, and therefore the more work involved in computing and applying separate overhead rates. The choice of cost centers in a particular situation depends on the balance between the increase in the equity of the overhead rates and the increased work involved. If all products spend approximately the same proportion of time in each department, the differences in indirect costs assigned by means of a series of rates for each department and indirect costs assigned by a plantwide rate will be small. In such a situation, little increase in equity is gained by using a number of rates.

A few companies compute what they call "actual" indirect costs by going through the process shown in Illustration 13–2 at the end of the period, rather than prior to the beginning of the period. At the end of the period the actual indirect cost and the actual level of activity are available, and these are used to calculate a rate that, when applied to products, will result in the exact absorption of indirect cost. Since under this procedure no jobs can be costed until the period has ended, it is rarely used. Furthermore, although this procedure does absorb indirect cost in total, it does not eliminate the judgment made with respect to the amount of costs applicable to the period, to the product center, or to the individual product, and hence the detailed indirect cost allocations cannot be said to be, literally, "actual" even under this procedure.

The following excerpts from publications of the National Association of Accountants are relevant:

A cost is joint when it is incurred for a group of segments as a unit and no portion of the cost can be traced exclusively to any of the individual segments. . . .[6]

---

[6] National Association of Accountants, *Concepts for Management Accounting*, 1966, p. 42.

To the extent that costs are joint, individual products in a combination have no objectively determinable separate costs.

Joint costs can be allocated, but all bases for allocation imply assumptions that cannot be objectively verified. . . . While a chosen basis can be rationalized, it cannot be proved more correct than another by any objective process. As a consequence, equally competent accountants may arrive at different costs for the same product.[7]

Product Line Reporting

Currently, there is considerable controversy over a proposal of the Securities and Exchange Commission to require disclosure of revenues and costs for each substantial product line or other segment of a conglomerate, that is, a company that operates in more than one industry. The controversy is symptomatic of the differences that exist among companies in their method of accounting for product costs. Opponents of the SEC proposal claim that these differences are so great that the reported figures would be meaningless to the reader of the financial statement, or to anyone not thoroughly familiar with the rules of product costing used in the company.

Selling and General Costs

Although, in accordance with generally accepted accounting principles, selling costs cannot be included in product costs for the purposes of measuring the amounts of inventory and cost of sales, a company may nevertheless assign selling costs to products for other purposes. The same approach is used as described above; that is, costs are classified as either direct (e.g., commissions on sales) or indirect, and products are charged with the direct selling costs and an equitable share of the indirect selling costs. Selling costs may also be collected by geographical regions or sales offices, or by channels of distribution.

Even though a company may decide to omit certain general and administrative costs from its inventory and cost-of-sales computations, it may decide to include these in its product costs for other purposes. If so, the approach is the same as that described above for manufacturing costs.

STANDARD COSTS

The basic objective of the system outlined above was to charge units of product with a fair share of the *actual* costs incurred in making these products. Many cost accounting systems, in contrast, are based wholly or

---

[7] National Association of Accountants, *Costing Joint Products* (Research Series No. 31), 1957, pp. 1 and 4.

in part on the principle that the costs charged to individual products are the costs that *should have been incurred* on those products rather than the costs that *actually were incurred*. Such a system is called a *standard cost system.*[8] The essential nature of standard costs, then, is that they represent costs that should have been incurred rather than costs that actually were incurred.

In a standard cost system, each unit of product has a standard material cost, a standard labor cost, and a standard overhead cost for each product cost center. The total standard cost for the month is obtained by multiplying these standard unit costs by the number of units flowing through the cost center in that month.

Illustration 13–3 shows the system for our pipe factory shifted to a standard cost basis. It is the same as the actual cost system shown in Illustration 7–2 except that three *variance accounts* have been added. Standard costs are usually different from the costs actually incurred, and variance accounts are a repository for these differences. For example, if actual labor costs for the month were $2,500, the credit to the liability account Wages Payable must be $2,500. If the standard labor costs of the operations performed totaled only $2,100, Goods in Process would be debited for $2,100, and the $400 difference would be debited to the Labor Variance account. Entries to variance accounts are debits if actual costs are greater than standard costs, and they are credits if actual costs are less than standard costs.

A standard cost system may have several advantages. First, it is often simpler and requires less work than an actual cost system. This is so because once the standard cost for a unit of product has been determined, this cost remains unchanged for relatively long periods, instead of being recalculated for each separate unit or job.

Second, a standard cost system produces the same costs for physically identical units of product, whereas an actual cost system may not. For example, in our pipe factory there may be two equally efficient men making identical sizes and shapes of pipe bowls. If one man, because of seniority or other reasons, has a higher wage rate than the other, under an actual job cost system the pipes that he makes will have a higher labor cost than the pipes the other man makes; yet realistically there is no difference in the finished pipes—no reason why one should be said to "cost" more than another. This fact also makes standard costs a better basis for estimating selling prices than are actual costs.

Third, a standard cost system provides the beginning of a mechanism for checking on the efficiency with which the work was done, in that the

---

[8] Some accountants limit the term "standard costs" to costs determined on the basis of engineering estimates and use the term "estimated costs" for costs determined on the basis of estimates made by persons who are not engineers. As a practical matter, the distinction is not of great significance.

Illustration 13–3

A STANDARD COST SYSTEM

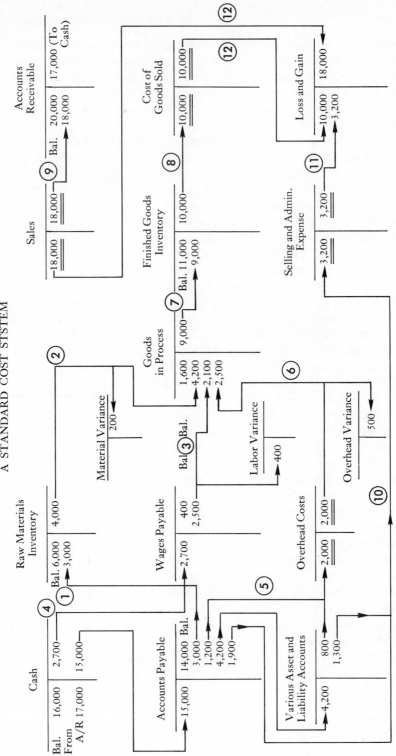

NOTE: Circled numbers refer to events described in Chapter 7.

Bal. = Net income before taxes.

balance in the variance account may be an indication of good or bad performance. The validity of this statement depends on the accuracy with which the standard cost actually measures what should have been incurred; this point is discussed in Chapter 17.

Companies which use standard costs do not necessarily use a *complete* standard cost system, that is, a system that treats all elements of cost on a standard basis. Some, for example, use standard direct labor and indirect costs but use actual material costs.

Standard costs may be inserted into the system at any one of several places. Thus, material may be taken up in Raw Materials Inventory at a standard price, with the difference between actual purchase price and the standard price being entered in a Raw Materials Price Variance account; in Illustration 13–3 this account would be placed to the left of the Raw Materials Inventory account. Another alternative is to charge all elements of cost into Goods in Process at actual; the conversion to a standard cost basis would then be made between Goods in Process and Finished Goods Inventory. In the latter system, the variance account would occur between Goods in Process and Finished Goods Inventory. The essential point is that one or more variance accounts are inserted in the system at whatever point the shift from actual to standard is made.

The variance accounts may or may not be closed at the end of the accounting period. The possibilities are the same as those already discussed with respect to under- or overabsorbed overhead, which is one type of variance account.

JOINT PRODUCTS AND BY-PRODUCTS

In some manufacturing plants, two or more dissimilar end products may be made from a single batch of raw material or from a single production process. The classic example of these *joint products* is the variety of end products—the hide, the many different cuts of meat, and so on—that are made from the single raw material, a steer. Beyond a certain point in the manufacturing process, which is called the *split-off point*, separate end products are identified, and costs are accumulated for each of them. The problem of joint costing is to find some reasonable basis for assigning to the joint products the material, labor, and indirect costs incurred up to the split-off point.

This problem is essentially the same as that of allocating indirect costs. In both cases, the objective is to assign a fair share of the joint or common costs to the separate end products, and in neither case can the results be scientifically accurate.

One common basis of allocating joint costs is in proportion to the *sales value* of the end products, adjusted for processing and marketing costs incurred beyond the split-off point. If the selling price depends on cost, this method involves a certain amount of circular reasoning, but there may be no better alternative. If gasoline sells for twice the price of kerosene, it is perhaps reasonable that gasoline should bear twice as much of the crude oil and joint refining costs. Another basis of allocation is weight; in the case of the steer, this would assume that the stew meat is as valuable as the tenderloin, which is unrealistic; but in other situations, this might be a reasonable assumption. In any event, the amount charged to each end product must be recognized as resulting from an allocation. If some scientifically correct method of assigning the cost were available, the product would not be a joint product, by definition.

By-products are a special kind of joint product. If management wishes to make Products A and B in some predetermined proportion, or if it wishes to make as much of each as possible from a given quantity of raw material, then they are ordinary joint products. If, on the other hand, management's objective is to make Product A, but some quantity of Product B inevitably emerges from the production process, then Product A is a main product and Product B is a by-product. The intention is to make from a given amount of joint material as much of the main product and as little of the by-product as possible. As management's intention changes, the classification changes. Kerosene was once the main product made from crude oil; subsequently, with the growth in consumption of gasoline, many petroleum companies considered kerosene a by-product; and currently it has become a main product again, because it is an important component of jet engine fuel. Certain tars and petrochemicals, once by-products, are now main products.

A number of alternative procedures are used in costing by-products. At one extreme, they may be assigned zero cost, with all costs being charged to the main products. At the other extreme, by-products may be assigned a cost equal to their sales value, with the result that no profit or loss is attributed to the by-product and the entire profit of the process is attributed to the main product.

DIRECT COSTING

Although not now a generally accepted financial accounting practice, mention should be made of the practice of *direct costing*, which is widely discussed and used by an increasing number of companies in their internal accounting systems.[9] "Direct costs," as used here, are costs that vary with changes in production volume; therefore they correspond to variable costs, and not to direct costs in the sense of traceable or separable costs as the term was used in the preceding section.[10]

---

[9] Of 365 respondents to a 1959 Financial Executives Institute survey, 77, or 21 percent, reported a use of direct costing, and nearly half of these had started using the system within the previous five years.

[10] This confusion in terminology is another example of the differences in the definition of cost that cause trouble in practice unless they are recognized.

In the conventional system, the basic concept is *full costing;* that is, products should bear a fair share of all the costs involved in making them. In the direct cost system, only the variable costs are charged to products and thus pass through inventory accounts; nonvariable costs are charged off as expenses in the period in which they are incurred. Consequently, nonvariable overhead costs affect net income more quickly in the direct cost system than in a full cost system. This effect can be seen in Illustration 13–4, in which it is assumed that one unit is manufactured each period, but that the unit manufactured in the first period is not sold until

Illustration 13–4

COMPARISON OF FULL COSTING AND DIRECT COSTING

	Under Full Costing		Under Direct Costing	
	Period No. 1	*Period No. 2*	*Period No. 1*	*Period No. 2*
Activity:				
Units manufactured.........	1	1	1	1
Units sold...............	0	2	0	2
Income Statement:				
Sales....................	$ 0	$200	$ 0	$200
Cost of goods sold.........	0	160	0	60
Manufacturing overhead....	0	0	50	50
Selling and administrative...	10	10	10	10
Net Income or Loss..........	$(10)	$ 30	$(60)	$ 80
Ending Inventory (Balance Sheet)..................	$ 80	$ 0	$ 30	$ 0

the second period. The sales price is $100 per unit, variable costs are $30 per *unit*, and nonvariable overhead is $50 per *period*. In the conventional full cost system, the entire manufacturing cost of $80 is held in inventory at the end of Period No. 1, and is released as cost of goods sold in Period No. 2, along with the cost of the unit made and sold in that period. In direct costing, only the $30 of variable cost is held in inventory at the end of Period No. 1, and the $50 of nonvariable overhead is charged as an expense of the period.

The conventional system is also called *absorption costing* because all costs are absorbed by products, in contrast with direct costing, in which nonvariable overhead is not absorbed by products.

In direct costing, nonvariable manufacturing indirect costs are viewed as being essentially the same as administrative costs; that is, these are costs associated with being in business rather than costs associated with the specific units of product manufactured. Proponents of direct costing assert that management can be misled by the income reported in a period if these costs are hidden away in inventory. Direct costing is the extreme case of differences of opinion about which costs are product costs and which are period costs.

Since direct costing is not a generally accepted practice for financial accounting, companies that use it for internal purposes recompute their inventory valuation and cost of goods sold for their published financial statements. They do this by computing an overhead rate, usually on a plantwide basis, which they use solely for this purpose.

RELATION TO FINANCIAL ACCOUNTING

It should be emphasized that the product costing systems described above are an integral part of financial accounting, with the same rules of debit and credit. The accounting entries described in this chapter are made for the same purpose as those described in Chapter 7. The only substantive difference is that in Chapter 7 we assumed that the company did not have a way of directly obtaining the cost of items moving from Raw Materials, through Goods in Process, to Finished Goods, and out to Cost of Goods Sold; we therefore had to find these amounts by the process of deduction. In the present chapter, a method of finding the amounts directly has been described. The other differences, such as the classification of goods in process into cost centers, are merely differences in detail.

Cost information is sometimes collected outside the debit and credit structure. Such a system is called a *statistical* cost system, in contrast with a *tied-in* cost system. A statistical system is simpler to operate but does not permit the checks on accuracy that are possible in the tied-in system.

RESPONSIBILITY ACCOUNTING

Product costing is one of the two principal types of management accounting. The other is responsibility accounting. The objective of product costing is to assign an equitable share of costs to products; the objective of responsibility accounting is to assign to responsibility centers the costs incurred by them. Product costing and responsibility accounting, although here described separately, are actually two aspects of a single management accounting system. They do not involve two "sets of books," but only two ways of aggregating the same detailed bits of information. Indeed, we need to refer to only two important distinctions between the two types of information:

1. In responsibility accounting, costs are assigned to responsibility centers rather than to products.

2. In responsibility accounting, a clear distinction must be made be-

tween costs that are controllable by the head of the responsibility center and costs that are not controllable by him.

Responsibility Centers

A responsibility center is an organization unit headed by a responsible person, its manager. It is responsible for performing some function, which is its *output*. In performing this function, it uses resources, or *inputs*. The costs assigned to a responsibility center are intended to measure the inputs that it consumes in a specified period of time, such as a week or a month.

Within a business there is a whole hierarchy of responsibility centers. At the top, there is the president or chief executive officer, who is held responsible by the owners for the overall profitability of the enterprise. Beneath him, the several operating and staff departments are each responsibility centers, and at still lower levels, responsibility centers may consist of sections, subsections, or even individuals. The delineation of responsibility centers is in practice a difficult task, and the installation of a control system often uncovers instances of overlapping responsibility which need to be corrected. If the company's organization chart reflected the actual lines of responsibility, this difficulty would not exist, but for various reasons the chart may not do this.

In a given company, responsibility centers are often synonymous with cost centers. This is because production departments are often defined as cost centers, and these departments are also responsibility centers since the department foreman is a responsible supervisor. When individual machines or other segments of a department are used as cost centers, costs for the responsibility center can be obtained simply by adding up the relevant costs of these separate cost centers. At the other extreme, if the whole factory is a single cost center (as is the case when a plantwide overhead rate is used), separate accounts are set up to collect the costs for the individual responsibility centers in the plant. Likewise, if cost centers are departments and responsibility centers are individual work shifts or other departmental subdivisions, separate accounts for these subdivisions are required.

In short, costs are collected for the cost center or the responsibility center, whichever is the smaller unit, and costs for the other are obtained by addition. Thus, the fact that a cost center is not necessarily the same as a responsibility center raises no particular problem of cost collection.

Service centers headed by responsible supervisors, such as the maintenance department, the personnel department, the accounting department, and so on, are also responsibility centers. Service centers that are mere aggregates of cost without reference to personal responsibility are not. An example of the latter is the Occupancy service center described in a preceding section, which is not in itself a responsibility center, although its costs are part of the responsibility center of the plant manager. All costs in a company are assigned to some responsibility center.

Controllable Costs

The costs incurred in a responsibility center are those associated with accomplishing its function, whatever that function may be. Some of these costs are controllable by the head of the responsibility center, and others are not so controllable. Since responsibility center costs are used principally in the control process, it is important that the controllable costs be shown separately from the noncontrollable costs. The line between controllable and noncontrollable costs is difficult to draw; it is discussed in Chapter 14.

Some companies collect only controllable costs by responsibility centers. Others collect both controllable and noncontrollable costs. When a responsibility center is synonymous with a cost center, the latter practice is often more convenient because the same set of costs can then be used for both purposes—the controllable costs for control, and the sum of controllable and noncontrollable costs for product costing.

In product costing, we need only to know the total cost to be charged to products, but for management control, the total must be broken down in a way that facilitates the analysis of performance. Thus, in responsibility accounting, costs are classified according to *type* (also called "object," or "natural element," or "function"). Indirect labor, supplies, power, heat, overtime premiums, and spoilage are examples from the long list of cost types that might be useful in a given situation.

For analysis purposes, it may also be useful to separate *variable costs* (which are costs that change proportionately with changes in production volume or other measure of activity) from nonvariable costs, but such separation usually requires only that each cost type be designated either as variable or as nonvariable. Variable costs are discussed further in Chapter 14.

In summary, *responsibility accounting* requires that costs be classified: (1) by responsibility centers; (2) within each responsibility center, by whether controllable or noncontrollable; and (3) within the controllable classification, by cost types, or natural elements, in a way that provides a useful basis for analysis.

As mentioned above, product costing and responsibility accounting are part of a single system, in which detailed cost information is aggregated in two different ways in different purposes. The lowest common denominator of the system is called the *account building block*, which consists of a single type of cost (e.g., direct material, supplies, overtime) incurred in the *smaller* of either a cost center or a responsibility center. All summaries of cost information are obtained by combining these building blocks in one of two principal ways: (1) according to products, or (2) according to the hierarchy of responsibility centers.

SUMMARY

A management accounting system consists of two principal parts, called respectively product cost accounting and responsibility accounting. In some companies, there is a third part, in order to conform to the requirements of regulatory agencies.

In product costing, each product worked on is charged with what is believed to be a fair share of the total manufacturing costs incurred. Products in inventory are valued at this cost, and this is the cost used in figuring the cost of goods sold. Direct labor and direct material costs applicable to each product can usually be measured with reasonable accuracy; for these costs, the principal problem is the mechanical one of accumulating the various labor and material costs that belong to the product. The remaining cost elements, collectively called overhead or indirect cost, cannot be traced directly to products. These costs are accumulated by cost centers, and the total costs of the cost center are allocated to products going through the center on some reasonable basis. *Whenever allocated costs are involved, the resulting product cost cannot be said to be accurate.*

Also, when joint or common costs are involved there can be no scientifically correct way of splitting them up among time periods, among cost centers, or among products passing through cost centers. A pig is a pig; there is no way of knowing how much of its cost belongs to the hide and how much to the bacon. This is *not* merely difficult; it is impossible.

But the objective of product cost accounting is not to ascertain a scientifically correct cost; rather it is to charge products with a *fair share* of the total costs incurred in the manufacturing process. This it can do.

Since costs are also used for management control, the elementary building blocks of cost are arranged by type in responsibility centers, and by proper combination and summarization they can serve both purposes.

SUGGESTIONS FOR FURTHER READING

DEARDEN, JOHN. *Cost and Budget Analysis.* Englewood Cliffs, N.J.: Prentice-Hall, Inc., 1962.

DICKEY, ROBERT I. (ed.). *Accountants' Cost Handbook.* 2d ed.; New York: Ronald Press Co., 1960.

MATZ, ADOLPH; OTHEL J. CURRY; and GEORGE W. FRANK. *Cost Accounting.* 4th ed.; Cincinnati: South-Western Publishing Co., 1967.

MOORE, CARL L., and ROBERT K. JAEDICKE. *Managerial Accounting.* 2d ed.; Dallas, Texas: Southwestern, 1967.

NEUNER, JOHN J. W., and SAMUEL FRUMER. *Cost Accounting: Principles and Practice.* 7th ed.; Homewood, Ill.: Richard D. Irwin, Inc., 1967.

NICKERSON, CLARENCE B. *Managerial Cost Accounting and Analysis.* 2d ed.; New York: McGraw-Hill Book Co., Inc., 1962.

SHILLINGLAW, GORDON. *Cost Accounting: Analysis and Control.* Rev. ed.; Homewood, Ill.: Richard D. Irwin, Inc., 1967.

THOMAS, WILLIAM E. (ed.). *Readings in Cost Accounting, Budgeting and Control.* 3d ed.; Cincinnati: South-Western Publishing Co., 1967.

CASES

CASE 13–1. BENNETT BODY COMPANY

Mr. Ralph Kern, the controller of the Bennett Body Company, received a memorandum from Mr. Paul Bennett, the company's president, suggesting that Mr. Kern review an attached magazine article and comment on it at the next executive committee meeting. The article described the Conley Automotive Corporation's cost accounting system. The Bennett Body Company was a custom manufacturer of truck bodies. Occasionally a customer would reorder an exact duplicate of an earlier body, but most of the time some modifications caused changes in design and hence in cost.

The Conley System

Mr. Kern learned from the article that Conley also manufactured truck bodies but that these were of standard design. Conley had 12 models that it produced in quantities based upon management's estimates of demand. In December of each year, a plan, or budget, for the following year's operations was agreed upon, which included estimates of costs and profits as well as of sales volume.

Included in this budget were estimated costs for each of the 12 models of truck bodies. These costs were determined by totaling estimated labor at an expected wage rate, estimated material at an expected cost per unit, and an allocation for overhead that was based on the proportion of estimated total overhead costs to estimated total direct labor dollars. This estimate for each model became the standard cost of the model.

No attempt was made in Conley's accounts to record the actual costs of each model. Costs were accumulated for each of the four direct producing departments and for several service departments. Labor costs were easily obtainable from payroll records, since all employees assigned to a producing department were classified as direct labor for that department. Material sent to the department was charged to it on the basis of signed issue slips. Overhead costs were charged to the department on the basis of the same percentage of direct labor as that used in determining the standard cost.

Since Conley's management also knew how many truck bodies of each model were handled by each department monthly, the total standard costs for each department could easily be calculated by multiplying the quantity of that model produced by its standard cost. Management watched closely the difference between the actual cost and the standard cost as the year progressed.

As each truck body was completed, its cost was added to Finished Goods Inventory at the standard cost figure. When the truck body was

Exhibit 1

SUMMARY OF COSTS, DEPARTMENT 4, NOVEMBER

Standard	Number of Bodies	Material		Labor		Overhead	
		Per Unit	Total	Per Unit	Total	Per Unit	Total
Model 101.........	10	$150	$ 1,500	$220	$ 2,200	$220	$ 2,200
109.........	8	200	1,600	175	1,400	175	1,400
113.........	11	305	3,355	210	2,310	210	2,310
154.........	20	95	1,900	194	3,880	194	3,880
Total..............	49		$ 8,355		$ 9,790		$ 9,790
Actual costs........			9,120		10,030		10,030
Variances..........			$— 765		$— 240		$— 240

The overhead rate for Department 4 was 100 percent of direct labor cost.

sold, the standard cost became the Cost of Sales figure. This system of cost recording avoided the necessity of accumulating detailed actual costs on each specific body that was built; yet the company could estimate, reasonably well, the costs of its products. Moreover, management believed that the differences between actual and standard cost provided a revealing insight into cost fluctuations that eventually should lead to better cost control. An illustrative tabulation of the costs for Department 4 is shown in Exhibit 1. No incomplete work remained in this department either at the beginning or at the end of the month.

The Bennett System

Because almost every truck body that Bennett built was in some respect unique, costs were accumulated by individual jobs.

When a job was started it received a code number, and costs for the job were collected weekly under that code number. When material (such as wood, metal tubing, steel forms or bars, canvas, paint, etc.) used for a particular job was issued to the workmen, a record of the quantity issued was obtained on a requisition form. This quantity of material—so many units, board feet, linear feet, weight, etc.—was multiplied by the purchase cost per unit to arrive at the actual cost of material used. Maintenance of cumulative records of these withdrawals by code number made the total material cost of each job easy to determine.

Likewise, all labor costs of making a particular truck body were recorded. If a man moved from job to job, a record was made of his time spent on each job, and his week's wages were divided among these jobs in proportion to the amount of time spent on each. Throughout the shop, the time of any person working on anything directly related to an order —Job No. 1375J, for example—was ultimately converted to a dollar cost and charged to that job.

Finally, Bennett's overhead costs that could not be directly associated with a particular job were allocated among all jobs on the proportional basis of direct labor hours involved. Thus, if in any month 135 direct labor hours were spent on Job No. 1375J, and this was 5 percent of the 2,700 direct labor hours spent on all jobs at Bennett, then Job No. 1375J received 5 percent of all the overhead costs—supplies, salaries, depreciation, etc.—for that month.

Under this system Bennett's management knew at the end of each month what each body job in process cost to date. They could also determine total factory cost and therefore gross profit at the completion of each job.

The note that Mr. Bennett attached to the magazine article read:

Ralph:

Please review the system of cost accounting described in this article with the view of possible applications to our company. Aside from the overall comparison, I am interested particularly in your opinion on—

1. Costs of paper work and record keeping, as compared with our system.
2. Possible reasons for cost differences between the actual and standard costs under Conley's system.
3. How do you think Conley develops the standard cost of factory overhead for a particular model for the purpose of preparing the budget?
4. Do you think that we should change our period for determining the overhead allocation rate from monthly to annually? If so, why?

These are just a few questions which might be helpful in your overall analysis. I would like to discuss this question at the next executive committee meeting.

Thank you.

Paul Bennett

Question

1. As Mr. Kern, what would you be prepared to say in response to Mr. Bennett's memorandum?

CASE 13–2.   TREYNOR COMPANY

The Treynor Company had a standard cost system with separate accounts established to record factory variances. Variance accounts were closed at the end of the month to the Loss and Gain account. Two products were made, each with a standard cost as follows:

	Product A	Product B
Direct material cost (at standard cost of $1 per pound)	$ 5	$ 8
Direct labor cost (at standard rate of $1 per hour)	20	12
Overhead cost	10	20
Total	$35	$40

Raw material cost was debited to the Raw Materials Inventory account at the standard cost of $1 a pound upon delivery, any discrepancy between actual and standard price going to a variance account. All debits to Goods in Process were at standard.

Following are statements relating to operations in September:

1. On September 1, balances in the accounts were as follows:

	Dr.	Cr.
Raw Materials	$ 12,600	
Goods in Process	35,000	
Finished Goods	43,000	
Other Assets	200,000	
Accounts Payable		$ 20,000
Wages Payable		8,000
Other Liabilities		100,000
Shareholders' Equity		162,600
Total	$290,600	$290,600

Raw material on hand, Sept. 1, 12,000 lbs.
2. During September, the company bought and received 20,000 pounds of material, paying $12,000 cash of the total bill of $23,000, leaving $11,000 still payable as of September 30.
3. The materials warehouse issued 15,000 pounds of material to the production department during the month.
4. Production schedules for September called for 800 units of A and 1,200 units of B to be started through production during the month, and the 15,000 pounds of material was all used for this purpose.

5. Direct labor expense incurred during September was $30,000. Indirect labor expense was $10,000. Wages paid were $38,000 (disregard taxes).

6. Overhead expenses for September other than indirect labor were $25,000. Of this amount, $19,000 was credited to Other Assets and $6,000 to Accounts Payable.

7. Administrative and selling expenses were $20,000. The offsetting entry was to Accounts Payable.

8. Standard cost sheets showed that standard costs were charged to products, representing work done on those products during the month, as follows: labor, $30,400; overhead, $32,000.

9. During September, 1,100 units of A and 1,000 units of B were delivered to the warehouse as finished goods, although some of this production had in fact been started in August.

10. September sales were 1,000 units of A for $53,000 and 1,200 units of B for $65,000. The offsetting entry was to Other Assets.

Questions

1. Set up T accounts and record the above transactions. Adjust and close the accounts, carrying the process through to the transfer of September's net profit to Retained Earnings.

2. Prepare an income statement for September.

3. Prepare a balance sheet as of September 30.

4. Why is your figure for the profit in September only a rough approximation at best?

CASE 13–3. LAREN MANUFACTURING COMPANY

Mr. James Laren, Jr., was asked to investigate the possibility of instituting new methods of cost control in the Laren Manufacturing Company, which was owned by his father. Mr. Laren, Sr., keenly felt the need for better cost control because his small plumbing and pipe fitting equipment firm competed on a price basis with large corporations that were firmly entrenched in the market.

James Laren, Jr., decided to start his investigation in the company's valve department, because this department produced almost one third of the company's total volume of sales. The valve department contained drilling and grinding machines, lathes, welding equipment, and assembly space. In this department all the operations necessary to produce and assemble valves were performed.

The valve department occupied almost one half the total floor space in the Laren Company's three-story plant. Section 1, the welding section, was located on the first floor of the plant and occupied about one sixth of the space on that floor. Sections 2, 3, and 4, as well as the office, toolroom and stock room were all located on the third floor. None of these sections occupied more than one fifth of the third floor's space. Section 5, the assembly section, occupied about one half of the second floor and one sixth of the third floor. Exhibit 1 describes the functions of these sections, each of which was under the supervision of a leadman.

Exhibit 2 indicates the flow of production through the various sections of the valve department. Valves in the standard line went through Sections 1, 2, 3, and 5. Special valves (i.e., valves not in the standard line) went through all five sections. Pieces produced for spare parts inventory did not go through Section 5 (assembly). In addition, any section of the

Exhibit 1

FUNCTIONS PERFORMED IN VALVE DEPARTMENT

Section 1 . . . . This section repairs casting defects, welds special fittings to valve bodies,
Welding   and performs other welding operations required in fabrication of valve
                     parts.

Section 2 . . . . Grinding is done to prepare castings for further machining. Also, various
Grinding   parts which make up valves are ground for precision fit.

Section 3 . . . . All the necessary machining operations to produce various standard
Machining   valves are done in this section.

Section 4 . . . . Here, the layout, drilling, tapping, and special machining needed on
Special Work   valves other than the standard line are done.

Section 5 . . . . This section is responsible for the assembly and testing of all valves
Assembly   produced in the department.

valve department might perform some operations on products for other departments of the Laren Manufacturing Company.

Mr. Laren's investigation showed that all factory costing in the valve department (except material costs) was done on a departmentwide, direct-labor-hour basis; that is, each lot of products going through the department was costed at a certain rate for each direct labor hour actually spent on the lot. Exhibit 3 shows the computation made to arrive at the cost figure of $5.76, which was the rate per labor hour in the whole department in August. Costs were accumulated and allocated to jobs each month.

Mr. Laren, Jr., did not feel that this method of obtaining and apportioning costs was accurate enough. He believed that problems could arise in trying to judge performance and in obtaining the true cost of different products by following this method. He proposed, therefore, that costs be collected monthly for each section of the department and that these costs be apportioned to jobs according to the amount of time spent in each section.

Exhibit 2

PRODUCTION FLOW THROUGH
VALVE DEPARTMENT

In order to study the effect of this proposal, Mr. Laren recomputed the costs for August so as to show the costs applicable to each section. Since direct labor charges were already being collected by sections, no change in procedures was necessary for the collection of labor costs. Some overhead items, such as the salary of a section chief, could be charged directly to the section in which they were incurred. Other overhead charges, such as heating and lighting, were allocated on bases that seemed

Exhibit 3

CALCULATION OF MANUFACTURING COST
PER DIRECT LABOR HOUR IN THE
VALVE DEPARTMENT*

(August)

Section	Labor Charge per Month	Burden	Total
1	$ 3,070		
2	1,860		
3	10,720		
4	4,100		
5	17,400		
Total	$37,150	$60,630	$97,780

Total number of hours worked: 16,970/month.
Average hourly charge: $97,780 ÷ 16,970 = $5.76.

* Does not include materials.

to Mr. Laren to be reasonable. He divided the total overhead costs charged to each section by the number of labor hours worked in the section, and arrived at costing rates for each section. These are shown in Exhibit 4.

Exhibit 4

PROPOSED COST PER DIRECT LABOR HOUR
FOR EACH SECTION OF THE
VALVE DEPARTMENT*

(August)

Section	Total Hours	Labor Charge per Hour	Burden Charge per Hour	Total Cost per Hour
1..............	1,370	$2.24	$3.32	$5.56
2..............	1,000	1.86	3.10	4.96
3..............	4,000	2.68	6.56	9.24
4..............	1,800	2.28	4.20	6.48
5..............	8,800	1.98	2.18	4.16
Total.......16,970				

* Does not include materials.

Mr. Laren made the following observations in support of his proposal for revising the costing rates.

One of the items produced in largest volume by the department was Valve 301. A standard production run of Valve 301 required the following hours in the different sections of the department:

Section	Hours
1......................	15
2......................	10
3......................	65
5......................	40

Mr. Laren said that there obviously was a wide difference between the cost for this valve as figured under the present system and the cost as figured under his proposed system. His contention was that the present method led to false conclusions as to the profitability of a line.

Mr. Laren also saw problems in the valuation of the spare parts inventory produced by the valve department. The company produced a wide line of valves, and it was necessary to maintain an inventory of spare parts in order to be able promptly to supply repair parts to customers. The following amounts of time were usually spent on producing spare parts for inventory each month:

Section	Hours
1......................	160
2......................	145
3......................	560

When Mr. Laren's proposal was explained to the heads of the operating departments, it met with immediate and strong opposition. First to voice disapproval were the heads of other departments that had work totaling the following amounts done by the valve department each month:

	Hours
Welding (Section 1)	350
Grinding (Section 2)	250
Machining (Section 3)	1,100

These supervisors thought that it was unfair to change a sizable part of their department's costs, especially since they had no control over the costs incurred in the valve department.

Mr. Ahearn, foreman of the pipe fixture department, was very much against the proposal:

The valve department does the machining work on all the jobs that my department can't handle. If you raise my costs on this work, I'll never be able to stay within my budget, because the valve department is already charging me more than I could do the work for in my own department if I had the capacity.

The sales manager was also against the proposal:

If you start monkeying around with our cost system, we'll have to start changing our prices, and we're having enough trouble with price competition from the major companies as it is. After all, our complete valve line is showing a profit. You have to carry some items for sales reasons, regardless of their profitability, so why worry about the very small variation in cost between different items.

The foreman of the valve department also opposed the change:

I'm too busy to fool with more paper work. It takes all my time to get the production out without trying to keep up with this stuff, section by section. And my lead men in the sections don't have time for it either. The department is carrying all its costs now, so why put in an extra gimmick?

Mr. Laren, Sr., remained neutral on the question. He was most interested in whether or not the added cost and trouble of the proposed system would be justified by the benefits the system would give.

Questions

1. What is the difference in the cost of Valve 301 under the proposed method as compared with that under the present method? In value of spare parts added to inventory each month? In the cost of work done for other departments? Are these cost differences significant?
2. What causes the difference in costs given by the proposed method as compared with the present method?

3. Suppose that the company purchased a new $72,000 machine for Section 4 that both reduced machining time and resulted in higher quality special valves. As a result, the total time required for valves in Section 4 is reduced by 30 percent. The extra labor is transferred to other departments. About 10 percent of the overhead in Section 4 is variable with respect to machining time. The engineer's best estimate of the life of the machine is about five years. During August only special valves were worked on in Section 4.

   a) Calculate what the total cost per hour would be after the new machine is in operation if there were only one cost center in the valve department. Assume that operations are the same as actual operations in August in all other respects.

   b) Calculate what the total cost per hour would be if Section 4 were a separate cost center.

   c) What would happen to the computed costs per month of producing special valves with a single cost center, after purchase of the machine, as compared with the cost before purchase of the machine?

   d) What would happen to the computed costs per month of producing special valves with five cost centers, after purchase of the new machine, as compared with the cost before purchase of the machine?

   e) What do you conclude about the relative usefulness of the two methods (single cost center versus five cost centers)?

4. What management benefits, if any, would you expect from the proposed system, that is, the collection and allocation of costs by sections? Consider this question from the standpoint of (*a*) product pricing, (*b*) cost control, (*c*) inventory valuation, and (*d*) charges to other departments. Do you think these benefits would outweigh the costs of collection of the necessary data?

CASE 13–4. BEALE COMPANY

Early in November the new president of the Beale Company was eagerly awaiting the completion of the income statement for October. He knew that October sales had exceeded those for September by more than $50,000, and he was anxious to see how much of this increased sales volume was reflected as extra profit. But when the report came in, it showed an overall loss of $5,015. (See Exhibit 1.) In September, profit had been $3,509.

The president immediately thought some mistake had been made and called in the controller for an explanation. The controller said the figures were correct, but that in October the company had not produced anywhere near its normal volume and hence the charge for unabsorbed burden had decreased the profit more than the added sales had increased it. He said that if the rate of sales were always the same as the rate of factory production, the kind of distortion that was bothering the president would not appear. When factory operations were out of phase with sales operations, however, such distortions were almost certain to result, so long as the company followed the commonly practiced accounting convention of charging or crediting periodic under- or overabsorbed factory overhead to the current profit and loss account.

The president reacted strongly to the controller's explanations: "I don't care a hoot for your accounting conventions. But I do know this: when our sales go up, with other things reasonably equal, I expect our profit to increase. If your reports can't show so simple a thing as that, why do we spend so much money on your department?"

As a matter of fact, the controller had been thinking about the problem that disturbed the president. He concluded that the solution was to take a radically different approach to the accounting treatment of overhead, namely, to charge all fixed overhead costs for the month to the current operating statement rather than to absorb them as a part of product costs. If this were done, there would be no problem of heavy over- or underabsorbed overhead as the volume of operations changed. Cost of goods sold would then reflect only the nonfixed factory costs, that is, variable costs, which the controller called "direct costs."

Exhibit 1

BEALE COMPANY

Condensed October Income Statement as Actually Prepared

Sales		$336,903
Cost of sales at standard		178,168
Standard gross margin		$158,735
Less: Manufacturing variances:		
Labor	$ 4,321*	
Material	3,972	
Overhead:		
Volume	26,870	
Spending	1,347	
Net manufacturing variances		27,868
Gross profit		$130,867
Selling costs:		
Selling expenses	$ 84,514	
Sales taxes	3,236	
Freight allowed	7,195	
Total selling costs		94,945
Operating profit before administration costs		$ 35,922
Administrative costs:		
General administrative expenses	$ 20,640	
Research expenses	5,879	
Total administrative costs		26,519
Operating profit		$ 9,403
Other income or charges		14,418
Loss, Current Month		$ 5,015

* Credit variance.

As an illustration of how his proposal would work out, the controller reworked the company's figures for October, with the startling result that instead of a loss of $5,015, the statement showed a profit of $11,028. (See Exhibit 2.) When this revised statement was shown to the president, he first exclaimed, "That's more like it." Then he hesitated and started to speculate: "But this means more taxes and more demands for wage increases and dividends and what-all. Maybe your idea isn't so good after all."

The controller was in favor of the new plan largely because of its simplified accounting procedures. For one thing there would be no fixed overhead costs in the standard cost figures for different products but only the three classes of direct costs: (*a*) raw materials, (*b*) direct labor, and (*c*) the portion of the outlay for manufacturing expenses which varied directly with productive activity. Omission of fixed overhead costs from the individual product costs would mean that the vexing and expensive task of working out an acceptable allocation of overhead to each product would be unnecessary. Inasmuch as many of these prorations had in fact become out of date, the controller was further attracted to his plan by the possibility that the expense of the needed overhauling of the figures might be avoided.

The controller also believed the proposed system would greatly increase management's focus on the *controllable* portion of costs by spot-

Exhibit 2

BEALE COMPANY

Condensed October Income Statement, Proposed Style

Sales..		$336,903	
Standard "variable" cost of sales.................		123,133	
Gross margin above variable costs...............			$213,770
Selling expenses............................		$ 84,514	
Sales taxes.................................		3,236	
Freight allowed.............................		7,195	
Total selling expenses......................			94,945
Merchandising margin.........................			$118,825
Administrative expenses:			
General administrative expenses...............		$ 20,640	
Research expenses...........................		5,879	
Total administrative expenses...............			26,519
Additional factory expenses:			
Fixed factory overhead......................		$ 65,862	
Manufacturing variances:			
Labor variance..........................$4,321*			
Material variance........................ 3,972			
Overhead variance (spending)............... 1,347		998	66,860
Operating margin.............................			$ 25,446
Other income or charges.......................			14,418
Profit, Current Month.........................			$ 11,028

* Credit variance.

lighting the variable elements. Since the fixed costs pertaining to factory operations tend to fall into quite a different category from that of the variable costs, he thought they should be segregated anyway. By way of analogy he suggested that, like a retail store, a manufacturing company "purchases" its product for a known "direct cost." Consequently the chief difference between the two kinds of business is that to make a profit the manufacturing company has to pay the fixed factory costs in addition to the selling salaries, administration costs, storage, etc. Furthermore, the fixed factory costs are like the occupancy costs (rent, maintenance, etc.) of a retail store. On such a basis the factory's direct costs, that is, variable costs, are similar to the retail store's cost of purchases.

The controller argued that a further advantage of his proposal would be the provision of a more satisfactory basis for making the usual monthly comparison of margin figures in the company's product-by-product gross margin statement. When recast in the new form, with fixed costs excluded, the figures would be much more meaningful. The new margin figures would be much higher all down the line, but the controller was confident that once the management adjusted its thinking to the new basis, the value of knowing how much each product was contributing to fixed costs and profit would be greatly appreciated.

One of the sales executives supported the controller's argument on the usefulness of the new margin figures. He pointed out that if there were two products sold by one of his divisions, Products A and B, and if the situation were as described in the following example, Product B would clearly *appear to be* the more desirable item to sell:

Product	Total Factory Cost per Pound (Std.)	Selling Price	Margin	Percentage of Sales
A	$0.897	$1.55	$0.653	42.1
B	1.015	1.80	0.785	43.6

If, however, the new margin figures were to work out something as follows, then Product A was by all odds the product on which the company's selling effort really should be concentrated:

Product	Variable Factory Cost	Selling Price	New Margin	Percentage of Sales
A	$0.413	$1.55	$1.137	73.6
B	0.809	1.80	0.991	55.6

The controller's proposed method of keeping records, the sales executive reasoned, would thus reveal the true opportunities for profit. He cited one company he knew that had adopted a system similar to that proposed by the controller and had so redirected its selling effort that in less than eight months it had shifted from an operating loss to an operating profit and had maintained good profits ever since.

At this point in the discussion the treasurer entered the argument. He observed, cynically, that the first thing anyone knew, the sales department, in its efforts to get business, would be selling at its usual markup over the new standard cost figures (variable costs only). "When that time comes," he snorted, "how are we going to cover the fixed costs? Where

Exhibit 3

BEALE COMPANY

Condensed Balance Sheets as Actually Prepared

	As of September 30	As of October 31
ASSETS		
Current Assets:		
Cash	$ 80,560	$ 95,553
Accounts receivable	150,428	178,610
Inventory	573,630	521,822
Total Current Assets	$ 804,618	$ 795,985
Plant and equipment (net)	2,120,450	2,108,788
Total Assets	$2,925,068	$2,904,773
LIABILITIES AND NET WORTH		
Current liabilities	$ 397,480	$ 382,200
Mortgage payable	560,000	560,000
Total Liabilities	$ 957,480	$ 942,200
Net Worth:		
Capital stock	$1,000,000	$1,000,000
Retained earnings	967,588	962,573
Total Net Worth	$1,967,588	$1,962,573
Total Liabilities and Net Worth	$2,925,068	$2,904,773

Effect of "Direct Cost" Method

Had the Beale Company used the direct cost method, its balance sheets would appear as above except for the inventory and retained earnings items. These would appear as shown below:

	As of September 30	As of October 31
Inventory	$401,541	$365,776
Retained earnings	795,499	806,527

NOTE: In both present and proposed statements, the effect of income taxes is not shown. The Beale Company recorded estimated income tax expense only at the end of the calendar year.

do we get our capital replacements? We'll have to pay the piper sooner or later."

Turning to the controller, who had talked of the desired focus of the new system on variable costs, the treasurer gave his opinion, based on long experience, that it was the lack of control of the long-run costs that really wrecked a company. "You can make mistakes on the direct costs," he said, "but because things in this area are constantly changing and because one never makes much of a commitment anyway, the life of the company is really not seriously hurt. If necessary, a new management could quickly reverse the trend. But once a company lets the long-run costs get out of control, then the fat really is in the fire. I'm opposed to anything that leads us to take a shortsighted view of cost." To this argument the controller had little to say, except that it was a matter of

Exhibit 4

BEALE COMPANY

Condensed Income Statement, September

	As Actually Prepared	Under Proposed Method
Sales...	$283,028	$283,028
Cost of sales at standard.............................	152,604	104,662
Gross margin..	$130,424	$178,366
Less: Manufacturing variances:		
Labor..	$ 5,426*	$ 5,426*
Material..	5,081	5,081
Overhead:		
Volume..	447*	....
Spending...	2,173	2,173
Fixed factory overhead.............................	....	65,862
Subtotal overhead and variances..................	$ 1,381	$ 67,690
Profit before administrative and selling expenses.........	$129,043	$110,676
Selling expenses (total)...........................	$ 85,482	$ 85,482
Administrative expenses (total).....................	26,026	26,026
Total administrative and selling expenses..........	$111,508	$111,508
Operating profit.....................................	$ 17,535	($ 832)
Other income or charges.............................	14,026	14,026
Net Profit or (Loss) Current Month..................	$ 3,509	($ 14,858)

* Credit variance.

emphasis, and that he still thought the variable costs the more important.[12]

All the group discussing the proposal were aware of the effect of the controller's scheme on the inventory item in the balance sheet. The treasurer, and the president too, were worried about this effect, and both wondered if the possible improvement to the operating statement was worth the price of distorting the balance sheet. The controller proposed that a footnote be carried in the balance sheet calling attention to the matter, and perhaps indicating the extent of the distortion.

When one of the officials asked about the income tax implications, the controller pointed out that the tax return was a special report, that it already differed from the company's operating reports in several respects,

---

[12] In the preceding year, variable costs were 67 percent of total costs.

and that the reports he was suggesting were monthly profit estimates largely for internal use and not annual reports. Furthermore, if the company wished to do so, it could have the annual reports computed on the more orthodox basis. "But," he insisted, "let's make these monthly reports so that they help us, not handicap us."

Balance sheets for the company are shown in Exhibit 3, together with an indication of how the balance sheet figures would appear had the company used the direct cost method. Income statements for September, under both the present and proposed methods, are shown in Exhibit 4. In this exhibit, nomenclature and arrangement have been changed somewhat in order to facilitate comparison between the present and proposed systems.

Questions

1. What do you recommend?
2. Approximately how busy (relative to normal volume) was the factory in October?
3. Could the problem in the case ever arise with respect to annual statements of profit?

CASE 13–5.   BLACK METER COMPANY

After his graduation from college, Richard Harrington was employed in the cost department of the Black Meter Company. His duties purposely were made light during the first few days so that he could have time to acquaint himself with the company in general and its cost system in particular. He had been taken on a complete plant trip before having been hired, and he had had a chance to see most of the operations again in the early days of his employment. Also, the assistant controller, Mr. Miller, who was his immediate supervisor, had spent several hours describing the Black cost system to him.

By combining the information gained from these trips and conversations, Mr. Harrington acquired the information summarized below. He expected that Mr. Miller would, in the near future, ask for his opinion about the cost system.

Product and Production Process

The Black Meter Company manufactured water meters in one standard design but in a wide range of sizes for industrial and residential applications. The water meters installed in the basements of most homes are an example of its product. The meters consisted basically of a hard rubber piston that was put in motion by the flow of water past it, a gear train that reduced this motion and registered it on a dial, and two heavy bronze castings which were bolted together around the measuring device.

The company was organized into several functional departments to manufacture almost all the parts for these meters. The casings and many interior parts were cast in the foundry and then were sent to one of the three machining departments, depending upon their size. The machining departments were equipped with most of the machines which are common to the metalworking industry. Many of the finished parts were sent to a subassembly department to be subassembled into gear trains. The other parts went directly to the meter assembly departments. There were also several departments that provided service to the producing departments.

The Standard Cost System

In describing the cost system to Mr. Harrington, Mr. Miller said:

The Black Meter Company uses a standard cost system to control costs and to obtain monthly operating statements. The basic difference between this standard cost system and an actual cost system lies in the way we value our inventories, from raw materials to finished goods. In an actual cost system the debits for the amounts of materials, direct labor, and manufacturing overhead added to the inventories are made at actual cost. In a standard cost system like ours, normal or standard costs are established for these elements, and every debit to the inventory account is made at standard cost. The fact that all the inventory items are valued at standard costs allows us to forget about the actual cost of every item, thereby greatly simplifying the accounting procedure.

During the month, actual costs are accumulating. Material is purchased, workers are paid, manufacturing overhead items such as water or electricity, are purchased and paid for at actual cost. But the *values* of these items are debited into inventory at predetermined standard costs for each cost factor. Often the actual cost varies from the standard costs, and this fact causes variations that we journalize and post to variance accounts. At the end of a month we examine the variations between actual and standard; consequently, we are able to control costs by focusing our attention on these variances, or *exceptions*, rather than on the bulk of the cost data.

Setting Up Standard Costs

The first step in setting up standard costs in this company was to establish a standard cost for every type of material that was purchased. This was done by adjusting the current market price for any irregularities that might not be expected to continue for the following year. For example, if copper at the end of a year cost 30 cents a pound and no change was predicted, the standard cost for copper for the next year would be 30 cents a pound. The same procedure was followed for every purchased item.

Having established standard costs for all materials, the accountants next calculated standard rates for direct labor and manufacturing overhead. They did this on a departmental basis, and set up the rates to be applied according to the number of standard direct labor hours incurred in the processing of each product.

From each department they obtained data for the past few years on the actual direct labor payroll and the number of direct labor hours worked. On the basis of these data and from estimates of future conditions, the accountants selected a figure for total labor cost and a figure of hours worked under normal conditions of activity in each department. By dividing this payroll figure by the normal number of hours, they obtained a standard direct labor rate per standard direct labor hour for each department.

The same type of calculation was made to determine standard manufacturing overhead rates for each department. The procedure was complicated by the necessity of allocating all service department costs to the producing departments. The first step had been to calculate from past records the total cost of each of the service departments at normal volume. Then various methods were used to allocate the service department costs to the producing departments. For example, the total cost of the boiler room was allocated to the producing departments according to the number of square feet of floor space taken up by each. The maintenance department expense was allocated on the basis of the number of hours the maintenance men normally worked for each producing department.

After the cost of the service departments had been allocated to the producing departments, it was necessary to calculate the manufacturing overhead costs that normally were incurred within each producing department. The sum of the allocated and the internal costs gave the total manufacturing overhead cost for each department under normal conditions. These totals were divided by the standard number of direct labor hours for each producing department, the same totals that had been used in calculating the labor rate. In this way, a manufacturing overhead rate per standard direct labor hour was obtained for each department, as shown in Exhibit 1.

The next step in setting up this standard cost system was to apply the standard rates to each of the items manufactured. This was accomplished on the manufacturing orders, examples of which can be seen in Exhibits 2 through 5. The part described was a ⅝-inch chamber ring that was manufactured for assembly into a ⅝-inch HF meter. The standard costs of most parts were calculated on the basis of 100 pieces.

Exhibit 1

STANDARD RATES EFFECTIVE JANUARY 1

Depart-ment No.	Department Name	Labor	Burden	Total Rate
103	Carpenter and pattern shop	$2.06	$1.07	$3.13/hour
104	Toolroom	2.35	1.26	3.61/hour
108	Pattern storage	--	--	0.02/pound
120A	Foundry -- molding	2.50	3.78	6.28/hour
120B	Foundry -- grinding and snagging	1.50	0.90	2.40/hour
122	Small parts manufacture	1.72	1.38	3.10/hour
123	Interior parts manufacture	1.68	1.73	3.41/hour
124	Case manufacture	1.98	4.02	6.00/hour
125	Plating -- rack	--	--	2.50/100 pcs.
130	Train, register, and interior assembly	1.70	1.97	3.67/hour
131	Small meter assembly	1.50	2.01	3.51/hour
132	Large meter assembly	1.90	3.98	5.88/hour
133	Meter testing	2.11	1.56	3.67/hour
134	Meter repair	1.50	1.66	3.16/hour

Exhibit 2

FOUNDRY ORDER

Rate Number	Std. Man Hrs. Per 100 Pcs.	Std. Basic Rate	Prod. Center	Opr. No.	Operation and Tools	Machine	Man No.	Std. Rate /Hr.	Man No.	Total Cost	Total
	1.76		120 A	1	Mold	Match Plate		·6.28		11.053	
	.45		120 B	2	Grind	Wheel		2.40		1.08	
	.68		120 B	3	Snag	Bench		2.40		1.632	
											$45.297

Drawing No. X-2408 Part 5/8" HF Chamber Rings Deliveries to Stores Order No.

Material Gov't Bronze 100 Pieces 91.00 At 0.3265/0 $29.712

Weight Plating Econ. Lot Pattern Cost 0.02 Quantity Ordered $1.82

The standard material cost was figured in the second line of the foundry order (Exhibit 2). These parts were cast from government bronze that had a standard cost of $0.3265 a pound. Since the standard weight of 100 pieces was 91 pounds, the standard material cost was $29.712 as shown in the deliveries-to-stores box. The $0.02 figure in the pattern cost box was a standard pattern cost per pound which resulted in a $1.82 standard pattern charge.

In order to apply the standard direct labor and manufacturing overhead rates to any part, it was necessary to calculate the standard time needed to perform the operations to make that part. This task was simplified for the Black Meter Company because all operations had been time-studied. Using the results of the time studies, the accountants could fill in the first column of the foundry order. For example, the standard time to mold 100 chamber rings was 1.76 hours, to grind them 0.45 hours,

Exhibit 3

RR-7						PARTS ORDER					
Drawing No. X-2408			Part 5/8" HF Chamber Rings				Deliveries to Stores			Order No.	
							$45.297				
Plating H.T. & E.T.			Material Gov't Bronze 100 Pieces 89¢		W'gt per 100		Date Wanted			Quantity Ordered	
Econ. Lot 2,000					L'gth per 100						

Rate Number	Hours per 100 pc.		Set-up St'd	Prod. C't'r	Opr. No.	Operation and Tools	Machine	Man No.	Std. Rate /Hr.	Total
	St'd	All'w'd								
	0.75			122	1	Broach out 1st ∅734	P.P.		3.10	2.325
	0.55			123	2	Finish tap plate bore & face	Heald		3.41	1.876
	0.93			123		Drill 6 holes	Drill		3.41	3.171
	0.47			123	3	C-Sink 3 holes tap plate side	Drill		3.41	1.603
	0.17			123		Tap 3 holes tap plate side	Heskins		3.41	0.560
	5.00			123	4	Rough & finish inside & outside	Heald		3.41	17.050
	0.20			123		C-Sink 3 holes on bottom	Drill		3.41	0.682
	0.30			123	5	Tap 3 holes on bottom	Drill		3.41	1.023
	0.47			123		Spline inside	Spliner		3.41	1.603
	0.50			123	6	Spline outside	Miller		3.41	1.705
	5.80			123		Dress	Bench		3.41	19.778
					7					96.673

Exhibit 4

ASSEMBLY ORDER

Drawing No. 2400		Assembly 5/8" Disc Interior						Sheet No. of			
Used on Assemblies of 5/8' HF & HD Meters								Order No.			
Parts of Assembly		Delivered	Parts of Assembly			Delivered		Quantity Ordered			
K-2408 Chamber Ring		96.673									
K-2414 Chamber Top Plate		43.550						Date Ordered			
K-2418 Chamber Bot. Plate		40.120									
X-2465 Disc Piston Assem.		79.010						Date Wanted			
K-2422 Disc Chbr. Diaphragm		3.660									
								Deliveries to Stores			
			K-4521 Chamber Screws (6)			7.000					

Rate Number	Std. Man Hrs. Per 100 Pcs.	Std. Basic Rate	Prod. Center	Oper. No.	Operation and Tools	Machine	Man No.	Std. Rate /Hr.	Man No.	Total Cost	Total
2.6			130	1	Assemble Top Plate to Ring	Bench		3.67		9.542	
0.9			130	2	Fit Abutment for Interior	Bench		3.67		3.303	
1.1			130	3	Mill & Scrape Diaphragm for Interior	Bench		3.67		4.037	
3.9			130	4	File Diaphragm Slots in Piston	Bench		3.67		14.313	
											301.208

and to snag them 0.68 hours. In the first column of figures on the right-hand side of the foundry order, the combined standard direct labor and manufacturing overhead (i.e., burden) rate per standard direct labor hour was recorded for the department in which the operation took place. For example, Exhibit 1 shows the labor and burden rate for molding in Department 120A as $6.28 per standard man-hour. This amount appeared on the foundry order for the molding operation, and multiplied by the standard time gave a standard cost of labor and burden of $11.053. The same procedure was followed for the three foundry operations, and the total standard foundry cost of 100 chamber rings was $45.297.

Exhibit 3 traces these 100 chamber rings through the interior parts manufacture department. They entered the parts department at the standard cost of $45.297—the same cost with which they left the foundry. After 11 operations had been performed on them, they became finished chamber rings with a standard cost of $96.673. As shown in Exhibits 4 and 5 these parts were assembled into ⅝-inch HF disc interiors, and finally, into the ⅝-inch meters. The total cost of the meters was $850.506.

Exhibit 5

ASSEMBLY ORDER

Drawing No. 2735				Assembly	5/8" HF Meter ET FB				Sheet No. of		
Used on Assemblies of									Order No.		
Parts of Assembly				Delivered	Parts of Assembly		Delivered				
									Quantity Ordered		
2761 Top Case				170.60	K-5030 5/8 HF Dur. Bolt (6)		32.880				
K-2776 Casing Gasket				3.25	K-4630 5/8 HF ac Nut (6)		25.440				
X-2770 Bottom Case				50.14	K-5068 5/8 HF Washers (6)		10.140		Date Ordered		
2779 Casing Strainer				6.95	2782 Chamber Pin		1.966				
3209 5/8 Closed Train				200.01	6172 Misc. Train Conn.		7.120				
2400 5/8 HF Int. Assem.				301.208					Date Wanted		
2412 5/8 HF Sand Plate				5.00							
									Deliveries to Stores		
Rate Number	Std. Man Hrs. Per 100 Pcs.	Std. Basic Rate	Prod. Center	Oper. No.	Operation and Tools	Machine	Man No.	Std. Rate /Hr.	Man No.	Total Cost	Total
4.6			131	1	Assem. Train & Strainer to Case	Bench		3.51		16.146	
5.6			131	2	Assem. Int. & Bottom to Meter			3.51		19.656	
										850.506	

In the same manner, standard costs had been calculated for all the meter sizes that the Black Meter Company manufactured. These standards were revised annually to recognize any significant changes in the costs of labor, materials, or overhead.

Accounting Entries

While talking about the uses of the standard cost system, Mr. Miller said:

Once the standards have been established, all material, direct labor, and manufacturing overhead are charged into the Inventory account at standard costs that do not change. This means that actual costs need only be collected in total for the period, and the actual cost of each individual item in inventory is forgotten. Therefore, the controlling of costs becomes a relatively simple matter.

MATERIAL. As soon as any material was purchased, the standard cost of that material was penciled on the vendor's invoice. Each purchase was journalized in an invoice and check register containing columns in which to credit the actual cost of the material to Accounts Payable, to debit an inventory account for the standard cost, and to debit or credit the difference to a variance account called "Purchase Loss or Gain." The company had a single inventory account in its general ledger which lumped together raw materials, work in process, and finished goods inventory; therefore no accounting entry was made when material was issued for use in production.

Exhibit 6

INCENTIVE JOB CARD

MACH. NO.	PROD. CENTER 130	QUANTITY ORDERED 3000 3000	ORDER NUMBER 2I - 86572 1 I - 86572		CLOCK NO. 337
TOTAL FIN. 1250 3000	PART NAME	5/8 " Cl. Trains.			
PREV. QUAN. FIN. 0 1150	OPR. NO. 9	OPERATION NAME Finish Assem.			
QUAN. FINISHED 1250 1850	STD. HOURS PER 100 1 75	STD. HOURS 54 25	STD. RATE 1 70	STANDARD LABOR 92 23	
QUAN. FINISHED 3,100	ALL'D HOURS PER 100 1 75	ALL'D HOURS 54 25	INCENTIVE JOB CARD		B. Harris NAME
	STOP Sept. 20 40.0	ACTUAL HOURS 40 0	D.W. RATE 1 65	EARNINGS 89 51	
	START Sept. 20 00.0		FOREMAN	GAIN OR LOSS 2 72	

LABOR. The basic document for controlling direct labor costs was the incentive job card. Each productive employee filled out a card for each order on which he worked during the week. The card reproduced as Exhibit 6 shows that Mr. Harris had worked all week on one order so that he had turned in only one card for that week. On the card he recorded the quantity finished, the actual hours worked, and the allowed hours, which were usually the same as the standard hours. A payroll clerk entered each employee's daywork rate, the standard direct labor rate for that department, and extended the actual and standard direct labor cost of the work completed.

By totaling all the incentive job cards, the payroll clerk obtained the actual wages accrued for each employee in each department, and the standard labor cost of the work done in each department. He credited accrued wages for the actual amount to set up the liability and debited the Inventory account for the standard amount of direct labor. The variance was closed out to a Direct Labor variance account.

MANUFACTURING OVERHEAD. The method of handling manufacturing overhead was very similar in each department. A cost clerk multiplied the standard direct labor hours worked by the manufacturing overhead rate for that department (Exhibit 1) to obtain the amount of manufacturing overhead to be absorbed by the department that month. He debited the Inventory account for the total amount of the absorbed manufacturing overhead. During the month actual manufacturing overhead expenses had been accumulating in the invoice and check register and in various adjusting entries. The difference between the sum of the actual expenses and the absorbed manufacturing overhead cost was the under- or overabsorbed manufacturing overhead variance, which was closed to the overhead variance accounts.

Exhibit 7

CARBON COPY OF SALES INVOICE

Village of Vernon, Att. Village Clerk, Vernon, N.Y.	41740 NY 931	9/11/-- 9/10/--			
Village of Vernon, Water Dept., Att: E. J. Blackburn, Mayor Vernon, N.Y.	7/31/-- 8/13/--	Boston			
STIBBS	Prepaid				
10	5/8 x 3/4 Model HF Meters SG SH ET FB & 3/4" Cons. #3015331-340 40%		21.80	218.00	
1	Charge Gear #46X -- shipped 8-10-		.25	130.80	
		Plus 10%	.03	.28	131.08
		Meters		130.80	85.05
		Parts		.28	.18
	Ship gear by P. Post				

When these transactions had been made, all material, direct labor, and manufacturing overhead were charged into the Inventory account at standard cost, and three variance accounts were debited or credited for the difference between actual and standard.

A physical inventory was taken every six months and was valued at standard cost. Any difference between this figure and the total value of the inventory as shown in the Inventory account was debited or credited to an Inventory Adjustment variance account.

COST OF SALES. Before monthly operating statements could be prepared, a cost clerk had to make an analysis of sales for the month. A duplicate copy of each invoice was sent to the cost office where a clerk entered in pencil the standard cost of the items sold (see Exhibit 7). At the end of the month the cost clerk simply totaled the figures on these duplicate invoices to get figures for sales and the standard cost of those sales for the month. The standard cost of sales was a credit to the inventory account and a debit to the Cost of Sales account. The total sales amount was a credit to Sales and a debit to Accounts Receivable. When this work had been completed, the cost department was in a position to obtain the monthly income statements (see Exhibit 8) by closing the ledger.

Exhibit 8

BLACK METER COMPANY

Income Statement, Six Months Ending June 30

Sales....................................		$3,148,234.13
Less: Cash discounts......................		3,030.13
Net sales.................................		$3,145,204.00
Standard cost...........................	$2,045,127.63	
Variances..............................	118,080.55*	$2,163,208.18
Gross manufacturing profit...................		$ 981,995.82
Selling expense............................		504,032.35
Operating profit...........................		$ 477,963.47
Administrative expense.....................		108,236.76
Adjusted operating profit...................		$ 369,726.71
Nonoperating profit........................		6,415.93
Net Profit................................		$ 376,142.64

*Variances

Deductions from gross profit:	
Direct labor variance....................................	$ 26,389.14
Factory burden unabsorbed..............................	48,137.61
Material price variance..................................	39,298.01
Unused space and equipment............................	210.00
Inventory adjustments..................................	12,875.30
Loss due to changes in manufacturing methods..............	10,146.50
Total deductions....................................	$ 137,056.56
Additions to gross profit:	
Cash discounts taken.....................................	$ 9,699.60
Gain from sale or salvage................................	9,276.41
Total additions.......................................	$ 18,976.01
Net Variances..	$ 118,080.55

A flow chart summarizing the above description appears in Exhibit 9.

Exhibit 9

FLOW CHART

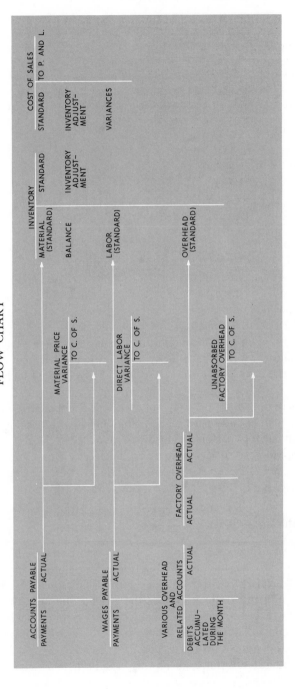

Questions

1. Assuming that you were Mr. Harrington, what evaluation would you have made of the standard cost system employed by the Black Meter Company? Would you have agreed with the statements made by Mr. Miller to the effect that this system made the controlling of costs "a relatively simple matter"?

2. What questions concerning this cost system would you have wished to ask Mr. Miller at your next conversation with him?

CASE 13–6.   CRAIK VENEER COMPANY

The sales manager of the Craik Veneer Company received from the Groton Company an offer to buy one million feet per month of sound "backs" of $\frac{1}{24}$-inch birch veneer[13] at $8 per thousand surface feet. The sales manager wanted to accept the offer, but the production manager argued that it should not be accepted because the cost of production was at least $10 per thousand feet and probably more.

The Craik company manufactured rotary cut birch veneer from high-grade yellow birch logs bought in Vermont. Selected sections called "blocks" were cut out of those logs, the length of the block varying from 84 inches to 98 inches, depending on the length along the grain of the veneer being produced. These blocks, as cut for the lathe, cost an average of $200 per thousand board feet. A thousand board feet, log measure, was an amount of logs which, being sawed, would produce a thousand board feet of lumber. (A board foot is one square foot one inch thick.) After being cut, the blocks were put in vats filled with hot water and left there for 24 to 48 hours until the entire log was heated through.

Manufacturing Process

In the rotary veneer process, a block was put in a lathe in which a knife longer than the block, with a heavy frame, guide bars, and pressure bars, was brought against the side of the block so that it cut off a thin slice of wood the entire length of the block. The process was similar to unrolling a large roll of paper held on a horizontal shaft. The process could be controlled with skillful operation so it would produce veneer of uniform thickness. The Craik company produced principally $\frac{1}{24}$-inch veneer, and for the purposes of this case it may be assumed that all of its product was $\frac{1}{24}$-inch.

---

[13] Veneer is a term applied to thin leaves or layers of wood. Generally veneer is made of valuable wood and is laid over a core of inferior wood.

The sheet of veneer from the lathe, for instance from a 98-inch block, was brought onto a clipping table approximately 60 feet long. This table had rubber belts on its upper surface which moved the veneer along to the clipper. At this point the veneer was like a long sheet of paper moving along the table, the veneer being 98 inches along the grain. The clipper was a long knife extending entirely across the table. The clipper operator was one of the most highly skilled men in the plant. Constantly inspecting the sheet of veneer, he first took one cut to get a straight edge. If the next section of the sheet was of high quality, he advanced the sheet not over 3 feet 8 inches, depending on customers' requirements. If the sheet showed a defect within 3 feet 8 inches, he made his cut just short of the defect. A man called the "off bearer" piled these sheets on a hand truck reserved for high-grade or "face" veneer. If the defect was a knot, the clipper operator then advanced the sheet enough to clear the knot and took another cut, making a piece of waste possibly 3 inches wide. If he decided that a section of the sheet was not of face quality, he cut it off for "backs," either 3 feet 8 inches or in lesser widths. Backs were put on another hand truck.

The clipper operator thus separated the whole sheet of veneer into faces, backs, and waste. The faces consisted of pieces of veneer 98 inches long along the grain and anywhere from 6 inches to 3 feet 8 inches wide. The sound backs were of the same size. The waste went to a chipper and was then burned. The term "faces" came from the fact that these veneer sheets were substantially perfect and could be used on the exposed parts of furniture or on the best face of plywood.[14] The backs had minor defects and were so called because they were used on the back of plywood panels. The quality required for faces was established by specifications and by the custom of the industry. The dividing line between sound backs and waste was similarly established. The Craik company had a reputation for using high-grade logs and for producing a high grade of veneer both on faces and backs.

Groton Company's Offer

The Groton Company's research and development department had developed two new lines of furniture, one in blond modern and one in colonial, in which the table tops, dresser tops and panels, drawer fronts, and other exposed parts were of birch veneer over lower-grade birch or poplar cores, with table legs, dresser frames, etc., of solid birch. The Groton research people knew that while all sheets of backs contained defects, 50 to 60 percent of the area of backs as produced by Craik were

[14] Veneer is a single thin sheet of wood. Plywood consists of several sheets (three, five, or nine) glued together with the grain of alternate courses at right angles to add to the strength.

of face quality. They had discovered that by buying backs 84 inches to 98 inches long they could cut clear face quality veneer in lengths that would match their use requirements: enough 54 inches for their longest dresser tops and enough of other lengths down to 14-inch drawer fronts. The remainder of the veneer that was not of face quality could be used for such purposes as making plywood for drawer bottoms. The methods developed in the research department had been tested by cutting up several carloads of backs bought from Craik and by the manufacture and sale of the furniture.

On the basis of this experience the Groton Company offered Craik $8 per thousand feet for one million feet per month of sound backs in $\frac{1}{24}$-inch birch veneer for the next 12 months.

Cost Information

The Craik company cut an average of 12,000 board feet of logs a day in one eight-hour shift. With the high quality of logs it bought, it got a yield of 18,000 surface feet of $\frac{1}{24}$-inch veneer per 1,000 board feet cut; this graded on the average 50 percent faces and 50 percent backs.

Labor and factory overhead costs together averaged $8 per thousand surface feet of veneer; selling costs averaged $1.50. Both the cost of the blocks and operating costs for the heating, lathe turning, and clipping operations were joint costs; backs had to be produced in order to get the faces. The remaining operations in drying, a slight amount of reclipping, storing, and shipping were in a sense separate costs as the operations were done on backs separately, although with the same equipment. The labor and factory overhead costs through clipping averaged $6.75 per 1,000 surface feet of veneer; those for drying and later operations, $1.25.

The selling price for $\frac{1}{24}$-inch birch faces 84 inches to 98 inches long was $40 per thousand surface feet. Face veneer 84 inches to 98 inches had a high price because it could be used on large surfaces, such as flush birch doors that require lengths up to eight feet. The shorter veneer in length along the grain, made from recutting backs, had a somewhat lower price because it could not be used for these purposes. Unlike faces, the price of backs fluctuated widely. Sometimes Craik could get $10 per thousand feet, but the insistence of the production manager on $10 had led to the accumulation of a heavy inventory of backs. Faces were easy to sell and were shipped substantially as fast as they were produced.

More effort was required to sell backs than to sell faces, although both were sold to the same customers by the same salesmen. Sometimes buyers of faces were required to take a percentage of backs in order to get a carload of faces. For these reasons the offer of the customer was attractive to the sales manager.

Discussion of Offer

When the production manager was first informed by the sales manager of the offer of $8 per thousand surface feet, the production manager contended that "Your salesmen are so lazy, they would give veneer away if nobody watched them." The production manager went on to say:

If a birch block cost $200 per thousand and we get 18,000 feet of $\frac{1}{24}$-inch-thick veneer from every thousand board feet of the block, the cost of the block to be allocated to a thousand feet of veneer, whether backs or faces, is $200 divided by 18,000 feet, or about $11.11 per thousand feet. Simple arithmetic proves that selling backs at $8 per thousand doesn't even pay for the material, let alone labor and overhead.

The sales manager countered that this argument was fallacious:

Allocating the cost of the block to the veneer in this manner implies that backs are as valuable as faces, which is not the case. The $11.11 material figure for a thousand feet of veneer that you get is merely an average of the value of faces and backs. The material for faces is worth considerably more per thousand feet than this figure; the material for backs is worth considerably less.

The sales manager suggested that the proper procedure was to allocate the cost of the block to faces and backs in proportion to the amounts for which the products were sold. Using this method, the ratio that the revenue of one of the two grades of veneer bore to the revenue received from both grades of veneer would be applied to the total cost of the block, the result representing the cost to be allocated to that particular grade. To illustrate this method, assume a block of a thousand board feet cost $200, and the selling prices and quantities of faces and backs are as shown in the following table:

Grade	$\frac{1}{24}$-Inch Veneer in Feet	Sales Revenue per 1,000 Feet	Net Value	Percent of Total	Cost Applicable to Each
Faces.............	9,000	$40	$360	83.3%	$166.67
Backs.............	9,000	8	72	16.6	33.33
	18,000		$432	100.0%	$200.00

The material cost applicable to each product, then, per thousand feet of $\frac{1}{24}$-inch veneer would be $166.67/9,000 feet × 1,000 feet, or $18.52, for faces; and $33.33/9,000 feet × 1,000 feet, or $3.70, for backs.

The production manager again argued that this did not represent the true material cost, which was the same for both products, and added:

Under your method the material cost allocated to either faces or backs would be a function of their relative selling prices. If the selling price of faces fell from $40 per thousand to $20 per thousand and the price of backs remained the same, you would then charge much more material costs to backs, and much less to faces. Your method of allocating cost doesn't make sense.

The sales manager at this point said:

O.K., if you don't think that method is justified, then let's treat backs as a by-product. I think you'll agree that we would prefer to be making faces all the time, yet we can't. As long as we manufacture faces, we're going to produce backs as an undesirable consequence. Now if we consider backs as a by-product, we can charge all block costs to faces. The net proceeds from the sale of backs, after allowing for all conversion, selling and administrative expenses, can be credited to the raw material cost of faces. All profits and losses of the business would be borne by the main product.

The production manager, however, pointed out again that the cost of material allocated to faces would still be a function of the selling price of backs and, furthermore, there would be some difficulty in trying to value inventories at the end of an accounting period; and that any profits arising from the sale of backs would be hidden, since it would be included in the credit to faces. "It is important to determine the profit or loss being realized on the sale of backs so we can establish a firm sales policy," he said.

Because of their inability to resolve this question, the production manager and the sales manager consulted the president of the Craik Veneer Company, who, in turn, asked the controller to examine the cost situation to determine whether the $8 per thousand surface feet of $\frac{1}{24}$-inch backs would, or would not, result in a profit.

Questions

1. As controller, what method of allocating raw material costs would you recommend? What similarities and differences would be encountered in allocating labor and overhead costs as compared to material costs?
2. Should the sales manager accept the $8 per thousand feet offer that he received for the $\frac{1}{24}$-inch backs?
3. If a group of blocks containing 1,000 board feet costs $205, what would be the cost applicable to faces and backs under each of the methods of allocating costs described in the case, and other methods that you may devise, if the following conditions existed:
   a) The current market price of $\frac{1}{24}$-inch faces is $40 per thousand feet; $\frac{1}{24}$-inch backs are currently selling at $9 per thousand.
   b) 10,000 feet of $\frac{1}{24}$-inch faces and 8,000 feet of $\frac{1}{24}$-inch backs were produced from a group of blocks.

c) Factory labor and overhead cost averaged $8 per thousand feet of veneer ($6.75 for operations through clipping and $1.25 for drying and later operations). Selling costs averaged $1.50 per thousand feet of veneer. If backs were not manufactured (i.e., if they were treated the same as waste), labor, overhead, and selling costs amounting to roughly $2 per thousand feet of backs might be saved.

CHAPTER **14**

THE MANAGEMENT CONTROL
PROCESS

One of the uses of accounting information is in the process called management control. This chapter gives an overview of that process. Aspects of it are discussed in more detail in succeeding chapters.

MANAGEMENT CONTROL

Management control is *the process by which managers assure that resources are obtained and used effectively and efficiently in the accomplishment of an organization's objectives.*

As this statement suggests, management control takes place within an organization that already exists and that already has a set of objectives or goals. Every organization has objectives, that is, it exists for some purpose, and these objectives are taken as given. The control process is not concerned with whether these objectives are good or bad; the process occurs both in the Roman Catholic Church and in the Cosa Nostra. It occurs in governments and other nonprofit organizations as well as in profit-seeking corporations.

The control process is facilitated when the objectives of the organization are clear-cut, but in most organizations objectives are by no means clear. The statement that the objective of a business corporation is "to make a profit" is both too simple and too vague to be of much use. It is an oversimplification because corporations usually have more than one objective. "Survival" is usually listed as an objective that is at least as important as making a profit. Fulfilling the organization's responsibility to society and being a good place in which to work are other possible objectives that, although not easily measurable, are often also important. The profit objective is too vague because for effective control one needs to know the strategies that the top management in a particular company has chosen: the products it has decided to manufacture, the scale and location of manufacturing activities, the markets in which these products are to be sold, the method of reaching these markets, the organizational structure, the sources of financing, and so on. The process of deciding on these policies is called *strategic planning*. Strategic planning establishes a framework within which management control takes place.

Characteristics of Management Control Systems

Ordinarily, a management control system is a *total* system in the sense that it embraces all aspects of the company's operation. It needs to be a total system because an important management function is to assure that all parts of the operation are in balance with one another; and in order to examine balance, management needs information about each of the parts.

With rare exceptions, the management control system is *built around a financial structure;* that is, resources and outputs are expressed in monetary units. Money is the only common denominator by means of which the heterogeneous elements of output and resources (e.g., hours of labor, type of labor, quantity and quality of material, amount and kind of products produced) can be combined and compared. Although the financial structure is usually the central focus, nonmonetary measures such as minutes per operation, number of persons, and reject and spoilage rates are also important parts of the system.

The management control process tends to be *rhythmic;* it follows a definite pattern and timetable, month after month and year after year. In budgeting, which is an important part of the management control process, certain steps are taken in a prescribed sequence and at certain dates each year: dissemination of guidelines, preparation of original estimates, transmission of these estimates up through the several echelons in the organization, review of these estimates, final approval by top management, dissemination back through the organization, operation, reporting, and the appraisal of performance. The procedure to be followed at each step in this process, the dates when the steps are to be completed, and even the forms to be used can be, and often are, set forth in a manual.

A management control system is, or should be, a *coordinated, integrated system;* that is, although data collected for one purpose may differ from those collected for another purpose, these data should be reconcilable with one another. In a sense, the management control system is a *single* system, but it is perhaps more accurate to think of it as a set of interlocking subsystems. In many organizations, for example, three types of cost information are needed for management control: (1) costs by responsibility centers, used for planning and controlling the activities of responsible supervisors; (2) full program costs, used for pricing and other operating decisions in normal circumstances; (3) direct program costs, used for pricing and other operating decisions in special circumstances, such as when management wishes to utilize idle capacity. ("Program" is here used for any activity in which the organization engages. In industrial companies, programs consist of products or product lines, and "product costs" can be substituted in the above statements.)

Line managers are the focal points in management control. They are the persons whose judgments are incorporated in the approved plans, and they are the persons who must influence others and whose performance is measured. Staff people collect, summarize, and present information that is useful in the process, and they make calculations that translate management judgments into the format of the system. Such a staff may be large in numbers; indeed, the control department is often the largest staff department in a company. However, the significant decisions are made by the line managers, not by the staff.

MOTIVATION

Management control involves human beings, from those in the lowest responsibility center of the organizational hierarchy up to and including members of top management. The management control process in part consists of inducing these human beings to do certain things and to refrain from doing others. Although for some purposes an accumulation of the costs of manufacturing a product is useful, management literally cannot "control" a product, or the costs of making a product. What management does—or at least what it attempts to do—is control the actions of the people who are responsible for incurring these costs.

Principles of Motivation

Since management control involves the behavior of human beings, the relevant principles are those drawn from such disciplines as social psychology and organizational behavior, rather than from economics, mathematics, or any discipline that focuses on impersonal relationships rather than on human behavior. An adequate discussion of psychological principles is outside both the scope of this book and the competence of its author. Furthermore, social psychologists regard the currently accepted principles of the behavior of individuals in groups as extremely tentative, since the evidence from which they are derived is both inconclusive and often contradictory. There are, however, generalizations relevant to the design of a management control system on which many behavioral scientists agree. Some of these are as follows:[1]

1. An individual has a number of basic motives or needs. He joins an organization and contributes toward the accomplishment of its objectives because in this way he believes he can satisfy at least some of his needs. Among these needs are:

a) Physiological considerations, such as food, bodily comfort, and sex, which are basic in the sense that these needs ordinarily must be satisfied before consideration is given to "higher" needs.

b) Realistic recognition of his abilities and achievements by his colleagues and superiors (need for achievement).

c) Status and social acceptance as a member of a group (need for affiliation).

d) Self-esteem, a sense of personal worth.

e) Security, including an understanding of what is expected of him and a belief that his performance will be judged fairly.

f) Autonomy, the freedom to exercise discretion.

g) The desire to change other people's behavior, leadership (need for power).

2. Individuals are influenced either by the expectation of reward or the fear of punishment. *Reward* is the satisfaction of a need, and *punishment* is the deprivation of satisfaction. Individuals tend to be more strongly motivated by reward than by punishment.

3. Monetary compensation is an important means of satisfying certain needs, but beyond the subsistence level the amount of compensation is not necessarily so important as nonmonetary rewards. Nevertheless, pay is often important indirectly as an indication of how achievement and ability are regarded. (A man earning $50,000 a year may be unhappy if a colleague of perceived equal ability receives $51,000 a year.)

4. The effectiveness of reward or punishment diminishes rapidly as the time elapses between an action and the reward or punishment administered for it.

---

[1] For further reading on this subject, see:

J. W. Atkinson, *An Introduction to Motivation* (Princeton, N.J.: D. Van Nostrand Company, 1964).

Edwin J. Caplan, "Behavorial Assumptions of Management Accounting," *Accounting Review*, July 1966, p. 496–509.

R. M. Cyert and J. G. March, *A Behavorial Theory of the Firm* (Englewood Cliffs, N.J.: Prentice-Hall, Inc., 1963).

G. C. Homans, *Social Behavior: Its Elementary Forms* (New York: Harcourt, Brace & World, 1961).

P. R. Lawrence and J. W. Lorsch, *Organization and Environment: Managing Differentiation and Integration* (Boston: Division of Research, Harvard Business School, 1967).

D. C. McClelland, *The Achieving Society* (Princeton, N.J.: D. Van Nostrand Company, 1961).

5. Needs may be unconscious, or they may be expressed as aspirations or goals. Motivation is weakest when the individual perceives a goal as either unattainable or too easily attainable. Motivation is strong when the goal can be attained with some effort and when the individual regards its attainment as important.

6. An individual tends to accept evidence of his performance more willingly and to use it more constructively when it is presented in a manner that he regards as objective, that is, without personal bias.

7. Individuals are receptive to learning better ways of doing things only when they personally recognize the inadequacies of their present behavior.

8. Beyond a certain point, pressure for improved performance accomplishes nothing. This optimum point is far below the maximum amount of pressure that conceivably could be exerted. (When the coach says, "Don't press; don't try too hard," he is applying this principle.)

9. Individuals differ greatly in the importance they attach to various need satisfactions. Their attitudes also change with time and circumstances and are heavily influenced by the attitudes of their colleagues and superiors.

In view of the differences among individuals mentioned in the ninth point above, precise rules for designing control systems could not be constructed even if the above list of generalizations were fully substantiated by experiment. They nevertheless seem to be sufficiently valid so that useful concepts for control can be derived from them. Some of these are described in the next section.

Management Sponsorship

A control system will probably be ineffective unless the organization is convinced that management considers the system to be important. Some systems are installed with no more management backing than the directive, "Let's have a good control system," and with no subsequent interest or action by managements. Such a system, instead of being a part of the management process, becomes a paper shuffling routine whose principal virtue is that it provides employment for a great many clerks. In a talk describing the remarkable reorganization of Ford Motor Company, Mr. Ernest R. Breech gave an excellent illustration of the importance of this point:[2]

In the course of reorganizing Ford Motor Company, by 1948 we had set up

---

[2] Ernest R. Breech, "Planning the Basic Strategy of a Large Business," *Harvard Business School Bulletin,* Summer 1955, pp. 28, 29. Mr. Breech was at that time Chairman of the Board.

a modern cost control system and a supplemental compensation plan. Having done so, we were startled to find that nothing in particular happened. We had built, or so we thought, a log fire under the company. But we had not, up to that point, applied the torch of internal competition.

In the fall of 1948 we called together several hundred of our top management men. We analyzed and compared the profit performance of each key operation, and showed how performance was reflected in the supplemental compensation fund. It was quite a show, and each man went out of that meeting determined to put his own house in order. Each man in turn set up similar meetings of his own supervisors and the process continued on down the line. These meetings were held, and still are, at regular intervals. The results were almost unbelievable.

Our direct labor costs were reduced from an off-standard of 65% in July of 1948 to only 6% off-standard in 1951, and manufacturing overhead improved 48 percentage points during the same period. We never could have achieved that performance without a real incentive system and internal competition that reached deep into our management structure.

Action is a sure signal, probably the only effective signal, that management is interested in the control system. Basically, this action involves praise or other reward for good performance, criticism of or removal of the causes for poor performance, or questions leading to these actions. If, in contrast, reports on performance disappear into executive offices and are never heard from again, the organization has reason to assume that management is not paying attention to them. And if management does not pay attention to them, why should anyone else?

Participation and Understanding

Control is exercised in part by setting up standards of expected performance and comparing actual performance with these standards. Whatever standard of good performance is adopted, it is likely to be effective as a means of control only if the person being judged agrees that it is an equitable standard. If he does not agree, he is likely to pay no attention to comparisons between his performance and the standard; and he is likely to resent, and if possible reject, an attempt by anyone else to make such a comparison.

The best way to assure this agreement is to ask the person whose performance is to be measured to participate in the process of setting the standard. This was not the usual practice some years ago. The earliest budgets were "imposed budgets"; that is, they were edicts promulgated by management, which said, in effect, to the organization: "Thou shalt do such and such." The results obtained from these imposed budgets were frequently unsatisfactory because the organization tended to resent and disregard them. The more recent trend is in the direction of permitting the person who is being held responsible for performance to have a considerable voice in the preparation of the budget. This trend is a manifestation of the general tendency to decentralize decision making to lower echelons in the organization.

Although the responsible supervisor participates in the budgeting process, he is not solely responsible for deciding on the budget allowances. Rather, the supervisor and his superior discuss the matter until they *jointly* agree.

In order to participate intelligently, the supervisor needs to understand clearly what the control system is, what he is expected to do, what basis he is going to be judged on, and so on. As illustrated by the remarks of Mr. Breech quoted above, such an understanding probably cannot be achieved by written communication. Frequent meetings of supervisors for discussion and explanation are required.

The process of educating the individuals involved in the system is necessarily a continuous one. Not uncommonly, a system is introduced with a loud fanfare, works well for a time, and then gradually withers away in effectiveness as the initial stimulus disappears.

Incentives

Many management control systems rely for the strength of their motivation on the attitude and actions that management takes in response to reported performance. Some tie the supervisor's compensation to his performance. In view of the importance which people attach to monetary compensation, this is a strong motivation indeed. In some cases it may be too strong, for unless the standards are very carefully worked out, incessant arguments will go on about the justice and equity of the reported results. If the system is being used only for praise or blame, inequities in the figures can be allowed for in interpreting the results, but this is not possible when a bonus is computed mechanically on the basis of reported performance. Thus, a bonus plan is most successful when there is general agreement that the basis of measurement is fair.

Individual Differences

As pointed out above, individuals differ in their needs and in their reactions to rewards and punishments of various types. An important function of the manager, at each level, is to adapt the system to the personalities of the individuals whom he supervises. Thus, the impersonal system can never be a substitute for personal management; rather, the system is a framework that is adapted by management to fit individual situations.

Goal Congruence

It is reasonable to expect that a person will act according to what he perceives his own best interests to be. Essentially, therefore, the control system should be designed so that actions that it leads people to take in accordance with their perceived self-interest are actions that are also in the best interests of the company. In the language of social psychology, the system should encourage *goal congruence;* that is, it should be structured so that the goals of people in the organization are, so far as feasible, consistent with the goals of the organization as a whole.

Perfect congruence between individual goals and organizational goals does not exist, but as a minimum the system should not encourage the individual to act *against* the best interests of the company. For example, if the system signals that the emphasis should be only on reducing costs, and if the individual responds by reducing costs at the expense of adequate quality, or by reducing costs in his own department by measures that cause a more than offsetting increase in some other department, he has been motivated, but in the wrong direction. It is therefore important to ask two separate questions about a control technique: (1) What will it motivate people to do in their own selfish interests? and (2) Is this action in the best interests of the company?

An Example: Maintenance Costs

As an illustration of this point, let us consider the problem of the control of maintenance costs in a factory that has a separate maintenance department. The maintenance function is that of insuring that the buildings and equipment are in good operating condition. This is partly the responsibility of the maintenance department, which incurs costs when it makes repairs or does other maintenance work; and it is partly the responsibility of the operating department foreman, who can influence the amount of required maintenance work by how well he takes care of his equipment. In addition, some maintenance work, such as outside painting, is required simply because of the uncontrollable forces of nature.

There are at least a dozen ways in which the costs of the maintenance department can be charged to the several operating departments, and each gives a different "message" to the foremen as to how they should view their responsibility for maintenance. Here are a few of the possibilities and the implications that each is likely to convey:

Method No. 1: Do not charge any maintenance costs to the operating departments.

Message: The operating foreman has no responsibility for maintenance costs. He requests the maintenance department to do whatever work he thinks needs to be done, and the maintenance department has the responsibility for doing this work. (Note that this system does not motivate the foreman to curb unnecessary requests for maintenance work.)

Method No. 2: Prorate total maintenance costs to the operating departments on the basis of the volume of activity in the department.

Message: Maintenance costs in total are expected to vary proportionately with plant activity. However, the foreman of each department has no direct responsibility for maintenance work, and the maintenance department, as in the first method, has full responsibility. The operating foreman is told what is his "fair share" of total maintenance costs incurred, which may make him interested in the magnitude of such costs.

Method No. 3: Charge departments for each maintenance job at a prescribed cost for each type of job.

Message: The operating foreman is responsible for situations that create the need for maintenance work, such as machine breakdowns. The maintenance department is responsible for the cost of doing a given maintenance job. The foreman therefore need not be concerned with the efficiency with which maintenance men work, once he has requested that the job be done, since he will be charged a prescribed amount no matter how much is actually spent in doing the job.

Method No. 4: Charge each department for maintenance work at a prescribed hourly rate for each hour that a maintenance man works in the department.

Message: The operating foreman is responsible both for situations that create the need for maintenance work and for the time taken by the maintenance people to do the work. Presumably, he has some control over the work of the maintenance men. In some situations, he may even be authorized to hire outside maintenance people if he believes that they will do the work less expensively than the rates charged by the maintenance department.

None of the above methods is necessarily better than the others. Each of them tends to motivate the foreman differently. The best method is the one that motivates the foreman to act most nearly as management wants him to act. Depending on what top management wishes to accomplish, any one of these methods, or other methods not listed, or some combination of them, may be best for a given company.

THE MANAGEMENT CONTROL SYSTEM

Much of the management control process is informal; it occurs by means of memoranda, meetings, conversations, and even by such signals as facial expressions. Such control devices are not amenable to a systematic description. Many companies also have a formal system, consisting of some or all of the parts described briefly below and in more detail in succeeding chapters.

Information in a management control system can be classified as (1) planned and (2) actual data on (*a*) outputs and (*b*) inputs. Prior to actual operations, decisions and estimates are made as to what outputs and inputs are to be; during actual operations, records are maintained as to what outputs and inputs actually are; and subsequent to operations, reports are prepared that compare actual outputs and inputs to planned outputs and inputs. The principal steps in the formal process are:

1. Programming.
2. Budgeting.
3. Accounting.
4. Reporting and analysis.

As indicated in Illustration 14–1, each of these steps leads to the next. They recur in a regular cycle, and together they constitute a "closed loop."

Programming

In the programming phase, decisions are made with respect to the major programs in which the organization is to engage during the coming period. These decisions either are made within the context of the objectives and strategies that have previously been decided upon, or they represent changes in strategy. (If the latter, they are part of the strategic planning process, rather than the management control process; the two processes merge into one another in the programming phase.) A few companies state their programs in the form of a "long-range plan" which shows planned outputs and inputs for a number of years ahead—usually 5 years, but possibly as few as 3 or (in the case of certain public utilities) as many as 20. The majority of companies do not have such a formal mechanism for recording their overall future programs; they rely instead on reports or understandings as to specific, important facets of the program, particularly the amounts to be invested in capital assets and the means of financing these assets.

In an industrial company, the "Programs" are usually products or product lines, plus activities (such as research) that are not relatable to specific products. The plans have to do with the amount and character of resources (i.e., inputs) that are to be devoted to each program, and with the ways in which these resources are to be used. The accounting information used as a basis for such plans therefore tends to be program or cost accounting data, rather than responsibility accounting data.

Illustration 14–1

SEQUENCE OF MANAGEMENT CONTROL TECHNIQUES

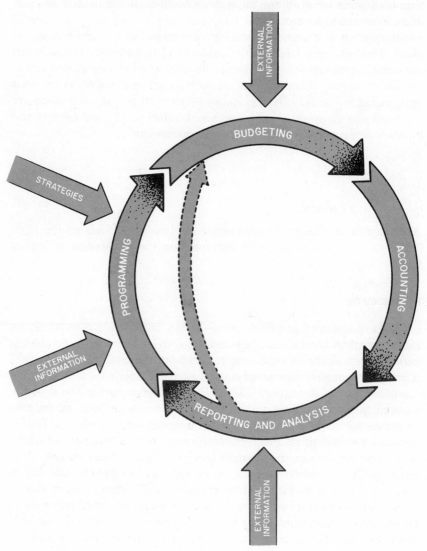

Budgeting

A budget is a plan expressed in quantitative, usually monetary, terms. It covers a specified period of time—usually a year, but in some companies six months or three months. In the budgeting process the program is translated into terms that correspond to the responsibility of those who are charged with executing it. Thus, although the plans are originally made in program terms, in the budgeting process they are translated into responsibility terms. The process of arriving at the budget is essentially one of negotiation between the managers of responsibility centers and their superiors. The end product of these negotiations is a statement of the outputs that are expected during the budget year and the resources that are to be used in achieving this output. The process is discussed more fully in Chapter 16.

Accounting

During the period of actual operations, records are kept of resources actually consumed and outputs actually achieved. As described in Chapter 13, the records of inputs (i.e., costs) are structured so that costs are collected both by product or programs and by responsibility centers. Costs in the former classification are used as a basis for future programming, and those in the latter are used to measure the performance of the heads of responsibility centers.

The degree to which outputs and inputs can be measured quantitatively varies greatly in different responsibility centers. In a department making a tangible homogeneous product (e.g., cement), the *quantity* of output often can be measured precisely; but when the products are heterogeneous (e.g., different styles and grades of shoes, parts produced by a machine shop), problems arise in summarizing the separate outputs into a meaningful measure of the total. Converting the disparate physical products to a monetary equivalent is one way of solving this problem. The *quality* of product also involves measurement problems, which often are solved by a "go, no-go" procedure: either the product is of satisfactory quality, or it is not.

When the outputs are services or other intangibles, the problem of measuring them becomes formidable. It is always difficult and often not feasible to measure, even approximately, the outputs of such staff units as the legal department or the research department of a company, or the outputs of hospitals, schools, government agencies, or churches. Nevertheless, these organizations *have* outputs; the difficulty of measurement does not alter this fact.

In addition to the products and services usually thought of as outputs, responsibility centers produce other intangible effects, some intentional and others unintentional. They may prepare employees for advancement; they may instill attitudes of loyalty and pride of accomplishment (or, alternatively, attitudes of disloyalty and indolence); and they may affect the image of the whole organization that is perceived by the outside world. Some of these outputs, such as better trained employees, are created in order to benefit operations in future periods; that is, they will become inputs at some future time. Such outputs are therefore "investments," since a business investment is a commitment of current resources in the expectation of deriving future benefits.

In the typical responsibility center, inputs are a heterogeneous mixture of resources: labor, materials, and services. Some common denominator must be found if these heterogeneous elements are to be aggregated into a measure of the total resources consumed by the responsibility center. Money is the most frequently used common denominator. The total resources consumed by a responsibility center, when measured in monetary terms, are the expenses of that responsibility center. Total recorded expenses are at best an approximation of the true inputs. Some inputs are not included as expenses, either because the effort required to translate them into monetary terms is not worthwhile (e.g., minor supplies and services, small amounts of borrowed labor) or because measurement is not possible (e.g., certain types of executive or staff assistance, training).

Reporting and Analysis

Accounting information, along with a variety of other information, is summarized, analyzed, and reported to those who are responsible for knowing what is happening in the company and for improving performance. As indicated above, these reports essentially compare planned outputs and inputs with actual outputs and inputs. Chapter 17 describes analyses that can be made of this information.

Need for Internal Consistency

It seems obvious that control is not possible unless actual performance and the standard against which it is being measured are comparable; yet instances of complete noncomparability do occur. This often happens when a management accounting system is separated from the financial accounting system, perhaps being operated by different staff organizations. An extreme case is that of the federal government, notably the Defense Department. For cost control purposes, an operating manager in the Defense Department should be judged on the basis of the costs *incurred* in doing his job. Nevertheless, until recently and despite the recommendations of two Hoover Commissions, the Congress attempted to exercise control through a limitation on obligations, which are essentially the cost of goods and services *purchased*. Since purchases are made by different persons from those who actually use the goods and services, and since they are made in different time periods from the time of consumption, this basis of control did not permit a matching of the control standard, the obligation, against the desired basis of control—costs incurred in responsibility centers. Although the practice is currently being corrected in the federal government, similar situations continue to exist in some businesses.

Inconsistencies between the standard desired by management and the standard as perceived by the organization also arise when aspects of performance are being measured in separate control systems. If a supervisor's performance as to quality is being measured in one system, his performance as to cost control in another, and his performance as to volume in a third, he may be uncertain as to the relative weights that he should attach to these three aspects of performance. He will tend to regard one of these aspects as more important than the others, but his choice may be different from what management actually intends.

RESPONSIBILITY CENTERS

In motivating and measuring performance, the control system is focused on the responsibility center, which is an organization unit headed by a responsible person. There are three types of responsibility centers: (1) expense centers, (2) profit centers (also called financial performance centers), and (3) investment centers.

Expense Centers

If the control system measures the expenses incurred by an organization unit, but does not measure the monetary value of its output, the unit is an expense center. Although every organization unit *has* outputs (i.e., it does something), in many cases it is neither feasible nor necessary to measure these outputs in monetary terms. It would be extremely difficult to measure the monetary value that the accounting department contributes to the whole business, for example, and although it would be relatively easy to measure the monetary value of the outputs of an individual production department, there is no reason for doing so if the responsibility of the factory foreman is simply to produce a stated *quantity* of output at the lowest feasible cost.

Thus most individual production departments and most staff units are expense centers. For these, the accounting system records expenses incurred, but not revenue earned.

Profit Centers

Revenue is a monetary measure of output, and expense is a monetary measure of inputs, or resources consumed. Profit is the difference between revenue and expense. Thus if performance in a responsibility center is measured in terms of both the revenue it earns and the cost it incurs, it is called a *profit center.*

Although in financial accounting, revenue is considered as being earned only when it is realized, in management accounting it is quite all right to define revenue as the value of the output of the center, whether realized or not. Thus, the factory may be a profit center, "selling" its production to the sales department; or service departments, such as the maintenance department, may "sell" their services to the departments receiving them.

Since the term "profit center" seems inappropriate in a nonprofit organization, the term "financial performance center" is used in such organizations for exactly the same concept.

The profit center concept is a powerful one. If properly operated, it has the effect of "putting the supervisor in business for himself," a business in which he can earn a profit. The development of this concept is one of the factors that has made possible the recent tendency for large companies to decentralize.

TRANSFER PRICE. A profit center is created by a conscious act of management. Usually, this requires that transfer prices be established. A transfer price is a price used to measure the exchange of products or services between responsibility centers within a company, as contrasted with a market price, which measures exchanges between a company and the outside world. Such internal exchanges result in revenue for the responsibility center furnishing the product or service and in cost for the responsibility center receiving the good or service. There are two general approaches to the construction of a transfer price: the market-based price, and the cost-based price.

If a market price for the product or service exists, such a price is usually preferable to a cost-based price. The "buying" responsibility center should not ordinarily be expected to pay more internally than it would have to pay if it purchased from the outside world, nor should the "selling" center ordinarily be entitled to more revenue than it could obtain by selling to the outside world. If the market price is abnormal, as for example when an outside vendor sets a low "distress" price in order to use temporarily idle capacity, then such temporary aberrations are ordinarily disregarded. The market price may be adjusted for cash discounts and for certain selling costs that are not involved in an internal exchange.

In a great many situations, there is no reliable market price that can be used as a basis for the transfer price, and in these situations, the transfer price is based on cost. Two general types of cost-based price are discussed in the literature: (1) marginal cost and (2) full cost plus profit. The marginal cost approach is consistent with the economic model of the firm that assumes that managers make decisions on the basis of complete knowledge of all factors affecting the firm, but it is not much used in practice.[3]

If the full cost approach is used, the method of computing cost and the amount of profit to be included is set by management in order to lessen

---

[3] For the argument for the marginal cost approach, see: Jack Hirshleifer, "On the Economics of Transfer Pricing," *Journal of Business* (July, 1956) pp. 172–84; and his "Economics of the Divisionalized Firm," *Journal of Business* (April, 1957) pp. 96–108.

arguments that would otherwise occur between the buying and the selling responsibility centers. If feasible, the cost should be a *standard* cost, for if it is an actual cost, the selling responsibility center can pass along its inefficiencies to the buying responsibility center; they will be included in the transfer price. The costs are not necessarily related to the costs actually incurred in the selling responsibility center; they may instead be built up from the costs that would be incurred by the most efficient producer, if these costs can be estimated. A transfer price based on such external costs may be a better measure of the output of the selling responsibility than a price based on the manufacturing practices and equipment actually being employed.

Whatever the approach to setting the transfer price, there is usually a mechanism for *negotiating* the price of actual transactions between the buying and the selling units. For example, the selling unit may be willing to reduce the normal market price in order to obtain the business, rather than having the buying unit take advantage of a temporarily low outside price, and the two parties negotiate such "deals." Unless the managers of responsibility centers have complete freedom to act, these negotiations will not always lead to an equitable result because the parties have unequal bargaining power; that is, the prospective buyer may not have the power of threatening to take his business elsewhere, and the prospective seller may not have the power to refuse to do the work. Thus, there usually needs to be an arbitration mechanism to settle disputes concerning transfer prices.

CRITERIA FOR PROFIT CENTERS. With some ingenuity, practically any expense center could conceivably be turned into a profit center, because some way of pricing its output can usually be found. Since the profit center concept is relatively new, its possibilities have by no means been fully exploited, and its use is growing rapidly. Its extension will be limited in accordance with criteria such as the following:

1. Extra record keeping is involved in a profit center to measure output, and in the receiving responsibility center to record costs. The gains in better information for decision making and in better motivation of managers must be important enough to offset these additional costs.

2. When top management *requires* responsibility centers to use a certain service (e.g., internal auditing), the service probably should be furnished at no charge, and the service unit therefore should not be a profit center.

3. If the manager of a responsibility center has little authority to decide on the quantity and quality of his outputs and on the relation of output to costs, then a profit center is usually of little value as a control device. This does not imply that the manager of a profit center must have complete control over outputs and inputs, for few if any managers have such authority.

4. If output is fairly homogeneous (e.g., cement), a nonmonetary measure of output (e.g., hundredweight of cement produced) may be adequate, and there may be no substantial gain in converting this to a monetary measure of revenue.

5. To the extent that a profit center puts a manager in business for himself, it promotes a spirit of competition. Up to a certain point, this is desirable, but beyond that point, the device may lead to too much friction between profit centers at the expense of the whole company's welfare, or too much interest in short-run "profits" to the detriment of long-run results (e.g., by undermaintaining his equipment). These difficulties are likely to arise when managers have an inadequate understanding of the management job, and they often can be overcome by education. If, however, they cannot be overcome, the profit center technique should be abandoned.

Investment Centers

An investment center is a responsibility center in which the manager is held responsible for the use of assets, as well as for revenues and expenses. It is therefore the ultimate extension of the responsibility idea. The manager is expected to earn a satisfactory return on *capital employed* in the responsibility center. Measurement of capital employed, or the *investment base*, poses many difficult problems, and the idea of the investment center is so new that there is considerable disagreement as to the best solution of these problems. For example, consider cash. The cash balance of the company is a safety valve, or shock absorber, protecting the company against short-run fluctuations in funds requirements. An investment center needs very little cash, however, since it can obtain funds on short notice from headquarters. Part of the headquarters cash balance therefore exists for the financial protection of the operating investment centers, and headquarters cash can therefore logically be allocated to the investment center as part of their capital employed. There are several ways of allocating this cash, just as there are several ways of allocating general overhead costs.

FIXED ASSETS. Perhaps the most controversial aspect of measuring capital employed has to do with fixed assets, both the machinery and other assets that are directly employed in the investment center, and an equitable share of the fixed assets that are allocated to the investment center (such as a building used by several investment centers). Assets may be valued at (1) replacement cost, which is usually measured by their insured value; (2) gross cost; or (3) net book value, which is gross cost less accumulated depreciation. Replacement cost, although conceptually sound, is rarely used because it cannot be substantiated by accounting records. Gross cost disregards differences in age, and hence in the accumulated depreciation; but it is widely used because the omission of depreciation may roughly counterbalance the omission of the effect of price inflation, which is not taken into account in the accounting records. Net book value has the advantage of being the figure that appears in the accounting records; but when this approach is used, an investment center with old, almost fully depreciated assets may show an extremely high rate of return solely for this reason.

DEPRECIATION METHODS. The method of depreciation affects not only the net book value of assets, but it also affects the amount of expense, and hence of profit, that is reported for the investment center. Various depreciation methods were discussed in Chapter 6. The annuity method, which was only briefly mentioned there because it is rarely used in financial accounting, appears to have merit in management accounting, although it is rarely used at present. The annuity method, coupled with profit calculated as a fixed percentage of the book value of assets, is the only method that provides a level charge each year, assuming no change in other costs, and it is a method that matches the method used to analyze proposed capital equipment acquisitions that will be described in Chapter 19.[4]

EFFECTIVENESS AND EFFICIENCY

The performance of the head of a responsibility center can be measured in terms of his "effectiveness" and his "efficiency." By effectiveness, we mean *how well* the manager does his job—that is (to quote the dictionary), "the extent to which he produces the intended or expected result." Efficiency is used in its engineering sense—that is, the amount of output per unit of input. An efficient machine generates a given quantity of outputs with a minimum consumption of inputs, or generates the largest possible outputs from a given quantity of inputs.

Effectiveness is always related to the organization's goals. Efficiency, per se, is not related to the goals. An efficient manager is one who does whatever he does with the lowest consumption of resources; but if what he does (i.e., his output) is an inadequate contribution to the accomplishment of the organization's goals, he is ineffective.

In many responsibility centers, a measure of efficiency can be developed that relates actual expenses to some standard—that is, to a number that expresses what expenses should be incurred for the amount of measured output. Such a measure can be a useful indication of efficiency, but it is never a perfect measure for at least two reasons: (1) recorded expenses are not a precisely accurate measure of resources consumed,

---

[4] For further discussion, see "Accounting for Capital Costs" in *Management Control Systems,* by Robert N. Anthony, John Dearden, and Richard F. Vancil (Homewood, Ill.: Richard D. Irwin, Inc., 1965), p. 343.

and (2) standards are, at best, only approximate measures of what resource consumption ideally should have been in the circumstances prevailing.

Effectiveness cannot be measured in financial terms in an expense center. Effectiveness is related to outputs, and in an expense center, by definition, outputs are not measured in financial terms. In some types of profit centers an approximate measure of effectiveness is possible. When one goal of the whole organization is to earn profits, then the contribution to this goal by a profit center is a measure of its effectiveness. This is so because in a profit center, by definition, the relationship between outputs and inputs is measured in monetary terms, and profit is a term describing such a relationship; that is, profit is the difference between revenue, which is a measure of output, and expense, which is a measure of input.

Actually, profit is influenced both by how effective a manager is and by how efficient he is; so profit measures both effectiveness and efficiency. When such an overall measure exists, it is unnecessary to determine the relative importance of effectiveness versus efficiency. When such an overall measure does not exist, it is feasible and useful to classify performance measures as relating either to effectiveness or to efficiency. In these situations, there is the problem of balancing the two types of measurements. For example, how do we compare the profligate perfectionist with the frugal manager who obtains less than the optimum output?

Profit is, at best, a crude measure of effectiveness and efficiency for several reasons: (1) monetary measures do not exactly measure either all aspects of outputs or all inputs, for reasons already given; (2) standards are not accurate; and (3) at best, profit is a measure of what has happened in the short run, whereas we are presumably also interested in the long-run consequences of decisions.

In view of the inadequacies of the profit measure, even under the best of circumstances, and in view of the absence of any profit measure in an expense center, many companies set other ways of measuring effectiveness. They may, for example, work out with the managers of responsibility centers a list of the objectives which are to be attained in the year—including such nonmonetary statements as, "Develop a new organization manual"; "Send three persons to management development programs"; "Reduce clerical errors by 50 percent"—and they then measure actual performance against these plans. This is called "management by objectives."

FUNCTION OF THE CONTROLLER

There is a tendency to regard the controller as the person who is primarily responsible for exercising control. Such an inference is natural because of the similarity between the two words, but it is erroneous. Generally, the controller is responsible for the design and operation of the *system* by means of which control information is collected and reported, but the *use* of this information in actual control is the responsibility of line management. The controller is something more than an accountant and something less than a chief executive. In addition to his responsibility for collecting figures, the controller may also be responsible for analyzing figures, for pointing out their significance to management, and for making recommendations as to what should be done. Moreover, he may police the adherence to limitations on spending laid down by the chief executive. He controls the integrity of the accounting system and is responsible for safeguarding assets from theft and fraud. In recent years the controllership function has become increasingly important in companies generally.

The controller does *not*, however (unless *de facto* he *is* the chief executive), make or enforce management decisions. The responsibility for control runs from the president down through the line organization, not through the controller, who is a staff officer.

Control of the Control System

Like a fruit tree, a management control system can become both unsightly and unproductive unless it is pruned periodically. What happens is that a new technique, usually in the form of a new report, is created to meet a particular problem, but once the problem has been solved, the report nevertheless continues. To avoid this result, companies either have a periodic overhaul of their control structure to eliminate such reports, or they have a person whose job is to ascertain that proposed new reports are likely to be worth the cost of preparing and using them and that existing reports continue to fill a real need. The work of keeping the system pruned is usually a function of the controller.

SUMMARY

Accounting information is useful in management control, a process that takes place after the objectives and strategies of an organization have been determined, and that is intended to assure managers that resources are used effectively and efficiently in the accomplishment of these objectives.

The scientific discipline most closely related to this process is social psychology, and its principles, rather than those of mathematics or economics, underlie the design of sound management control systems. Of these principles, the most important are those relating to motivation. The control system should be goal-congruent; that is, it should be designed so that when members of the organization are working in their own perceived self-interest they are also working toward the organization's objectives.

The control process involves the following sequential steps: (1) programming (which is also related to the process of strategic planning); (2) budgeting, which involves preparing and agreeing upon a plan for a specific time period, usually a year; (3) accounting, or the collection of information about what actually transpired during the period; and (4) reporting and analyzing performance, which essentially involves a comparison of actual outputs and inputs with planned outputs and inputs.

Management control focuses on responsibility centers. There are three types of responsibility centers: (1) expense centers, in which only inputs are measured in monetary terms; (2) profit centers (also called financial performance centers), in which both inputs and outputs are measured in monetary terms, the difference between them being profit—a recent development of great significance in control; and (3) investment centers, in which both profits and assets employed are measured in monetary terms—an even more recent and significant development.

In the measurement of performance, the focus is on effectiveness, which means how well the job was done, and on efficiency, which has to do with the amount of resources consumed in doing the job.

The control system is designed and operated by the controller, but he is not responsible for the acts of control; these are the responsibility of line management.

SUGGESTIONS FOR FURTHER READING

BARNARD, CHESTER I. *The Functions of the Executive.* Cambridge, Mass.: Harvard University Press, 1968.

BONINI, CHARLES P. et. al., eds. *Management Controls.* New York: McGraw-Hill Book Co., 1964.

JEROME, WILLIAM TRAVERS. *Executive Control; The Catalyst.* New York: John Wiley & Sons, Inc., 1961.

MARCH, JAMES G., and HERBERT A. SIMON. *Organizations.* New York: John Wiley & Sons, Inc., 1958.

TANNENBAUM, ARNOLD S. *Control in Organizations.* New York: McGraw-Hill Book Co., 1968.

CASES

CASE 14–1. GILLETTE SAFETY RAZOR COMPANY

On the morning of March 5, Miss Ruth Fillipetti, an employee of the Gillette Safety Razor Company, reported for work in the buffing room of the South Boston plant. At the stock cage she picked up a tray containing handles for one of the current models of the Gillette safety razor. These stamped copper handles had been sent to the buffing department for smoothing and polishing. After being polished, the handles went to the plating department for the final stage in their manufacture.

Miss Fillipetti's job was to smooth and polish the end of the razor handle. In this work she used a power-driven buffer wheel, against which she held the handle. The operation was not a difficult one, but it was not automatic; that is, she was required to place the end of the handle against the buffer wheel manually. For certain models, an automatic machine could be used that required only that the handles be placed on a moving belt of spindles. This belt carried the handles automatically across a buffer wheel. Miss Fillipetti spent the full day of March 5 buffing razor handle ends and by 5 o'clock had completed the smoothing and polishing of 2,100 pieces.

A close check was kept on the amount of work given to Miss Fillipetti and also on the amount of time she spent doing it. Although none of the employees of the Gillette Safety Razor Company was paid on a piece-rate basis, a daily comparison was made of the actual and standard times required to do the work assigned. On the morning of March 6 the timecard for Miss Fillipetti, together with timecards of other employee in the buffing room, was sent upstairs to the accounting department, where work and time requirements were posted and compared with previously established standard times. By 4 o'clock that afternoon—that is, the afternoon of March 6—the complete record of gains and losses with reference to standard times for work done on March 5 was reported back to the foreman in the buffing room. A procedure similar to that used for the buffing department was followed for each of the production departments of the razor division. In some departments the reports were

Exhibit 1. DAILY REPORT OF PRODUCTION BY OPERATORS

GILLETTE SAFETY RAZOR COMPANY
DAILY REPORT OF PRODUCTION BY OPERATORS

490 BUFFING DEPARTMENT

DATE March 5

Total Expected Hours	181 9/—
" Productive Hours Not Measured	48 6/—
Lost Hours	13 3/—
Gained Hours	5
Nonproductive Hours Charged to This Dept.	50 4/—
" " Not Charged to This Dept.	2
Loaned Hours	48
Total Actual Hours Worked incl. Loaned	343 10/—

		Operation Number	Acct.	Production Total Actual	Expected per Hour	Hours Expected	Actual	Diff. Red-Loss R / Bl.-Gain B
4126	MOORE, STELLA	195 D 20	502	2800	375	7 6/—	8	6/—
4126	MOORE, STELLA							
4127	MACCAREY, ELEANOR	1001 DG 25	502	2800			7	
4127	MACCAREY, ELEANOR	195 DG 25	502	400	400	1	1	9/—
4128	MURPHY, ELLEN	1005 R 200	502	200			1	9/—
4128	MURPHY, ELLEN	1005 RG 26	502	100			6/—	6/—
4129	LEIGH, VIRGINIA	139 B 204	502	20000	2250	8	8	11/—
4129	LEIGH, VIRGINIA					11/—		
4130	FILLIPETTI, RUTH	195 D 20	502	2100	375	5 7/—	7 10/—	2 3/—
4130	FILLIPETTI, RUTH					7	7	
4131	LURRELLO, HELEN	139 B 24	502	14000	1750	8	8	
4131	LURRELLO, HELEN							

Operation Number	Acct.	Production Total Actual	Expected per Hour	Hours Expected	Actual	Diff. Red-Loss R / Bl.-Gain B
195 D 20	502	450	375	1	2 1/—	6 1/— ... 4/—
194 H 20	522	600	300	2	3 3/—	1 3/—

4132	CONRAD, HORTENSE	Loaned										
4132	CONRAD, HORTENSE								8			
4133	OLEARY, KATHARINE	1005 AG 210	502	76						3|		
4133	OLEARY, KATHARINE	195 D 20	502	2275	375	6	1|	7	9|	1 8|	
4134	WOODROW, ESTHER	139 B 206	502	20000	2250	8	11		8			
4134	WOODROW, ESTHER										11	
4135	ROVETA, MILDRED	195 C 24	502	12000	1750	6	10	8		1 2		
4135	ROVETA, MILDRED											
4136	CAPRA, JOSEPHINE	1004 A 20	522	500			3|	3	5|		
4136	CAPRA, JOSEPHINE	195 D 20	502	1600	375	4	3|	4	7|	4|	
4137	CASSIDY, ELINOR	195 D 20	502	2400	375	6	5|	8		1 7|	
4137	CASSIDY, ELINOR											
4138	LOVITT, MARION	Group										
4138	LOVITT, MARION											
4139	LESLIE, ALTHEA	1004 A 20	522	1100				8			
4139	LESLIE, ALTHEA											
4140	SMITH, MARY	139 B 29	502	14000	1750	8		8			
4140	SMITH, MARY											
4141	GRADY, ANNE	Loaned										
4141	GRADY, ANNE											
4142	LAMB, ELIZABETH	1001 D 211	502	23000	3500	6	7|	8		1 5|	
4142	LAMB, ELIZABETH											

referred to by the foreman when talking privately with operators, but in other departments the reports were posted daily. A portion of the March 5 report for the buffing department is reproduced as Exhibit 1.

The time standard set up for the operation of buffing the ends of the razor handles was 375 handles an hour.[5] The normal time to produce 2,100 units at the rate of 375 an hour was 5 hours and 36 minutes. The time records were kept in 5-minute units; and, therefore, the expected time for the work done by Miss Fillipetti on March 5 was listed on the report as $5\frac{7}{12}$ hours. Her day's work actually took $7\frac{10}{12}$ hours, so that a loss of $2\frac{3}{12}$ hours in standard time was indicated. When actual time exceeded standard allowable time, the amount lost was reported on the daily record sheet in red pencil; when actual time was under standard time, the gain was shown in black. A summary for the whole department was shown at the top of each report form.

Once a week the daily summary reports were combined into a weekly report that was furnished each of the foremen and the plant superintendent. From these weekly reports a continuous tabulation was maintained by the plant superintendent. The departmental labor control record for the buffing room shown in Exhibit 2 contains data for the three-month period beginning with the week ending December 23, through and including the week ending March 16.

The first column of the departmental labor control record (Exhibit 2) gives the normal or standard allowable hours for the volume of work done. Normal hours were the daily average of the "expected" hours shown on the daily report. Columns 2 and 3 of Exhibit 2 show the average daily hours lost and gained. Column 4 gives the daily average of actual hours required to do the same work for which the normal operating time is given in column 1. It will be noted that column 1 plus column 2 minus column 3 equals column 4. The entries in column 5, "General Ledger," refer to hours spent on special work ordered by the general office and therefore not part of the normal production flow. Column 6 gives the number of hours' work that was not measured and for which no normal times were available for comparison. Columns 7 and 8 relate to nonproductive time devoted to the work of maintenance and similar work not directly resulting in produced goods. The final column gives the total number of hours worked in the department.

A report similar to that shown in Exhibit 2 was prepared weekly for each of the departments engaged in manufacturing razors. Exhibit 3 shows for the weeks ending March 9 and March 16 the hours lost in each of six

---

[5] This operation was coded as 195 D 20; the "195" refers to the model, the "D" to the handle of the razor, and the "20" to the operation. A similar code number was given every other operation. The letter "B" was used to refer to the cap of the razor, "C" to the guard, and "A" to the complete razor. The operation on which Miss Fillipetti was engaged, 195 D 20, was known as "cut down and color."

Exhibit 2

DEPARTMENTAL LABOR CONTROL, DEPARTMENT 490—BUFFING

Average Daily Hours

Week Ending	Normal Hours (1)	Hours Lost (2)	Hours Gained (3)	Actual Measured Hours (4)	General Ledger (5)	Productive Hours Not Measured (6)	Nonproductive Hours (7)	Ratio to Normal Hours (8)	Total Hours (9)
December 9..	212.9	8.0	8.1	212.8	6.4	30.1	50.8	23.86	300.1
16..	183.8	10.5	5.6	188.7	12.7	23.4	51.3	27.91	276.1
23..	192.0	5.5	5.2	192.3	11.9	22.7	51.4	26.77	278.3
January 6..	174.7	9.2	5.0	178.9	2.0	39.8	57.6	32.97	278.3
13..	196.4	24.4	4.9	215.9	1.5	28.2	54.2	27.60	299.8
20..	194.9	14.6	6.1	203.4	4.0	54.5	50.3	25.80	312.2
27..	194.7	11.3	7.5	198.5	8.0	63.0	54.8	28.15	324.3
February 3..	160.8	10.5	4.5	166.8	6.0	106.9	56.7	35.26	336.4
10..	153.8	14.5	3.4	164.9	5.8	86.1	41.7	27.11	298.5
17..	168.4	19.7	5.4	182.7	3.6	72.7	50.9	30.23	309.9
24..	177.1	13.2	3.7	186.6	2.5	72.7	57.5	32.47	319.3
March 2..	192.5	10.6	3.5	199.6	1.8	68.3	54.8	28.47	324.5
9..	201.1	13.2	3.2	211.1	0.4	46.7	54.1	26.90	312.3
16..	169.6	5.4	4.8	170.2	...	17.7	56.3	33.20	244.2

Exhibit 3

EXCERPTS FROM PRODUCTION CONTROL REPORT, SELECTED DEPARTMENTS

Average Daily Hours

Department	Hours Lost Week Ending March 9	Hours Lost Week Ending March 16	Measured Hours Week Ending March 9	Measured Hours Week Ending March 16	Total Hours Week Ending March 9	Total Hours Week Ending March 16
Cap and guard.......	0.3	0.7	167.9	208.5	297.2	279.2
Buffing.............	13.2	5.4	211.1	170.2	312.3	244.2
Handle inspection	6.0	2.8	143.2	135.7	157.4	146.2
Wire and plating:....	0.1	...	79.3	86.3	181.7	188.1
Handle packing......	34.5	50.9	440.2	546.5	535.9	683.4
Auto-strop and probak department........	13.2	7.9	64.4	60.4	186.4	156.1

departments. The exhibit also shows the total number of hours reported for the departments and the number of measured hours for which losses were computed.

The daily report comparing actual and normal times by operators was prepared for the department foremen. The personnel department did not receive copies of the daily report and, therefore, could not make the operator's performance a formal part of his personnel record. It was estimated that the time of two clerks was required to prepare the daily and weekly reports for the entire razor division.

Questions

1. What is the source, so far as you can judge, of the entries in each of the columns of Exhibit 1? If you were handed this report, what would you look for first? Should the plant superintendent request that the daily production report be put on his desk?

2. If Miss Fillipetti's record on operation 195 D 20 continued to be poor, should the department manager refer the matter to the personnel department? Before taking such action, what should the department manager consider?

3. Rank, from best to poorest, the performance of Stella Moore, Ellen Murphy, Ruth Fillipetti, and Esther Woodrow.

4. What purpose could be served by the operating report illustrated in Exhibit 1? Is it worth the cost? Should the cost be shared by other reports, perhaps not shown in the case?

5. What is Exhibit 2? Why is this type of report called a comparative report? Why are the figures in Exhibit 2 in terms of daily averages instead of weekly totals?

6. Look at Exhibit 2, *not Exhibit 3*, and decide what items you would select to be included in a summary report comparing performance in various departments in the factory.

7. What do Exhibits 2 and 3 tell other than the number of hours put in by employees? Doesn't management really want to know whether any work was done during those hours?

8. If you were receiving these control reports, what standards would you develop?

CASE 14–2. BENTLEY CORPORATION

The management of the Bentley Corporation, manufacturer of corrugated paper, was aware that the company would soon face intense competition. For several years, its mills had been operating at capacity, but demand appeared to be slackening. Consequently, the management started an intensive program to find means of reducing costs.

As one of the first steps in the economy program, the main office cut costs by eliminating unnecessary personnel in the staff departments, dropping unused reports, and tightening controls on administrative expenses. At the same time top management and the various plant managers had conferences on the need for cost reduction at the factory level.

The company operated seven mills scattered throughout the northern part of the United States. In each mill, there were four processing departments, with the product moving in succession through Departments 1, 2, 3, and then 4. Up to this time, the managers of the seven mills had been given monthly reports that compared costs of the different processing departments in the seven mills. The costs were compiled according to a uniform accounting system. It was recognized that mill costs differed because of size, technology, local cost situations, current volume of output, and so forth. Nevertheless, top management believed that all factors affecting a plant's costs were controllable by someone, either plant management or top management.

In an attempt to dramatize the cost differences among mills and the opportunities for cost reductions, the controller's office held several con-

Exhibit 1

COMPARATIVE COST REPORT, JUNE

	Department 1			Department 2			Department 3	
Mill	Unit Cost	Loss over Best	Mill	Unit Cost	Loss over Best	Mill	Unit Cost	Loss over Best
A	$0.655	$ 0	D	$3.89	$ 0	C	$ 6.74	$ 0
B	0.772	2,210	C	4.09	235	F	7.15	176
C	0.781	2,146	A	4.26	502	G	7.42	391
D	0.855	3,785	E	4.95	3,160	B	7.54	712
E	0.965	10,001	F	5.80	1,755	A	8.01	775
F	1.129	4,100	B	5.85	2,885	E	8.39	2,724
G	1.220	9,790	G	5.96	2,849	D	14.39	2,360

	Department 4			Total Waste			Cost Standing	
Mill	Unit Cost	Loss over Best	Mill	Percentage	Loss over Best	Mill	Total Loss over Best	
G	$ 5.00	$ 0	F	7.4	$ 0	F	$ 6,499	
B	6.71	525	B	8.4	1,985	B	8,317	
F	6.86	468	E	8.8	6,420	C	9,527	
D	7.32	3,798	D	9.0	4,070	A	9,558	
C	7.65	995	C	10.5	6,151	D	14,013	
A	8.41	1,881	A	11.0	6,400	E	30,155	
E	10.51	7,850	G	14.8	18,510	G	31,540	

ferences on the subject with plant managers. As a follow-up on such discussions, a new report, based on the old comparative cost reports, was prepared and sent to the plant managers. An accompanying letter, signed by the controller, closed with a request for comments or suggestions on the report.

A copy of the new report is given in Exhibit 1. It shows unit products costs in each of the four departments, with a separate tabulation of the cost of waste in the whole mill.

Questions

1. Comment on the strong and weak points of the comparative cost report.
2. What would you do next to examine and reduce costs?

CASE 14–3.   DAY COMPANY

The president of the Day department store has received the facts tabulated in Exhibit 1 from one of the operating executives. He has asked you to comment on the significant points revealed by these data.

Exhibit 1

COMPARATIVE OPERATING STATISTICS FOR DEPARTMENT A AND
SIMILAR DEPARTMENTS OF COMPARABLE STORES

	1964	1965	1966	1967	1968
Department A:					
Sales......................	$100,000	$104,400	$109,600	$98,800	$100,600
Gross margin...............	$ 25,900	$ 28,814	$ 38,250	$35,469	$ 36,517
Direct expenses.............	$ 8,264	$ 8,601	$ 9,024	$ 8,861	$ 8,980
Indirect expenses...........	20,000	20,880	21,920	24,700	25,150
Total expenses............	$ 28,264	$ 29,481	$ 30,944	$33,561	$ 34,130
Net Profit (Loss).......	$ (2,364)	$ (667)	$ 7,306	$ 1,908	$ 2,387
Percentages, Department A:					
Sales (1964 = 100).........	100%	104.4%	109.6%	98.8%	100.6%
Gross margin..............	25.9	27.6	34.9	35.9	36.3
Transactions (1966 = 100)...	96	98	100	95	96
Percentages, Similar Departments of Other Stores:					
Sales (1964 = 100).........	100%	106.1%	111.3%	112.7%	114.2%
Gross margin..............	25.1	27.2	29.4	30.1	34.6
Transactions (1966 = 100)...	....	....	100	97	98
Published index of retail prices of products sold in Department A (1966 = 100).........			100	102	103

The data relate to the operating results of Department A, which handles gloves and ladies' hosiery. The president is interested in the results of your analysis because the department adopted a higher markup percentage in pricing goods sold in this department beginning in 1966. The effect of this policy may be noted clearly in the percentage gross margin figures.

CASE 14–4. BIRCH PAPER COMPANY

"If I were to price these boxes any lower than $480 a thousand," said Mr. Brunner, manager of Birch Paper Company's Thompson division, "I'd be countermanding my order of last month for our salesmen to stop shaving their bids and to bid full cost quotations. I've been trying for weeks to improve the quality of our business, and if I turn around now and accept this job at $430 or $450 or something less than $480, I'll be tearing down this program I've been working so hard to build up. The division can't very well show a profit by putting in bids which don't even cover a fair share of overhead costs, let alone give us a profit."

Birch Paper Company was a medium-sized, partly integrated paper company, producing white and kraft papers and paperboard. A portion of its paperboard output was converted into corrugated boxes by the Thompson division, which also printed and colored the outside surface of the boxes. Including Thompson, the company had four producing divisions and a timberland division, which supplied part of the company's pulp requirements.

For several years each division had been judged independently on the basis of its profit and return on investment. Top management had been working to gain effective results from a policy of decentralizing responsibility and authority for all decisions except those relating to overall company policy. The company's top officials felt that in the past few years the concept of decentralization had been successfully applied and that the company's profits and competitive position had definitely improved.

Early in 1957 the Northern division designed a special display box for one of its papers in conjunction with the Thompson division, which was equipped to make the box. Thompson's package design and development staff spent several months perfecting the design, production methods, and materials that were to be used; because of the unusual color and shape, these were far from standard. According to an agreement between the two divisions, the Thompson division was reimbursed by the Northern division for the cost of its design and development work.

When the specifications were all prepared, the Northern division asked for bids on the box from the Thompson division and from two outside companies. West Paper Company and Erie Papers, Ltd. Each division manager normally was free to buy from whichever supplier he wished; and even on sales within the company, divisions were expected to meet the going market price if they wanted the business.

Early in 1957 the profit margins of converters such as the Thompson division were being squeezed. Thompson, as did many other similar converters, bought its board, liner or paper; and its function was to print, cut, and shape it into boxes. Though it bought most of its materials from other Birch divisions, most of Thompson's sales were to outside customers. If Thompson got the order from Northern, it probably would buy its linerboard and corrugating medium from the Southern division of Birch. The walls of a corrugated box consist of outside and inside sheets of linerboard sandwiching the corrugating medium.

About 70 percent of Thompson's out-of-pocket cost of $400 a thousand for the order represented the cost of linerboard and corrugating medium. Though Southern division had been running below capacity and had excess inventory, it quoted the market price, which had not noticeably weakened as a result of the oversupply. Its out-of-pocket costs on both liner and corrugating medium were about 60 percent of the selling price.

The Northern division received bids on the boxes of $480 a thousand from the Thompson division, $430 a thousand from West Paper Company, and $432 a thousand from Erie Papers, Ltd. Erie Papers offered to buy from Birch the outside linerboard with the special printing already on it, but would supply its own inside liner and corrugating medium. The outside liner would be supplied by the Southern division at a price equivalent to $90 a thousand boxes, and would be printed for $30 a thousand by the Thompson division. Of the $30, about $25 would be out-of-pocket costs.

Since this situation appeared to be a little unusual, Mr. Kenton, manager of the Northern division, discussed the wide discrepancy of bids with Birch's commercial vice president. He told the commercial vice president, "We sell in a very competitive market, where higher costs cannot be passed on. How can we be expected to show a decent profit and return on investment if we have to buy our supplies at more than 10 percent over the going market?"

Knowing that Mr. Brunner had on occasion in the past few months been unable to operate the Thompson division at capacity, the commercial vice president thought it odd that Mr. Brunner would add the full 20 percent overhead and profit charge to his out-of-pocket costs. When he asked Mr. Brunner about this over the telephone, his answer was the statement that appears at the beginning of the case. Mr. Brunner went on to say that having done the developmental work on the box, and having received no profit on that, he felt entitled to a good markup on the production of the box itself.

The vice president explored further the cost structures of the various divisions. He remembered a comment the controller had made at a meeting the week before to the effect that costs that for one division were variable could be largely fixed for the company as a whole. He knew that in the absence of specific orders from top management, Mr. Kenton would accept the lowest bid, namely, that of the West Paper Company for $430. However, it would be possible for top management to order the acceptance of another bid if the situation warranted such action. And though the volume represented by the transactions in question was less than 5 percent of the volume of any of the divisions involved, other transactions could conceivably raise similar problems later.

Questions

1. Does the system motivate Mr. Brunner in such a way that actions he takes in the best interests of the Thompson division are also in the best interests of the Birch Paper Company? If your answer is "no," give some specific instances related as closely as possible to the type of situation described in the case. Would the manager of *other* divisions be correctly motivated?
2. What should the vice president do?

CASE 14–5. BULTMAN AUTOMOBILES, INC. (A)

William Bultman, the part owner and manager of an automobile dealership, felt the problems associated with the rapid growth of his business were becoming too great for him to handle alone. (See Exhibit 1 for current income statement.) The reputation he had established in the community led him to believe that the recent growth in his business would continue. His long-standing policy of emphasizing new car sales as the principal business of the dealership had paid off, in Mr. Bultman's opinion. This, combined with close attention to customer relations so that a substantial amount of repeat business was available, had increased the company's sales to a new high level. Therefore, he wanted to make organizational changes to cope with the new situation. Mr. Bultman's three "silent partners" agreed to this decision.

Accordingly, Mr. Bultman divided up the business into three departments: a new car sales department; a used car sales department; and, the service department. He then appointed three of his most trusted employees as managers of the new departments: John Ward was named manager of new car sales; Marty Ziegel, manager of used car sales; and, Charlie Lassen, manager of the service department. All of these men had been with the dealership for several years.

Each of the managers was told to run his department as if it were an independent business. In order to give the new managers an incentive,

Exhibit 1

BULTMAN AUTOMOBILES INC. (A)

Income Statement for the Year Ended December 31, 1964

Sales of new cars............................		$764,375
Cost of new sales..........................	$631,281	
Sales remuneration........................	32,474	
		663,755
		$100,620
Allowances on trade*.....................		23,223
		$ 77,397
Sales of used cars.........................	$479,138	
Appraised value of used cars................$381,455		
Sales remuneration........................ 18,312		
	399,767	
	$ 79,371	
Allowances on trade*.....................	12,223	
		67,148
		$144,545
Service sales to customers..................	$ 69,502	
Cost of work.............................	51,397	
	$ 18,105	
Service work on reconditioning:		
Charge...............................$ 47,316		
Cost................................. 48,862	(1,546)	
		16,559
		$161,104
General and administrative expenses..........		98,342
Profit before Taxes.......................		$ 62,762

* Allowances on trade represents the excess of amounts allowed on cars taken in trade over their appraised value.

their remuneration was calculated as a straight percentage of their department's profit.

Soon after taking over as the manager of the new car sales department, John Ward had to settle upon the amount to offer a particular customer who wanted to trade his old car as part of the purchase price of a new one with a list price of $3,600. Before closing the sale, Mr. Ward had to decide the amount of discount from list he would offer the customer and the trade-in value of the old car. He knew he could deduct 15 percent from the list price of the new car without seriously hurting his profit margin. However, he also wanted to make sure that he did not lose out on the trade-in.

During his conversations with the customer, it had become apparent that the customer had an inflated view of the worth of his old car, a far from uncommon event. The new car had been in stock for some time, and the model was not selling very well, so Mr. Ward was rather anxious to make the sale if this could be done profitably.

In order to establish the trade-in value of the car, the manager of the used car department, Mr. Ziegel, accompanied Mr. Ward and the customer out to the parking lot to examine the car. In the course of his appraisal, Mr. Ziegel estimated the car would require reconditioning work costing about $200, after which the car would retail for about $1,050. On a wholesale basis, he could either buy or sell such a car, after reconditioning, for about $900. The wholesale price of a car was subject to much greater fluctuation than the retail price, depending on color, trim, model, etc. Fortunately, the car being traded in was a very popular shade. The retail automobile dealers' handbook of used car prices, the "Blue Book," gave a cash buying price range of $775 to $825 for the trade-in model in good condition. This range represented the distribution of cash prices paid by automobile dealers for that model of car in the area in the past week. Mr. Ziegel estimated that he could get about $625 for the car "as is" (that is, without any work being done to it) at next week's auction.

The new car department manager had the right to buy a trade-in at any price he thought appropriate, but then it was his responsibility to dispose of the car. He had the alternative of either trying to persuade the used car manager to take over the car, accepting the used car manager's appraisal price, or he himself could sell the car through wholesale channels. Whatever course Mr. Ward adopted, it was his primary responsibility to make a profit for the dealership on the new cars he sold, without affecting his performance through excessive allowances on trade-ins. This primary goal, Mr. Ward said, had to be "balanced against the need to satisfy the customers and move the new cars out of Inventory—and there is only a narrow line between not allowing enough on the used car and allowing too much."

After weighing all these factors, with particular emphasis on the personality of the customer, Mr. Ward decided he would allow $1,200 for the used car, provided the customer agreed to pay the list price for the new car. After a certain amount of haggling, during which the customer came down from a higher figure and Ward came up from a lower one, the $1,200 allowance was agreed upon. The necessary papers were signed, and the customer drove off.

Mr. Ward returned to the office and explained the situation to Ronald Bradley, who had recently joined the dealership as an accountant. After listening with interest to Mr. Ward's explanation of the sale, Mr. Bradley set about recording the sale in the accounting records of the business. As soon as he saw the new car had been purchased from the manufacturer for $2,500, he was uncertain as to the value he should place on the trade-in vehicle. Since the new car's list price was $3,600 and it had cost $2,500, Mr. Bradley reasoned the gross margin on the new car sale was $1,100. Yet Mr. Ward had allowed $1,200 for the old car, which needed $200 repairs and could be sold retail for $1,050 or wholesale for $900. Did this mean that the new car sale involved a loss? Mr. Bradley was not at all sure he knew the answer to this question. Also, he was uncertain about the value he should place on the used car for inventory valuation purposes.

Question

1. How should this transaction be recorded?

CASE 14–6. BULTMAN AUTOMOBILES, INC. (B)

Ronald Bradley, the recently appointed accountant of Bultman Automobiles, Inc., was unable to resolve the problem he faced as to the valuation of a trade-in car. The car had been taken in trade at an allowance of $1,200 against the list selling price of the new car of $3,600. The cost of the new car to the company had been $2,500. The old car could be sold wholesale or retail, at prices of about $900 and $1,050 respectively. Bradley decided that he would put down a valuation of $1,200, and then await instructions from his superiors.

When Marty Ziegel, manager of the used car department, found out what Mr. Bradley had done, he went to the office and stated forcefully that he would not accept $1,200 as the valuation of the used car. His comment went as follows:

My used car department has to get rid of that used car, unless John [new car department manager] agrees to take it over himself. I would certainly never have allowed the customer $1,200 for that old tub. I would never have given any more than $700, which is the wholesale price less the cost of repairs. My department has to make a profit too, you know. My own income is dependent on the gross profit I show on the sale of used cars, and I will not stand for having my income hurt because John is too generous toward his customers.

Mr. Bradley replied that he had not meant to cause trouble, but had simply recorded the car at what seemed to be its cost of acquisition, because he had been taught that this was the best practice. Whatever response Mr. Ziegel was about to make to this comment was cut off by the arrival of William Bultman, the general manager, and Charlie Lassen, the service department manager. Mr. Bultman picked up the phone and called John Ward, the new car sales manager, asking him to come over right away.

"All right, Charlie," said Mr. Bultman, "now that we are all here, would you tell them what you just told me."

Mr. Lassen, who was obviously very worried, said:

Thanks, Bill; the trouble is with this trade-in. John and Marty were right in thinking that the repairs they thought necessary would cost about $200.

Unfortunately, they failed to notice that the rear axle is cracked, which will have to be replaced before we can sell the car. This will use up materials and labor costing about $150.

Besides this, there is another thing which is bothering me a good deal more. If I did work costing $350 for an outside customer, I would be able to charge him about $475 for the job. The Blue Book[6] gives a range of $460 to $490 for the work this car needs, and I have always aimed for the middle of the Blue Book range. That would give a contribution to my department's gross profit of $125, and my own income is based on that gross profit. Since it looks as if a high proportion of the work of my department is going to be the reconditioning of trade-ins for resale, I figure that I should be able to make the same charge for repairing a trade-in as I would get for an outside repair job. In this case, the charge would be $450.

Messrs. Ziegel and Ward both started to talk at once at this point. Mr. Ziegel, the more forceful of the two, managed to edge Mr. Ward out:

This axle business is unfortunate, all right, but it is very hard to spot a cracked axle. Charlie is likely to be just as lucky the other way next time. He has to take the rough with the smooth. It is up to him to get the cars ready for me to sell.

Mr. Ward, after agreeing that the failure to spot the axle was unfortunate, added:

This error is hardly my fault, however. Anyway, it is ridiculous that the service department should make a profit out of jobs it does for the rest of the dealership. The company can't make money when its left hand sells to its right.

William Bultman, the general manager, was getting a little confused about the situation. He thought there was a little truth in everything that had been said, but he was not sure how much. It was evident to him that some action was called for, both to sort out the present problem and to prevent its recurrence. He instructed Mr. Bradley, the accountant, to "work out how much we are really going to make on this whole deal," and then retired to his office to consider how best to get his managers to make a profit for the company.

Question

1. How should this transaction be recorded?

---

[6] In addition to the Blue Book for used car prices, there is a Blue Book which gives the range of charges for various classes of repair work. Like the used car book, it is a weekly, and is based on the actual charges made and reported by motor repair shops in the area.

CASE 14–7. BULTMAN AUTOMOBILES, INC. (C)

A week after the events described in Bultman Automobiles, Inc. (B) had occurred, William Bultman, part owner and manager of the business, was still far from sure what action to take to motivate his managers to make a profit for the business. During the week, Charlie Lassen, the service manager, had reported to him that the repairs to the used car had cost $387, of which $180 represented the cost of those repairs which had been spotted at the time of purchase, and the remaining $207 was the cost of supplying and fitting a replacement for the cracked axle.

To support his case for a higher allowance on reconditioning jobs, Lassen had looked up the duplicate invoices over the last few months, and had found other examples of the same work that had been done on the trade-in car. The amount of these invoices totaled $453, which the customers had paid without question, and the time and materials that had gone into the jobs had been costed at $335. This included an allocation of departmental overhead, but no charge for general overhead.

In addition, Lassen had obtained from Mr. Bradley, the accountant, the cost analysis shown in Exhibit 1. Lassen told Bultman that this was a fairly typical distribution of the service department expense.

Exhibit 1

BULTMAN AUTOMOBILES, INC. (C)

Analysis of Service Department Expenses for the Year Ended December 31, 1964

	Customer Jobs	Recondition- ing Jobs	Total
Number of jobs..............................	183	165	348
Direct labor...................................	$21,386	$19,764	$ 41,150
Supplies.......................................	7,412	6,551	13,963
Department overhead (fixed)....................	6,312	5,213	11,525
	$35,110	$31,528	$ 66,638
Parts...	16,287	17,334	33,621
	$51,397	$48,862	$100,259
Charges made for jobs to customers or other departments................................	69,502	47,316	116,818
Profit (Loss).................................	$18,105	($ 1,546)	$ 16,559
General overhead proportion.................			11,416
Departmental profit for the year..............			$ 5,143

Questions

1. In view of the new information, how should the complete transaction relating to the cars described in the (A), (B), and (C) cases be recorded?
2. Does the system motivate the department managers properly? If not, what changes would you recommend?

CHAPTER 15

CHARACTERISTICS OF COST

This chapter discusses some additional aspects of the nature and behavior of costs that are relevant in management accounting. A number of cost concepts have been described in previous chapters, viz, the distinction between:

—Capital costs and operating costs, i.e., between assets and expenses, in Chapter 6.
—Product costs and period costs, in Chapter 7.
—Historical costs and current costs, in Chapter 9.
—Direct, or traceable, costs and indirect (allocated, common, joint) costs, in Chapter 13.
—Actual costs and standard costs, in Chapter 13.
—Direct costs and full costs, in Chapter 13.
—Program, or product, costs and responsibility costs, in Chapter 13.

To this list, we add, in the current chapter, the distinction between:

—Variable and nonvariable costs.
—Controllable and noncontrollable costs.
—Engineered, discretionary, and committed costs.

Different Costs for Different Purposes

We emphasize again the point that the word "cost" is slippery. It is used indiscriminately with quite different meanings, and the reader or listener often has difficulty in deducing which meaning is intended. In particular, it is important to remember that there is no such thing as "the" cost of something in any situation in which joint or common costs are involved, and they are involved in most situations. When someone refers to "cost" under such circumstances, he may mean full costs, direct costs, variable costs, controllable costs, or whatever.

The appropriate definition depends on the purpose for which the cost

451

is to be used. Consider the factory superintendent's salary. In costing a product for inventory purposes, some fraction of the superintendent's salary is usually included. For overall planning purposes, it is the whole amount of the salary, and not the fractions allocated to individual products, that needs to be studied. As the basis for certain specific decisions (such as whether to buy a new machine), the salary is completely excluded from the figures; for other types of decisions (such as whether to shut down the factory), the salary is an important consideration. In the evaluation of performance, only those costs for which the person being judged is responsible should be taken into account. Thus, in an appraisal of the performance of a departmental foreman, the superintendent's salary is not an element of cost, but in an appraisal of the performance of the whole company, it is. In summary, some of these purposes require the full amount of the actual salary, some require a fraction of that amount, some require an estimate of what the amount (full or fractional) will be in the future, and some require that the amount be completely omitted.

The fact that different purposes require different cost constructions is obvious, but failure to appreciate this fact is perhaps the most important cause both of the misuse of cost figures and of the common but unwarranted criticism that cost accountants can't be pinned down to a definite statement on what "the" cost is.

RELATION OF COSTS TO VOLUME

In general usage, the word "variable" means simply "changeable," but in accounting "variable" has a more restricted meaning. It refers not to changes that take place over time, or to changes associated with the seasons, but only to changes associated with the *level of activity*, that is, with volume. If a cost goes up as volume goes up, it is a variable cost; otherwise, it is not. More specifically, we can distinguish three types of cost patterns: variable, nonvariable, and semivariable (or partly variable).

Variable costs vary directly and proportionately with volume; that is, as volume increases by 10 percent, the cost also increases by 10 percent. Direct labor, direct material, lubricants, power costs, and supplies often are examples of variable costs.

Nonvariable costs do not vary at all with volume. Building depreciation, property taxes, supervisory salaries, and occupancy costs (heat and light) often behave in this fashion. These costs are incurred with the passage of time, and are independent of the level of activity within a time period. They are sometimes called "fixed" costs, but this term implies that they cannot be changed, which is not so.

Semivariable costs vary directly, but less than proportionately, with volume; that is, as volume increases by 10 percent, the cost increases, but by less than 10 percent. Examples may be indirect labor, maintenance, and clerical costs.

Illustration 15–1

A generalized picture of the behavior of these types of cost is shown in Illustration 15–1. The nonvariable cost is $300 regardless of the level of activity; the variable cost is $0.80 per unit of volume; and the semivariable cost starts at $200 and increases at a rate of $0.20 per unit of volume. Note that the semivariable cost can be decomposed into two elements, a non-variable element of $200 and a variable element of $0.20 per unit.

Cost-Volume Diagrams

A characteristic of the cost-volume diagrams shown in Illustration 15–1 should be noted, since it is common to all diagrams showing the relationship between cost and volume: cost is always plotted on the vertical, or *y*, axis, and volume is plotted on the horizontal, or *x*, axis. A conventional rule in geometry is that the "dependent variable" is plotted on the *y* axis and the "independent variable" is plotted on the *x* axis. In the above diagrams, therefore, cost is implicitly assumed to be the "dependent variable" and volume the "independent variable." In these diagrams, the measure of volume is not defined; various possibilities will be described in a subsequent section.

Behavior of Total Costs

If the separate cost elements behave according to one of the three patterns shown above, then the total cost, which is the sum of these separate elements, must vary with volume, as shown in Illustration 15–2, which was constructed simply by merging the separate elements shown in Illustration 15–1.

Since the semivariable item can be split into nonvariable and variable components, the *behavior of total costs can be described in terms of only two components—a total amount, and an amount per unit of volume.* In Illustration 15–2, the nonvariable amount is $500 and the variable amount is $1 per unit of volume. There is therefore no need to consider semivariable costs as a separate category; from this point on, we shall consider only the nonvariable and variable components.

Illustration 15–2

Cost Assumptions

Illustration 15–2 is based on several implicit assumptions as to the behavior of costs, two of which are discussed below. The first is usually a reasonable one, but the second is actually quite unrealistic.

THE LINEAR ASSUMPTION. One cost behavior assumption is that all costs behave according to one of the three patterns described above. Actually, some costs may vary in steps, as in Illustration 15–3. This happens when the cost occurs in discrete "chunks," as when one indirect worker is added for every 160 additional hours of direct labor per week. Others may vary along a curve rather than a straight line, and others, such as maintenance of idle machines, may actually decrease as volume increases.

In most situations, however, the effect of these discontinuities and nonlinear cost functions on total costs is minor, and the assumption that

Illustration 15–3

total costs vary in a linear relationship with volume is a satisfactory working approximation. This is a most fortunate fact. Many theoretical treatises discuss cost functions with various types of complicated curves. The formulas for these functions are difficult to understand and to work with. Such complicated curves are rarely used in practice, for it is usually found that the simple straight line, although perhaps not a perfect representation of cost-volume relationships, is close enough for practical purposes.

FULL-RANGE ASSUMPTION. A second cost behavior assumption implicit in Illustration 15–2 is that costs move along a straight line throughout *the whole range* of volume. This is unrealistic. At zero volume, for example, when the factory is shut down, a special set of conditions operate, and these may make costs considerably higher or considerably lower than the $500 shown in the diagram. When production gets so high that a second shift is required, costs may behave quite differently from the way in which they behave under one-shift operations. Even within the limits of a single shift, it is to be expected that costs will behave differently when the factory is busy, from the way they do when it is operating at low volume levels. In short, a single straight line gives a good approximation of the behavior of costs *only within a certain range of volume*. We can indicate this fact by using a straight line for the range within which the relationship is valid, and using a dotted line simply to indicate where an extension of the line crosses the *y* axis, as shown in Illustration 15–4.

Illustration 15–4 shows the same cost pattern as Illustration 15–2, but the solid line representing total costs now extends only over a selected range of volume, here 600 units to 1,200 units. The dotted line extending back to zero does not imply that costs will behave in this fashion at low

Illustration 15–4

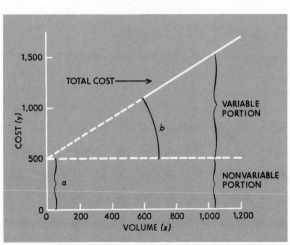

volumes; rather it is drawn on the diagram solely as a means of finding the nonvariable component of total costs.

Formula for the Cost Line

As already pointed out, cost at any volume is the sum of the nonvariable component ($500) and the variable component ($1 per unit). For example, at a volume of 1,000 units, cost is $500 + ($1 per unit times 1,000 units) = $1,500. Designating cost as y, volume as x, the nonvariable component as a, and the variable component as b, the cost at any volume can be found from the formula, $y = a + bx$; this is simply the general formula for a straight line.[1] For example, $1,500 = 500 + (1) (1,000)$.

If the values of a and b for a given line are not known, they can be deduced provided total costs are known for any two points or volume levels on the line. One method of doing this is as follows:
1. Subtract total cost at the lower volume from total cost at the higher volume, and subtract lower volume from higher volume.
2. Divide the difference in cost by the difference in volume, which gives b, the amount by which cost changes with a change of one unit of volume.
3. Multiply either of the volumes, x, by b and subtract the result from the total cost at that volume, thus removing the variable component and leaving the nonvariable component, a.

Unit Costs

It should be emphasized that the line we are studying shows *total* costs at various volumes. This line should not be confused with a line showing *unit* costs. If total costs have a linear relationship with volume, then unit costs will be a curve, showing how unit costs decrease as volume increases. Illustration 15–5, is a unit cost curve derived from Illustration 15–4.

Estimating Cost-Volume Relationship

In many practical situations costs are expected to vary with volume in the straight-line relationship shown in Illustration 15–4. The formula for this line of expected costs can be estimated by any of the following methods:

1. Estimate the cost at any two volumes in order to establish two points on the line. Find the values of a and b by the method described above. (This is sometimes called the "high-low" method because one of

---

[1] In many geometry texts, the notation used is: $y = mx + b$. In such a notation, m represents the slope, or cost per unit, and b represents the nonvariable component.

Illustration 15–5

$$\text{UNIT COST} = \frac{500 + (\$1)(X)}{X}$$

the volumes selected is likely to be high, and the other is likely to be low.)

2. Estimate the cost at one volume, and estimate how cost will change with a given change in volume. This gives b directly, and a can be found by subtraction, as described above.

3. Build up separate estimates of the behavior of each of the elements that make up total cost.

4. Make a "scatter diagram" in which actual costs recorded in past periods are plotted against the volume levels in those periods, and draw a line that best fits these observations. Such a diagram is shown in Illustration 15–6. A statistical technique, called the "method of least squares" may be used to find the line of best fit (see Appendix), but in many cases a line drawn by visual inspection is just as good as, and in some cases it is better than, a mathematically fitted line.

Illustration 15–6

PROBLEMS WITH SCATTER DIAGRAMS. Estimating cost-volume relationships by means of a scatter diagram is a common practice, but the results can be misleading. In the first place, this technique shows, at best, what the relationship was in the past, whereas we are interested in what it is now or what it will be in the future. The past is not necessarily a mirror of the present or the future. Also, the relationship we seek is that obtaining under a *single set of conditions,* whereas each point on a scatter diagram may represent changes in factors other than the two being studied, namely, cost and volume.

Illustration 15–7 shows a common source of difficulty. In this scatter diagram, volume is represented by sales revenue, as is often the case. Each

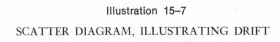

Illustration 15–7

SCATTER DIAGRAM, ILLUSTRATING DRIFT

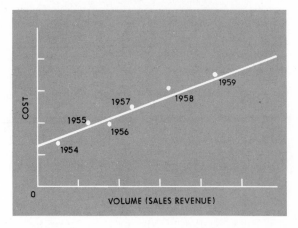

dot is located by plotting the cost for one year on the *y* axis and the sales revenue for that year on the *x* axis. The dots lie along a well-defined path, which is indicated by the straight line, but this line may *not* indicate the present relationship between cost and volume. It may, instead, indicate nothing more than the tendency for both revenue and cost to increase over the past six years because of inflationary factors. If this is the case, then the line shows the trend, or *drift,* of costs *through time,* not the probable relationship between cost and volume *at a given time.* Any scatter diagram covering a period of years in which sales were generally increasing each year, or generally decreasing each year, is likely to have this characteristic, and the longer the period covered, the more unreliable the diagram becomes.

If, in order to avoid this difficulty, the figures for only the most recent years are plotted on the diagram, there may not be enough difference in the volumes of the several periods to indicate a reliable line of relation-ship. The choice of a series of observations that are recent enough so that they do not reflect an obsolete set of conditions, yet which cover a wide enough volume range to permit the drawing of a satisfactory line, is a difficult matter.

Sometimes, statistical techniques are used to adjust, or "deflate," histor-ical observations so as to allow for changes in price and other factors. As a minimum, the historical relationship should be adjusted for anticipated changes in the underlying conditions.

Whatever the method used for estimating the relationship, the result is a line, described by the formula $y = a + bx$, which shows how costs are expected to vary with volume.

We have described the line as referring to total costs. The same tech-nique can be used to study various parts of the total. In fact, it is common to restrict analyses of this type to overhead costs, since direct material and direct labor are presumed to be purely variable.

Measures of Volume

Thus far, "volume" has been used as an abstract concept. In a real situation, it must be measured in some concrete fashion. The best measur-ing stick of volume is one that most closely reflects the conditions that cause costs to change. Two basic questions must be answered: (1) Should the measuring stick be based on input or should it be based on output? and (2) Should the measuring stick be expressed in monetary terms or should it be expressed in physical quantities? Within each general cate-gory, there are many specific possibilities. The following discussion is limited to indirect costs, for it is here that the choice of the best measure of volume is especially important.

Input measures relate to the resources being used in the cost center; examples are the number of actual direct labor hours worked, actual ma-chine-hours operated, or the pounds of raw material used. *Output meas-ures* relate to the amount of product coming out of the center; examples are units of product completed or the standard direct labor costs absorbed by products worked on. Since indirect cost is itself an element of input, in many situations it tends to vary more closely with other input factors than with output. For example, it is reasonable to expect that indirect cost items associated with direct labor, such as fringe benefits, social security taxes, and payroll accounting, tend to vary more closely with the actual quantity of direct labor used than with the standard labor content of products produced. In general, an input measure is likely to be more accurate than an output measure. Some overhead costs, such as inspection costs and plant transportation, however, might vary more closely with the quantity of products produced.

A measuring stick expressed in physical quantities, such as direct labor hours, is often better than one expressed in dollars, such as direct labor cost, because the former is unaffected by changes in prices. A wage increase would cause direct labor costs to increase, even if there were no actual increase in the volume of activity. On the other hand, if price changes are likely to affect both labor and overhead to the same degree, the use of a monetary measuring stick may be a means of allowing implicitly for the effect of these price changes.

These theoretical considerations must be tempered by practicality. Total direct labor costs are often available in the cost system without extra calculation, whereas the computation of total direct labor hours, or machine-hours, may require considerable additional work. Also, since the measuring stick of volume for control purposes is often (but not always) the same as that used in allocating overhead costs to products for the purpose of financial accounting, the appropriateness of the measure for the latter purpose must also be taken into account.

The Overhead Rate and Standard Volume

It will be recalled from Chapter 13 that the overhead rate for product costing purposes is found by dividing total overhead costs by a measure of activity. When the same measure of activity is used in a cost-volume diagram, such as that in Illustration 15–4, this total overhead cost is one point on the cost line. This point is the total cost expected at *standard volume* (or *normal volume*).

Standard volume is defined in one of three ways. In some companies, it is the volume anticipated for the next year or other short period of time; in other companies, it is the average volume expected over a number of years in the future, and in still other companies it is the volume at capacity operations. Overhead costs *per unit* (i.e., the overhead rate) decrease as volume increases because the same amount of nonvariable cost is spread over a larger number of units. Therefore, the overhead rates resulting from the application of one of these three concepts of standard volume can differ substantially from one another.

When the standard volume is taken as the volume expected next year, total overhead costs incurred in the year will be approximately absorbed onto products if the estimates are made with reasonable accuracy. This method therefore meets the objective of financial accounting. It may, however, cause difficulty if the costs are being used as a basis for pricing, for unit costs will tend to be high in a year of low volume. If the low volume implies a business recession, the high unit cost may lead to an increase in selling prices at the very time when it is probably most unwise to attempt such an increase.

A standard volume based on an average of several years is used by automobile manufacturers and by a number of other leading companies. It avoids the pricing paradox mentioned above, but does result in a large variance in a year of abnormally high or abnormally low volume.

A measure based on capacity is not widely used, except by companies that expect to operate at capacity, and in these situations it is the same as the first method. "Capacity" means, not the theoretical maximum amount of product that can be produced if everything goes perfectly, but rather "practical capacity," which is a reasonably attainable amount. It may mean the capacity of 40 hours a week, or 168 hours a week, or anywhere in between.

THE PROFITGRAPH

The cost/volume diagram in Illustration 15–4 can be turned into a useful device called the *profitgraph* (or "Profit-Volume graph," or "P/V graph") simply by the addition of a revenue line to it, for a profitgraph is a diagram showing the expected relationship between cost and revenue at various volumes.[2] On a profitgraph, the measure of volume may be the number of units produced and sold, or it may be sales revenue. We have already stated the formula for the cost line: $y = a + bx$.

Revenue is plotted on the assumption of a constant selling price per unit. Assuming that volume is to be measured as units of product, and designating the unit selling price as p, total revenue (y) at any volume (x) equals the unit selling price (p) times the number of units of volume (x); or, for revenue $y = px$. For example, if the unit selling price is $2, the total revenue from 1,000 units will be $2,000.

A profitgraph of these relationships is shown in Illustration 15–8. Note that as on Illustration 15–4, the lines are dotted at very low volumes to emphasize the fact that the relationships are expected to hold only within a limited volume range (in practice, the lines are usually drawn solid throughout, and it therefore is easy to overlook the fact that the relationship is not valid outside the normal range).

At the *break-even volume*, cost equals revenue. (This is simply a geometric fact; the break-even point is of little practical interest in a profitable company, since attention is focused on the profit area considerably above it.) At lower volumes, a loss is expected; and at higher volumes, a profit is expected. The amount of loss or profit expected at any volume is the difference between points on the cost and revenue lines at that volume. The break-even volume is not the same as the "normal" volume used as a basis for determining the overhead rate. In a profitable business, normal volume is considerably higher than the break-even volume.

---

[2] This device is also called a "break-even chart," but such a label has the unfortunate implication that the objective of a business is merely to break even.

Illustration 15–8

A PROFITGRAPH

Construction of a Profitgraph

If volume (the x axis) is expressed in terms of sales revenue, the revenue line on a profitgraph is simply the straight line $y = x$. If volume is expressed as number of units sold, revenue at any volume is found from the formula $y = px$, as described above. Sometimes several revenue lines are drawn on a profitgraph, each one showing what revenue would be at that selling price. This procedure helps to show how a change in selling price affects the profit at any given volume.

Interpretation of the Profitgraph

The profitgraph is a useful device for analysis of the overall profit characteristics of a business. To illustrate such an analysis, assume the following situation, which is the same as that shown in previous diagrams:

Nonvariable costs................................$500
Variable costs....................................$1 per unit
Normal volume...................................1,000 units
Selling price......................................$2 per unit

In this situation, total costs at normal volume will be $500 (nonvariable) plus $1,000 (variable), or $1,500. The cost of the product as shown on the accounting records will therefore be $1,500 ÷ 1,000 units, or $1.50 per unit. At a selling price of $2 per unit, the normal profit will be $0.50 per unit.

COMPUTATION OF BREAK-EVEN VOLUME. Recall that the break-even volume is the volume at which cost equals revenue.

Since revenue (y) at any volume (x) is $y = px$
And cost (y) at any volume (x) is $y = a + bx$
And since at the break-even volume, cost = revenue:
Therefore the break-even volume is the volume at which $px = a + bx$

If we let x equal the break-even volume, then for the above situation, we have

$$\$2x = \$500 + \$1x$$
$$x = \ \ 500 \text{ units.}$$

At the break-even volume of 500 units, revenue equals 500 units × \$2 per unit, which is \$1,000, and cost equals \$500 + (500 units × \$1 per unit), which is also \$1,000.

MARGINAL INCOME. From the relationships of cost and revenue at various volumes, an important conclusion can be drawn: although the normal profit is \$0.50 per unit, this unit profit will be earned *only* at the normal volume. At lower volumes the profit will be less than \$0.50 per unit, and at higher volumes it will be more than \$0.50 per unit. The relationship between cost, revenue, and volume can be summed up by the statement that for each change of one unit in volume, profit will change by \$1. This \$1 is the *marginal income*, the difference between selling price and *variable cost* per unit. Below the break-even point, losses will be incurred at the rate of \$1 for each unit decrease in volume.

The break-even volume can also be determined by the relationship between nonvariable costs and marginal income. In the illustrative situation where the marginal income is \$1 per unit and nonvariable costs are \$500, 500 units must be sold before enough revenue will be earned to cover nonvariable costs. After that, a profit of \$1 per unit will be earned.

Improving Profit Performance

These revenue-cost-volume relationships suggest that a useful way of studying the profit factors of a business is to consider, not the profit per unit (which is different at every volume), but rather the nonvariable costs and the marginal income, which is the difference between selling price and marginal cost. In these terms, there are four, and only four, ways in which the profit of a business can be increased:

1. Increase selling prices per unit.
2. Decrease variable costs per unit.
3. Decrease nonvariable costs.
4. Increase volume.

The separate effects of each of these possibilities are shown in the following calculations and in Illustration 15–9. Each starts from the current situation, assumed to be "normal" (selling price, \$2; variable costs,

Illustration 15–9

EFFECT OF 10 PERCENT CHANGE IN PROFIT FACTORS

A. Increase Selling Price   B. Decrease Variable Cost

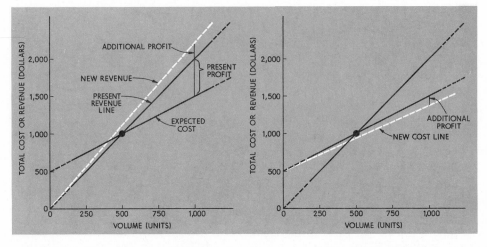

C. Decrease Nonvariable Cost   D. Increase Volume

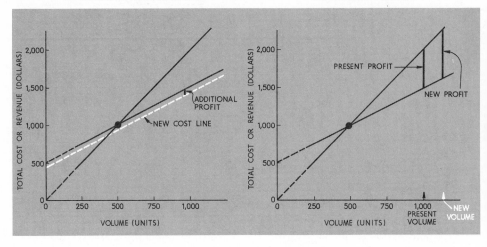

$1 per unit; nonvariable costs, $500; and volume, 1,000 units). The effect of a 10 percent change in each factor is calculated:

A. A 10 percent increase in selling price would add $200 to revenue and would therefore increase the current profit of $500 by 40 percent.

B. A 10 percent decrease in variable cost would reduce variable costs by $100 and would therefore increase profit by 20 percent.

C. A 10 percent decrease in nonvariable cost would amount to $50, and would result in an increase in profit of 10 percent.

D. A 10 percent increase in volume would increase profit by the marginal income of $1 per unit times an additional 100 units, or $100, an increase of 20 percent.

If we look at some of the interrelationships, we can calculate, for example, that a 20 percent (i.e., $100) increase in nonvariable costs could be offset by a 5 percent increase in selling price, a 10 percent increase in volume, or a 10 percent decrease in variable costs.

Another calculation made from a profitgraph is the *margin of safety*. This is the amount or ratio by which the current volume exceeds the break-even volume. Assuming current volume is 1,000 units, the margin of safety in our illustrative situation is 500 units, or 50 percent, of current volume. Sales volume can decrease by 50 percent before a loss is incurred, other factors remaining equal.

Limitations on Profitgraph Analysis

The foregoing calculations assume that each of the factors is independent of the others, a situation that is rarely the case in the real world. An increase in selling price often is accompanied by a decrease in volume, for example. Changes in the factors must therefore usually be studied simultaneously rather than separately as was done above.

Also, the diagram assumes that the company, in effect, sells only one product. If several products with different marginal incomes are sold, the profitgraph for the whole company shows the average marginal income for all products, and is affected by changes in the mix of products. Under these circumstances, profitgraphs for each product, or for each group of approximately homogeneous products, are more useful for analysis than is the single overall diagram.

The profitgraph analysis also implicitly assumes that changes in the four factors are not accompanied by changes in the amount of capital employed. If a decrease in variable cost arises because of the purchase of a new machine, for example, the effect on the return on investment is not given by the profitgraph. In part, the effect shows up as an increase in the nonvariable depreciation cost, but one cannot tell from this alone what the effect is on the overall rate of return.

MARGINAL INCOME ANALYSIS STATEMENT

The marginal income idea suggests a way of recasting the conventional income statement so as to provide more useful information to management. Illustration 15–10 shows such a recasting for a dry cleaning and laundry business. The top section is the conventional income statement. The lower section shows the same basic information in the form of a "Marginal Income Analysis Report."

Illustration 15–10

MARGINAL INCOME ANALYSIS STATEMENT

A. Conventional Income Statement for June

Sales..		$3,540
Salaries...	$1,640	
Supplies...	900	
Heat, light, power...	210	
Employer's payroll tax..	89	
Advertising..	88	
Telephone...	66	
Rent..	100	
Depreciation...	483	
Amortization of leasehold improvements.............................	140	
Insurance..	95	
Total expenses..		3,811
Net Loss..		$(271)

B. Same Data Recast in Format of a Marginal
Income Analysis Report

	Dry Cleaning		Laundry	
Sales.......................................	$2,800		$740	
Variable costs:				
Salaries.................................	$ 790		$200	
Supplies.................................	760		140	
Heat, light, power.....................	150		25	
Employer's payroll tax.................	43	1,743	10	375
Contribution to nonvariable costs.............		$1,057		$365
Less: Depreciation on equipment..............		200		100
Contribution to unassigned nonvariable costs....... $1,122		$ 857		$265
Unassigned nonvariable costs:				
Salaries........................... $650				
Advertising....................... 88				
Telephone......................... 66				
Heat, light, power................ 35				
Employer's payroll tax............ 36				
Rent.............................. 100				
Depreciation...................... 183				
Amortization...................... 140				
Insurance......................... 95	1,393			
Net Loss for the Period..................	$ 271			

SOURCE: Adapted from material collected by Professor W. W. Haynes, University of Kentucky, and Professor J. L. Gibson, Arlington State College, for the Small Business Administration.

To construct this report, the cost elements are first segregated into variable and nonvariable categories. For some items (e.g., heat, light, and power in the illustration), part of the cost is variable and part is nonvariable. For each activity, the variable costs relating to the activity are subtracted from revenue, giving the marginal income, or, as labeled here, "contribution to nonvariable costs." In the illustration, nonvariable costs assignable to each activity (i.e., depreciation on equipment) are also shown, although this is not always done. Then the other nonvariable costs are listed, but they are not allocated among activities.

The message given by the conventional statement is quite different from that given by the marginal statement. In the conventional statement, the message is that the business as a whole was operated at a loss; a breakdown into its two elements, dry cleaning and laundry, would show that on a full-cost basis, each of them was operating at a loss, and the argument could easily be made that one or the other of these elements should be discontinued in order to reduce losses. The marginal statement shows that each of the elements made a contribution to nonvariable costs, and that losses would therefore not be reduced by discontinuing either of them. Indeed, other things being equal, the loss would be $1,057 greater if the dry cleaning segment were discontinued and $365 greater if the laundry segment were discontinued.

In the illustration, the revenue and variable costs are broken down by revenue-earning activities. Marginal income analysis statements are also prepared in which the breakdown is by products or product groups.

LEARNING CURVES

Cost-volume diagrams and profitgraphs are two-dimensional; they show only what happens to cost when volume changes. Actually, costs change for a variety of other reasons, such as (1) changes in price levels (e.g., inflation), as already noted; (2) changes in efficiency (e.g., Parkinson's first law: "Costs tend to increase, regardless of the work done"); and (3) productivity. Many studies have shown that the change in cost associated with a change in productivity has, in many situations, a characteristic curve that can be estimated with reasonable accuracy. This is called the *learning curve*, or the *experience curve*.

The phenomenon was first observed in the aircraft industry, where it was found that certain costs tend to decrease, per unit, in a predictable pattern as the workers and their supervisors become more familiar with the work; as the flow of work, tooling, and methods improve; as less scrap and rework result; as fewer skilled workers need to be used; and so on. The decreasing costs are a function of the learning process, which results in fewer and fewer man-hours being necessary to produce a unit of product as more units of the same product are completed. It should be noted, however, that not all costs decrease; for instance, material costs are not usually subject to the learning process, although they may decrease to the extent to which waste is eliminated. Packaging and trucking costs are other examples of costs that usually are not subject to the learning process.

The research done in the aircraft industry indicates that there is probably an average learning curve rate that can be applied to the increase in production efficiency, insofar as costs subject to the learning function are concerned. This rate approximates an "80 percent curve," which means that when quantities of production are doubled on an item, cumulative average man-hours per unit should be reduced 20 percent. As an illustration of this concept, assume that a company has purchased 250 machined castings at $50 each from XYZ Company. To simplify this case, assume further that material costs are insignificant and that the elements of labor, overhead, selling, and administration expense and profit, which make up the $50 per unit price, all vary in relation to the man-hours

Illustration 15-11

EIGHTY PERCENT LEARNING CURVE—MACHINED CASTINGS

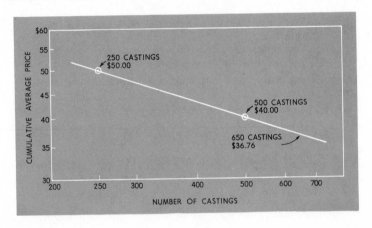

required to produce one machined casting; that is to say, all the elements of the $50 price are subject to the learning curve. Before production of the 250 castings has been completed, another 400 castings of the same type are ordered from the XYZ Company. What should the additional 400 castings cost?

Assuming that an "80 percent curve" can be applied in this situation, the $50 price is plotted at the 250-unit quantity level on log-log graph paper (see Illustration 15–11). The second point on the graph is established at double the quantity and 80 percent of the price of the first order. A straight line is drawn through and extended past these two points. (Log-log graph paper shows the 80 percent curve as a straight line, whereas arithmetic graph paper shows the 80 percent curve as a complex curve that is difficult to plot.) The point on this line that locates the sum of the quantities of the old and new orders (250 plus 400 units) indicates also the cumulative average unit price for the total units, or $36.76.

Multiplying the total quantity of 650 units by the new cumulative average price of $36.76 gives the *total cost* for *both* orders, $23,894. Because the first order of 250 castings cost $12,500 in total, this is subtracted from the total price of both orders. The remaining $11,394 is divided by the number of units to be purchased in the new order (400) to give the estimated unit cost of $28.48 for the new castings.

This characteristic decline in unit costs as an increasing number of units are produced does not come about automatically; rather, it depends on management efforts to force costs down. It is important that the existence of the learning phenomenon be recognized and exploited; otherwise, management may be satisfied with cost performance as indicated on a cost-volume graph, whereas such costs may be significantly too high.

CONTROLLABLE COSTS

An element of cost is controllable if the amount of cost incurred in (or charged to) a responsibility center is significantly influenced by the actions of the manager of that responsibility center. Otherwise, it is noncontrollable. There are two important implications of this definition: (1) it refers to a specific responsibility center, and (2) it suggests that controllability results from *some* influence, rather than *complete* influence.

The word "controllable" must be used in the context of a specific responsibility center, rather than as an innate characteristic of a given cost element; because when the organization is viewed as a complete entity, all costs are controllable. For any element of cost, there is someone, somewhere in the company, who can take actions that influence it. In the extreme case, costs for any segment of the business can be reduced to zero by closing down that segment; costs incurred in manufacturing a component can be changed by purchasing that component, and so on. Thus, the important question is not what costs are controllable in general, but rather what costs are controllable in a given responsibility center, for it is these costs on which the management control system must focus.

Degree of Influence

The definition refers to a "significant" influence rather than to "complete" influence because only in rare cases does one individual have complete control over *all* the factors that influence a given cost element. The influence of the foreman of a manufacturing department over labor costs may actually be quite limited, since wage rates may be established by the personnel department or by union negotiations; the amount of labor required for a unit of product may be largely determined by the engineers who designed the product and who specified how it was to be manufactured; and the number of units produced, and hence total labor costs, may be influenced by the output of some other department, by the ability of the purchasing department to obtain materials, or by a variety of other factors. Nevertheless, the foreman usually has a significant influence on the amount of direct labor cost incurred. He has some control over the amount of idle time in his department, the speed and efficiency with which work is done, and other factors which to some extent affect labor costs.

The use of a *standard cost* is one way of distinguishing between those parts of a cost element for which a person is responsible and those for which he is not. A standard labor cost, for example, presumably states what the cost should be, considering the influence of wage rates, product design, and other factors over which the foreman has no control. Ideally, the difference between standard cost and actual cost incurred represents the effect of actions by the foreman, and it is this difference for which the foreman is held responsible. As explained in Chapter 17, there are many reasons why this concept does not work out precisely in practice, but it nevertheless may work well enough to provide an acceptable basis for control.

Direct material and direct labor costs are usually controllable. With respect to the overhead costs in a cost center, some are controllable and others are not. Indirect labor, supplies, and electricity are usually controllable. So are charges from service centers based on services actually rendered by the service center. By definition, *an allocated cost is not controllable;* the amount of the charge varies in accordance with the formula used for allocation, not with the actions of the supervisor. This is so unless the cost is actually a direct cost that is allocated only for convenience, as in the case of social security taxes on direct labor that are as controllable as other elements of the direct labor cost.

CONTRAST WITH DIRECT COSTS. Controllable costs are not synonymous with direct costs. All controllable costs are direct since by definition an allocated cost is not controllable, but not all direct costs are controllable. For example, depreciation on departmental equipment is a direct cost of the department, but the depreciation charge is often noncontrollable by the departmental supervisor since he may have no authority to acquire or dispose of equipment. The rental charge for rented premises is another example of a direct but noncontrollable cost.

CONTRAST WITH VARIABLE COSTS. Neither are controllable costs necessarily the same as *variable costs*. Variable costs vary with volume. Some costs, such as indirect labor, heat, light, and magazine subscriptions, may be unaffected by volume, but they are nevertheless controllable. Conversely, some variable costs are noncontrollable. Raw material and parts, whose consumption varies directly with volume, may be entirely outside the influence of the departmental supervisor. For example, in an automobile assembly department, the fact is that the car requires an engine, a body, five wheels, and so on, and there is nothing the supervisor can do about it. He is responsible for waste and spoilage of material, but not for the main flow of material itself.

Similarly, direct labor, which is usually thought of as the prime example of a controllable cost, may be noncontrollable in certain types of responsibility centers. If, for example, an assembly line has 20 work stations and cannot be operated unless it is manned by 20 persons of specified skills and hence specified wage rates, direct labor cost on that assembly line may be noncontrollable. Situations of this type must be examined very carefully, however, in order to insure that the noncontrollability is real. Supervisors tend to argue that more costs are noncontrollable than actually is the case, in order to avoid being held responsible for them.

Converting Noncontrollable Costs to Controllable Costs

A noncontrollable element of cost can be converted to a controllable element of cost in two related ways: (1) by changing the management control system; and/or (2) by changing the locus of responsibility for decisions.

Converting Allocated Costs to Direct Costs. By definition, allocated costs are noncontrollable. Many elements of costs that are allocated to responsibility centers could be made into controllable costs simply by devising a method of charging the cost that reflects actions taken by the head of the responsibility center. To take the simplest situation, if all electricity coming into a plant is measured by a single meter, there is no way of measuring the actual electrical consumption of each department in the plant, and the electrical cost is therefore necessarily allocated for each department and is noncontrollable. This cost element can be changed to a controllable cost for the several departments in the plant simply by installing electrical meters in each department.

Similarly, services that a responsibility center receives from service units can be converted to controllable costs by charging these costs to the responsibility center on some basis that measures the services actually rendered.

> Example: As described in Chapter 14, if maintenance costs are charged to responsibility centers as a part of an overhead rate, they are noncontrollable; but if responsibility centers are charged on the basis of an hourly rate for each hour that a maintenance man works there and if the head of the responsibility center can influence the requests for maintenance work, then maintenance is a controllable element of cost.

As pointed out in Chapter 13, practically any element of overhead cost could conceivably be converted to a direct cost, but for some (such as charging the president's salary on the basis of the time he spends on the problems of various parts of the business), the effort involved in doing so clearly is more than the benefit that would be derived. There are nevertheless a great many unexploited opportunities in most companies.

The same principle applies to costs actually incurred in a responsibility center but which are not charged to the responsibility center at all, even on an allocated basis. Under these circumstances, the material or services are "free" insofar as the head of the responsibility center is concerned, and since he does not have to "pay" for them (as part of the costs for which he is held responsible), there is little reason to expect him to be concerned about careful use of the resources that these costs represent.

DECENTRALIZATION. The most important decisions affecting costs are made at or near the top of an organization, both because people at the top presumably have more ability and because they have a broader viewpoint. On the other hand, the farther removed these decisions are from the "firing line," the place where resources are actually used, the less responsive they can be to conditions currently existing at the point of spending. Although there is no way of drawing a precise line, an organization in which a relatively high proportion of decisions are made at the top is said to be *centralized*, and one in which lower level managers can make relatively more decisions is said to be *decentralized*.

In the context of our present discussion, a decentralized organization is one in which a relatively large fraction of costs are controllable in the lower levels of responsibility centers. Many companies have found that, given a good system for controlling performance, they can safely delegate responsibility for many decisions affecting cost and thus take advantage of the knowledge of the man who is on the spot where spending actually occurs. Perhaps the most dramatic example of a shift from centralized to decentralized management is the change that has taken place in Communist countries. Beginning with Yugoslavia in the 1950's, and later extending to the U.S.S.R., there has been a recognition that the highly centralized planning and control process envisioned by Lenin simply does not work well in practice; consequently, individual plant managers have been given much more authority to make decisions affecting the costs of their plants.

Recording Noncontrollable Costs

In control reports, it is obviously essential that controllable costs be distinguished from noncontrollable costs. Some people argue that the *separation* of controllable from noncontrollable costs is not enough; they insist that noncontrollable costs should not even be recorded in a management accounting system. Actually, there may be good reasons for charging all, or certain types of, noncontrollable costs to responsibility centers.

One reason is that management may want the supervisor to be concerned about such costs, the expectation being that his concern may indirectly lead to better cost control. For example, an operating unit may be charged with part of the costs of the personnel department, even though the foreman of the unit has no direct responsibility for that department. Such a charge can be justified either on the ground that the foreman will be careful about making unnecessary requests of the personnel department if he is made to feel some responsibility for personnel department costs, or on the ground that the foreman may in various ways influence the head of the personnel department to exercise good cost control in his own department.

Another reason for charging all costs is that the collection of all costs in responsibility centers may facilitate the calculation of selling prices, a topic to be discussed in Chapter 18. A third reason is that if the supervisor is made aware of the total amount of costs that are incurred in the operation of his unit, he may have a better understanding of how much the company contributes to the operation. Such a practice may boomerang, however, for the supervisor may conclude that his controllable costs are so small, relative to the costs that he cannot control, that they are not worth worrying about.

ENGINEERED, DISCRETIONARY, AND COMMITTED COSTS

The final classification of costs to be discussed in this chapter is that between (1) engineered, (2) discretionary, and (3) committed costs. Although both engineered and discretionary costs are controllable, the approach to the control of one is quite different from that of the other. Committed costs are not controllable in the short run, but they are in the long run.

Engineered Costs

These are elements of cost for which the *right* or *proper* amount of costs that should be incurred can be estimated. Direct labor is an example. Given the specifications for a product, engineers can determine the necessary operations to be performed and can estimate, within reasonably close limits, the time that should be spent on each operation. The total amount of direct labor costs that should be incurred can then be estimated by translation of these times into money by means of a wage rate and multiplication by the number of units of product produced. Since production engineering is not an exact science, these amounts are not necessarily the exact amount that should be spent, but the estimates can usually be made close enough so that there is relatively little ground for disagreement as to what the cost should be. In particular, there can be no reasonable ground for denying that there is a direct relationship between volume and costs; two units require more direct labor than does one unit.

Discretionary Costs

These costs are also called "programmed" or "managed" costs. They can be whatever management wants them to be, within wide limits. There is no scientific way of deciding what the "right" amount should be, or at least there is no scientific basis that the management of the particular company is willing to rely on. How much should we spend for research and development? for public relations? for employees' parties and outings? for donations? for the accounting department? No one knows. In most companies, the discretionary cost category includes all general and administrative functions, all order-getting costs, and a great many items of factory overhead cost.

In the absence of an engineering standard, the amount to be spent must be a matter of judgment. Usually, this judgment is arrived at by joint agreement between the supervisor concerned and his superior, as part of the budgeting process. Indeed most of the discussion in the budgeting process occurs with respect to the permitted level of discretionary costs.

Although there is no "right" level for the total amount of a discretionary cost item, there may be usable standards for controlling some of the detail within it. Although no one knows the right amount to spend for accounting, it is nevertheless possible to measure the performance of individual clerks in the accounting department in terms of number of postings or number of invoices typed per hour. And although we cannot know the "right" amount of total travel expense, we can set standards for the amount that should be spent per day or per mile.

Furthermore, new developments in management accounting result in a gradual shift of items from the discretionary cost to the engineered cost categories. Several companies have recently started to use what they believe to be valid techniques for determining the "right" amount that they should spend on advertising in order to achieve their sales objectives, or the "right" number of salesmen.

ANALYSIS OF PERFORMANCE. With respect to engineered costs, the general rule is "the lower they are, the better." The objective is to spend as little as possible, consistent with quality standards, safety standards, and so on. The supervisor who reduces his engineered costs usually should be congratulated.

With respect to discretionary costs, the situation is quite different and much more complicated. Often, optimum performance consists of *spending the amount agreed on*, for spending too little may be as bad as, or worse than, spending too much. A factory supervisor can easily reduce his costs by skimping on maintenance or on training; a marketing manager can reduce his advertising or sales promotion expenditures; top management may eliminate research. None of these actions may be in the overall best interest of the company, although all of them result in lower costs on the current income statement.

Committed Costs

Committed costs are those that are the inevitable consequences of commitments previously made. Depreciation is an example; once a company has purchased a building or a piece of equipment, there is an inevitable depreciation charge so long as the building continues to be owned.

In the short run, committed costs are noncontrollable. They can be changed only by changing the commitment, for example, by disposing of the building or equipment whose depreciation is being recorded.

Spurious Relationships

The decision on how much to spend for a discretionary cost item may take several forms, such as "spend the same amount as we spent last year," or "spend *b*. percent of sales," or "spend *b*. dollars plus *a* percent of sales." These decision rules result in historical patterns which, when plotted against volume, have the same superficial appearance as the patterns of engineered cost. The first rule gives a nonvariable cost line, the second a variable cost line, and the third a semivariable cost line.

These relationships are fundamentally different from those observed for engineered costs, however. For engineered costs, the pattern is inevitable; as volume increases, the direct labor cost *must* increase. For discretionary costs, the relationship exists only because of the management decision, and it can be changed simply by changing the management decision. For example, a company may decide that research and development cost should be 3 percent of sales. There can be no scientific reason for such a decision, for no one knows the optimum amount that should be spent for research; in all probability, such a rule exists primarily because management thinks that this is what the company can afford to spend. In such a situation there will be a linear relationship between sales volume and research/development costs. There is, however, little significance to such a relationship, and no reason to believe that research/development costs in the future should follow the same pattern.

ORDER-GETTING COSTS. Order-getting costs are those incurred in order to make sales. They include the costs of the selling organization, advertising, sales promotion, and so on. These costs may vary with sales volume, but the relationship is the reverse of that for factory costs: order-getting cost is the independent variable, and sales volume is the dependent variable. Order-getting costs vary not in response to sales volume but rather *in anticipation of* sales volume, according to decisions made by management.[3] They are therefore discretionary costs.

If management has a policy of spending more for order-getting activities when sales volume is high, then a scatter diagram of the relationship between selling costs and sales volume will have the same appearance as the diagram for production costs and production volume, Illustration 15–6. The two diagrams should be interpreted quite differently, however. The production cost diagram indicates that cost *necessarily* increases as volume increases, while the selling cost diagram shows that cost has been *permitted* to increase with increases in volume; there is no necessary relationship in the latter case. Further, subject to some qualifications, it may be said that for total factory overhead costs, the lower they are the better; but lower selling costs may reflect inadequate selling effort. The "right" level of selling costs is a judgment made by management.

Nor is there always a direct relationship between order-getting cost and sales volume. Take advertising as an example. Management may decide either (1) to increase advertising expenditures when sales *increase*, on the theory that the company can afford to spend more when revenue is high; (2) to spend the same amount for advertising, regardless of sales volume; or (3) to increase advertising expenditures when sales *decrease*, in the belief that additional effort is necessary to regain lost volume. Each of these policies gives a different line of relationship, and the pattern is further obscured by the fact that sales volume is influenced not only by advertising, or indeed sales effort in total, but also by general business conditions and other factors outside the company's control.

SUMMARY

The word "cost" has many meanings, and care must always be taken to make sure that the context applying to a given situation is understood.

Variable costs are those that vary with volume. Although some costs are semivariable, they usually can be decomposed into variable and non-variable components. The relationship between costs and volume is usually linear within a normal range of volume.

When a revenue line is added to a diagram showing the cost-volume relationship, the diagram is called a profitgraph, an important tool in analysis of the factors that affect profit. Marginal income, which is the difference between revenue and variable cost, is a significant concept in such an analysis.

Controllable costs in a responsibility center are those that can be

---

[3] Exceptions are salesmen's commissions and other payments related to sales in that sales is the basis of figuring the cost. These of course vary directly with sales.

significantly influenced by the head of the responsibility center. This does not mean that the head of the responsibility center has complete responsibility, because few cost elements are the complete responsibility of any single person in an organization. Noncontrollable costs often can, and should, be converted to controllable costs by changing either the control system or the amount of authority delegated to lower responsibility centers, or both.

Controllable costs may be further classified as either engineered costs or discretionary costs. Methods of estimating and analyzing the former are basically different from those applicable to the latter.

APPENDIX

Fitting a Straight Line by Least Squares

If the variable measured on the vertical axis is designated y and that on the horizontal axis x, then *any* straight line is described by the general formula, $y = a + bx$. In order to describe a *specific* straight line, we must assign specific numerical values to the two constants (or "parameters"), a and b.

EXAMPLE: Illustration 15–12 shows the line $y = 2 + \frac{1}{2}x$. Notice that the line cuts the y axis at a value of 2, and that for each unit increase in x, y increases $\frac{1}{2}$ unit.

The technique of fitting a straight line by the method of least squares makes use of this formula for a straight line. We assume here that the distances from the point to the line are measured *vertically*, that is, parallel to the y axis. We write down in two adjacent columns every value of x and beside each value of x the corresponding actual value of y.

Illustration 15–12

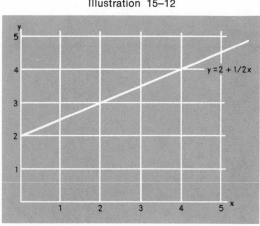

In a third column we put the square of each value of x, and in the fourth, the product of each x times the corresponding y. We total each column and use the symbol Σx^2 to denote the total of the squares of the x values, Σxy to denote the total of the products of x times the corresponding y, etc. (Notice that Σx^2 does *not* denote the square of the sum of the x's, nor does Σxy denote the total of the x's times the total of y's.) We then determine the constants a and b in the equation for a straight line by solving the two simultaneous "normal equations":

$$Na + b(\Sigma x) = \Sigma y$$
$$a(\Sigma x) + b(\Sigma x^2) = \Sigma xy$$

N is the number of items, that is, the number of x, y pairs.

Suppose we have the following data (simplified for the purpose of illustration):

Visits	*Sales*
0	10
1	12
2	13
3	15

We write the figures:

(1) x	(2) y	(3) x^2	(4) xy
0	10	0	0
1	12	1	12
2	13	4	26
3	15	9	45
6	50	14	83

Therefore,

$$\Sigma x = 6, \ \Sigma y = 50, \ \Sigma x^2 = 14, \ \Sigma xy = 83, \ N = 4;$$

and the normal equations given above become

$$50 = 4a + 6b$$
$$83 = 6a + 14b.$$

To solve for a and b, multiply the first equation by 3 and the second equation by 2 and get—

$$150 = 12a + 18b$$
$$166 = 12a + 28b.$$

Subtract the first equation from the second and get—

$$16 = 10b$$
$$b = 1.6.$$

Therefore, $50 = 4a + 9.6$ (from the first normal equation with 9.6 written in place of $6b$):

$$4a = 40.4$$
$$a = 10.1.$$

Therefore, the equation of the least-squares regression line is:

$$y = 10.1 + 1.6x.$$

SUGGESTIONS FOR FURTHER READING

ANTHONY, ROBERT N. *Planning and Control Systems: A Framework for Analysis.* Boston: Harvard Graduate School of Business Administration, 1965.

ANTHONY, ROBERT N., JOHN DEARDEN, and RICHARD F. VANCIL. *Management Control Systems: Cases and Readings.* Homewood, Ill.: Richard D. Irwin, Inc., 1965.

BEYER, ROBERT. *Profitability Accounting for Planning and Control.* New York: Ronald Press, Co., 1963.

CYERT, RICHARD M., and JAMES G. MARCH. *A Behavioral Theory of the Firm.* Englewood Cliffs, N.J.: Prentice-Hall, Inc., 1963.

LEWIS, RALPH F. *Management Uses of Accounting.* New York: Harper & Bros., 1961.

SOLOMONS, DAVID. *Divisional Performance: Measurement and Control.* New York: Financial Executives Institute, 1965.

CASES

CASE 15–1. BILL FRENCH

Bill French picked up the phone and called his boss, Wes Davidson, controller of Duo-Products Corporation. "Say, Wes, I'm all set for the meeting this afternoon. I've put together a set of break-even statements that should really make the boys sit up and take notice—and I think they'll be able to understand them, too." After a brief conversation about other matters, the call was concluded and French turned to his charts for one last check-out before the meeting.

French had been hired six months earlier as a staff accountant. He was directly responsible to Davidson and, up to the time of this case, had been doing routine types of analysis work. French was an alumnus of a liberal arts undergraduate school and graduate business school, and was considered by his associates to be quite capable and unusually conscientious. It was this latter characteristic that had apparently caused him to "rub some of the working guys the wrong way," as one of his co-workers put it. French was well aware of his capabilities and took advantage of every opportunity that arose to try to educate those around him. Wes Davidson's invitation for French to attend an informal manager's meeting had come as some surprise to others in the accounting group. However, when French requested permission to make a presentation of some break-even data, Davidson acquiesced. The Duo-Products Corporation had not been making use of this type of analysis in its review or planning programs.

Basically, what French had done was to determine the level at which the company must operate in order to break even. As he phrased it,

The company must be able at least to sell a sufficient volume of goods so that it will cover all the variable costs of producing and selling the goods; further, it will not make a profit unless it covers the fixed, or nonvariable, costs as well. The level of operation at which total costs (that is, variable plus nonvariable) are just covered in the break-even volume. This should be the lower limit in all our planning.

The accounting records had provided the following information that French used in constructing his chart:

Plant capacity—2 million units.
Past year's level of operations—1.5 million units.
Average unit selling price—$1.20.
Total fixed costs—$520,000.
Average variable unit cost—$0.75.

From this information, French observed that each unit contributed $0.45 to fixed overhead after covering the variable costs. Given total fixed costs of $520,000, he calculated that 1,155,556 units must be sold in order to break even. He verified this conclusion by calculating the dollar sales volume that was required to break even. Since the variable costs per unit were 62.5 percent of the selling price, French reasoned that 37.5 percent of every sales dollar was left available to cover fixed costs. Thus, fixed costs of $520,000 require sales of $1,386,667 in order to break even.

When he constructed a break-even chart to present the information graphically, his conclusions were further verified. The chart also made it clear that the firm was operating at a fair margin over the break-even requirements, and that the profits accruing (at the rate of 37.5 percent of every sales dollar over break-even) increased rapidly as volume increased (see Exhibit 1).

Shortly after lunch, French and Davidson left for the meeting. Several representatives of the manufacturing departments were present, as well as the general sales manager, two assistant sales managers, the purchasing officer, and two men from the product engineering office. Davidson introduced French to the few men whom he had not already met, and then the meeting got under way. French's presentation was the last item

Exhibit 1

BREAK-EVEN CHART—TOTAL BUSINESS

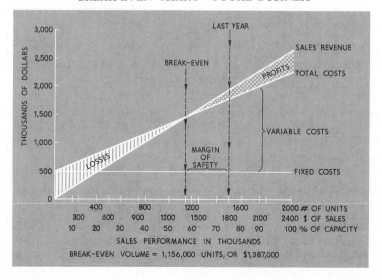

on Davidson's agenda, and in due time the controller introduced French, explaining his interest in cost control and analysis.

French had prepared enough copies of his chart and supporting calculations for everyone at the meeting. He described carefully what he had done and explained how the chart pointed to a profitable year, dependent on meeting the volume of sales activity that had been maintained in the past. It soon became apparent that some of the participants had known in advance what French planned to discuss; they had come prepared to challenge him and soon had taken control of the meeting. The following exchange ensued (see Exhibit 3 for a checklist of participants with their titles):

COOPER (production control): You know, Bill, I'm really concerned that you haven't allowed for our planned changes in volume next year. It seems to me that you should have allowed for the sales department's guess that we'll boost sales by 20 percent, unit-wise. We'll be pushing 90 percent of what we call capacity then. It sure seems that this would make quite a difference in your figuring.

FRENCH: That might be true, but as you can see, all you have to do is read the cost and profit relationship right off the chart for the new volume. Let's see—at a million-eight units we'd . . . .

WILLIAMS (manufacturing): Wait a minute, now!!! If you're going to talk in terms of 90 percent of capacity, and it looks like that's what it will be, you had better note that we'll be shelling out some more for the plant. We've already got okays on investment money that will boost your fixed costs by 10 thousand dollars a month, easy. And that may not be all. We may call it 90 percent of plant capacity, but there are a lot of places where we're just full up and we can't pull things up any tighter.

COOPER: See, Bill? Fred Williams is right, but I'm not finished on this bit about volume changes. According to the information that I've got here—and it came from your office—I'm not sure that your break-even chart can really be used even if there were to be no changes next year. Looks to me like you've got average figures that don't allow for the fact that we're dealing with three basic products. Your report here (see Exhibit 2) on costs, according to product lines, for last year makes it pretty clear that the "average" is way out of line. How would the break-even point look if we took this on an individual product basis?

FRENCH: Well, I'm not sure. Seems to me that there is only one break-even point for the firm. Whether we take it product by product or in total, we've got to hit that point. I'll be glad to check for you if you want, but . . . .

BRADSDHAW (assistant sales manager): Guess I may as well get in on this one, Bill. If you're going to do anything with individual products, you ought to know that we're looking for a big swing in our product mix. Might even start before we get into the new season. The "A" line is really losing out and I imagine that we'll be lucky to hold two thirds of the volume there next year. Wouldn't you buy that Arnie? [Agreement from the general sales manager.] That's not too bad, though, because we expect that we should pick up the 200,000 that we lose, and about a quarter million units more, over in "C" production. We don't see anything that shows much of a change in "B." That's been solid for years and shouldn't change much now.

WINETKI (general sales manager): Bradshaw's called it about as we figure it, but there's something else here too. We've talked about our pricing on "C" enough, and now I'm really going to push our side of it. Ray's estimate of maybe half a million—450,000 I guess it was—up on "C" for next year is on the basis of doubling the price with no change in cost. We've been priced so low on this item that it's been a crime—we've got to raise, but good, for two reasons. First, for our reputation; the price is out of line class-wise and is completely inconsistent with our quality reputation. Second, if we don't raise the price, we'll be swamped and we can't handle it. You heard what Williams said about capacity. The way the whole "C" field is exploding, we'll have to answer to another half million units in unsatisfied orders if we don't jack that price up. We can't afford to expand that much for this product.

At this point, Hugh Fraser (administrative assistant to the president) walked up toward the front of the room from where he had been standing near the rear door. The discussion broke for a minute, and he took advantage of the lull to interject a few comments.

FRASER: This has certainly been enlightening. Looks like you fellows are pretty well up on this whole operation. As long as you're going to try to get all the things together that you ought to pin down for next year, let's see what I can add to help you:

Number One: Let's remember that everything that shows in the profit area here on Bill's chart is divided just about evenly between the government and us. Now, for last year we can read a profit of about $150,000. Well, that's right. But we were left with half of that, and then paid out dividends of $50,000 to the stockholders. Since we've got an anniversary year coming up, we'd like to put out a special dividend about 50 percent extra. We ought to hold $25,000 in for the business, too. This means that we'd like to hit $100,000 *after* the costs of being governed.

Number Two: From where I sit, it looks like we're going to have a talk with the union again, and this time it's liable to cost us. All the indications are—and this isn't public—that we may have to meet demands that will boost our production costs—what do you call them here, Bill—variable costs—by 10 percent across the board. This may kill the bonus-dividend plans, but we've got to hold the line on past profits. This means that we can give that much to the union only if we can make it in added revenues. I guess you'd say that that raises your break-even point, Bill—and for that one I'd consider the company's profit to be a fixed cost.

Number Three: Maybe this is the time to think about switching our product emphasis. Arnie Winetki may know better than I which of the products is more profitable. You check me out on this Arnie—and it might be a good idea for you and Bill French to get together on this one, too. These figures that I have (Exhibit 2) make it look like the percentage contribution on line "A" is the lowest of the bunch. If we're losing volume there as rapidly

Exhibit 2

PRODUCT CLASS COST ANALYSIS

(Normal Year)

	Aggregate	"A"	"B"	"C"
Sales at full capacity (units)........	2,000,000			
Actual sales volume (units)........	1,500,000	600,000	400,000	500,000
Unit sales price................$	1.20	$ 1.67	$ 1.50	$ 0.40
Total sales revenue..............$1,800,000		$1,000,000	$600,000	$200,000
Variable cost per unit............$	0.75	$ 1.25	$ 0.625	$ 0.25
Total variable cost..............$1,125,000		$ 750,000	$250,000	$125,000
Fixed costs....................$	520,000	$ 170,000	$275,000	$ 75,000
Net profit.....................$	155,000	$ 80,000	$ 75,000	......
Ratios:				
Variable cost to sales...........	0.63	0.75	0.42	0.63
Variable income to sales........	0.37	0.25	0.58	0.37
Utilization of capacity..........	75.0%	30.0%	20.0%	25.0%

as you sales folks say, and if we're as hard pressed for space as Fred Williams has indicated, maybe we'd be better off grabbing some of that big demand for "C" by shifting some of the facilities over there from "A."

That's all I've got to say. Looks to me like you've all got plenty to think about.

DAVIDSON: Thanks, Hugh. I sort of figured that we'd get wound up here as soon as Bill brought out his charts. This is an approach that we've barely touched, but, as you can see, you've all got ideas that have got to be made to fit here somewhere. I'll tell you what let's do. Bill, suppose you rework your chart and try to bring into it some of the points that were made here today. I'll see if I can summarize what everyone seems to be looking for.

First of all, I have the idea buzzing around in the back of my mind that your presentation is based on a rather important series of assumptions. Most of the questions that were raised were really about those assumptions; it might help us all if you try to set the assumptions down in black and white so that we can see just how they influence the analysis.

Then, I think that Cooper would like to see the unit sales increase taken up, and he'd also like to see whether there's any difference if you base the calculations on an analysis of individual product lines. Also, as Bradshaw suggested, since the product mix is bound to change, why not see how things look if the shift materializes as sales has forecast?

Arnie Winetki would like to see the influence of a price increase in the "C" line; Fred Williams looks toward an increase in fixed manufacturing costs of 10 thousand a month, and Hugh Fraser has suggested that we should consider taxes, dividends, expected union demands, and the question of product emphasis.

I think that ties it all together. Let's hold off on our next meeting, fellows, until Bill has time to work this all into shape.

With that, the participants broke off into small groups and the meeting disbanded. French and Wes Davidson headed back to their offices and

Exhibit 3

LIST OF PARTICIPANTS IN THE MEETING

Bill French.....................staff accountant
Wes Davidson.................controller
John Cooper..................production control
Fred Williams................manufacturing
Ray Bradshaw.................assistant sales manager
Arnie Winetki................general sales manager
Hugh Fraser..................administrative assistant to president

French, in a tone of concern asked Davidson, "Why didn't you warn me about the hornet's nest I was walking into?"

"Bill, you didn't ask!"

Questions

1. What are the assumptions implicit in Bill French's determination of his company's break-even point?
2. On the basis of French's revised information, what does next year look like:
   a) What is the break-even point?
   b) What level of operations must be achieved to pay the extra dividend, ignoring union demands?
   c) What level of operations must be achieved to meet the union demands, ignoring bonus dividends?
   d) What level of operations must be achieved to meet both dividends and expected union requirements?
3. Can the break-even analysis help the company decide whether to alter the existing product emphasis? What can the company afford to invest for additional "C" capacity?
4. Is this type of analysis of any value? For what can it be used?

CASE 15–2. DAVIGO FOODS COMPANY

The Davigo Foods Company, located in a tomato-growing section, had for many years produced tomato specialties such as tomato juice cocktail, tomato paste, and ketchup. In 1953, it was able to extend its production season from four to nine months by the addition of various types of prepared spaghetti dinners and ravioli. In order to keep certain skilled personnel, the company had found a place for five men in the shipping department during the three months when the remainder of the plant was closed.

These men had been earning a wage of $1.30 an hour at their regular work, but they were willing to accept $0.97 an hour for the time they were in the shipping department. This meant that during the three months that they were in the shipping department the five men had collectively received $860 less than they would have received at their regular rate of pay. However, the regular wage rate in the shipping department was $0.80 an hour, and the shipping department therefore had been charged with $440 more than it ordinarily would have paid for this type of work.

The head of the shipping department was indignant that his costs were increased by this amount and contended that he should be charged at a rate not higher than the regular $0.80 rate for his department and that a fairer rate would be the beginners' rate of $0.65, since these men were not so efficient as his experienced work force.

Question

1. How would you account for the $0.97 an hour paid the five men when they worked in the shipping department?

CASE 15–3.   AZIENDA VINICOLA ITALIANA

Azienda Vinicola Italiana produced and bottled wines. A large percentage of its sales were of special table wine. Most of its customers, located in the principal Italian cities, were served through local representatives. Its prices were in line with those of competitors.

In 1956 the firm sold 704,000 liters[4] of wine, in 871,850 bottles. In recent years demand had been increasing, and the firm had approached the limit of its productive capacity, which was estimated to be 900,000 bottles a year.

The production process was not complicated, since the firm did not buy grapes but rather bought either mosto[5] or bulk wine. This policy had the disadvantage that the firm could not assure itself of a consistently high-quality product. Moreover, it was estimated that if grapes were purchased, the price of raw material would be reduced by about Lit.[6] 10 per bottle. On the other hand, the purchase and installation of equipment needed for pressing grapes would require an additional investment of about Lit. 50 million. No significant increase in labor costs was anticipated under such a practice.

---

[4] One liter is slightly more than one United States liquid quart.

[5] Mosto is the juice of grapes before the fermentation process takes place. The fermentation process takes about one month. During this process carbon dioxide develops, and the sugar is converted into alcohol. Therefore, mosto is an unstable product, and wine is a stable product.

[6] In 1956, 100 Italian lira (abbreviated "Lit.") equaled approximately U.S. $0.16.

In the production department there were 40 employees who worked a total of about 90,000 hours in 1956 and whose average wage per hour, including fringe benefits, was Lit. 365. The administrative manager was of the opinion that 40 percent of this labor expense should be considered as being fixed, while the remainder could be considered as varying proportionally with production volume.

In 1956, production had required 700,000 liters of mosto and bulk wine, purchased at a total cost of Lit. 54,752,000. The average cost incurred for auxiliary materials (bottles, stoppers, neckbands, labels, etc.) was about Lit. 41 per bottle.

The income statement for 1956 is shown in Exhibit 1.

Exhibit 1

AZIENDA VINICOLA ITALIANA

Income Statement for 1956 in Lira

Sales...............................		174,670,000
Costs:		
Labor............................32,467,000		
Raw materials.........................54,752,000		
Auxiliary materials....................35,774,000		
General manufacturing expenses		
(including pay of two cellar foremen).... 4,795,000		127,788,000
Manufacturing gross profit...............		46,882,000
General administrative expenses (including the salary of a person skilled in the art of making and preserving wine).......16,745,000		
Depreciation...........................10,540,000		
Interest............................. 7,500,000		
Advertising........................... 7,900,000		42,685,000
Net Profit............................		4,197,000

The administrative manager wished to reorganize the firm in order to exploit its productive capability to the utmost and, above all, to increase the net profit, which the owners did not consider satisfactory. They were of the opinion that a net profit of 8 percent or 9 percent of sales could be realized.

As a basis upon which to make decisions, the administrative manager intended to use charts of costs and revenues that he had seen other firms use and that he considered helpful. The first step in this graphic analysis was a study of costs, separating fixed costs from variable costs. For that purpose, he examined the income statements of preceding years and came to the conclusion that the figures for 1956 were representative. He also noticed that the different types of wine had been sold in more or less the same relative proportions each year, despite large fluctuations in the total volume of business, and this fact confirmed his belief that the figures for 1956 were representative. He therefore prepared the following analysis:

a) *Fixed Costs:*

40% of labor cost	12,987,000
Staff salaries	10,745,000
General manufacturing expenses	4,795,000
General administrative expenses	6,000,000
Advertising expenses	7,900,000
Interest	7,500,000
Depreciation	10,540,000
	60,467,000

b) *Variable Costs*

60% of labor cost	19,480,000
Raw materials	54,752,000
Auxiliary materials	35,774,000
	110,006,000

The administrative manager assumed a maximum capacity of 900,000 bottles a year. At current prices he estimated this would produce sales revenue of Lit. 180 million.

With the present structure of costs and revenue, the profits resulting from an annual production of 900,000 bottles would be small. The administrative manager decided, therefore, to try to discover a way to change costs and revenue so as to obtain a profit of Lit. 16 million a year, which would be 9 percent of sales of Lit. 180 million.

Questions

1. Accepting the distribution between fixed and variable elements as estimated by the administrative manager, prepare a chart of costs and revenues. Determine the volume of production at which the firm reaches its break-even point and the profit at capacity operation.
2. Draw three other charts, each constructed so that a production of 900,000 bottles will produce a profit of Lit. 16 million, one in which selling price is assumed to increase, another in which fixed costs are assumed to decrease, and a third in which variable costs are assumed to decrease. What are the break-even points in each of these situations?
3. What are the most likely alternatives to consider so as to achieve a profit of Lit. 16 million?

CASE 15–4.   TRACY MANUFACTURING COMPANY

In the summer of 1947 there was considerable feeling among the executives of the Tracy Manufacturing Company that costs were out of line. The company had made good profits for several years, and it was believed that under such conditions, laxity in cost control had developed.

Exhibit 1

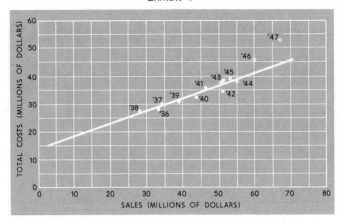

The end of World War II in 1945 and the sharp increases in prices in 1946 also had created problems.

The Tracy Manufacturing Company made a variety of tools. Although the company concentrated on small tools that it sold through mail-order houses and hardware stores, it also manufactured larger tools sold directly to manufacturers. The company used a well-developed cost accounting system.

In an effort to determine whether the cost-sales relationship had changed, the treasurer had an assistant plot the total cost of sales for each of the years 1936–45, taken from income statements, against net sales for each of those years. (See Exhibit 1.) A trend line was then fitted to these points by the method of least squares; that is, the line was drawn in such a way that the squares of all deviations of actual points from the line were at a minimum. When, however, the actual cost for 1946 and the budgeted cost for 1947 were plotted against actual and projected sales, the points were found to fall well above the previous line of relationship. On seeing the chart, some of the executives were quick to point out that here was proof of the company's growing inefficiency. The treasurer, however, believed that more study was needed before any such conclusion could be reached.

The treasurer asked his assistant to initiate a study that would, among other things, answer the following questions:

1. Are the 1946 and 1947 points out of line?
2. If so, why are they out of line?
3. If volume declines, what line of relationship can cost be expected to follow? What has happened to the break-even point?

Questions

1. What was the approximate break-even point under the 1936–45 relationship?
2. What are some of the possible reasons why the 1946 and 1947 points departed from the 1936–45 line of relationship?
3. What steps would you take in order to answer the treasurer's questions?

CHAPTER 16

BUDGETING

All managements make plans. One cannot conceive of an organization of any kind whose leaders were not giving some thought to what the organization's objectives should be and to the best way of reaching those objectives. A group of people not operating under some sort of plan is merely an incoherent, directionless mob, not an organization.

Although all managements plan, there are considerable differences in the way in which they plan. Some people do their planning entirely in their heads, others make notes and rough estimates on the backs of old envelopes, and still others express their plans in quantitative terms and commit these to paper in some orderly, systematic fashion. The process engaged in by the latter group is called "budgeting," for a *budget* is merely a plan expressed in quantitative terms. We are here primarily concerned with budgets that are expressed in monetary terms, although some budgets are expressed in units of product, number of employees, units of time, or other nonmonetary quantities. In addition to its use in planning, the budget is also used for control and for coordination.

Types of Budgets

There is a considerable diversity of practice in budgeting, much greater than the diversity in accounting practice. Most companies except the smallest have some sort of budget, but a great many do not have a truly comprehensive budgeting system. Such a system consists of three types of budgets: an *operating* budget, showing planned operations for the forthcoming period; a *cash* budget, showing the anticipated sources and uses of cash; and a *capital* budget, showing planned changes in fixed assets.

These types of budgets, the relationships between them, and the principal segments of which they are composed, are shown in Illustration 16–1.

The illustration shows only one of the large number of ways in which budgets are structured in various companies.

Illustration 16–1

TYPES OF BUDGETS

THE OPERATING BUDGET

An operating budget usually consists of two parts, a "program" budget and a "responsibility" budget. These represent two ways of depicting the overall operating plan for the business, two different methods of slicing the pie; therefore, both arrive at the same figure for projected net income and return on investment.

The *program budget* describes the major programs the company plans to undertake. Such a budget might be arranged, for example, by products lines and show the anticipated revenue and costs associated with each product. This type of budget is useful to an executive examining the overall balance among the various programs of the business. It helps to answer such questions as these: Is the profit margin on each product line satisfactory? Is production capacity in balance with the size and capability of the sales organization? Can we afford to spend so much for research?

Are adequate funds available? And so on. A negative answer to any of these questions indicates the necessity for revising the plan.

The *responsibility budget* sets forth plans in terms of the persons responsible for carrying them out. It is therefore primarily a control device, since it is a statement of expected or standard performance against which actual performance can later be compared. In the factory, for example, there may be a responsibility budget for each department, showing the costs that are controllable by the foreman of the department. There may also be a program budget showing costs for each product, including both direct costs and allocated costs. The figures on both sets of budgets add up to total factory costs, but the product-cost budget would not be useful for control purposes, since the costs shown on it could not ordinarily be related to the responsibility of specific individuals.

If the costs in a responsibility center are expected to vary with volume, as is the case with most production departments, the responsibility budget may be in the form of a *variable budget* or *flexible budget*. Such a budget shows the expected behavior of costs at various volume levels. The variable budget may be expressed in terms of the cost-volume equation described in Chapter 15, that is, a nonvariable amount and a variable amount per unit of volume, or $y = a + bx$. It may also be expressed as the costs that are expected at discrete levels of volume; that is, there may be a column for the costs expected at 60 percent of normal volume, another at 70, 80, 90, 100, 110, 120, 130, and 140 percent. In the latter case, a comparison of actual costs with budgeted costs requires an interpolation when actual volume is between two of the specified levels.

In addition to the responsibility budgets for costs, there also may be budgets showing planned inventory levels of finished products and raw materials; a budget of the planned purchases of materials; personnel budgets showing planned manpower levels, and plans for promotions, participation in training programs, and retirements; and budgets for a variety of other special purposes.

Relationships among the Budgets

The budget should constitute a coherent whole; therefore, the pieces should be consistent with one another. The costs in the individual production centers in the responsibility budget should add up to the same amount as the total product costs in the program budget, for example. If variable budgets are used, then one point on the cost-volume line must be selected as the volume at which product costs are to be calculated. This point is the expected volume for the year, and the costs at this volume are used in preparing the estimated income statement.

The program budget ordinarily cannot be used for control purposes, since the costs shown on it cannot ordinarily be related to the responsibilities of specific individuals. The costs of a product, for example, include a fraction of the costs of all the production departments through which the product passes during the manufacturing process. In some situations, however, individual responsibility can be related to specific programs, and in these situations, the program budget serves as a means of control. The producer of a motion picture or a television "special," for example, has a budget for his particular program, and control is exercised in terms of that budget. This is also the case in the construction of major capital assets: buildings, dams, roads, bridges, ships, weapons systems, and the like. Within such a program, the budget may be subdivided according to the organizational units responsible for various aspects of it, and these units are responsibility centers.

The Budget Process

The preparation of a budget can be studied both as an accounting process and as a management process. From an accounting standpoint, the procedures are essentially the same as those described in Part I, and the end result of the recording and summarizing operations is a set of financial statements—a balance sheet and an income statement—identical in format with those resulting from the process of recording historical events. The only difference is that the budget figures are estimates of what will happen in the future rather than historical data on what has happened in the past.

From a management standpoint, the budgeting process is so closely associated with the operation of the business that a complete description of the factors and considerations involved would take us far beyond the scope of this book. Rather than attempt such a description, we shall merely indicate some of the important general considerations in the budget process.

Choice of Time Periods

The majority of companies prepare budgets once a year. For control purposes, the annual totals may simply be divided by 12 to obtain monthly budgets, but if seasonal influences are important, separate budget estimates are made for each month or each quarter. In many companies data are shown by months only for the next three months or the next six months, with the balance of the year being shown by quarters.

Some companies follow the practice of preparing a new budget every quarter, but for a full year ahead. Every three months the estimates for the quarter just completed are dropped, the figures for the succeeding three quarters are revised if necessary, and estimates for the fourth succeeding quarter are added. This is called a *rolling budget*.

Organization for Preparation of Budgets

A *budget committee*, consisting of several members of the top management group, may oversee the work of preparing the budget. This committee will set the general guidelines that the organization is to follow, coordinate the separate budgets prepared by the various organizational units, resolve differences among them, and submit the final budget to the president and to the board of directors for approval. In a small company, this work is done by the president himself, or by his immediate line subordinate. Instructions go down through the regular chain of command, and the budget comes back up for successive reviews and approvals through the same channels. The essential point is that decisions about the budget are made by the line organization, and the final approval is given by the head of that organization, the president or the board.

The line organization usually is assisted in its preparation of the budget by a staff unit headed by the *budget director*, preferably reporting to the controller. If he reports to the president, as is sometimes the case, he is likely to be performing the functions described above for the budget committee and therefore acting in a line, rather than a staff, capacity.

As a staff man, the budget director's functions are to disseminate instructions about the mechanics of budget preparation (the forms and how to fill them out), to provide data on past performance that are useful in preparation of the budget, to make computations on the basis of decisions reached by the line organization, to assemble the budget figures, and to see that everyone submits his figures on time. Thus, the budget organization may do a very large fraction of the budget work. It is not the crucial part, however, for the significant decisions are always made by the line organization. Once the members of the line organization have reached an agreement on labor productivity and wage rates, for example, the budget man can calculate all the detailed figures for labor costs by products and by responsibility centers; this is a considerable job of computation, but it is entirely based on the judgments of the line supervisors.

The budget organization is like a telephone company, operating an important communication system; it is responsible for the speed, accuracy, and clarity with which messages flow through the system, but not for the content of the messages themselves.

The Budget Timetable

As indicated in Illustration 16–1, "the" budget for a typical company consists of several parts: the sales budget, the sales expense budget, the inventory and purchases budget, the production budget, the administrative budget, the research and development budget, the budgeted income statement and balance sheet, and the cash budget, among others. Some of these pieces are affected by decisions or estimates made in constructing other pieces. Most of them are affected by the estimate of sales volume. The factory budget is affected by estimated sales volume and decisions as to inventory levels. The purchases budget is affected by estimated production volume and decisions as to material inventory levels, and so on. Thus, there has to be a carefully worked out timetable specifying the order in which the several parts of the budget are to be prepared and the time when each must be completed. In general, the steps covered by this timetable are as follows:

1. Setting guidelines.
2. Making the sales estimate.
3. Initial preparation of the other parts of the budget.
4. Negotiation of agreed estimates.
5. Coordination and review.
6. Final approval.

In a company of average complexity, the elapsed time for the whole process is approximately three months, with the most hectic part (steps 4, 5, and 6 above) requiring approximately one month. In highly complex organizations, the elapsed time may be six months, or occasionally even longer. At the other extreme, a small business may go through the whole process in one afternoon.

Setting Guidelines

Ideally, the budget process is *not* the mechanism by which major policy decisions are made, but rather a means of implementing these decisions. These major decisions are made whenever the need or the opportunity arises. (In practice, there are exceptions to this statement, because the act of preparing the budget may uncover a need to make new major decisions.)

In any event, when budget preparation begins, a great many decisions affecting the budget year already have been made, some of which are irrevocable and some of which are subject to modifications. The maximum scale of manufacturing operations is set by the available facilities, for example, and if an expansion is to take place during the budget year, the decision would ordinarily have to have been made a year or more previously because of the time required to build buildings and to acquire and install machinery. If a new product is to go into volume production, considerable time would have already been spent prior to the budget year on product development, design, testing, and initial promotional work. Thus, the budget is not a *de novo* creation; it is built within the context of the ongoing business.

LONG-RANGE PLANNING. The decisions described above are part of the *programming* process. In a small, but growing, number of companies programming decisions are incorporated in a formal long-range plan. Such a plan shows the estimated revenues and expenses (and possibly asset acquisitions and other information) over each of the next several (i.e., three, four, or five) years that are implied in policy decisions that have already been taken. When such a plan exists, the revenue and expense estimates for the budget year column of the long-range plan provide a starting point in preparing the budget. They do not by any means provide the budget automatically, for they must be refined and be brought up to date; the other steps in the process must be followed even when a long-range plan exists.

The long-range plan, if one exists, is a guideline that governs the preparation of the budget. Alternatively, or in addition, top management may describe in more general terms the policies that are to govern budget preparation. These guidelines vary greatly in detail. At one extreme, there may be only a brief general statement, such as, "Assume that volume will be 5 percent greater than the current year." More commonly, detailed information and guidance is given on such matters as projected general economic conditions, allowance to be made for price increases and wage increases, changes in the product line, changes in the scale of operations, allowable personnel promotions, anticipated productivity gains, and a variety of other topics. In addition, detailed instructions will be issued as to what information is required for the budget, and how this information is to be recorded on the budget documents.

These guidelines are of great interest to competitors, so they are circulated only to those who need to know them. If it is particularly important that a new strategy be concealed, it may be omitted from the statement, with necessary adjustments in the budget being made subsequently at the headquarters level. In the absence of statements to the contrary, the organization customarily assumes that the budget year will be similar to the current year.

An example of a guideline statement is given below. It was prepared by a large bank, and is relatively general and brief:

It is customary for the committee to summarize for your general guidance current thinking regarding deposits, loans, and loan rates. The expectations outlined below are for the overall bank. Therefore, it is important that the head of each earning unit analyze the impact of expected general economic trends on the conditions peculiar to his own area of activity in order to project specific goals which he may reasonably expect to attain.

DEPOSITS

There is every indication that money market conditions will be such that demand deposit levels in our area will expand. In our judgment, we anticipate at least a 5 percent growth in demand deposits for all banks. Our overall goal, however, should be set somewhat higher to reflect an improvement in our relative position. Savings deposits will continue to climb moderately. Current rates for time and savings deposits should be used to project interest costs.

LOANS AND LOAN RATES

In all probability loan demand will slacken seasonally in the early months of next year; in fact, many economists believe that the decline may continue through the second quarter of the year. We firmly believe that sometime between the March tax date and early in the third quarter, loan demand should strengthen.

For the most part, the recent decline in the prime rate is reflected in the loan rate structure at this time. Accordingly, except where necessary rate adjustments are still anticipated, the existing rate structure should prevail.

EXPENSES

Before preparing the budget, it is imperative that each supervisor closely evaluate every controllable expense in his area and consider all means of economizing and reducing costs, particularly in such areas as personnel staffing, overtime, entertainment, stationery, etc. The salary administration policies explained on pages 19 and 20 in the Budget Instructions[1] should be strictly followed.

In order to complete the budget for the entire bank by year-end, your full cooperation is necessary in meeting the deadlines which appear in the attached General Instructions.

BUDGET COMMITTEE

---

[1] The policies referred to are as follows:

Your current appraisal of each employee's performance as E (excellent), AA (above average), A (average), or P (poor) is to be shown immediately following the individual's name on schedule 4A, as a guide for your own budgeting and for the subsequent review by the budget committee.

Salary administration policies, as expressed in Bulletin III of the Personnel Policies Manual are not expected to change. Our salary rates are competitive, and as in recent years, any projected increases should be based solely on merit or, where plans are sufficiently advanced, on anticipated bona fide promotions.

In general, the budget committee anticipates that we will be able to maintain our competitive position with total bankwide increases to deserving employees, averaging no more than 5 percent of their salaries. In order to achieve this purpose, all departments must cooperate in observing the following guides:

a) In all cases, *merit* and not length of service is to be the basis for the forecasting of increases.

b) Individual merit increases should be roughly 5 to 5½ percent of the range midpoint with no increase less than $156 nor more than 10 percent of the range midpoint, ($500 maximum), and in multiples of $1.00 weekly.

c) Individual increases exceeding the guidelines in (*b*) above should be thoroughly documented both in budget submittal and in subsequent actual review for salary purposes.

d) An employee rated average should not receive appreciably more than the midpoint of his salary range. The top half of the range is reserved for those employees who demonstrate above-average performance.

e) In case of promotion, the increase or increases to be scheduled should normally bring the salary within a reasonable period to the minimum for the new job.

The Sales Estimate

In almost all companies, the most difficult estimate to make is that of sales revenue. There are in general two ways of proceeding: to make a *statistical* forecast on the basis of an analysis of general business conditions, market conditions, product growth curves, and the like; or to make an *internal* forecast, by collecting the opinions of executives and salesmen. In some companies salesmen are asked to estimate the sales of each product made to each of their customers; in others, they estimate total sales in their territory; in still others, salesmen do not participate in the estimating process. There are advantages and weaknesses in both the statistical and the internal methods; both are often used together, but neither can be guaranteed to yield an even reasonably close estimate in view of the inevitable uncertainties of the future.

The sales budget is more than a sales *forecast*. A forecast is merely passive, while a budget should reflect the positive actions that management plans to take in order to influence future events. For example, this may be the sales forecast: "With the present amount of sales effort, we expect sales to run at about the same level as currently." By contrast, the sales *budget* may show a substantial planned increase in sales, reflecting management's intention to add salesmen, increase advertising and sales promotion, or redesign the product.

The sales estimate may or may not be disseminated as part of the budget guidelines. It is a piece of information in which competitors are greatly interested, particularly as it relates to new products, so its distribution may be restricted for that reason. Instead of disseminating the detailed estimate, some companies send only summaries of it, with enough information to permit necessary planning of material purchases, additional personnel, and other needed resources.

Initial Budget Preparation

The budget guidelines prepared by top management are sent down through the successive levels in the organization, and the management at each level may add other, more detailed, information for the guidance of its subordinates.

When the guidelines arrive at the lowest responsibility centers, the heads of these responsibility centers make the budget estimates, working within the guidance and restraints specified in the guidelines. The respective roles of the line supervisor and the staff budget man in this process are as described above; that is, the accounting and budget staff assist the line supervisor by making detailed calculations, by providing historical data, and by summarizing and recording the estimates, but the line supervisor, not the accountant, is responsible for the estimates themselves.

For each expense center, the supervisor makes an estimate of each significant element of controllable expense. If noncontrollable expenses are reported, these estimates are usually added subsequently by the budget staff.

Whenever feasible, estimates for quantities and for unit prices should be shown separately in order to facilitate the subsequent analysis of performance. Material cost is preferably shown as number of pounds times cents per pound, labor costs as number of hours times the hourly wage rate, and so on. The basic reason for doing this is that different factors, and often different people, are responsible for changes in the quantity component and the price component, respectively. The purchasing officer is responsible for the cost per pound of material, but the factory foreman is responsible for the quantity used, for example. For similar reasons, the estimates are broken down by product lines, by significant items of cost, and in other ways that will facilitate subsequent analysis of actual performance.

Usually, the current level of expenses is used as a starting point in making these estimates. The guidelines may provide specific instructions as to the permitted changes that can be made from current expenses, such as, "Assume a 3 percent increase for purchased materials and services." In addition to following these instructions, the person who prepares the budget, i.e., the budgetee, expresses his judgment as to the behavior of costs not covered by the instructions.

Negotiation

Now comes the crucial stage in the process from a control standpoint, the negotiation between the budgetee and his superior. The value of the budget as an estimate of what is going to happen, as a motivating device, and as a standard against which actual performance will be measured, depends largely on how skillfully this negotiation is conducted.

Several recent studies have shown that the budget is most effective as a motivating device when it represents a tight, but attainable, goal. If it is too tight, it leads to frustration; if it is too loose, it leads to complacency. The budgetee's superior therefore seeks to arrive at this desirable middle ground.[2]

As did the budgetee, the superior usually must take the current level of expense as a starting point. There simply is not enough time during the budget review to reexamine each of the elements of expense and insure

---

[2] The policy of some companies is to set the responsibility budget slightly tighter than the performance that reasonably can be expected. Under these circumstances, the responsibility budgets will not jibe with the program budget unless a specific allowance is subsequently added for the difference between the budget goals and expected performance.

that the current level is optimum. It is a fact, however, that the operation of Parkinson's first law ("Costs tend to increase regardless of the work done") strongly suggests that costs do drift out of line over a period of time, and that the current level of spending is therefore probably too high. One way of addressing this problem is to make an arbitrary cut, say 5 percent, in the budget estimates, but this is not satisfactory simply because of its arbitrariness; it affects the efficient and the inefficient alike. Furthermore, if the budgetees know that such a cut is going to be made, they can counter it by inflating the original estimates by a corresponding amount.

Zero-Base Review.   Another approach to this problem is the zero-base review, a periodic study of the responsibility center made by a staff group, or by outside experts. Such a study builds up the costs from zero, rather than starting with the current level of costs. These studies are especially important when costs are of the discretionary cost type. Basic questions are raised, such as: (1) Should the function be performed at all? (2) What should the quality level be? Are we doing too much? (3) Should it be performed in this way? (4) How much should it cost?

One way of examining costs is to make a comparison with similar functions in other parts of the company, or with information obtained from trade associations and similar sources about the cost of performing similar functions in other companies. Although there are problems of comparability; although, by definition, there is no way of finding a "correct" relationship between cost and output in a discretionary cost situation; although there is a danger in taking an outside average as a standard; and although many other criticisms can be raised about such comparisons, they nevertheless can be useful. For example, they often lead to the following interesting question: If other companies can get the job done for $X, why can't we?

The zero-base review is time consuming, and it is also likely to be a traumatic experience for the heads of responsibility centers. It therefore cannot be made every year, but rather is scheduled so that all responsibility centers are covered once in four or five years. This review establishes a new base for the budget, and the annual budget review attempts to keep costs reasonably in line with this base for the intervening four or five years.

The superior has various tactics for doing this. He asks for a full justification of any proposed cost increases. He seeks reasons why costs may be expected to decrease, such as a decrease in the work load of the responsibility center, an increase in productivity, or the operation of the learning phenomenon described in Chapter 15, recognizing that these prospective decreases may not willingly be disclosed by the budgetee. (Some managements, knowing that overall productivity in America increases by approximately 3 percent per year, expect similar productivity gains within their companies. As a rough rule of thumb, some companies expect productivity gains to offset inflationary price increases, and so expect total expenses to show a net change of zero from one year to the next.)

For his part, the budgetee defends his estimates. He justifies proposed cost increases by additional work that he is expected to do, by the effect of inflation, by the need for better quality output, and so on.

THE COMMITMENT. The end product of this negotiation[3] is an agreement which represents an implicit commitment by each party. By agreeing to the budget estimates, the budgetee says to his superior, in effect: "I can and will operate my department in accordance with the plan described in the budget." By approving the budget estimates, the superior says to the budgetee, in effect: "If you operate your department in accordance with this plan, you will do what we consider to be a good job." Both of these statements contain the implicit qualification of "adjusted for changes in circumstances" since both parties recognize that actual events, such as price levels and general business conditions, may not correspond to those assumed when the budget was prepared and that these changes will inevitably affect the plans set forth in the budget. In judging whether the commitment is in fact being carried out as the year progresses, management must take these changes into account.

The nature of the commitment, both as to individual elements of expense and as to the total expense of the responsibility center, may be one of three types: (*a*) It may represent a *ceiling* (e.g., "Not more than $X should be spent for books and periodicals"); (*b*) it may represent a *floor* (e.g., "At least $Y should be spent for employee training"); or (*c*) it may represent a *guide* (e.g., "Approximately $Z should be spent for overtime"). Often, the individual items are not explicitly identified as to which of these categories they belong in, but it is obviously important that the two parties have a clear understanding as to which item belongs in which category.

Coordination and Review

The negotiation process is repeated at successively higher levels of responsibility centers in the organizational hierarchy. The subsequent negotiations may, of course, result in changes in the detailed budgets that have been agreed to at lower levels, and if these changes are significant, the budget may have to be recycled back down the organizational chain. If, however, the guidelines are carefully described, and if the budget process is well understood and conducted by those who participate in it, such recycling is not ordinarily necessary. In the successive stages of

---

[3] In a perceptive study, D. H. Hofstede describes this process as a "game"; see *The Game of Budget Control* (Assen, The Netherlands: Van Gorcum & Co., N.V., 1967). A negotiation is a game, in the formal sense.

negotiation, the person who has the role of supervisor at one level becomes the budgetee at the next higher level. Since he is well aware of this fact, he is strongly motivated to negotiate budgets with his budgetees that he can defend successfully with his superiors. If his superior demonstrates that the proposed budget is loose, this is a reflection on the budgetee's ability as a manager.

As the individual budgets move up the organizational hierarchy, they are also examined in relationship to one another, and this examination may reveal aspects of the plan that are out of balance. If so, certain of the underlying budgets may need to be changed. Major unresolved problems are submitted to the budget committee for resolution. The individual responsibility budgets may also reveal the need to change estimates in the program budget, and these changes may in turn disclose parts of the program that appear to be out of balance. Various summary documents, especially the budgeted income statement and the budgeted balance sheet, are also prepared at this time.

Final Approval

Just prior to the beginning of the budget year, the proposed budget is submitted to top management—usually to the board of directors—for approval. If the guidelines have been properly set and adhered to, the proposed budget should contain no great surprises to top management, and approval should therefore be forthcoming after a relatively brief discussion. This approval is by no means perfunctory, however, for it signifies the official agreement of top management to the proposed plans for the year. The approved budget is then transmitted down through the organization.

Variations in Practice

The preceding is a "textbook" description of the budget process. Not all companies have a budget for each responsibility center, and some of those that do have complete budgets treat the process more casually than is implied in the above description. Some companies formulate their budgets in a process that is the reverse of that described; that is, instead of having budget estimates originate at the lowest responsibility centers, the budget is prepared by a high-level staff, blessed by top management, and then transmitted down to the organization. This *imposed* budget is an unsatisfactory motivating device, and it is becoming less common.

Revisions

The budget is formulated in accordance with certain assumptions as to conditions that will be prevailing during the budget year. Actual conditions will never be exactly the same as those assumed, and the differences may be significant. The question then arises as to whether or not the budget should be revised to reflect what is now known about current conditions. There is considerable difference of opinion on this question.

Those who favor revising the budget point out that the budget is supposed to reflect the plan in accordance with which the company is operating, and that when the plan has to be changed because of changing conditions, the budget should reflect these changes. If the budget is not revised, it is no longer a statement of plans.

The opponents of revising the budget argue that the process of revision not only is time consuming, but also may obscure the goals that the company originally intended to achieve and the reasons for departures from these goals, especially since a revision may reflect the budgetee's skill in negotiating a change that hides his inefficiency, rather than one that reflects an actual change in the underlying assumed conditions. They refer disparagingly to a frequently revised budget as a "rubber standard." Many companies therefore do not revise their budgets during the year, and take account of changes in conditions when they analyze the difference between actual and budgeted performance.

Other companies solve this problem by having two budgets, a *baseline* budget set at the beginning of the year, and a *current* budget, reflecting the best current estimate of revenue and expenses. A comparison of actual performance with the baseline performance shows the extent of deviation from the original goals, and a comparison of the current budget with the baseline budget shows how much of this deviation has been attributed to changes in current conditions from those originally assumed.

Some managers use current budgets in lieu of reports of actual performance. Such a manager says: "I am not interested in actual costs because I literally can't do anything to control them; they have already happened. What I am interested in is a comparison of how we now think we are going to come out, compared with how we originally planned to come out, as expressed in the baseline budget. If this comparison is not satisfactory, I can at least investigate what can be done to bring the situation back into line." As Charles F. Kettering said, "We should all be concerned about the future because we will have to spend the rest of our lives there."

Such an approach is particularly useful in the case of a program budget for the construction of a building or other capital equipment. Presumably the program was undertaken because the originally foreseen relationship between its costs and the benefits to be achieved was deemed to be satisfactory. If current estimates indicate that this relationship has been significantly changed with the passage of time—for example, that it is now estimated that the program will cost significantly more than originally contemplated—then the whole program needs to be reexamined, and possibly redirected or even discontinued.

Uses of the Budget

From the above description, it should be apparent that the budget is useful: (1) as a device for making and coordinating plans, (2) for communicating these plans to those who are responsible for carrying them out, (3) in motivating managers at all levels, and (4) as a standard with which actual performance subsequently can be compared.

Although basic planning decisions are usually made prior to the beginning of the budget cycle, the process of formulating the budget leads to a refinement of these plans, and, when it discloses inbalances or unsatisfactory overall results, may lead to a change in plans.

As a communication device, it should be recognized that management's plans will not be carried out (except by accident) unless the organization understands what the plans are. Adequate understanding includes not only a knowledge of programs and objectives (e.g., how many units are to be manufactured, what methods and machines are to be used, how much material is to be purchased, what selling prices are to be) but also a knowledge about policies and restrictions to which the organization is expected to adhere. Examples of these kinds of information follow: the maximum amounts that may be spent for such items as advertising, maintenance, administrative costs; wage rates and hours of work; desired quality levels; and so on. A most useful device for communicating quantitative information concerning these objectives and limitations is the approved budget.

If the atmosphere is right, the budget process can be a powerful force in motivating managers to work toward the goals of the overall organization. Such an atmosphere is created when heads of responsibility centers understand that top management regards the process as important, and when they participate in the formulation of their own budgets in the manner described above.

A carefully prepared budget is the best possible standard against which to measure actual performance, and it is increasingly being used for this purpose. Until fairly recently, the general practice was to compare current results with results for last month or with results for the same period a year ago; and this is still the basic means of comparison in many companies. Such a historical standard has the fundamental weakness that it does not take account either of changes in the underlying forces at work or of the planned program for the current year.

EXAMPLE: In a favorable market situation, a certain company increased its volume and its selling prices and hence increased its net income in 1968 by 25 percent over the net income of 1967. If 1968's results are compared with 1967's, there is an apparent cause for rejoicing. However, the company had *planned* to increase profits by 35 percent, and performance when measured against the plan was not so good. The company quite properly took steps to find out, and if possible to correct, the factors accounting for the difference between actual and budgeted results.

In general, it is more significant to answer the question, "Why didn't we do what we planned to do?" than the question, "Why is this year different from last year?" Presumably, the principal factors accounting for the difference between this year and last year were taken into consideration in the preparation of the budget.

The foregoing discussion presupposes a carefully prepared budget. If management does not trust the budget, then there is good reason to use last year's performance as a benchmark, for it at least has the merit of being a definite, objective figure.

THE CASH BUDGET

The operating budget is usually prepared in terms of revenues and expenses. For financial planning purposes, it must be translated into terms of cash receipts and cash disbursements. This translation results in the *cash budget.* The financial people use the cash budget to make plans to insure that the company has enough, but not too much, cash on hand during the year ahead.

There are two approaches to the preparation of a cash budget:

1. Start with the budgeted balance sheet and income statements and adjust the figures thereon to reveal the sources and uses of cash. This procedure is exactly the same as that described for the cash flow statement in Chapter 12, except that the data are estimates of the future rather than historical. It therefore is not described again here.

2. Project directly each of the items that results in cash receipts or cash disbursements. A cash budget prepared by this means is shown in Illustration 16–2. Some useful points in connection with this technique are mentioned below.

Collections of accounts receivable is estimated by applying a "lag" factor to estimated sales or shipments. This factor may be based simply on the assumption that the cash from this month's sales will be collected next month; or there may be a more elaborate assumption, for example, that 10 percent of this month's sales will be collected this month, 60 percent next month, 20 percent in the second month, 9 percent in the third month, and the remaining 1 percent will never be collected.

The estimated amount and timing of *raw materials purchases* is obtained from the purchases budget, and is translated into cash disbursements by applying a lag factor for the time interval that ordinarily elapses between the receipt of the material and the payment of the invoice.

Illustration 16–2

CASH FORECAST, 1969
(in thousands)

	January	February	March	April	May	June	July	Totals for Year
Gross shipments	1,200	1,987	2,063	1,387	2,363	2,325	1,575	21,000
Cash balance beginning of month	375	396	222	150	257	160	192	375
Add: Cash receipts:								
Collections of accounts receivable	1,380	1,350	1,605	1,635	1,680	2,055	2,205	19,305
Miscellaneous receipts	66	81	70	105	105	97	97	1,050
Total receipts	1,446	1,431	1,675	1,740	1,785	2,152	2,302	20,355
Total cash available	1,821	1,827	1,897	1,890	2,042	2,312	2,494	20,730
Less: Cash disbursements:								
Operating expenses	810	915	1,035	885	975	1,020	960	10,730
Raw materials purchases	503	570	1,050	600	607	555	345	7,140
Taxes		60	412	13		395	3	1,310
Equipment purchases					100			100
Dividends	112			135			135	517
Pension contribution		210						247
Total disbursements	1,425	1,755	2,497	1,633	1,682	1,970	1,443	20,044
Cash balance or (deficiency) end of month before bank loans or (repayments)	396	72	(600)	257	360	342	1,051	686
Bank loans or (repayments)		150	750		(200)	(150)	(450)	0
Cash Balance End of Month	396	222	150	257	160	192	601	686

Other *operating expenses* are often taken directly from the expense budget, since the timing of cash disbursements is likely to correspond closely to the incurrence of the expense. Depreciation and other noncash expenses are excluded from this item.

The bottom of the cash forecast in Illustration 16–2 shows how cash plans are made. In February, for example, cash on hand would drop to $72,000, which is considered to be too low for safety; so the company plans to borrow $150,000 to provide a better safety margin. It plans to borrow $750,000 more in March and to start repaying these bank loans in May, when cash receipts exceed cash disbursements.

A monthly cash forecast, as in Illustration 16–2, is especially useful in planning for short-term, seasonal needs of cash. In order to estimate needs for more permanent capital, such as that obtained from the issuance of stock or bonds, the same general procedure would be followed, but with longer time intervals.

It should be noted that the figures in Illustration 16–2 are rounded. This procedure is customary in budgets. The amounts could be shown to the last penny, but the users of the report do not need such precise estimates. Furthermore, such figures tend to give a spurious impression of accuracy. Two or three significant digits are usually adequate.

THE CAPITAL BUDGET

The capital budget is essentially a list of what management believes to be worthwhile projects for the acquisition of new capital assets together with the estimated cost of each project. Proposals for such projects may originate anywhere in the organization. The capital budget is usually prepared separately from the operating budget, and in many companies it is prepared at a different time and cleared through a capital appropriations committee that is separate from the budget committee.

Each proposal, except those for minor amounts, is accompanied by a justification. For some projects, the expected return on investment can be estimated by methods to be described in Chapter 19. For others, such as the construction of a new office building or remodeling of employee recreation rooms, no estimate of return is possible, and these are justified on the basis of improved morale, safety, appearance, convenience, or other subjective grounds. A lump sum usually is included in the capital budget for projects that are not large enough to warrant individual consideration by top management.

In the capital budget, projects are often classified under headings such as the following:

1. Cost reduction and replacement.
2. Expansion of existing product lines.

3. New products.
4. Health and safety.
5. Other.

The first three categories usually are susceptible to an economic analysis in which the return on investment can be estimated.

As proposals come up through the organization, they are screened at various levels, and only the sufficiently attractive ones flow up to the top and appear in the final capital budget. On this document, they are often arranged in what is believed to be the order of desirability, and the estimated expenditures are broken down by years, or by quarters, so that the funds required in each time period are shown. At the final review meeting, which is usually at the board-of-director level, not only are the individual projects discussed but also the total amount requested on the budget is compared with total funds available. Many apparently worthwhile projects may not be approved, simply because the funds are not available.

Approval of the capital budget usually means approval of the projects *in principle*, but does not constitute final authority to proceed with them. For this authority, a specific authorization request is prepared for the project, spelling out the proposal in more detail, perhaps with firm bids or price quotations on the new assets. These authorization requests are approved at various levels in the organization, depending on their size and character. For example, each foreman may be authorized to buy production tools or similar items costing not more than $100 each, provided the total for the year does not exceed $1,000; and at the other extreme, all projects costing more than $500,000 and all projects for new products, whatever their cost, may require approval of the board of directors. In between, there is a scale of amounts that various echelons in the organization may authorize without the approval of their superiors.

An increasing number of companies are instituting procedures to follow up on capital expenditures. These include both checks on the spending itself and also an appraisal, perhaps a year or more after the project is completed, as to how well the estimates of cost and earnings actually turned out.

SUMMARY

Budgets are used as a device for making and coordinating plans, for communicating these plans to those who are responsible for carrying them out, for motivating managers at all levels, and as a standard with which actual performance subsequently can be compared. In a fully developed budget system, there is a package of interrelated budgets, including the program operating budget, the responsibility operating budget (and its subcategory, the variable budget), the cash budget, and the capital budget.

The operating budget is prepared within the context of basic policies and plans that have already been decided upon. The principal steps are as follows: (1) the dissemination of guidelines stating the overall plans and policies and other assumptions and constraints that are to be observed in the preparation of budget estimates; (2) the preparation of a sales estimate; (3) the preparation of other estimates by the heads of responsibility centers, assisted by, but not dominated by, staff budget men and accountants; (4) the negotiation of an agreed budget between the budgetee and his superior, which gives rise to a bilateral commitment by these parties; (5) coordination and review as these initial estimates move up the organizational chain of command; and (6) approval by top management and dissemination of the approved budget back down through the organization.

The *cash budget* translates revenues and expenses into receipts and disbursements and thus facilitates financial planning.

The *capital budget* is a priced list of presumably worthwhile projects for the acquisition of new capital assets. Often it is prepared separately from the operating budget. Approval of the capital budget constitutes only approval in principle, and a subsequent specific authorization is usually required before work on the project can begin.

SUGGESTIONS FOR FURTHER READING

CHAMBERLAIN, NEIL W. *The Firm: Micro-Economic Planning and Action.* New York: McGraw-Hill Book Co., Inc., 1962.

HEISER, HERMAN C. *Budgeting, Principles and Practices.* New York: Ronald Press Co., 1959.

HOFSTEDE, D. H. *The Game of Budget Control.* Assen, The Netherlands: Van Gorcum & Co., N.V., 1967.

STEINER, GEORGE A. (ed). *Top Management Planning.* New York: The Macmillan Co., 1969.

WELSCH, GLENN A. *Budgeting: Profit Planning and Control.* 2d ed.; New York: Prentice-Hall, Inc., 1963.

CASES

CASE 16–1. SANTA INEZ POULTRY COMPANY

In 1948, George Russo, a recent graduate of the state agricultural college, took over the management of his father's small poultry hatchery. Up to that time, the hatchery had been merely one of his father's many, not very successful, agricultural operations. Through the combination of good management and a booming market for poultry, George Russo had developed the hatchery into the largest of its kind in the region.

In 1954, George decided to expand his operations by entering into the production of broilers for his own account. This expansion proved very successful. By 1960, however, southern producers with lower labor costs and a better climate had reduced prices to the point where an independent grower was merely an adjunct to a feed mill which could offset profits from the highly volatile poultry market with profits from feed sales.

As a result, in 1960, the Santa Inez Poultry Company constructed a 40,000-ton feed mill. In order to utilize fully the output of this mill, chick and broiler production was further expanded. By 1967, annual broiler production had risen to 8 million birds which required about 90 percent of the output from the feed mill.

Several facts had convinced Mr. Russo in 1966 that his feed production was not adequate. The original mill had been poorly located with regard to receipt of shipments of grains, and he estimated that if he constructed a new mill on a railroad siding, he could save $5 a ton in handling and freight alone. Further, since the currently low prices of broilers had practically wiped out the profits in broiler production, his only chance of maintaining his present profit level was to produce and sell more feed. He decided to build another feed mill, using the best technological developments, with an 80,000-ton capacity on a site contiguous to the railroad. He decided that rather than continue operation of the old feed mill when the new mill went into production, he would scrap it, even though it was not fully depreciated.[4]

---

[4] Scrapping the mill would give the company an $80,000 tax write-off in 1968 over and above depreciation on the mill for the full year.

Exhibit 1

SANTA INEZ POULTRY COMPANY

Balance Sheets, December 31

(in thousands of dollars)

	1967		1966		*Net Increase*
ASSETS					
Cash............................		$ 438		$ 394	$ 44
Accounts receivable..............		261		250	11
Inventories:					
Own broilers..................	$ 427		$379		
Other.......................	75		10		
Total Inventories............		502		389	113
Prepaid items...................		7		9	(2)
Total Current Assets.........		$1,208		$1,042	$166
Mortgages......................		84		50	34
Note receivable (unsecured).......		32		28	4
Land and improvements...........	$ 179		$ 17		$162
Machinery and equipment.........	363		304		59
Buildings......................	166		186		(20)
Construction in progress*........	379		0		379
	$1,087		$507		$580
Less: Depreciation.............	247		202		45
Total Net Fixed Assets.......		840		305	535
Reserve fund for construction.....		0		200	(200)
Total Assets..............		$2,164		$1,625	$539
LIABILITIES					
Notes payable bank..............		$ 292		$ 165	$127
Accounts payable...............		158		216	(58)
Accrued liabilities...............		150		62	88
Accrued taxes..................		250		179	71
Total Current Liabilities......		$ 850		$ 622	$228
Capital stock and surplus:					
Stock.......................	$ 600		$500		$100
Retained earnings.............	714		503		211
Total Equity		$1,314		$1,003	
Total Liabilities..........		$2,164		$1,625	$539

* New feed mill.
( ) = decrease.

In early 1968, the company had already paid out $379,000 for the new mill plus $40,000 for additional farm land.[5] (See Exhibit 1.) It was estimated that an additional $75,000 would be required to finish the feed mill and put it in production. Considering that the new mill would permit slightly more than double his present broiler production of 8 million

[5] The remaining new investment in land was for farm land owned by Russo's father.

Exhibit 2

SANTA INEZ POULTRY COMPANY

Income Statements
(in thousands of dollars)

	1967		*1966*	
Net sales:				
Broilers............................	$4,983		$4,768	
Feed..............................	302		260	
Supplies...........................	177		122	
Chicks............................	318		375	
Other.............................	18		23	
Total sales.......................		$5,798*		$5,548
Cost of goods sold:				
Materials..........................	$3,916		$3,998	
Operating expense†.................	1,305		1,042	
Total............................		5,221		5,040
Gross income......................		$ 577		$ 508
Operating ratio....................		90%		91%
Selling, general, and administrative expense....		179		174
Income before taxes...............		$ 398		$ 334
State and federal taxes............		187		154
Net Income.......................		$ 211‡		$ 180

* $4,159,000 of own feed, chicks, and other supplies used in broiler operations. These cancel out through broiler sales on own account. Figures not available for 1966.

† Operating expense includes annual depreciation charge of $65,000. Straight-line method on all depreciable assets. The average life was 10 years.

‡ The breakdown of profit from the divisions of the company shows that 73 percent of profit was contributed by the feed mill and 18 percent by the hatchery. Broiler production and other sales contributed the remainder.

birds, hatchery production would have to increase to keep pace. Mr. Russo thought that eight new incubators at $9,000 each plus a new hatchery building costing $50,000 would be adequate to handle this additional production. These additional facilities could be in operation by the end of June.

The problems that Mr. Russo had to decide in early 1968 were how much money he needed and how he should raise this money. Of course, his financial needs were dependent upon what additional level of broiler production he attained and how fully he utilized his new feed mill. Mr. Russo thought that he might be able to reach full capacity, or a rate of 16,000,000 birds per year, by the end of 1968. He believed that he could sell the additional production to several buyers if he would agree to a long-term contract at prevailing low prices.

In addition to his financial problems, Mr. Russo was bothered by the fact that the size of his organization was growing beyond his ability to control it directly. In 1967, he had over 150 employees. He had as executives under him an executive vice president, a feed mill superintendent, a hatchery superintendent, a sales manager, a supervisor of field service men, and an office manager–controller. He was looking for a young man trained in animal husbandry with financial or business experience who could act as his executive assistant. He was willing to offer a salary of $10,000 to the right man, but found that he could not get any takers at this price. He himself drew $35,000 a year as salary, and his father, as chairman of the board, drew $20,000 but did not contribute to the management of the business. Other Santa Inez executives were drawing from $12,000 to $16,000 a year, and Mr. Russo feared that if he brought a new man in at a salary of $12,000 or over, the other executives who had worked up in the company would resent the new man.

Questions

1. Prepare a statement showing how much the company will need to finance increased production at an annual rate of 16,000,000 birds by the end of 1968.
2. What do you recommend as a means of improving the management of the enlarged company?

CASE 16–2.   REED PAINT COMPANY

C. H. Macrae had recently been elected president of the Reed Paint Company to fill the vacancy created by the retirement from active business life of the former chief executive. Mr. Macrae had been with the company for 15 years, and for the preceding 6 years he had been vice president in charge of manufacturing. Shortly after taking over his new position, Mr. Macrae held a series of conferences with the controller in which the general subject under discussion was budgetary control technique. The new president thought that the existing method of planning and checking on selling costs was particularly unsatisfactory, and he asked the controller to devise a system that would provide better control over these costs.

The Reed Paint Company manufactured a complete line of paints that its branch office salesmen sold to wholesalers, retailers, builders, and industrial users. Most of the products carried the Reed brand name, which was nationally advertised. The company was one of the largest in the industry.

Current Budgeting Procedure

Under the procedure then being used, selling expenses were budgeted on a "fixed" or "appropriation" basis. Each October the accounting department sent to branch managers and to the other executives in charge of selling departments a detailed record of the actual expenses of their departments for the preceding year and for the current year to date. Guided by this record, by estimates of the succeeding year's sales, and by his own judgment, each department head drew up and submitted an estimate of the expenses of his department for the succeeding year, detailed as to main items of expense. The estimates made by the branch managers were sent to the sales manager, who was in charge of all branch sales. He determined whether or not they were reasonable, and cleared up any questionable items by correspondence. Upon approval by the sales manager, the estimates of branch expenses were submitted to the manager of distribution, Mr. Campbell, who was in charge of all selling, promotional, and warehousing activities.

The manager of distribution discussed these figures and the expense estimates furnished by the other department heads with the executives concerned, and after differences were reconciled, he combined the estimates of all the selling departments into a selling expense budget. This budget was submitted to the budget committee for final approval. For control purposes, the annual budget was divided into 12 equal amounts, and actual expenses were compared each month with the budgeted figures. Exhibit 1 shows the form in which these monthly comparisons were made.

Mr. Macrae believed that there were two important weaknesses in this method of setting the selling expense budget:

1. It was impossible for anyone to ascertain with any feeling of certainty the reasonableness of the estimates made by the various department heads. Clearly, the expenses of the preceding year did not constitute adequate standards against which these expense estimates could be judged, since selling conditions were never the same in any two years. One obvious cause of variation in selling expenses was the variation in the "job to be done," as defined in the sales budget.

2. Selling conditions often changed substantially after the budget was adopted, but there was no provision for making the proper corresponding changes in the selling expense budget. Neither was there a logical basis for relating selling expenses to the actual sales volume obtained or to any other measure of sales effort. The chief executive believed that it was reasonable to expect that sales expenses would increase, though not proportionately, if actual sales volume were greater than the forecast volume, but that with the existing method of control it was impossible to determine how large the increase in expenses should be.

Proposed Procedure

As a means of overcoming these weaknesses the president suggested setting standards for the selling cost budget on a fixed and variable basis, a method similar to the techniques used in the control of manufacturing

Exhibit 1

BUDGET REPORT CURRENTLY USED

BRANCH SALES AND EXPENSE PERFORMANCE					
DATE: October		BRANCH A		Mgr: H. C. Obermeyer	
	This Month				*Over*—Under Year to Date*
	Budget†	*Actual*	*Over* Under*	*Per-centage of Sales*	
Net sales	190,000	160,000			
Executive salaries	2,000	2,000	. . . .	1.25	. . . .
Office salaries	1,150	1,134	16	0.71	1,203
Salesman's compensation	11,400	9,600	1,800	6.00	2,802*
Traveling expense	3,420	3,127	293	1.95	1,012*
Stationery, office supplies, and expense	1,042	890	152	0.56	360
Postage	230	262	32*	0.16	21
Light and heat	134	87	47	0.05	128
Subscriptions and dues	150	112	38	0.07	26
Donations	125	. . . .	125	0.00	130
Advertising expense (local)	1,900	1,800	100	1.12	1,200*
Social security taxes	291	205	86	0.13	27*
Rental	975	975	. . . .	0.61	. . . .
Depreciation	762	762	. . . .	0.48	. . . .
Other branch expense	2,551	2,426	125	1.52	247*
TOTAL	26,130	23,380	2,750	14.61	3,420*
† $\frac{1}{12}$ of annual budget.					

costs. The controller agreed that this approach seemed to offer the most feasible solution to the problem, and he therefore undertook, with the cooperation of the sales department, a study of selling expenses for the purpose of devising a method of setting reasonable standards. In recent years, the accounting department had made many analyses of selling costs, the results of which had been used to determine the proper bases for allocating costs to products, customers, functions, and territories. These studies also were used in the solution of certain special problems, such as that of determining how large an individual order must be to yield a profit for the company. Many of the data that had been accumulated for these purposes were helpful in the controller's current study.

The controller was convinced that the fixed portion of selling expenses —in other words, the portion that was independent of any fluctuation in volume—could be established by determining the amount of expenses that had to be incurred at the minimum sales volume at which the company was likely to operate. He therefore asked Mr. Campbell to suggest a minimum volume figure and the amount of expenses which would have to be incurred at this volume. A staff assistant was assigned the task of studying the past sales records of the company over several business cycles, the long-term outlook for sales, and sales trends in other companies in the industry. From the report prepared by his assistant, Mr. Campbell concluded that sales volume would not drop below 45 percent of the current capacity of the factory.

Mr. Campbell then attempted to determine the selling expenses that would be incurred at the minimum volume. With the help of his staff assistant, he worked out a hypothetical selling organization that in his opinion would be required to sell merchandise equivalent to 45 percent of factory capacity, complete as to the number of persons needed to staff each branch office and the other selling departments, including the advertising, merchandise, and sales administration departments. Using current salary and commission figures, the assistant calculated the amount of money that would be required to pay salaries for such an organization. The manager of distribution also estimated the other expenses, such as advertising, branch office upkeep, supplies, and travel, that he thought would be incurred by each branch and staff department at the minimum sales volume.

The controller decided that the variable portion of the selling expense standard should be expressed as a certain amount per sales dollar. He realized that the use of the sales dollar as a measuring stick had certain disadvantages in that it would not reflect such important influences on costs as the size of the order, the selling difficulty of certain territories, changes in buyer psychology, etc. The sales dollar, however, was the measuring stick most convenient to use, the only figure readily available from the records then being kept, and also a figure that all the individuals concerned thoroughly understood. The controller believed that a budget that varied with sales would certainly be better than one that did not vary at all. He planned to devise a more accurate measure of causes of variation in selling expenses after he had had an opportunity to study the nature of these factors over a longer period.

As a basis for setting the initial variable expense standards, the controller prepared a series of charts on which the actual annual expenditures for the principal groups of expense items for several preceding years were correlated with sales volume for the year. Using these charts, which showed to what extent the principal expense items had fluctuated with sales volume in the past, and modifying them in accordance with his own judgment, the controller determined a rate of variation for the variable portion of each item of selling expense. The controller thought that after the new system had been tested in practice, it would be possible to refine these rates, perhaps by the use of a technique analogous to the time-study technique employed to determine certain expense standards in the factory.

At this point the controller had both a rate of variation and one point (i.e., at 45 percent capacity) on the selling expense curve for each expense item. He was therefore able to construct a formula for each item by extending a line through the known point at the slope represented by the rate of variation. He determined the height of this line at zero volume and called this amount the fixed portion of the selling expense formula. The diagram in Exhibit 2 illustrates the procedure, although the actual computations were mathematical rather than graphic.

The selling expense budget for the following year was determined by adding to the new standards for the various fixed components the indicated flexible allowances for the year's estimated sales volume. This budget was submitted to the budget committee, which studied the fixed amounts and the variable rates underlying the final figures, making only minor changes before final approval.

The controller planned to issue reports each month showing for each department actual expenses compared with budgeted expenses. The variable portion of the budgeted allowances would be adjusted to correspond to the actual volume of sales obtained during the month. Exhibit 3 shows the budget report that he planned to send to branch managers, with figures for the same month as those in Exhibit 1.

One sales executive privately belittled the controller's proposal. "Anyone in the selling game," he asserted, "knows that sometimes customers

Exhibit 2

BUDGET FOR "OTHER BRANCH EXPENSE," BRANCH A

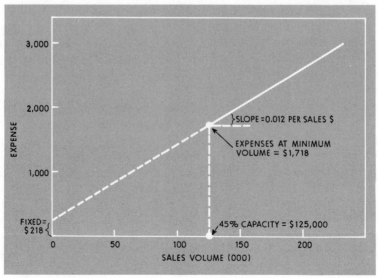

Exhibit 3

BUDGET REPORT PROPOSED BY CONTROLLER

			EXPENSE BUDGET REPORT		BRANCH: A MANAGER: H. C. Obermeyer DATE: October		

	Budget Factors		This Month			Year to Date
	Fixed	Variable	Budget	Actual	Over* Under	Over* Under
Net sales				160,000		†
Executive salaries	2,000	. . . . .	2,000	2,000	. . .	
Office salaries	110	0.0051	926	1,134	208*	
Salesman's compensation	. . . .	0.0600	9,600	9,600	. . .	
Traveling expense	568	0.0142	2,840	3,127	287*	
Stationery, office supplies, and expense	282	0.0042	954	890	64	
Postage	47	0.0010	207	262	55*	
Light and heat	134	. . . . .	134	87	47	
Subscriptions and dues	10	0.0008	138	112	26	
Donations	20	0.0005	100	. . . .	100	
Advertising expense (local)	150	0.0100	1,750	1,800	50*	
Social security taxes	42	0.0013	250	205	45	
Rental	975	. . . . .	975	975	. . .	
Depreciation	762	. . . . .	762	762	. . .	
Other branch expense	218	0.0120	2,138	2,426	288*	
TOTAL	5,318	0.1091	22,774	23,380	606*	

† The controller had not recalculated budgets for previous months, and figures were therefore not available for this column.

fall all over each other in their hurry to buy, and other times, no matter what we do, they won't even nibble. It's a waste of time to make fancy formulas for selling cost budgets under conditions like that."

Questions

1. From the information given in Exhibits 1 and 3, determine, insofar as you can, whether each item of expense is (a) nonvariable, (b) partly variable with sales volume, (c) variable with sales volume, or (d) variable with some other factor.
2. What bearing do your conclusions in Question 1 have on the type of budget that is most appropriate?
3. Should the proposed sales expense budget be adopted?
4. If a variable budget is used, should dollar sales be used as the measure of variation?

CASE 16–3. THOMPSON METAL WORKS COMPANY

Thompson Metal Works Company was founded in 1947 by Mr. Lee Thompson to fabricate and sell tin and aluminum products. Among the items made and sold by the company were duct work for home and industrial heating and air conditioning, ventilation louvers for various types of buildings, and paneling for any need whatever. In addition the company followed the practice of taking orders for any special items a customer requested, provided the company was capable of filling the order. Most work was done on a job-lot basis, and inventories of finished goods were practically nil.

The company showed a rapid and steady growth and, until 1959, was very profitable. From 1959 to 1961 profits declined, and in 1962 there was a small operating loss, even though the volume of business in each of these years showed a slight increase. Mr. Thompson felt certain that this trend was caused by higher priced materials and wage increases, while at the same time the selling prices of most products, because of increasing competition, had gone up very little or, in some instances, not at all over the past several years. By 1962 sales amounted to some $750,000 annually.

At the end of 1962 the company had 6 employees in sales; 30 employees in the fabrication department; and two installation crews, each consisting of an in-charge man and two helpers. Because of the diversity of jobs undertaken, the investment in tools and equipment had become quite sizable. Mr. Thompson, after talking the situation over with his key employees, decided that the problem was poor cost control. He hired Mr. Bruce Keys, CPA, as controller and office manager, and it was agreed a budgetary system was needed. Mr. Keys went to work on the problem and by the end of 1963 had installed a profit planning and reporting system.

With the aid of Mr. Keys, Jake Brown, shop foreman, was able to cut out some waste in the shop. The men were given written assignments and schedules, and the work stations of the shop were rearranged to provide for a better flow of goods through the processes. In addition, punctuality rules were strictly enforced and coffee breaks or rest periods were permitted only at scheduled times. By the end of 1964 some improvement in cost control was evident and the company was out of the red, but Mr. Thompson felt the results should be better and decided to get his key employees together and see if anything more could be done to improve the profits of the company. A summary of the meeting follows:

Mr. THOMPSON (president): Gentlemen, as you know I have been concerned about the low profit margin the company has shown over the past few years. I am not blaming you for the unfavorable profit margins, but it is certain we are going to have to work together in order to remedy the situation or possibly go out of business before too long. Jake, since you are in charge of the shop, what do you think we could do to further lower our costs?

JAKE BROWN (shop foreman): Well, as far as I'm concerned the real problem is that we make too many different products and in too small quantities. I believe Mr. Keys will agree that this is a costly way to manufacture anything. We lose entirely too much time in setting up for the various jobs, and also we usually have a lot of idle equipment since some of the equipment is required only for special jobs or for a small amount of time.

TIM WILDE (commercial and industrial salesman): I can certainly appreciate Jake's situation, but the salesmen have got to make sales when they can or there won't be any business. You all know that this is a competitive market and individual jobs call for small quantities. Mr. Keys will agree that we've got to make sales. I know our actual sales don't necessarily agree with our forecast, especially by types of products, but I'm sure all will agree that we face a peculiar situation. We have discussed this with Mr. Keys and he understands our problem and, I believe, is convinced we are doing our best to meet our quotas.

BRUCE KEYS (controller): I think we have hit on some important problems here. I'm not sure of how to solve them. One way sometimes available to a company is to manufacture for inventory. However, in our case I feel this is out because most of our work is of a custom nature. Do you installation men have any comments?

KEITH ALLEN (installation crew supervisor): We review each job with Mr. Keys prior to doing it and he approves our estimates of installation costs. So far, we've been doing the work within these approved budgets. I don't know what else we could do.

MR. THOMPSON: Gentlemen, I believe I have discovered our primary problem. Right now the salesmen are estimating sales; Brown is estimating and planning the shop work; and the installation men plan their work. Each of you has indicated that Mr. Keys helps you considerably in your planning. Since Mr. Keys is so familiar with all aspects of the business and understands the problems completely, it appears to me that he should be responsible for all forecasting and planning. This would give us better coordination and, after all, what's a budget director for if he doesn't provide a budget from which the rest of us can get our quotas and work schedules?

Questions

1. If you were Mr. Keys, what would be your reply to Mr. Thompson's last comment?
2. What impression do you get as to the adequacy of the budgetary system installed by Mr. Keys?
3. Do you feel that the company might need to change some of its operating policies? If so, in what way and why?
4. Is there a possibility that this company is too small, or that production is too unstable, to require a formal system of profit planning and control? Explain.

CHAPTER 17

THE ANALYSIS
OF PERFORMANCE

This chapter describes some of the concepts and techniques that are useful in analyzing the performance of a responsibility center. Essentially, such an analysis involves comparing actual performance with what performance should have been under the circumstances prevailing, in such a way that reasons for the difference between actual and expected performance are identified, and, if feasible, quantified.

The appraisal of performance involves a paradox. A man's performance can be measured only *after* he has performed; but at that time the work has already been done, and nothing management does later can change what was done. Of what value, therefore, are techniques for judging performance?

There seem to be two valid answers to this question. First, if a person knows in advance that his performance is going to be judged, he tends to act differently from the way he will if he believes no one is going to check up on him. (Anyone who has received grades in school should appreciate the importance of this point.)

The second reason why the appraisal of performance is valuable is that even though it is literally impossible to change an event that has already happened, an analysis of how well a person has performed in the past may indicate, both to the person and to his superior, ways of obtaining better performance in the future. Corrective action taken by the person himself is of prime importance; the system should "help the man to help himself." Action by the superior is also necessary. Such action may range in severity from giving criticism or praise or suggesting specific means of improving future performance, to the extremes either of firing or of promoting the person.

STRUCTURE OF ANALYSIS

Inputs and Outputs

For the purpose of this analysis, it is useful to visualize the work of a responsibility center as in Illustration 17–1. The responsibility center uses resources, which are its *inputs*. These resources can be classified as material, labor, and services, and their consumption is measured in terms of cost. In the operation of the responsibility center, these resources are used to produce *outputs*. These outputs are supposed to help achieve the objectives of the organization of which the responsibility center is a part. Information on outputs can be divided into: (1) quantity, that is, how much was done, and (2) quality, that is, how well it was done. For a customer invoicing unit, for example, the *quantity* of output may be measured by the number of invoices processed, and the *quality* of output

Illustration 17–1

WORK OF A RESPONSIBILITY CENTER

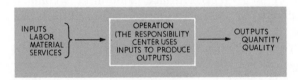

by the percentage of invoices that have no errors. Usually, it is easier to measure quantity than to measure quality; for example, it is easier to count the number of invoices processed than to detect and count those that contain errors.

As described in Chapter 13, performance can be measured along two dimensions: (1) *effectiveness*, which is how well the responsibility center does its job, and which is therefore related to its outputs; and (2) *efficiency*, which is the ratio of outputs to inputs.

This structure suggests that three key questions need to be considered: (1) How much was accomplished? (2) How well was the work done? and (3) How much did it cost? In some situations, the analysis can be simplified by answering the second question on a "go, no go" basis; that is, quality was either satisfactory or it was not satisfactory. When this simplification is feasible, the analysis is reduced to a problem of comparing quantity of output with costs.

In still other situations, the analysis can be limited to only one of these questions. For example, if the manager of a production department has no control over the volume of production and if the quality of work is indicated by the amount of rework costs, his performance may be judged primarily on the basis of cost alone.

In the typical situation, however, all three questions need to be considered together, and mistakes are made when one facet of performance is given undue emphasis as compared with the others. For example, until recently the Soviet management control system emphasized the quantity of output, with substantial bonuses being paid to managers for exceeding volume quotas. This emphasis on volume led to inadequate attention being paid to quality and cost, and the system was consequently redesigned to give a more balanced emphasis to these factors.

The Search for a Standard

As described in Chapter 11, the task of analyzing performance is, essentially, to compare what a person *actually did* with what he *should have done* under the circumstances. In many cases, actual performance can be ascertained without difficulty. The trick is to find a *standard*, or basis of comparison, that states what performance should have been under the conditions existing at the time.

The task of judging performance in business is complicated because results are affected by a complex set of factors, and the net influence of all these factors is never identical at two different times or on two different jobs done at the same time. A man who runs the mile in 4:04 minutes has done an excellent job, but what can we say about a foreman who spent $404 on supplies? First of all, we are not even sure of the *direction* that represents good performance. Offhand, one might conclude that spending $404 is "better" than spending $504, but there are many situations in which such a conclusion would be incorrect. If the foreman had spent another $100, for example, the department might have been able to turn out a much larger quantity of products, or the quality of the products might have been better, or safety conditions might have been improved, or other results worth more than $100 might have been achieved. Secondly, the actual spending of $404 may have been occasioned by any of a large number of factors over which the foreman has no control—company policies, an accident, orders from a superior, and a long list of others. Unless we recognize these factors and measure their impact, we cannot obtain a good measurement of the phenomenon we are trying to measure: the performance of the foreman himself.

Despite these difficulties, judgments about performance must be made, and some kind of standard, imperfect though it may be, is used as a guide in making such judgments. The four possible types of standards have been described in Chapter 11 in connection with the specific problem of analyzing financial statements, and are repeated in more general terms below. They can be used either separately or jointly.

1. STANDARDS BASED ON EXPERIENCE.   Although the techniques to be described in this chapter will generally focus on formal standards expressed in quantitative terms, the importance of intuitive, informal standards derived from a person's experience and expressing his feel for what is "right" in a given situation should not be minimized. Such standards may well be more valid than those derived from any of the other sources listed below, and they are not described more fully here simply because of the difficulty of fitting them into the context of a formal framework.

2. PREDETERMINED STANDARDS OR BUDGETS.   These are statements of expected performance under an assumed set of circumstances. Although actual events will never exactly match the assumed conditions, the standard may nevertheless be an adequate approximation to what should have been done.

3. PERFORMANCE OF OTHERS IN COMPARABLE JOBS.   Department A may be compared with Department B, and if conditions in the two departments are reasonably similar, the comparison may provide a useful basis for judging performance.

4. PERFORMANCE IN THE PAST.   Results this month may be compared with results last month, or with results in the same month a year ago. In addition to the need to allow for circumstances that may have changed between the two periods, this comparison has the weakness that when a man is measured against his own record, there may be no way of knowing whether the prior period's performance was acceptable to start with. A foreman whose spoilage cost is $100 a week, week after week, is consistent, but we do not know, without other evidence, whether he is consistently good or consistently poor.

DIFFICULTIES IN PERFORMANCE MEASUREMENT

It is unfortunately true that the more relevant a piece of information is, the more difficult it is to measure. An estimate of future performance is more difficult to make than a record of past performance, but it is more useful. A timely report, that is, one furnished shortly after the events reported on, is more difficult to compile than a report submitted long after the period has ended, but it is more useful. A measurement requiring judgment is more useful than one obtained by reading meters or other objective information, but it is more difficult. Thus, in designing a performance measurement system, a balance must be drawn between what management would like to have and what it is feasible to furnish.

Difficulty in Measuring Outputs

In a responsibility center that produces a physical product, the quantity of output can often be measured in physical terms: so many pairs of shoes, hundredweights of cement, and so on. When the outputs are so heterogeneous that they cannot be summarized by any physical measure, as in a job shop making many different types of products, output can be expressed by a monetary measure, such as the total standard cost of all products produced. In a profit center, the revenue of the center is a measure of its output.

For a great many responsibility centers, however, there is no reliable way of expressing the quantity of output, much less the quality of output, by any numerical measure. This is the case with most staff departments of a company, such as the research and development department, the personnel department, the controller department, the treasurer's office, and the general administrative offices. It is also the case generally with nonprofit organizations, that is, organizations whose objective is to perform some service rather than to earn a profit. Such organizations include government bodies of all types, schools, hospitals, foundations, churches, and social welfare organizations.

If output cannot be measured, there is obviously no way of making a formal appraisal of effectiveness or of comparing outputs with inputs, and the formal analysis must be restricted to an analysis of inputs, i.e., costs. Such an analysis is often better than not attempting any analysis at all, but its validity is necessarily narrower than the analysis that can be made of a responsibility center for which there is a reliable measure of outputs. When the analysis is thus restricted to imputs, there is a temptation to overlook or minimize the importance of the elements that have not been reduced to numbers. Every responsibility center has outputs, even though they cannot be measured, and performance appraisal must always take appropriate account of the effectiveness of these outputs, even if this has to be done in an entirely subjective manner.

It should also be recognized that most measures of output do not encompass all the outputs of a responsibility center. Even in the case of a production department, its total output—its contribution to the objectives of the company of which it is a part—is only partially measured by the quantity and quality of the products it produces, for its outputs may also include training personnel for advancement, employee morale, contribution to the community, and other elements that are either unmeasurable or at best measurable as rough approximations.

Conversely, in responsibility centers for which there is no overall measure of the dominant element of output, there may be ways of measuring certain aspects of output. The number of patient days is a crude measure of output for a hospital, even though it takes no account of the quality of service rendered or of the variations in the complexity of care required for different patients. Such a crude measure is often useful, provided its limitations are recognized.

Long-Run versus Current Performance

Management control systems tend to measure current performance, rather than long-run performance; that is, they measure the profit earned this year, rather than the effect on future profits of actions taken this year.

> EXAMPLE: The manager of a profit center can improve his current profits by reducing the amounts spent on research and development, advertising, training, or maintenance. Any of these actions may have an adverse effect on future profits. Since the company's goal is presumably to earn satisfactory profits over the long run, such actions may be dysfunctional. Reports of current profits may therefore be misleading.

It is important that this limitation of the management control system be kept in mind both in analyzing performance and in deciding on the amount of emphasis that should be given to current performance measures. If too much emphasis is given to current performance, as may happen when there is a sizable bonus based on current profits, managers may take actions that are detrimental in the long run in order to make current performance look good.

The Special Problem of Investment Centers

Investment centers (i.e. centers in which both profit and investment are measured) pose a special problem that is not present in profit centers or expense centers. This is the problem of measuring the assets employed. The problem relates to all assets, but it is most difficult with respect to depreciable assets, such as buildings and equipment. For reasons that are given elsewhere,[1] the most conceptually sound basis of measurement seems to be that based on the annuity method of depreciation although this method is rarely used in practice.

PERFORMANCE REPORTS

Control reports vary widely in format, and only a few general comments are in order. They should be *objective;* that is, they should report what actually happened without bias. They should be *timely;* if they are to be the basis of action, they must be received before the time for effective action has passed. They should be *clear and easily understood,*

---

[1] "Accounting for Capital Costs" in *Management Control Systems: Cases and Readings,* by Anthony, Dearden, and Vancil (Homewood, Ill.: Richard D. Irwin, Inc., 1965), p. 343. See also articles by John Dearden in the *Harvard Business Review* of May–June, 1960, May–June, 1961, and July–August, 1962.

although clarity should not be achieved by oversimplifying an inherently complicated situation. They should indicate, if possible, the *reasons why*, not only the facts about performance itself.

Control reports, in the literal sense, are intended as a basis for action. Copies of the same reports together with other data on performance may be used for *information*, even though the person receiving them is not expected to take action.

The Time Interval of Control

The proper control period is the shortest period of time in which management can usefully intervene and in which significant changes in performance are likely. The period is different for different responsibility centers and for different items within responsibility centers. Spoilage rates in a production operation may be measured hourly, or oftener. Other key cost elements of the center may be measured daily. Reports on overall performance, particularly those going to top levels of management, are often on a monthly basis, and sometimes for quarterly or longer intervals, since top management does not have either the time or the inclination to explore local, temporary problems.

Performance for a short period of time is influenced by random factors that tend to average out over longer periods; a system with a short time interval costs more to operate and consumes more time of the participants at all levels than a system with longer intervals; and frequent reports may be associated with unduly restrictive supervision. These considerations may be offset, of course, by the necessity for detecting serious trouble quickly: a change in the behavior of a continuous chemical processing operation must be known as soon as it occurs, or there may be an explosion.

Content of Reports

Costs should be collected and measured only to the extent that they are *significant*. Reporting a long list of cost elements, many of which have only minor amounts, tends to obscure the few really significant ones. This can happen when the report is a standard form containing a long list of cost items that are reported uniformly for each responsibility center. Preferably, the control system is tailor-made to the situation in each responsibility center, having in mind also the probable uses of the information for purposes other than control.

The significance of an item is not necessarily proportional to its size. Management may be interested in a cost item of relatively small amount if this cost is one which is largely discretionary and therefore warrants close attention (such as travel expense, professional dues, books and periodicals), or if costs incurred for the item may be symptomatic of a larger problem (such as spoilage and rework costs, which may indicate problems of quality control.)

Management by Exception

A management control system operated on the exception principle is one in which management's attention is focused on the relatively small number of items in which actual performance is significantly different from the standard; when this is done, little or no attention need be given to the relatively large number of situations where performance is satisfactory.

No control system makes a perfect distinction between the situations that warrant management attention and those that do not. For example, it is the usual practice to "red flag" those items for which actual spending significantly *exceeds* the budgeted amount, but an investigation of these items may reveal that a difference between actual and budgeted spending was entirely warranted. On the other hand, even though actual spending for an item exactly matches the budget allowance, an unsatisfactory situation may exist. The exception principle is thus tricky to apply in practice. It is nevertheless a useful starting point for indicating the significance of what would otherwise be a bewildering mass of data, provided that the need for some examination of the superficially unexceptional situations is not overlooked. Conforming precisely to the budget is not necessarily good, and departing from the budget is not necessarily bad.

The distinction between significant and insignificant results is usually a matter of judgment. Attempts are being made to define "significant" in statistical terms, and these new techniques will probably have applications to business problems in the future.

Feedback

In engineering, when information about what has actually happened is used to change the performance of a machine, the process is called *feedback*. If the temperature of a room drops below a prescribed level, the thermostat activates the furnace. Control reports are, in a sense, feedback devices, for they contain information that is used by management to alter future actions of the organization.

Although the analogy with thermostats is useful, an important difference between thermostats and control reports must be recognized. In the former, the action is automatic; in the latter, it is far from automatic. In an organization, action occurs only when management has recognized the need for action and when it has persuaded the person responsible to take the action desired.

FORMAL ANALYTICAL TECHNIQUES

All analyses of performance involve comparisons. We make judgments about current performance, not by using some abstract or absolute criterion, but rather by comparing data on current performance with some other data.

We shall refer to the data we are analyzing as the *actual* data, and to the data used as a basis for comparison as the *standard* data. As used here, therefore, the word "standard" has a broader connotation than in the phrase "standard cost"; it includes *any* figure with which actual performance is compared.

In cost accounting, the difference between actual and standard is called a *variance*.[2] We shall use the words "variance" and "difference" interchangeably. It is of little use to know only the amount by which actual profit differs from standard profit. In order to take effective action, we need to know what factors accounted for the difference. In this section techniques for decomposing a total difference into the elements that account for it are described.

In a given company the techniques actually used will depend on management's estimate of the value to be derived from them. Some companies use no formal techniques, others use only a few of those described here, and still others use even more complicated techniques. There is no prescribed pattern beyond the general rule that any technique should be worth more than the costs involved in using it.

Validity of the Standard

Presumably, we choose a certain standard because it is the best measure we can find of the job that should have been done; yet a standard is rarely, if ever, perfect. Thus, although it is often convenient to refer to "favorable" and "unfavorable" variances, these words imply value judgments that are valid only to the extent that the standard is a valid measure of what should have been done. Some of the limitations of various types of standards have been discussed in Chapter 11.

Even a standard cost may not be an accurate estimate of what costs "should have been under the circumstances." This situation can arise for either or both of two reasons: (*a*) the standard was not set properly, or (*b*) although set properly in the light of conditions existing at the time, those conditions have changed so that the standard has become obsolete.

An essential first step in analysis of a variance, therefore, is an examina-

---

[2] Note that this word has quite a different meaning in statistics.

tion of the validity of the standard. Judgments made on the basis of the variance must be tempered by the results of this examination. The importance of this first step cannot be overemphasized, but we must assume for the purpose of describing other analytical techniques that the standard has been properly set.

It should also be recognized that for the whole category of discretionary costs, the standard or budgeted amount represents not what should have been done, in any cause-and-effect sense, but rather what has been agreed to as the permitted level of spending. For discretionary costs, a variance between standard and actual indicates only that the manager spent more or less than the agreed upon amount. In particular, actual spending that is less than standard does not imply "good" performance. Presumably, good performance is spending approximately the amount budgeted, neither more nor less.

Even though the standard is valid, a variance may not reflect the performance of a responsible supervisor since it may result from a combination of causes, some of which he can control and some of which he cannot control. Analytical techniques make it possible to separate out, at least approximately, the controllable portion. These techniques are strictly mechanical, and at best provide a starting point for solution of the problem of performance evaluation.

FACTORS TO BE CONSIDERED

The operations of a business can be examined in terms of its outputs and its inputs. Outputs are measured in terms of revenue, and inputs in terms of cost or expense; profit is the difference between them. The difference between actual and standard profit is explainable principally by the existence of some or all of the following factors:

1. Noncomparable data.
2. Price per unit of input.
3. Quantity of inputs.
4. Mix of inputs.
5. Quality of outputs.
6. Price per unit of output.
7. Volume.
8. The measuring stick.
9. Assets employed in investment centers. (This factor will not be discussed further here.)

These factors explain the profit variance for a whole company. Some or all of them also explain the variance for any department or other responsibility center within the company.

Noncomparable Data

For many reasons, the data used as the standard may not be strictly comparable with the actual data. Possible differences in the accounting rules used and in the definition of terms have been discussed at length in previous chapters. It is also possible that simple arithmetic errors have crept into one or the other set of data. Before proceeding with the detailed analysis, therefore, it is important that one examine the data carefully, and adjust them to remove such sources of noncomparability whenever possible.

Price and Quantity of Inputs

In order to decompose variances in input factors into price and quantity elements, we must have available, for both standard and actual, the number of units and the price per unit. The procedure will be discussed first in terms of direct labor and then in terms of direct material.

DIRECT LABOR. The standard labor cost of a unit of product is constructed essentially by multiplying the standard time (e.g., number of hours) required to produce that unit by a standard rate per unit of time (e.g., standard wage rate per hour). Total standard labor cost for an accounting period is found by multiplying the standard labor cost per unit by the number of units of product produced. When employees are paid on an hourly basis, actual labor cost for the period is the product of actual hours worked times the actual labor rate per hour. These relationships suggest that it is possible to break the variance between actual and standard labor costs into two components: (1) the variance caused by the fact that actual *time* differed from standard time, and (2) the variance caused by the fact that actual *rates* differed from standard rates. The former is the input quantity variance, and the latter is the input price variance.

A commonly used pair of rules for isolating the effects of these components follows:

1. The *time* variance is the difference between standard hours and actual hours, priced at the standard rate per hour. (This variance is also known as a "usage," "spending," or "efficiency" variance, although the latter two terms connote too strong an inference as to the meaning of the results.)
2. The *rate* (or "price") variance is the difference between the standard rate per hour and the actual rate per hour, multiplied by the actual numbers of hours.

The *net* variance (or *total* variance) in labor costs is the algebraic sum of the time and rate variances. It follows that having found one variance, the other can be found by subtracting this variance from the net variance.

The net variance is also the difference between actual cost and standard cost.

The application of these rules is illustrated in Illustration 17–2 which is a diagram of this situation:

	Actual	*Standard*
Hours to produce one unit....................	6	8
Wage rate per hour.........................	$ 3	$ 2
Cost of one unit (rate times hours)............	$18	$16

Illustration 17–2

ILLUSTRATION OF COMPUTATION OF TIME
AND RATE VARIANCES

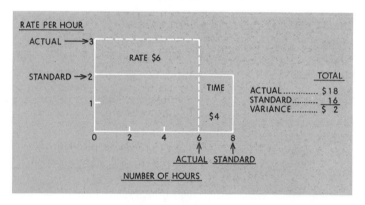

In the diagram, the solid rectangle indicates the standard cost (8 hours × $2 per hour = $16), and the dotted rectangle indicates actual cost (6 hours × $3 per hour = $18). The variances are the areas where the two rectangles do not coincide. The *time* variance is 2 hours times $2 per hour or $4; it is favorable because actual time is less than standard time. The *rate* variance is $1 per hour times 6 hours, or $6; it is unfavorable because the actual wage rate exceeds the standard rate. The net variance is the algebraic sum of these two variances, or $2, unfavorable; this is also the difference between actual cost and standard cost.

The calculations are repeated in terms of the rules given above:

1. (Std. Hours − Actual Hours) × Std. Rate   = Time Variance
   (8   −   6   ) × $2   = $4
2. (Std. Rate − Actual Rate) × Actual Hours = Rate Variance
   ($2   − $3   ) ×   6   =   −$6
3. Std. Cost − Actual Cost   = Net Variance
        $16   − $18   =   −$2

These equations are set up in such a way that a plus answer means a favorable variance and a minus answer means an unfavorable variance, but it often is easier to find by inspection whether the variance is favorable or unfavorable than to remember this fact.

THE GRAY AREA. When both the time and rate variances are favorable, or when both are unfavorable, the above rules do not give so clear-cut a result. The difficulty is demonstrated in Illustration 17–3, which shows the following situation:

	Actual	*Standard*
Hours to produce one unit....................	10	8
Wage rate per hour........................	$ 3	$ 2
Cost of one unit............................	$30	$16

In this situation, the unfavorable net variance of $14 is partly the result of the high wage rate and partly the result of the longer time required.

Illustration 17–3

COMPUTATION OF TIME AND RATE VARIANCES

Clearly, at least $8 of the variance is a rate variance resulting because the work was done at a rate that was $1 per hour higher than standard, and at least $4 results because actual hours exceeded standard hours. But the remaining $2 is a *gray area;* it is an inextricable combination of the influence both of the high rate and the long time. The above rules have the effect of assigning the entire $2 as *rate variance.* Other possibilities would be just as logical, but in practice the rules given are usually used. The calculation is:

> 1. (Std. Hours − Actual Hours) × Std. Rate   = Time Variance
> (8   −   10   ) × $2   =   −$4
> 2. (Std. Rate − Actual Rate) × Actual Hours = Rate Variance
> ($2   − $3   ) ×   10   =   −$10

INTERPRETATION OF THE LABOR VARIANCE. The reason for attempting to break down the total labor variance as described above is that the rate variance is often evaluated differently from the time variance. The rate variance may arise because of a change in wage rates for which the foreman cannot be held responsible, whereas the foreman may be held entirely responsible for the time variance, because he should control the time spent on a given job.

This distinction cannot be made in all cases, for there are many situations in which the two factors are interdependent. For example, the foreman may find it possible to complete the work in less than the standard time by using men who earn a higher than standard rate, and he may be perfectly justified in doing so. Even so, the use of the technique described above may lead to a better understanding of what actually happened.

The technique described provides only a partial explanation of the cause of the labor variance. It does not isolate any of a great number of other factors that may cause a difference between actual and standard labor costs. An incomplete list of such factors follows:

1. A standard labor cost per unit is valid only if labor costs vary proportionately with the number of units produced. Labor costs, in fact, may not vary proportionately with volume at all levels of production.
2. The measure of volume (e.g., number of units, pounds of product, etc.) may not be an accurate indication of the amount of direct labor required. For example, a standard labor cost of $1 a pound implies that each pound of product requires the same amount of labor, which, in fact, may not be the case.
3. The volume figure used to compute total standard costs may not correspond exactly to the volume figure that generated the actual labor costs, because of the nature of the system.
4. The elements included in standard cost (e.g., overtime, fringe benefits, shift premium) may differ from the elements included in actual costs.
5. Spoilage may not have been allowed for properly (see below).
6. Quality may have suffered or improved.
7. Labor performance may have affected, or may have been affected by, factors that are reflected in material or overhead costs.
8. There may have been changes in morale that have not affected current costs but which may have an important effect on future costs.
9. The total actual costs and total standard costs for a period may be influenced by offsetting forces for individual products or individual responsibility centers. The totals conceal these underlying forces.

Since the objective is to isolate that portion of the variance that is the result of efficiency or inefficiency and to hold the supervisor responsible for this portion, factors of the type mentioned above must be considered.

MATERIAL COST VARIANCES.   The variance between actual and standard direct material costs can be broken down into what are commonly called *material usage variance* and *material price variance* by the same technique as that described above for direct labor. The diagram in Illustration 17–2 is made applicable to material costs simply by changing the names:

	Actual	Standard
Quantity (pounds) used to produce one unit.....	6	8
Price per pound............................	$ 3	$ 2
Material cost for one unit...................	$18	$16

The *usage* variance, or *yield* variance, is 2 pounds times $2 a pound, or $4; and the *price* variance is $1 a pound times 6 pounds, or $6.

In some companies, the cost accounting system is constructed so that the price variance is removed as a part of the regular accounting entries; if such a system is used, there may be no need to separate out the price variance by the method described above. For example, if a company takes raw material into inventory at a standard price, the price variance is set up at the time the purchase is recorded. Raw Materials Inventory is debited at standard cost, Accounts Payable (or Cash) is credited at actual cost, and the difference is debited or credited to Material Price Variance. Even in such a case, a kind of price variance may later appear if material of a different *quality* from standard (hence, with a different standard cost) is used in the production process.

SPOILAGE AND REWORK. The material usage variance shows the difference between the actual and standard quantities of material *put into* the manufacturing process. If the product itself does not pass inspection at the end of the process or at some intermediate stage, it must either be discarded or sent back to have the defect corrected. If discarded, the labor, material, and overhead costs accumulated on it up to that point constitute *spoilage*. If sent back for correction, the extra *rework* cost is also a cost associated with substandard products.

There are several ways of accounting for spoilage and rework costs, only one of which is described here. A budgeted amount of spoilage is agreed on for each responsibility center. The actual cost of spoilage charged to the responsibility center is the cost of the defective products for which the responsibility center is responsible. This cost includes the material, labor, and overhead costs that have been accumulated on the defective product up to the point where the defect is discovered; thus, it may be the total cost of the product if the defect is not discovered until final inspection, or it may be a lesser amount if the defect is discovered during the manufacturing process. The costs of reworking products are charged to the responsibility center that caused the defect. Note that both spoilage costs and rework costs are charged to the responsibility center that *caused* the spoilage or rework, which is not necessarily the same as the responsibility center in which the defect was discovered ِ_ the responsibility center in which the rework was actually done.

The difference between the budgeted amount of spoilage and rework and the spoilage and rework costs charged to the responsibility center is the amount of variance attributable to the fact that actual spoilage and rework differed from the amount assumed in the budget.

Mix of Inputs

When the process uses several different materials, or several grades of the same material, that are supposed to be combined in a standard proportion, it is possible to compute a *mix variance* that shows the effect on cost of variations from the standard proportion. The mix variance for each item of material is the difference between the actual quantity of material used and the standard proportion (i.e., the quantity that would have been used if the standard proportions were adhered to), priced at the standard price. If a mix variance is calculated, the price variance is also calculated for each item of material separately.

To illustrate the calculation of the mix variance, we shall use a situation similar to that described in Illustration 17–2. We shall shift the situation from labor costs to material costs, simply to highlight the fact that the technique applies equally well to either type of cost; and instead of a single quantity and a single unit price, we shall assume that there are three items of material, each with its own quantity and unit price. The total amounts for the three items correspond to the totals shown in Illustration 17–2, signifying that the mix variance is a further decomposition of the differences analyzed there.

The calculation of the mix variance is shown in Illustration 17–4. As shown in the top block of the Illustration, a standard unit of product consists of Materials A, B, and C in the proportions $\frac{4}{8}$, $\frac{2}{8}$, and $\frac{2}{8}$, respectively. In the next block, these fractions are applied to the *actual* total quantity, 6 pounds, to give the standard mix of the three materials in such a quantity: namely, 3 pounds of A, 1.5 pounds of B, and 1.5 pounds of C. The difference between the actual quantity of each material and its standard mix, priced at its standard price and totaled, is the mix variance.

The price variance on each material is computed according to the rule already given: the difference between standard price and actual price, times the actual quantity. Note that the *sum* of the mix variances and price variances computed in this manner equals the price variance computed from the total quantity and average price given above, that is $(-\$4) + (-\$2) = -\$6$. The usage variance and the net variance are not affected.

Computation of the mix variance and price variance in this manner, although a little complicated, reveals information that might otherwise be concealed. It shows the effect of changes in the price of each material, which is hidden if averages are used. It also shows the effect of varying the mix of materials. These two may be interrelated; for example, it is

Illustration 17–4

MIX, PRICE, AND USAGE VARIANCES

A. Assumed Situation

	Standard			Actual		
	Quantity (Lbs.)	Unit Price	Total	Quantity (Lbs.)	Unit Price	Total
Material A.............4		$1.00	$ 4.00	2	$3.50	$ 7.00
Material B.............2		2.00	4.00	1	2.00	2.00
Material C.............2		4.00	8.00	3	3.00	9.00
Total...............8		$2.00	$16.00	6	$3.00	$18.00

B. Computation of Mix Variance

	Standard* Mix	−	Actual Quantity	=	Differ- ence	×	Std. Price	=	Mix Variance
Material A...............3			2		+1		$1.00		$1.00
Material B...............1.5			1		+0.5		2.00		1.00
Material C...............1.5			3		−1.5		4.00		− 6.00
Total.................6			6						−$4.00

* This is the standard proportions ⁴⁄₈, ²⁄₈, and ²⁄₈ applied to the actual total quantity.

C. Computation of Price Variance

	Std. Price	−	Actual Price	=	Differ- ence	×	Actual Quality	=	Price Variance
Material A.................$1.00			$3.50		−$2.50		2		−$5.00
Material B................. 2.00			2.00		...		1		...
Material C................. 4.00			3.00		+ 1.00		3		+ 3.00
Price Variance............									−$2.00

D. Computation of Usage Variance

$$(\text{Standard Quantity} - \text{Actual Quantity}) \times \text{Standard Price} = \text{Usage Variance}$$
$$(\qquad 8 \qquad - \qquad 6 \qquad) \times \qquad \$2 \qquad = \qquad \$4$$

quite possible that a higher than standard proportion of one material was used in an attempt to offset the effect of an increased price of another material. The mix variance may also be related to the quality of the product, although this does not appear in the calculation; if one material is a low grade and another is a high grade, then the increase in the proportion of the lower grade material may have had an adverse effect on quality.

GENERAL USE OF THE MIX CONCEPT.   The mix phenomenon arises whenever a cost or revenue item is analyzed by components, rather than in total. The price and quantity variances obtained from an analysis of each of the components will not add up to the price and quantity variance of the whole item if the actual proportions of the components differ from the standard proportions. Thus, if labor cost is being analyzed by employee skill classifications, if revenue is analyzed by individual products, or by individual geographic regions, a mix variance inevitably arises. Failure to appreciate this fact can lead to great frustration in trying to make the figures add up properly.

Quality of Output

In many situations, there is no numerical way of measuring the differences in quality or other characteristics between the standard and the actual output, the significance of this factor must therefore be judged intuitively. In some cases, it can be brought into the analysis explicitly. For example, if we are analyzing the differences between two bids to build a house, the fact that one contractor includes certain features that the other omits is an obvious factor to be taken into account.

Output Price and Volume

The sales revenue variance can be decomposed into a price factor and a quantity or volume factor. The *price variance* is the difference between the standard price per unit and the actual price per unit multiplied by the actual quantity sold. The *quantity variance* is the difference between standard quantity and actual quantity sold priced at the standard price per unit. Note the similarity between these rules and the rules for deriving the labor time and rate variances; whenever a total variance is to be broken down into a quantity element and a price element, the same general approach is used.

If revenue is analyzed by individual products or product lines, a mix variance will emerge, as described in the preceding section.

In many situations, it is more informative to analyze output in terms of gross margin, rather than in terms of sales revenue. The procedure is the same, except that gross margin per unit is used instead of selling price per unit. Such an analysis implies that the output of the sales organization is more usefully viewed as dollars of gross margin, rather than as dollars of sales revenue.

Volume and Overhead Costs

Direct labor and direct material costs usually vary directly and proportionately with volume. Consequently, *unit* direct labor and direct material costs are the same at all volume levels within the normal range; they are unaffected by volume. By contrast, overhead costs vary with volume but less than proportionately, as we saw in the diagrams presented in Chapter 15. This being so, *unit* overhead costs are inevitably higher at low volumes than they are at high volumes.

EXAMPLE: If the formula for the overhead cost line is $500 plus $1 per unit, overhead costs at various volumes are expected to be as follows:

Volume (in Units)	Total Overhead Cost	Unit Overhead Cost
800	$1,300	$1.62
900	1,400	1.56
1,000	1,500	1.50
1,100	1,600	1.45
1,200	1,700	1.42

Since the unit selling price presumably does not fluctuate with volume, whereas unit costs change with volume as seen above, unit profits are different at different volumes. Thus, if actual volume is different from standard volume, a volume variance results.

In order to measure this variance, we shall make use of the cost-volume relationship developed in Chapter 15. In Illustration 17–5, the line marked "budgeted" cost shows this direct, but less than proportional, relationship between costs and volume. Costs at any volume are expected to be the nonvariable amount, a, plus the variable rate, b, times the number of units of volume.

Recall that the overhead rate was set by choosing one level of volume, the *normal volume*, and dividing total costs at that volume by the number of units of volume. Thus, if the formula for the budgeted cost line is

Illustration 17–5

BUDGETED, ABSORBED, AND ACTUAL COSTS

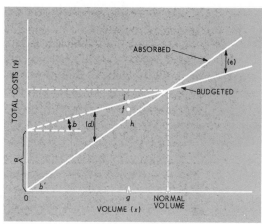

$500 + $1 per unit, and if normal volume is 1,000 units, total budgeted costs at 1,000 units are $1,500, and the overhead rate is $1.50 per unit.

At any volume, overhead costs would be *absorbed* into products at the rate of $1.50 per unit. The line of "absorbed" cost on the diagram shows the total costs that would be absorbed at any volume. At normal volume, budgeted costs equal absorbed costs, but at any other volume budgeted costs are different from absorbed costs, as indicated by the spread between the two lines. At lower volumes, costs are expected to be *underabsorbed*, as indicated by the amount *d*, and at higher volumes they are expected to be *overabsorbed*, as indicated by the amount *e*. They are underabsorbed or overabsorbed *because* actual volume differs from normal volume; hence, this amount is the volume variance. The volume variance results solely from the fact that actual volume in a given period differed from the normal volume that was used, *prior to the beginning of the year*, in setting the overhead rate.

If everything went as expected during an accounting period, actual costs incurred would coincide with budgeted costs at the level of activity prevailing in the period. For a variety of reasons, actual costs will probably be different from budgeted costs; the difference is called the *spending variance*. For control purposes, the spending variance is of particular interest as a starting point in appraising the supervisor's performance. It is only a starting point, since the variance may be the result of any of a number of uncontrollable factors, such as changes in prices, the method of overhead allocation, the rate and direction of change in volume, and changes in methods.

The overhead variance, as shown in the accounting records, is the algebraic sum of the volume variance and the spending variance. It is therefore useful to break down this *net variance* into its two components. The method for doing this is shown in Illustration 17–5 in a period when actual costs are at the point marked *f* and actual volume is *g*. Absorbed cost at this volume is the amount *h*, and budgeted cost the amount, *i*. Note that budgeted cost is the amount of cost budgeted for the volume level actually attained in the period. The following relationships will hold:

The *net variance* is the difference between absorbed cost, *h*, and actual cost, *f*. In the example, cost is underabsorbed.

As is stated above, this variance is also the algebraic sum of the volume variance and the spending variance. (The "favorable" and "unfavorable" variances can be designated by plus or minus signs, but it is usually easier to insert the proper signs from a consideration of the relationships than by memorizing the algebraic formulas.)

The *volume variance* is the difference between absorbed cost, *h*, and budgeted cost, *i*. In the example, this variance is unfavorable.

The *spending variance* is the difference between budgeted cost, *i*, and actual cost, *f*. In the example, this variance is favorable.

EXAMPLE: Assume that—
  Actual volume in an accounting period is 900 units.
  Actual cost is $1,380.
  The budget formula is $500 plus $1 per unit.
  The overhead rate is $1.50 per unit.
Then:
  Budgeted cost at the actual volume = $1,400
  Absorbed cost at the actual volume = 1,350
  Net variance (underabsorbed)   = 1,350 − $1,380 = −$30
  Volume variance (unfavorable)   = 1,350 − 1,400 = − 50
  Spending variance (favorable)   = 1,400 − 1,380 =   20

INTERPRETATION OF THE VARIANCES. Presumably, the supervisor is responsible for the spending variance that arises in his responsibility center. Because the budgeted cost line cannot take account of all the noncontrollable factors that affect cost, there may be a reasonable explanation for the spending variance. The existence of an unfavorable variance is therefore not, by itself, grounds for criticizing performance. Rather, it is a signal that investigation and explanation are required.

In some situations the supervisor may also be responsible for the volume variance. Failure to obtain standard volume may result from his inability to keep products moving through his department, for example. The volume variance is more likely to be someone else's responsibility, however. It may result because the sales department was unable to obtain the planned volume of orders, or because some earlier department in the manufacturing process failed to deliver materials as they were needed.

In appraising spending performance, the analyst will go behind the total spending variance and examine the individual overhead items of which it consists. The total budgeted cost is the sum of the allowances for each of the separate items. A spending variance can be developed for each item, as the difference between actual cost incurred and the budget allowance for the item; attention is focused on significant spending variances for individual items.

In terms of the structure established at the beginning of this section, the spending variance is a composite of input price and input quantity factors. After it has been separated from the volume variance, it could conceivably be broken down into its price and quantity elements, as was done for direct labor, but in practice the analysis is usually not carried this far.

It should be emphasized that the volume variance arises only from differences in the *level* of volume. The *speed* of change in volume from one level to another also can have an effect on costs. So can the *direction* of change, for actual costs often tend to be below the line of budgeted costs when volume is increasing and above the line when volume is decreasing. This phenomenon, which is called *lag* or *hysteresis*, shows up in the spending variance, not the volume variance.

Measuring Stick Variance

If the measure of volume is an input factor, such as actual direct labor hours, rather than an output factor, such as units of products produced or the standard direct labor hours in these products, then an additional complication arises. To illustrate it, let us assume that the unit of volume in Illustration 17–5 was *actual* direct labor hours, but that overhead costs were absorbed into products on the basis of $1.50 per *standard* labor hour in these products.

Assume further that actual direct labor in a month totaled 900 hours and that standard direct labor totaled only 860 hours, other conditions remaining as in the above illustration. The amount of overhead costs absorbed will then be 860 hours times $1.50 per hour, or $1,290. If standard hours had totaled 900, then $1,350 (= 900 × $1.50) would have been absorbed. The difference of $60 between this $1,350 and the $1,290 actually absorbed arises because the direct labor force worked at less than standard efficiency. This variance is therefore called the *efficiency variance*, although it can be seen that the word "efficiency" relates to the ultilization of direct labor, and not to overhead itself. It is the difference between actual hours and standard hours, priced at the standard rate per hour.

> EXAMPLE: The complete analysis of this new situation is as follows:
> Actual overhead cost incurred   = $1,380.
> Budgeted cost at actual volume   = 1,400.
> Absorbed cost, 860 standard hours × $1.50 = 1,290.
> Net variance (underabsorbed)   = $1,290 − $1,380 = −90.
> Volume variance (unfavorable)   = 1,350 − 1,400 = −50.
> Spending variance (favorable)   = 1,400 − 1,380 =   20.
> Efficiency variance (unfavorable)   = (860 − 900) × $1.50 = −60.

The efficiency variance is not present in many situations, but only in those in which there is a difference in the way volume is measured for control and the way costs are absorbed for product costing.

AN ILLUSTRATIVE ANALYSIS

As a way of summarizing the techniques described above, the complete analysis of a simple hypothetical situation is shown in Illustration 17–6. Although the company in this example manufactures three products, we have simplified the calculation of manufacturing variances by making standard unit manufacturing cost the same for all products; this is simply for the purpose of avoiding numerous computations of mix variance. For further simplification of the arithmetic, we have assumed that only one kind of material and one class of labor are used. In the examination of revenue variances, we have carried through the three-product analysis in order to illustrate the calculation of a mix variance.

The income statement (Section A) shows a variance between actual and standard profit of $55. The question is: What accounts for this variance? The answer to this question is given in Section B, which decomposes the total variance into elements. The remainder of the illustration shows how these elements were found.

Illustration 17–6

COMPUTATION OF VARIANCES

A. Income Statements

	Standard	Actual	Variance
Sales......................................	$540	$555	
Less: Standard cost of sales................	440	418	
Gross margin at standard cost...............	$100	$137	$ 37
Less: Manufacturing variances.............	0	82	(82)
Gross margin.............................	$100	$ 55	$(45)
General and admin. expense.................	40	50	(10)
Operating Profit before Taxes...............	$ 60	$ 5	$(55)

B. Summary of Variances

Sales volume.............................	$(5)
Sales mix................................	3
Sales price...............................	39
Net marketing............................	$ 37
Material price............................	$(16)
Material usage............................	4
Labor time...............................	(24)
Labor price...............................	(8)
Overhead volume.........................	(15)
Overhead spending........................	(23)
Net manufacturing........................	$(82)
General and admin........................	$(10)
Net Profit Variance.......................	$(55)

( ) = unfavorable

C. Underlying Data, Marketing Area

	Standard			Actual		
	Quantity	Unit Price	Total	Quantity	Unit Price	Total
Product A..................	100	$2.60	$260	80	$2.50	$200
Product B..................	60	2.80	168	60	3.00	180
Product C..................	40	2.80	112	50	3.50	175
Total..................	200	$2.70	$540	190		$555

Illustration 17–6 (Continued)

D. Computation of Marketing Variances

(1) Volume Variance

Actual Vol.	−	*Std. Vol.*	=	*Diff.*	×	*Std. Gross Margin*		
190	−	200	=	−10	×	$0.50	=	−$5.00

(2) Mix Variance

Actual Quantity	−	*Std. Quantity**	=	*Diff.*	×	*Std. Gross Margin*	=	*Variance*
80	−	95	=	−15	×	$0.40	=	−$6.00
60	−	57	=	+ 3	×	0.60	=	+ 1.80
50	−	38	=	+12	×	0.60	=	+ 7.20
Total 190		190				Mix Variance =		+$3.00

* Based on standard proportions of $\frac{100}{200}$, $\frac{60}{200}$, $\frac{40}{200}$.

(3) Selling Price Variance

Actual Selling Price	−	*Std. Selling Price*	=	*Diff.*	×	*Actual Quantity*	=	*Variance*
$2.50	−	$2.60	=	−0.10	×	80	=	−$ 8.00
3.00	−	2.80	=	+0.20	×	60	=	+ 12.00
3.50	−	2.80	=	+0.70	×	50	=	+ 35.00
						Price Variance =		+$39.00

E. Underlying Data, Manufacturing Area

Item	*Standard*	*Actual*
Volume..................	200 units	170 units
Direct material...........	2 lbs./unit at $0.20/lb.	320 lbs. at $0.25 = $ 80
Direct labor..............	0.4 hrs./unit at $2.00/hr.	80 hrs. at $2.10 = 168
Overhead................	$100 + $0.50 per unit	$208

F. Computation of Manufacturing Variances

(1) Material Price Variance

Std. Price	−	*Actual Price*	=	*Diff.*	×	*Actual Quantity*	=	*Material Price Variance*
$0.20	−	$0.25	=	−$0.05	×	320	=	−$16

(2) Material Usage Variance

Std. Quantity	−	*Actual Quantity*	=	*Diff.*	×	*Std. Price*	=	*Material Usage Variance*
340	−	320	=	20	×	$0.20	=	+$4

Illustration 17–6 (Continued)

(3) Labor Time Variance

Std. Hours		*Actual Hours*	=	*Diff.*	×	*Std. Rate*	=	*Labor Time Variance*
68	−	80	=	− 12	×	$2.00	=	− $24

(4) Labor Price Variance

Std. Rate		*Actual Rate*	=	*Diff.*	×	*Actual Hours*	=	*Labor Price Variance*
$2.00	−	$2.10	=	− $0.10	×	80	=	− $8

(5) Overhead Variances

Net Variance   = $170–$208 = − $38
Volume Variance = $170–$185 = − 15
Spending Variance = $185–$208 = − 23

Marketing Variance

The first step in the computation is to make a breakdown of the variance for which the marketing department is held accountable. The basic data required for this part of the analysis are shown in Section C, and the computations are made in Section D. Mix, volume, and price variances are calculated, their algebraic sum totaling the $37 shown as a revenue variance on the income statement. In calculating marketing variances, notice that gross margin, not selling price or total revenues, is used. This is because the contribution of the marketing department is best measured by the gross margin it generates, rather than by sales revenue. Gross margin is found by subtracting *standard* cost of sales (which is $2.20 per unit) from selling prices. Using the *standard* cost of sales figure means that the marketing department is not held accountable for any manufacturing expense variances; rather, these are the responsibility of the manufacturing organization.

The volume variance is the loss or gain in gross margin that results from a difference between actual and standard sales volume. The mix variance is figured by multiplying the standard gross margin for each product by the difference between the actual and standard quantity. The selling price variance is determined by multiplying the actual sales quantities for each product by the difference between actual and standard selling price.

Note that revenue variances are favorable when actual is greater than standard, which is of course the opposite situation from expense variances.

EXAMPLE: In Illustration 17–6, the $37 excess of actual gross margin over standard gross margin is favorable, but the $82 excess of actual manufacturing variances over standard manufacturing variances is unfavorable.

It is advisable to use parenthesis (or red ink or asterisks) for unfavorable variances, i.e., those that decrease net profit, rather than to use them for excesses of actual over standard. This provides a clearer signal to the reader, for if the latter practice is followed, increases in cost, which are unfavorable, will have the same appearance as increases in revenue, which are favorable.

Manufacturing Variances

Next we turn to an analysis of the manufacturing expense variances. Note that, as shown in Section E, actual production volume is less than actual sales volume, the difference being made up out of inventory which is carried at standard cost. Carrying the inventory at standard cost means that expense variances are treated as period costs and charged directly to cost of sales during the period in which they occur and not put into inventory.

The labor, material, and overhead variances described earlier in the chapter are calculated in Section F. Their algebraic sum equals the $82 unfavorable variance noted on the income statement. This is charged directly to cost of sales.

An examination of the $10 unfavorable variance in general and administrative expenses completes the analysis of the net profit variance. This is not shown; it would consist of an analysis by class of expense of the amount of and reasons for differences between the budgeted expense and the actual expense.

ATTACKING AN APPRAISAL PROBLEM

Some or all of the techniques described above may be useful if the necessary data are available. The unfortunate fact is, however, that one rarely has all the data he would like to have in order to reach a sound judgment on performance. Under these circumstances, the analyst simply does the best he can with what he has. Everyone would agree that both the Union and Confederate leaders made mistakes at the battle of Gettysburg; but despite volumes of analysis by military experts and historians, there is not unanimous agreement, even today, as to what these mistakes were or who was responsible for them. Nevertheless, the field commanders at the time, without the benefit of any historical research, had to make judgments on the performance of those participating in this battle and take action on the basis of these judgments.

In view of the inevitable incompleteness of the data, the following guides may suggest a useful way of attacking a problem that involves the appraisal of performance:

1. From the information available or obtainable, decide on the best possible standard or basis of comparison.

2. Define the factors that are not included in the standard; attempt to estimate the importance of these factors; and either modify the standard to take them into account or reduce the degree of certainty attached to the comparison of actual against standard.

3. Find, and attempt to estimate the importance of, nonquanitative considerations that cannot be included in a standard (e.g., morale, quality, intangible future benefits).

4. Make a judgment and be prepared to act on it. (One possible judgment is that no action should be taken until more information is available. This judgment should be made only if one is reasonably confident that it is both feasible and necessary to obtain additional facts.)

SUMMARY

Conceptually, the performance of a responsibility center is judged by measuring the effectiveness of its outputs and the efficiency of its inputs. Effectiveness can be divided into quality and quantity, suggesting two key questions: (1) How much was accomplished? and (2) How well was the work done? Efficiency is measured by the ratio of outputs to inputs, that is, by the ratio of work done to resources used in doing the work.

In making judgments on effectiveness and efficiency, actual outputs and inputs are compared with standard outputs and inputs. These standards presumably represent what should have happened under the circumstances prevailing. They are derived from experience, from past performance of the responsibility center, from the performance of similar responsibility centers, or from predetermined standards or budgets.

Even the best standard is unlikely to be a perfectly valid measure of what should have happened. In many situations there is no way of expressing in numbers what output actually was, let alone what it should have been. Moreover, the analysis tends to focus on current performance, whereas the impact of current decisions on future performance may be as important, or even more important.

Formal techniques are available for decomposing the difference between actual performance and standard performance and showing the magnitude of the difference attributable to each factor. These techniques provide clues as to the reason for the variance, but they never provide a complete answer to the question, "Why did the variance occur?" At best, they show the areas in which further investigation should be concentrated in order to find the answer to this vital question.

CASES

CASE 17–1. DAVISON MANUFACTURING COMPANY

The Davison Manufacturing Company, manufacturer of electric light fixtures, operated under a standard cost accounting system. Labor data for the four production departments for the month of June (with numbers slightly rounded for ease of computation) were as follows:

Department	Direct Labor Cost		Hours of Direct Labor		Rate per Hour	
	Actual	Standard	Actual	Standard	Actual	Standard
A.............	$2,227.50	$2,231.00	990	970	$2.25	$2.30
B.............	1,056.00	1,071.00	480	510	2.20	2.10
C.............	1,935.50	2,132.00	790	820	2.45	2.60
D.............	1,828.50	1,650.00	690	660	2.65	2.50
Total.......	$7,047.50	$7,084.00	2,950	2,960		

Questions

1. Prepare a journal entry recording the direct labor cost. The company used an account called Work in Process, and direct labor was charged to this account at standard. The difference between actual cost and standard cost was carried to an account called Labor Variance.
2. For each department, determine how much of the difference between actual and standard cost was caused by differences between actual and standard hours, and how much was caused by differences between actual and standard rates of pay.
3. What additional information, if any, would be required in order to explain the significance of the differences?

CASE 17–2.   PROBLEMS IN THE ANALYSIS OF OVERHEAD COST

Problem A

The overhead rate is $2 a ton. Budgeted overhead cost at 3,000 tons a month is $8,000 and at 7,000 tons is $12,000. Actual overhead cost in September is $9,000, and actual volume is 5,000 tons.

Required:
1. On a graph, show absorbed costs and expected costs.
2. State the following:
    a) Standard volume.
    b) Budgeted nonvariable cost.
    c) Budgeted variable cost per ton.
    d) Costs absorbed in September.
    e) Volume variance in September.
    f) Spending variance in September.
    g) Net variance in September.

Problem B

The formula for budgeted overhead costs is $y = \$5,000 + \$1$ per unit. Standard volume is 5,000 units a month. Actual overhead expense in March is $11,500, and output in March is 6,000 units.

Required:
1. Standard volume.
2. Budgeted nonvariable cost.
3. Budgeted variable cost per unit.
4. Cost absorbed in March.
5. Volume variance in March.
6. Spending variance in March.
7. Net variance in March.

Problem C

The forecast year's overhead expense for an expected volume of 180,000 pounds of a product is as follows:

Nonvariable overhead	$ 36,000
Variable overhead	108,000

In May, output was 10,000 pounds and actual overhead expense was $7,700. Determine (*a*) the budget line, (*b*) standard volume, (*c*) standard overhead per unit, and (*d*) the overhead variances.

Problem D

In June overhead volume variance was 0 and "spending" variance was a debit of $600. In July overhead volume variance was a debit of $800, but "spending" variance was 0. June actual overhead expense was $7,000 for an output of 800 tons. July's expense was $5,600, and output was 600 tons. In August output was 900 tons and actual overhead expense was $7,100. What was the budget figure for August? How much was absorbed in August? What can you say of variances for August?

Problem E

Overhead was charged to product at 75 percent of direct labor dollars. According to the budget, overhead should be $5,600 for a direct labor payroll of $8,000 and $6,800 for a direct labor payroll of $10,000. If actual overhead costs turned out to be $6,000 and $7,000, respectively, at these two volumes, what were the variances? What was standard volume for the company?

Problem F

Budgeted overhead costs per month are $2,000 plus $0.60 per actual direct labor hour. The overhead rate is $0.80 per standard direct labor hour. In November, standard direct labor hours totaled 11,000, actual direct labor hours totaled 11,500, and actual overhead costs totaled $9,000. Compute the overhead variances.

Problem G

Department 12 of the Hudson Company manufactured rivets and no other products. All rivets were identical. In August Department 12 made four million rivets. The company used a standard cost system plus a variable budget for overhead expense. Standard unit overhead charges (i.e., standard unit costs for overhead) were determined by dividing budgeted costs at an expected average volume by the number of rivets (in thousands) which that volume level (i.e., rate of capacity) represented.

Certain cost information is shown in the following table, and you are requested to fill in the blank spaces. The clue to the expected average volume necessary to fill in the blanks in line 3 can be found by a close analysis of the relationships among the figures given for allocated service and general overhead.

Dept.12	Actual Cost, August	Std. Chg. per 1,000 Rivets	Total Std. Cost, August*	Overhead Budget, August	Overhead Budget Formula
Direct labor	$10,500	$3.00	$	Not Used	
Direct material	22,000	5.00	20,000	" "	
Department direct overhead expense	9,500	...	.....	$ 9,200	$6,000 per month plus $0.80 per thous. rivets
Allocated service and general overhead	5,000	1.00	4,000	5,000	$5,000 per month
Total	$47,000	$ ...	$	$14,200	

* Standard charge per thousand rivets times August volume of 4,000,000 equals total standard cost.

Required:

1. Fill in the blanks.
2. What was the expected average volume (in terms of rivet output) at which the standard unit overhead charge was determined?
3. Explain as much of the difference between total actual costs and total standard costs as you can on the basis of the information given.

CASE 17–3.   LOTSACAL SUGAR COMPANY

The Lotsacal Sugar Company produced a compound which was sold as a "body-builder." The standard cost card per 100 pounds of this product, Lotsacal, is given in Exhibit 1. These standard costs were established at a

Exhibit 1

STANDARD COST CARD

Lotsacal—100 Lbs.

Materials:

Refined sugar	50 lbs. at $0.05	$ 2.50	
Dextrose	40 lbs. at $0.09	3.60	
Malt	10 lbs. at $0.07	0.70	
			$ 6.80

Labor:

Mixing	8 hrs. at $2.00	$16.00	
Cooking	8 hrs. at $1.50	12.00	
			28.00

Overhead:

Mixing	8 hrs. at $1.25	$10.00	
Cooking	8 hrs. at $1.50	12.00	
			22.00
Total Standard Cost per 100 lbs			$56.80

normal volume for the year of 220,000 pounds of Lotsacal. At this level of volume, variable overhead costs should amount to $11,440 in the mixing department and $10,560 in the cooking department. Fixed overhead costs amount to $10,560 in the mixing department and $15,840 in the cooking department.

During the week of May 22, 1961, 4,400 pounds of Lotsacal were produced. Actual costs for this production were accumulated as follows:

```
Refined sugar used.....................2,350 lbs. at $0.04
Dextrose used........................1,850 lbs. at $0.08
Malt used...........................  400 lbs. at $0.08
```

Direct labor hours worked in the mixing department: 350 hours at $2.05 an hour.

Direct labor hours worked in the cooking department: 370 hours at $1.40 an hour.

At December 31, 1961, production records revealed that 200,000 pounds of Lotsacal had been produced during the year with 15,000 hours of direct labor in the mixing department and 16,500 hours of direct labor in the cooking department. The actual overhead costs for the year amounted to $20,300 in the mixing department and $25,000 in the cooking department.

Question

1. Prepare an analysis of actual and standard costs reflecting a price and mix variance for each material, a total material usage variance, a time and rate variance for labor in each department, and as complete an analysis of overhead costs as you can.

CASE 17–4. RETALLACK COMPANY

The Retallack Company manufactured pennants on a customer-order basis for local organizations, such as schools, fraternities, and yacht clubs. Because there was considerable variation in the quantities ordered, the quality of material used, and the sizes and patterns, the company prepared a separate job cost sheet for each order.

Costs of materials and direct labor applicable to each order were recorded directly on the appropriate job cost sheet. Manufacturing overhead was allocated to each order on the basis of a standard overhead rate per unit. The standard overhead rate was determined before the beginning of each year for each size of pennant by dividing the estimated overhead costs for the coming year chargeable to that size by the estimated sales of units of that size. Overhead costs were divided into two components, variable and fixed.

In December 1967, the accountant was working out for the following year the overhead rates to be applied per unit for each of the four sizes of pennants manufactured by the company. The estimated number of pennants of each size to be sold in 1968 was as follows:

Size	Estimated Quantity to Be Sold
A.	15,000
B.	20,000
C.	10,000
D.	5,000
Total.	50,000

On the basis of the sales forecast, the accountant estimated that the overhead costs chargeable to each size of pennant would probably be as follows:

1968 Estimated Components of Overhead Cost

Size	Fixed*	Variable (per Pennant)
A.	$3,300	$0.08
B.	4,000	0.06
C.	1,500	0.05
D.	850	0.03
Total.	$9,650	

* Fixed overhead costs, both estimated and actual, were allocated to each size of pennant on the basis of direct labor-hours, raw material quantity, floor space required, and other reasonable bases of allocation.

Questions

1. What is the estimated total overhead cost per pennant (i.e., the standard overhead rate) for each of the four sizes?
2. Using the standard overhead rate found in Question 1, determine the overhead variances attributable to volume and the variances attributable to "spending" or "efficiency" if the actual units produced and sold in 1968 and actual overhead costs were as follows:
    a) 15,000 units of size A produced and sold. Actual overhead cost was $4,700.
    b) 18,000 units of size B produced and sold. Actual overhead cost was $5,080.
    c) 9,000 units of size C produced and sold. Actual overhead cost was $1,825.
    d) 7,000 units of size D produced and 6,500 units sold. Actual overhead cost was $975.
3. When the accountant calculated the overhead per pennant to be allocated on customers' orders for the following year, should he have included the fixed element of the overhead?

CASE 17–5.   STALCUP PAPER COMPANY

In March, 1935, the president of the Stalcup Paper Company, while examining a group of charts regarding unit costs submitted to him by the cost department, noted that the unit costs of sorting rags had been rising for approximately two years. In order to determine the reason for this increase, he invited the foreman of the rag-sorting department and the head of the cost department to his office to discuss the matter. The head of the cost department submitted three exhibits, shown as Exhibits 1, 2, and 3, giving the details of the upward trend in costs shown in the charts. The foreman of the rag-sorting department said that his costs were lower rather than higher than they had been in past years, and that the basis of

Exhibit 1

OUTPUT OF RAG-SORTING DEPARTMENT IN POUNDS

	1932	*1934*	*Change*
Old rags....................	3,220,000	2,460,000	− 23.6%
New rags....................	810,000	2,520,000	+211.1
	4,030,000	4,980,000	+ 23.6%
Percentage old rags............	79.9%	49.4%	
Percentage new rags............	20.1	50.6	

Exhibit 2

EXPENSES OF RAG-SORTING DEPARTMENT

	1932	*% of Direct Labor*	*1934*	*% of Direct Labor*
Direct labor..............		$20,965		$17,185
Rag-sorting department burden:				
Indirect labor...........$ 8,533			$ 9,540	
Repair labor............ 610			508	
Repair materials........ 123			271	
Supplies................ 156			160	
Power.................. 612			553	
Investment............ 15,549			15,204	
		25,583	122%	26,236	153%
General overhead..........		19,128	91	15,186	88
		$65,676		$58,607	

Exhibit 3

RAG-SORTING DEPARTMENT, COSTS OF SORTING OLD AND NEW RAGS

(As Shown in Cost Records)

	1932		1934	
	Dollars	*Cents per Pound*	*Dollars*	*Cents per Pound*
Old rags:				
Wages.........................	$20,475	0.636	$15,645	0.636
Department overhead.............	24,985*	0.776	23,885†	0.971
General overhead...............	18,681	0.580	13,825	0.562
	$64,141	1.992	$53,355	2.169
Increase.....................				0.177
New rags:				
Wages.........................	$ 490	0.0605	$ 1,540	0.0611
Department overhead.............	598*	0.0738	2,351†	0.0933
General overhead...............	447	0.0552	1,361	0.0540
	$ 1,535	0.1895	$ 5,252	0.2084
Increase.....................				0.0189

* 122 percent of wages.
† 153 percent of wages.

the cost department's estimates was unsound. He submitted Exhibit 4 in support of this contention.

The Stalcup Paper Company used old rags, new rags, and pulp in manufacturing its papers. The proportions in which these materials were

Exhibit 4

RAG-SORTING DEPARTMENT,
COSTS OF SORTING OLD AND NEW RAGS

(As Estimated by Foreman)

	1932		1934	
	Dollars	*Cents per Pound*	*Dollars*	*Cents per Pound*
Old rags:				
Wages.........................	$20,475	0.636	$15,645	0.636
Department overhead............	20,441	0.635	12,960	0.527
General overhead...............	15,285	0.475	7,502	0.305
	$56,201	1.746	$36,107	1.468
Decrease...................				0.278
New rags:				
Wages.........................	$ 490	0.060	$ 1,540	0.061
Department overhead...........	5,142	0.635	13,276	0.527
General overhead...............	3,843	0.475	7,684	0.305
	$ 9,475	1.170	$22,500	0.893
Decrease...................				0.277

mixed were varied in accordance with the requirements for different grades and types of paper. New rags, which were purchased from textile converters, cost substantially more per pound than did old rags, which were purchased from junk dealers. The old rags usually were received in the form of garments, from which it was necessary to remove carefully all foreign materials such as buttons, rubber, and metal. New rags were mostly remnants containing only a small percentage of foreign matter requiring removal; consequently, they could be sorted much more rapidly than could old rags.

The sorters sat at benches. Their task was to remove all foreign matter from the material placed before them and to distribute the usable cloth, according to quality, into containers placed beside them. The sorters processed, on the average, 55 pounds of old rags per hour or 575 pounds of new rags per hour. They were paid on a day-rate basis, the management having discovered by experience that payment on a piece-rate basis resulted in their picking over rags less carefully.

Between 1932 and 1934 the composition of rags purchased by the Stalcup Paper Company changed considerably, as shown in Exhibit 1. The percentage of old rags to the total dropped from approximately 80 to approximately 50 percent. During the same interval the total quantity of rags handled increased by nearly 25 percent. In spite of the large increase in total volume, labor costs declined over the period because of the smaller quantity of old rags handled.

Costs charged to the rag-sorting department were of three types: first, direct labor in the department; second, overhead charged directly to the department; and third, general factory overhead. The amount of general factory overhead charged to a department was obtained by multiplying the direct labor in the department by the ratio of total general overhead to total direct labor in the entire plant.

Both departmental overhead and the department's share of general factory overhead were charged to products processed by the department as a percentage of the direct labor applied to these products. This percentage was obtained by dividing total overhead by total direct labor in the department.

The items included in the overhead of the rag-sorting department were as shown in Exhibit 2. The most important of these were indirect labor, including the salary of the foreman and wages of employees engaged in taking material to and from the sorters, and investment, which included the charge against the department for taxes, depreciation, and insurance on the premises and equipment it used. General overhead included miscellaneous factory labor, building repair labor and materials, manufacturing executive salaries, and expenses of functional departments, such as planning, costing, and research.

The head of the cost department pointed out to the president that between 1932 and 1934 the overhead charge of the rag-sorting department had increased from 122 percent of direct labor to 153 percent, and that the difference in the cost of rag sorting in the two years was, as shown in Exhibit 3, almost entirely attributable to this increase.

The foreman differed with the cost department's estimated unit costs and pointed out that it was hard to conceive of unit costs increasing while total costs were diminishing and while volume of output was rising. He stated that the cost department was not charging the proper proportion of overhead charges to the new rags and that therefore old rags were taking more than their share of total department overhead. He said that, in his opinion, a much sounder method of allocating overhead charges would be on a per-pound basis rather than on the percentage-of-direct-labor basis previously used, and he recommended that costs in the rag department in the future should be calculated on the basis shown in Exhibit 4.

The unit costs for old and new rag sorting, as calculated by the cost department, were used in setting up standard costs. These standard costs, however, were used only rarely in setting prices of finished paper, since most of the company's paper was sold in a competitive market at prices established by competition. The company used the standard costs mostly to determine the relative profitability of the various lines of paper manufactured. When the plant was being operated at capacity and orders were being refused, the relative profitability of lines was a factor in determining what lines should be discontinued. In 1935, the Stalcup Paper Company was operating at about 55 percent of capacity.

Questions

1. What is your assessment of performance in 1934?
2. Discuss the validity of the points made by the foreman and by the head of the cost department.

CASE 17–6. STORROW COMPANY

Mr. George Jessup was one of the junior managers in an operating division of Storrow Company, which did a mail-order business in women's clothing. Mr. Jessup was supervisor of a unit engaged in the inspection and preparation for stock of women's coats. It was his job to see that the work of his Examination and Preparation Unit, as it was called, was done carefully yet efficiently and economically.

Functions of the Examination and Preparation Unit

The procedure of examining and checking shipments of new merchandise in Mr. Jessup's unit was elaborate, particularly in the early part of each season. For a period of two or three weeks a thorough examination was conducted of all coats received, regardless of the manufacturer of the type of coat. The examination routine consisted of a careful inspection of the stitching, the condition of the cloth and lining, the evenness of hems, and other features. Comparison was made with a sample approved by the Storrow buyer. Each coat was placed on a model so that inspectors could see if it fitted properly; sometimes live models were used. If a manufacturer's shipments were consistently satisfactory as the season progressed, a less thorough examination of each coat, called a spot check, was made. The spot check was a quick, overall inspection of the quality of the garment and a check on the presence of all accessories. Substantially the same procedure was followed for merchandise returned by customers.

In the Examination and Preparation Unit, operators were stationed at work tables, and floor boys were employed to bring in merchandise and later to remove it to stock, or wherever it was to go. Every afternoon each girl reported, on a specified form, the number of coats she had handled and the number of hours she had spent on the work. Each girl filled out her daily report at about half an hour before closing time, including thereon her estimate of work for the remainder of the day. These forms were then countersigned by the floor supervisor, whose responsibility it was to see that the work was done by the close of the day.

There were three classes of employees in Mr. Jessup's unit. The first was a group of "basic regular" operators, who were guaranteed 38 hours a week for 50 weeks in the year. This group was ordinarily limited to the minimum number of employees required to handle the lowest weekly volume in the year. The second group of workers, known as "nonbasic," were guaranteed 30 hours of work a week. Finally, there were temporary workers who were employed to meet peak demands. The only requirement of their use was that if a girl was taken on, she had to be given at least four hours of work for that day.

Budget Procedure

At the beginning of the spring season, which ran from February through July, the company prepared a six-month key budget of revenue, expense, and net profit by months. This general budget was based on all known factors, including national and local economic conditions, anticipated trends, and planned company policies. Based on the sales estimate in this budget, Mr. Jessup made up a budget for his unit showing the number of hours of labor that would be required in the various activities under his charge and also the expected rate of output per man-hour. In addition, on the 15th of each month Mr. Jessup prepared a budget for each week of the coming month. In preparing these weekly budgets he used the estimates of the merchandisers as to the volume of shipments to be received into the examination and preparation unit, and also the recorded performance for the corresponding period in the preceding year. Both the semiannual budget and the weekly budgets were submitted to the expense controller, who either approved them as presented or discussed revisions with Mr. Jessup.

Every Wednesday morning Mr. Jessup prepared a revised weekly budget for the coming week, again showing the expected hours of work to be spent in the several lines of activity in his department. This revised weekly budget, which also had to be approved by the expense controller, set the standard against which the performance of Mr. Jessup's unit would be judged by his superiors. After his weekly budget had been approved, Mr. Jessup divided his week's estimate according to days, in order to follow daily performance. Whereas he might be in the red on any one day, it was expected that at the end of the week the total hours spent would not exceed his budget.

The expense control department maintained a budget book that showed for each unit the total hours worked each day and the budgeted hours for that day, with summary figures for each week. A copy of this book was in the office of the superintendent of operations, and a copy of his own record, day by day and week by week, was also available to the head of each unit. The management believed that effective control required good planning and a careful watch on daily performance, and it therefore wanted results and not excuses. It approved prompt corrective action taken in order to attain an objective; it did not approve the use of unproductive time spent in explanation of why the objective had not been reached.

Performance Reports

For comparison with his budget, daily performance reports of output and hours worked in Mr. Jessup's unit were compiled by one of his clerks from the daily work reports filed every afternoon by each of the operators. The ratio of total output to total hours worked provided a measure of output per man-hour, after an adjustment had been made by applying a weighting factor that reflected the amount of work involved in the several operations.

Exhibits 1 and 2 show budgeted and actual performance reports, respectively, for the week ended May 15. In column 1 is listed the budgeted or actual output, in number of coats, of Mr. Jessup's unit. In column 2 is listed the budgeted or actual number of hours worked.

Lines 1–6 and 10 relate to direct labor used in the examination and the preparation for stock of both new and returned merchandise. Other lines relate to the activities of floor boys and other service employees, clerical

Exhibit 1

LABOR BUDGET FOR EXAMINATION AND PREPARATION UNIT
WEEK ENDING MAY 15

(Revised Figures in Parentheses)

APPROVED BUDGET ESTIMATES

		1	2	3	4	5	6
		ACTUAL OUTPUT	HOURS WORKED	OUTPUT PER MAN HOUR (1 ÷ 2)	WEIGHTING FACTOR	WEIGHTED OUTPUT (1x4)	CARRY-OVER
1	EXAMINATION OF NEW MERCHANDISE	(10000) 5970	(286) 171	35.0	.63	(6300) 3761	
2	PREPARATION OF NEW MERCHANDISE	(9000) 4220	(300) 141	30.0	.73	(6570) 3081	
3	INSPECTION OF CUSTOMER RETURNS	(3100) 3600	(140) 163	22.0	1.00	(3100) 3600	
4	PREP. & LISTING OF CUSTOMER RETURNS	(3100) 3600 (2790) 3240	(12) 14 (96) 112	257.0 29.0	.09 .76	(279) 324 (2118) 3462	
5	IRREGULARITY HANDLING	(700) 520	(30) 23	22.6	.94	(658) 489	
6	R.G. & JOB SALE MDSE. HANDLING	(1000) 880	(20) 18	48.9	.44	(440) 387	
7	UTILITY		(148) 105				
8	CLERICAL		(79) 63				
9	SUPERVISION · INSTRUCT. TIMEKEEPING		(90) 78				
10	Sign-up	(1860) 2160	(124) 144	15.0	1.47	(2734) 3175	
11	Additional	100	(3) 3	35.0	.63	63	
12	TOTAL		(1328) 1035	16.76		(22262) 17342	

help, and the various supervisors including Mr. Jessup. Since supervisors on the floor were required to do some of the routine work themselves when they were not busy otherwise, Mr. Jessup was restricted in the number of hours he could budget for supervision. When the department was busy, it was presumed that there would be more time spent in supervision than when work was slack.

The weighting factors in column 4 reflect the relative amounts of time normally required to do the several operations. The figures are not in units of time but are in relative units, the activity taking the longest time (excluding "sign up") being expressed as 1.00. For example, the activity reported on line 1 was supposed to take 63 percent as much time as the activity reported on line 3. The entries in column 5 are the measures of weighted output obtained by multiplying output figures by the weighting factors. The outputs per man-hour in column 3 are the simple ratios of output to hours worked. The overall output per man-hour figure (16.76 budgeted and 15.6 actual) is derived from the total weighted output figure of column 5.

Column 6 was used to record the quantity of work on hand, that is, carry-over, at the end of the week. Inasmuch as shipments of new

Exhibit 2

ACTUAL LABOR PERFORMANCE, EXAMINATION AND PREPARATION UNIT, WEEK ENDING MAY 15

ACTUAL PERFORMANCE

Receipts 6463	1 ACTUAL OUTPUT	2 HOURS WORKED	3 OUTPUT PER MAN HOURS (1 ÷ 2)	4 WEIGHTING FACTOR	5 WEIGHTED OUTPUT (1x4)	6 CARRY-OVER
1 EXAMINATION OF NEW MERCHANDISE	7042	224 6/12	31.2	.63	4427	12991
2 PREPARATION OF NEW MERCHANDISE	9023	278 3/	32.4	.73	6587	11620
3 INSPECTION OF CUSTOMER RETURNS	4046	156 7/	26.0	1.00	4046	
4 PREP. & LISTING OF CUSTOMER RETURNS	4603 5219	12 9/ 160 9/	358. 32.6	.09 .76	414 3967	
5 IRREGULARITY HANDLING	120	3 10/	31.7	.94	113	
6 R.G. & JOB SALE MDSE. HANDLING	2833	65 4/	43.3	.44	1247	
7 UTILITY		167 3/				
8 CLERICAL		164 10/				
9 SUPERVISION - INSTRUCT. TIMEKEEPING		119 9/				
10 Sign-up	1761	122 5/	14.4		2589	
11 Additional		19				
12 TOTAL		1495 3/	15.6		23390	

merchandise did not arrive every day, a stock of unexamined merchandise was ordinarily kept in Mr. Jessup's unit in order to even out his daily work load. Ordinarily this unexamined stock amounted to one or two days' work. As indicated on Exhibit 2, the unit received 6,463 new coats during the week ended May 15.

The reports shown in Exhibits 1 and 2 were sent to Mr. Phillips, superintendent of Division 10 of Storrow, who was Mr. Jessup's immediate superior. Since performance of the Examination and Preparation Unit for the week was below the budget, Mr. Jessup was required to make a written explanation. This accompanied the reports and read as follows:

The following factors were responsible for the failure to meet budget requirements:

The transfer to the division of the handling of even exchanges (customers' returns). Time had to be spent explaining the new procedure to all sign-up clerks as well as the additional time required to handle the added activity.

The transfer to the examination and preparation payroll of two employees (Brown and Swenson). Since no provision had been made for training during this week, examination output suffered. Assuming that the new examiners produced 50 percent of normal output, 40 hours additional were required, plus instruction time.

Twenty-four hours spent by Jones preparing drawings of the new preparation and examination fixtures and having them priced by the plant engineer.

Questions

1. What aspects of Mr. Jessup's job (speed, quality, cost, etc.) should Mr. Phillips be interested in controlling?
2. Insofar as you can determine, how well did Mr. Jessup perform in each of these aspects during the week ended May 15? With respect to his cost performance:
   a) What exactly was the standard to which Mr. Jessup was expected to adhere? (Hint: Trace through exactly how the figures in Exhibit 1 were reached; the process was *not* that of working from left to right.)
   b) By how many *hours* was actual performance over or under standard on each line?
3. Are you satisfied with Mr. Jessup's explanation of his performance?
4. What action, if any, should Mr. Phillips take?
5. Can you suggest a better way of presenting the information on performance?

CASE 17–7. PHILIP HENRY

"It's darn tough for an old dog like me to have to keep learning new tricks!" exclaimed Mr. Philip Henry in some exasperation. Mr. Henry, president of the PH Manufacturing Company, explained that he had given his son full responsibility for the operations of one branch of the business a few months previously. "Since then," he said, "it's been one dad-blamed thing after another!"

The most recent cause for complaint was the latest monthly profit and loss statement received from the plant run by his son:

Profit and Loss Statement, April 1961

	Loss	Gain	
Sales:			
14,000 X frames @ $7.50		$105,000	
12,000 H frames @ $8.00		96,000	$201,000
Standard cost of goods sold:			
26,000 × $4.50			117,000
Standard gross profit			$ 84,000
Materials variance		$1,500	
Labor variance	$3,100		
Overhead variance		3,700	
	$3,100	$5,200	2,100
Gross profit			$ 86,100
Selling and administrative expenses			40,000
Net Profit before Income Tax			$ 46,100

Exhibit 1

PROFITGRAPH

Standard Costs at Normal Volume:

Prime costs at standard..................... $3.00/Frame
Plant overhead:
    Indirect labor........................... 0.20   "
    Power.................................... 0.03   "
    Supervision and inspection................ 0.27   "
    Depreciation............................. 0.20   "
       Total plant overhead.................. 0.70   "
    General burden........................... 0.80   "
    Total Standard Cost...................... $4.50/Frame

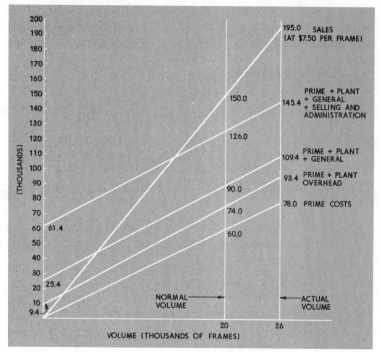

Mr. Henry explained that at the beginning of the year his son had prepared a "profitgraph" (Exhibit 1) which showed for various levels of sales volume what his plant's sales income, various categories of expense and profit should be. "As nearly as I can figure out that thing, he should have showed a profit of just under $50,000, even at our regular price of $7.50 per frame. Since it looks as if he got a better rate on his H frames this month, doesn't it look to you as if he should have cleared almost $56,000?" demanded Mr. Henry.

Further investigation disclosed that the plant under consideration made two types of metal frames which were used in the construction industry. The X frame, though larger than the H frame, was less complex and required less welding than did the H frame. At the beginning of the year when standards were set, it so happened that the extra material cost of the X frame was exactly offset by the extra labor cost of the H frame, so that the prime cost (direct labor plus materials) of each frame was $3. This greatly facilitated the preparation of volume-cost-profit estimates such as the profitgraph.

At that time, it was estimated that each X frame required two units of metal stripping and one unit of welding supplies. The H frame, on the other hand, required one unit of metal stripping and two units of welding supplies. Metal stripping normally cost $1 per unit and the welding supplies were purchased at a price of $0.60 per unit.

The direct labor requirement was the opposite of that for raw material. The X frame required approximately half as much time to fabricate as did the H frame. It was estimated that under normal working conditions, 5 H frames per man-hour could be assembled and one welder could keep up with two assemblers; that is, H frames could be welded at the rate of 10 per welder-hour. Assemblers normally received $2.50 per hour and welders received $3 per hour. Failure to schedule work properly and failure to provide adequately for absenteeism sometimes resulted in overtime or night work, which, of course, was paid for at premium rates. For purposes of variance computation such extra pay was shown as a labor cost, not an overhead cost, since it was felt that this more nearly placed the responsibility where it belonged.

The term "plant overhead" was used to describe a series of expenses actually incurred at the plant where the frames were manufactured. Indirect labor mainly consisted of the wages paid to several material handlers employed at the plant. At the time the standards were set, power was purchased at the rate of $0.008 per kw.-hr. Since that time the rate had gone up to $0.009, although no change had been made in the standards. For control purposes it was considered to be sufficiently accurate to assume that the power requirements would vary directly with the total number of frames produced. Supervision and inspection made up a fairly expensive item which tended to be reasonably constant over quite a wide range of output. Depreciation was computed on a straight-line basis and naturally depended upon the valuation placed on the production facilities of the part of the firm under consideration.

An examination of the general overhead revealed that this cost was an allocated cost. It was the practice of the PH Manufacturing Company to assign the general administrative overhead (the cost of such departments as accounting, engineering, etc., which were grouped at a central location) to the various operating branches of the firm. It was the policy of the company to anticipate this category of expense and assign a fixed sum monthly to each of the operating plants. However, when, as occasionally happened, the expenses of these central departments exceeded the amount anticipated, larger sums were assigned to the operating branches in order that such costs might be fully allocated by the year's end.

Selling and administrative expense was budgeted at a fixed sum per month since this expense was regarded as a direct result of management decision making and did not vary in direct relation with any of the standard parameters by which business activity might be judged.

Mr. Henry pointed out that in general, apart from the change in power rate noted above, only one change from standard had been made in the base rate paid for any input to the plant. He explained that the plant was now paying less than formerly for their supply of welding rod. "I'm really tickled to death at the interest the boy has taken in every part of the operation," he confided. "As you can see, he's managed to raise the price we're getting for H frames. Not only that, he looked around until he found a fellow who'd sell us welding rod at a lower price. Rod that used to cost us 60 cents we're now getting for only 50. I guess we have to burn a little more, but you can see from that materials variance that we're money ahead in the long run.

"Not only that," he continued, "a couple of months ago he talked me into buying some portable conveyors which he put in the plant and cut the cost of materials handling quite a bit. They weren't cheap, but they'll last 10 years and I expect they'll pay for themselves several times before that.

"Still and all," Mr. Henry grumbled, resuming the earlier trend of his conversation, "I wish I could get a little more accurate estimate of how well he's doing. When I got lost on that P.&L., I asked for a little more dope, and here are the actual figures for his April operations:

Production: 12,000 X frames; 12,000 H frames

Raw materials consumed:		
Metal stripping, 36,300 units	$	36,300
Welding supplies, 39,600 units		19,800
Direct labor:		
Assemblers, 3,450 hours		9,000
Welders, 2,160 hours		8,500
Plant overhead:		
Supervision and inspection		5,400
Power		900
Depreciation		7,000
Indirect labor		1,000
General burden		18,000
Total		$105,900

"In spite of the fact that his P.&L. doesn't show him making as much as he ought to from the profitgraph, it looks to me as if the actual cost for the average frame he's turned out this month is only about $4.41, almost a dime less than standard. It's all pretty confusing," concluded Mr. Henry. "I'd like you to explain a few things to me in plain English. First of all, how come the P.&L. doesn't agree with the profitgraph? Is it only because of the rate changes from standard? Secondly, how well is he doing? Is he making progress or is he just making changes? Thirdly, is there some less confusing (and not too expensive) way of reporting on how well he's making out? Finally, he says because of the changes he's made, some of our standards should be changed. What does he mean by that?"

Question

1. Answer Mr. Henry's questions as completely and clearly as possible.

CASE 17–8. TREFLAZ COMPANY

Treflaz Company was a large distributor of a wide range of consumer and industrial products. Products were sold to wholesalers, retailers, and directly to large institutional consumers (such as hospitals and laboratories). The organization was divided into 11 product sales departments, each responsible for the sale of a particular group of products, and 12 service and administrative departments.

Sales department X reported the following sales, cost of goods sold, and operating expenses for the month of September:

Net sales	$340,400
Cost of goods sold	191,000
Operating expenses	95,400

Each sales department prepared a budget at the beginning of each year. Because of seasonal factors, department X's September budget differed slightly from one twelfth of the annual budget for the year. The figures were:

Budgeted net sales, entire year	$3,900,000
Budgeted net sales, September	318,000

Cost of goods sold was budgeted on an annual basis by multiplying budgeted annual physical unit sales of each product by standard cost or purchase price per unit. This was then expressed as a percentage of budgeted net sales for the department. The resulting ratio was multiplied by budgeted monthly sales to compute budgeted costs of goods sold for each month. For department X the annual figures were:

Budgeted cost of goods sold, entire year, percent of budgeted net sales	54.4%
Budgeted cost of goods sold, September (54.4% × budgeted net sales)	$173,000

Exhibit 1

DEPARTMENT X

Budgeted Operating Expenses for the Year
and Actual Expenses for September

	Budgeted			
	Fixed Amount per Year	*Variable % of Sales*	*Basis for Charging Department*	*Actual Expenses September*
Net sales..........................	$3,900,000			$340,400
Direct Cost of Department A:				
Salaries and premiums........... $	84,000		Traceable	$ 6,900
Commission of representatives...	....	3.0%	"	10,200
Fringe benefits.................	16,800		"	300
Office supplies.................	12,000		"	1,900
Depreciation on equipment and furniture....................	9,200		"	800
Price lists, brochures...........	3,600		"	1,300
Travel and entertaining expense..	24,000		"	1,900
Postage, telephone, and telegraph...................	24,000		"	2,300
Cost of demonstration and models....................	2,400		"	....
Quality control and research......	54,000		"	4,500
General selling expense.........	18,000		"	2,600
Subtotal.................... $	248,000	3.0%		$ 32,700
Cost Allocated to Department A:				
Buildings (depreciation, maintenance, etc.)............ $	67,200		Fixed sum	$ 5,600
Management...................	....	2.0%	Fixed %	6,800
Data processing................	....	2.8	" "	9,500
Inventory handling.............	....	4.4	" "	15,000
Subtotal.................... $	67,200	9.2%		$ 36,900
Freight........................	....	1.8%	Traceable	$ 3,300
Reserves, Interest:				
Provision for advertising........	....	4.2%	Fixed %	$ 14,400
Provision for bad debts.........	....	0.5	" "	1,700
Provision for unsalable inventories....................	....	0.2	" "	700
Provision for free replacement of goods sold................	....	0.5	" "	1,700
Interest on inventories.......... $	27,300		*	2,900
Intetest on accounts receivable....	19,500		*	1,100
Subtotal.................... $	46,800	5.4%		$ 22,500
Total.................. $	362,000	19.4%		$ 95,400

*Charge based on fixed percent of departmental inventories and receivables; all other "fixed percent" charges
are based on actual net sales.

Operating expenses were divided into four categories:

Direct .... Traceable to specific sales departments.

Allocated .... Allocated to sales departments by
formula.

Freight .... Traceable to specific sales departments.

Reserves and interest .... Provisions for costs that will not be
known with certainty until some
future period, plus imputed interest on working capital.

Flexible budgets were prepared for expenses in each of these four
categories, on the bases described in Exhibit 1. These budgets for the
current year can be summarized in the formula:

Budgeted Operating Expense = $30,200 per Month + 19.4% × Net Sales.

The budget allowance for the year was:

Entire year (budgeted net sales of $3,900,000)....................$1,118,600
September (budgeted net sales of $318,000)....................... 91,900

Actual operating expenses charged against department X's revenues for
September totaled $95,400, as detailed in the right-hand columns of
Exhibit 1.

Budgeted net sales were stated on the basis of standard list prices[3] in
force at the beginning of the year. Actual net sales were recorded on the
basis of the amounts actually billed customers, but a supplementary
record was kept of the standard list prices of all goods sold. For September, actual net sales at standard list prices amounted to $355,500.

Questions

1. Prepare a summary report analyzing department X's profit variance for the
month of September, in as clear and as concise a form as possible. This
report should show, among other things, the total variance from budgeted
profit, the effect of deviations from budgeted physical sales volume, the
effect of deviations from budgeted or standard list prices, and the amounts
due to ineffective cost control and other causes, to the extent that these
effects can be identified. (Note: you need not accept the company's classifications into direct, allocated, etc., if you feel that some other classification
would be more meaningful.)

2. Do you agree with the company's methods of charging expenses to department X? Give your reasons.

3. What variances should be reported to the department managers?

---

[3] The company actually kept a record of sales at gross or dealer prices and *computed* standard net prices by multiplying these by a predetermined average discount
percentage. The result is approximately the same as that described here.

CASE 17–9.   MOULDING MOTORS, INC.

Mr. Richard Todd, the chief purchasing agent for the Mercobile Division of Moulding Motors, called in one of his buyers, Mr. Tom Roswald, to discuss Mr. Roswald's purchasing performance. Mr. Todd had just received the January report of buyers' performances, which indicated that Mr. Roswald had incurred a $500,000 loss on a seat-spring-assembly contract. This report was prepared by the estimators of the parts cost control department, who measured a buyer's performance by differences between negotiated prices and the so-called "price objectives" for purchased parts.

Organization of the Company

Moulding Motors, Inc., was a large, decentralized, multiplant manufacturer of automobiles and trucks. Each division manager was considered to be operating an autonomous unit, and was responsible to an executive vice president for his division's profitability.

Sales of the Mercobile Division, which assembled and sold the medium-priced line of Mercobiles, had been approximately $1.8 billion the previous year. The division operated several assembly plants located throughout the country. Parts and subassemblies, amounting to about $1.2 billion, were purchased either from other divisions of Moulding Motors or from outside vendors. The division had no facilities for manufacturing these parts and subassemblies.

Parts Cost Control System

The highly competitive automobile market required that Mercobile maintain close control over costs. Annually Moulding's top management established total price objectives for the new Mercobile models based on the price bracket in which they were to be sold and on anticipated market conditions. Mercobile Division management then broke down the total price objective for each model into percentages for material, assembly, distribution and other costs, and profit.

To control material costs, a system had evolved of continual cost and price estimates through the annual cycle of planning new models and engineering, developing, and procuring the parts for these models. Mr. Todd's parts cost control department was responsible for this task. Of the 97 employees in the department, 80 were estimators or supervisors, each of whom had several years of machine shop or time-study experience. These men maintained their familiarity with production processes, material market information, price trends, labor rates, and other pertinent data through reading a number of current periodicals in these fields. The estimators were responsible for providing cost estimates for important body and chassis parts, which, although they comprised only 21 percent of the total number of such parts, amounted to 94 percent of the cost of the body and chassis. They were also responsible for cost estimates for the tooling. Virtually all the tooling necessary for the fabrication of body and chassis parts was designed and purchased by the Mercobile Division. This tooling was provided the division's suppliers once contracts were signed. Cost control of engine parts was not the Mercobile Division's responsibility. This work was performed by an engine engineering division.

Each year the estimators provided tentative cost estimates of future models based upon clay models. Working only with what they could see of the interior and exterior body mock-ups and their knowledge of current costs, they developed detailed estimates of the cost *differences* between the proposed model's parts and the same parts for the current model. These "variance estimates" were based on operational changes that the estimators thought would be necessary, that is, changes in either the type, quantity, or cost of the material or labor required, and changes in labor times, labor rates, and overhead rates.

After the clay model had been approved, parts-cost estimates of the variances were refined, based first on broad structural drawings and, later, on detailed engineering drawings. During these development and engineering phases, variances for one item were typically estimated from five to seven times.

In the final phase, that of actual procurement, the estimators provided the buyers with individual part price objectives, which were the actual costs of the part on the current model plus or minus the estimated variances based upon the final engineering drawings.

The Buyer's Use of Estimates

Once a buyer received notification to purchase specific parts, he initiated requests for bids for the parts from suppliers, stating the specifications and anticipated monthly demand; at the same time he requested a price estimate from the parts cost control department.

The parts cost control department then completed and sent back to the buyer a price estimate sheet showing the part number, the actual price currently being paid for the same part, and the price that the estimating department thought should be paid in the coming year. The price estimate sheet did not show a detailed cost breakdown but indicated the extent to which the estimated price varied from the actual price as a result of either a design change or a change in the anticipated price level. Thus, if the current actual price for a particular part was $0.75 per unit and the estimated price was $0.72 per unit, the price estimate sheet would show whether a design change and/or price level change caused the difference. In this case, the estimate sheet might show that a design change was expected to decrease the unit price by $0.04 and that an increase in price levels was expected to increase the unit price by $0.01, resulting in a net unit cost decrease of $0.03.

In negotiations with vendors, the buyer used the estimate as his target price, although he attempted to negotiate a lower price. The estimates were particularly useful to the buyers when only one or two vendors supplied particular parts and components. In these cases, the buyers were handicapped by not being able to undertake comparative price analyses. Since the Mercobile Division bought parts or components from the manufacturing divisions of Moulding Motors, and since in some cases these divisions were the only possible suppliers, the Mercobile buyers found the estimates of particular help in negotiating the price at which to procure parts from these divisions.

When the buyer completed a transaction, he recorded the price he paid for the part or component on the price estimate sheet. The estimate sheet was then returned to the parts cost control department, where a record was kept, showing for each buyer the past month's negotiated savings or losses compared with the estimated price objectives. Once a month a report of each buyer's performance was sent to Mr. Todd, the Mercobile Division's chief purchasing agent.

Special Pricing Studies

Whenever a buyer or a member of the parts cost control department thought that an estimated price was out of line, as occurred when over a period of three or four years the accumulated variances for annual changes did not accurately reflect the current manufacturing costs, a special estimate was made that resulted in a new cost figure and price objective. Such studies differed from the typical estimates of variances in that the latter merely considered the cost variances attributable to design or price level changes.

In making a special pricing study, the estimator studied the engineering prints and then carefully defined each operation required for the fabrication. When possible, the estimator visited the manufacturer of the part or component. During these visits the estimator gathered as much information as possible about the operations performed, the type of equipment used, the operating time, and so on. However, even the manufacturing divisions of Moulding Motors refused to permit estimators to time operations or to obtain cost information; the manufacturing divisions, being autonomous, were in the same position as that of other vendors in selling their products to the Mercobile Division.

After he had picked up as much information as he could from the plant visit, the estimator proceeded to fill out a work sheet, entering the type, quantity, and price of material; the labor time, allowances, and rate; and the overhead charges. After he had estimated the costs for each part, he estimated the costs for any assembly operations. Finally, the cost of the individual parts and the cost of any assembly operations were totaled. To this total were added freight costs, general and administrative expenses, and profit, to give a final price.

The prices developed from these special studies were then sent to the buyer as his price objective.

The Seat-Spring Study

In the previous December, when the procurement of parts for the next year's Mercobiles was being initiated, Mr. Tom Roswald, a buyer of special assemblies, received a price objective from the parts cost control department of $14 a set for front- and back-seat-spring assemblies, one of the many items that he procured. Mr. Roswald decided that, since no new estimates of this assembly had been made for several years, the price might possibly be out of date. He therefore requested the parts cost control department to study the seat-spring-assembly manufacturing processes and determine a new price objective.

After a careful study of engineering drawings for the seat-spring assembly, the section supervisor of the body cost estimating section and two of his estimators spent a day at the plants of each of the two suppliers of these assemblies. The three men were particularly interested in the vendors' facilities, their method of fabricating and assembling the seat springs, the manpower required, and the time of the production cycle. After they had concluded these plant visits, the two estimators, with some assistance from their supervisor, spent three weeks in developing a new price objective. Work sheets were made out detailing each fabrication operation for the several side members of the frames, for the springs, and for the assembly of side members and springs into a completed unit. The estimators used as a basis the same production processes and equipment the two vendors were using. (Only in exceptional instances when the vendor was grossly inefficient would an estimator suggest changes in production methods.) Exhibit 1 is a work sheet showing in detail the material, labor, and overhead cost for each operation in the fabrication of one of the side members for the seat-spring assembly.

Once the detailed work sheets had been completed, they were summarized on a final work sheet to which was added freight, general administrative expenses, and profit, to arrive at the purchase price objective. The revised purchase price objective for the seat-spring assemblies indicated that each set should cost $11.50, in contrast to the prior estimated cost of $14 a set.

Exhibit 1

ESTIMATED COST ANALYSIS

		MATERIAL COST SUMMARY						
DATE OF EST.	MATERIAL DESCRIPTION AND SPECIFICATION	ROUGH PIECE WEIGHT	% SCRAP REJECT	MATERIAL COST		F.C.A. DEDUCTION	
				PER UNIT OF WEIGHT	$ PER PIECE	%	$
1-12	.075 C.R.C.Q. 21" Coil x 14⅜" = 2	3.289	—	.0602	.1980	—	—

		DESCRIPTION OF EQUIPMENT AND OPERATIONS					LABO
DATE OF ESTI-MATE	OPER. NO.	EQUIPMENT	OPERATION	NO. OF MEN	HOURLY PROD.	BASIC MINUTES	EX OFF
1-12	10		Blank (R.H. + L.H. Attached)	1	1,667	.036	
1-12	20		First form (R. + L. Attached)	1	950	.063	
1-12	30		Separat + partial trim (R. + L.)	1	950	.063	
1-12	40		Restrike (R. + L.)	1	732	.082	
1-12	50		Pierce (R. + L.)	1	732	.082	
1-12	60		Cam pierce pin holes (R. + L.)	1	732	.082	
1-12	70		Flange rear (R. + L.)	1	732	.082	
			TOTAL			.490	

PART NUMBER BAC-7060356-7-A

PART NAME Member- Frt. Seat Cushion Frame Side - Upper

SOURCE ___ **MAKE** ___ **BUY** ___

AUTHORITY AH I # 621 (12-16-55)   **PPC CODE** 3D46

NEXT ASSEMBLY BAC-7360336-A   **SHEET** 1 **OF** 1

NET MATERIAL PIECE COST .1980

MODEL YEAR	ALL	6	8	70A	70D	73A		70B	73B		70C	73C	58A	58B	64A	64B
		✓	✓			1 EA			1 EA					1EA	1EA	
	64C	63A	57A	78B	51A	57B	79F	59A	59B	59C	79B	79C	79D	79E	77A	78A	40A	40B
			1EA			1EA	1EA					1EA	1EA	1EA			

F.100 63-110 | F.100 82-110 | F.250 83-118 | F.350 93-130 | F.500 81-154 | F.600 81-154 | C.600 81-156 | B.600 84-192 | F.750 81-144 | F.800 81-144 | C.800 81-116 | T.800 81-144 | F.900 81-144

TIME AND COST

ALLOWANCE RPT TD.	OFF STD.	MINUTES INCL. ALL ALLWS.	LABOR RATE PER MINUTE	LABOR COST	BURDEN %	BURDEN $	TOTAL MFG. COST $	TOTAL COST INCLUDING A & C RATE	$	TOTAL COST INCLUDING PROFIT RATE	$
5		.040	.0333	.0013	300	.0039	.0052				
5		.069	.0333	.0023	300	.0069	.0092				
5		.069	.0333	.0023	300	.0069	.0092				
5		.090	.0333	.0030	300	.0090	.0120				
5		.090	.0333	.0030	300	.0090	.0120				
5		.090	.0333	.0030	300	.0090	.0120				
5		.090	.0333	.0030	300	.0090	.0120				
		.538		.0179		.0537	.0716				

When Mr. Roswald received the new purchase price objective, he contacted the two vendors and explained that the price his division was willing to pay for the seat springs in the coming year would be substantially less than the price paid in the past year. The larger vendor of the two, the Bornley Company, agreed to review its past year's price. In mid-January, the buyer and four estimators visited the Bornley Company and spent two days comparing their material, labor, and overhead cost data with data of the Bornley Company. On the basis of this review, the Bornley Company representatives agreed that they could reduce the price of seat-spring assemblies to $13.35 a set. At the same time, the purchase price objective developed by the Mercobile estimators was adjusted upward to $11.60 a set on the basis of the additional information they had received during the talks.

Because of the still existing spread in price, further negotiations were conducted the following week at the Mercobile Division's buying offices. After two days of negotiations, the Bornley Company finally reached an agreement with Mr. Roswald to supply the seat-spring assemblies for $12.50 a set. In the meantime, the Mercobile Division estimators had increased their purchase price objective to $11.75 a set.

Once the Bornley Company had agreed to the $12.50 figure, Mr. Roswald reached a quick settlement with the second vendor to supply seat-spring assemblies at the same price.

Meeting with Mr. Todd

In February, after he had received the January report showing the performance of his buyers, Mr. Todd, the Mercobile Division's chief purchasing agent, called in Mr. Roswald. Mr. Todd explained to Mr. Roswald that his purchasing performance for the month of January had been fine except for the seat-spring-assembly procurement. "According to my monthly report on buyers' performance," Mr. Todd said, "on the seat-spring assembly you lost over $500,000 compared with your purchase price objective. What I want to know is how this happened? Was it a poor job of estimating or was it a poor job of buying?"

Questions

1. Appraise the parts cost control system at the Mercobile Division of Moulding Motors.
2. How effective is the system of reporting negotiated gains or losses in procurement as a means of appraising buyers' performance?
3. Is Mercobile's system of providing price objectives to buyers applicable to other industries?
4. Did Mr. Roswald do a poor job of procuring the seat-spring assemblies, or was there a poor job in estimating the price?

PART IV

Accounting in Business
Decisions

CHAPTER 18

DECIDING AMONG ALTERNATIVE COURSES OF ACTION

Businessmen are many times called upon to make decisions by choosing what they believe to be the best one of several possible alternative courses of action. Problems in this area are therefore called "alternative choice problems."

In a great many business problems, the decision is made intuitively; that is, there is no systematic attempt to define, measure, and weigh the advantages and disadvantages of each alternative. A person who makes an intuitive decision may do so simply because he is not aware of any other way of making up his mind, or he may do so, and with good reason, because the problem is one in which a systematic attempt to weigh alternatives is not useful, too difficult, too expensive, or simply not possible.

No mathematical formula will aid in solving a problem in which the attitudes or emotions of the individuals involved are the dominant factors, nor is there any point in attempting to make calculations if the available information is so sketchy or so inaccurate that the results are completely unreliable.

In many other situations, however, it is useful to reduce at least some of the anticipated consequences of the alternatives to a quantitative basis and to weigh these consequences in a more or less systematic manner. Usually, this process involves a consideration of accounting data, with particular attention to cost data. Some of the problems which managers are likely to face in using cost data as an aid in making these business decisions are discussed in this chapter.

APPROACH TO ALTERNATIVE CHOICE PROBLEMS

Criteria

In earlier chapters, we assumed that, insofar as it is measured quantitatively, the dominant objective of a business is to earn a satisfactory return on its investment. We now expand this concept by adding the common-sense idea that if two alternative courses of action are being considered, the management will select the one that is likely to lead to the higher return on investment, or if no investment is involved, the one with the higher profit.[1]

The fact that this criterion is limited to measurable objectives should again be emphasized. In many practical problems, personal satisfaction, friendship, patriotism, self-esteem, or other considerations may be much more important than return on investment. Or, the company may have other measurable objectives, such as maintenance of its market position, stabilization of employment, or avoidance of undue risk. When these considerations are important or dominant, the solution to the problem cannot be reached by the techniques discussed here. The most these techniques can do is show the effect on return on investment of seeking some other objective. The problem then becomes one of deciding whether the attainment of the other objective is worth the cost.

Outline of Approach

Return on investment may be expressed as the ratio:

$$\frac{\text{Revenue} - \text{Costs}}{\text{Investment}}.$$

Although the general approach to all alternative choice problems is similar, it is useful to discuss three types separately. First, there are problems that involve only the cost element of the ratio. Since revenue and investment are unaffected, the best alternative is the one with the lowest cost. Problems of this type are discussed in the next section. Second, there are problems in which both revenue and costs are involved. These are discussed in the latter part of this chapter. Third, there are problems that involve both the numerator and the denominator of the ratio. These are discussed in Chapter 19.

---

[1] "Profit" in this context is usually defined as in the ordinary accounting sense, but there are exceptions, because profit does not always measure the "well-offness" of a business, particularly in the short run. A more accurate, but also more vague, criterion is that the management will select the alternative that makes the business the "best off."

STEPS IN ANALYSIS. Before a separate discussion of these types is given, some general comments about approaching alternative choice problems are in order. Following is a list of steps that are useful for most problems:

1. Define the problem.
2. Define the most likely alternative solutions.
3. Measure and weigh those consequences of each alternative that can be expressed in quantitative terms.
4. Evaluate those consequences that cannot be expressed in quantitative terms and weigh them against each other and against the measured consequences.
5. Reach a decision.

The discussion in this chapter has to do primarily with costs, which are the best means of measuring those consequences that can be expressed in quantitative terms. Thus, we focus primarily on step 3. Brief mention will be made of the other steps, but in no sense is this a comprehensive discussion of the art of decision making.

Definition of the Problem and of Alternative Solutions

Unless the problem is clearly and precisely defined, quantitative figures that are relevant to it cannot be computed. In many situations, the definition of the problem, or even the recognition that a problem exists, may be the most difficult part of the whole process.

Quite often, the possible alternative solutions to the problem are by no means clear at the outset. For example, suppose that a factory manager is considering a machinery salesman's proposal that a certain machine should be used to perform an operation now done by hand methods. At first glance, there may appear to be two alternatives: (*a*) continue to perform the operation by hand or (*b*) buy the new machine. Actually, however, several additional alternatives should perhaps be considered, such as these: (*c*) buy a machine other than the one recommended by the salesman, (*d*) improve the present method of making the part, or even (*e*) eliminate the manufacturing operation altogether and buy the part from an outside source. Some thought should be given to these other possibilities before attention is focused too closely on the original proposal.

On the other hand, the more alternatives that are considered, the more complex the analysis becomes. For this reason, having thought about all the possible alternatives, the analyst should eliminate without more ado those that are clearly unattractive, leaving only a few for detailed analysis. In the simplest situation, only two alternatives are examined closely. These can be described in general terms as follows: (*a*) the continuation of what is now being done, or (*b*) the adoption of a proposed change—a new machine, a new process, a new selling price, and so on. Note that there must always be at least two alternatives. If only one course of action is open, the company literally has "no choice," and hence no analytical problem. In most problems one of the alternatives is to keep on doing what is now being done. This "no-change" alternative is often used as a bench mark against which other alternatives are compared.

Weighing and Measuring the Quantitative Factors

There are usually a number of advantages and a number of disadvantages associated with each of the alternative solutions of a problem. The task of the analyst is to evaluate each of the relevant factors and to decide, on balance, which alternative has the largest *net* advantage.

If the factors are stated solely in words, such an evaluation is an exceedingly difficult task. For example, consider the statement that a proposed manufacturing process will save labor but that it will result in increased power consumption and require additional insurance protection. Such a statement provides no way of weighing the relative importance of the saving in labor against the increased power and insurance costs. If, by contrast, the statement is made that the process will save $1,000 in labor, that increased power will cost $200, and that increased insurance will cost $100, the net effect of these three factors can easily be estimated; that is, $1,000 - $200 - $100 is a net advantage of $700 for the proposed process.

The reason why we try to express as many factors as possible in quantitative terms is made clear in the above illustration: once we have done this, it becomes easy to find the net effect of these factors by the simple arithmetic operations of addition and subtraction.

Evaluating and Weighing the Unmeasured Factors

For most problems there are important factors that are not measurable; yet the final decision must take into account *all* differences between the alternatives being considered, both those that are measured and those not measured. The process of weighing the relative importance of these unmeasured factors, both as compared with one another and as compared with the net advantage or disadvantage of the measured factors, is solely a judgment process.

It is easy to underestimate the importance of these unmeasured factors. The numerical calculations for the measured factors often require hard work, and they result in a figure that has the appearance of being definite and precise; yet all the factors that influence the final number may be collectively less important than a single factor that has not been measured. For example, there are many persons who could meet their transportation needs less expensively by using public conveyances rather than by operating an automobile, but who nevertheless own an automobile for reasons of prestige, convenience, or other unmeasured factors.

As another example, an analysis of trucking costs and freight movements indicated that a company could save $14,260 a year by operating its own truck instead of using common carriers. Nevertheless, the decision was made to continue using common carriers, and the reasons given were as follows:[2]

1. The difference in the densities of the products carried would complicate the truck loading.
2. The problem of scheduling the routing of the truck to insure maximum utilization would be difficult.
3. The length of the round trip would result in the truck's visiting some locations after working hours, thus missing the pickup or delivery.
4. Our company is not unionized. The question of unionization of the truck driver would be troublesome.
5. It may be possible to have the suppliers absorb the freight, thus eliminating the transportation cost entirely.
6. Who will administer the operation of the truck? The traffic manager has only one clerk.
7. How are the common carriers going to treat the company on the remainder of the items that cannot be carried on the company truck?
8. Freight rates and truck operating costs are subject to change.
9. The supply points may change.
10. Since there is only one truck and one driver, the risk of truck breakdown and illness of the driver would be too great.

Note that this list includes both factors that probably were unmeasurable (e.g., the consequences of unionization) and factors that could have been measured, but in fact were not (e.g., the cost of administering the operation of the truck).

Cost calculations make it possible to express as a single figure the net effect of many factors bearing on the decision. They therefore reduce the number of factors that must be considered separately in the final judgment process that leads to the decision; or, as is often said, they narrow the area within which judgment must be exercised. Rarely, if ever, do they eliminate the necessity for this crucial judgment process.

Reaching a Decision

Having gone through the above process, the analyst has only two choices: to seek additional information or to reach a decision and act on it. Most decisions could be improved by making the former choice; in a

---

[2] From "Norwalk Screw Company," a case prepared by Professor Harold Bierman, Jr.

complicated business situation, it is usually possible to obtain more information than is available when the analysis begins. However, obtaining this
information always involves effort and, what is more important, it involves time. There comes a point, therefore, when the analyst concludes
that he is better off to act than to defer a decision until more data have
been collected.

PROBLEMS INVOLVING COSTS

In the first class of problems we shall discuss, the difficult part of the
quantitative analysis involves costs; that is, revenue is either unaffected by
the alternative or is affected in such an obvious way that no analytical problems are involved. Illustrative of these problems are the following questions: Will a proposed new method of doing something cost less than the
present method? Which of several proposed methods is the best? Should
we manufacture a certain part or buy it from an outside vendor? Shall
we discontinue a department that is apparently losing money? Shall we
produce on one shift or two shifts? Shall we shut down the plant temporarily? Problems of this type are often called *trade-off problems:* we
wish to find out whether one alternative has an acceptable trade-off
compared with another in terms of its costs and the advantages that we
hope to obtain from adopting it.

The types of cost that are relevant in problems of this kind can be
summed up in two brief statements: (1) they are *future* costs and (2)
they are *differential* costs.

Future Costs

No decision made by man can change what has already happened. The
past is history; decisions made now can affect only what *will* happen in
the future. It follows that the only relevant cost figures are estimates of
what costs will be in the future.

The difficulty in applying this obvious statement arises from the fact
that in many instances our best information about future costs is derived
from an analysis of historical costs. One can easily lose sight of the fact
that historical costs per se are irrelevant. These historical costs, often
obtained from the accounting records, may be a useful guide as to what
costs are likely to be in the future, but using them as a guide is basically
different from using them as if they were statements of what the future
costs are in fact *going* to be.

Except where future costs are determined by long-term contractual
arrangements, such costs are necessarily estimates, and they usually cannot
be close estimates. An estimated labor saving of $1,000 a year for five
years, for example, implies assumptions as to future wage rates, future

fringe benefits, future labor efficiency, future production volume, and other factors that cannot be known with certainty at the time the estimate is prepared. Consequently, there is ordinarily no point in carrying computations of cost estimates to several decimal places; in fact, there is a considerable danger of being misled by the illusion of precision that such meticulous calculations give.

BOOK VALUE OF FIXED ASSETS.   An historical cost that seems to cause considerable difficulty is the book value of fixed assets. Suppose that a new production process is proposed as a substitute for operations now performed on a certain machine. The machine was purchased six years previously for $10,000, and depreciation on it has been charged at $1,000 a year, a total of $6,000 to date. The machine therefore has a book value of $4,000. Assume that it has no market value, that is, the cost of removing it just equals its value as scrap metal, and assume that it would be of no further use to the company. If the new process requires additional labor and related costs of $600 a year, one could argue that in spite of this increase, adoption of the process would save a net of $400 a year, since the depreciation charge of $1,000 a year would no longer be a cost. The fact is, however, that the remaining book value must be written off the books; and this amount, of course, exactly offsets the total depreciation charge over the remaining life of the machine. Thus the depreciation charge is *not* relevant to the problem. It is a *sunk cost*, arising from actions taken in the past, and unaffected by any subsequent decision. Adoption of the proposed process would in fact result in a *loss* of $600 a year.

The cost of an asset is supposed to be written off over its useful life. In the above example, we know, by hindsight, that this was not done, for if it had been done, the book value of the machine would be zero at the time it became obsolete. This was an error, but it was an error made in the past, and no current decision can change it.

The irrelevance of sunk costs can be demonstrated by comparison of two income statements for the complete time periods of the remaining life of the machine, one showing the results of operations if the new process is adopted and the machine is scrapped, and the other showing the results if the process is continued on the present equipment, as in Illustration 18–1. This illustration demonstrates that there would be a loss of $2,400 over a four-year period if the new process were adopted.

If the machine had a *market value*, this fact would be a relevant consideration, since its disposal would then bring in additional cash. If the *tax effect* of writing off the loss on disposal were different from the tax effect of writing off depreciation over the four-year period, which is often the case, the effect on taxes is relevant. The book value of the machine itself is not relevant. Ultimately, the book value is going to be charged against income, but whether this is done through the annual depreciation charge or through a lump-sum write-off makes no ultimate

Illustration 18–1

COMPARATIVE INCOME STATEMENTS ILLUSTRATING
IRRELEVANCE OF SUNK COSTS

(For Four Years)

	A. If New Process Is Adopted		B. If New Process Is Not Adopted
Sales...............................		$1,000,000	$1,000,000
Cost and expenses:			
Costs unaffected by the decision.......$700,000			$700,000
Additional labor, etc..................	2,400		0
Depreciation on machine.............	0		4,000
Book loss on disposal of machine......	4,000		0
Total costs and expenses...........		706,400	704,000
Profit before income taxes..............		$ 293,600	$ 296,000
			−293,600
Loss if New Process Is Adopted.........			$ 2,400

difference. The facts given indicate that the new process should not be adopted.

Differential Costs

A great many cost items will be unaffected by the alternatives under consideration, and these may be disregarded. Attention is focused on items whose costs will be *different* under one alternative from what they will be under the others. Suppose, for example, that a company is considering the possibility of buying Part No. 101 from an outside supplier instead of manufacturing the part as it is now doing. In this case the alternatives are either: (*a*) to continue manufacturing Part No. 101, or (*b*) to purchase Part No. 101 from the outside supplier. All revenue items, all selling and administrative expenses, and all production costs other than those directly associated with the manufacture of Part No. 101 will probably be unaffected by the decision. If so, there is no need to consider them.

In some calculations, a listing of some or all of these unaffected costs may be useful, so as to insure that all relevant cost items have been considered. This was done, in Illustration 18–1, and there is no harm in doing so, provided the unaffected costs are treated exactly the same way under each of the alternatives. The *net difference* between the costs of the two alternatives, which is the figure we seek, is not changed by adding equal amounts to the cost of each alternative.

Costs from a Cost Accounting System.   In considering "costs that make a difference," figures drawn from a cost accounting system may be misleading, since differences in such figures may not reflect actual differences in cost arising because of the alternative under consideration. For example, for cost accounting purposes, the "cost" of Part No. 101 may include charges for rent, heat, light, and other occupancy costs that are prorated to this product on the basis of the number of square feet of floor space occupied by the department in which it is manufactured. If Part No. 101 were purchased from an outside vendor, the floor space formerly used in its manufacture would be saved. It does not necessarily follow, however, that the *costs* prorated to Part No. 101 on the basis of floor space used would actually be saved. The costs for rent, heat, light, and so on might not be changed at all by the decision not to manufacture the part. Unless there is some real saving in cash outlays (or their equivalent) or some real additional revenue possibilities resulting from the use of the freed floor space (e.g., renting it, or manufacturing some revenue-producing item in it), the "cost" of floor space should be ignored.

In general, when estimating differential costs, *allocated or prorated accounting charges should be viewed with skepticism.* In a cost accounting system, each unit of product manufactured is charged with its fair share of all manufacturing costs, including costs that are not directly caused by or traceable to the product. Such cost figures are not intended to show, and in fact do not show, the differential costs that are relevant in most alternative choice problems. A company may allocate overhead as 100 percent of direct labor; but this does *not* mean that if direct labor cost is decreased $575 by purchasing Part No. 101, there will be a corresponding decrease of $575 in overhead costs. Overhead costs may not decrease at all; they may decrease, but by an amount less than $575; or they may even increase, as a result of an increased procurement and inspection work load resulting from the purchase of Part No. 101. In order to estimate what will happen to overhead costs, we must go behind the overhead rate and analyze what will actually happen to the various elements of overhead under each of the alternatives being considered.

Fringe Benefits. Labor costs are one of the important considerations in many business decisions. In many problems an allowance for fringe benefits should be added to the actual amount of wages earned for the work done. Fringe benefits include such items as taxes for old-age and unemployment compensation; insurance, medical, and pension plans; vacation and holiday pay; and the like. For business in general, these benefits average about 25 percent of wages earned, although there is so wide a variation among different companies that an overall average is unlikely to be reliable in a specific situation. To the extent that the cost of these fringe benefits varies directly with wages paid, they are relevant when costing an alternative that involves a change in labor costs.

Opportunity Costs. Most, but not all, relevant cost figures are represented by actual cash outlays. In some cases, however, the concept of cost should be broadened to include sacrifices that are not immediately reflected in the cash account. Such amounts are called *imputed* costs or *opportunity* costs. Opportunity cost is measured by the sacrifice involved in accepting the alternative under consideration rather than the next best opportunity. The floor space item mentioned above provides an example. If the floor space required to make Part No. 101 can be used for some other revenue-producing purpose, then the sacrifice involved in using it for Part No. 101 is a cost of making that part. Note that this cost is measured by the income sacrificed if the floor space is used for Part No. 101; this is not necessarily the same as the allocated cost per square foot of floor space as developed in the cost accounting system.

In general, if accepting an alternative requires that facilities or other resources must be devoted to that alternative that otherwise could be used for some other purpose, there is an opportunity cost, and it is measured by the profit that would have been earned had the resources been devoted to the other purpose.

VARIABLE COSTS.   The term "differential costs" does not have quite the same meaning as the term "variable costs." Variable costs are those that vary directly with, and roughly proportionately to, changes in the *volume of output;* that is, if output increases 50 percent, variable costs will increase approximately 50 percent. Differential costs are related to the specific alternatives that are being analyzed. If, in a specific problem, one of the alternatives involves a change in output, then differential costs may be the same as variable costs. Depending on the problem, however, the differential costs may include nonvariable items. A proposal to change the number of plant watchmen and their duties, for example, involves no elements of variable cost.

MARGINAL AND INCREMENTAL COSTS.   The terms "marginal" and "incremental" cost are usually used in a sense that makes them synonymous with differential cost. A semantic problem can arise when these terms are used as general labels for cost elements, rather than with reference to the specific set of alternatives being analyzed, and caution is necessary before accepting such general statements as, "This cost is incremental." The proper question is, "Is it incremental in the specific problem being analyzed?"

IMPORTANCE OF THE TIME SPAN.   The question of what costs are relevant depends to a considerable extent on the time span of the problem. If the proposal is to make only one unit of Part No. 101, only the direct material costs may be relevant; the work could conceivably be done without any differential labor costs if, for example, workers were paid on a daily basis and had some idle time. At the other extreme, if the proposal involves a commitment to make Part No. 101 over the foreseeable future, practically all the elements of manufacturing costs may be affected. In general, *the longer the time span of the proposal, the more items of cost are differential.* In the very long run, all costs are differential. Thus, in very long-run problems, differential costs include the same elements as the conventional accounting "full costs," for in the long run one must consider even the replacement of buildings and equipment, which are sunk costs in the short run. (Although the *elements* are the same, the amounts are different, since alternative choice problems involve future costs, not historical costs.) In the short run, relatively few cost elements may be subject to change by a management decision.

GENERAL CHARACTERISTICS OF DIFFERENTIAL COSTS. Few specific suggestions can be made as to what costs should be included in an alternative choice calculation. In general, we are looking for costs that *would* be incurred if the alternative were adopted but that *would not* be incurred if the alternative were not adopted. Labor costs are relevant in many problems; but if in a specific situation people are going to be employed regardless of which alternative is adopted, labor costs may not be relevant. For example, it can be demonstrated that a given quantity of material can be typed in less time with an electric typewriter than with a nonelectric typewriter, but an actual saving in labor costs will result from the purchase of an electric typewriter only if the time thus freed is used productively for some other purpose.

Mechanics of the Calculation

Any of several devices can be used for combining the various cost elements that are relevant to each alternative. Costs may, for example, be listed separately under each alternative, viz:

	If Part No. 101 Is Manufactured	*If Part No. 101 Is Purchased*
Purchased material...............	$ 572	$1,700
Labor.........................	600	25*
Power.........................	98	0
Other costs....................	150	0
Total.....................	$1,420	$1,725
		1,420
Difference (Disadvantage of Purchasing)...............		$ 305

* Estimated handling cost.

Or, exactly the same result can be obtained by figuring the net differences between the alternatives, viz:

	If Part No. 101 Is Purchased
Purchase price of Part No. 101......................	$1,700
Costs saved by not manufacturing Part No. 101:	
Raw material.....................................$572	
Labor.. 575	
Power.. 98	
Other costs................................... 150	
Total costs saved............................	1,395
Net Disadvantage in Purchasing....................	$ 305

The same result also can be obtained by preparing a complete income statement for each alternative for the total time period involved in the proposal, as was done in Illustration 18–1. This requires more work than either of the other two types of calculations shown above, but it provides assurance that some cost or revenue elements have not been overlooked, and it may also provide a useful format for explaining the calculations to someone else.

The Margin of Error

Cost figures used in alternative choice problems are estimates, and in many cases they are very rough estimates. In some calculations, an attempt is made to express the margin of error in these estimates by making two sets of calculations, one in which costs are estimated on the high side and the other in which they are estimated on the low side. Even though the range between these two estimates is wide, the rough estimates may be more useful than none at all, since they set boundaries on the net influence of the factors that are contained in them.

Sometimes the high and low estimates are combined into a single "compromise" figure by averaging them. This is often a useful device, but it should be recognized that the compromise is not necessarily a more correct estimate than either the high or the low figure. The reliability of the estimate depends on the uncertainties involved, and there may be no way of eliminating or minimizing these uncertainties.

Example: Operating an Automobile

As an example of the fact that the cost elements that are relevant in an alternative choice problem vary with the nature of the problem, let us consider the costs that are relevant for various decisions that may be made about owning and operating an automobile. A study made by Runzheimer and Company and published by the American Automobile Association gives the national average cost in 1969 of operating a 1969 eight-cylinder Chevrolet Impala four-door hardtop (equipped with standard accessories —radio, automatic transmission, and power steering) as follows:

Variable Costs:	*Average per Mile*
Gasoline and oil	2.76 cents
Maintenance	0.68
Tires	0.51
Total	3.95 cents

Nonvariable Costs:	*Annual*
Fire and theft insurance	$ 44
Other insurance	256
License and registration	24
Depreciation	729
Total	$1,053

What costs are relevant? In answering this question, we shall assume that the car in question is comparable with that for which the averages were computed; that gasoline prices, insurance rates, and the like are "average" in the locality in which the automobile is to be operated; that the AAA figures are reliable; that the classification of certain costs as variable and others as nonvariable is valid; and that costs during the period in which the automobile will be operated will be the same as they were in 1969. Unless each of these assumptions is reasonable, the figures given above cannot be used. Accepting these assumptions, we can make the following statements about relevant costs:

1. When a person owns an automobile, already has it registered, and is deciding whether it is worthwhile to make a proposed trip, the relevant costs are 3.95 cents a mile times the estimated mileage of the trip. The nonvariable costs are not relevant since they will continue whether or not the trip is made. (Costs are shown here exactly as reported in the AAA table above; actually, you would undoubtedly round off the numbers rather than showing them to hundredths of a cent.)

2. When a person owns an automobile and is deciding whether to (*a*) register it for a year or (*b*) leave it idle and use some other form of transportation, the relevant costs are the insurance and fees of $324 plus 3.95 cents a mile times the number of miles he expects to travel by automobile during the year. The $324 has become a cost because it is affected by the decision as to registration.

3. When a person is deciding whether to (*a*) buy an automobile or (*b*) use some other means of transportation, the relevant costs are $1,053 a year plus 3.95 cents a mile times the number of miles he expects to travel. (Actually, in this case one probably would have a closer estimate for depreciation for the specific automobile under consideration than the average figure of $729.)

Other statements can be made for the costs relevant to other contemplated uses of the automobile. These illustrations may help to clarify the basic point that the relevant costs for a given decision are the costs affected by that decision; other costs can be ignored.

Example: Economic Lot Size

When manufacture of a product involves setup costs that are incurred once for each lot manufactured, the question arises of how many units should be made in one lot. If the demand is predictable and if sales are reasonably steady throughout the year, the optimum quantity to manufacture at one time, called the *economic lot size* or *economic order quantity*, is arrived at by considering two offsetting influences—setup costs and inventory costs. Consider an item with annual sales of 1,200 units. If the whole 1,200 were manufactured in one lot, only one setup a year would be necessary, but inventory costs would be high, since the inventory would start with 1,200 units and would average 600 units over the year.[3] By contrast, manufacture of 12 lots of 100 units each (i.e., one lot a month) would involve 12 setups but a low inventory carrying cost, since there would be an average of 50 units in inventory at any one time, that is, $\frac{1}{2}(100 + 0) = 50$.

Given this set of relationships, the mathematician can easily construct a formula from which the economic lot size can be found. His reasoning is as follows. Let:

Q = Economic lot size (number of units in one lot).
S = Setup costs, for one setup.
R = Annual requirements in units.
K = Inventory carrying charge, expressed as a percentage of average inventory value.
C = Factory cost per unit.

Then:

Number of lots made in one year $= \dfrac{R}{Q}$.

Annual setup cost = setup cost for one lot times number of lots made per year

$$= S\left(\frac{R}{Q}\right) = \frac{SR}{Q}.$$

Average number of units in inventory $= \dfrac{Q}{2}$.

Average value of inventory = average units in inventory times unit cost

$$= \left(\frac{Q}{2}\right)C = \frac{QC}{2}.$$

Annual carrying cost = K times average inventory value

$$= \left(\frac{QC}{2}\right)K = \frac{QCK}{2}.$$

Total cost will be at a minimum when the increase in carrying cost resulting from adding one more unit to a lot is equal to the corresponding

---

[3] Inventory is 1,200 units immediately after the lot has been manufactured and declines to zero a year later. Assuming that the decline is at a roughly even rate throughout the year, the average inventory for the year is one half the sum of the beginning plus ending inventories; thus: $\frac{1}{2}(1,200 + 0) = 600$.

decrease in setup costs. Using calculus, we can show that this minimum occurs when annual setup cost equals annual carrying cost,[4] or when:

$$\frac{SR}{Q} = \frac{QCK}{2}.$$

Solving for Q gives the desired formula:

$$Q = \sqrt{\frac{2SR}{CK}}.$$

At this point, the mathematician loses interest. As far as he is concerned, the problem has been solved, and all that remains is to insert the relevant numbers in the formula and do the arithmetic. But the important practical question is: what numbers? What are the setup costs that are relevant to this problem? Clearly, they include the differential labor costs involved in making the setup, they include fringe benefits on this labor, they include any differential overhead costs, and they also include such costs as moving the products to inventory if these are a function of the number of lots manufactured, even though these are not labeled as setup costs. Deciding which costs vary with the number of lots produced and are therefore differential setup costs is a difficult matter. Similarly, the unit cost used in valuing the inventory involves problems. Essentially, we need to know how much money will be tied up in inventory, and for this purpose it may be necessary to adjust the cost-accounting unit cost of the products to eliminate elements such as depreciation that do not represent current outlays of funds. Finally, the calculation of the inventory carrying charge includes an estimate of interest costs, and of the costs associated with the occupancy of warehouse space.

The point is that in this and many other types of business problems involving costs, the general approach to the problem may be quite simple and definite, but estimating the relevant cost figures may be exceedingly difficult.

PRICING

The second class of problems involves revenue considerations as well as cost considerations. The discussion here will focus on the pricing problem; that is, how much should we charge for our products? This is the most common problem in this category.

---

[4] It is not *generally* true that when it is desired to find a minimum total cost point for two costs, one of which is increasing and the other decreasing, the minimum will be found at the point where the two totals are equal. It happens to be true for the specific cost functions being considered here.

Theoretical Considerations

Some economics texts state that the selling price of a product should be set so as to maximize the difference between revenue and costs. In order to do this, one needs to be able to estimate (1) the demand schedule, which is the number of units that would be sold at each possible selling price; and (2) *marginal* costs. Marginal costs, which in this context are the same as differential costs, can be estimated by techniques already discussed, but estimating the demand schedule is a much more difficult matter. Who can estimate what quantity of product will be sold at one price, let alone at all possible prices? Indeed, the difficulty is so great that few companies ever attempt to estimate a demand schedule, and few managers have ever even seen one. Without a demand schedule, the elaborate diagrams and equations that economists have built up cannot be used to solve real-world pricing problems (although they are useful for classroom analysis).

Not only is the maximization approach to pricing unworkable, but also it leads to "gouging," "profiteering," "charging all the traffic will bear," and other unethical practices. A discussion of pricing that is built on the maximization foundation would therefore be both impractical and ethically indefensible.

This fact is one of the reasons why this book is not based on the profit maximization concept. (A second reason has to do with the cost-of-capital approach to investment decisions, discussed in Chapter 19.) But if we do not use profit maximization as an underlying premise, we must have an alternative concept. Some have advocated "long-run profit maximization," but this is too vague to serve as a basis for the solution of practical problems.

The concept that probably underlies the actions of most responsible businessmen is that of *satisfactory profit*, or satisfactory return on investment; that is, they have a notion of a fair or reasonable profit that should be earned in their business, and they strive to earn such a profit. This is the concept we shall use.

The satisfactory profit concept leads to what is called *full-cost pricing* as the normal approach to pricing problems, and to *contribution pricing* in certain unusual situations.

Full-Cost Pricing

Many companies have no pricing problem. A market price exists, customers will not pay more than this price, and there is no reason why the product should be sold for a lower price. Wheat and other products traded on commodity markets are the classic examples, but the situation also exists for companies in many other industries, such as small companies in industries where one or a few large companies exercise price leadership. Under such circumstances, a company makes no pricing calculations; it simply charges the market price.

If a company does have the problem of determining its selling prices, the usual practice is to compute the full cost of the product and add to this a profit margin, figured either as a percentage of cost or preferably as a percentage return on the investment involved in making the product. Note that the relevant costs are *full costs*, which are the direct costs plus a fair share of allocated costs; they are not the differential costs discussed in the preceding section.

The result of this calculation is a *first approximation* to the price; it is modified to take into account the strength of competition, the necessity of fitting the price into customary price lines (such as $9.98 dresses), and many other marketing considerations. Consequently, actual prices and hence actual profit margins on specific products may differ widely from this first approximation. The company plans, however, that overall it will obtain the desired profit, with extra profits on high-margin products offsetting thin profits on low-margin products. It will achieve this goal if a fair share of total costs is allocated to each product, and if it obtains a satisfactory profit margin above this cost, on the average, for the products it actually sells.

Adjustments to this first approximation may take the form of changing costs as well as changing profit margins. If it is thought that the computed price is too high, then the product may be redesigned to bring its costs down so that a satisfactory profit can be made at the attainable price. In this process, it is full costs rather than differential costs that are considered.

PROFIT MARGIN. In many companies, the profit margin is expressed as a percentage of cost. Increasingly, however, companies are figuring the profit margin as a return on the assets employed in manufacturing and selling the product. This newer practice relates prices to the overall objective of earning a satisfactory return on investment.

Assume, for example, that a company manufactures two products, A and B, the manufacturing cost of each being $6 per unit. At a mark-on of 50 percent of cost (33 percent of selling price), the normal selling price of each product would be $9, and if 100,000 units of each are sold, the total margin would be $600,000. Under return-on-investment pricing, the company would first estimate the total assets employed for the two products. Assume that this works out to $3 million, or $30 per unit, for Product A and $1 million, or $10 per unit, for Product B. If the company desires 15 percent return on its investment, the normal margin would be $4.50 for Product A and $1.50 for Product B, making the normal selling prices $10.50 and $7.50 respectively. These prices produce the same total margin, $600,000, as the alternative prices calculated as a 50 percent mark-on on cost. Product A's higher price reflects the fact that more assets are required to make a unit of Product A than a unit of Product B.

ADDING OR DROPPING PRODUCTS.   In making decisions about whether or not to add a new product and whether or not to discontinue an existing product, similar considerations normally govern. A new product is normally added to the line only if it is expected to produce a satisfactory return on the investment. If an existing product has a low margin, and if the situation cannot be corrected by increasing prices or reducing costs, then the product normally is replaced with a more profitable one. Again, marketing considerations may dictate departures from the normal procedure. Many low-margin products are retained so that the company may offer its customers a full line; equipment may be sold at a low margin in order to induce the sale of high-margin accessories and supplies;[5] no replacement product with an adequate margin may be known; and so on.

PRICE REGULATIONS.   A further reason for basing price on full costs rather than on differential costs is the fact that the Robinson-Patman Act prohibits differentials in the prices charged competing customers unless these differentials "make due allowance for differences in the cost of manufacture, sale, or delivery resulting from the differing methods or quantities in which commodities are to such purchasers sold or delivered." The Federal Trade Commission and the courts have interpreted these "due allowances" as related to full costs, and they have rejected defenses that are based on differential cost calculations. Many states prohibit the sale of certain products or services below cost, with "cost" either specified as, or interpreted as meaning, the full cost.

TIME AND MATERIAL PRICES.   One of the commonly used pricing formulas based on full costs is the *time and material* price. This price consists of a charge for material plus a charge per labor hour. Profit may be included as part of the material element, or the labor element, or both of them. The usual price for repairing an automobile consists of the material priced at cost plus a profit margin, plus labor priced at an hourly rate. The hourly rate includes the direct labor cost, a fair share of overhead, and profit. Most other service work (television repair, plumbing, carpentry, electrical work, etc.) is priced on this basis. In job shops, where each job is done according to the customer's specifications, this is a common basis for pricing.

Contribution Pricing

Although the full cost is the normal basis for pricing, and although a company must recover its full cost or eventually go out of business, there

---

[5] A company cannot *compel* its customers to buy its own accessories and supplies. Such "tie-in" agreements are illegal.

are many situations where differential (i.e., marginal, or incremental) costs are appropriately used. In general, these may be described as *crisis* situations. In normal times, a company may refuse to take orders at prices that will not yield a satisfactory profit, but if times are bad, such orders may be accepted if the differential revenue obtained from them exceeds the differential costs involved. The company is better off to receive some revenue above its outlays than to receive nothing at all. Such orders make some contribution to profit,[6] and the selling price is therefore called a *contribution price*, to distinguish it from a normal price. Here, differential costs are the same as those discussed in the preceding section; that is, the costs that will be incurred if the order is accepted and that will not be incurred if it is not accepted.

Dumping, which is the practice of selling surplus quantities of a product in a selected marketing area at a low price, is another version of the contribution idea. However, dumping may violate the Robinson-Patman Act in domestic markets, and may be prohibited or unwise for other reasons in foreign markets.

In times of crisis a product may be retained in the line if it makes some contribution to profits, even though it has such a low profit margin that in normal times it would be dropped.

It is difficult to generalize on the circumstances that determine whether full costs or differential costs are appropriate. Even in normal times, an opportunity may be accepted to make some contribution to profit by using temporarily idle facilities. Conversely, in crisis times the contribution concept may be rejected on the grounds that the low price may "spoil the market," or that orders can in fact be obtained at normal margins if the sales organization works hard enough. Finally, it must be recognized that some companies do not price on the basis of full costs simply because they do not know what their full costs are. Dun & Bradstreet's annual analysis of bankruptcies invariably lists inadequate knowledge of costs as one of the principal factors responsible for business failure.

ADVANCED TECHNIQUES

The foregoing is an introductory description of approaches to the analysis of alternative choice problems. In recent years, a number of techniques have been developed for increasing the power of such an analysis. They are described in the books listed at the end of this chapter, but a brief description of some of these techniques is given here as an indication of the possibilities.

---

[6] Some prefer to regard this as a contribution to *overhead*, which is merely another way of looking at it.

Probability Theory

All the figures used in making business decisions are estimates of what will happen in the future. In the foregoing, we have assumed that these estimates were "single valued," that is, that each of them was a single number representing someone's best guess as to the future situation. Some companies are experimenting with estimates made in the form of probability distributions. For example, instead of stating, "I think sales of Item X will be $100,000 next year," the estimator states a range of possibilities, together with his estimate of the probability that each will occur. The sum of these separate possibilities, weighted by the probability that each will occur, is called the *expected value* of the probability distribution. It is computed as in the following example:

Possible Sales (a)	Estimated Probability (b)	Weighted Amount (a × b)
$ 60,000	0.1	$ 6,000
80,000	0.1	8,000
100,000	0.4	40,000
120,000	0.2	24,000
140,000	0.2	28,000
	Expected Value....$106,000	

The probability 0.1 means that there is 1 chance in 10 that sales will be about $60,000. The sum of the probabilities always adds to 1.

Businessmen do not find it easy to state their estimates in the form of probability distributions; but if they can do so, the usefulness of the estimates can be greatly increased. For one thing, probability distributions tend to fall into a limited number of patterns. Many of them are the familiar "normal," or bell-shaped, curves. These patterns are described by mathematical equations, and important characteristics of the distributions may be inferred from them. Historical data can often be fitted into the same patterns, and used more powerfully than hitherto to improve the accuracy of the estimates.

Mathematical Models

A mathematical model is a set of equations or other expressions that states what are believed to be the significant factors in a situation and the relationships among them. A balance sheet is a mathematical model, with the relationships among the balance sheet items being governed by the principles of financial accounting. A budget is also a model, and probably a more useful one than a balance sheet.

In the budget, individual revenue and expense items are combined by the arithmetic operations of addition and subtraction to give anticipated net income. The newer models attempt to describe or *simulate* the basic forces at work in the business (or, rather, as many as can be reduced to quantitative terms) and the interrelationships among them in much more elaborate manner. For example, whereas the variable budget may state that a $10,000 increase in sales will result in a $4,000 increase in labor costs, the more sophisticated model may relate labor costs not solely to sales volume but also to the desired level of inventory, the cost of hiring and training an additional worker, other costs associated with changing the level of production, and so on. Furthermore, the model may take into account the delay, or lag, that occurs between the receipt of a sales order and the actual incurrence of labor costs to fill the order.

As these models become more accurate simulations of the real situation, they can provide an effective way of testing the effect on profits of proposed alternatives, because the model incorporates interrelationships and secondary consequences of proposed actions which are often otherwise overlooked. This type of model serves the same function as a pilot plant; it permits inexpensive experimentation with various proposals so that mistakes in full-scale operation can be avoided. Since a single experiment often involves many millions of separate calculations, these models require the use of a computer.

A model is necessarily a simplification of the real situation because the real situation is too complex to be handled on even the largest computers, but if it is *over*simplified, it is useless. Very few companies have, up to the present, devised a model of their overall situation that is both sufficiently simple to be manipulated and also sufficiently realistic so that they trust it as an aid for making decisions. Many companies are working on this problem however.

Model building will become increasingly important to business. As Dr. Oskar Morgenstern has said: "The penetration of mathematics into new fields has, without exception, brought about profound changes. Whenever mathematics has entered, it has never again been pushed out by other developments."

Linear Programming

One of the models developed in recent years is the *linear programming* model. It is useful when the alternatives under consideration interact with one another.

> EXAMPLE: A company makes two products, each of which has to go through two departments, the daily capacity of each department being as follows if only one of the products is made in it:

	Capacity in Units	
	Dept. 1	*Dept. 2*
Product A	200	120
Product B	100	200

Any amount of Product A can be sold, but a maximum of 90 units of Product B can be sold per day. The contribution margin (i.e., difference between revenue and variable costs) of Product A is $2 per unit, and for Product B it is $2.50 per unit. How many units of each product should be produced?

A "commonsense" solution to the above problem would be to make the maximum 90 units of Product B, since it has the higher contribution margin, and to use the remaining capacity for Product A. By the use of linear programming, however, it can be demonstrated that a higher profit will result with a combination of 86 units of Product A and 57 units of Product B.[7]

Linear programming involves a great deal of arithmetic, but a standard program for doing this arithmetic is available on most computers. The analyst need only know enough about these programs to permit him to plug in the proper numbers; he does not need to know the equations themselves.

NONPROFIT ORGANIZATIONS

Since the criterion underlying the analysis described in this chapter was profit, there may be a tendency to conclude that the techniques are not applicable in organizations that do not have a profit objective, such as government agencies, universities, hospitals, and the like. Indeed, these techniques are not used in some nonprofit organizations. This is a mistake.

Many alternative choice problems involve a choice between two ways of reaching the same objective. Neglecting nonquantitative considerations, the one with the lower cost is the better alternative. It is better in a profit-seeking company because it leads to higher profits, and it is better in a nonprofit organization because it means that the objective of the organization, whatever it may be, can be accomplished with fewer resources. Thus, the techniques described in this chapter can be applied to problems of this type in nonprofit organizations.

Cost-Benefit Analysis

For problems involving both outputs and inputs, however, the problem of quantifying the factors is usually quite difficult in a nonprofit organization. In a profit-seeking company, outputs are measured by revenue, and the best alternative is the one with the greatest difference between differential revenue and differential costs, that is, the one that adds the most to profit. In a nonprofit organization, there often is no feasible way of

---

[7] For the solution, see Charles T. Horngren, *Cost Accounting: A Managerial Emphasis* (Englewood Cliffs, N.J., Prentice-Hall, Inc., 1967) pp. 828–33.

measuring output in monetary terms, and hence no way of using the above criterion.

Nevertheless, formal analytical techniques can be used in many such alternative choice problems in nonprofit organizations. Two general approaches are coming into common use, and both are described as techniques of *cost-benefit analysis.*

In one approach, the outputs, or benefits, anticipated under each alternative are expressed in some quantitative way, and a cost per unit of benefit is then computed. Neglecting nonquantitative considerations, the alternative with the lowest cost per unit is the best alternative. For example, the Department of Defense evaluates various strategic postures by estimating the "cost per delivered megaton of destruction"; the Department of Transportation evaluates alternative highway safety measures by the "cost per reduced fatality"; the amount of research funds to be allocated to various diseases can be roughly studied in terms of cost related to reduction in mortality; alternative ways of providing new recreational facilities are gauged by the cost per person benefited; and so on.

In the other approach, no attempt is made to quantify the benefits. A careful estimate of the cost is made, and the decision maker arrives at a judgment by asking: "Are the benefits worth *at least* the cost?" Or, if two alternatives are being considered, the differential costs of one over the other are estimated, and the question then becomes: "Are the incremental benefits likely to be worth the differential costs?"

These calculations rarely, if ever, provide the solution to the problem by themselves, because they do not include the effect of all the relevant considerations. But, as has been emphasized throughout this chapter, this is characteristic of all such calculations. If they help to reduce significantly the area within which judgment must be exercised, then they are worthwhile.

SOME PRACTICAL POINTERS

The following points may be helpful in attacking specific problems:

1. Use imagination in choosing the possible alternatives to be considered, but don't select so many alternatives that you bog down before you begin. There is only a fine line between the alternative that is a "stroke of genius" and the alternative that is a "harebrained idea," but it is a crucial one.

2. Don't yield to the natural temptation to give too much weight to the factors that can be reduced to figures, even though the figures have the appearance of being definite and precise.

3. On the other hand, don't slight the figures because they are "merely" approximations. A reasonable approximation is much better than nothing at all.

4. Often, it is easier to work with total costs rather than with unit costs. Unit cost is a fraction in which total cost is the numerator and number of units the denominator, that is,

$$\frac{\text{Total Cost}}{\text{Number of Units}} = \text{Unit Cost}.$$

Changes in either the numerator or the denominator result in changes in unit costs. An error is made if one of these changes is taken into account and the other is overlooked.

5. There is a tendency to underestimate the cost of doing something new because all the consequences often are not forseen.

6. The *number* of arguments is irrelevant in an alternative choice problem. A dozen reasons may be, and often are, advanced against trying out something new, but all these reasons put together may not be so strong as a single argument in favor of the proposal.

7. Be realistic about the margin of error in any calculation involving the future. Fancy figures cannot be made out of rough estimates, nor is an answer necessarily precise or valid just because you spent a long time calculating it.

8. Despite uncertainties, a decision should be made if as much information is available as you can obtain at reasonable cost and within a reasonable time. Postponing action is the same as deciding to perpetuate the existing situation, which may be the worst possible decision.

9. Show clearly the assumptions you made and the effect of these on your estimates so that someone going over your analysis can substitute his own judgments if he wishes.

10. Do not expect that everyone will agree with your conclusion simply because it is supported with carefully worked-out figures. Think about how you can sell your conclusion to those who must act on it.

SUMMARY

Differential costs are the costs that are incurred if a project is undertaken but that would not be incurred if it is not undertaken. When an alternative choice problem involves changes in costs but not changes in revenue or investment, the best solution is the one with the lowest differential costs, insofar as cost information bears on the solution.

When the problem involves both cost and revenue considerations, full costs are often a useful first approximation in normal times, but differential costs are used in times of crisis. Managements differ as to their opinion of the circumstances under which each is appropriate.

Cost calculations alone rarely provide the answer to any business problem, but they facilitate comparisons and narrow the area within which judgment must be applied.

SUGGESTIONS FOR FURTHER READING

BIERMAN, H.; C. P. BONINI; L. E. FOURAKER; and R. JAEDICKE. *Quantitative Analysis for Business Decisions.* Rev. ed.; Homewood, Ill.: Richard D. Irwin, Inc., 1965.

RAIFFA, HOWARD. *Decision Analysis.* Reading, Mass.: Addison-Wesley, 1968.

SIMON, HERBERT A. *The New Science of Management Decision.* New York: Harper and Row, 1960.

CASES

CASE 18–1. HARCORD WHOLESALE GROCERS, INC.

Prior to 1962, Harcord Wholesale Grocers, Inc., had kept no departmental income statements. In order to control operations more effectively, the management decided at the beginning of that year to install departmental cost accounts. At the end of 1962, the new accounts showed that although the business as a whole had a gross margin of 13.1 percent and a net profit of 1.1 percent on net sales of $2,408,000, the fresh fruit and produce department had shown a substantial loss, with a gross margin of only 9.8 percent of its $416,000 net sales, against an expense rate of 12.3 percent. The income statement for this department is shown in Exhibit 1.

Exhibit 1

HARCORD WHOLESALE GROCERS, INC.

Income Statement, Fresh Fruit and Produce Department

		Percent
Net sales..	$416,016	100.0
Cost of sales..	375,246	90.2
Gross margin.......................................	$ 40,770	9.8
Expenses:		
Payroll, direct labor, and supervision in the department..	$ 20,640	
Salesmen's commissions (fruits sold by general salesmen selling for all departments on straight, uniform, commission basis)....................................	6,396	
Rent (charged to department on basis of yearly rental per square foot occupied; the company rented and occupied an entire building)...............................	16,440	
Taxes (assessed by state on average value of inventory)...	600	
Insurance (for protection of inventory)................	480	
Depreciation (basis: 5 percent on departmental equipment)	1,560	
Administration and general office (allocated on basis of departmental sales).............................	12,824	
Interest on inventory (an accounting charge; actually there was no outside borrowing for working capital)..	235	
Total expenses..................................	$ 59,175	14.2
Net Loss..	$ 18,405	4.4

This loss led one executive to argue that the department should be discontinued. The executives agreed that, so far as the factor of customer satisfaction with the completeness of the company's line was concerned, it was not essential to continue selling fresh fruits and produce. Elimination of this department, in other words, was not expected to result in loss of sales by other departments.

After several protracted discussions of the proposal, one of the executives sought to end the controversy by saying that the company should discontinue either the department or the new accounting system.

Question

1. What action should be taken?

CASE 18–2. LIQUID CHEMICAL COMPANY

The Liquid Chemical Company manufactured and sold a range of high-grade products throughout Great Britain. Many of these products required careful packing, and the company had always made a feature of the special properties of the containers used. They had a special patented lining, made from a material known as GHL, and the firm operated a department especially to maintain its containers in good condition and to make new ones to replace those that were past repair.

Mr. Walsh, the general manager, had for some time suspected that the firm might save money, and get equally good service, by buying its containers from an outside source. After careful inquiries, he approached a firm specalizing in container production, Packages, Ltd., and asked for a quotation from it. At the same time he asked Mr. Dyer, his chief accountant, to let him have an up-to-date statement of the cost of operating the container department.

Within a few days, the quotation from Packages, Ltd., came in. The firm was prepared to supply all the new containers required—at that time running at the rate of 3,000 a year—for £12,500[8] a year, the contract to run for a guaranteed term of five years and thereafter to be renewable from year to year. If the required number of containers increased, the contract price would be increased proportionally. Additionally, and irrespective of whether the above contract was concluded or not, Packages, Ltd., undertook to carry out purely maintenance work on containers, short of replacement, for a sum of £3,750 a year, on the same contract terms.

Mr. Walsh compared these figures with the cost figures prepared by Mr. Dyer, covering a year's operations of the container department of the Liquid Chemical Company, which were as follows:

[8] At the time of this case, one British pound (£) was worth about $2.80.

	£	£
Materials..		7,000
Labour..		5,000
Department overheads:		
Manager's salary.............................	800	
Rent..	450	
Depreciation of machinery......................1,500		
Maintenance of machinery......................	360	
Other expenses................................1,575		
		4,685
		16,685
Proportion of general administrative overheads........		2,250
Total Cost of Department for Year..........		18,935

Walsh's conclusion was that no time should be lost in closing the department and in entering into the contracts offered by Packages, Ltd. However, he felt bound to give the manager of the department, Mr. Duffy, an opportunity to question this conclusion before he acted on it. He therefore called him in and put the facts before him, at the same time making it clear that Duffy's own position was not in jeopardy; for even if his department were closed, there was another managerial position shortly becoming vacant to which he could be moved without loss of pay or prospects.

Mr. Duffy looked thoughtful and asked for time to think the matter over. The next morning, he asked to speak to Mr. Walsh again, and said he thought there were a number of considerations that ought to be borne in mind before his department was closed. "For instance," he said, "what will you do with the machinery? It cost £12,000 four years ago, but you'd be lucky if you got £2,000 for it now, even though it's good for another four years at least. And then there's the stock of GHL (a special chemical) we bought a year ago. That cost us £10,000, and at the rate we're using it now, it'll last us another four years or so. We used up about one fifth of it last year. Dyer's figure of £7,000 for materials probably includes about £2,000 for GHL. But it'll be tricky stuff to handle if we don't use it up. We bought it for £50 a ton, and you couldn't buy it today for less than £60. But you wouldn't have more than £40 a ton left if you sold it, after you'd covered all the handling expenses."

Walsh thought that Dyer ought to be present during this discussion. He called him in and put Duffy's points to him. "I don't much like all this conjecture," Dyer said. "I think my figures are pretty conclusive. Besides, if we are going to have all this talk about 'what will happen if,' don't forget the problem of space we're faced with. We're paying £850 a year in rent for a warehouse a couple of miles away. If we closed Duffy's department, we'd have all the warehouse space we need without renting."

"That's a good point," said Walsh. "Though I must say, I'm a bit worried about the men if we close the department. I don't think we can find room for any of them elsewhere in the firm. I could see whether Packages can take any of them. But some of them are getting on. There's Walters and Hines, for example. They've been with us since they left school 40 years ago. I'd feel bound to give them a small pension— £150 a year each, say."

Duffy showed some relief at this. "But I still don't like Dyer's figures," he said. "What about this £2,250 for general administrative overheads. You surely don't expect to sack anyone in the general office if I'm closed, do you?" "Probably not," said Dyer, "but someone has to pay for these costs. We can't ignore them when we look at an individual department, because if we do that with each department in turn, we shall finish up by convincing ourselves that directors, accountants, typists, stationery, and the like don't have to be paid for. And they do, believe me."

"Well, I think we've thrashed this out pretty fully," said Walsh, "but I've been turning over in my mind the possibility of perhaps keeping on the maintenance work ourselves. What are your views on that, Duffy?"

"I don't know," said Duffy, "but it's worth looking into. We shouldn't need any machinery for that, and I could hand the supervision over to a foreman. You'd save £300 a year there, say. You'd only need about one fifth of the men, but you could keep on the oldest. You wouldn't save any space, so I suppose the rent would be the same. I shouldn't think the other expenses would be more than £650 a year." "What about materials?" asked Walsh. "We use about 10 percent of the total on maintenance," Duffy replied.

"Well, I've told Packages, Ltd., that I'd let them know my decision within a week," said Walsh. "I'll let you know what I decide to do before I write to them."

Questions

1. Assuming no additional information can be readily obtained, what action should be taken?
2. What, if any, additional information do you think is necessary for a sound decision?

CASE 18–3. HANSON MANUFACTURING COMPANY

In February, 1967, Mr. Herbert Wessling was appointed general manager by Mr. Paul Hanson, president of the Hanson Manufacturing Company. Mr. Wessling, age 56, had wide executive experience in manufacturing products similar to those of the Hanson Company. The appointment of Mr. Wessling resulted from management problems arising from the death of Mr. Richard Hanson, founder and, until his death early in 1966, president of the Hanson Company. Mr. Paul Hanson, who then was 34 years old, had only four years' experience with the company. His father had hoped to train him over a 10-year period, but his untimely death had cut this seasoning period short. The younger Hanson became president when his father died and exercised full control until he hired Mr. Wessling.

Mr. Paul Hanson knew that during 1966 he had made several poor decisions and noted that the morale of the organization had suffered, apparently through lack of confidence in him. When he received the profit and loss statement for 1966 (Exhibit 1), the net loss of over

Exhibit 1

HANSON MANUFACTURING COMPANY

Profit and Loss Statement for Year Ending December 31, 1966

Gross sales...............................		$10,589,405
Less: Cash discount....................		156,578
Net sales................................		$10,432,827
Cost of manufacturing....................		7,529,758
Manufacturing profit.....................		$ 2,903,069
Less: Selling expense..................	$1,838,238	
General administration............	653,020	
Depreciation.....................	458,440	2,949,698
Operating loss...........................		$ 46,629
Less: Other income....................		21,065
Net loss before bond interest..............		$ 25,564
Add: Interest on bonds.................		145,283
Net Loss after All Charges................		$ 170,847

$170,000 during a good business year convinced him that he needed help. He attracted Mr. Wessling from a competitor by offering him a stock option incentive in addition to salary, knowing that Mr. Wessling wanted to acquire a financial competence for his retirement. The two men came to a clear understanding that Mr. Wessling, as general manager, had full authority to execute any changes he wished. In addition, Mr. Wessling would explain the reasons for his decisions to Mr. Hanson and thereby train him for successful leadership upon Mr. Wessling's retirement.

The Hanson Manufacturing Company made only three industrial products, 101, 102, and 103. These were sold by company salesmen for use in the processes of other manufacturers. All the salesmen, on a salary basis, sold the three products but in varying proportions. The Hanson Company sold throughout New England and was one of eight companies with similar products. Several of its competitors were larger and manufactured a larger variety of products than did the Hanson Company. The dominant company was the Samra Company, which operated a branch plant in the Hanson Company's market area. Customarily, the Samra

Exhibit 2

HANSON MANUFACTURING COMPANY

Analysis of Profit and Loss by Departments, Year Ending December 31, 1966

	Product 101		Product 102		Product 103		Total			Basis of
	(Thousands)	¢ per Cwt.	(Thousands)	¢ per Cwt.	(Thousands)	¢ per Cwt.	(Thousands)	Direct	Allocated	Allocation
Rent	$ 587	27.55	$ 457	44.43	$ 388	39.25	$ 1,432		x	Sq. ft.
Property taxes	62	2.93	50	4.85	40	4.05	152		x	Sq. ft.
Property insurance	52	2.45	40	3.87	53	5.33	145		x	Val. of equip.
Compensation insurance	152	7.13	105	10.20	81	8.20	338		x	Direct labor
Direct labor	1,293	60.63	890	86.42	687	69.65	2,870	x		
Indirect labor	398	18.65	273	26.48	212	21.52	883		x	Direct labor
Power	22	1.05	25	2.42	30	3.05	77		x	Machine hrs.
Light and heat	15	0.70	13	1.23	10	1.02	38		x	Sq. ft.
Building service	10	0.47	8	0.75	7	0.75	25		x	Sq. ft.
Materials	909	42.59	232	22.58	251	25.47	1,392	x		
Supplies	52	2.45	48	4.62	35	3.55	135	x		
Repairs	18	0.83	15	1.45	10	1.03	43	x		
Total	$ 3,570	167.43	$ 2,156	209.30	$ 1,804	182.87	$ 7,530			
Selling expense	910	42.70	458	44.45	470	47.62	1,838		x	$ Val. of sales
General administrative	345	16.17	130	12.63	178	17.98	653		x	$ Val. of sales
Depreciation	165	7.75	127	12.37	165	16.73	457		x	Val. of equip.
Interest	52	2.45	40	3.88	53	5.32	145		x	Val. of equip.
Total cost	$ 5,042	236.50	$ 2,911	282.63	$ 2,670	270.52	$10,623			
Less: Other income	10	0.48	5	0.50	5	0.50	20		x	$ Val. of sales
	$ 5,032	236.02	$ 2,906	282.13	$ 2,665	270.02	$10,603			
Sales (net)	5,167	242.35	2,599	252.28	2,667	270.27	10,433			
Profit or loss	$ 135	6.33	$ 307†	29.85†	$ 2	0.25	$ 170†			
Unit sales (in cwts.)	2,132,191		1,029,654		986,974					
Quoted selling price	$ 2.45		$ 2.58		$ 2.75					
Cash discounts taken (% of sales)	1.08%		2.03%		1.72%		1.48%			

† Loss.

NOTE: Figures may not check exactly because of rounding.

Company announced prices annually, and the other producers followed suit.

Price cutting was rare, and the only variance from quoted selling prices took the form of cash discounts. In the past, attempts at price cutting had followed a consistent pattern: all competitors met the price reduction, and the industry as a whole sold about the same quantity but at the lower prices. This continued until the Samra Company, with its strong financial position, again stabilized the situation following a general recognition of the failure of price cutting. Furthermore, because sales were to industrial buyers and because the products of different manufacturers were very similar, the Hanson Company was convinced that it could not individually raise prices without suffering a volume decline.

During 1966 the Hanson Company's share of industry sales was 12 percent for type 101, 8 percent for 102, and 10 percent for 103. The industrywide quoted selling prices were \$2.45, \$2.58, and \$2.75, respectively.

Mr. Wessling, upon taking office in February 1967, decided against immediate major changes. Rather he chose to analyze 1966 operations and to wait for results of the first half of 1967. He instructed the accounting department to provide detailed expenses and earnings statements by products for 1966 (see Exhibit 2). In addition, he requested an explanation of the nature of the costs including their expected future behavior (see Exhibit 3).

Exhibit 3

ACCOUNTING DEPARTMENT'S COMMENTARY ON COSTS

Direct Labor: Variable. Union shop at going community rates. No abnormal demands foreseen.

Compensation Insurance: Variable. Nine percent of direct and indirect labor is an accurate estimate.

Materials: Variable. Exhibit 2 figures are accurate. Includes waste allowances. Purchases are at market prices.

Power: Variable. Rates are fixed. Use varies with activity. Averages in Exhibit 2 are accurate.

Supplies: Variable. Exhibit 2 figures are accurate. Supplies bought at market prices.

Repairs: Variable. Varies as volume changes within normal operation range. Lower and upper limits are fixed.

General Administrative, Selling Expense, Indirect Labor, Interest, and Other Income: These items are almost nonvariable at levels of operation between \$5 and \$15 million.

Cash Discounts: Almost nonvariable. Average cash discounts taken are consistent from year to year. Percentages in Exhibit 2 are accurate.

Light and Heat: Almost nonvariable. Heat varies slightly with fuel cost changes. Light is a fixed item regardless of level of production.

Property Taxes: Almost nonvariable. Under the lease terms Hanson Company pays the taxes; assessed valuation has been constant; the rate has risen slowly. Any change in the near future will be small and independent of production volume.

Rent: Nonvariable. Lease has 12 years to run.

Building Service: Nonvariable. At normal business level variances are small.

Property Insurance: Nonvariable. Three-year policy with fixed premium.

Depreciation: Nonvariable. Fixed dollar total.

Exhibit 4

HANSON MANUFACTURING COMPANY

Profit and Loss Statement by Departments, at Standard, Showing Variations from January 1 to June 30, 1967

	Product 101		Product 102		Product 103		Total Standard (Thousands)	Total Actual (Thousands)	Variations + = Standard Exceeds − = Actual Exceeds
	Unit* Standard	Total at Standard (Thousands)	Unit* Standard	Total at Standard (Thousands)	Unit* Standard	Total at Standard (Thousands)			
Rent	27.55¢	$ 275	44.43¢	$ 316	39.25¢	$ 197	$ 788	$ 715	+$ 73
Property taxes	2.93	29	4.85	35	4.05	20	84	77	+ 7
Property insurance	2.45	25	3.87	28	5.33	27	80	73	+ 7
Compensation insurance	7.13	71	10.20	73	8.20	41	185	185	
Direct labor	60.63	604	86.42	615	69.65	349	1,568	1,582	− 14
Indirect labor	18.65	186	26.48	188	21.52	108	482	448	+ 34
Power	1.05	10	2.42	17	3.05	15	42	42	
Light and heat	0.70	7	1.23	9	1.02	5	21	20	+ 1
Building service	0.47	5	0.75	5	0.75	4	14	10	+ 4
Materials	42.59	425	22.58	161	25.47	128	714	705	+ 9
Supplies	2.45	24	4.62	33	3.55	18	75	75	
Repairs	0.83	8	1.45	10	1.03	5	23	25	− 2
Total	167.43¢	$1,669	209.30¢	$1,490	182.87¢	$ 917	$4,076	$3,957	+$119
Selling expense	42.70	426	44.45	317	47.62	239	982	923	+ 59
General administrative	16.17	161	12.63	90	17.98	90	341	328	+ 13
Depreciation	7.75	77	12.37	88	16.73	84	249	227	+ 22
Interest	2.45	25	3.88	28	5.32	26	79	73	+ 6
Total cost	236.50¢	$2,358	282.63¢	$2,013	270.52¢	$1,356	$5,727	$5,508	+$219
Less: Other income	0.48	5	0.50	4	0.50	2	11	11	
	236.02¢	$2,353	282.13¢	$2,009	270.02¢	$1,354	$5,716	$5,497	+$219
Actual sales	242.35	2,416	252.28	1,796	270.27	1,355	5,567	5,567	
Profit or loss	6.33¢	$ 63	29.85¢†	$ 213†	0.25¢	$ 1	$ 149†	$ 70	+$219
Unit sales		996,859		712,102		501,276			

* Unit = cwt.
† Loss.

To familiarize Mr. Hanson with his methods, Mr. Wessling sent him copies of these exhibits, and they discussed them. Mr. Hanson stated that he thought Product 102 should be dropped immediately as it would be impossible to lower its expenses as much as 30 cents per cwt. In addition, he stressed the need for economies on Product 103.

Mr. Wessling relied on the authority arrangement Mr. Hanson had agreed to earlier and continued production of the three products. For control purposes he had the accounting department prepare monthly statements using as standard costs the costs per cwt. taken from the analytical profit and loss statement for 1966 (Exhibit 2). These monthly statements were his basis for making minor sales or production changes during the spring of 1967. Late in July, 1967, Mr. Wessling received from the accounting department the six months' statement of cumulative standard costs including variances of actual costs from standard (see Exhibit 4). They showed that the first half of 1967 was a successful period.

During the latter half of 1967 the sales of the entire industry weakened. Even though the Hanson Company retained its share of the market, its profit for the last six months was small. In January, 1968, the Samra Company announced a price reduction on Product 101 from $2.45 to $2.25 per cwt. This created an immediate pricing problem for all its competitors. Mr. Wessling forecast that if the Hanson Company held to the $2.45 price during the first six months of 1968, its unit sales would be 750,000 cwt. He felt that if it dropped its price to $2.25 per cwt., the six months' volume would be 1,000,000 cwt. Mr. Wessling knew that competing managements anticipated a further decline in activity. He thought a general decline in prices was quite probable.

The accounting department reported that the standard costs in use would probably apply during 1968, with two exceptions: materials and supplies would be about 5 percent below standard; and light and heat would decline about one third of 1 percent.

Mr. Wessling and Mr. Hanson discussed the pricing problem. Mr. Hanson observed that even with the anticipated decline in material and supply costs, a sales price of $2.25 would be below cost. Mr. Hanson therefore wanted the $2.45 price to be continued, since he believed that the company could not be profitable while selling a key product below cost.

Questions

1. Is Exhibit 4 the most useful form in which to present information to management?
2. Was Mr. Wessling correct in his decision not to drop Product 102 in the spring of 1967?
3. In January, 1968, should the company have reduced the price of Product 101 from $2.45 to $2.25 or to an intermediate figure?

CASE 18–4.   ATHERTON COMPANY

Early in January, 1956, the sales manager and the controller of the Atherton Company met for the purpose of preparing a joint pricing recommendation for Item 345. After the president approved their recommendation, the price would be announced in letters to retail customers. In accordance with company and industry practice, announced prices were adhered to for the year unless radical changes in market conditions occurred.

The Atherton Company was the largest company in its segment of the textile industry; its 1955 sales had exceeded $6 million. Company salesmen were on a straight salary basis, and each salesman sold the full line. Most of the Atherton competitors were small. Usually they waited for the Atherton Company to announce prices before mailing out their own price lists.

Item 345, an expensive yet competitive fabric, was the sole product of a department whose facilities could not be utilized on other items in the product line. In January 1954, the Atherton Company had raised its price from $1.50 to $2 a yard. This had been done to bring the profit per yard on Item 345 up to that of other products in the line. Although the company was in a strong position financially, it would require considerable capital in the next few years to finance a recently approved long-term modernization and expansion program. The 1954 pricing decision had been one of several changes advocated by the directors in an attempt to strengthen the company's working capital position so as to insure that adequate funds would be available for this program.

Competitors of the Atherton Company had held their prices on products similar to Item 345 at $1.50 during 1954 and 1955. The industry and Atherton Company volume for Item 345 for the years 1950–55, as estimated by the sales manager, is shown in Exhibit 1. As shown by this

Exhibit 1

ITEM 345, PRICES AND PRODUCTION, 1950–55

	Volume of Production (Yards)		Price	
			Charged	
	Industry		by Most	Atherton
Year	Total	Atherton	Competitors	Company
1950	610,000	213,000	$2.00	$2.00
1951	575,000	200,000	2.00	2.00
1952	430,000	150,000	1.50	1.50
1953	475,000	165,000	1.50	1.50
1954	500,000	150,000	1.50	2.00
1955	625,000	125,000	1.50	2.00

exhibit, the Atherton Company had lost a significant portion of its former market position. In the sales manager's opinion, a reasonable forecast of industry volume for 1956 was 700,000 yards. He was certain that the company could sell 25 percent of the 1956 industry total if it adopted the $1.50 price. He feared a further volume decline if it did not meet the competitive price. As many consumers were convinced of the superiority of the Atherton product, the sales manager reasoned that sales of Item 345 would probably not fall below 75,000 yards, even at a $2 price.

During the pricing discussions, the controller and sales manager had considered two other aspects of the problem. The controller was con-

Exhibit 2

ESTIMATED COST PER YARD OF ITEM 345 AT VARIOUS VOLUMES

OF PRODUCTION

	75,000	100,000	125,000	150,000	175,000	200,000
Direct labor	$0.400	$0.390	$0.380	$0.370	$0.380	$0.400
Material	0.200	0.200	0.200	0.200	0.200	0.200
Material spoilage	0.020	0.020	0.019	0.019	0.019	0.020
Department expense:						
Direct*	0.060	0.056	0.050	0.050	0.050	0.050
Indirect†	0.400	0.300	0.240	0.200	0.180	0.150
General overhead‡	0.120	0.117	0.114	0.111	0.114	0.120
Factory cost	$1.200	$1.083	$1.003	$0.950	$0.943	$0.940
Selling and administrative expense§	0.780	0.704	0.652	0.618	0.613	0.611
Total Cost	$1.980	$1.787	$1.655	$1.568	$1.556	$1.551

* Indirect labor, supplies, repairs, power, etc.
† Depreciation, supervision, etc.
‡ 30 percent of direct labor.
§ 65 percent of factory cost.

cerned about the possibility that competitors would reduce their prices below $1.50 if the Atherton Company announced a $1.50 price for Item 345. The sales manager was confident that competitors would not go below $1.50 because they all had higher costs and several of them were in tight financial straits. He believed that action taken on Item 345 would not have any substantial repercussions on other items in the line.

The controller prepared estimated costs of Item 345 at various volumes of production (Exhibit 2). These estimated costs reflected current labor and material costs. They were based on past experience except for the estimates of 75,000 and 100,000 yards. The company had produced more than 100,000 yards in each year since World War II, and prewar experience was not applicable because of equipment changes and increases in labor productivity.

Questions

1. How, if at all, did the company's financial condition relate to the pricing decision?
2. Should $1.50 or $2 have been recommended?

CASE 18–5. HELVIN BLANKET COMPANY

The Helvin Blanket Company was a large producer of cotton blankets. Since the company performed all the operations from the baled cotton to the finished blankets, and since a market existed for cotton in various stages of manufacture, an ever-present problem before its management was, at what point in the manufacture of a blanket the alternative of selling the uncompleted product was more profitable than continuing with the manufacturing process toward a later market. In the spring of 1956, during a period of undercapacity operations, an incident occurred that raised the question of the validity of using the familiar total average cost accumulations and prorations of the accounting department as a basis for deciding at which point to terminate manufacturing and to sell the product in process.

At a meeting of the principal executives in the spring of 1956, the sales manager proposed that the carding and spinning capacity of the mill be used to produce warp yarn which, he said, the company could sell currently at a profit. The production manager, on the other hand, contended that the loom capacity of the plant rendered it desirable to continue all yarn operations through to the stage of blankets. The sales manager defended his position with the following figures, which the cost office had prepared for him on the basis of current standard costs:

	Cost per Pound, Warp Yarn	Cost per Blanket
Labor	$0.1316	$0.2937
Overhead	0.1053	0.2327
Processing materials	0.0083	0.0521
Raw materials	0.3812	1.1436
Cost at standard	$0.6265	$1.7221
Current selling price	0.6450	1.7000
Profit or (Loss)	$0.0185 per lb.	($0.0221) per blanket

Each blanket contained one pound of warp yarn and two pounds of filling yarn. The figures for cost per blanket were cumulative. Thus, the $0.2937 labor item under cost per blanket included the $0.1316 labor cost of making one pound of warp yarn, plus the labor cost of making two pounds of filling yarn and the labor cost of weaving the blanket.

The production manager challenged the validity of any figures that indicated that the optimum move for the management was to shut down the greater part of the mill in the face of a reasonably favorable market demand for blankets. He argued that the plant was set up to manufacture blankets, not yarn, and to sell yarn was, in effect, to get out of the blanket business, in which the company had made its name. Moreover, he wasn't sure but that the company, despite the generally weak market, might do better financially by keeping the blanket room open.

The head of the cost office stated that the figures presented by the sales manager had been based on painstaking studies of labor and material costs and of methods of distributing overhead to products. He admitted that certain allocations were rough and that different kinds of costs were reported together. On being questioned, he said that for both yarn and blankets about 15 percent of the labor cost was fixed and that about 60 percent of overhead was fixed.

The executives had to reach a decision on the issue. The sales manager was opposed to selling blankets at a loss when he could be selling yarn at a profit. The production manager certainly did not want to close his blanket mill.

Questions

1. What different courses of action might be taken, and what arguments can be made to support them?
2. What information or forecasts might be useful to round out the story?
3. On balance, and in the light of the probable state of affairs, what would you decide?
4. If the current selling price of warp yarn was $0.725 a pound, instead of $0.645, as given in the case, would your decision be changed?

CASE 18–6.   MARTALL BLANKET COMPANY

In the spring of 1941, the Martall Blanket Company was negotiating a large contract for blankets with the U.S. Navy. A question arose as to the method that the company should use in estimating the price that it would ask for these blankets.

In January 1941, the production manager prepared an estimate of production for the 1941–42 season. This estimate, shown in Exhibit 1, was made on the assumption that the mill would be operated at three-shift capacity. There was general agreement in the company that demand was strong enough to warrant capacity operations for the foreseeable future. Production facilities could be used to make any of the blankets shown on Exhibit 1 interchangeably.

Exhibit 1

PRODUCTION ESTIMATE 1941–42

Style	Size	Quantity
Ashmont	72 × 90	12,000
Velona	72 × 90	26,000
Fairfax	72 × 90	22,000
Total domestic		60,000
Army	66 × 84	75,000
Navy	66 × 90	25,000
Total		160,000

The production estimate was sent to the cost department, which prepared cost and selling price estimates for each blanket appearing thereon. Raw material prices were obtained by averaging the prices of wool on hand and the prices of expected purchases for the period of the budget. Standard costs for labor, factory expense, and processing materials were added to raw material costs so as to arrive at a total manufacturing cost per blanket. These standard costs had been estimated in 1938 but had been corrected subsequently for actual cost experience through ratios applied to labor, factory expense, and processing materials. Selling, advertising, administrative, and interest charges were added at $24 per loom.[9] (At $24 a loom it was possible to absorb these charges at 85 percent of three-shift capacity.)

Profit was also computed on a similar loom basis at $60 a loom. This $60 rate was set so as to return to the blanket division $162,000 profit for the year at three-shift operations. This was considered a "reasonable return" on investment and management. Thus the cost and pricing sheet submitted by the cost department, Exhibit 2, furnished the prices at which the various types of blankets would have to be sold in order to realize the budgeted total profit.

The Units per Loom column in Exhibit 2 showed the number of blankets that could be produced on one loom running for 40 hours.

The vice president in charge of government contracts questioned the selling price that the cost department had calculated for Navy blankets. He pointed out that at this price, profit on Navy blankets would be 13.5 percent of cost, whereas the profit on Army blankets would amount to only 12.3 percent of cost. Furthermore, the profit margin on Navy blankets was higher, both in absolute terms and as a percentage of cost, than the profit on any of the domestic blankets. The Army contract had already been negotiated at $7.83 per blanket, and the vice president knew that the Navy would be most reluctant to pay a price that was out of line

---

[9] As a measure of output, a "loom" meant the number of blankets that could be produced on one loom running for 40 hours.

Exhibit 2

COMPUTATIONS OF COSTS AND SELLING PRICES FOR 1941-42

| Style | Size (Inches) | Weight (Pounds) | Raw Material | Labor | Expense | Processing Materials | Total Mfg. Cost | Units per Loom | Selling, Admin. Interest, Adv. | | Total Cost Sold | Profit per Loom | Profit per Blanket | Net Selling Price | Invoice Selling Price | Retail Price 40% |
									Per Loom	Per Blanket						
Ashmont...	72 × 90	3.75	$4.12	$0.93	$0.66	$0.58	$6.29	64	$24.00	$0.38	$6.67	$60.00	$0.94	$7.61	$7.76	$12.94
Velona....	72 × 90	4.00	4.39	0.94	0.66	0.58	6.57	60	24.00	0.40	6.97	60.00	1.00	7.97	8.13	13.55
Fairfax....	72 × 90	5.00	5.43	1.03	0.74	0.59	7.79	56	24.00	0.43	8.22	60.00	1.07	9.29	9.48	15.80
Army......	66 × 84	3.75	4.83	0.99	0.63	0.18	6.63	70	24.00	0.34	6.97	60.00	0.86	7.83		
Navy......	66 × 90	4.25	5.85	1.08	0.64	0.19	7.76	54	24.00	0.44	8.20	60.00	1.11	9.31		

with the price the Army paid. The company gave the government negotiators full access to all its cost information.

The vice president realized that the difference in profit margins arose because of the manner in which selling and administrative cost and profit were allocated. He asked the controller either to provide an adequate justification of the price computed in Exhibit 2 or to recalculate the price. The controller replied with a memorandum, which included the following:

The problem of overhead (used hereafter to include selling, administrative, advertising, and interest charges) and profit distribution is probably the most important source of possible error. While the loom basis of allocation of these items is arbitrary in certain respects and may therefore be misleading, it is certainly not without logical foundation.

The fair basis of allocating profit and overhead apparently depends upon the market conditions existing at the time. If the division can produce more than can be sold, profit and overhead may well be distributed on a per-blanket basis; that is, we could add a certain percent to each type of blanket for overhead and profit, as you suggested. On the other hand, if the mill is operating at capacity in the sense that total capacity can be sold, the distribution on some measure of capacity, such as loom hours, will provide the fair answer, for such a method takes into account the time required to produced each blanket.

In allocating overhead and profit on a loom basis we have assumed that total blanket division capacity would be completely sold out for the coming fiscal year. For this reason I feel that the blanket prices previously submitted to you are justified.

Questions

1. Assume that Martall was considering the possibility of making Blanket X, on which the following information was available. (Items correspond to column headings in Exhibit 2.)

Size...........72 × 90 inches		Expense...............$0.59	
Weight.......3.75 lbs.		Processing materials.....$0.57	
Raw material...$4.38		Total manufacturing cost..$6.37	
Labor........$0.83		Units per loom..........84	

Complete the columns in Exhibit 2 for Blanket X, including the retail price necessary to give the desired markup.

2. At what price should Navy blankets be sold?
3. How should the vice president explain this price in his contract negotiations?

CASE 18–7. LACKLIN AIRCRAFT COMPANY

On several occasions since late 1950 the Lacklin Aircraft Company had renewed contracts with the government for the manufacture of BF 2C bombers. In March 1953, Mr. Fred Hill, one of the buyers for the Lacklin Aircraft Company, was trying to decide upon a fair price to offer the Heyler Company, a subcontractor, for the manufacture of guide strips for the bomb-bay doors, one of the many parts for the BF 2C bomber.

The guide strips, made of a special alloy steel, required difficult machining operations, first, to fit the guide strips to the contour of the plane's fuselage; second, to provide a groove along which rollers traveled; and third, to cut down the weight of the guide strips by boring holes. Unusual accuracy was demanded in order to prevent the bomb-bay doors from jamming.

The Heyler Company had been subcontracting the manufacture of the guide strips since December 1950, at which time its bid of $253 per ship set[10] for the 120 ship sets required was the lowest of the several bids considered. With each new order for the BF 2C bomber that the Lacklin company received from the government, Mr. Hill successfully negotiated new contracts for the manufacture of the guide strips with Mr. Wright, the Heyler Company salesman. During this period the Heyler Company continued to meet all quality standards and delivery schedules.

On each successive contract after the original one signed in December 1950, Mr. Hill had applied an 80 percent learning curve to the price of the previous order, excluding the cost of raw material and also excluding profit. Mr. Hill assumed that the tooling cost incurred by the Heyler Company in manufacturing the guide strips was amortized over the cost of the original contract, and therefore he made no allowance for tooling cost in estimating the price of subsequent contracts. Although it appeared to Mr. Hill that Mr. Wright was not familiar with the use of learning curves in purchase contracting, Mr. Wright agreed to manufacture the guide strips at the prices quoted by Mr. Hill. As a result, the price paid per unit for the guide strips was lowered on each successive contract. The Heyler Company's production rate of guide strips was held essentially constant at eight ship sets a month. Application of the learning curve would not be valid if production was not reasonably steady.

In making his calculations of the price to offer the Heyler Company for the guide strips after the first contract had been fulfilled, Mr. Hill had to rely on his own estimates of the raw material price, the tooling cost, and the Heyler Company's profit. Mr. Hill knew from his previous experiences with the Heyler Company that this company would refuse to reveal its cost and profit figures. Because of his past experience in purchasing and the use of the learning curve, however, Mr. Hill was confident that his estimates were fairly accurate. The Lacklin Company's own man-hour records showed that an 80 percent curve was appropriate for the production of similar guide strips for another type of bomber made in

---

[10] A "ship set" is the set of guide strips required for one bomber.

the immediate postwar period, and this led Mr. Hill to conclude that the same 80 percent curve was applicable to the Heyler Company.

Breaking down the original bid of $253 per ship set, Mr. Hill estimated the profit was around $23, which was 10 percent of total cost, and the raw material was about $40 per ship set. He estimated that the Heyler Company's tooling cost was in the neighborhood of $3,600 and that this had probably been amortized over the 120 ship sets ordered under the first contract.

In order to set up his 80 percent curve to find the cumulative average price on which he could base his future price offers, Mr. Hill made the following calculations:

Original price..............................		$253 per ship set
Less: Profit at 10 percent of cost.............$23		
Tooling cost on first order $3,600 ÷		
120 units........................... 30		
Raw material cost per unit.............. 40		
Items not subject to learning curve.......	93	
Costs Subject to Learning Curve..............	$160	

The adjusted costs of $160 per ship set for 120 units was plotted on log-log graph paper (see Exhibit 1). Mr. Hill then took double the

Exhibit 1

EIGHTY PERCENT LEARNING CURVE—
BF 2C BOMBER GUIDE STRIPS

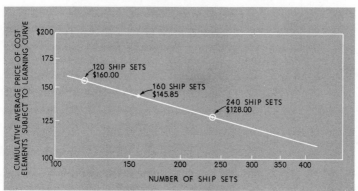

quantity of the original order (or 240 units) and 80 percent of the unit price ($128) and plotted his second point on the log-log graph paper. Through these two points he drew a straight line.

When the Lacklin company signed the second contract calling for 40 more BF 2C bombers, Mr. Hill looked at his graph to find the new cumulative average price of cost elements subject to the learning curve for the total quantity of the old and new orders, which amounted to 160 ship sets. The new cumulative average price, as indicated by the graph, was $145.85 per ship set (see Exhibit 1). Using this information, Mr. Hill continued his calculations:

```
160 ships sets at $145.85 per set average for cost elements
    subject to learning curve...........................$23,336
Less: 120 units purchased at $160 per set average for cost
    elements subject to learning curve....................  19,200
    Total Price to Be Paid on New Order for Cost Ele-
        ments Subject to Learning Curve................$ 4,136
```

The new average price per ship set to be paid on the new order for the cost elements subject to the learning curve was found to be $4,136 ÷ 40 new ship sets, or $103.40. To this new price of $103.40 per ship set Mr. Hill added back in the cost items not subject to the curve which previously had been subtracted:

```
Cost elements subject to learning curve.................$103.40
Plus: Raw material.................................   40.00
Average price per unit before profit....................$143.40
Plus: Profit at 10 percent of cost......................   14.34
    Total Price per Ship Set on the New Order.........$157.74
```

Mr. Hill believed that this figure of $157.74 per ship set was quite adequate, and he used it in his negotiations with Mr. Wright, who finally, but grudgingly, accepted this figure.

In subsequent negotiations, the prices Mr. Hill offered to the Heyler Company on successive contracts for the guide strips became lower and lower. Mr. Wright became more emphatic in his objections and warned Mr. Hill that "this learning curve business is going too far." However, each time Mr. Hill asked to see the Heyler Company's cost data to justify some other price, Mr. Wright would give the same answer: "Our cost data is none of your business!"

On February 2, 1953, about one month before the final delivery of the latest order of guide strips, which had been contracted for in November 1952, Mr. Wright complained that the Heyler Company had recently experienced an increase in raw material cost which added $2 to the cost per ship set. Furthermore, Mr. Wright stated that modifications in the design of the guide strips since the original contract had been signed had increased the raw material cost per ship set by another $3. These modifications in design, however, had not increased labor or overhead costs. Mr. Wright stated that because of these increased costs and the low $148 per ship set price paid by the Lacklin company for the currently produced guide strips, he was quite skeptical as to whether his company would take on any further contracts for guide strips, especially since at that time it could get all the business it wanted. He went on to say that his company was "sick and tired of producing guide strips at a loss for Lacklin and having to make up these losses out of contracts with other companies." While Mr. Hill believed that the raw material cost increases mentioned by Mr. Wright were correct, he did not have any way of appraising the validity of Mr. Wright's statements about the Heyler Company's losing money on this contract with the Lacklin Aircraft Company.

Two weeks after this conference between Mr. Hill and Mr. Wright, the Lacklin Aircraft Company negotiated a new contract with the government for additional BF 2C bombers, which would require 100 more ship sets of guide strips. Again Mr. Hill was confronted with the task of securing more guide strips. From December 1950 to March 1953, the Heyler Company would have produced 210 ship sets of guide strips. Over this period the price paid for the guide strips had decreased from $253 per ship set on the first order to $148 per ship set on the current order contracted for in November 1952 and scheduled for completion within the next two weeks. The total price of the 210 ship sets *for the cost elements subject to the learning curve* was $28,060.20. This sum compares to $33,600 which would have been paid on 210 ship sets for these same cost elements if the learning curve had not been applied. A further saving to the Lacklin Company was realized because the profit which the Heyler Company received per unit was a fixed percentage of cost. Thus with the lower calculated cost per ship set based on the learning curve, the profit to the Heyler Company was cut correspondingly.

Mr. Hill realized that it was important to continue dealing with the Heyler Company for the additional 100 ship sets of guide strips. Mr. Hill recalled that at 1950 price levels the Heyler Company's first bid of $253 per ship set was the lowest of the several bids submitted; the next lowest bid at that time was $272. If the Heyler Company refused to accept any more orders, dealing with a new subcontractor would probably result in a substantial increase in price. Mr. Hill estimated that the lowest price for which he could currently purchase guide strips from another subcontractor would be in the neighborhood of $280 per ship set (including the amortized cost, over 100 ship sets, of new tooling). Furthermore, Mr. Hill considered the Heyler Company an excellent source of supply because it produced a satisfactory product and always met its delivery schedule.

On the other hand, Mr. Hill knew that the validity of the learning curve had been widely accepted in the aircraft industry and that it was especially applicable to the manufacture of parts such as guide strips, for which direct labor was the major cost component. Furthermore, it was his job as a purchasing agent for the Lacklin Aircraft Company to get as low a price as possible commensurate with a satisfactory product.

Mr. Hill had an appointment with Mr. Wright the next day, at which time they would open negotiations for the 100 additional ship sets of guide strips. Mr. Hill knew that Mr. Wright would suggest a substantial upward revision in the price.

Questions

1. If he used the 80 percent learning curve, what price would Mr. Hill calculate for the new order of 100 ship sets?
2. What is the highest price that the Lacklin Company should pay to the Heyler Company for the guide strips?
3. What price *should* Mr. Hill use as a basis for his negotiations?
4. What are the implications of the use of learning curves in purchase contracting to both the prime contractor and the subcontractor?
5. In what situations would the use of the learning curve in purchase contracting not be appropriate?

CHAPTER 19

PLANNING CAPITAL
ACQUISITIONS

Of the several types of alternative choice problems, those involving proposed investments in new assets, i.e., *capital budgeting* problems, are both the most important and the most difficult. These problems are important not only because they involve large sums of money but also because the decision may influence the whole conduct of the business for years to come. A decision to build a new plant, for example, tends to commit a company to a certain locality and to a certain character and scale of manufacturing activity for the life of the plant. Investment problems are difficult because they require that estimates be made of conditions several years in the future, and also because allowances must be made for differences in timing of the relevant inflows and outflows of funds.

Any investment involves the commitment of funds *now* with the expectation of earning a satisfactory return on these funds over a period of time in the future. The word "investment" immediately calls to mind the commitment of funds to stocks or bonds. The commitment of funds to land, building, equipment, inventory, and other types of assets has the same essential characteristic as these financial investments: namely, that the commitment is made with the expectation of earning a satisfactory return on the investment in the future.

Illustrative of these capital budgeting problems are the following:

1. *Expansion.* Shall we build or otherwise acquire a new plant? (The expected earnings on this investment are the profits from the products produced in the new plant.)
2. *Replacement.* Shall we replace existing equipment with more efficient equipment? (The expected earnings on this investment are the savings

resulting from lower operating costs, or the profit from additional volume produced by the new equipment, or both.)

3. *Cost Reduction.* Shall we buy equipment to perform an operation now done manually, i.e., shall we spend money in order to save money? (The expected earnings on this investment are the savings resulting from lower operating costs.)

4. *Choice of Equipment.* Which of several proposed items of equipment shall we purchase for a given purpose? (The choice often turns on which item is expected to give the largest return on the investment made in it.)

5. *Buy or Lease.* Having decided to acquire a building or a piece of equipment, should we lease it or should we buy it? (The choice turns on whether or not the investment required to purchase the asset will earn an adequate return as compared with leasing.)

Investment problems fall into two broad categories; they are either screening problems or preference problems. In a *screening* problem, the issue is whether or not a proposed investment is likely to earn a satisfactory return; that is, the problem is to screen out the satisfactory proposals from all the investment proposals that are made. In a *preference* problem, also referred to as a *ranking* or *rationing* problem, the task is to decide which of several proposals is the best, which is the next best, and so on. The screening problem is conceptually simpler, and the first part of this chapter will be restricted to a discussion of this problem. The preference problem will be discussed in the last section of the chapter.

The comments in Chapter 18 about the types of costs and revenues that should be used in alternative choice problems are equally relevant in capital budgeting problems. As also noted in that chapter, the techniques are applicable only to those problems or parts of problems for which quantitative information is available and important. In nearly every problem, there are important unmeasured considerations that must be weighed in order to make a final decision, and in many problems these considerations are so important that calculations of the type described here are not worth making. Decisions regarding investments in employee recreational facilities, or in research equipment, or in office furniture, ordinarily are not based on an estimate of the return on investment.

FRAMEWORK OF ANALYSIS

Essentials of a Business Investment

If the company purchases a machine, the funds so invested are initially tied up, or frozen, and they are gradually liquidated through the profitable operation of the machine. Any investment involves a risk, and even if the money to finance the purchase is borrowed, it is the owner of the machine who incurs the risk. A businessman will ordinarily not risk funds in an investment unless he believes that he will obtain a satisfactory return on these funds.

Since the purchase of proposed equipment will presumably result in additional earnings, the issue to be resolved in an investment problem is *whether the proposed investment is justified by the earnings it will create over its life.* The techniques to be described are methods for comparing these essentially unlike elements: (1) a single lump-sum investment made now, and (2) a stream of future earnings.

Concept of Return on Investment

When a bank lends $1,000 and receives interest payments of $80 at the end of each year for five years, with the $1,000 loan being repaid at the end of the fifth year, the bank is said to earn a return of 8 percent on its investment of $1,000. Note that the percentage is always expressed on an

Illustration 19–1

DEMONSTRATION OF MEANING OF RETURN ON INVESTMENT

Year	Total Earnings (a)	Return at 8% of Investment Outstanding (b)	Balance, to Apply against Investment c = (a − b)	Investment Outstanding End of Year (d)
0..............	$...	$..	$...	$1,000
1..............	250	80	170	830
2..............	250	66	184	646
3..............	250	52	198	448
4..............	250	36	214	234
5..............	250	19	231	3

annual basis and that it is found by dividing the annual return by the amount of the investment outstanding during the year.

If a bank lends $1,000 and is repaid $250 at the end of each year for five years, the problem of finding the return becomes more complicated. In this situation, only part of the $250 annual payment represents interest, and the remainder is a repayment of the principal. By a method to be described below, it turns out that this loan also has a return of 8 percent, in the same sense as the loan described in the preceding paragraph: namely, the $250 annual payments will repay the loan itself and in addition will provide a return of 8 percent of the *amount still outstanding each year.* The fact that the return is 8 percent is proved in Illustration 19–1. Of the $250 earned in the first year, $80, or 8 percent of the $1,000 then outstanding, is the return, and the remainder, or $170, goes to reduce the investment, making it $830. In the second year, $66 is a return of 8 percent on the $830 then outstanding, and the remainder, $184, reduces the investment to $646. And so on. (The residual of $3 at the end of the fifth year arises because the true return is not exactly 8.000 percent.)

Thus, when an investment involves annual interest payments with the full amount of the investment being repaid at its termination date, the computation of the return is simple and direct; but when the annual payments combine both principal and interest, the computation is more complicated. Some business problems are of the simple type. If a business buys land for $1,000, for example, and rents it for $80 a year for five years, selling the land for $1,000 at the end of five years, the return is 8 percent. Many business investment decisions, on the other hand, relate to depreciable assets, whose characteristic is that they have no, or very little, resale value at the end of their useful life. The earnings on these investments must therefore be large enough for the investor both to recoup the investment itself during its life and to earn a satisfactory return on the amount not yet recouped, just as in the situation shown in Illustration 19–1.

Concept of Present Value

A businessman will not invest $1 today unless he expects to get back somewhat more than $1 later on; that is, he expects to earn a return on the investments he makes. By the same token, if a certain proposal will produce earnings of $1 at the end of one year, the businessman will be willing to invest only somewhat less than $1 in it today. The expectation of receiving $1 one year hence therefore has a *present value*, a value today, of somewhat less than $1. How much less depends on how much the businessman expects to earn on money he invests. If he expects to earn 10 percent, for example, the expectation of receiving $1 a year from now has a present value of $0.909, since if he invested $0.909 today for one year at a rate of 10 percent, he would earn $0.091 on the investment and have $1 at the end of the year.

The present value for a payment of $1 to be received n years hence at any rate of return (i) can be found with the formula:

$$\frac{1}{(1 + i)^n}.$$

The formula itself need not be used, however, since present values computed from it are given in Table A (p. 777). It is important that the meaning of the numbers in this table be clearly understood. Note, for example, that the first figure in the 10 percent column is the same $0.909 used in the preceding paragraph. It means that, at a rate of 10 percent, the expectation of receiving $1 a year from today has a present value of $0.909.

The next figure in the 10 percent column, $0.826, means that the expectation of receiving $1 *two* years from today has a present value of $0.826. This can be checked, as follows: if $0.826 is invested today, at 10 percent, $0.0826 would be earned during the first year, and the total amount would therefore increase to $0.9086; during the second year, 10 percent of the $0.9086, or $0.09086, would be earned, so that by the end of the second year, the total would have increased to $0.99946, or practically $1.[1] Tracing through any other figure in Table A will produce the same result; namely, the final figure will be practically $1.

Table A shows the present value of $1. The present value of any amount other than $1 can be found simply by multiplying that amount by the appropriate figure in the table. Thus the present value of $1,000 to be received two years hence at a rate of 10 percent is $826.

Present Value Method

The foregoing concepts can be used to construct methods for making decisions about investment proposals, always keeping in mind the fact that these methods are necessarily limited to those aspects of the proposal that can be reduced to money amounts. One such method is called the *present value* method. The rule here is: *Neglecting nonmonetary considerations, an investment proposal should be accepted if the present value of its earnings equals or exceeds the amount of the investment required.* Earnings are *cash flow* earnings; that is, they are the cash or cash equivalent amounts which are relevant in alternative choice problems, as explained in Chapter 18. To find the present value of these earnings, they are *discounted* at a specified rate of return, using the numbers in Table A. This rate will henceforth be referred to as the *required earnings rate*.

> EXAMPLE 1. Should a proposed investment of $1,000 with expected earnings of $1,080 one year hence be accepted if the required earnings rate is 8 percent? In Table A, we find that the present value of $1 to be received one year hence at 8 percent is $0.926. The present value of $1,080 is therefore $1,080 × $0.926 = $1,000. The proposal should be accepted.

> EXAMPLE 2. Should a proposed investment of $1,000 with expected earnings of $250 a year for five years be accepted if the required earnings rate is 8 percent? The present value of the earnings is found as follows:[2]

---

[1] The difference of $0.00054 arises from rounding.

[2] Calculations in all examples are rounded to emphasize the fact that the numbers are only estimates. In real problems, results that came so close as those in these two examples would certainly be decided on other grounds than the results of the arithmetic calculations, because of the inevitable margin of error in the estimates.

Year	Earnings (a)	Present Value of $1 at 8% (b)	Total Present Value (a × b)
First..........$250		0.926	$230
Second......... 250		0.857	214
Third.......... 250		0.794	198
Fourth......... 250		0.735	184
Fifth.......... 250		0.681	172
		Total Present Value..	$998

The present value being slightly less than $1,000, the proposal is not acceptable, neglecting nonquantitative considerations.

Present Value of a Stream of Payments

Table B (p. 778) has, for many problems, a more convenient set of present value figures than those in Table A. It shows the present value of $1 to be received annually for *each* of the next *n* years. Each figure on Table B was obtained simply by cumulating, that is, adding together, the figures for the corresponding year and all preceding years in the same column on Table A. Table B can be used directly to find the present value of a stream of equal payments received annually for any given number of years, and therefore reduces considerably the arithmetic required in problems of the type worked in Example 2 above.

EXAMPLE: Same question as in Example 2 above. The present value of $1 *a year* for five years at 8 percent, as shown in Table B, is $3.993; therefore the present value of $250 a year for five years is 250 × $3.993 = $998, which is the same result as in Example 2.

Although the values in Table B are cumulative from year 1, they can be used to find the present value of a stream of earnings between any two points in time. The procedure is to subtract the value for the year *preceding* the first year of the flow from the value for the last year of the flow.

EXAMPLE: What is the present value of $1,000 a year to be received in years 6 through 10, if the discount rate is 8 percent? Solution:

Present value of $1 a year for 10 years at 8 percent....$6.710
Less: Present value of $1 for years 1–5 at 8 percent....–3.993
Difference (equals present value years 6-10)..........$2.717
$1,000 × $2.717 = $2,717

Other Present Value Tables

Tables A and B are calculated on the assumption that earnings are received once a year and on the last day of the year. For many problems this is not a realistic assumption because earnings in the form of increased revenues and lower costs are likely to be incurred throughout the year. Nevertheless, annual tables are customarily used in business investment problems, on the grounds that they are easier to understand than tables constructed on other assumptions, and that they are good enough considering the inevitable margin of error in the basic estimates.

Annual tables *understate* the present value of earnings if earnings are in fact received throughout the year rather than entirely on the last day of the year. The amount of the understatement can be seen in Illustration 19–2. Tables are available showing the present values of earnings flows

Illustration 19–2

EFFECT OF RAPID RECEIPTS

Approximate Ratio of Present Value of Faster Receipts to Present
Value of Annual Receipts at Various Discount Rates

Frequency of Receipt	Discount Rates			
	6%	*10%*	*15%*	*25%*
Semiannually	1.01	1.03	1.04	1.06
Monthly	1.03	1.05	1.07	1.11
Continuously	1.03	1.05	1.08	1.12

that occur quarterly, monthly, or even continuously, but they are not commonly used. Close results often can be obtained from a table that is based on the assumption that the amount is received at the *middle* of the year rather than at the *end* of the year.

The calculations in this chapter will use only the annual tables: Table A for a single amount to be received *n* years from now, and Table B for a stream of uniform amounts to be received for each of the next *n* years. The two are often used in combination, as illustrated in the next example, which also relates the mechanism discussed here to the basic meaning of return on investment discussed at the beginning of this section.

EXAMPLE: Should a proposed investment of $1,000 with annual earnings of $80 a year for the next five years with the $1,000 to be repaid at the end of five years be accepted if the required earnings rate is 8 percent? Solution: As shown by the following calculation, the earnings have a present value of $1,000, so the proposal is acceptable:

Year	Payment	8% Discount Factor	Present Value
1–5	$80/year	3.993 (Table B)	$ 319
End of 5	$1,000	0.681 (Table A)	681
		Total Present Value...	$1,000

Unadjusted Return on Investment

Since the depreciation mechanism provides, in a sense, for the recovery of the cost of a depreciable asset, one might suppose that the return on an investment could be found by relating the investment to its income after depreciation, but such is *not* the case.[3] In our illustrative situation, if a depreciation allowance of $200 a year is subtracted from the gross annual earnings of $250, and the net amount of $50 is divided by the investment of $1,000, the indicated return is 5 percent. Note that this is substantially less than the 8 percent that we now know to be the true return. The return of 5 percent, calculated as above, is called the "accounting" return or the "unadjusted" return. It is unadjusted in the sense that it makes no allowance for the differences in present values of the earnings of the various years; that is, it treats each year's earnings as if they were as valuable as those of every other year, whereas actually the prospect of earning $250 next year is more attractive than the prospect of earning $250 two years from now, and *that* $250 is more attractive than the prospect of earning $250 three years from now, and so on.

The unadjusted return method, computed as above, will always understate the true return. The shorter the time period involved, the more serious is the understatement. For investments involving very long time periods, the understatement is insignificant. An unadjusted return can be computed in other ways, such as using one half the investment as the divisor. All these variations have the same conceptual error, although some of them yield a close approximation to the true return under certain conditions.

ESTIMATING THE VARIABLES

In order to make the calculation described above, four types of estimates must be made: (1) the required earnings rate; (2) the amount of earnings in each year; (3) the economic life, which is the number of years for which earnings are anticipated; and (4) the amount of investment. Each is discussed below. The examples will be limited to the *equipment replacement* problem, although the same considerations apply to problems of all types. Essentially, the alternatives in this problem are (*a*) to continue to use the present equipment, or (*b*) to replace it, with the expectation that savings in operating costs or other factors will be sufficient to recoup the investment and earn a satisfactory return on the funds that have been frozen in the new equipment.

---

[3] Unless depreciation is calculated on the annuity method, which is rare in practice.

Required Earnings Rate

The selection of the appropriate earnings rate is a crucial matter of top-management judgment. The problem can usefully be subdivided into two parts: (1) selection of the average rate required on the average investment and (2) consideration of factors that make a specific proposed investment different from the average.

AVERAGE EARNINGS RATE.   In many companies, the choice of an average required earnings rate is largely subjective. Management decides that a sufficient number of investment opportunities can be found that will earn 10 percent, 15 percent, or some other number, and this percentage becomes the prescribed minimum below which the company refuses to make investments of average risk and uncertainty.

COST OF CAPITAL.   Some people argue that the required earnings rate should be equal to the company's *cost of capital*, which is the aftertax cost of debt capital plus the cost of equity capital, weighted by the relative amount of each in the normal capital structure (the aftertax cost of debt is used because interest on debt is a tax deductible expense); thus:

Type	*Cost*	*Weight*	*Weighted Total*
Debt (bonds)...............	3%	0.4	1.2%
Equity (stock)............	15	0.6	9.0
Total...................		1.0	10.2%

The indicated cost of capital is 10.2 percent or, rounded, 10 percent. The trouble with the cost-of-capital approach is that the cost of equity capital is extraordinarily difficult to estimate.[4] One starts with the market price of the stock, and then tries to estimate what fraction of the market price is attributable to the market's judgment of profits on the present equity, and what fraction is attributable to the market's judgment of future profits that will be earned on retained earnings. Few people have much confidence in the results of such estimates. The discussion here has been cursory for this reason.

PRO FORMA APPROACH.   A less exact but more feasible approach is to construct a *pro forma* (i.e. hypothetical) balance sheet and income statement for a "satisfactory" future situation. The balance sheet will show the real values of the assets (as distinguished from their book value), perhaps using half the current cost of fixed assets as an indication of their average

---

[4] See Hunt, Williams, and Donaldson, *Basic Business Finance: Text and Cases* (3d ed.; Homewood, Ill.; Richard D. Irwin, Inc., 1966). The economists' profit maximization model requires that a cost-of-capital figure be estimated. This is the second reason why this book is not based on the profit maximization assumption. The other reason was discussed on page 594.

future value. It will show a proportion of fixed debt to equity capital that management considers satisfactory. The income statement will show the income that management considers as being an acceptable and attainable level of earnings for such assets. The required earnings rate is calculated as follows:

1. Find the aftertax interest cost. This is the actual interest cost of long-term debt multiplied by one minus the income tax rate; it is approximately one half the actual interest cost.

2. Add this to the net income after taxes.

3. Divide the amount obtained in step 2 by the sum of long-term debt plus owners' equity.

The procedure is shown in Illustration 19–3.

Illustration 19–3

ESTIMATING THE REQUIRED EARNINGS RATE

A. "Satisfactory" Balance Sheet
(in thousands)

ASSETS			EQUITIES	
Working capital....		$ 2,000	Long-term debt (6%)........	$ 3,000
Fixed assets, gross..	$16,000		Owners' equity.............	7,000
Less: Average				
depreciation.	8,000	8,000		
Total Assets...		$10,000	Total Equities.........	$10,000

B. "Satisfactory" Income Statement

Revenue...	$11,000
Less: All costs except interest and taxes.................	9,000
Income before interest and taxes.........................	$ 2,000
Interest...	180
Income before taxes..................................	$ 1,820
Income taxes (50%)..................................	910
Net Income...	$ 910

C. Calculation of Required Earnings Rate

$$\frac{\text{Aftertax Interest} + \text{Net Income}}{\text{Debt} + \text{Equity}} = \frac{90 + 910}{4,000 + 6,000} = 10 \text{ Percent}$$

OTHER APPROACHES. Many companies arrive at the average required earnings rate by a process that is essentially trial and error. If a given rate results in the rejection of projects that management intuitively feels are desirable, there is an indication that the rate is too high, and it is lowered. An average required rate of 10 percent after taxes is found in many industrial companies and government agencies, with lower rates in public utilities (say, 8 percent) and higher rates (15 or 20 percent) in companies in industries where profit opportunities are unusually good or risks are unusually high.

Sometimes income taxes are ignored, in which case the rate is a pretax rate, which is higher than the aftertax rate in the same company.

INTEREST RATE. Whatever the rate selected, it is almost certain to be considerably higher than an *interest* rate, that is, the rate for borrowing money (say, 5 to 8 percent before taxes). The required earnings rate includes interest, but it also includes an additional allowance for risks that are borne by the business rather than by the lender of money, and for which the business expects compensation.

ADJUSTMENT OF THE AVERAGE RATE. The required earnings rate for the whole business reflects the average risk of investments in various classes of assets. This average results from a composite of many different types of risks, ranging from investments in government bonds, where the risk is very low, to investments that may be almost pure gambles, such as those in untried new products. The earnings rate required on the particular investment under consideration should reflect, if feasible, the relative risk of this investment compared to the average.

It may also reflect the uncertainty that the estimated savings will actually be realized. The figures on costs, savings, and economic life are *estimates* of what will happen in the future. Often, a higher than average earnings rate is used when these uncertainties are believed to be great. (Uncertainty can also be allowed for by arbitrarily shortening the estimate of economic life. Care should be taken not to *overallow* for uncertainty by using both a short life and a high required earnings rate.)[5]

Finally, the required earnings rate is sometimes adjusted to compensate for the "administrative bother" that may be entailed in going into the venture—the unmeasured, but sometimes significant, cost of the additional management headaches and worry that may be a consequence of making the proposed investment.

PROFIT CENTER RATES. If the company has several profit centers or divisions it may or may not use the same required earnings rate for all profit centers. If it uses different required earnings rates in different profit centers, the rates chosen will tend to influence the flow of corporate funds to the various profit centers; for the higher the required rate, the fewer proposed investments will be accepted. It is erroneous to derive these profit center rates from the actual earnings of the profit centers; for example, it is erroneous to assign a low rate to a division that currently has

---

[5] Uncertainty can also be taken into account by mathematical techniques. These include (*a*) *sensitivity analysis,* that shows the change in the present value of earnings that results from systematically varying each of the main elements of the earnings calculations, and (*b*) calculation of a large number of earnings estimates, each based on different estimates of the main elements of the earnings calculation, and study of the resulting frequency distribution. These techniques are not difficult if a computer is available.

a low return on its investment. Such a practice would tend to perpetuate, or even enlarge, mature divisions whose profit potential is low, at the expense of young divisions that have a high profit potential and need large investments to exploit that potential.

FINANCIAL PROBLEMS.   In some problems, the issue is not whether to acquire an asset, but rather the manner in which to finance it; in other problems, a certain method of financing may be an integral part of the proposal. In these situations, the relevant required earnings rate must be tailored to the facts of the problem. If a company has already decided to acquire a building, and the issue is whether to buy it with borrowed funds or to acquire it through a long-term noncancelable lease, the required earnings rate is close to the cost of borrowing funds rather than the overall earnings rate for the whole company.

Unless the method of financing is closely related to the proposition itself, it is usually better to consider the means of obtaining the funds as a separate problem. Ordinarily, the question as to whether the proposed investment is or is not desirable is an operating matter, decided by operating people; the question of how to finance it is a financial matter, decided by financial people.

Earnings

The earnings from an investment are essentially the additional cash that the company estimates it will earn from the investment as compared with what the company's earnings would be if it did not make the investment. The *differential* concept emphasized in Chapter 18 is therefore equally applicable here. Consider, for example, a proposal to replace an existing machine with an even better machine. We note first that the existing machine must still be usable, for if it can no longer perform its function, there is no analytical problem; it *must* be replaced. The existing machine has a certain set of labor, material, power, repair, maintenance, and other costs associated with its future operation. If the alternative machine is proposed as a means of reducing costs, there will be a different, lower set of costs associated with its use. The difference between these two sets of cost is the *earnings* anticipated if the new machine is acquired. These earnings are figured on an annual basis.

If the proposed machine increases the company's productive capacity, and if the increased output can be sold, the incremental profit on this increased volume is the earnings anticipated from acquisition of the proposed machine. Incremental profit is the difference between added sales revenue and incremental costs, which usually include direct material, direct labor, direct selling costs, and any other costs that will not be incurred if the increased volume is not manufactured and sold.

Depreciation on the proposed equipment is not a relevant cost item; the present value tables automatically provide for recouping the investment itself, and to include a depreciation charge would be counting this recoupment twice. Depreciation on the existing equipment is likewise not relevant because, as explained in Chapter 18, this represents a sunk cost that is unaffected by the present decision.

The earnings stream in a capital budgeting problem usually must be estimated for a considerable period of time in the future. Such estimates are fraught with uncertainty and must be treated accordingly. A particularly troublesome aspect of these estimates is what assumption to make about changes in price levels. If the analyst believes, as many people do, that labor rates and material prices will generally tend to move upward, it may be desirable to incorporate in the calculation of earnings an explicit assumption about inflation.

In general, the earnings are cash flows. As explained in Chapter 18, changes in prorated or allocated costs are not relevant unless they actually represent differential costs.

INCOME TAXES. Presumably, the purpose of making an investment is to increase the owners' equity. Owners' equity will not be increased by the full amount of the cost savings or additional income resulting from the investment, however, since a substantial fraction of these savings or income usually will be paid to the government in the form of additional income taxes. Owners' equity will be increased only by the amount remaining after these additional taxes have been deducted.

If "earnings," as defined above, were the same as "additional profit subject to income tax," then profit after taxes could be found simply by multiplying the profit by the complement of the estimated future tax rate (i.e., one minus the tax rate). Thus, if 50 percent is accepted as a reasonable estimate of future applicable tax rates, the profit after taxes would be one half the profit before taxes.

In estimating earnings, however, depreciation was intentionally omitted from the calculations. Since depreciation is an allowable expense for tax purposes, "additional profit subject to income tax" will not correspond to earnings in any problem where depreciation is a significant factor. In effect, the depreciation on the equipment being purchased provides a "tax shield"; it shields earnings from the full impact of income taxes.

EXAMPLE: A proposed machine costing $1,000 is expected to result in cash savings of $320 a year for five years. Assuming a required earnings rate of 10 percent, is this a good investment?

The additional income subject to taxes will be, not the whole $320, but rather $320 less the depreciation charge. If straight-line depreciation is used, this will be $200 a year ($1,000 ÷ 5 years). The additional income subject to tax will be $320 − $200 = $120. At a tax rate of 50 percent, income taxes will be increased half of this, or $60, so the net savings will be $320 − $60 = $260. Savings of $260 a year for 5 years at 10 percent has a present value of 260 × $3.791 = $986. Since this is less than the $1,000 investment, the machine is not a good investment.

ACCELERATED DEPRECIATION. In the preceding example we assumed that depreciation would be calculated on a straight-line basis for tax purposes. Many companies use one of the accelerated bases of depreciation, however (see Chapter 6 for description). Assuming the sum-of-years' digit basis is used, the tax deductible depreciation and the earnings after taxes for the proposal described in the preceding example would be as follows:

Year	Cash Earnings (a)	Depreciation (b)	Earnings Subject to Tax (c = a − b)	Tax at 50% (d)	Cash Earnings after Tax (e = a − d)
1..........	$ 320	$ 333	$ −13	$ −6	$ 326
2..........	320	267	53	26	294
3..........	320	200	120	60	260
4..........	320	133	187	94	226
5..........	320	67	253	126	194
Total.....	$1,600	$1,000	$600	$300	$1,300

We could then find the present value of the earnings by discounting each of the five after-tax cash earnings amounts in the last column, as follows:

Year	Earnings after Tax	Discount at 10%	Present Value
1..................	$ 326	0.909	$ 297
2..................	294	0.826	243
3..................	260	0.751	195
4..................	226	0.683	154
5..................	194	0.621	121
Total............	$1,300		$1,010

TABLE C. There is a way of greatly simplifying the above calculation. It involves the use of Table C, page 779, which shows the present value of a stream of depreciation charges figured by the sum-of-years' digit method. (Double declining balance, which is the other commonly used accelerated method, gives practically the same results.) Using this table, the total present value of the depreciation tax shield can be figured easily in a single computation, and this amount can then be added to the present value of the aftertax cash earnings to give the total present value of the earnings.

The procedure is as follows:

1. Multiply the annual cash earnings, neglecting depreciation, by the complement of the tax rate to find the aftertax cash earnings.

2. Multiply the aftertax cash earnings by the appropriate discount amount from Table B, to find their present value.

3. Multiply the depreciable investment by the appropriate amount from Table C to find the present value of the stream of depreciation charges.

4. Multiply this present value by the tax rate to find the present value of the depreciation tax shield.

5. Add the amounts in steps 2 and 4 to find the aftertax present value of earnings.

> EXAMPLE: Same problem as above, but using Table C.
>
> The cash earnings after taxes, but *neglecting depreciation*, are 50 percent of $320, or $160 a year. The present value of $1 a year for five years at 10 percent is $3.791; therefore the present value of the cash earnings is 160 × $3.791   = $ 607
>
> The present value of depreciation of $1 of investment spread over five years is, from Table C, $0.806. For an investment of $1,000, it is therefore 1,000 × $0.806 = $806. The present value of the depreciation tax shield is $806 times the tax rate, 50 percent,   =   403
>
> The total present value therefore equals $1,010

Note that the result in the above example is exactly the same as in the year-by-year calculation given above. Note also how the use of accelerated depreciation increases the attractiveness of the investment; its present value rises from $986 under straight-line depreciation to $1,010, and the proposal now meets the criterion that the present value of its earnings exceeds the investment. This result occurs because a larger fraction of the depreciation tax shield occurs in the early years, where present values are relatively high; it is the reason why accelerated depreciation has become so popular for tax purposes.

If the proposed machine is to replace a machine that has not been fully depreciated for tax purposes, then the tax shield is only the differential depreciation, that is, the difference between depreciation on the present machine and that on the new machine, because if the new machine is purchased, the old machine will presumably be disposed of, so its depreciation will no longer provide a tax shield. In this case, the present value of the tax shield of the remaining depreciation on the old machine must be calculated (usually year by year), and this amount must be subtracted from the present value of the depreciation tax shield on the proposed machine.

OMISSION OF TAX CALCULATION. In many types of alternative choice problems, the question of income taxes may be omitted entirely, since the alternative that produces the most profit *before* taxes will also produce the most profit *after* taxes. This is the case with pricing problems and many make-or-buy problems. In problems involving depreciable assets, however, there is unlikely to be a simple relationship between savings before taxes and savings after taxes, and the above calculation is therefore necessary.

TAX EFFECT OF INTEREST. Interest actually paid (as distinguished from imputed interest) is an allowable expense for income tax purposes; therefore, if interest costs will be increased as a result of the investment, it could be argued that interest provides a tax shield similar to depreciation and that its impact should be estimated by the same method as that shown for depreciation, above. Customarily, however, interest is *not* included anywhere in the calculations either of earnings or of taxes. This is because we usually seek the overall rate of return on the investment, without regard for whether the funds required for the investment are borrowed (which involves interest) or whether they come from the shareholders (which does not involve interest).

In problems where the method of financing is an important part of the proposal, the tax shield provided by interest may appropriately be considered. In these problems, the rate of return that results from the calculation is a return on that part of the investment which was financed by the shareholders' equity, not a return on the total funds committed to the investment.

> EXAMPLE: Suppose a company is considering an investment in a parcel of real estate, and intends to finance perhaps 70 percent of the investment by a mortgage loan on the property. It may wish to focus attention on the return on its own funds, namely, the remaining 30 percent. It would be appropriate to include in the calculation of such a return both the interest on the mortgage loan and the effect of this interest on taxable income.

Economic Life

The cash flow analysis is carried out for the time period corresponding to the life of the proposed project, the period over which benefits can be estimated. The end of this period is called the *horizon* for the project, the word suggesting that beyond this point earnings are not visible. When the proposed project involves the purchase of equipment, this time period corresponds to the economic life of the equipment.

There are at least three ways of defining the "life" of equipment:

1. Its physical life.
2. Its technological life.
3. Its product-market life.

The economic life is the *shortest* of these three types of life. Economic life can rarely be estimated exactly; nevertheless, making the best possible judgment of the economic life is extremely important.

PHYSICAL LIFE.   There is a tendency, when thinking about the life of a machine, to consider primarily its physical life; that is, the number of years the machine will probably be of use to the company in performing the technical job for which it was acquired. This concept of life is sometimes used in calculating depreciation for accounting purposes and for income tax purposes. It is of little use in investment decisions.

TECHNOLOGICAL LIFE.   This refers to the period of time that elapses before a new machine comes out that makes the present machine obsolete. It is this life that, for most companies, corresponds to the economic life. Improvements will almost certainly be made sometime in all machines now in existence, but the question of *which* machines will be improved and *how soon* the improved machines will be on the market is a most difficult one to answer. Unless special information is available, the answer can be little more than a guess. Yet it is a guess that must be made, for the investment in a machine will cease to earn a return when and if this machine is replaced by an even better machine.

PRODUCT-MARKET LIFE.   Although the machine may be in excellent physical condition, and although there may be no better machine available, its economic life has ended, as far as the owner is concerned, as soon as the company ceases to market the product made on the machine. The "product-market" life of the machine may end because the particular operation performed by the machine is made unnecessary by a change in style or a change in process, or because the market for the product itself has vanished. A machine for making buggy whips may last physically for 100 years, and there may be no possibility of making technological improvements in it; yet such a machine cannot earn a return on its investment if the buggy whips produced on it cannot be sold.

The product-market life of a machine also ends if the company goes out of business. Most managements quite properly operate on the premise that the company will be in business for a long time to come. There are instances, however, when a businessman foresees an end to his business, or to a particular part of it, in the relatively near future. In such a case, the economic life of a machine *to him* is limited to the period during which he believes his business is going to operate.

UNEVEN LIVES.   For many types of equipment, it is reasonable to assume that the present machine can be used, physically, for a period of time at least as long as the economic life of the proposed machine. In situations in which this assumption is not valid, however, earnings on a proposed machine purchased now will not in fact occur each year of the period being considered, for a new machine must be purchased anyway when the physical life of the present machine ends. Thereafter, there may be no difference in the annual cost of the two alternatives (buy now versus don't buy now), since the same machine will be involved in both of them.

If the expected physical life of the present machine is significantly shorter than the expected economic life of the proposed machine, some way must be found of making an equivalence between the time periods covered by the two alternatives. For example, if the proposed machine has an economic life of 10 years but the present machine has a remaining physical life of only 6 years, the relevant earnings will occur for only 6 years. This fact raises the difficult question of treating the situation that will exist at the end of the sixth year.

Since the purchase now of a new machine eliminates the need of purchasing another one six years from now, this future purchase price will have been saved and its present value can therefore be counted as a cash inflow in the sixth year. However, the machine purchased now presumably will have to be replaced at the end of 10 years; whereas if a machine is not purchased until 6 years from now, it will last until 16 years from now. So, if the proposal is accepted, there will be an additional cash outflow at the end of the 10th year. This intricate reasoning can be extended indefinitely through later replacement cycles. Estimates of these distant values are tenuous, and this whole procedure is based on the assumption that there will be no further changes in technology or price levels; but the roughness of the estimates is somewhat mitigated by the fact that the present values become less significant as the time span increases, so that the calculations need not be carried out indefinitely.

Another approach is to estimate the remaining value of the new machine at the end of the sixth year of its life. The analysis would then cover only the six-year period, with this remaining value being treated as a residual value, or implicit cash inflow at the end of the period. Such an estimate is extremely difficult to make, however.

The problem of uneven lives does not arise often, and this is fortunate, because the timing and consequences of the future replacements under each alternative are difficult to visualize.

Investment

The amount of the investment is the amount that the company risks if it accepts the proposal. The relevant investment costs are the differential or incremental costs. These are the outlays that will be made if the project is undertaken and that will not be made if it is not undertaken. The cost of the machine itself, its shipping costs, cost of installation, and the cost of training operators are examples. These outlays are part of the investment, even though some of them are not capitalized in the accounting records.

INVESTMENT CREDIT. At present (mid 1969) a company may receive an "investment credit" of up to 7 percent of the cost of a new machine as a reduction in its income taxes. The amount of company funds involved may therefore be only 93 percent of the invoice cost of the machine.

EXISTING EQUIPMENT. If the purchase of new equipment makes possible the sale of existing equipment, the proceeds from the sale may reduce the amount of incremental investment. In other words, the investment represents the total amount of *additional* funds that must be committed to the operation. To subtract this resale value from the gross investment, however, is to assume implicitly that (*a*) if the proposed machine is not purchased, the present machine will continue to be used, and its resale value will decrease to zero through its continued use; and (*b*) if the proposed machine is purchased, the present machine will in fact be sold or converted to some other productive use. If either of these assumptions is not valid, and if the amount involved is significant, the resale value of the present machine should be treated separately as a cash inflow in some future year, not netted against the gross investment in the proposed machine.

TAX EFFECTS. The disposition of the present machine may involve a write-off of undepreciated book values or a sale at a price above book value. In either of these cases, special tax considerations may apply, since the write-off may give rise to a capital loss and the sale to a capital gain. The capital gains rate is, in effect, 25 percent. Nevertheless, under most circumstances, gains and losses on the disposition of machinery and equipment (not buildings) are taxed at the regular rate of approximately 50 percent. No tax gain or loss arises if the new machine replaces one of "like kind." Expert tax advice is needed on problems involving gains and losses on the sale of depreciable assets, for the line between the assets giving rise to capital gains or losses and other assets is difficult to define. In any event, when existing assets are disposed of, the relevant amount by which the net investment is reduced is the proceeds of the sale, adjusted for taxes.

RESIDUAL VALUE. A machine may have a salvage or resale value at the end of its useful life. In a great many cases, the estimated residual value is so small and occurs so far in the future that it has no significant effect on the decision. Moreover, any salvage value that is realized may be almost, or completely, offset by removal and dismantling costs.

In situations where residual value is significant, the net residual value (after removal costs) is a cash inflow in the year of disposal, and is included with the other cash inflows. Other assets, such as repair parts or inventory, may also be released at the end of the project, and these are treated in the same fashion.

SUNK COSTS. As emphasized in Chapter 18, sunk costs are irrelevant. If $100,000 has been sunk in research leading to a new product, and if the new product will require an additional investment in new facilities of $10,000 and is expected to generate profits of $5,000 a year for five years, the relevant investment figure is $10,000, not $110,000. The $100,000 may be regretted, but it cannot be recouped.

INVESTMENTS IN WORKING CAPITAL.   An investment is the commitment, or locking up, of funds in any type of asset. Although a machine has here been used as an example, land and buildings also are investments, and so are commitments of funds to additional inventory and other current assets. In particular, if the new equipment is to produce a new product, additional funds will probably be tied up in inventories, accounts receivable, and increased cash needs. Part of this increased working capital will be supplied from increased accounts payable and accrued expenses. The net increase in working capital is as much an investment as the equipment itself, although in a more liquid state.

Often it is reasonable to assume that the residual value of investments in working capital items is approximately the same as the amount of the investment; that is, that at the end of the project, they can be liquidated at their cost. Under these circumstances, the amount of working capital is treated as a cash inflow in the last year of the project, and its present value is found by discounting at the required earnings rate.

SEVERAL ALTERNATIVES.   Some proposals involve a choice among several alternatives, each involving a different amount of investment. A useful way of approaching such problems is to start with the alternative that requires the smallest investment and to analyze the next most expensive alternative in terms of its *incremental* investment and its *incremental* earnings above those of the least expensive alternative. This question is asked: Is the *additional* investment in the second alternative justified by the *additional* earnings that are expected from it, over and above the earnings expected from the least expensive alternative? If it is not, the proposal with the smaller investment should be accepted.

DEFERRED INVESTMENTS.   Many projects involve a single commitment of funds at one moment of time, which we have called "the present." For some projects, on the other hand, the commitments are spread over a considerable period of time. The construction of a new plant may require disbursements over several years, or it may involve the construction of one unit now and a second unit five years later. In order to make the return-on-investment calculations, these investments must be brought to a common point in time, and this is done by the application of discount rates to the amounts involved. In general, the appropriate rate depends on the uncertainty that the investment will be made; the lower the uncertainty, the lower the rate. Thus, if the commitment is an extremely definite one, the discount rate may be equivalent to the interest rate on bonds (which also represents a definite commitment) whereas if the future investments will be made only if earnings materialize, then the rate can be the required earnings rate. In effect, in the latter case, the future investment is treated as a cash outflow.

Summary of the Process

Following is a summary of the steps involved in using the present value method:

1. Select a required earnings rate. Presumably, once selected, this rate will be used for all proposals in the same risk category.

2. Estimate the differential cash inflows, or "earnings," for each year or sequence of years including:

   a) The cash earnings, neglecting depreciation, after taxes, for each year of the economic life.

   b) The depreciation tax shield, using Table C.

   c) Residual values at the end of the economic life, consisting of disposal value of equipment plus working capital that is to be released.

3. Estimate the cash outflows other than the investment itself, if there are any, for the year in which they occur.

4. Find the net present value of all future inflows and outflows by discounting them at the required earnings rate, using Table A or Table B.

5. Find the net investment, which includes the additional outlays made at "the present time," less the proceeds from disposal of existing equipment (adjusted for tax consequences), plus the present value of investment outlays made at some time other than the present. Use a low discount rate if these future outlays are quite certain to be made.

6. If the present value of the cash flows exceeds the amount of the net investment, decide that the proposal is acceptable, insofar as the monetary factors are concerned. This comparison is often made by treating the net investment as a cash outflow in year 0; i.e., with a present value of 1.000. When this is done, adding the numbers algebraically gives the result directly. A positive sum indicates an acceptable proposal; a negative sum, an unfavorable one.

7. Taking into account the nonmonetary factors, reach a final decision. (This part of the process is at least as important as all the other parts put together, but there is no way of generalizing about it, other than to offer the list of suggestions given in Chapter 18.)

As an aid to visualizing the relationship, it is often useful to make a rough diagram of the flows such as that shown in Illustration 19–4.

The diagram is for the same situation given in the example on page 637, with the addition of an estimated residual value of $200; namely, a machine costing $1,000, and estimated cash earnings (say, from savings in labor costs) of $320 a year for five years. As an illustration of the whole process, the analysis of this proposal will be described, arranged according to the steps given above.

1. The required earnings rate is 10 percent. (The company has arrived at this rate by one of the methods described above.)
2. The differential cash inflows are:
   a) The cash earnings of $320 a year, which, after adjustment for an estimated income tax of 50 percent, becomes $160 a year for five years.
   b) The depreciation tax shield, which, assuming the whole investment of $1,000 is subject to depreciation for tax purposes, has a present value of $403, as calculated in the preceding example.
   c) The residual value at the end of the fifth year, which is $200. (Note that this differs from the assumption of zero residual value made for tax purposes.)

Illustration 19–4

CASH FLOW DIAGRAM

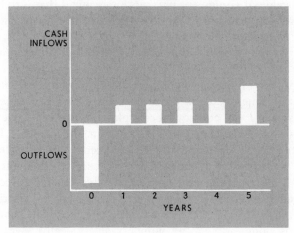

3. There are no noninvestment cash outflows in this problem.
4. The net present value of the cash flows, other than the investment are the sum of (*a*) the aftertax cash earnings of $160 a year for five years, which has a present value, already calculated, of $607; plus (*b*) the present value of the depreciation tax shield of $403; plus (*c*) the present value of the residual value of $200, which, discounted at 0.621 (from Table A), amounts to $124. These amounts total $1,134.
5. The net investment is the gross investment of $1,000, less the investment credit, here assumed to be 2 percent, a net of $980. (The investment credit is not always 7 percent; the amount varies, depending principally on the estimated life of the asset.)
6. Since the present value of the inflows, $1,134, exceeds the net investment, $980, the indication is that the proposal is acceptable insofar as the monetary factors are concerned.

7. The final decision would also take into account nonmonetary factors which, although not discussed here, may be as important as or more important than the monetary factors.

OTHER METHODS

Time-Adjusted Return

With the present value method, the required earnings rate must be selected in advance. There exists an alternative method, which finds the earnings rate at which the present value of the earnings equals the amount of the investment. This rate is called the *time-adjusted return*, or *internal rate of return*, or *project rate of return*. The method is called by one of the above names and also by the terms "discounted cash flow method" and "investor's method." We shall refer to it as the time-adjusted return method.

LEVEL EARNINGS. If the earnings are level—that is, the same amount each year—the process is simple. It will be illustrated by a proposed investment of $1,000 with estimated earnings of $250 a year for five years. The procedure is as follows:

1. Divide the investment, $1,000, by the annual earnings, $250. The result, 4, is called the "factor."
2. Look across the five-year row of Table B. The column in which the figure closest to 4 appears shows the rate of return. Since the closest figure is 3.993 in the 8 percent column, the return is slightly less than 8 percent.
3. If management is satisfied with a return of slightly less than 8 percent, then it should accept this project (neglecting nonquantitative considerations); if it requires a higher return, then it should reject the project.

The factor 4 is simply the ratio of the investment to the annual earnings. Each figure on Table B shows the ratio of the present value of a stream of earnings to an investment of $1 made today, for various combinations of discount rates and numbers of years. The number 4 opposite any combination of years and discount rates means that the present value of a stream of earnings of $1 a year for that number of years discounted at that rate is $4. The present value of a stream of earnings of $250 a year is in the same ratio; therefore it is $250 times 4, or $1,000.

In this procedure, it is usually necessary to interpolate, that is, to estimate the location of a number that lies between two figures appearing in the table. There is no need to be precise about these interpolations because the final result can be no better than the basic data, and the basic data are ordinarily only rough estimates. A quick interpolation, made visually, is usually as good as the accuracy of the data warrants. Computations of fractions of a percent are rarely, if ever, warranted.

COMPUTING SEVERAL RETURNS. Since the most uncertain estimate of all is often the number of years during which there will be earnings, it is often useful to locate several combinations of years and rates that have the specified factor. For example, an investment of $20,000 and annual earnings of $4,000 give a factor of 5. Some of the combinations found on Table B for a factor of 5 are as follows:

If the Life Is:	*Then the Rate of Return Is about:*	*Or figured another way:*	*If the Required Rate of Return Is:*	*Then the Life Must Be at Least:*
6 years	6%		6%	6 + years
8 years	12%		10%	7 + years
10 years	15%		15%	10 years
12 years	17%		18%	14 years

If the proposed investment is expected to have a longer life, *and* if the required earnings rate is lower than any one of the combinations selected, the investment is attractive; otherwise, it is not attractive.

PAYBACK. The figure referred to above as the "factor" is also called the "payback" because it is the number of years over which the investment outlay will be recovered or paid back from earnings *if* the estimates turn out to be correct; that is, the project will "pay for itself" in this number of years. The payback figure is often used as a quick but crude method of appraising investments. If the payback period is equal to or only slightly less than the estimated life of the project, then the proposal is obviously a poor one. If the payback period is considerably less than the estimated life, then the project begins to look attractive.[6]

If several investment proposals have the same general characteristics, then the payback period can be used as a valid way of screening out the acceptable proposals. For example, if a company finds that production equipment ordinarily has a life of 10 years, and if it requires a return of at least 15 percent, then the company may specify that new equipment will be considered for purchase only if it has a payback period of 5 years or less; Table B shows that this payback period is equivalent to a return of approximately 15 percent if the life is 10 years. Stating the criterion in this fashion avoids the necessity of explaining the present value concept to the members of the operating organization.

The danger of using the payback figure is that it gives no consideration to differences in the lives of various projects. There may be a tendency to conclude that the shorter the payback period, the better the project;

---

[6] Professor Myron Gordon has shown that the reciprocal of the payback (i.e., 1/payback period) is a close approximation of the time-adjusted return IF the estimated life of the project is somewhat more than twice the payback period and IF earnings are level. The return found by this simple method slightly overstates the true return (*Journal of Business,* October 1955, p. 253).

whereas the project with the longer payback may actually be better if it will produce satisfactory earnings for a longer period of time.

UNEVEN EARNINGS. If earnings are not the same in each year, the time-adjusted return must be found by trial and error; that is, the earnings for each year and the residual values are listed, and various discount rates are applied to these amounts until a rate is found that makes their total present value equal to the amount of the investment. This rate is the time-adjusted return.

This method is illustrated by a problem in which it is assumed that the net investment is $1,000 and that earnings are estimated to be $300 a year for the first 5 years but only $100 a year for the 6th through the 10th year.

As a first trial, the present value of these earnings will be computed at an earnings rate of 18 percent. From Table B, we find that the present value of $1 a year for the next five years at 18 percent is $3.127. Table B does not tell us directly the present value of an amount to be received from the 6th through the 10th year, but, as already explained, this can easily be found by subtraction. The amount for 10 years is $4.494, and the amount for the first 5 of these years is $3.127; therefore, the amount for the 6th through the 10th years must be the difference between these figures, or $1.367. The present value of the estimated earnings can be computed by use of these factors, as follows:

Time Period	Earnings	Factor at 18%	Present Value
Years 1– 5............	$300/year	3.127	$ 938
6–10............	100/year	1.367	137
		Total......	$1,075
		Investment..	1,000
		Difference..+$	75

When the present value exceeds the net investment, a higher earnings rate is used on the next trial; when the present value is less than the net investment, a lower rate is used.

In this case, therefore, a higher rate must be used, and 20 percent is selected. Another trial is made, as follows:

Time Period	Earnings	Factor at 20%	Present Value
Years 1– 5............	$300/year	2.991	$ 897
6–10............	100/year	1.201	120
		Total......	$1,017
		Investment..	1,000
		Difference..+$	17

This calculation gives a present value slightly above the net investment, which indicates that the time-adjusted return is slightly more than 20 percent.

In a similar fashion, all the elements involved in an investment can be compared with all the elements involved on the earnings side of the equation, with the difference in the timing of the money flows being recognized by the application of a trial discount rate. Eventually a rate will be found that makes the present value of the outflows approximately equal to the present value of the inflows. Usually, a satisfactory approximation to this rate can be found in two or three trials.

MAPI Method

Dr. George Terborgh of the Machinery and Allied Products Institute (MAPI) has developed a method that is specifically intended to help decide whether a machine should be replaced now or whether replacement should be deferred until some future time. Special forms and charts make this method quite easy to use. The charts are constructed in accordance with certain assumptions, the most important of which is that earnings will decline each year as the machine ages, in accordance with a prescribed pattern. Doctor Terborgh asserts that this is the typical situation with respect to replacement equipment, both because equipment becomes less efficient and requires higher maintenance costs with the passage of time and because the probability of obsolescence increases as time goes on.

If this and the other assumptions built into the method fit facts of the situation being analyzed, then the "urgency rating," which is the end product of the MAPI method, is a close approximation to the time-adjusted return. This method is fully described in a reference at the end of this chapter.

Comparison of Methods

Given the same set of raw data, the time-adjusted return method will produce the same results at the present value method in the class of problems we have called screening problems; that is, if one method signals that a proposal is acceptable, so will the other. Under most circumstances, the MAPI method will also give the same signal if the special assumptions built into this method are used in the other methods. As will be seen, this similarity of results does not hold true in the other class of problems, called preference problems.

PREFERENCE PROBLEMS

So far, the discussion has been limited to *screening* or "go, no go" problems, where this is the question: Is the proposal acceptable, or isn't it? We turn now to the more difficult *preference* problem, where we must decide which of two competing proposals is preferable, or where we must rank a series of proposals in order of their attractiveness. Both the time-adjusted return and the present value methods are used for this purpose.

If the time-adjusted return method is used, the preference rule is as follows: the higher the return, the better the project. A project with a return of 20 percent is said to be preferable to a project with a return of 19 percent.

Profitability Index

If the present value method is used, the present value of the earnings of one project cannot be compared directly with the present value of the earnings of another unless the investments are of the same size. Most people would agree that a $1,000 investment that produces earnings with a present value of $2,000 is better than a $1,000,000 investment that produces earnings with a present value of $1,001,000. In order to compare two proposals, we must relate the size of the earnings to the amount of money that is risked. This is done simply by dividing the present value earnings by the amount of investment, to give a ratio that is called the *profitability index*. The preference rule is as follows: the higher the index number, the better the project.

Comparison of Preference Rules

Conceptually, the profitability index is superior to the time-adjusted return as a preference device, for the time-adjusted return method will not always give the correct preference as between two projects with different lives or with different patterns of earnings.

As an example, consider two proposals. Proposal A involves an investment of $1,000 and earnings of $1,200 received at the end of one year; its time-adjusted return is 20 percent. Proposal B involves an investment of $1,000 and earnings of $300 a year for five years; its time-adjusted return is only 15 percent. But Proposal A is *not* necessarily preferable to Proposal B. It is preferable only if the company can expect to earn a high return during the following four years on some other project in which the funds released at the end of the first year are reinvested. Otherwise, Proposal B, which earns 15 percent over the whole five-year period, is preferable.[7]

The error illustrated above is not present in the profitability index

---

[7] Note that this problem arises when a choice must be made between two competing proposals, only one of which can be adopted. If the proposals are noncompeting and the required earnings rate is less than 15 percent, then *both* of them are acceptable.

method. Assuming a required earnings rate of 10 percent, the two proposals described above would be analyzed as follows:

Proposal (a)	Earnings (b)	Discount Factor (c)	Present Value (d = b × c)	Investment (e)	Index (f = d ÷ e)
A.........$1,200—1 yr.		0.909	$1,091	$1,000	1.09
B.........$ 300—5 yrs.		3.791	1,137	1,000	1.14

The index signals that Proposal B is better than Proposal A, which is in fact the case if the company can expect to reinvest the money released from Proposal A so as to earn only 10 percent on it.

Although the profitability index method is conceptually superior to the time-adjusted return method, and although the former is also easier to calculate since there is no trial-and-error computation, the time-adjusted return method is widely used in practice. There seem to be two reasons for this. First, the profitability index requires that the earnings rate be established before the calculations are made, whereas many analysts prefer to work from the other direction; that is, to find the return and then see how it compares with their idea of the earnings rate that is appropriate in view of the risks involved. Second, the index is an abstract number that is difficult to explain; whereas the time-adjusted return is similar to interest rates and earnings rates with which every businessman is familiar.

Concluding Comment

Not every businessman uses a discounting technique in analyzing investment proposals. In some cases, this is because the businessman is not familiar with the techniques. But there is a much better reason than this in many instances. Some businessmen, having studied the approach carefully, have concluded that it is like trying to make a silk purse out of a sow's ear; that is, in their opinion the underlying estimates are so rough that the refinement of discounting them is more work than it is worth. They therefore use a payback method or some alternative that does not involve discounting.

Those who do use one of the discounting methods argue that the extra work involved is small, and that the results, although admittedly rough, are nevertheless better than not even attempting to allow for the time element.

SUMMARY

The capital investment problem is essentially that of determining whether the anticipated earnings from a proposed project are sufficiently attractive to warrant risking the investment of funds in the project. The investment is typically made at one moment of time, whereas earnings flow in over a period of time in the future. The analysis technique must take this difference in timing into account.

For screening purposes, that is, for deciding whether a proposal is or is not attractive, two techniques are available. In the present value method, the *present value* of the earnings is found by discounting earnings at a required rate. If this present value equals or exceeds the amount of the investment, the proposal is acceptable. In the *time-adjusted return* technique, a discount rate is found that makes the present value of the earnings equal to the investment. If this rate equals or exceeds the required earnings rate, the proposal is acceptable.

Similar techniques may be used to establish preferences. The *profitability index* derived from the present value method is conceptually superior to the time-adjusted return method in signaling preferences, but both methods are widely used in practice.

These techniques can be used only to the extent that the facts of a proposal can be reduced to dollar amounts for investment and earnings. For many proposals, nonquantitative considerations are dominant, and the techniques are not applicable. In nearly every problem there are some nonquantitative considerations, and these must be used to temper the numerical result.

SUGGESTIONS FOR FURTHER READING[8]

GRANT, EUGENE L., and WILLIAM G. IRESON. *Principles of Engineering Economy*. 4th ed.; New York: Ronald Press Co., 1960.

SOLOMON, EZRA (ed.). *The Management of Corporate Capital*. Glencoe, Ill.: Free Press, 1959.

TERBORGH, GEORGE. *Business Investment Policy*. Washington, D.C.: Machinery and Allied Products Institute, 1958.

WESTON, J. FRED and DONALD H. WOODS. *Basic Financial Management: Selected Readings*. Belmont, Calif.: Wadsworth Publishing Co., 1967.

---

[8] See also "Suggestions for Further Reading" for Chapter 18.

CASES

CASE 19–1. REEQUIPMENT PROBLEMS

A. Equipment Replacement

The Parsons Company is considering the purchase of new equipment to perform operations currently being performed ·on different, less efficient equipment. The purchase price is $10,000, delivered and installed.

A Parsons production engineer estimates that the new equipment will produce savings of $2,000 in labor and other direct costs annually, as compared with the present equipment. He estimates the proposed equipment's economic life at 10 years, with zero salvage value. The present equipment is in good working order and will last, physically, for at least 20 more years.

The company can borrow money at 5 percent, although it would not plan to negotiate a loan specifically for the purchase of this equipment. The company requires a return of at least 20 percent before taxes on an investment of this type. Taxes are to be disregarded.

Questions

1. Assuming the present equipment has zero book value and zero salvage value, should the company buy the proposed equipment?
2. Assuming the present equipment is being depreciated at a straight-line rate of 10 percent, that it has a book value of $4,800 (cost, $8,000; accumulated depreciation, $3,200), and has zero net salvage value today, should the company buy the proposed equipment?
3. Assuming the present equipment has a book value of $4,800 and a salvage value today of $3,000, and that if retained for 10 more years its salvage value will be zero, should the company buy the proposed equipment?
4. Assume the new equipment will save only $1,000 a year, but that its economic life is expected to be 20 years. If other conditions are as described in (1) above, should the company buy the proposed equipment?

654

B. Replacement Following Earlier Replacement

The Parsons Company decided to purchase the equipment described in Part A (hereafter called "Model A" equipment). Two years later, even better equipment (called "Model B") comes on the market and makes the other equipment completely obsolete, with no resale value. The Model B equipment costs $20,000 delivered and installed, but it is expected to result in annual savings of $5,000 over the cost of operating the Model A equipment. The economic life of Model B is estimated to be 10 years. Taxes are to be disregarded.

Questions

1. What action should the company take?
2. If the company decides to purchase the Model B equipment, a mistake has been made somewhere, because good equipment, bought only two years previously, is being scrapped. How did this mistake come about?

C. Effect of Income Taxes

Assume that the Parsons Company expects to pay income taxes of 50 percent and that a loss on the sale or disposal of equipment is treated as an ordinary deduction, resulting in a tax saving of 50 percent. The Parsons Company expects to earn 10 percent on its investment after taxes. Depreciation for tax purposes is computed on the sum-of-years' digits basis.

Questions

1. Should the company buy the equipment if the facts are otherwise as described in Part A (1)?
2. If the facts are otherwise as described in Part A (2)?
3. If the facts are otherwise as described in Part B?

D. Change in Earnings Pattern

Assume that the savings are expected to be $2,500 in each of the first five years and $1,500 in each of the next five years, other conditions remaining as described in Part A (1).

Questions

1. What action should the company take?
2. Why is the result here different from that in Part A (1)?
3. What effect would the inclusion of income taxes, as in Part C, have on your recommendation?

CASE 19–2.   ECONOMY MANUFACTURING COMPANY

The Economy Manufacturing Company owned a truck that was six years old. The production vice president decided to replace the old truck with a new truck, since he felt that it was uneconomical to operate equipment older than six years. The truck was fully depreciated as of December 31, 1966. It could, though, be sold for $500. Its estimated operating expenses for the next five years (excluding depreciation and income taxes) were:

Year	Operating Expense
1967	$2,800
1968	2,800
1969	2,850
1970	2,850
1971	2,900

By December 31, 1971, the truck would have a scrap value of $50.

The operating expenses of the new truck, which would cost $4,000, were estimated to be (exclusive of depreciation and income taxes):

Year	Operating Expenses
1967	$1,800
1968	1,800
1969	1,900
1970	1,900
1971	2,000

The estimated resale value of the new truck was $500 at December 31, 1971.

The company also was considering leasing the new truck on either of two plans. Under both plans, the company would have to pay all license and registration fees and be responsible for all costs incurred in the operation and maintenance of the truck. Additionally, Economy would be required to assume all risk of loss or damage to the truck and provide adequate insurance coverage for losses from property damage, collision, personal injury, and fire and theft.

From Leasing Company A, Economy could lease the truck for $1,000 a year for five years with an option to buy the truck for $300 at the end of the fifth year. From Leasing Company B, Economy would incur monthly charges of 2 percent of the acquisition cost of the truck for the first 50 months of the lease period (called a depreciation reserve) plus monthly charges based on a percentage of the acquisition cost as follows:

(a) 1.0% for the first 12 months.
(b) 0.8% for the next succeeding 12 months.
(c) 0.6% for the next succeeding 12 months.

(*d*) 0.4% for the next succeeding 12 months.

(*e*) 0.25% for all succeeding months.

Leasing Company B believed that the desired truck could be acquired for a cost of $3,800 because it was similar to other trucks that Company B purchased in large volume. In either case, the leases would be noncancelable.

The company had a required earnings rate of 10 percent and an estimated income tax rate of 50 percent. If the truck were purchased, the company would be able to write off in the year of purchase 20 percent of the cost of the truck. It would take depreciation on the remainder of the truck cost on a declining-balance method, using a rate of twice the straight-line rate, based on an estimated useful life of six years from January 1, 1967. Assume that salvage value need not be considered in computing depreciation.

Questions

1. Should the company acquire the new truck?
2. If the new truck is acquired, should it be purchased, leased from Company A, or leased from Company B?

CASE 19–3. STANDEEN MANUFACTURING COMPANY

The Standeen Manufacturing Company, which produced oil burners, had followed a policy of purchasing the metal cabinets required in the assembly of its burners. Currently, however, the executives were considering whether the company should continue to purchase the metal cabinets or whether it should make them. The cost of the cabinets represented about 15 percent of the total cost of the completed oil burners.

The cabinets were purchased from a single supplier, who had always made delivery on time. Early in the spring the company contracted for a full year's requirement, ordinarily between 1,500 and 2,000 units. The Standeen Company did not pay for the cabinets until delivery, but it was financially committed for the number ordered.

The cabinet supplier made the cabinets during the off-peak season and held them until Standeen asked for them. Then the supplier crated the cabinets and sent them directly to the Standeen dealers for installation with the Standeen burner that was on the customer's premises. Standeen's peak production was in August, September, and October. As a result of this method of off-peak production and the large volume of business that the cabinet manufacturer obtained from Standeen and others, he had quoted a price lower than that of any competitors that Standeen's purchasing agent had discovered.

Nevertheless, in the opinion of the management of the Standeen Manufacturing Company, the purchase arrangement had certain unsatisfactory aspects. For one thing, the supplier did not provide full inspection at the time of crating; occasionally not all necessary parts were included, or the cabinets had defects such as scratches that had developed during storage in the supplier's warehouse. The supplier made good any defects, but in order to provide full inspection at the factory at the time of shipment, the supplier estimated that he would have to charge $1 more for each cabinet.

Another difficulty arose from the method of mass production used by the cabinet supplier. Each cabinet was composed of several pieces, including side panels and top. In order to obtain low costs, the manufacturer made large lots of each individual piece. These pieces were painted and baked in lots, and often there were some slight variation in the color of different lots. Thus, when the individual pieces were assembled into a cabinet, the side panels did not always match the top.

One Standeen executive believed the present purchasing arrangements slowed up the adoption of new cabinet models. The company first had to submit the specifications to the cabinet manufacturer and have a model made. This model then had to be inspected by the Standeen company's sales department, a process that necessitated either shipping the model cabinet to the company or sending a Standeen representative to the supplier's plant. Additional negotiations often were necessary after the model had been inspected.

In the event that the Standeen Manufacturing Company did decide to manufacture its own cabinets, the executives expected that certain disadvantages of the present arrangement would be overcome. They were of the opinion that a better inspection job would be possible at a total cost not much more than now was being paid to the supplier. They were not bothered by the fact that the general practice in the industry was to purchase finished cabinets. One executive argued that if Standeen withdrew its business, the supplier's costs would rise and so would the price at which Standeen's competitors bought cabinets.

If the company were to produce its own cabinets, it would have to take certain steps. It would be necessary to clear space in the factory, and to purchase some new equipment. Experienced men would have to be obtained and trained in the company's methods. Detailed production plans would have to be developed.

Investigation revealed that sufficient factory space could be made available for the needed equipment by means of plant rearrangement. This was true despite the fact that the company had recently started to produce equipment for the United States Army. There was adequate capital to meet the anticipated financial requirements. The corporation was currently estimating its income tax expenses as 25 percent of its net income before taxes. The manufacturing processes required for the cabinets were somewhat similar to those already familiar to the company's workers, and some of the needed equipment was already at hand. It was estimated that other needed skilled and semiskilled men could be hired and trained within 30 days.

The experience of the company was that if it purchased cabinets on the basis of annual contracts for 1,000 or more, it could obtain them at a price of $35 a unit. The company's accounting department made cost estimates for making cabinets on the basis of a volume of 1,000 units. Estimated costs for a unit were as follows:

Material...	$17.30
Direct labor.......................................	11.25
Overhead, at 100 percent of direct labor.............	11.25
Total Unit Cost..............................	$39.80

The Standeen Manufacturing Company followed the practice throughout its operations of charging overhead at a standard rate of 100 percent of direct labor; it was roughly estimated that half the overhead represented variable costs. Executives estimated that the company would have to spend $10,000 for new equipment and for the rearrangement of the plant in order to make cabinet production possible. This new equipment would be subject to depreciation at a rate of 15 percent a year.

Question

1. Should the Standeen Manufacturing Company manufacture its cabinets?

CASE 19–4. THURBER COMPANY

In November 1962 the executive committee of the Thurber Company was considering the addition of a new superwidget to its product line. It had before it an unfavorable report from the assistant treasurer which read as follows:

1. It is recommended that the Thurber Company *not* add the superwidget to its current product line. This is largely based on a consideration of the quantity we can sell annually versus that required to break even. According to our market research department, we can anticipate sales of about 45,000 units per year. My calculations show that the break-even sales volume is 50,000 units per year, as follows:

2. The marketing department has indicated that the best selling price

would be $10 per superwidget. The cost department has prepared the following estimate of costs:

```
Per unit:
    Materials...................................$3.00
    Direct labor: 1 hour @ $2 per hour.................  2.00
    Variable overhead @ 25% of direct labor...........  0.50
    General factory overhead @ 25% of direct labor.....  0.50
    Selling and administrative expense @ 20% of
        selling price.................................  2.00
    Total cost per unit............................$8.00
```

Apart from the overhead costs specified above, it is expected that the new superwidget department will incur fixed costs of $100,000 per year. This includes $50,000 per year for depreciation and the remainder for supervision, indirect labor, and light and power.

The sales volume at which the unit contribution of $2 ($10 selling price less $8 variable cost) will just cover the $100,000 fixed departmental expenses is 50,000 units per year.

3. The rates used for determining the unit charges for variable overhead, general factory overhead, and selling and administrative expense are standard for all of the company's product lines.

4. The estimated depreciation expense is based on $500,000 of new equipment and an economic life of 10 years. Straight-line depreciation will be used on this investment.

5. A total of $300,000 was spent last year on product development and market research for the superwidget. This has already been expensed for tax purposes, but we still have this on our books as an asset. It was planned to write this off over the first five years of superwidget sales. An additional $20,000 will be required to clean up the factory area in which the new superwidget department will go. This can probably be expensed for book and tax purposes. Since the $20,000 represents a one-shot expenditure, it has been excluded from the break-even analysis.

6. Our working capital needs will be about 25 percent of the expected annual sales volume, or $112,500 (25 percent of 45,000 units times $10 per unit). Since this will be recovered any time we want to drop superwidgets from our product line, this has not been included in the break-even analysis.

7. I doubt that the company will want to incur a loss on the superwidget even though the marketing people say it would be a desirable addition to the company product line and can be handled without any increase in the sales force.

8. Setting up the new department for the manufacture of superwidgets would also provide some administrative problems for the factory management. This would be the only factory department at Thurber whose personnel cannot be used in other departments or vice versa. In effect, the

"direct labor" would become a fixed cost for the company, raising the break-even point still higher than that calculated in this memorandum.

9. Certainly this project will not earn the 10 percent return after taxes that you have specified as desirable for investments in new product introduction.

Questions

1. Evaluate the assistant treasurer's report and suggest ways, if any, in which it might be improved.
2. What will the company's accounting net income after taxes be if the new superwidget is introduced?
3. What volume of new superwidgets would be required to make this a desirable investment?
4. On the basis of the information provided, what should the Thurber Company do? What additional information is required, if any?

NOTE: Use a 55 percent tax rate for your calculations.

CASE 19–5. WILSON COMPANY (A)

In March, 1960, the Wilson Company was considering a proposal to replace four hand-loaded transmission case milling machines with one automatic machine. The company operated a large machine shop that did machining work on a subcontract basis for local industries in the Detroit area. One of the contracts was to machine transmission cases for truck engines for the Maynard Automobile Company. The Wilson Company had negotiated such a contract with the Maynard Automobile Company for each of the previous 14 years. For the last few years, the contract had been for 60,000 transmission cases annually.

The unfinished cases were supplied by Maynard. With a hand-loaded machine, all the faces could not be machined at the same time. Each machine required the constant attention of one skilled machine operator.

The machines used by Wilson were only three years old. Each had an annual output of approximately 15,000 cases on a two-shift, five-day week basis; therefore, four machines had been purchased at a total cost of $147,500.

The useful life of a hand-loaded machine on a two-shift, five-day week basis was estimated to be 15 years. Its salvage value at the end of its useful life was estimated to be $1,000. Depreciation of $29,500 had been built up for the four machines, representing three years' accumulation. The purchase of the machines had been financed by a 5 percent bank loan, and $45,000 of this loan had not yet been repaid. It was estimated that the four machines could be sold in their present condition for a total of $60,000, net, after dismantling and removal costs. The book loss resulting from the sale would be a deductible expense for income tax purposes and would therefore result in a tax saving of 52 percent of the loss.

The machine being considered in 1960 was a fully automatic transfer-type milling machine, equipped with four machining stations. Automatic transfer equipment on this machine moved the part progressively from one station to the next and indexed at each station, finishing a complete case with each cycle of the machine. One skilled machine operator was required to observe the functioning of the machine and make any necessary adjustments.

An automatic transfer-type machine with an annual output of 60,000 transmission cases on a two-shift basis would be specially built by a machine tool manufacturer at an estimated cost of $170,000, delivered and installed. The useful life of this machine was estimated to be 15 years. No

Exhibit 1

WILSON COMPANY

Condensed Income Statement, 1959

Net sales...	$5,364,213
Less: All costs and expenses..................	4,138,647
Profit before taxes............................	$1,225,566
Provision for income taxes.....................	622,715
Net Income....................................	$ 602,851

Condensed Balance Sheet, December 31, 1959

Current assets............	$3,051,349	Current liabilities........	$ 930,327
Fixed assets (net)........	4,239,210	4% mortgage bonds.......	500,000
Other assets.............	151,491	Capital stock............	1,000,000
		Surplus.................	5,011,723
Total Assets..........	$7,442,050	Total Liabilities.......	$7,442,050

reliable estimate of scrap value could be made; a rough estimate was that it would approximate the removal costs.

The Wilson Company's engineering department was asked to prepare a study for the executives to use in deciding what action to take. Its findings were as follows: The direct labor rate for milling machine operators was $2.50 an hour, including provision for social security taxes and fringe benefits, which varied with the payroll. There would be a saving in floor space amounting to $400 annually on the basis of the charge made in 1960 for each square foot of floor space used. However, the factory layout was such that it would be difficult to use this freed space for some other purpose, and no other use was planned. Out-of-pocket savings of $5,000 a year for other cost items were estimated if the automatic machine was purchased.

The Wilson Company planned to finance any new equipment purchase with a bank loan at a rate of 5 percent.

Selected financial data for the company are shown in Exhibit 1. The company considered the picture given by these statistics to be normal and expected the same general pattern to prevail in the foreseeable future.

Question

1. What action, if any, would you recommend? Why?

CASE 19–6. BISBO A. G. (A)

Mr. Aschinger, managing director of Bisbo A.G., a large German manufacturer of biscuits, was concerned about sales of two types of cream-filled crackers, "Cocktail" and "Picknick." Although Bisbo's total sales volume had been growing steadily for the last several years, the sales volume of Cocktail and Picknick had remained static for some time. Moreover, recent cost calculations indicated that the company was losing money on both items. In 1956 total Bisbo sales amounted to DM 49,740,000,[9] of which sales of Cocktail and Picknick were approximately DM 320,000 each.

The sales manager, Mr. Stark, believed that the poor sales record on Cocktail and Picknick resulted from the fact that competing firms had recently introduced crackers similar in quality and taste but wrapped in cellophane rolls, 10 crackers to a roll. Cocktail and Picknick were at present sold loose. Mr. Stark was convinced that Bisbo A.G. could increase sales considerably if it offered Cocktail and Picknick packed in cellophane rolls. On the basis of a careful analysis of dealers' reports and market research information, he estimated that if the products were so wrapped, 1957 sales of the two items would increase to DM 1,045,000.

Mr. Stark had been with Bisbo A.G. for eight years and was thoroughly familiar with the German biscuit market. He made sales estimates for each product annually by months, based on dealers' reports and recommendations of his market analyst. In a typical recent monthly forecast, covering 87 items, actual sales of 72 items were within 20 percent of his estimate, sales of 11 were 20 to 70 percent below the forecast, and sales of 4 exceeded the forecast by from 20 to 100 percent. Mr. Stark considered that his market analyst, who had been with the company for three years, was very competent.

The technical department made a study of the wrapping proposed by Mr. Stark. A new packing machine costing DM 31,000 and having a physical life of 10 years would be required. Installation costs would add a further DM 1,200. At the volume of 376,000 kg. of crackers with the new

---

[9] In 1957 one deutsche mark (DM) equaled approximately U.S. $0.24. One kilogram (kg.) equals 2.2 pounds. One square meter (m²) equals 1.2 square yards.

cellophane wrapper predicted by Mr. Stark for 1957, operating costs were estimated to be DM 7,866 a year, as shown in Exhibit 1.

Exhibit 1

ESTIMATED OPERATING COSTS OF NEW MACHINE

For Annual Production of 376,000 kg.
(in DM)

```
Labor.........................................1,000
Material (48,200 m² of cellophane at 0.13 DM/m²).....6,266
Electricity, maintenance.......................... 600
        Total....................................7,866
```

At the same time, the cost department prepared an estimate of the 1957 product costs of Cocktail and Picknick. With the present method of packaging, annual sales for 1957 had been estimated at DM 325,000 (117,000 kg.) of each of the two items. The manufacturing direct cost of this quantity was estimated to be DM 299,617 for Cocktail and DM 320,158 for Picknick. Overhead, allocated at the plantwide rate of 14.38 percent of estimated sales, was DM 46,735 for each item. Thus total costs of the two items in 1957 were expected to exceed total revenue by DM 63,245, or 9.73 percent of sales (see Exhibit 2).

Exhibit 2

ABSORPTION OF FIXED OVERHEAD BY COCKTAIL AND PICKNICK
AT A PRODUCTION OF 117,000 KG. EACH
(in DM)

	*Manufacturing Cost**	*Total Cost*	*Estimate of Sales*	*Unabsorbed Fixed Overhead*		*Absorbed Fixed Overhead*	
Cocktail............	299,617	346,352	325,000	21,352	6.57%	25,383	7.81%
Picknick............	320,158	366,893	325,000	41,893	12.89	4,842	1.29
Total............	619,775	713,245	650,000	63,245	9.73%	30,225	4.65%

* Manufacturing direct cost included all costs of production, with the exception of fixed factory overhead and other overhead costs listed in Exhibit 3.

Exhibit 2 also indicates that Cocktail and Picknick together would absorb overhead only at a rate of 4.65 percent (14.38 − 9.73 percent) at a production rate of 117,000 kg. each.

Mr. Sager, head of the costing department, explained the method of allocating overhead. Prior to the beginning of the year, sales estimates for all products were collected. Fixed costs for the total forecast volume were then estimated. These two estimates were used to calculate the plantwide overhead rate, which was allocated to individual products on the basis of actual individual sales. For 1957, total fixed costs were estimated at DM 7,967,000, as shown in Exhibit 3, and total sales were estimated to be DM 55,400,000; thus the overhead rate was 7,967,000 ÷ 55,400,000, or 14.38 percent.

Mr. Aschinger, who did not usually see complete cost figures for individual products, was surprised to learn that Cocktail and Picknick

Exhibit 3

ESTIMATE OF TOTAL FIXED OVERHEAD, 1957

(in DM)

Fixed plant overhead.	2,554,000
Sales force.	1,245,000
Advertising.	410,000
Interest.	80,000
Depreciation.	976,000
General costs.	2,702,000
Total.	7,967,000

were not covering their full costs. He discussed with Mr. Stark the possibility of dropping these items entirely, but they agreed this was not feasible, because the products were essential to Bisbo's full product line. Nevertheless, Mr. Aschinger questioned whether it was prudent to buy a new machine, since this would result in additional costs that would have to be charged against an already unprofitable line.

However, since he knew that increased production volume meant an increase in the absorbed amount of overhead, Mr. Aschinger continued his investigation. His calculations were based on the estimates of Mr. Stark, which he agreed were the best that could be made, that sales of Cocktail and Picknick if offered in the new cellophane rolls would go up to a total of 376,000 kg., or DM 1,045,000. Mr. Aschinger reasoned that the expected increased sales of DM 395,000 would result in a considerable increase in the amount of overhead absorbed. Even if this was not at the rate of 14.38 percent, which was the rate needed to cover the fixed overhead, but only at the rate of 4.65 percent, which was the rate at which overhead currently was being absorbed, his calculations showed an increase in fixed overhead absorption of DM 18,370 (4.65 percent of DM 395,000).

The company wished an average return of at least 20 percent before taxes on investments in capital assets.

Question

1. What action should Mr. Aschinger take?

CASE 19–7.   BISBO A. G. (B)

Before proceeding with the project described in the (A) case, Mr. Aschinger thought that it would be desirable to test-market the cellophane-wrapped Cocktail and Picknick crackers to get additional data on prospective demand. In past instances of this sort, Mr. Aschinger had retained Kurtz and Company, a marketing research organization, to supervise the test. For a flat fee of DM 10,000, Kurtz would select a random sample of 50 stores from the 1200 retail outlets which sold the crackers, arrange for the delivery of the product during a three-month test period, perform necessary clerical functions, and provide a detailed report on the test results. The report would include, in addition to more detailed information, the average incremental DM sales of the crackers per sample store for the three-month period over prior sales levels.

The chief statistician of Kurtz and Company pointed out to Mr. Aschinger that the average incremental sales per sample store could be considered as an estimate of the mean quarterly incremental sales per store in the entire population of 1200 stores and this figure would be helpful in verifying the predicted sales gain from wrapping Cocktail and Picknick crackers in cellophane. Based on previous studies with similar products, the statistician advised Mr. Aschinger that the standard error of estimate of the sample mean (the standard deviation) for a sample of 50 store quarters would be about DM 3.

A characteristic of normal distributions is that 68 percent of the observations are within one standard deviation of the mean, 95.5 percent are within two standard deviations, and 99.7 percent are within three standard deviations. Thus, approximately 68 percent of the average incremental quarterly sales per store of the 1200-store population would lie between plus and minus DM 3 about the sample mean; approximately 95 percent would lie within plus and minus DM 6; and almost 100 percent would lie within plus and minus DM 9.

Question

1. Should Mr. Aschinger test-market the cellophane-wrapped crackers?

CASE 19–8.   BURTON CHEMICAL COMPANY

The Burton Chemical Company was a medium-sized producer of industrial chemicals. In November, 1958, the company was in the process of expanding its production. This expansion created the need for additional capacity for an intermediate product that was currently being manufactured in the company's plant. The required increment was 300,000 pounds a year, which the plant could produce only if it installed additional facilities. On the other hand, the increment could be purchased from the major supplier of the raw materials which went into the intermediate product. Mr. Burton, the president, asked the company's controller, Mr. Scott, to investigate these alternatives and to determine the return on investment that could be expected if additional facilities were installed.

Mr. Scott gathered the data shown in Exhibit 1. An increase in the

Exhibit 1

INITIAL CALCULATION OF RETURN ON INVESTMENT

Additional quantity of intermediate product required: 300,000 lb./year
Investment required to manufacture:

Equipment...	$100,000
Inventory (raw materials)...........................	50,000
Total......................................	$150,000

Manufacturing costs, per pound of intermediate product:

Raw materials (current prices)........................	$ 0.50
Labor..	0.04
Utilities and supplies................................	0.01
Depreciation......................................	0.05
Total......................................	$ 0.60

Analysis of savings, per pound of intermediate product:

Purchase price from supplier (estimated)................	$ 0.70
Less: Manufacturing costs..........................	0.60
Saving..	$ 0.10
Less: Tax at 50%.................................	0.05
Net Saving.....................................	$ 0.05

$$\text{Return on Investment:} \frac{\text{Net Saving per Pound}}{\text{Investment per Pound}} = \frac{\$0.05}{\$0.50} = 10\%.$$

plant's manufacturing capacity to produce the 300,000-pound annual increment would require an investment of $100,000 in equipment (to be depreciated at a rate of 15 percent) and $50,000 in raw materials inventory. On a unit basis, therefore, Mr. Scott figured the investment to be 50 cents a pound. Manufacturing costs, including depreciation, would be 60 cents a pound. If the product were purchased from the supplier, Mr. Scott estimated the price at 70 cents a pound. Thus by manufacturing the increment, the company would realize an aftertax saving of 5 cents a pound. The controller's final calculation—saving per pound over investment per pound—indicated an expected return on investment of 10 percent. He considered this return to be barely sufficient to justify the installation of facilities.

Before reporting to the president, Mr. Scott asked the purchasing department to solicit a bid price on the intermediate product from the supplier. To the controller's surprise, the price quoted was 55 cents a pound. Since this was below the company's own manufacturing costs, it now appeared more advantageous to purchase the 300,000-pound increment. However, Mr. Scott could not see why the raw material supplier should be able to produce and sell the intermediate product at such a low price. He ran a check on his manufacturing cost estimates and found them to be quite accurate. This led him to conclude that the price the company was currently paying for raw materials might be excessive. Further negotiations with the supplier confirmed this conclusion, and the com-

Exhibit 2

REVISED CALCULATION OF RETURN ON INVESTMENT

Current production of intermediate product: 900,000 lb./year
Raw material price saving on current level of annual production
    of intermediate product (900,000 × $0.07).............$63,000
    Less: Additional costs to produce 300,000-pound increment—
      labor, supplies and utilities, depreciation
      (300,000 × $0.10)............................ 30,000
Net saving...$33,000
    Less: Tax at 50%.................................. 16,500
Net Saving after Tax................................$16,500

Investment required to manufacture 300,000-pound increment: $150,000

$$\text{Return on Investment:} \frac{\text{Net Saving after Tax}}{\text{Investment}} = \frac{\$\ 16,500}{\$150,000} = 11\%.$$

pany was able to secure a price reduction on raw materials of 7 cents a pound of intermediate product.

Under these new circumstances, Mr. Scott prepared a revised calculation of the return on investment that could be expected if the company were to manufacture the 300,000-pound increment. His calculations, shown in Exhibit 2, indicated a return of 11 percent on the $150,000 investment required to increase plant capacity. His reasoning was as follows: Current annual production of the intermediate product was 900,000 pounds. The 7-cent price reduction in raw materials would generate annual savings of $63,000. From these savings he subtracted the additional costs to manufacture a 300,000-pound increment (i.e., labor, utilities and supplies, and depreciation) at 10 cents a pound, or $30,000. This produced net savings of $33,000, or $16,500 after tax. The ratio of net annual savings after tax to the initial investment showed a return of 11 percent.

Mr. Scott reported the results of his investigation to Mr. Burton and recommended that the company increase plant capacity to produce the 300,000-pound increment of intermediate product. He stated that the anticipated 11 percent return in investment would justify such a decision.

Questions

1. Comment on the strengths and weaknesses of the approach used by Mr. Scott.
2. Should the product in question be purchased or manufactured?

CASE 19–9. FEDERAL MAKE-OR-BUY POLICIES

This case consists of the substantive portions of U.S. Bureau of the Budget Circular A–76 dated August 30, 1967, subject "Policies for acquiring commercial or industrial products and services for government use," and applicable to all departments and agencies of the federal government.

2. POLICY. The guidelines in this Circular are in furtherance of the Government's general policy of relying on the private enterprise system to supply its needs.

* * * * *

No executive agency will initiate a "new start" or continue the operation of an existing "Government commercial or industrial activity" except as specifically required by law or as provided in this Circular.

3. DEFINITIONS. For purposes of this Circular:

a) *A "new start"* is a newly established Government commercial or industrial activity involving additional capital investment of $25,000 or more or additional annual costs of production of $50,000 or more. A reactivation, expansion, modernization or replacement of an activity involving additional capital investment of $50,000 or more or additional annual costs of production of $100,000 or more are, for purposes of this Circular, also regarded as "new starts." Consolidation of two or more activities without increasing the overall total amount of products or services provided is not a "new start."

(Sections 4 and 5, omitted here, set forth exceptions to the general application of the policy. They are not to be applied to management functions, managerial advisory services, products or services obtained from other government agencies, situations inconsistent with the terms of treaties, cases in which an agency's program would be disrupted or delayed, etc.)

6. COST COMPARISONS. A decision to rely upon a Government activity for reasons involving relative costs must be supported by a comparative cost analysis which will disclose as accurately as possible the difference between the cost which the Government is incurring or will incur under each alternative.

* * * * *

The determination as to whether to purchase or to lease equipment or to construct buildings or acquire their use under lease-construction arrangements involves a determination of the difference in costs under the alternatives, and the principles set forth in this Circular should be applied to the extent relevant in making such determinations.

a) *Costs of obtaining products or services from commercial sources* should include amounts paid directly to suppliers, transportation charges, and expenses of preparing bid invitations, evaluating bids, and negotiating, awarding, and managing contracts. Costs of materials furnished by the Government to contractors, appropriate charges for Government-owned equipment and facilities used by contractors and costs due to incentive or premium provisions in contracts also should be included. If discontinuance of a Government commercial or industrial activity will cause a facility being retained by the Government for mobilization or other reasons to be placed in a standby status, the costs of preparing and maintaining the facility as standby also should be included. Similarly, if such a discontinuance is expected to result in premature retirement of Government employees which will cause a significant increase in retirement costs to the Government, such increased cost should be added to the cost of procurement from commercial sources. Costs of obtaining products or services from commercial sources should be documented and organized for comparison with costs of obtaining the product or service from a Government activity.

b) For purposes of economy and simplicity in making cost comparison studies, generally agreed costs that would tend to be the same under either alternative need not be measured and included (for example, bid and award costs and operating costs under lease-purchase alternatives).

c) *Costs of obtaining products or services from Government activities* should include all costs which would be incurred if a product or service were provided by the Government and which would not be incurred if the product or service were obtained from a commercial source. The objectives should be to compute, as realistically as possible, the incremental or additional cost that would be incurred by the Government under the alternatives under consideration. In making such determinations it is important that recognition be given to the full amount of additional or incremental direct and indirect cost to be incurred in providing the products or services required. Under this general principle, the following costs should be included, considering the circumstances of each case:

(1) *Personal services and benefits.* Include costs of all elements of compensation and allowances for both military and civilian personnel, including the full cost to the Government of retirement systems, calculated on a normal cost basis, Social Security taxes where applicable, employees' insurance, health, and medical plans, (including services available from Government military or civilian medical facilities), living al-

lowances, uniforms, leave, termination and separation allowances, travel and moving expenses, and claims paid through the Bureau of Employees' Compensation.

(2) *Materials, supplies, and utilities services.* Include costs of supplies and materials used in providing a product or service and costs of transportation, storage, handling, custody, and protection of property, and costs of electric power, gas, water, and communications services.

(3) *Maintenance and repair.* Include costs of maintaining and repairing structures and equipment which are used in providing a product or service.

(4) *Damage or loss of property.* Include costs of uninsured losses due to fire or other hazard, costs of insurance premiums and costs of settling loss and damage claims.

(5) *Federal taxes.* Include income and other Federal tax revenues (except Social Security taxes) received from corporations or other business entities (but not from individual stockholders) if a product or service is obtained through commercial channels. Estimates of corporate incomes for these purposes should be based upon the earnings experience of the industry, if available, but if such data are not available, *The Quarterly Financial Report of Manufacturing Corporations*, published by the Federal Trade Commission and the Securities and Exchange Commission, may be consulted. Assistance of the appropriate Government regulatory agencies may be obtained in estimating taxes for regulated industries.

(6) *Depreciation.* Compute depreciation as a cost for any new or additional facilities or equipment which will be required if a Government activity is started or continued. Depreciation will not be allocated for facilities and equipment acquired by the Government before the cost comparison study is started. However, if reliance upon a commercial source will cause Government-owned equipment or facilities to become available for other Federal use or for disposal as surplus, the cost comparison analysis should include as a cost of the Government activity, an appropriate amount based upon the estimated current market value of such equipment or facilities. The Internal Revenue Service publication, *Depreciation Guidelines and Rules* may be used in computing depreciation. However, rates contained in this publication are maximums to be used only for reference purposes and only when more specific depreciation data are not available. Accelerated depreciation rates permitted in some instances by the Internal Revenue Service will not be used. In computing the depreciation cost of new or additional facilities or equipment to be acquired if a Government activity is started or continued and in determining comparative costs under lease-purchase alternatives, appropriate recognition should be given to estimated residual or salvage values of the facilities or equipment.

(7) *Interest.* Compute interest for any new or additional capital to be

invested based upon the average rate of yield for long-term Treasury bonds as shown in the current monthly Treasury Bulletin. The method of computation should provide for reduction in the capital investment to which interest is applied over the useful life of the asset on a straight-line basis.

(8) *Indirect costs.* Include any additional indirect costs incurred resulting from a Government activity for such activities as management and supervision, budgeting, accounting, personnel, legal and other applicable services.

7. ADMINISTERING THE POLICY. . . .

*   *   *   *   *

b) *"New starts."*. . .

*   *   *   *   *

(3) A "new start" should not be proposed for reasons involving comparative costs unless savings are sufficient to outweigh uncertainties and risks of unanticipated losses involved in Government activities.

The amount of savings required as justification for a "new start" will vary depending on individual circumstances. Substantial savings should be required as justification if a large new or additional capital investment is involved, or if there are possibilities of early obsolescence or uncertainties regarding maintenance and production costs, prices and future Government requirements. Justification may be based on smaller anticipated savings if little or no capital investment is involved, if chances for obsolescence are minimal, and if reliable information is available concerning production costs, commercial prices and Government requirements. While no precise standard is prescribed in view of these varying circumstances, a "new start" ordinarily should not be approved unless costs of a Government activity will be at least 10 percent less than costs of obtaining the product or service from commercial sources. It is emphasized that 10 percent is not intended to be a fixed figure. . . .

c) Existing Government activities. . . .

*   *   *   *   *

(3) An activity should be continued for reasons of comparative costs only if a comparative cost analysis indicates that savings resulting from continuation of the activity are at least sufficient to outweigh the disadvantages of Government commercial and industrial activities. No specific standard or guideline is prescribed for deciding whether savings are sufficient to justify continuation of an existing Government commercial activity, and each activity should be evaluated on the basis of the applicable circumstances.

*   *   *   *   *

9. EFFECTIVE DATE.   This Circular is effective on October 2, 1967.

PHILLIP S. HUGHES
Acting Director

Question

1. Will these policies lead executive agencies to make decisions that are in the national interest? If not, suggest changes that should be made.

CASE 19–10. PHILLIPS LAUNDRY

In January 1968, the Phillips Laundry installed a new shirt-pressing unit. The results obtained from operation of this unit were so satisfactory that early in 1969 Mr. Howard Phillips, president of the laundry, was considering the purchase of a second new shirt-pressing unit.

For the preceding several years Phillips' sales had amounted to roughly $260,000 each year. Mr. Phillips, owner of the laundry, thought that sales probably would not change much during 1969, but he hoped eventually to increase sales volume. The business was subject to slight seasonal fluctuations, which necessitated employment of part-time labor during parts of the year.

The laundry had always operated profitably, although in recent years the shirt-laundering section had done no better than break even. Inasmuch as shirts made up an important part of the laundry's business, Mr. Phillips was extremely anxious to make this operation profitable. He had considered the possibility of raising shirt-laundering prices to the customer but had rejected this alternative because of the intense competitive conditions that existed in the area.

In order to determine where costs might be reduced, Mr. Phillips in 1967 had made a careful analysis of the operations performed on shirts. He concluded that high costs in the pressing department were his principal problem. At that time the shirt-pressing department included three separate but similar pressing units, called here Units A, B, and C. Each unit consisted of four presses. In each of Units A and B, a cuff and collar press and a front press were operated by one girl, a back press and a sleeve press were operated by a second girl, and two other girls did touch-up ironing and the folding of the finished shirts. Each of these two pressing units had a capacity of 90 shirts an hour. Unit C had four basically similar presses, but it was operated only when there were more shirts to be pressed than the other two units could handle. Two girls employed on a part-time basis operated Unit C and turned out 40 shirts an hour.

Both the full-time and part-time employees were paid $1.70 an hour; social security taxes and fringe benefits increased this expense to almost exactly $2 an hour. The company did not have a piecework incentive plan, but the girls were free to leave the plant when they finished a day's work. Full-time girls were guaranteed and paid for a 40-hour week. In practice, however, they averaged only 27.5 hours of actual work in a week; they had one hour off for lunch and two 15-minute rest periods daily. The remaining five hours a week was accounted for by their practice of leaving early. Part-time help was employed to operate the third unit rather than work the full-time girls over 27.5 hours.

In order to reduce shirt-pressing costs, Mr. Phillips made a major change in the shirt-pressing department in January 1968. At that time, he replaced Unit A with a new pressing unit, the Beager Model 70.

Each of the old units had cost $2,400 when purchased, and installation charges for all three units had amounted to $400. They were 18 years old, however, and had been fully depreciated on the laundry's books. With periodic replacement of parts and routine maintenance, they probably could have been kept in operating condition indefinitely, but Mr. Phillips thought that the new type of press had made them obsolete. The old presses had no resale value.

The new Beager pressing unit consisted of only three presses. It occupied only about half the space of one of the old four-press units. Building depreciation, light, and other space costs allocated to each press unit were approximately $2,000 a year. Thus, this saving in space was worth $1,000 a year.

On the Beager pressing unit, one girl operated both a collar and cuff press and also another machine that pressed the bosom and body of the shirt in one operation. This girl was able to operate these two presses simultaneously because of automatic timers that made it unnecessary to watch one press while inserting or removing a shirt from another press. A second girl operated the sleeve press and did all the folding for the unit. The touch-up, hand-ironing operation was completely eliminated. Even without this touch-up operation, there was a marked improvement in the appearance of shirts turned out by the new Beager unit as compared with those turned out on the old units. The capacity of the Beager unit operated by two girls was 70 shirts an hour.

Under the revised setup, then, the shirt-pressing department consisted of (*a*) the new Beager unit, which was operated by two girls on a full-time basis and which had a capacity of 70 shirts an hour; (*b*) one old unit, which was operated by four girls on a full-time basis and had a capacity of 90 shirts an hour; and (*c*) a second old unit, which was operated only when needed by two girls on a part-time basis, with a capacity, when operated in this manner, of 40 shirts an hour. Mr. Phillips continued his policy of using Unit C on a part-time basis rather than have his employees work over 27.5 hours a week. Exhibit 1 shows the number of hours the presses of each unit were in operation in 1968, the number of shirts each unit pressed, and the number of hours for which the operators of each unit were paid.

The cost of the three new presses of the Beager unit was $16,325 f.o.b. the factory. Freight to the Phillips Laundry was $455, and installation charges were $200. There was no disruption of work while the presses were being installed over a weekend, but there was some slowdown while the girls became accustomed to the new methods and procedures used. The slowdown resulted in an increase in labor cost for the period of about $200. Power costs were increased by the cost of electricity for a five-horsepower motor that powered the bosom and body press. The motor used one kilowatt of electricity an hour at a cost of 9 cents a kilowatt-hour. Also, it was estimated that costs of operating the boiler and air compressor used to produce steam would increase about $10 a month.

Exhibit 1

SELECTED DATA FROM THE PRESSING DEPARTMENT FOR 1968

Type of Unit	*Capacity in Shirts/ Hour*	*No. of Hours in Operation in 1968*	*No. of Shirts Pressed in 1968*	*No. of Hours for which Each Operator Was Paid*
A. 2-girl unit (full-time basis) 70		1,375*	96,250	2,080
B. 4-girl unit (full-time basis) 90		1,375*	123,750	2,080
C. 2-girl unit (part-time basis) 40		900	36,000	1,350†

* There were 250 working days in 1968. The presses were actually in operation about 5.5 hours a day.
† Part-time employees were paid for their lunch hours and rest periods.

During 1968 the Beager unit performed much as expected. Mr. Phillips was pleased with the results and therefore was led to consider a second change in February 1969. At about that time, the manufacturer of Beager machines brought out a new model, Model 85, which was equipped with an automatic folding table. The capacity of this unit, which also was operated by two girls, promised to be 85 shirts an hour. In the new setup, as Mr. Phillips conceived it, a Model 85 unit would replace Unit B, the pressing unit then being operated by four girls. The two Beager units would then be operated on a full-time basis, 1,375 hours each a year, and the remaining old unit, Unit C, would be operated only when necessary by two girls on a part-time basis. This arrangement would give Mr. Phillips one Beager unit with a potential capacity of 85 shirts an hour, one Beager unit with a capacity of 70 shirts an hour, and one old unit with a capacity of 40 shirts an hour when operated by two girls, or 80 shirts an hour when operated by four girls.

The Beager Model 85 would cost $18,585 f.o.b. the factory; freight would be $525; and the installation cost would be $240. The bosom and body press of the second Beager unit would have its own five-horsepower motor. Costs of operating the boiler and air compressor would be increased about $10 a month by use of the Beager Model 85 in place of the old equipment in Unit B.

A year-end balance sheet and an income statement for 1968 are shown in Exhibits 2 and 3.

Exhibit 2

PHILLIPS LAUNDRY

Balance Sheet, December 31, 1968
(figures rounded to hundreds of dollars)

ASSETS

Current Assets:

Cash..	$ 8,200
Accounts receivable............................	11,000
Prepaid expenses................................	5,400
Total current assets............................	$ 24,600

Fixed Assets:

Machinery and equipment (net)...................	120,800
Building (net)...................................	91,600
Total Assets...............................	$237,000

LIABILITIES AND NET WORTH

Current Liabilities:

Accounts payable...............................	$ 6,400
Accrued expenses...............................	2,200
Total current liabilities......................	$ 8,600

Long-Term Liabilities:

Mortgage loan.................................	62,800
Total Liabilities............................	$ 71,400

Net Worth:

Capital stock..................................	80,000
Surplus..	85,600
Total Liabilities and Net Worth...........	$237,000

Exhibit 3

PHILLIPS LAUNDRY

Income Statement, Year Ending December 31, 1968
(figures rounded to hundreds of dollars)

Net sales..............................			$262,000
Laundry operating costs:			
Productive labor....................	$93,000		
Productive supplies..................	24,800		
Power............................	8,400		
Pland overhead.....................	34,200		
Total operating costs..............		$160,400	
Collection and delivery.................		36,400	
Sales promotion........................		9,000	
Executive salaries.....................		14,200	
Office and administrative...............		16,800	
Total costs.....................			236,800
Net profit before taxes.................			$ 25,200
Federal income tax (30%).............			7,600
Net Profit after Taxes.................			$ 17,600

Question

1. Should the Phillips Laundry buy an Beager Model 85 for use in Unit B?

CHAPTER 20

AUTOMATED DATA PROCESSING

Automated data processing is, as the name suggests, the processing of data without human intervention. It was made possible by the development of electronic computers. Although the first computer for business purposes began operation as recently as 1951, growth has been extremely rapid, and computers now have a significant impact on management accounting. The purpose of this chapter is to describe what automated data processing is, what its impact is currently, and what its impact is likely to be in the future.

For this purpose a detailed understanding of what goes on inside the computer is not required, any more than one needs a detailed knowledge of what goes on under the hood in order to understand how to use an automobile.

DESCRIPTION OF ELECTRONIC COMPUTERS[1]

A general purpose, digital computer (hereafter, simply "computer") performs these operations:

1. It stores data.
2. It performs arithmetic operations on data.
3. It compares two pieces of data and determines whether or not they are equal.
4. It rearranges stored data.
5. It prepares reports or otherwise displays all or any desired part of the data stored within it.

---

[1] This description is limited to general purpose, digital computers, thereby omitting (a) special purpose and (b) analog computers. Neither special purpose nor analog computers are now, nor are they likely to be, of major consequence in the field of management accounting. *Special purpose* computers are designed to perform a single task, such as calculating the course of an aircraft or missile. *Analog* computers work with approximations rather than with cardinal numbers; a slide rule is a manually operated analog computer.

The components of a computer are shown schematically in Illustration 20–1. They are: input, storage, processing, and output. Each is described below.

Illustration 20–1

SCHEMATIC OF AN ELECTRONIC COMPUTER

Input

COMPUTER CODES. In the computer each numerical digit, alphabetical letter, or other symbol (e.g. $, %, #, *) is represented by a combination of electrical impulses. Each such combination is called a *character*. Illustration 20–2 shows part of this code for one computer system (not all

Illustration 20–2

COMPUTER CODES

Code	Represents
0●0●0000●	1
0●0●000●0	2
0●0●00●●	3
0●0●●000	9
●0●0000●	A
●0●000●0	B
●0●000●●	C

SOURCE: American Standard Code for Information Exchange, as used in the IBM 360 computers.

computers use exactly the same code). On the printed page, the code is represented by a combination of black and white dots. Inside the computer, it is represented by a combination of electrical states, such as the presence or absence of an electrical charge (e.g., "on" or "off"). These electrical states can be manipulated almost with the speed of electricity (which is the speed of light), and this is the basic reason that the computer operates so rapidly. A computer works on one character at a time, so the usual way of describing the capacity of a computer is in terms of the number of characters it can store, and the usual way of describing its speed is in terms of the number of characters it can process in a second or other unit of time.[2]

INPUT DEVICES. In the input operation, data are fed into the computer and translated electrically into the code that the computer will use in all subsequent operations. Instructions which tell the computer what to do with these data, called the *program,* are also fed in. In the earliest computers, this step involved preparing a punched card for each item of data, and these cards were then fed into the computer. This is still the most common input method, but the preparation of punched cards is relatively expensive; in the typical business data processing situation, it is many times more expensive than all the succeeding operations combined. Punched-card input is also relatively slow, the maximum speed being approximately 1300 characters per second.[3] The usual practice therefore is to convert the original data to computer code in a preliminary operation, often with an inexpensive computer, and to hold it temporarily on magnetic tape. The magnetic tape is used subsequently as input to the main computer. A 2,400-foot reel of magnetic tape can hold 40 million characters, and these can be inputted to the computer at a maximum rate of 300,000 characters per second.

MACHINE-READABLE INPUT. Not only is the preparation of punched cards expensive and slow, but it also is an operation that is susceptible to errors, since the cards are prepared by human beings. Much work has therefore been done to develop input mechanisms that eliminate most of this manual process. The first such machine-readable input to come into widespread use is magnetic ink character recognition (MICR), which is now used on most bank checks and deposit slips. On such documents, a number identifying the depositor and his bank appears in a form that can be read by humans, viz:

⑈0511⑈0003⑈ 07⑈0511149⑈

The printing ink contains a metallic substance which permits these characters to be read automatically by the computer. The computer does this by comparing the characteristics of each MICR character with a file

---

[2] Another unit of measurement is called the *byte.* In some computers, one byte equals one character. In other computers, two numerical characters are included in a single byte.

[3] All computer characteristics given in this chapter are rough approximations. There is considerable variation between computers, and speed also varies with the nature of the work being done.

of characteristics contained in its memory. When it obtains a match, it creates the corresponding computer code for the character.

Some success has also been achieved with optical devices that will permit the computer to read characters that are printed with ordinary ink. Currently, most of these devices work only with characters that conform to a fairly rigid format and are positioned in a prescribed area of the document, but a few computer input devices are able to read ordinary typewritten material, and these devices will soon be widely used.

DIRECT INPUT. Another solution to the input problem is to have input information created automatically by a machine that is located at the point where the transaction originates; this information is then transmitted by wire directly to the computer. For example, in a job shop, there may be input devices in each department or section. When an employee begins a job, he inserts in the device one card containing his own employee number and another card containing the number of the operation he is about to perform. He does the same thing when the job is completed. The input device notes the beginning and ending time from a clock and sends all this information by wire to the computer.

Storage

The processing unit of the computer works on only one or a few characters at one time. It is therefore necessary that a means of storing data be provided. Since the data are represented by combinations of electrical states, the storage medium can be anything in which there are two states and which can be changed from one state to the other electrically. The earliest computers used vacuum tubes, which are either on or off, or switches, which are either open or closed. In more recent developments, the two-state characteristic is obtained by coatings which can be either magnetized or not magnetized, or by cores or metallic film, in which the two states are represented by the clockwise or counterclockwise direction of a magnetic field.

The storage medium consists of cells, each containing the code for one or a few characters, much like letter boxes in a post office contain the mail of one box holder. There must be a means of identifying the cell in which a given character is stored. This is called the *address*. Since the stored data are in the form of electrical impulses, they are invisible. When a new piece of data is entered into a storage cell, any data previously in the cell are automatically erased. Thus, unlike an accounting ledger page, which is also a means of storing information, computer storage can be reused indefinitely.

There are two general categories of storage, internal and external, and several types within each category. They essentially represent different trade-offs between cost and access time. *Access time* is the time required to locate a character in storage and transfer it to the place where it will be used.

INTERNAL STORAGE. Internal storage or *memory* is used in the computing process, to be described next. Since hundreds of thousands of computations are made each second, and since, for each computation, data must be moved out of memory, worked on, and then returned to memory, it is essential that access time of internal storage be very short in order not to slow down the computations any more than is absolutely necessary.

Storage devices with fast access time are much more expensive per character stored than storage devices with slow access time. Because of the high cost, internal storage is relatively small, with a capacity on the order of 50,000 to one million characters, which is about the amount of input data that can be received in a second or so.

EXTERNAL STORAGE. Until shortly before they are needed in a computation, data are stored in external storage devices. Various combinations of these devices may be used in a given computer. At one extreme, there are fast-access but expensive devices similar to those used for internal storage. In the middle are the magnetic tapes already described. In a moderately large computer at least four *tape drives*, each of which handles one reel of tape, will be connected to the computer, and in large computers the number can be ten tape drives or more. Large quantities of information can also be stored on magnetic disks, which resemble phonograph records in appearance. Typical disk devices have a storage capacity of from 3 million to 100 million characters.

When magnetic tape is used, the tape must be used sequentially, which makes the process of searching for a desired piece of information very slow—as long as several minutes, if its general location on the tape is not known. In magnetic disks, the search process can be random, and much faster—from $\frac{1}{20}$ to $\frac{1}{2}$ second (i.e., 50 to 500 milliseconds) to locate one character. At the other extreme are mass storage devices which hold tremendous quantities of information, but which have a relatively long access time. An IBM "Data Cell," for example, weighs about five pounds; it contains 200 strips of magnetic tape, on which 400 million characters can be stored. About 200 of these data cells can be used in a medium-sized computer system.

Processing

The processing section consists of (1) an *arithmetic unit*, which performs the computations, and (2) a *control unit*, which contains the program and which directs the movement of characters out of and back to storage and the manipulation of these characters in the arithmetic unit. The arithmetic unit does only two things: (1) it computes, that is, performs the arithmetic operations of addition, subtraction, multiplication and division; and (2) it compares two characters and determines whether or not they are equal; in some computers, if the characters are unequal, the computer determines which one is larger. If a computer only computed, it would be nothing more than a very fast, accurate calculating machine (up to three million additions per second.) It is the second operation, that of comparison, that gives the computer its extraordinary power. In order to understand why this is so, a description of the programming process is necessary.

PROGRAMMING. A program is a set of instructions specifying each operation that the computer is to perform. If the computer is to add two numbers, *a* and *b*, stored in addresses *x* and *y*, the control unit must give the following instructions:

1. Transfer the contents of address *x* from storage to the arithmetic unit.
2. Transfer the contents of address *y* from storage to the arithmetic unit.
3. Add.
4. Transfer the sum to address *z*.

Most data processing procedures consist not of a single operation, such as adding two numbers together, but rather of a series of operations performed one after the other, and the rules for performing each of these operations may vary with the circumstances. For example, in computing an employee's pay, a certain percentage must be deducted for social security taxes if, *but only if*, the total of such deductions for the year to date has not exceeded a certain amount (in 1969, $374.40). Thus, for a given employee, the social security deduction may or may not be made, depending on the circumstances. The instructions to the computer will provide for these circumstances by something like the following (which is condensed by eliminating the details of moving data to and from storage):

1. Are this employee's social security deductions to date less than $374.40?
2a. If no, do not make a social security deduction; go to the next operation.
2b. If yes, multiply his gross pay by 0.048, record this as his social security deduction for this week, and add it to his accumulated social security deduction for the year.
3. Does the total deduction now exceed $374.40?
4a. If yes, subtract the difference and to go the next operation.
4b. If no, go to the next operation.

The first and third of these instructions illustrates the comparison feature. It is this feature that permits the computer to handle any conceivable set of circumstances, *providing* these circumstances have been foreseen and instructions for handling them have been incorporated in the program. This is a large proviso, for one of the great difficulties that the programmer must contend with is to visualize in advance every contingency that might arise in the procedure that he is programming.

As an indication of the possibilities opened up by this comparison feature, a greatly simplified portion of an order processing program is given in Illustration 20–3. The illustration is in the form of a *block*

Illustration 20–3

BLOCK DIAGRAM OF ORDER
PROCESSING PROCEDURE

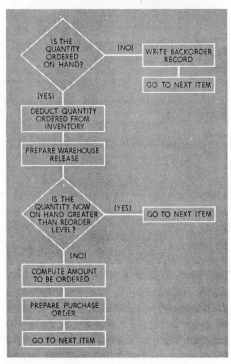

diagram and shows, not the detailed instructions, but rather the main steps in the procedure, for each of which there will be a detailed set of instructions. Note that at various points the program *branches* into either of two directions, depending on the conditions found to exist at that point.

The comparison or logic feature also enables the computer to sort records into numerical, alphabetical, or any desired order; to merge two or more sets of records together; to update a set of records, and indeed to manipulate the data in any conceivable way that can be reduced to a written instruction. "Data" as used here means letters as well as numbers. Some computer programs operate on straight textual material; for example, the U.S. Code and all the laws of many states are now available on magnetic tape so that references to specific topics can be located quickly.

COMPUTER LANGUAGES.   In the earliest computers, the programmer had to write down each step that the computer was to take, in as much detail as that given for the addition operation above. This is no longer necessary in most cases. Instead, the programmer uses a computer language, such as BASIC, COBOL, or FORTRAN. He writes his instructions in the vocabulary and grammar of that language, which closely resembles ordinary English and the symbols of algebra. The simplest of these languages, BASIC, can be learned by high school students in a few hours. The program written in this language is inputted to the computer, and the computer, using a special compiler program, translates this program into the detailed instructions that it requires.

> EXAMPLE: In Chapter 19, the formula for finding the present value of a future payment of $1 was given as $P = 1 \div (1 + r)^n$. With CAL, which is a widely used computer language, the user would simply input the following instruction:
>
> TYPE 1/ $(1 + R)$ ↑ N FOR R = .1 FOR N = 1 TO 50.
>
> The computer would then compute the 10 percent column of the present value Table A (p. 777), the whole operation requiring less than a minute. (Actually, only a fraction of a second of this is computation time; most of the time is required to get data into and out of the computer.)

The users of a computer language also have access to standardized instructions for many procedures, such as "sort in alphabetical order," "raise to the nth power," and also whole routines, such as those for linear programming, payroll, and order processing. Some of these routines they can use "as is"; others require modification to fit the needs of a particular company. All these developments simplify and speed up the task of preparing programs for computers.

Output

The results of the computations are stored initially in computer code. If the results are to be printed on a form or a report, they are often first transferred to magnetic tape, and this tape actuates a separate machine that does the printing. Since printing is slow relative to computation speed, this procedure avoids tying up the computer's processing unit during the printing operation. The program instructs the computer how to "format" these reports, that is, the program will cause the computer to arrange the data in rows and columns in any desired format. Some computers will print the results in the form of dots at prescribed locations on the page, thus producing graphs automatically. The output can also be displayed on a cathode-ray tube (a television screen is a cathode-ray tube). The computer can even be connected to a tape file containing a spoken sound for each number and for certain common words, and this permits its output to be communicated audibly over an ordinary telephone.

Processing Modes

Computers operate basically in one of two modes, on-line or off-line.

In the *on-line* mode, the computer is kept loaded with a program and related data file. The user is connected directly to the computer with an input-output device. He inputs his specific problem or question, and the computer solves this problem or answers the question and communicates the output to the user in a few seconds. The first extensive application of on-line processing was for airline seat reservations. The computer storage contains the number of seats still available on each flight for the next month or so. A ticket agent at any ticket counter in the country who wishes to inquire whether space is available on a certain flight simply pushes a few buttons or writes his query on an electric typewriter. This query is transmitted to the computer over ordinary telephone wire, and the computer, in a second or so, responds with information on whether the space is available on the desired flight or on alternative flights. If the ticket agent then sells the space, he makes another input, and the computer automatically adjusts its record of seats available. Similarly, many banks are doing deposit accounting on an on-line basis; that is, each teller has an input-output device that he uses both to find the balance in a customer's account and to record deposits and withdrawals at the instant they are made.

In the *off-line* mode, users are not connected directly to the computer. They submit their problems to the computer center, which processes these, together with routine, recurring programs, on a predetermined schedule. This method of operation is called *batch processing*. Instructions and data in internal storage are removed from the computer after each job has been completed, and the computer therefore starts fresh with each new job. Thus, the payroll computation might be run weekly; order processing work, once a day; financial statements, monthly; and so on. The off-line mode is much less expensive than the on-line mode, so it is used for those data processing jobs where an immediate response is unnecessary. For example, individuals are paid once a week or once a month, so payroll programs are run off-line.

TIME SHARING. Large computers are constructed so that the processing unit can work on several problems practically simultaneously. Many users can enter their problems into the computer, where they are held in storage until time on the processing unit becomes available. This usually happens within a few seconds, because the processing unit makes several hundred thousand computations a second. The computer then processes the problem and transmits the output back to the user. The airline reservation and bank deposit applications mentioned above are examples of one type of time sharing, using the on-line mode.

With time sharing, a user with an input-output console in his office can, at relatively small cost, have access to the largest computer at the same time that any of a hundred or more other users are connected to it.

SUMMARY OF CAPABILITIES. It is difficult for anyone to comprehend the power of the computer compared with alternative ways of processing data. One example must suffice: In February 1968, enemy rockets demolished a warehouse at Da Nang Air Base in South Vietnam and destroyed its contents, which consisted of 16,000 items of spare parts for F–4 aircraft. The attack occurred at midnight. By 8 o'clock the next morning, the computer had located the records of each of the 16,000 items stored in that warehouse (out of the several hundred thousand items stored on the whole base), had corrected these records, had computed the quantity to be reordered in accordance with its economic order quantity rules, and had prepared 10,000 requisitions for these amounts.

COMPUTER ECONOMICS

Some conclusions about the type of work for which the computer is suitable can be deduced from the above description and from the following facts:

1. Computers can compute faster and more accurately than human beings.

2. The computer itself, the "hardware," is expensive. A large computer with its associated input, output, and external storage equipment costs several million dollars. A medium-sized computer costs several hundred thousand dollars.

3. The preparation of programs, or "software," for business data processing is also expensive. Companies typically spend at least half as much on software as they spend on the hardware.

4. If input data must be prepared manually, this is a relatively expensive operation; as automatic inputs become increasingly available, input costs will decrease.

5. The incremental cost of processing data once it is in machine-readable form is trivial.

6. Rapid-access storage is much more expensive than slower storage.

7. The cost per calculation is much less for large computers than for small computers, assuming each is used at capacity.

8. Developments in technology are reducing both storage costs and processing costs rapidly. The cost per calculation for computers intro-

duced in the early 1960's was roughly one tenth that of those in use in 1955, and the cost in the late 1960's is roughly one tenth of that in the early 1960's. Developments anticipated in the relatively near future will reduce storage costs still further.

9. Development of better program languages and the increased availability of standard programs or sections of programs will reduce software costs.

Conclusions

These facts would seem to lead to the following conclusions:

1. Because of the high investment cost, both in hardware and in software, and the low operating cost, it is desirable to operate computers, especially large computers, close to capacity. Most large computers operate around the clock, except for necessary maintenance work and a safety margin for unexpected jobs and breakdowns.

2. Time sharing permits users with relatively small requirements to obtain the benefits of large computers. It should grow rapidly.

3. Most business data processing involves rather simple arithmetical calculations. Because of the relatively high programming cost, the computer is most advantageous when used in repetitive, high-volume work. (In scientific problems, by contrast, the calculations are typically long, so the computer pays for itself in reducing calculating costs, even for nonrepetitive problems.) However, as new technological developments lead to still lower processing and storage costs, and as programming becomes even simpler, there will be a corresponding increase in the number of tasks that can be performed less expensively by the computer than by humans.

4. As machine-readable input supersedes punched-card input in more and more applications, the number of economical uses of computers will increase. The high payoff from such developments is a strong incentive for manufacturers to bring them to fruition quickly.

5. Since the processing of data is very inexpensive once it has been converted to computer code, businesses will seek additional ways to use the same raw data.

6. A program is expensive to prepare, and it is also expensive to revise. There may therefore be a tendency for an undesirable rigidity in programs, a reluctance to change them as conditions change.

SOME IMPLICATIONS FOR MANAGEMENT ACCOUNTING

In 1961, ten years after the first business computer was delivered, total industry revenue from the sale or lease of general-purpose digital computers was approximately $600 million. In 1967, six years later, revenue was more than $3 billion.[4]

This $3 billion is equal to 5 percent of the total purchases of new plant and equipment in that year. The number of business computers in use rose from 1 in 1951, to 1,000 in 1956, to 31,000 in 1966. This growth will undoubtedly continue. Clearly, computers have already had a significant effect on business data processing, and they are likely to have an increasing effect in the future. Some of these implications are discussed below, arranged roughly in the order in which topics were presented in the preceding chapters.

First, as an overall observation, it seems clear that almost all companies will make some use of computers. The individual physician's office, with perhaps a nurse and a secretary, is a small business entity, but an increasing number of physicians have their billing and accounts receivable done at computer service centers.

Although most companies will use computers, it is by no means clear that most companies will have their own computers. Because of the great advantage that large computers have over small computers in terms of cost per calculation, it is quite possible that all but the large companies will use time on computers owned by someone else. A few such "computer utilities" are already in existence.

Financial Accounting

One of the criteria used in arriving at accounting principles is feasibility, and with the widespread use of computers it can no longer be argued that a proposed principle should not be adopted because the computations that it requires are too complicated to be feasible. This consideration is dominant in only a few situations, however. The possibility of calculating depreciation on individual items of fixed assets, rather than on a group or composite basis, is one example, but there are not many others. With this exception, it seems unlikely that the widespread use of computers will have much effect on accounting *principles*.

Financial accounting *procedures*, by contrast, are changing rapidly. The journal and the ledger, in the form described in Chapter 4, are disappearing, although the basic concepts are unchanged: the journal concept is now computer input, the ledger concept is computer storage. The work sheets and other devices described in Chapter 4 as mechanical aids to bookkeeping are replaced by computer programs. Indeed, of all the topics discussed in Part 1, the only significant changes are likely to be those relating to the material of Chapter 4 on bookkeeping.

One interesting development is the tendency to record more data than

---

[4] These estimates appear in the suit filed by the U.S. Justice Department against International Business Machines Corporation, January 17, 1969. Other experts put 1967 revenue as high as $6 billion.

was feasible under manual methods. Thus, in a manual accounts receivable record, it is customary to record the name and address of the customer company, its credit rating, and the dollar amount of each sale and cash receipt. It is now feasible to record a variety of additional information about the customer company, including information about its product line, its sales potential, and the details of individual sales transactions. Such information is useful in market analysis, statistics on sales of individual items, and so on.

Financial Analyses

As mentioned in Chapter 11, the computer is already a powerful tool in the analysis of financial statements. Voluminous financial data are available in machine-readable form; they can be purchased for a fee and used for comparative analyses. Furthermore, all sorts of ratios can now be computed as a matter of routine, at trivial cost. These computations provide better information on which to base judgments about financial performance, but they do not lessen the need for sound judgment.

Cost Accounting

If there are advantages in more sophisticated allocations of cost to cost centers and to products, such allocations can now be made automatically and at low cost. Shortcuts in the calculation of direct material and direct labor costs that may have been used on the ground that more exact methods were too costly, are no longer necessary.

Management Control

The mechanics of programming, budgeting, and measurement of performance are facilitated by the use of computers. Computers help to insure that the calculations are accurate. More importantly, they shorten the time required to compile and disseminate information and thus speed up corrective action if it is required. Computers also make it feasible to take into account many more variables in analyzing the difference between planned and actual performance, and to use more sophisticated analytical techniques in this process. The management control process is, however, fundamentally a behavioral process, and the computer does not eliminate the manager nor alter the basic fact that managers obtain results by working with other human beings.

Alternative Choice Problems

The fact that computers can be programmed to perform a long sequence of operations rapidly, inexpensively, and without human intervention, means that it is now feasible to use quantitative techniques for many types of problems for which their use has not hitherto been practical; and the fact that the computer can be programmed to make choices means that machines can now make certain types of decisions formerly made by humans. For example, the computer can be programmed to decide when a purchase order should be placed to replenish a routine item carried in inventory, the quantity that should be ordered, and the date when the new stock should arrive; and it can even write the purchase order without human intervention, although humans are necessary to supervise the operation and to make certain that the transaction is actually "routine." The computer can do this job better than people can do it; "better" in the sense that if its program truly expresses what management intends to be done, the computer will carry out these intentions more accurately and more consistently than the humans normally employed for these routine operations.

Companies have developed computer programs that handle, as a routine matter, make-or-buy problems, buy-or-lease problems, production scheduling, product pricing strategies, capital budgeting analyses, and other problems of the types discussed in Chapters 18 and 19. These practically eliminate the drudgery of the calculations required for such problems, and make obsolete the argument that a certain procedure should not be used because it is too complicated.

Fortunately for us humans, the computer is limited to operations that can be precisely described. It does not eliminate the need for judgment in defining the problem and specifying and evaluating the factors that have not been quantified, nor can these calculations produce results that are more accurate than the validity of the data fed into them. Thus, the computer provides great assistance to managers and analysts, but it replaces only the computational part of their work; it does not replace the people themselves.

Integrated Data Processing

The dream of every system builder is a system in which every relevant piece of raw data is recorded once, and only once, and is then combined, summarized, and analyzed automatically in a variety of ways to produce all the reports and other output documents that the business needs. Such a system can easily be described in general terms, but to develop it in practice is a far more complicated task than any group of mortals has so far been able to accomplish. It now appears that the computer may make feasible such an integrated data processing system, if not for all the data in a business, at least for substantial chunks of it. Such a system will not be developed overnight, but it is a goal that is not now completely fanciful.

Integrated data processing implies a blurring of the distinction that hitherto has existed among different categories of data, and this is a development that is indeed occurring. There is no longer a sharp distinction between the system for financial accounting data and that for management accounting data, or between input data and output data, or between accounting data and nonmonetary data, or even between numbers and words. The computer processes them all. Thus it may soon be undesirable to define management accounting as being restricted to monetary information; it may be more useful to view it as encompassing all recurring information that is of use to management.

There is a temptation to be too enthusiastic about the future of the computer. The fact is that at present computers tend to spew out too much information, and this tends to hinder rather than help the management process. But this is almost certainly a temporary condition, symptomatic of the haste with which computer programs have been developed, and the necessity for learning how best to use the computer's power. As time goes on, it is reasonable to expect that outputs will be better organized and more relevant to management's needs.

SUMMARY

A computer basically does only a few things: it stores data, makes computations, makes comparisons, rearranges data, and produces reports; but it does these things a million times faster than a human being can do them, it can perform a long and involved sequence of such operations without human intervention, and it does its work with virtually perfect accuracy. Thus computers are rapidly taking over the routine data processing work of business. It seems likely that they will take over such work in all businesses except the smallest, and those without a number of recurring transactions.

Computers also provide a powerful way of analyzing the data relevant to management problems of all types. They thus improve the quality of such analyses, although the results can be no better than the quality of the raw data, nor can the computer substitute for management judgment.

SUGGESTIONS FOR FURTHER READING

BLUMENTHAL, SHERMAN. *Management Information Systems.* Englewood Cliffs, N.J.: Prentice-Hall, 1969.

DEARDEN, JOHN and F. WARREN McFARLAN. *Management Information Systems.* Homewood: Richard D. Irwin, Inc., 1966.

MEIER, ROBERT C., W. NEWELL, and H. POZER. *Simulation in Business and Economics.* Englewood Cliffs, N.J.: Prentice-Hall, 1969.

CASE

CASE 20–1. WILSON COMPANY (B)

In 1969 the Wilson Company installed a remote terminal in an office that was readily accessible to members of the controller organization. This terminal was rented from a "computer utility" company and connected to a large computer owned by that company. The terminal was viewed as an experiment. If profitable uses were found, and if sufficient interest developed, there were plans to install similar terminals in other offices.

Mr. Bruce Carroll, controller of the Wilson Company, discussed possible uses of the computer with the salesman of the computer utility. One of these was the equipment replacement calculation of the type described in the Wilson Company (A) case (Chapter 19). The next day, the salesman brought Mr. Carroll a program called PINDX, which he said would aid in solving such problems.

Exhibit 1 is a flow chart of this program, and Exhibit 2 is a sample of the actual operation of the program as it appeared on the terminal in the Wilson Company office, typed on a continuous roll of paper.

As indicated in Exhibit 2, the user activated the program by typing the phrase "RUN PINDX" on the terminal keyboard. The computer then asked whether the user wanted instructions printed out. (Presumably, this would be desirable until such time as the user was thoroughly familiar with the program.) Upon receiving a "YES" the computer printed five paragraphs of instructions, and then requested the first piece of information, the "interest rate." On the next line after this request, the computer printed a "?" and the user typed the desired information, in this case 15. The computer continued with its requests, and after each "?" the user typed the requested information. The computer then typed the solution.

The problem solved in Exhibit 2 is as follows: the proposed machine cost $185,000 and had an economic life of five years. It was estimated to increase costs by $10,000 per year, and to produce benefits of $70,000 in Year 1, $90,000 in Year 2, and $110,000 in each of Years 3, 4, and 5. The required earnings rate was 15 percent. There was zero residual value. According to the computer, the profitability index was 1.459.

Exhibit 1

LOGICAL FLOWCHART FOR PROFITABILITY INDEX PROGRAM

Exhibit 2

COMPUTER DIALOGUE

```
RUN PINDX

PINDX

DO YOU DESIRE USER INSTRUCTIONS (YES OR NO)
? YES

PINDX CALCULATES THE PROFITABILITY INDEX (PV BENEFITS/PV COSTS) FOR A SET OF
CASH FLOWS WHICH THE USER INPUTS.

PINDX WILL FIRST ASK FOR THE INTEREST RATE.  (E.G. IF YOU WISH TO USE 10% ENTER
10) NEXT PINDX PROMPT LIFE.  ENTER THE LIFE OF THE SYSTEM IN YEARS TO THE NEAREST
YEAR.

PINDX WILL NOW REQUEST THE COSTS AND BENEFITS FOR TIME = 0 (E.G. CASH FLOWS AT
THE BEGINNING OF THE FIRST YEAR.)  THE FORMAT FOR THIS INPUT IS THE COST
FOLLOWED BY A COMMA FOLLOWED BY THE BENEFIT.

A LOOP IS NOW SET UP TO RUN THE NUMBER OF TIMES YOU HAVE ENTERED AS THE LIFE.
IN THIS LOOP PINDX WILL PROMPT THE YEAR NUMBER AND REQUEST THE COST AND BENEFIT
FOR THAT YEAR.  ALL CASH FLOWS ARE ASSUMED TO OCCUR AT THE YEAR END.  THE INPUT
FORMAT IS THE SAME AS ABOVE--COST, BENEFIT.

ONCE THE LOOP IS FINISHED, PINDX WILL PRINTOUT THE PRESENT VALUE OF THE COSTS,
THE PRESENT VALUE OF THE BENEFITS, AND THE PROFITABILITY INDEX.

NOW GIVE IT A TRY!

ENTER INTEREST RATE
? 15
ENTER LIFE
? 5

ENTER INITIAL COSTS AND BENEFITS FOR TIME = 0
? 185000,0

YEAR = 1
COSTS, BENEFITS
? 10000, 70000

YEAR = 2
COSTS, BENEFITS
? 10000, 90000

YEAR = 3
COSTS, BENEFITS
? 10000, 110000

YEAR = 4
COSTS, BENEFITS
? 10000, 110000

YEAR = 5
COSTS, BENEFITS
? 10000, 110000

PRESENT VALUE OF COSTS = 218522
PRESENT VALUE OF BENEFITS = 318830
PROFITABILITY INDEX = 1.459

END PINDX 8 MIN ELAPSED TIME, 6 CPU SECONDS
```

As noted on Exhibit 2, the total elapsed time required for running this problem (i.e., from the time Mr. Carroll typed the word PINDX to the printout of the solution) was 8 minutes, of which 6 seconds was actually used in making the computations. The charge made for this time was approximately $1.25.

Questions

1. Did the PINDX program compute the profitability index accurately for the sample problem? (How many minutes did it take you to answer this question?)
2. Set up the information given in Wilson Company (A) (Chapter 19) in a form suitable for use with the PINDX program, or, if this is not possible, point out how the program should be changed to accommodate this type of problem.
3. Should the PINDX program be used as submitted, should it be modified, or should it not be used? If you recommend modifying it, suggest the nature of the modifications.

CHAPTER 21

REVIEW CASES

CASE 21–1. C. F. CHURCH MANUFACTURING COMPANY

The C. F. Church Manufacturing Company was established in 1898 for the purpose of manufacturing toilet seats. The executives had devoted considerable effort to the development of a quality product, to widespread advertising of the product, and to the realization of economical manufacturing methods.

The manufacturing processes were quite simple. First, the seats were shaped out of wood at a branch plant. They were then shipped to the main plant, where they underwent the particular finishing processes required. Some units were sprayed with paint, but the best seats were coated with cellulose nitrate sheeting. After the seats were coated, the rough edges were filed and the seats were sanded, buffed, and polished. Finally, hinges and rubber bumpers were added, and the seats were packed for shipment. Most operations were performed by hand with the aid of small machines, such as paint spray guns and buffing wheels.

1. Accounting

COLLECTION OF MATERIAL AND LABOR COST. A major part of the work required in the cost system was the orderly accumulation of data on actual and standard costs. The procedure in regard to materials used was as follows. When an order for a particular style of finish was started through the factory, the foreman of the department that performed the first operation received a manufacturing order. On the basis of this order, the foreman filled out a stores requisition slip for the materials necessary to manufacture this order. Items listed on this requisition subsequently were priced, and their purchase cost was entered on the requisition by the cost department on a last-in, first-out basis. (Inasmuch as raw material

Exhibit 1

ASSEMBLY ORDER No. 6291

Coated

Date __August__ Plate No. __2000__

Shipping Order No. _____ Quantity __100__

Work Order No. _____

Seats 2,000 – 917

Covers 2,000 – 917

Hinges 2,000

Special Instructions

FOR COST DEPT. ONLY	UNIT COST		AMOUNT		✓
Material	5	51	551	00	
Labor		92	92	00	
Burden	1	90	190	00	
Total Cost	8	33	833	00	

REQUISITION No. 6291

Hinges – Screws – Bumpers

Date __August__

DESCRIPTION		QUANTITY
Hinges 2,000		100
Screws 3/4 x 7		
Screws 5/8 x 7		400
1 1/4 x 8		200
Brass Ferrules		200
Bar Bumpers		200
Tack Bumpers		

Delivered by

	UNIT COST	AMOUNT	✓
Hinges			
Screws			
Screws			
Ferrules			
Bar Bumpers			
Tack Bumpers			

REQUISITION No. 6291

Cartons – Fillers

Date __August__

DESCRIPTION		QUANTITY
Cartons 25		100
Fillers	800	200
	214	
	105	100
Blocks		

Delivered by

	UNIT COST	AMOUNT	✓
Cartons			
Filler No. 1			
No. 105			
No. 800			
No. 214			
Blocks			

was purchased infrequently in large contract lots, this procedure was not difficult.) When seats were ready to be assembled and packed, the foreman in the assembly department made out an assembly order (Exhibit 1), which included a requisition for hinges, screws, bumpers, cartons, and fillers. These issues of materials were also costed at last-in, first-out. The totals of the requisition slips for the month served as the basis for credits to the respective materials inventory accounts and a debit to the Work in Process account for the cost of material put into process.

The direct labor debit to Work in Process was equally straightforward. Daily, each productive employee made out a time and production report (Exhibit 2) on which he recorded the factory order number, the

Exhibit 2

FORM C-STR7918								
C. F. CHURCH MFG. CO.								
Employee No. **3/3**			Name	**Time and Production**		Date August —		
Order No.	Oper. No.	TIME			Labor or Piece Rate	No. Pieces	Cost	✓
		Started	Finished	Elapsed				
2068	*31*	*7:20*	*12:00*	*4.8*	*2.30*	*350*	*8 05*	
2068	*31*	*1:00*	*4:20*	*3.4*	*2.30*	*250*	*5 75*	
							13 80	

operation, the time spent on each operation, and the number of pieces that he had finished. A clerk in the payroll department entered the correct piece rate or hourly rate and made the proper extension. The total of the direct labor thus computed provided the credit to the Accrued Wages account and the debit (for direct labor) to Work in Process.

STANDARD BURDEN SCHEDULE (ANNUAL). The debit to Work in Process for manufacturing expense was based on annual estimates of the relation of burden expenses to direct labor costs for each department. These annual estimates were made so that for each department there was available a schedule of standard burden expenses at varying possible rates of capacity utilization. Exhibit 3 illustrates such a schedule for the coating department, Department No. 3.

The process used to prepare the standard burden schedules was as follows:

1. Determine 100 percent capacity of each department in terms of direct labor hours and direct labor dollars by theoretically loading each unit of productive machinery and equipment with the number of men required to operate it, together with the necessary productive employees on floor or bench work. Consider, however, the normal sales volume of different types of products and limitations as to type of equipment in any one department that affect the capacity of the plant as a whole. For example, output might be limited to the capacity of the coating and spraying departments.

2. Establish burden expense allowances for each department, considering four general classifications: indirect labor, indirect supplies, fixed charges, and charges from nonproductive departments.

3. Base allowance for indirect labor and indirect supplies on the past year's experience, making adjustments if necessary for changes in wage rates and the prices of supplies. Compute these projections first for the 100 percent capacity determined above, and from this point use a sliding or graduated scale for the lower percentages of capacity. Give due recognition to the fact that some of these costs do not vary at all with production, that others vary in the same ratio as production, and that others, although variable, do not move proportionately with the rate of actual plant activity.

4. Prorate power expense according to the number of horsepower hours used and metered in the respective departments; water expense (after consideration is given to any special demands for water in particular departments, such as steam) according to the number of employees; insurance, taxes, and depreciation with reference to the net book value of buildings and equipment. Charge directly to the department involved specific insurance that definitely can be allocated to an individual department, such as automobile insurance on trucks in the shipping department or boiler indemnity for the steam department.

5. Distribute the total expense of nonproductive departments such as steam, general plant, shipping, and plant administration to the productive departments on the most logical basis: steam according to floor area, general plant and plant administration according to direct labor hours, and shipping according to direct labor dollars. The estimated cost of defective work for the whole plant was distributed to operating departments on the basis of the expected distribution of direct labor dollars. This item of expense was included in the total of "Charges from other departments," shown at the bottom of Exhibit 3.

6. Revise the standard burden schedules only for a general increase or decrease in wage rates or material costs or an important change in the manufacturing processes.

Exhibit 3

BURDEN DEVELOPMENT, DEPARTMENT NO. 3

	100%	95%	90%	85%	80%	75%	70%	65%	60%	50%	40%
Indirect labor:											
01 Supervision	775.00	775.00	775.00	775.00	775.00	775.00	775.00	775.00	775.00	775.00	775.00
08 General labor	625.00	595.00	565.00	530.00	500.00	470.00	440.00	405.00	375.00	315.00	250.00
10 Idle and lost time											
11 Guaranteed rate cost	375.00	356.00	338.00	319.00	300.00	281.00	263.00	244.00	225.00	188.00	150.00
16 Overtime bonus	100.00	100.00	95.00	90.00	85.00	85.00	80.00	75.00	50.00	25.00	25.00
19 Repairs and maint.—M and E	175.00	175.00	165.00	165.00	160.00	160.00	160.00	150.00	150.00	100.00	100.00
Total indirect labor	2,050.00	2,001.00	1,938.00	1,879.00	1,820.00	1,771.00	1,718.00	1,649.00	1,575.00	1,403.00	1,300.00
Indirect supplies:											
31 Repairs and maint.—M and E	25.00	25.00	25.00	20.00	20.00	20.00	20.00	20.00	15.00	15.00	10.00
35 Acetone and isotone	1,625.00	1,545.00	1,465.00	1,380.00	1,300.00	1,220.00	1,140.00	1,055.00	975.00	815.00	650.00
37 Sandpaper and sand-belts	11.00	10.00	10.00	9.00	9.00	8.00	8.00	7.00	7.00	5.00	4.00
38 Glue and cement	775.00	736.00	700.00	660.00	620.00	580.00	540.00	500.00	465.00	385.00	310.00
41 Consumable supplies	125.00	120.00	112.00	106.00	100.00	94.00	88.00	81.00	75.00	63.00	50.00
42 Loose and hand tools	50.00	48.00	45.00	43.00	40.00	38.00	35.00	33.00	30.00	25.00	20.00
46 Miscellaneous	15.00	14.00	14.00	13.00	12.00	11.00	10.00	9.00	9.00	7.00	6.00
Total indirect supplies	2,626.00	2,498.00	2,371.00	2,231.00	2,101.00	1,971.00	1,841.00	1,705.00	1,576.00	1,315.00	1,050.00
Fixed charges:											
65 Insurance—bldgs. and equip.	21.58	21.58	21.58	21.58	21.58	21.58	21.58	21.58	21.58	21.58	21.58
66 Insurance—L. and C.	161.00	152.00	145.00	137.00	128.70	121.00	113.00	105.00	97.00	80.00	64.00
68 Power	27.00	26.00	24.00	23.00	21.60	21.00	19.00	18.00	16.00	14.00	11.00
69 Water	17.25	17.25	17.25	17.25	17.25	17.25	17.25	17.25	17.25	17.25	17.25

70 Taxes—city and town.	28.68	28.68	28.68	28.68	28.68	28.68	28.68	28.68	28.68	28.68	28.68
71 Taxes—social security.	212.00	265.00	318.00	345.00	371.00	398.00	424.27	450.00	477.00	504.00	530.00
72 Depreciation.	81.25	81.25	81.25	81.25	81.25	81.25	81.25	81.25	81.25	81.25	81.25
73 Provision for vacations.	725.40	725.40	725.40	725.40	725.40	725.40	725.40	725.40	725.40	725.40	725.40
78 Group insurance.	112.70	112.70	112.70	112.70	112.70	112.70	112.70	112.70	112.70	112.70	112.70
80 Pensions.	420.36	420.36	420.36	420.36	420.36	420.36	420.36	420.36	420.36	420.36	420.36
Total fixed charges.	1,694.22	1,766.22	1,838.22	1,875.22	1,910.22	1,947.22	1,981.79	2,017.22	2,053.22	2,089.22	2,125.22
Total direct expense.	4,044.22	4,484.22	4,989.22	5,229.22	5,469.22	5,689.22	5,902.79	6,127.22	6,362.22	6,588.22	6,801.22
Charges from other departments.	8,235.38	8,440.11	8,630.42	8,751.83	8,826.90	8,945.27	9,032.28	9,140.56	9,240.12	9,333.33	9,435.37
Total expense.	12,279.60	12,924.33	13,619.64	13,981.05	14,296.12	14,634.49	14,935.07	15,267.78	15,602.34	15,921.55	16,236.59
Direct labor dollars.	3,750.00	4,687.00	5,625.00	6,094.00	6,562.00	7,031.00	7,500.00	7,969.00	8,437.00	8,906.00	9,375.00
Burden rate.	327%	276%	242%	229%	218%	208%	200%	191%	185%	179%	173%

STANDARD BURDEN RATE. After the burden expense schedule was prepared, executives estimated the percentage of capacity utilization expected during the coming year. The standard burden rate was the rate shown on Exhibit 3 for the estimated percentage of capacity. For example, it was estimated that during the year the coating department would operate at an average of 80 percent of capacity. The standard burden rate for the coating department was therefore 200 percent of direct labor, as shown at the bottom of the 80 percent column in Exhibit 3. The other columns in Exhibit 3 were used for control purposes, as described subsequently.

ACTUAL BURDEN COSTS (MONTHLY). Actual burden costs incurred during the month were charged to the Burden account in the general ledger and to an appropriate detail account in a burden subsidiary ledger. There was a detail account for each item listed in Exhibit 3 (supervision, general labor, etc.) in each department. Service department and other overhead costs were allocated to the producing departments. At the end of the month, the amount of "absorbed burden" was calculated by multiplying the burden rate for each department by the actual direct labor cost of the department for the month. In the coating department, for example, the actual direct labor for August was $5,915.60, and this multiplied by 200 percent gave $11,831.20, the absorbed burden. (Note that the rate used was the burden rate determined annually, *not* the burden rate under the column in Exhibit 3 that relates to the actual volume of the current month.)

The absorbed burden for all departments was debited to Work in Process and credited to the Burden account. Any balance remaining in the Burden account was then closed to Loss and Gain. In August, for example, actual burden was $45,914.98, absorbed burden was $45,904.44, so $10.54 was debited to Loss and Gain.

STANDARD PRODUCT COSTS. Deliveries from work in process to finished goods were recorded by completion in the factory of the assembly order (Exhibit 1). On the lower left corner of that form there was space for the cost department to fill in the standard cost per unit and the total amount of standard cost for the order, and the total of these standard costs entries for a month was credited to the Work in Process account and debited to Finished Goods Inventory.

The standard costs per unit mentioned in the previous paragraph were prepared for each product in the form illustrated in Exhibit 4. Because the lines on the standard cost sheets were arranged by successive operations, they showed the cumulative cost of a product at the completion of every operation as well as the final cost at which the product was delivered to finished goods inventory. For each operation and for the total cost there was a breakdown that showed separately the standard costs of materials, labor, and burden. The method of arriving at these costs is described below.

Standard materials costs consisted of a predetermined physical amount per unit priced at the expected purchase price for each classification of raw stock or of finished parts stock. Standard labor costs for the various piece-rate operations were simply the current piece rates; in the case of daywork operations, they were the quotients obtained by dividing the

Exhibit 4

STANDARD COST				
DATE January 1			PLATE NO. 2000	
Description	*Material*	*Labor*	*Burden*	*Total*
Receive woodwork	1.17	0.004	0.008	1.182
Insp. and hand sand		0.012	0.024	1.218
Bottom coat	0.542	0.038	0.076	1.874
Trim T.B. and O.F. seats		0.011	0.022	1.907
Sand edges T.B.C.F. out		0.003	0.008	1.918
Sand edges T.B.C.F. in		0.003	0.008	1.929
Inspect		0.012	0.024	1.965
Top coat	0.543	0.079	0.158	2.745
Shave		0.010	0.020	2.775
Sand edges—upright belt		0.005	0.014	2.794
Sand seats and covers		0.039	0.107	2.940
Inspect and file		0.015	0.030	2.985
Dope		0.004	0.008	2.997
Buff seats and covers		0.108	0.208	3.313
Inspect		0.012	0.024	3.349
Buff repairs		0.044	0.085	3.478
Trademark		0.007	0.014	3.499
Drilling		0.004	0.008	3.511
Total seat	2.255	0.410	0.846	3.511
Total cover No.	1.983	0.399	0.826	3.208
Total seat and cover	4.238	0.809	1.672	6.719
Assemble		0.032	0.064	6.815
Cleanup polish		0.033	0.066	6.914
Seal end of carton		0.006	0.012	6.932
Inspect and wrap		0.034	0.068	7.034
Seat, label, and pack		0.010	0.020	7.064
Bar bumpers	0.043			7.107
Tack bumpers	0.019			7.126
Screws 1¼–8	0.047			7.173
Hinge	1.04			8.213
Carton and filler 2—No. 1	0.125			8.338
Total Cost	5.512	0.924	1.902	8.338

daywork rate by an estimated attainable average output. Standard burden costs were found by multiplying the departmental burden rate selected for the year by the standard labor cost for the operation concerned. For example, the standard cost sheet for a style calling for a coated finish might show for an operation in the coating department a standard labor charge of $0.079. As indicated above, operations in the coating department for the year were estimated to be at 80 percent of capacity, which for the coating department meant a burden rate of 200 percent of productive labor. Thus, the standard burden cost for the operation with a labor charge of $0.079 was set at 200 percent of this amount, or $0.158.

These standard product costs were used to price deliveries into finished stock, to cost work in process inventory, and to transfer production between accounts. Once the standard costs were prepared, it was expected that they would remain constant except for alterations necessary to reflect a significant change in the manufacturing process, a change in wage rates or in the price of materials, or the selection of a new normal percentage of operating activity that determined the unit allowance for burden.

VARIANCES.   At the end of each month's accounting period, a physical inventory of raw materials, supplies, work in process, and finished goods was taken. For this inventory, raw materials and supplies were priced on the basis of last-in, first-out purchase cost, and work in process and finished goods were priced according to the standard cost sheets described above. The difference between the inventory thus determined and the book balance of each inventory account was closed into Cost of Goods Sold. The most important of these differences was for work in process inventory.

A work in process statement (Exhibit 5) was prepared each month. This report showed the beginning inventory at standard cost plus actual direct materials, actual labor, and actual absorbed burden added during the period in each department. From this total cost figure, there were subtracted the actual deliveries to finished goods as indicated on the completed assembly orders, less products transferred from Finished Goods back to Work in Process for reworking, both costed at standard cost. The resulting Balance in Process was the book value of work in process and was compared with the figure obtained by valuing, at standard, the results of the physical inventory. Any difference indicated by this comparison constituted the variance of actual cost from standard and was closed to Cost of Goods Sold. The physical inventory balance at standard constituted the debit to Work in Process at the beginning of the next month. If this Work in Process variance was large, its causes were investigated and action was taken accordingly.

A descriptive summary of the inventory accounts is given in Exhibit 6.

2. Control of Burden Expenses

BUDGETED BURDEN EXPENSES.   The Church company used the departmental burden schedules to set bogeys for the foremen and supervisors who were responsible for incurring expenses. A knowledge of the actual amount of direct labor for each productive department made it a simple

Exhibit 5

WORK IN PROCESS

Period Ending August   **Order No. GENERAL**

Detail	Amount				
Balance from Last Period			158	597	19
DIRECT MATERIALS			76	338	21
DIRECT LABOR					
1 Varnish					
2 Spray	2	990	25		
3 Coating	5	915	60		
4 Filing		998	83		
5 Sanding	1	637	53		
6 Buffing & Polishing	6	175	78		
8 Assembling and Packing	4	788	60		
Total Direct Labor			22	506	59
BURDEN					
1 Varnish					
2 Spray	6	180	50		
3 Coating	11	831	20		
4 Filing	1	937	73		
5 Sanding	4	489	05		
6 Buffing & Polishing	11	888	76		
8 Assembling and Packing	9	577	20		
10 Shipping					
Total Burden			45	904	44
TOTAL COST			303	346	43
Less Deliveries at Cost			222	386	74
BALANCE IN PROCESS			80	959	69

DELIVERIES AT COST

Date		Amount		Date		Amount		Date		Amount	
8/31	Del.	220	876	63							
	Var.	1	259	07							
	Defect.		251	04							
	Net	222	386	74							

matter to determine which column of figures to use as the bogey standard for evaluating the spending performance of each foreman. For example, the coating department (Exhibit 3) might be expected to operate, on the average, at 80 percent of capacity, but in any one month the actual

Exhibit 6

SUMMARY OF ENTRIES TO INVENTORY ACCOUNTS FOR AUGUST

Raw Materials

(Several accounts according to nature of material)

$151,204 Balance
$343,640.19
Purchases at invoice cost (credit to Accounts Payable).

$1,101.67
Materials salvaged from returned goods (credit to Cost of Goods Sold).

$76,318.21
Requisitions, priced at last-in, first-out cost (debit to Work in Process).

$138.32
Adjustment to physical inventory (Dr. or Cr.)

A physical inventory of all raw materials was taken each month and the difference between inventory and book balance written off to Cost of Goods Sold.

Work in Process

$158,597.19 Balance
$76,318.21
Direct materials from requisitions priced at last-in, first-out cost (credit to Raw Materials).

$22,506.59
Direct labor from payroll summary (credit to Accrued Wages).

$20.00
Materials purchased not usually carried in inventory (credit to Accounts Payable).

$17.61
Transfers from finished goods for reworking or alteration, at standard cost (credit to Finished Goods).

$45,904.44
Absorbed expense (earned burden) from burden summary sheet (credit to Burden).

$220,894.24
Deliveries to finished goods at standard costs (debit to Finished Goods).

$251.04
Defective work, from defective work order (debit to Burden).

$1,259.07
Adjustment to physical inventory (Dr. or Cr.)

A physical inventory was taken of all work in process every month. This was priced and totaled according to standard costs at last operation performed; the difference between the inventory and balance in the Work in Process account, representing the cost variation, was written off to Cost of Goods Sold.

Finished Goods

$429,682.73 Balance
$220,894.24
Deliveries to finished goods at standard costs (credit to Work in Process).

$400,954.09
Shipment at standard costs (debit to Cost of Goods Sold).

$17.61
Transfers to work in process for reworking or alteration at standard cost (debit to Work in Process).

operations might vary considerably from this average. Thus, if direct labor dropped to $7,031, the foreman would be expected to spend only $580 for glue and cement rather than the $620 allowable at the average operating level. For nonproductive departments, the column selected was the one that listed the expenses expected for the percentage of capacity nearest the average operating level of all productive departments.

COMPARISON OF ACTUAL AND BUDGET. The departmental comparisons of the actual burden expenses, by accounts, with the appropriate budgeted allowance for that volume, are illustrated in the departmental budget sheet, Exhibit 7. The August budgeted expense figures for the coating department are based upon an output level of 65 percent of capacity. This figure was arrived at by comparing the actual direct labor expense for the month, amounting to $5,915.60, to the closest corresponding direct labor expense, $6,094, which is under the 65 percent column shown on Exhibit 3. (Exhibit 7 is a standard form, and only those lines that are pertinent to the operations of the coating department are filled in on the example shown.)

Exhibit 7 also showed two items over which the foreman had no control. Other Overhead expenses was the total amount of fixed charges allocated to the department on the basis of the percentage distributions described earlier. Defective Work was the total amount of defective work budgeted ($600) and actual ($251.04) for the *entire plant*, and it bore no relation to the work done in the coating department. The amount allocated to each department for defective work was not shown on Exhibit 7 because the basis of allocation was considered too arbitrary. The amounts for both Other Overhead expenses and for Defective Work were shown in the Analysis of Overhead Expenses principally as a matter of information for the foreman. They were not considered as being controllable by the foreman.

Each month the accounting department prepared Exhibit 8, summarizing the actual, budgeted, and absorbed burden costs for each operating department. The amount shown as Actual Expense was obtained by adding the Charges from Other Departments ($8,362.13 for the coating department) to the other burden items shown in Exhibit 7 (excluding defective work). The Budgeted Expense was the total burden for each department as shown on the burden development sheets (Exhibit 3) at the applicable level of operations (65 percent for the coating department in August).

The amount of Absorbed Expense was computed by applying the *annual* burden rate to the direct labor in each productive department, as explained in the preceding section.

In the opinion of the management the entries in the column headed Loss or Gain on Budget could be considered a measure of the effectiveness of departmental supervision, whereas the amount Over- or Underab-

Exhibit 7

			Budget	Actual Expense	Over or Under Actual	
		C. F. CHURCH MFG. CO.				
		HOLYOKE				
		Analysis of Overhead Expenses				
		DEPARTMENT #3 Coating			Month August	
1		INDIRECT LABOR				1
2	01	Supervision	775 00	756 00	19 00	2
3	04	Truck Drivers & Helpers				3
4	06	Shipping				4
5	08	General Labor	405 00	171 22	233 78	5
6	09	Repair and Rework				6
7	10	Idle and Lost Time		1 77	(1 77)	7
8	11	Guaranteed Rate Cost	244 00	28 14	215 86	8
9	16	Overtime Bonus	75 00	32 98	42 02	9
10	19	Repairs & Maint. & Mchy. & Equip.	150 00	38 26	111 74	10
11	17	Vacations		46 00	(46 00)	11
12	21	Paid Holidays				12
13		Total	1649 00	1074 37	574 63	13
14		INDIRECT SUPPLIES				14
15	31	Repairs & Maint.--Mchy. & Equip.	20 00	360 18	(340 18)	15
16	33	Repairs & Maint. Trucks				16
17	35	Acetone & Isotone	1055 00	739 48	315 52	17
18	36	Buffing Compounds & Buffs				18
19	37	Sandpaper & Sandbelts	7 00	9 60	(2 60)	19
20	39	Labels, Tape, etc., Glue & Cement	500 00	734 71	(234 71)	20
21	40	Shipping Cartons				21
22	41	Consumable Supplies	81 00	55 54	25 46	22
23	42	Loose & Hand Tools	33 00	13 55	19 45	23
24	46	Miscellaneous	9 00	7 51	1 49	24
25		Total	1705 00	1920 57	(215 57)	25
26		OTHER OVERHEAD expenses:				26
27		Insurance, power, taxes, social				27
28		security, depreciation, group				28
29		insurance & pension	1875 22	1472 46	402 76	29
30						30
31		DEFECTIVE WORK	600 00	251 04	348 96	31
32						32
33		DIRECT LABOR	6094 00	5915 60	178 40	33
34						34
35						35
36						36
37						37
38						38
39						39
40						40

sorbed was influenced both by efficiency and by the volume of production.

The departmental overhead budget constituted the point of real control over expenditures. At the end of each month, the president met with the cost supervisor and the foremen to discuss spending. At these meet-

Exhibit 8

BURDEN SUMMARY AND STATISTICS

Plant—Holyoke   Period Ending—August 31

Dept. No.	Description	Direct Labor	Actual Expense	Budgeted Expense	Loss or Gain on Budget	Absorbed Expense	Over- or Under- absorbed
1							
2	Spray	2,990.25	6,464.64	7,103.64	639.00	6,180.50	(284.14)
3	Coating	5,915.60	12,829.53	13,981.05	1,151.52	11,831.20	(998.33)
4	Filing	998.83	2,590.83	2,190.20	(400.63)	1,937.73	(653.10)
4-I							
4-C							
4-5							
5	Sanding	1,637.53	3,907.74	5,243.47	1,335.73	4,489.05	581.31
6	Buffing	6,175.78	11,275.76	10,750.25	(525.51)	11,888.76	613.00
7							
8	Assemble and pack	4,788.60	8,846.48	8,998.58	152.10	9,577.20	730.72
9							
10							
11							
12							
14							
15							
	Total Plant	22,506.59	45,914.98	48,267.19	2,352.21	45,904.44	(10.54)

YEAR TO DATE

Dept. No.	Description	Direct Labor	Actual Expense	Budgeted Expense	Loss or Gain on Budget	Absorbed Expense	Over- or Under- absorbed
1							
2		22,071.46	44,718.50			45,643.78	925.28
3		50,512.16	104,611.39			101,024.32	(3,587.07)
4		9,077.03	21,509.51			17,618.52	(3,890.99)
4-I							
4-C							
4-5							
5		13,660.61	35,648.86			37,443.73	1,794.87
6		51,978.12	98,119.96			100,057.88	1,937.92
7							
8		30,878.48	62,125.19			61,756.96	(368.23)
9							
10							
11							
12							
14							
15							
	Total Plant	178,177.86	366,733.41			363,545.19	(3,188.22)

ings the foremen were encouraged to discuss their performance as indicated by the budget report. When the system was first installed, the cost supervisor did most of the talking, but with increasing familiarity with the costs for which he was responsible, each foreman gradually became "cost conscious," and after a short time each foreman knew approximately what his monthly performance would be, even before he saw the budget comparison report.

The foreman in charge of the coating department was particularly

Exhibit 9

SUMMARY OF PERFORMANCE IN THE COATING DEPARTMENT

	April		May		June		August	
	Actual	(Over) or Under	Actual	(Over) or Under	Actual	(Over) or Under	Actual	(Over) or Under
Indirect labor:								
01 Supervision	811	(36)	782	(7)	756	19	756	19
08 General labor	654	(124)	558	(28)	418	22	171	234
10 Idle and lost time	...	...	...	...	...	...	2	(2)
11 Guaranteed rate cost	313	6	154	165	50	213	28	216
16 Overtime bonus	63	27	45	45	37	43	33	42
19 Repairs and maint.—mchy. and equip.	89	76	30	135	35	125	38	112
17 Vacations	...	...	...	...	...	...	46	(46)
Total	1,930	(51)	1,569	310	1,296	422	1,074	575
Indirect supplies:								
31 Repairs and maint.—mchy. and equip.	5	15	85	(65)	176	(156)	360	(340)
33 Repairs and maint.—trucks	...	...	...	...	...	...	...	...
35 Acetone and isotone	1,300	80	1,134	246	1,031	109	739	316
36 Buffing compounds and buffs	...	...	...	...	...	...	...	...
37 Sandpaper and sandbelts	10	(1)	14	(5)	5	3	10	(3)
39 Labels, tape, etc., glue and cement	575	85	462	199	182	358	735	(235)
40 Shipping cartons	...	...	...	...	...	...	...	...
41 Consumable supplies	66	40	116	(10)	48	40	56	25
42 Loose and hand tools	37	6	14	29	10	25	14	19
46 Miscellaneous	27	(14)	9	3	9	1	8	1
Total	2,020	211	1,834	397	1,461	380	1,922	(217)
Other overhead expenses: Insurance, power, taxes, social security, depreciation, group insurance, and pension	1,456	561	2,014	3	1,836	74	1,472	403
Defective work	391	209	656	(56)	594	6	251	349
Direct labor	7,812	157	8,024	(55)	6,599	(36)	5,916	178

interested in controlling the overhead costs under his jurisdiction. Every month he discussed the analysis of overhead expenses with the factory manager and the cost supervisor to evaluate with them the performance of his department. During the first week of September, he received the analysis of overhead expenses for August (Exhibit 7), and he checked all the items carefully to learn if there were any costs out of line with his expectations for that month. He copied the August figures onto a sheet (Exhibit 9) on which he had previously summarized the figures for recent months (except for July, which included a vacation shutdown). After he felt that he had a good idea of his cost position, he arranged for a meeting with the factory manager and the cost supervisor to review the situation with them.

Questions

1. What are the major purposes of the standards developed by the company?
2. How does the company develop standard burden rates? How often do *you* think they should be changed?
3. What steps are involved in the development of the standard cost sheet (Exhibit 4)? How accurate do you judge the figures to be?
4. What are the possible causes of the $1,259.07 credit to Work in Process labeled "adjustment to physical inventory" in Exhibit 6?
5. Explain so as to distinguish them clearly from one another, the figures $12,829.53, $13,981.05, and $11,831.20 shown for the coating department on Exhibit 8.
6. If you were the cost supervisor, what evaluation would you make of the performance of the foreman in the coating department in controlling his overhead costs? About which items in Exhibits 7–9 would you be likely to question him?
7. In the coating department for the month of August, what is the variance attributable to "Charges from Other Departments"? Of what significance is this variance to (*a*) the coating department, and (*b*) the service departments that created these charges? Should this variance be included in the burden summary and statistics report?

CASE 21–2. CLIMAX SHIPPING COMPANY

In the spring of 1950, the controller of the Climax Shipping Company, located near Pittsburgh, was preparing a report for the executive committee regarding the feasibility of repairing one of the company's steam riverboats or of replacing the steamboat with a new diesel-powered boat.

The Climax Shipping Company was engaged mainly in the transportation of coal from the nearby mines to the steel mills, public utilities, and other industries in the Pittsburgh area. The company's several steamboats also, on occasion, carried cargoes to places as far away as New Orleans. The boats owned by Climax were all steam-powered. All were at least 10 years old, and the majority were between 15 and 30 years old.

The steamboat the controller was concerned about, the Cynthia, was 23 years old and required immediate rehabilitation or replacement. It was estimated that the Cynthia had a useful life of another 20 years provided that adequate repairs and maintenance were made. Whereas the book value of the Cynthia was $39,500, it was believed that she would bring somewhat less than this amount, possibly around $25,000, if she were sold in 1950. The total of immediate rehabilitation costs for the Cynthia was estimated to be $115,000. It was estimated that these general rehabilitation expenditures would extend the useful life of the Cynthia for about 20 years.

New spare parts from another boat, which had been retired in 1948, were available for use in the rehabilitation of the Cynthia. An estimate of their fair value, if used on the Cynthia, was $43,500, which was their book value. Use of these parts would, in effect, decrease the immediate rehabilitation costs from $115,000 to $71,500. It was believed that if these parts were sold on the market they would bring only around $30,000. They could not be used on any of the other Climax steamboats.

Currently, the Cynthia was operated by a 20-man crew. Annual operating costs for the 20-man crew would be approximately as follows:

Wages	$110,200
Vacation and sickness benefits	1,880
Social security payments	2,400
Life insurance	1,800
Commissary supplies	15,420
Repairs and maintenance	24,400
Fuel	34,500
Lubricants	550
Miscellaneous service and supplies	12,000
Total	$203,150

It was estimated that the cost of dismantling and scrapping the Cynthia at the end of her useful life after the overhaul would be offset by the value of the scrap and used parts taken off the boat.

An alternative to rehabilitating the steamboat was the purchase of a diesel-powered boat. The Quapelle Company, a local boat manufacturer, quoted the price of $325,000 for a diesel boat. An additional $75,000 for a basic parts inventory would be necessary to service a diesel boat, and such an inventory would be sufficient to service up to three diesel boats. If four or more diesels were purchased, however, it was estimated that additional spare parts inventory would be necessary.

The useful life of a diesel-powered boat was estimated to be 25 years, at the end of which time the boat would be scrapped or completely rehabilitated at a cost approximating that of a new boat. The possibility of diesel engine replacement during the 25-year life was not contemplated by the controller, since information from other companies having limited experience with diesel-powered riverboats did not indicate that such costs needed to be anticipated; but a general overhaul of the engines, costing at current prices $60,000, would be expected every 10 years.

One of the features the Quapelle Company pointed out was the 12 percent increase in average speed of diesel-powered boats over the steamboats. The controller discounted this feature, however, because the short runs and lock-to-lock operations involved in local river shipping would prohibit the diesel boats from taking advantage of their greater speed since there was little opportunity for passing and they would have to wait in turn at each lock for the slower steamboats. In 1950 only two diesel boats, out of about 40 boats, were operating on the river. The controller felt it would be many years, if at all, before diesel boats displaced the slower steamboats.

After consulting the Quapelle Company and other companies operating diesel-powered boats, the controller estimated that the annual operating costs of a diesel-powered boat would total $156,640, broken down as follows:

Wages for a 13-man crew	$ 77,300
Vacation and sickness benefits	1,320
Social security payments	1,680
Life insurance	1,170
Commissary supplies	10,020
Repairs and maintenance*	21,700
Fuel	28,800
Extra stern repairs	2,000
Miscellaneous service and supplies	12,650
Total	$156,640

* Excluding possible major overhaul of diesel engines.

Although the Climax controller had not considered the matter, the reader of this case may assume that at the end of the 20th year the diesel boat would have a realizable value of $32,500 and the inventory of parts of $37,500.

The controller was also concerned at this time with a city smoke ordinance which had been signed in 1948, to take effect in 1952. To comply with the regulations of the ordinance, all hand-fired steamboats had to be converted to stoker firing. Several of the Climax steamboats were already stoker-fired; the Cynthia, however, was hand-fired. The additional cost of converting the Cynthia to stoker firing was estimated to be $40,000, provided it was done at the same time as the general rehabilitation. This $40,000 included the cost of stokers and extra hull conversion and was not included in the $115,000 rehabilitation figure. The controller also knew that if $115,000 were spent presently in rehabilitating the

Cynthia and it was found out later that no relief, or only temporary relief for one or two years, was to be granted under the smoke ordinance, the cost of converting to stoker firing would no longer be $40,000, but around $70,000. The higher cost would be due to rebuilding, which would not be necessary if the Cynthia was converted to stoker firing at the time of her general rehabilitation.

Conversion would reduce the crew from 20 to 18, with the following details:

Wages..	$100,650
Vacation and sickness benefits........................	1,650
Social security payments...............................	2,200
Life insurance..	1,620
Commissary supplies....................................	13,880
Repairs and maintenance*..............................	24,400
Fuel*..	34,500
Lubricants*...	550
Miscellaneous service and supplies*..................	12,000
Total..	$191,450

* These costs would remain the same, whether the crew was 20 or 18 men.

All operating data the controller had collected pertaining to crew expenses were based on a two-shift, 12-hour working day, which was standard on local riverboats. He had been informed, however, that the union representing crew members wanted a change to a three-shift, eight-hour day. If the union insisted on an eight-hour day, accommodations on board the steamers or the diesels would have to be enlarged. The controller was perturbed by this fact, because he knew the diesels could readily be converted to accommodate three crews whereas steamers could not. How strongly the union would insist on the change and when it would be put into effect, if ever, were questions for which the controller could get no satisfactory answers. He believed that the union might have a difficult time in getting acceptance of its demands for three eight-hour shifts on steamers, since it would be very difficult, if not impossible, to convert the steamers to hold a larger crew, because of space limitations. The controller thought that the union might succeed in getting its demands accepted, however, in the case of diesel-powered boats. One of the diesel boats currently operating in the Pittsburgh area had accommodations for three crews, although it was still operating on a two-shift basis. The diesel boats that the Quapelle Company offered to build for Climax could be fitted to accommodate three crews at no additional cost.

Another factor the controller was considering at this time was alternative uses of funds. In the spring of 1950, Climax had sufficient funds to buy four diesel-powered boats; however, there were alternative uses for these funds. The other projects which the management was considering at this time had an estimated return of at least 10 percent after taxes. The income tax rate at the time was 48 percent.

The company was conservatively managed and, in 1950, had no long-term debt outstanding. Its net worth exceeded $2 million. The company occasionally used unsecured bank loans to provide working capital during seasonal periods of peak need. In the spring of 1950 the company's liability for bank loans amounted to $150,000, which had been borrowed at 3 percent interest. The "prime" loan rate in New York City at the time was 2 percent.

As a further inducement to have a contract to build a diesel boat, the Quapelle Company offered to rent a diesel boat to Climax. The rental terms offered by the Quapelle Company called for annual payments of $21,700 for 15 years plus $5,700 per year for an interest charge. At the end of 15 years, when the Quapelle Company had in effect recovered the value of the boat, it would charge a nominal rental of $2,850 a year. Title to the boat would continue to remain in the hands of the Quapelle Company. Climax would incur all costs of operating and maintaining the boat, including general overhaul every 10 years, and would still need to invest $75,000 in a basic spare parts inventory.

Question

1. What action do you recommend?

CASE 21–3. EASTERN LOCK COMPANY

Robert Burns, production engineer of the Eastern Lock Company, asked one of his assistants, John Hawkins, to write a report analyzing the advisability of purchasing some new drilling equipment. Mr. Burns told him that this equipment might be valuable in reducing the cost of manufacturing bases and plungers[1] for certain styles of padlocks. The management of the company was anxious to make cost reductions wherever possible. Mr. Burns told Mr. Hawkins that he expected the report to include specific recommendations supported by a concise but comprehensive analysis. The report would be used as a basis for further study of the proposal by officials responsible for equipment purchases and would serve as the file record of the plan.

Over a period of 70 years the Eastern Lock Company had become known as a large and dependable manufacturer of high-quality locks of several hundred styles. Currently, sales amounted to over $4 million. Eastern Lock Company was the only lock-making plant in the area. It was

---

[1] The base (also called the shell) is the body to which the main working parts of the lock are attached. The base is inserted into the outside case of the lock. The plunger (also called the bolt) is the small piece that moves against the notch in the shackle and holds it locked.

operating close to capacity, whereas other metal products concerns in the vicinity were laying off workers. Business conditions were generally uncertain throughout the country.

The new machinery could be used to make parts for 13 standard styles of padlocks that the company had been manufacturing for more than 40 years. It sold these locks largely to organizations that required the same style of lock throughout all their plants and buildings. The sale of styles of locks was fairly steady throughout the year; annual sales of the 13 styles of locks in recent years had been approximately as follows:

Style A,	3,000 units		Style G,	12,000 units	
B,	12,000	"	H,	6,000	"
C,	18,000	"	I,	6,000	"
D,	60,000	"	J,	4,000	"
E,	48,000	"	K,	4,000	"
F,	42,000	"	L,	30,000	"
			M,	12,000	"
			Total...	257,000	"

The equipment that Mr. Burns was considering was of two types. One type was semiautomatic equipment for performing the 12 drilling operations required on lock bases. The other type was automatic equipment for drilling lock plungers. For many years, lock bases and plungers both had been drilled on general-purpose machines.

Drilling Bases

Under the company's existing method, the drilling operations on the bases were performed by semiskilled men who on piecework earned an average of $1.32 an hour for a 40-hour week. Output per man varied somewhat with the particular style of lock base being drilled. On the basis of total annual production figures for the 13 styles of lock bases, output had averaged 33 pieces per worker per hour, exclusive of the setup time. Setup of the machines required very little time and was performed by the operatives, who received no payment for this work.

The semiautomatic machine being considered for the drilling of the lock bases could perform 6 of the 12 drilling operations at a rate of 225 units an hour; after another setup, the other 6 drilling operations could then be performed. Or two machines could perform the 12 drilling operations simultaneously, at the rate of 225 completed units an hour; these two machines would easily provide capacity for all 13 styles. Each machine could be operated by a girl who would be paid about $0.80 an hour. Changing the setup of a machine from the drilling (six holes) of one style of lock base to the drilling of another style would require a skilled mechanic and would take an average of five hours. Skilled mechanics in the Eastern Lock Company received $1.80 an hour. In addition, a charge of 100 percent of the mechanic's wages was made against setup operations to allow for overhead; this charge was included in the standard overhead for the valuation of inventories and the cost of goods sold.

To operate the machines advantageously, the company would have to produce each style of lock in large lots in order to spread the setup costs over a large number of units. On the other hand, the larger the lot produced, the larger would be the inventory of bases and the longer would be the average time a base remained in inventory. Thus, the inventory-carrying costs per unit would increase. In figuring overhead, Eastern Lock charged 4 percent a year for capital tied up in inventories and 4 percent of the value of inventories for space, handling, and so forth. Since the company was operating close to capacity, storage space was limited. It was believed, however, that if some rearranging were done in the stock room, sufficient space would be available to store the additional inventory. The handling of the additional inventory was expected to require extra labor, and although no close estimate had been made of the cost of this labor, it was estimated that perhaps a half (i.e., 2 percent) of the 4 percent space and handling charge might represent out-of-pocket costs of handling the inventory.

If large lots were manufactured, the parts would have to be moved into the stock room, entered on the inventory cards, tagged, and shelved. When these parts were removed from inventory, it would be necessary to record their withdrawal on the inventory cards and then move them out of the stock room to the place where they would be needed. Under the company's current method of operation, bases and lock plungers were drilled only as required by the assembly line. They were then moved directly over to the next operation without going through the extra handling and record-keeping procedures of the stock room.

The company could purchase from the Thompson Machine Company two identical semiautomatic machines for drilling lock bases at a cost of $8,000 each. A separate set of tools and fixtures would be required for the drilling of each of the 13 styles of lock bases. The Thompson company would produce sets of tools and fixtures at a cost of $2,500 a set. Thus, to buy complete equipment for drilling the 13 base styles would require $16,000 for machines and $32,500 for tools and fixtures.

Drilling Plungers

Although the drilling of plungers consisted of only one operation, this operation could not be performed on automatic equipment as long as the present general-purpose machines were used for the 12 drilling operations on the bases. The positions of the holes drilled in the lock bases by general-purpose machines frequently varied slightly, and plungers had to be inserted in lock bases and drilled with general-purpose machines in order that all holes in the finished lock might be in correct alignment. The use of semiautomatic equipment would enable the company to maintain much closer tolerances in the drilling of bases, and plungers could be drilled on automatic equipment prior to their insertion without the danger that the holes in the finished lock would be out of alignment.

If the lock plungers were drilled on automatic machinery, the direct labor cost of this operation could be reduced from the existing figure of $1 per 100 plungers to $0.20 per 100. The automatic equipment, which could be quickly set up for the drilling of any type of lock plunger, would cost $11,000. This price included fixtures for drilling all types of plungers used by the company. Drilling was the last one of three machining operations performed on plungers; total labor cost of the three operations was $1.45 per 100.

Other Considerations

Thompson Machine Company was the only concern represented in Eastern Lock's area that sold this type of equipment. Over the years, Eastern Lock had bought considerable equipment from Thompson and had always been satisfied with the quality of the machinery and with Thompson's service.

Eastern Lock was currently short of cash because of recent expenditures made in connection with a cost-reduction program, and for this reason Mr. Hawkins thought that new equipment would have to be financed through bank loans. Mr. Hawkins, on consulting with the company treasurer, thought that Eastern Lock could arrange a bank loan at an interest rate of around 6 percent.

Thompson listed the expected life of the new drilling equipment as 20,000 to 25,000 hours. Eastern Lock's policy was to depreciate such machinery over 15 years. Though he had no evidence of a high obsolescence rate on this equipment, Mr. Hawkins knew that the management would expect it to pay for itself in less than the expected usable life. The company expected to earn at least 15 percent before taxes on its investments.

The five general-purpose machines being used to drill bases and plungers were about 10 years old. They were originally worth $2,000 each and currently had a depreciated value of $675 each. Their scrap value was $50 each. The plant recently had been largely reequipped, so that there was little chance that this equipment could be used elsewhere or that excess time on new equipment could be used. The new equipment would be suitable for only a few other operations in the plant.

Mr. Hawkins realized that the drilling of lock bases with semiautomatic machinery and the drilling of lock plungers with automatic equipment might increase the amount of waste. If a machine was not properly adjusted, a large number of bases or plungers might be drilled before the error was recognized. Under the company's existing method of production, waste had amounted to not more than 1 or 2 percent of total production cost.

For the 13 styles A–M, the average manufacturing cost of locks was computed to be as follows:

Manufacturing Costs per 100 Units

	Bases*	Plungers*	Others	Complete Locks
Material...................	$14.30	$0.98	$ 11.42	$ 26.70
Direct labor.................	4.40	1.45	37.95	43.80
Factory overhead.............	4.80	1.45	33.14	39.40
Total factory cost..........	$23.50	$3.89	$ 82.51	$109.90
General overhead............	9.40	0.86	19.34	29.60
Total Cost.................	$32.90	$4.75	$101.85	$139.50

* Up to and including the drilling operation only.

Questions

1. What would be the most efficient lot size for the production of base styles A, B, and D using the semiautomatic drilling equipment for bases, and assuming that only one machine is purchased?

2. Assume that the economic lot sizes of the other base styles are as follows:

Style C, 6,600 units
E, 10,700 "
F, 10,000 "
G, Same as B
H, 3,800 units

Style I, 3,800 units
J, 3,100 "
K, 3,100 "
L, 8,500 "
M, Same as B

What action do you recommend?

CASE 21–4. MOLECULAR COMPOUNDS CORPORATION

Molecular Compounds Corporation manufactured a wide variety of products in the chemical field and related areas, ranging from industrial chemicals through consumer goods. During the 1950's, MOCOM's sales had grown over 60 percent, reaching a level in excess of $700 million in 1962. The corporate executive group was extremely anxious to match or exceed this growth record in the decade from 1960 to 1970. Toward this end, it had instructed the financial and planning staff to reevaluate the methods of financial analysis to insure that adequate investments were being made.

Capital Budgeting Procedures

The fundamental objective of the company's current capital budgeting process was to maximize corporate growth and especially the growth of earnings per share. Although each division was responsible for generating projects, all divisions were expected to abide by the 12 percent minimum return on investment which was applied by the divisional financial analyst following procedures set by the central planning staff. Projects below that rate were actively discouraged and usually rejected.

The corporation had installed a standard method of computing return on investment. After experimentation with several financial measures, management chose a net aftertax cash-flow present value technique. In this measurement present valued cash outflows were subtracted from present valued cash inflows (including an estimate for recovery) to arrive at a net present value figure. From alternative investments, the one showing the highest net present value was selected, all other factors being equivalent.

Returns were also measured on an expected value basis. Division personnel were supposed to consider various alternative outcomes and calculate related cash flows. They then assigned probabilities to the flows and used the probabilities as weights to obtain an expected present value figure. This adjustment was intended to correct the "most likely" estimate for skewed probability distributions in which the "expected" result differed from the most likely estimate.

One of the problems with the present procedure, as the financial and planning group saw it, was the extent of the risk to the division or plant managers. A central staff analyst said:

It is hard to get a division manager to commit himself and his division to a project which requires new assets equal to a major percent of the assets he has allocated to him at present. The risk (probability of success or failure) to him and to his division is the same as the risk to the corporation, but the extent of the risk (the seriousness of failure) is greater. If he guesses wrong and the project is a dud, he's got to do some explaining to show why his return on assets has dropped. But the potential returns are so great that the company could afford to have several duds for each one which pans out and still come out ahead.

Sample Study

When the central financial office staff began to investigate the capital budgeting procedure, they decided to look for samples of projects which had not been submitted to the capital budget review committee but which, they felt, should have been submitted. It was difficult to locate such projects, since few detailed records existed for most projects that had not been submitted. In addition, divisional managements were naturally reluctant to admit that they might have rejected desirable opportunities. Eventually, several projects were found. One of these was a project that was proposed in the industrial products division. Excerpts from a report by the division planning manager to the division general manager follow:

SUBJECT: *Proposed plant for the manufacture of water soluble resins, to be constructed in several stages with initial capacity of 15.5 million pounds per year requiring an initial fixed investment of $7.37 million.*

BASIS OF THE STUDY

Sales Justification. About 3 billion pounds of water soluble or water dispersal resins are sold today in the United States. By 1970 the sales of these products (which include such natural products as starches and modified starches, glue, casein, and locust bean gum, and organic substitutes similar to our product) are expected to be about 4 billion pounds.

Our product, because of its potentially low price and desirable properties, should permit us to sell about 15.5 million pounds per year by 1963, as estimated by the following schedule:

Grade	Expected Sales Est.1963 (lbs.)	Est. Potential Market (lbs.)	% of Potential Market
A	5,250,000	100,950,000	5.2
B	1,250,000	25,440,000	4.9
C	7,300,000	130,000,000	5.6
D	1,700,000	55,420,000	3.1

We have an excellent, but of course not invulnerable, patent position. Although several patents are held by competitors, out patent program covering process, composition, and uses—as well as our advanced research position in the industry—should give us a very strong position in the market for this resin for many years. We believe that the company is relatively invulnerable to backward integration by potential customers since, in general, the use of the product by any one firm is not large enough to justify the required capital investment.

In reaching our estimates of potential sales volume for this product, we have been in contact with a number of possible users for the compound. On the basis of their test applications and uses, we have customers who have expressed interest in purchasing about 4 million pounds a year, assuming that all quality specifications can be met. Our projections of volume are based on our estimates of the markets in which our tests have shown our product to offer effective substitutability, because of either a significant price saving, or because of important superior qualities on a competitive pricing basis.

Our most optimistic sales estimates assume only that we will sell 155 million pounds per year by 1970 (Exhibit 1). This is a little less than 4 percent penetration into the 4 billion pound market. Our sales of 15.5 million pounds in

Exhibit 1

MOLECULAR COMPOUNDS CORPORATION

Price and Volume Ranges for Proposed Plant for
Manufacture of Water Soluble Resins

	Volume Sold			Price		
	(thousands of pounds)					
	Probable	*High*	*Low*	*Probable*	*High*	*Low*
1962	7,500	15,000	2,800	$0.69	$0.83	$0.65
1963	15,500	31,400	4,650	0.65	0.81	0.59
1964	25,500	53,000	6,700	0.60	0.77	0.53
1965	38,250	73,500	9,500	0.58	0.72	0.48
1966	49,700	92,300	11,650	0.54	0.71	0.45
1967	59,100	108,100	13,900	0.52	0.70	0.40
1968	68,500	125,800	16,250	0.47	0.65	0.38
1969	76,900	135,400	18,800	0.46	0.64	0.36
1970	85,300	155,000	21,150	0.46	0.64	0.35
1971–76	”	”	”	”	”	”

1963 will be the base on which we will build to make our product the major synthetic water soluble resin.

Cost Justification. Our analysis shows that the most economical plant alternative is to build a plant for an expected annual volume of 15.5 million pounds in such a manner that expanded facilities can be easily added up to a total of 60 million pounds annual capacity. The initial cost of the 15.5 million pound plant is estimated at $7.37 million, with the expansion possible in two stages. The first stage would bring capacity up to 25.5 million pounds per year at a cost of $1 million, and the second stage would be to full expansion of 60 million pounds at a cost of $3.5 million.

In preparing our operating costs, we have estimated that the per unit manufacturing cost would vary from $0.31 at a volume of 3 million pounds per year down to $0.20 at a volume of 50 to 60 million pounds. Distribution costs have been estimated to be relatively constant at $0.015 per pound, since we anticipate selling this product with our existing sales force and most of the incremental cost will be for shipping and packaging. The overhead costs on an incremental basis are expected to be $250,000 per year at a minimum and a maximum of $375,000 when capacity is reached.

Working capital investment (based on one month's receivables and one month's inventory) has been estimated at about 20 percent of the cost of goods sold.

Depreciation is calculated on the sum-of-the-years'-digits method.

CONCLUSIONS

Using the proposed facilities and operating schedule, comparisons were made between a number of possible marketing results. We worked with a most probable case, a conservative sales volume with high prices and one with low prices. Price and volume estimates are included in Exhibit 1. Calculations for

Exhibit 2

MOLECULAR COMPOUNDS CORPORATION

Most Probable Present Value, at 12%, of Proposed Plant for Manufacture of Water Soluble Resins
(all figures in thousands)

Calendar year: Project year:	1961 0	1962 1	1963 2	1964 3	1965 4	1966 5	1967 6	1968 7	1969 8
New fixed investment	$(2,800)	$(4,570)	.....	$(1,000)	.....	$(3,500)	.....	.....	.....
Working capital (20% cost of goods sold)	(50)	(465)	$ (310)	(500)	$ (408)	(305)	$ (376)	$ (36)	$ (36)
Total investment	$(2,850)	$(5,035)	$ (310)	$(1,500)	$ (408)	$(3,805)	$ (376)	$ (36)	$ (36)
Volume (lbs.)		7,500	15,500	25,500	38,250	49,700	59,100	60,000	60,000
Sales		$ 5,175	$10,075	$15,300	$22,185	$26,838	$30,732	$28,200	$27,600
Cost of goods sold		$ 2,325	$ 3,875	$ 6,375	$ 8,415	$ 9,940	$11,820	$12,000	$12,000
Distribution at $15 per thous. lbs.		113	233	383	574	746	887	900	900
All other costs		250	275	300	350	350	375	375	375
Total costs		$ 2,688	$ 4,383	$ 7,058	$ 9,339	$11,036	$13,082	$13,275	$13,275
Operating income		$ 2,487	$ 5,692	$ 8,242	$12,846	$15,802	$17,650	$14,925	$14,325
Depreciation (sum-of-the-years'-digits)		921	860	941	869	1,380	1,254	1,129	1,004
Income before tax		$ 1,566	$ 4,832	$ 7,301	$11,977	$14,422	$16,396	$13,796	$13,321
Income after tax		$ 752	$ 2,319	$ 3,504	$ 5,749	$ 6,923	$ 7,870	$ 6,622	$ 6,394
Annual cash income		$ 1,673	$ 3,179	$ 4,445	$ 6,618	$ 8,303	$ 9,124	$ 7,751	$ 7,398
Annual cash flow	$(2,850)	$(3,362)	$ 2,869	$ 2,945	$ 6,210	$ 4,498	$ 8,748	$ 7,715	$ 7,398
12% present value factors	1.000	0.893	0.797	0.712	0.636	0.566	0.507	0.452	0.404
Annual present values	$(2,850)	$(3,002)	$(2,287)	$ 2,097	$ 3,950	$ 2,550	$ 4,435	$ 3,487	$ 2,989

Capacity: 1961, 15.5 million lbs.; 1964, 25.5 million; 1966, 60 million.

Unit Cost: 1962, $0.31; 1963, $0.25; 1964, $0.25; 1965, $0.22; 1966, $0.20.

NOTE: Because of space limitations, figures for 1970–76 are omitted. In each of these years, operating income is $14,325; depreciation declines, so the income before tax, income after tax, and annual cash flow change each year. The annual cash flow decreases from $7,333 in 1970 to $6,941 in 1976, and the present value decreases from $2,647 in 1970 to $1,270 in 1976.

the most probable case are included as a sample in Exhibit 2. Our most probable estimate produced a net present value cash flow of $29,555,000 at 12 percent and a discounted cash flow return of about 50 percent. The results of the various calculations are summarized below and have been assigned relative probabilities.

Case	Net PV at 12% (000)	Internal Rate of Return	Probability	Expected Net PV at 12% (000)	Expected Internal Rate of Return
Most probable...............	$29,555	50+%	.40	$11,822	20%
Conservative sales volume— high price.................	10,006	33	.10	1,001	3
Conservative sales volume— low price.................	(1,170)	9	.25	(293)	2
Optimistic sales volume— high price.................	68,260	100+	.10	6,826	10
Optimistic sales volume— low price.................	24,904	50+	.15	3,736	8
Total expected amounts.......			1.00	$23,092	43%

All our estimates were well above the demanded cutoff rate except the one instance when a low volume would be combined with a low price. Even weighting this likelihood heavily did not alter the final figure significantly, since the expected return is over 40% and the net expected PV is over $23 million.

RECOMMENDATIONS

The planning department believes that the substantial returns this project offers make the investment of $7,370,000 well worth the risk and recommends that this facility be included in the annual appropriations request.

The division general manager, industrial products division, replied to the division planning manager as follows:

SUBJECT: *Memorandum report on water soluble resin plant.*

I am returning your proposal to you for further analysis. I do not feel that the market potential and objectives for the market share and sales volume have been evaluated thoroughly enough. To extrapolate to 155 million pounds on the basis of a few containers sent to potential customers seems more than slightly unrealistic. It also seems clear that to compare this volume with the four billion pound total market is unrealistic.

To advance with a $7 million project on the basis of guesses as to the market seems to me unreasonable. The desirability of the project is no better than the accuracy of the guesses! Thus, I am not willing to proceed with the project until I am sure that it can be counted on to be of advantage to the company's return on investment.

Questions

1. Do you agree with the division general manager's reaction to the proposed project?
2. What steps could the company take to insure that worthwhile projects come to management's attention?
3. What changes, if any, do you recommend in the analytical procedures used by the company?

CASE 21–5. POLLARD APPLIANCE CORPORATION

Sitting in the controller's office of the Pollard Appliance Corporation was Austin Frederick, the company's pricing policy manager. The situation which Frederick was discussing with Controller Will Packer involved a pricing dispute between the corporation's chrome products division (manufacturing) and its electric stove division (marketing). The dispute centered on which division should be charged for costs associated with a quality improvement in the tops of the company's electric stoves.

The Pollard Appliance Corporation was a large integrated manufacturer of all types of home appliances. The company had a decentralized divisional organization, consisting of four product (marketing) divisions, four manufacturing divisions, and six staff offices. An organization chart appears in Exhibit 1.

Each division and staff office was headed by a vice president. The staff offices had functional authority over their counterparts in the divisions, but they had no direct line authority over the divisional general managers. The company organization manual stated: "All division personnel are responsible to the division manager. Except in functional areas specifically delegated, staff personnel have no line authority in a division."

The product divisions designed, engineered, assembled, and marketed various home appliances. They manufactured very few component parts; rather, they assembled the appliances from parts purchased either from the manufacturing divisions or from outside vendors.

As for the manufacturing divisions, they made most of their sales (about 75 percent) to the product divisions. Parts made by a manufacturing division were generally designed by a product division; the manufacturing divisions merely produced the part to specifications provided to them.

Interdivisional pricing was an important element in divisional profitability because of the high proportion of the manufacturing divisions' production that was sold to the product divisions. The divisions were

Exhibit 1

POLLARD APPLIANCE CORPORATION

Organization Chart

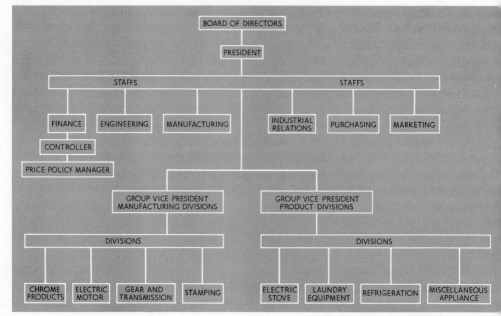

expected to deal with one another as though they were independent companies, and parts were to be transferred at competitive prices arrived at by negotiations between the divisions. Competitive price levels were generally determined from actual prices paid to outside suppliers for the same or comparable parts. These outside prices were adjusted to reflect differences in the design of the part bought from a supplier from that of the part made by Pollard. Also, if the outside price was based on purchases made at an earlier date, it was adjusted for changes in the general price level since that date.

In general, the divisions established prices by negotiations among themselves. If the divisions could not agree on a price, they could submit the dispute to the finance staff for arbitration. Responsibility for settling pricing disputes rested with the pricing policy manager, who reported to the company's controller.

Negotiations between divisions were not always conducted as though divisions were independent companies. This was true because the product division doing the buying did not have the power to decide whether to buy from within the company or from an outside supplier. Once a manufacturing division began to produce a part, the only way the buying division could change to an outside supplier was to obtain permission of the manufacturing division, or in case of disagreement, to appeal to the purchasing staff. The purchasing staff had the authority to settle disputes of this kind between the product and manufacturing divisions. In nearly every case of dispute the purchasing staff had decided that the part would continue to be manufactured within the company. When the buying divisions were instructed to continue buying a part inside, the manufacturing division had to price the part at the level that the buying division could purchase the part from an outside vendor.

In the case of new parts, the buying division had the authority to decide on the source of supply. However, a manufacturing division could appeal to the purchasing staff to reverse a decision of a product division to purchase a part from an outside vendor.

Stove-Top Problem

The dispute between the chrome products division and the electric stove division had been going on for several months, and concerned the chrome-plated unit which fitted on top of the company's stoves. Pricing policy manager Frederick explained the situation to the controller, Packer.

FREDERICK: As you know, our chrome products division produces chrome-plated stove tops for the electric stove division. They have been making them since the beginning of last year, when the electric stove division stopped buying them from outside.

PACKER: Were there problems that led to our wanting to make the top ourselves?

FREDERICK: Well, the unit has to be corrosion and stain resistant, and it must remain bright and new looking. I suspect that having it made inside the company meant better quality control.

PACKER: Was the stove-top unit affected by President Pollard's quality improvement program?

FREDERICK: Actually, that's what gave birth to the problem. After Mr. Pollard got Hind's staff into the quality improvement business, quality control standards on the stove-top unit were changed.

[About the middle of 1962, President Pollard became concerned over customer and dealer complaints about the quality of the company's products. A consumer survey indicated that in the previous year the company's reputation as a producer of quality products had deteriorated. Although this deterioration in reputation was caused principally by the poor performance of a new electric motor—a fault which was soon corrected—the president had come to the conclusion that the overall quality of the company's products had been deteriorating for the past several years. Furthermore, he believed it was essential for the company to reestablish itself as a leader in the production of quality products. Accordingly, in early 1963 the president called in Lee Hind, the manufacturing staff vice president, and told him that for the next six months his most important job was to bring the quality of all Pollard products up to a satisfactory level.]

PACKER: What were the changes?

FREDERICK: As I understand it, when the stove-top unit was first manu-factured by the chrome products division, it went through a five-step process —buffing, nickel plating, more buffing, chrome plating, and a final buffing. The quality control standards for rejection or acceptance were a corrosion test and an appearance test. And . . .

PACKER: . . . the appearance had to be improved!

Exhibit 2

ARGUMENTS IN CHROME PRODUCTS—ELECTRIC STOVE DISPUTE

Chrome Products Division believes it is entitled to the increased price:

1. We have been required by the manufacturing staff to add operations to our manufacturing processing at a cost of 40¢ a unit; we did not institute the change, and should not be forced to pay for it.

2. These operations have resulted in improved quality that could benefit only the Electric Stove Division. Since the payoff is in the market place, the Electric Stove Division should pay for these benefits.

3. The present price of $5 is based on old quality standards. Had the outside supplier been required to meet these new standards, its price would have been 45¢ higher.

Electric Stove Division believes it should not pay the increased price:

1. There was no change in engineering specifications, only a change in what was purported to be "acceptable appearance." This is a subjective matter which cannot be measured with any degree of precision.

Moreover, this case could establish a precedent: if we were to pay for any change in quality standards not accompanied by a change in engineering specifications, we would be opening up a Pandora's box. Every division would request higher prices because of giving us better quality based on some subjec-tive standard. Every request by this division to a manufacturing division to improve quality would be accompanied by a price increase, even though we were requesting only that the quality be brought up to competitive levels. If we are to maintain control over costs, we cannot have every complaint about quality result in higher costs.

2. The Electric Stove Division did not request that quality be improved. In fact, we were *not even consulted* on the change. Thus, the division should not be responsible for paying for a so-called improvement which it neither reviewed nor approved.

3. Even if the division had been consulted, we probably would have rejected the change. It is doubtful that there is any improvement in quality *from the customer's viewpoint*. Perhaps to the highly trained eye of the quality control personnel there may have been an improvement. But the customer would not notice a significant difference between the appearance of the part before and after the change in quality standards.

4. Furthermore, even if there were an improvement in quality perceptible to the consumer, we believe strongly that it is not worth 45¢. For 45¢ per unit, we could add features that would be far more marketable than this quality improvement.

5. Any improvement in quality only brought the part up to the quality level that the former outside producer had provided. The cost of the improved quality, therefore, was already included in the $5 price.

FREDERICK: Exactly. Hind apparently decided the appearance was unsatisfactory. He selected several of the better looking units as standards of minimum appearance quality, and the reject rate started to skyrocket. So the divisional and plant staff, together with Hind's staff, studied the operation and added copper plating and buffing steps at the beginning of the manufacturing process and a hand-buffing operation at the end of the cycle.

PACKER: I assume that this solved the quality problem, and at the same time created the pricing problem.

FREDERICK: Right. The appearance quality rejections dropped to under 1 percent, and the chrome products division proposed to add the 40-cent per unit cost of the new operations to the price of the stove-top unit, as well as a 5-cent profit markup. That brought the price per unit from $5 [$4.50 was the outside supplier's price when the chrome products division took over, plus $0.25 for design changes and $0.25 for price increases since then] to $5.45.

You can guess the rest: the electric stove division objected to the proposed price increase (the wailing was audible for miles), and after three weeks of fruitless negotiations the dispute was submitted to us two weeks ago.

PACKER: What's happened since then?

FREDERICK: Well, first we examined the arguments of each side. I've summarized them in this memorandum [Exhibit 2]. We also instituted a review of the added operation by the engineering department and the quality control department of the manufacturing staff. The former reported that the proposed costs were reasonable and represented efficient processing; the latter stated that the quality of the stove-top unit's appearance was definitely improved and that the new units were superior in quality to those purchased from outside sources 18 months ago.

PACKER (reading through arguments): This sure looks like a tough one . . .

FREDERICK: . . . and either way, as it always is in these pricing disputes, someone's going to be plenty annoyed!

Question

1. How should this dispute be resolved?

CASE 21–6.   HARRYMAN MANUFACTURING COMPANY

In January, 1961, Mr. Henry Harryman, president and principal stockholder of Harryman Manufacturing Company, was reviewing the results of recent periods' operations in preparation for a staff meeting the following week at which plans for 1961 were to be discussed.

By specializing in a single product and emphasizing quality, Harryman Manufacturing Company had established and maintained an excellent reputation among the industrial purchasers of its product. Henry Harryman had founded the company, and it was a matter of great pride and satisfaction to him that in the past five years there had been a significant increase in the demand for his product. He was convinced that the primary reason for this increased demand was his determination to maintain high quality without increasing his selling price, which had been held at $7.95 per unit for several years. His basic philosophy was that increased costs of factors of production should be and could be offset by increased efficiencies. In this way, the workers (directly or indirectly) could earn and rightfully share the benefits of increased efficiencies, the shareholders would share the benefits of growth in demand and investment, and the community would share the benefits of a secure and growing work force.

As the founder of the company, Mr. Harryman had been continuously

Exhibit 1

HARRYMAN MANUFACTURING COMPANY

A. Comparative Income Statements

	1958 $	1958 %	1959 $	1959 %	1960 $	1960 %
Sales...............	$1,168,650	100.0	$1,462,800	100.0	$1,550,250	100.0
Cost of sales........	900,007	77.0	1,117,462	76.4	1,188,343	76.7
Gross margin..... $	268,643	23.0	$ 345,338	23.6	$ 361,907	23.3
Selling expenses..... $	185,400	15.9	$ 209,600	14.3	$ 217,060	14.0
General and administrative expense*...	116,000	9.9	129,250	8.8	139,730	9.0
	$ 301,400	25.8	$ 338,850	23.1	$ 356,790	23.0
Income (Loss)†..... $	(32,757)	(2.8)	$ 6,488	0.5	$ 5,117	0.3

* General and administrative expense includes $2,600 depreciation of office furniture and equipment in each of the three years.

† Because there were not more than 10 shareholders, they had been able to elect "partnership-type taxation" under the provisions of the Internal Revenue Code. No corporate income tax was imposed.

B. Comparative Statements of Working Capital, December 31

	1958	1959	1960
Cash.................................	$ 51,460	$100,940	$107,510
Accounts receivable.....................	238,270	289,440	304,880
Finished goods inventory*................	128,541	78,871	182,880
Raw materials inventory*................	57,240	53,000	81,700
Total Current Assets.................	$475,511	$522,251	$676,970
Accounts payable.......................	$169,580	$184,610	$204,930
Note payable (due Dec. 1)..............	......	......	100,000
Total Current Liabilities...............	$169,580	$184,610	$304,930
Working Capital......................	$305,931	$337,641	$372,040

* The raw materials inventory was valued at the average purchase price experienced that year. The finished goods inventory was valued at the average manufacturing cost experienced that year. There was no work in process at the end of the year. Accordingly, at the end of the year, raw materials used and cost of goods sold were determined by a simplified form of Fifo. The inventory at the beginning of the year was costed out first; subsequent raw material usage and product sales were costed at the average cost for the year. For example for 1959:

			Finished Goods
Beginning inventory................	21,000 units at $6.121	....	$ 128,541
Produced and sold.................	163,000 units at 6.067	....	988,921
Cost of sales....................	184,000 units	....	$1,117,462
Ending inventory..................	13,000 units at 6.067	....	$ 78,871

and intimately involved in all its affairs. Indeed, it was not uncommon to find him in the plant, with sleeves rolled up, actively supervising and participating in various manufacturing problems. Because of his close personal relationship, control procedures had been either nonexistent or very informal. However, by January 1961, Mr. Harryman was fearful that at the current level of operations things were getting out of hand. The year 1960 had been a record year in terms of sales, but the profit picture was discouraging (see Exhibit 1).

Mr. Harryman noted that manufacturing costs had remained reasonably constant in spite of some cost increases. For example, a general wage increase which averaged $0.10 per hour went into effect January 1, 1960, yet the total manufacturing cost per unit of product, which included a total of about one hour of direct labor, increased only about $0.03. In addition, purchase price of raw materials had been creeping up year by year. During 1958, the purchase price of enough raw materials for one unit of finished product amounted to $2.12; during 1960, it was up to $2.15. Under the circumstances, Mr. Harryman was pleased that manufacturing cost per unit had declined from $6.121 in 1958 to $6.096 in 1960 (see Exhibit 2). Furthermore, selling expense as a percent of sales had been declining, and general and administrative expense as a percent of sales was up only slightly over 1959. Mr. Harryman was puzzled over the failure to show increased profits with increased sales.

Upon commenting to this effect to Mr. Jeffry Barrington, treasurer-controller, Barrington argued that the average manufacturing cost per unit was misleading. Barrington reasoned that some of the manufacturing costs were fixed and some were only semivariable. Accordingly, he suggested that a more detailed analysis of 1960 operations was required in order to determine the reasons for poor profit performance and to identify the best sources of future cost savings.

Mr. Harryman countered by suggesting that the relationship between 1958 and 1959 represented a reasonable and desirable trend and that if Barrington felt it would reveal anything, "Why not 'analyze' 1960 in relationship to 1959?"

Another matter of some concern to Mr. Harryman was also discussed with Mr. Barrington:

Every year you tell me our working capital has increased, yet, in spite of the general soundness of our operations and two profitable years, we had to borrow $100,000 during 1960 merely to meet normal operating expenses. Can you look into your crystal ball and tell me if we are going to be able to repay that $100,000 next December when the note becomes due, or will I have to ask for an extension, or possibly borrow additional cash?

Bill Dunbar (sales manager) says that next year we are going to have our biggest year of all. He says that he has worked it out very carefully and that he expects sales of 250,000 units during 1961. We had better try to look ahead

Exhibit 2

HARRYMAN MANUFACTURING COMPANY

A. Comparative Manufacturing Statements

	1958		1959		1960	
	total	unit	total	unit	total	unit
Raw materials.........	$316,040	$2.135	$ 378,130	$2.148	$ 456,640	$2.154
Direct labor...........	$378,880	2.560	$ 447,040	2.540	$ 555,440	2.620
Factory overhead:						
Indirect labor........	$119,200		$ 131,920		$ 154,530	
Supervision...........	31,800		31,800		35,000	
Power..............	19,400		21,310		23,450	
Maintenance.........	12,600		29,570		35,110	
Depreciation.........	22,600		22,600		26,750	
Insurance and taxes....	5,400		5,400		5,500	
Total overhead......	$211,000	1.426	$ 242,600	1.379	$ 280,340	1.322
Total manufacturing costs	$905,920	$6.121	$1,067,770	$6.067	$1,292,420	$6.096

B. Sales, Production, and Inventory Statistics
(in units of product)

	1956	1957	1958	1959	1960
Sales forecast.....................	120,000	125,000	140,000	160,000	200,000
Actual sales......................	114,000	130,000	147,000	184,000	195,000
Actual sales/sales forecast..........	95%	104%	105%	115%	97.5%
Actual production.................	120,000	124,000	148,000	176,000	212,000
Raw materials inventory, Dec. 31...	30,000	34,000	27,000	25,000	38,000
Finished goods inventory, Dec. 31...	26,000	20,000	21,000	13,000	30,000

and see what that means. This outfit is getting to be quite an operation. When we get together next week we had better plan more carefully than we ever have before.

We have an awful time with our inventories, too, don't we! We always seem to end up with too much or too little. Why can't we get Bill Dunbar and Andy Pitman (production manager) together and see if we can't improve our coordination? For a long time we have been striving to maintain about 60 days' supply of finished goods and 90 days' supply of raw materials. We haven't any seasonal problems to speak of, so it shouldn't be difficult, but we seldom seem to accomplish our goal.

A few days before the scheduled planning meeting, Bill Dunbar (sales manager) entered Mr. Harryman's office with an air of obvious elation and said,

I finally sold Lind Company! I have spent five years trying to convince them that they should be buying our product and I finally succeeded. They drive a hard bargain, however. They want a firm contract for 25,000 units per year for the next five years at a flat $7 per unit. That makes them our second best customer, right next to Huntington Machine Works.

Lind knows that $7 is below our standard selling price, but there would be no chance to get them to switch to us on any other basis. Anyhow, I am convinced we can make money on the deal. The only additional selling expenses will be the regular 5 percent commission. There shouldn't be any increase in G.&A.—after all, they pay their bills promptly, and it is a five-year contract. Pitman (production manager) tells me that we have the capacity to produce 300,000 units a year without expanding the building or buying more machines, so we will only have to pay for additional materials and labor. Surely that will run well below $6 per unit, won't it? And just think, this 25,000 units plus the 250,000 which I have calculated as a reasonable expectation for our regular demand, ought to really make a killing for us next year!

Questions

1. Comment upon each expense and manufacturing cost in terms of the difference in performance in 1960 as compared to 1959. In what areas, if any, might corrective action be taken during 1961?
2. Assuming that during 1961 the level of both sales and production will be 250,000 units, prepare an answer for Mr. Harryman's question concerning cash needs. Support your conclusion with adequate calculations and explanations.
3. Given the greater need for more careful planning and control as Harryman Manufacturing Company increases its production, what level of production would you recommend for 1961 (exclusive of Lind's proposal)? Justify your answer.
4. What kinds of costs or losses are apt to be associated with plans which are based on a predicted level of sales which is too high? Too low? (Calculations are not expected in answers to this question.)
5. What should Harryman Manufacturing Company do about the five-year contract with Lind Company for 25,000 units per year at $7 per unit? Justify your decision.

CASE 21–7. C. R. HAYES, INC.

Mr. F. W. Walker, the personnel manager of C. R. Hayes, Inc., a department store doing a business of approximately $40 million annually, was charged with the responsibility for all matters relating to personnel in the store. He arranged for the hiring and the firing of all the store salespeople and also considered all salary increases and decreases of both selling and nonselling employees.

It was the policy of the store to review a salesperson's record every 12 months on the anniversary of his entrance into the store. On the anniversary date the salesperson's department manager received a form raising the question of whether or not the weekly rate should be increased. If this form was returned with the approval of the department manager, a salesperson's record would be examined in detail. Recommendations for increases required the approval of the store manager and the personnel manager as well as the department head. A salesperson could ask the personnel manager directly for an increase in salary at any time, but such requests were not very common.

While most of the salespeople were compensated with a salary, it was the practice of the store in a few departments to pay commissions instead. These departments included men's and women's better shoes, men's clothing, furniture, and appliances. Commission percentages varied among the departments, depending on the average sale price and time required to sell an item in the department. Every salesperson in a particular department received the same commission percentage, so no individual compensation reviews were required of personnel in commission departments. The department commission rates were reviewed periodically and adjusted when the mix or prices of goods sold in the department changed significantly. In general, these commission departments were staffed with senior salespeople of proved ability who had begun working for the store on a salary in another department and had then been transferred.

Early in March 1966, Mr. Walker had on his desk, awaiting action, three requests for increases in salary resulting from anniversary reviews. The applicants were from different departments of the store, one being from the women's shoe department, another from the stationery department, and the third from the silverware department. In addition to these three, Mr. Walker had received a personal request for a raise from Mr. Perrin, who sold boys' shoes.

In considering the merits of requests for increases, Mr. Walker examined first the sales performance of the salespersons. The store maintained records of the salaries and sales of all salespersons in order to facilitate fair judgment of their accomplishments, since clearly the store could afford to pay higher salaries only to salespeople maintaining a high volume of sales. Greatest attention was paid to the direct selling expense ratios, that is, selling salaries or commissions divided by sales volume, since pressure was constantly maintained to reduce the selling costs of the store. This expense ratio was recorded monthly for each salesperson. Store executives regularly examined this ratio for departments and for the store as a whole. In 1965, the sales expense ratio for the store as a whole had been 6.8 percent.

Sales and Expense Data

Of the four salespeople whose salaries were under review, the lowest expense ratio was that of Miss Marsten, who was employed in the silverware department. In the year ended January 31, 1966,[2] Miss Marsten sold $92,819 worth of merchandise. Her salary payments during the year totaled $3,196. Thus, her selling costs were 3.1 percent of sales. Miss Young, in the women's shoe department, had been paid $3,510 during the same period, which was 6.9 percent of her sales volume of $50,836. Salary payments to Mr. Dagmar, in the stationery department, amounted to $2,800, translating to 6.1 percent of his selling volume of $45,960. Mr. Perrin, who was selling boys' shoes, was paid a salary of $3,666, which in 1965 was 12.1 percent of his sales volume of $30,096.

In addition to salary or commission, shoe salespeople were able to gain extra pay by selling merchandise that the store wished to move. These special bonuses for sales of "premium merchandise" were called P.M.'s. Such premium payments were not classed with salaries or commissions in calculating expense ratios and therefore had no bearing on the performance record of the various salespeople. In 1965 Miss Young received $132 in P.M.'s and Mr. Perrin received $130.

In terms of service, Mr. Perrin had been with the store the longest, having come on December 4, 1937; Miss Marsten joined the store in January 1947; Miss Young came in January 1956; and Mr. Dagmar had been with the store only since December 1964.

The sales records of these four salespeople for the three years, 1963, 1964, and 1965, are shown in Exhibit 1 with similar records for other salespeople in the respective departments and in three additional departments. The sales figure for each department as a whole is in every instance larger than the sum of the sales of the salespeople listed, for several reasons. C. R. Hayes, Inc., in common with many other department stores, was open for business more than 50 hours a week, whereas the regular full-time salespeople were employed for a 40-hour workweek. This required the use of short-hour and extra people, a group in which there was considerable turnover. Members of the store's flying squad also were used to supplement the regulars when additional salespeople were required. The selling expense ratio for each department reflected wage payments for all the selling man-hours used in relation to total departmental sales. Wage payments included vacation pay for regular employees.

The Departments Involved

In examining the merits of the four applicants, Mr. Walker had to consider other information. For one thing, the physical arrangements for selling were by no means the same in all departments. In the shoe

---

[2] Like many department stores, C. R. Hayes, Inc., maintained records for fiscal years running from February 1 through January 31, rather than for the calendar year from January 1 through December 31. The term "1965" as used in this case refers to the year ended January 31, 1966.

Exhibit 1

DIRECT SELLING EXPENSE RATIO AND RELATED DATA

Department	Direct Selling Expense Ratio			Sales			Entrance Date	Date of Last Raise	Current Weekly Salary
	1963	1964	1965	1963	1964	1965			
Women's Shoes:									
Entire department	9.4	8.7	9.5	$510,506	$536,328	$538,774			
Miss Clark	9.3	8.5	8.5	34,930	40,274	40,833	2/50	2/63	$66.00
Mr. Enders	9.3	9.0	9.2	39,673	42,805	43,024	9/62	9/65	78.50
Mr. Elliot	8.8	8.3	9.1	42,386	46,066	44,168	10/53	10/65	78.50
Miss Aspinwald†	8.3	8.0	8.2	33,885	35,982	35,009	9/32	9/62	55.00
Mr. Smith	8.2	7.9	8.2	45,366	47,306	47,805	2/52	2/65	76.00
Miss Sanders	7.8	7.4	7.4	52,108	54,233	54,593	12/55	12/62	77.50
Mr. Hanking	9.0	9.0	9.5	40,280	41,355	41,878	5/62	5/65	78.50
Miss Johnson	8.6	8.0	7.9	40,707	45,147	47,108	11/51	11/63	71.50
Miss Young*	7.5	7.2	6.9	45,995	48,472	50,836	1/56	1/63	73.00
Boy's Shoes:									
Mr. Perrin*	12.7	12.4	12.2	29,107	29,745	30,096	12/37	10/59	70.50
Women's Better Shoes:									
Entire department	7.9	7.9	7.9	231,296	291,370	288,794			
Mrs. Green		7.9	7.9	......	50,037	49,780	10/40	....	#
Mrs. Bourgeois	7.9	7.9	7.9	57,685	55,814	59,514	3/39	....	#
Miss Ransom	7.9	7.9	7.9	52,110	55,732	54,290	3/34	....	#
Mr. Cotton	7.9	7.9	7.9	50,776	50,709	52,712	2/50	....	#
Miss McNeil	7.9	7.9	7.9	54,248	58,021	56,009	7/43	....	#
Stationery:									
Entire department	9.0	7.8	7.2	341,137	381,184	449,940			
Miss Bard	10.1	10.1	9.0	29,828	29,346	32,794	11/62	11/63	57.00
Miss Cox	9.0	8.1	7.4	34,112	37,096	39,993	3/44	3/62	57.00

Mr. Dagmar*	..	..	6.1	......	......	45,960	12/64	....	56.00
Miss Dorn	7.1	7.0	6.4	......	43,747	47,442	9/63	....	58.50
Miss Gordon	6.3	6.3	5.6	40,564	45,584	52,143	8/51	8/63	56.00
Miss Scott	8.3	7.4	6.6	36,239	39,560	45,355	3/56	3/62	57.50
Miss Seick	6.4	6.4	5.5	45,325	46,909	53,626	4/62	4/63	57.00
Silverware:									
Entire department	6.1	4.9	5.1	220,948	302,518	325,202			
Miss Hitchcock	5.2	4.5	4.3	67,232	78,049	80,173	1/46	1/62	67.00
Miss Marsten*	4.2	3.6	3.1	80,902	88,561	92,819	1/47	1/63	68.00
Miss Santos	..	7.1	6.1	......	41,014	48,001	1/64	....	56.00
Miss Morse	..	..	5.8	......	......	36,743	4/65	....	56.00
Women's and Children's Hosiery:									
Entire department	6.3	7.0	7.2	475,087	460,011	405,255			
Miss Austin†	7.1	7.9	10.2	29,395	26,333	20,370	3/62	....	56.00
Miss Banter	6.5	5.9	5.6	46,237	51,649	54,511	12/61	12/63	58.50
Mr. Boyle	5.3	5.2	5.9	55,826	56,866	49,188	10/62	....	56.00
Mrs. Epstein	7.1	7.6	8.1	45,513	42,316	39,971	8/52	8/62	62.00
Mrs. Hawkes	6.0	5.6	5.7	50,200	53,770	53,118	3/62	....	58.00
Miss Moore	6.1	6.4	7.2	49,496	46,345	41,858	10/53	10/63	58.00
Miss Oppenheimer	5.7	6.1	6.8	51,120	48,815	43,544	12/61	12/63	57.00
Entire store: All selling departments	7.1	6.6	6.8						

† Part-time worker.
* Salary under review.
# Commission compensation.

departments, salespeople could serve any customer at any point on the floor. Shoe salespeople were not behind counters, as were the salespeople in the silverware department. Also, since selling shoes required a good knowledge of proper fitting, styles, and so forth, the customer frequently would ask for the services of a particular person.

The silverware department, manned regularly by four full-time salespeople, sold hollow ware, flatware, and small novelty and gift items. Whereas everyone was allowed to sell any of the merchandise, the position of the cash drawers operated by the several persons was such that as a practical matter the situation was one of "station selling," with the old-timers responsible for the flatware and hollow ware, and the newer people taking care of the novelty items. This department was particularly busy at certain times of the year when special promotions were made.

In the stationery department a variety of goods were sold, ranging from card tables to cameras. The arrangement of selling space in this department was not particularly good. On one side of the department were two long counters, back to back, with stationery displayed and sold on both sides. Access to the position behind the counters was at the ends only. To the right of this double counter were several aisle tables from which department items were sold. In addition, a facing wall counter beyond the aisle tables was provided, this position being used in 1965 for the sales of greeting cards at one end and cameras and related equipment and supplies at the other. Mr. Dagmar, in charge of the cameras, was the employee here whose compensation was up for review. The camera section of the stationery department had been established February 1, 1965.

Mr. Perrin was the only regular salesman in the boys' shoe department, which was a small department located next to the boys' clothing department. If a customer was waiting to be sold boys' clothing and Mr. Perrin was not busy, he often stepped across the aisle and made the sales in the other department, although he received no credit for such sales. When Mr. Perrin had first joined the store, he had sold men's clothing. During World War II and the years following, he had been working on a straight commission basis, which in a period of high consumer demand yielded a substantially larger income than did the salaries received in many of the other departments. In 1961 he had been transferred to the boys' shoe department, where salary compensation was employed. Thus his earnings had been considerably reduced, and he was anxious to obtain a salary increase. Mr. Walker, on inquiring of a noncompeting department store, found that its expense ratio was 11 percent in the boys' shoe department, where two people were employed.

Merchandise sold in the various departments was priced at different levels, and the unit sales usually varied accordingly. The dollar amount per sales check in the silverware department averaged $17.40 in 1965; in the stationery department, the average sales check was $1.50; in the women's shoe department, it was $15.20; and in the boys' shoe department, it was $8.60.

Miscellaneous Information

The personnel department had the full history of each salesperson's performance. Records were kept on absences, tardiness, and on any infringements of the store rules. In addition, the department managers were asked to rate the salespeople in their department as to sales ability, stock care, cooperation, and general suitability. The rating of sales ability was supposed to take into account sales volume, credits (merchandise returned), merchandise knowledge, and service. "Stock care" referred to the salesperson's method of handling merchandise and keeping stock in good order. In judging cooperation the managers were supposed to consider the salesperson's record in carrying out store rules, compliance with instructions, punctuality, adaptability, judgment, helpfulness to others, and special effort. In rating suitability the managers considered the fitness, by personality, appearance, attendance, interest in job, and so forth, of the salesperson for the particular department and position from the point of view of both the customer and the store. The records on these points for the four people whose salaries were under review were satisfactory.

The employees of C. R. Hayes, Inc., had been organized into a store union since the middle of 1945. This was an independent union, not affiliated with any other labor organization, and was the outgrowth of an old cooperative union which had been established in the store. The union had taken no position in regard to the four cases being reviewed by Mr. Walker.

Questions

1. There are many yardsticks against which the performance of the four employees being considered for raises can be measured. For example, their selling expense ratios can be compared with the overall ratio for the store, with the average ratio for the department, with ratios for prior years, and so on. Which of these yardsticks is of most significance to Mr. Walker?
2. What action should Mr. Walker recommend with respect to each of the four employees being considered for raises?

CASE 21–8. CANTON COMPANY

The Canton Company, a manufacturer of office supplies, sold to wholesalers and retailers. The company wished to establish standards by which the efficiency of the packers in the shipping room could be judged each week. If the standards proved satisfactory, the company expected to put packing on a piecework basis.

The company carried about 5,000 items in its warehouse. Items ordered were picked from the warehouse shelves, assembled in metal containers, and sent by gravity conveyors to the shipping room. There the goods were transferred to another gravity conveyor that ran between two lines of packers. Each packer was located next to a side track leading off from the main conveyor. The space occupied by a packer was called a "pocket." There were six pockets on one side of the conveyor and four pockets on the other side, as shown n Exhibit 1. The manager rotated the

Exhibit 1

CANTON COMPANY

Diagram of Conveyor Used in Packing Room

men from pocket to pocket, so that a man occupied each pocket one week and usually did not occupy the same pocket again until he had occupied every other pocket. The men usually occupied the pockets in the following order: 6, 5, 4, 3, 2, 1, 7, 8, 9, 10.

As the metal containers of merchandise to be packed came slowly down the conveyor, the packers pulled them onto the side tables that formed their pockets. There they packed the merchandise in corrugated cardboard cartons, and shipping labels were affixed. Within limits, the management found it possible to adjust the number of packers to the amount of work to be done. Ordinarily there was work for 10 packers; if not, one of the packers was temporarily withdrawn.

The time-study department worked out a method for giving a standard time allowance quickly for packing each shipment. This standard time varied according to the number of packages going into each carton and the numbers of cartons per order. This method of assigning standards necessarily was rough, but it was felt that since an average man packed about 18 cartons an hour, each man would get the same chance at the various types of packing in the course of a week. Before putting into effect a system of piecework based on such standards, however, the company decided to test it by trial. The manager of the packing department kept a record showing, for each man, the percentage of standard

Exhibit 2

PERCENTAGE OF EFFICIENCY ATTAINED BY PACKERS IN SHIPPING ROOM

Week Ending	A		B		C		D		E		F		G	
	Pocket	Per-centage	Pocket	Per-centage	Pocket	Per-centage	Pocket	Per-centage	Pocket	Per-centage	Pocket	Per-centage	Pocket	Per-centage
July 5	2	72	6	70	9	69	8	119	5	91			1	80
12	1	70	5	76			9	102	4	83			7	108
19	7	75	4	75	6	67	10	91	3	76			8	79
26	8	63	3	82	5	66	6	74	2	77			9	67
Aug. 2	9	56	2	92	4	74	5	80	1	85	8	95		
9	10	68	1	95	3	81	4	96	7	89	9	76	6	46
16	6	57	7	120	2	79	3	103			10	90	5	64
23	5	71	8	81	1	90	2	90	9	63	6	76	4	72
30	4	69	9	65	7	106	1	115	10	74	5	80	3	73
Sept. 6	3	71	10	81	8	68	7	121	6	64	4	88	2	74
13	2	77	6	71	9	75	8	113	5	83	3	98	1	91
20	1	79	5	79	10	66			4	90	2	91	7	94
27	7	86	4	85	6	66	10	90	3	84	1	104	8	61
Oct. 4	8	74	3	93	5	71	6	79	2	101	7	119	9	62
11	9	70	2	99	4	75	5	86	1	110	8	106	10	60
18	10	74	1	122	3	71	4	94	7	92	9	98	6	70
25	6	61	7	115	2	80	3	101	8	88	10	93	5	68
Nov. 1	5	66	8	103	1	86	2	103	9	75	6	85	4	71
8	4	80	9	88	7	107	1	114	10	84	5	90	3	72
15	3	91	10	78	8	86	7	120	6	81	4	104	2	84
22	2	89	6	83	9	73	8	103	5	92	3	103	1	83
29	1	98	5	81	10	68	9	98	4	90	2	96	7	107
Total		1,617		1,934		1,624		2,092		1,772		1,692		1,586
No. of Weeks		22		22		21		21		21		18		21
Average		73.5		87.9		77.2		99.6		84.4		94.0		75.5

time to actual time. He called this the percentage of efficiency. The packers were told that they would be judged according to this percentage of efficiency.

Exhibit 2 summarizes the percentages of efficiency for seven of the packers, called A, B, C, D, E, F, G, by weeks, for a five months' period. The average performance ratings ranged from 73.5 for Packer A to 99.6 for Packer D. The position of the label writer was believed to have no effect upon efficiency in any pocket.

Questions

1. What are the facts of the situation learned from a close examination of Exhibits 1 and 2? Make a list of the various points discovered and note their significance to management.
2. What possible explanations can you find for these facts?
3. What would you do if the responsibility for action were yours?

CASE 21–9. RIVERSIDE FUEL COMPANY

On the morning of January 10, 1968, Mr. Paul Newman appeared at the office of his accountant, Walter Dunn. Newman was disturbed, and explained his concern to Dunn in the following words:

When you started handling my accounts last May you said that my books seemed to be in pretty good shape. Since then we've been doing about the same volume of business as last year—maybe a little more. I've been thinking about the informal reports you've been giving me on how we're doing, and from what you say it looks like we've doubled last year's profit. I can't see how that can be right. Don't you think we ought to check this out before you make up our 1967 reports?

Mr. Newman, with his son-in-law, Peter Flint, operated Riverside Fuel Company. The company delivered heating oil to residential customers. It had been registered as a partnership on July 1, 1966, after having been operated as a sole proprietorship by Paul Newman for 20 years. The company operated from the Flint home. Mrs. Flint and her mother kept the records of deliveries (sales), receipts, and disbursements; Mrs. Newman billed all customers monthly. In addition to these members of the family, the company had recently taken on one full-time and two part-time workers to handle residential service work and to operate the company's second truck, acquired December 1, 1967. Peter's younger brother was frequently paid for performing such tasks as washing the trucks or answering the telephone.

Prior to the formation of the partnership, the firm needed records only for billing and tax requirements. With the formation of the partnership and the employment of driver servicemen, it became necessary to determine the partners' share of profits and to report payroll information to state and federal offices. Peter Flint was also somewhat more businesslike than his father-in-law and pressed for more formal handling of the company's records. For these reasons Newman and Flint decided that they would no longer depend on a "friend of the family" to figure their annual profit and income tax. Walter Dunn, a local accountant, was engaged to review the records of transactions monthly, to post to a set of accounts in a general ledger, to prepare quarterly statements and payroll reports, and to prepare the annual tax returns.

When Mr. Dunn first visited the Newman home he was given the income statement and balance sheet for the company's last full business year which ended December 31, 1966 (see Exhibits 1 and 2). He discussed the operations of the firm at some length with the principals and was reasonably well satisfied that the affairs of the company were fairly presented in the statements.

Exhibit 1

BALANCE SHEET, DECEMBER 31, 1966

ASSETS

Current Assets:			
Cash in bank			$15,392
Accounts receivable			13,735
Inventory of parts			6,039
Deposits on commercial bids			900
Total Current Assets			$36,066
Fixed Assets:			
Furniture and fixtures	$ 1,629		
Less: Depreciation allowance	623	$ 1,006	
Delivery and service equipment	$26,165		
Less: Depreciation allowance	10,766	15,399	
Total Fixed Assets			16,405
Total Assets			$52,471

LIABILITIES AND CAPITAL

Liabilities:			
Accounts payable			$ 4,820
Other liabilities			281
Total Liabilities			$ 5,101
Capital:			
Paul Newman, capital, January 1		$34,874	
Less: Drawings for the year		11,400	
		$23,474	
Add: Half share of profit for year		12,423	
Paul Newman, capital, December 31			35,897
Peter Flint, capital, January 1		$ 9,250	
Less: Drawings for the year		10,200	
		$ (950)	
Add: Half share of profit for year		12,423	
Peter Flint, capital, December 31			11,473
Total Liabilities and Capital			$52,471

Exhibit 2

INCOME STATEMENT FOR 1966

Revenue from sales and services:

Fuel oil, nonbudget accounts		$107,345
Budget plan income		88,985
Burner service and repairs		16,364
Installations		12,078
Total revenue		$224,772
Cost of sales and services:		
Fuel oil delivered	$167,703	
Burner parts and supplies	4,264	
Installation costs	5,741	
Subcontractor charges	1,619	
Total cost of sales		179,327
Gross profit on sales		$ 45,445
Operating expenses:		
Depreciation expense	$ 685	
Wages	7,426	
Vehicle expense	2,745	
Telephone	241	
Advertising	3,367	
Office and printing	1,121	
Utilities	481	
Taxes (other than payroll)	979	
Professional fees	1,460	
Payroll taxes	371	
Miscellaneous expense	1,723	
Total operating expense		20,599
Net Profit from Operations		$ 24,846

On the basis of his initial interview and his monthly visits, Dunn observed the general manner in which the records were maintained. Briefly stated, his observations follow:

Cash Receipts. A record of all receipts, entered chronologically by the name of the payer, was maintained by Mrs. Newman.

Cash Disbursements. A record of all checks issued was maintained by Mrs. Flint. She reconciled the cash balance each month with the bank statement and noted any errors or discrepancies.

Cash Records. The Receipts and disbursements journals (above) were completely transcribed, totaled, and balanced each month prior to Mr. Dunn's visit.

Payroll Records. A record of hours worked by each employee was maintained by Peter Flint. This record was the basis for issuance of payroll checks and preparation of payroll reports.

Sales. Although customers were billed monthly on the basis of metered delivery tickets, no entry in the sales accounts was made to reflect either the delivery or the billing. Instead, all cash recepts were recorded as sales when Mrs. Newman entered them in the cash receipts journal. She also prepared a list of accounts receivable on December 31 of each year; this list was used as the basis for year-end adjustment of the sales and receivables accounts.

Budget Accounts. Approximately half of the annual gallonage was sold to customers participating in the company's Budget Account Plan. Each of these customers made equal monthly payments for nine months of the year (September through May) and in June balanced the account. If the customer's account showed a credit balance in June, he could choose either to receive a refund check at that time, or to apply the credit against the next following payment.

Budget Plan customers paid neither a service charge nor a carrying charge. They were required, however, to purchase an annual service contract for which a $25 charge was the initial entry against their account. The contract covered cleaning and inspection of heating apparatus once during the year, usually in the July or August preceding the budget period, and expired each year at the end of the budget period. It also guaranteed free service and parts according to terms and conditions specified in the agreement.

Mr. Newman's experience was that it was virtually impossible to tell when he would have to provide repair service. The dollar cost had not varied greatly, however, for several years. Cleaning service, on the other hand, was much simpler to plan for; it involved a fixed commitment which could be scheduled conveniently and discharged under predictable conditions of cost and time.

Mr. Newman was particularly enthusiastic about the cleaning portion of the service contracts. Except for incidental costs of replacing filters, labor time was his only real cost. He maintained that the cleaning work done under the Budget Plan service contract was at least as good as the work billed to noncontract customers. These customers were charged $15 for cleaning and inspection. Although relatively few non-contract accounts called for cleaning service, Newman denied that his rate was established to induce customers to enroll in the Budget Account Plan. Competing firms offered similar cleaning services for $10 to $12.

The foregoing is a reasonably complete summation of Walter Dunn's knowledge of the company up to the time of Mr. Newman's visit to his office. He did, of course, have a complete file of data on the 1967 operations (see Exhibit 3) and was about to prepare the annual statements for the partners. Now that Newman had questioned the profit figures, Dunn felt obliged to spend a little more time before releasing any statements.

Dunn discussed the matter briefly with Newman and then agreed to meet with him and the other members of the family the following evening at the Newman home. At the meeting, attention soon centered on the marked difference in accounts receivable at the end of the two years in question. Mrs. Newman recalled, then, that there was some problem in setting up the balance of receivables at the end of last year. The friend who had been helping with the books had completed preparation of the tax returns before Mrs. Newman had totaled all of the accounts. She said, "He had only the tape on the budget accounts.[3] When I called him and

---

[3] Under the system used by this company, receipts on budget accounts had been recorded as budget plan income when received. The excess of delivery values over budget recepts had not been formally recorded. It was these amounts that Mrs. Newman calculated so that they could be added to budget plan income for the year.

Exhibit 3

OPERATING DATA 1967

Cash receipts journal:

Received from regular customers	$117,125
Received from budget plan customers	107,578
Received for burner service and repairs	13,985
Received for installation work	4,906
Received deposit refunds	750
Total receipts	$244,344

Cash payments journal:

Paid 1966 accounts payable	4,820
Withdrawn by Newman	12,250
Withdrawn by Flint	11,275
Paid for fuel purchases	160,886
Paid for burner parts	6,495
Paid for installations	2,322
Paid for utilities	466
Paid for new truck	12,185
Paid for telephone	255
Paid for advertising	2,571
Paid office and printing costs	1,231
Paid fees for professional services	1,672
Paid 1966 other liabilities	281
Paid payroll taxes (1967)	540
Paid for vehicle operation	2,543
Paid wages*	10,797
Paid miscellaneous expenses	2,144
Total disbursements	$232,733

Accounts payable, 12/31/67:

For fuel oil purchases	$ 4,358
For utility bills	40
For burner parts	482
For advertising	174

Other liabilities, 12/31/67:

Employers payroll taxes unpaid	108

Accounts receivable, 12/31/67:

Regular accounts	20,504
Budget accounts	13,389

Depreciation for 1967:

Furniture and fixtures	162
Delivery and service equipment	523
Inventory of burner parts, 12/31/67	9,075

* Withholding taxes not to be considered.

told him that I had the tape on all the other accounts, he said that he'd already finished the work and that it would all balance out." Mrs. Newman searched her desk and found the listing of accounts receivable that had not been recorded on December 31, 1966. The adding machine tape showed a total of $25,815.

Questions

1. Using the data that Dunn had prior to Newman's visit on January 10, prepare the income statement and balance sheet for Riverside Fuel Company.

2. How shall Mr. Dunn explain the situation to the Newmans and Flints? Will it "all balance out"? Why?

3. What accounts, if any, were misstated on December 31, 1966? December 31, 1967?

4. What corrections, if any, would you make in the two sets of statements?

5. Do you have any recommendations for the handling of the record of customers' accounts in the future?

6. How should Dunn reflect Newman's year-end liability on service contracts?

CASE 21–10. DIXON COMPANY

The Dixon Company made metal parts and subassemblies for approximately a dozen manufacturers in the Detroit area. Prior to 1960, it had done all this work on a fixed-price basis. In 1960 the company negotiated a contract with the Mayer Company, a large manufacturing company. Under the terms of this contract, the Dixon Company would devote roughly 40 percent of its output to parts for the Mayer Company. The exact nature and volume of these parts were to be determined subsequently. Payment was to be made on a basis of cost plus a fixed fee. "Cost" was to be the sum of the direct material, direct labor, and overhead cost of the parts. The overhead cost was to be calculated as that percentage of direct labor that total overhead in the plant bore to total direct labor. A tentative overhead rate was to be set for billing purposes, and an adjustment was to be made at the end of each year after actual overhead costs and actual direct labor costs for the year had been determined.

The Dixon Company used a simple cost accounting system under which most payments to employees were classified as direct labor. This classification was not satisfactory to the representative of the Mayer Company, and he suggested that the classification should be governed by the *Armed Services Procurement Regulation,* which is the principal regulation relating to the determination of costs under U.S. Defense Department contracts. Excerpts from this regulation are quoted below.[4]

15–201.1. Composition of Total Cost. The total cost of a contract is the sum of the allowable direct and indirect costs allocable to the contract, incurred or to be incurred, less any allocable credits. In ascertaining what constitutes costs, any generally accepted method of determining or estimating costs that is equitable under the circumstances may be used, including standard costs properly adjusted for applicable variances.

* * * * *

15–201.2 Factors Affecting Allowability of Costs. Factors to be considered in determining the allowability of individual items of cost include (i)

---

[4] *Armed Services Procurement Regulation,* Section XV, revised November 2, 1967.

reasonableness, (ii) allocability, (iii) application of those generally accepted accounting principles and practices appropriate to the particular circumstances, and (iv) any limitations or exclusions set forth in this Part 2, or otherwise included in the contract as to types or amounts of cost items.

15–201.3. Definition of Reasonableness.

(a) *General.* A cost is reasonable if, in its nature or amount, it does not exceed that which would be incurred by an ordinarily prudent person in the conduct of competitive business. The question of the reasonableness of specific costs must be scrutinized with particular care in connection with firms or separate divisions thereof which may not be subject to effective competitive restraints. What is reasonable depends upon a variety of considerations and circumstances involving both the nature and amount of the cost in question. In determining the reasonableness of a given cost, consideration shall be given to—

(i) whether the cost is of a type generally recognized as ordinary and necessary for the conduct of the contractor's business or the performance of the contract;

(ii) the restraints or requirements imposed by such factors as generally accepted sound business practices, arm's-length bargaining, Federal and State Laws and regulations, and contract terms and specifications;

(iii) the action that a prudent business man would take in the circumstances, considering his responsibilities to the owners of the business, his employees, his customers, the Government and the public at large; and

(iv) significant deviations from the established practices of the contractor which may unjustifiably increase the contract costs.

15–201.4 Definition of Allocability. A cost is allocable if it is assignable or chargeable to a particular cost objective, such as a contract, product, product line process, or class of customer or activity, in accordance with the relative benefits received or other equitable relationship. Subject to the foregoing, a cost is allocable to a Government contract if it

(i) is incurred specifically for the contract;

(ii) benefits both the contract and other work, or both Government work and other work, and can be distributed to them in reasonable proportion to the benefits received; or

(iii) is necessary to the overall operation of the business, although a direct relationship to any particular cost objective cannot be shown.

*   *   *   *   *

15–202 Direct Costs. (a) A direct cost is any cost which can be identified specifically with a particular cost objective. Direct costs are not limited to items which are incorporated in the end product as material or labor. Costs identified specifically with the contract are direct costs of the contract and are to be charged directly thereto. Costs identified specifially with other work of the contractor are direct costs of that work and are not to be charged to the contract directly or indirectly. When items ordinarily chargeable as indirect costs are charged to Government work as direct costs, the cost of like items applicable to other work of the contractor must be eliminated from indirect costs allocated to Government work.

(b) This definition shall be applied to all items of cost of significant amount unless the contractor demonstrates that the application of any different current practice achieves substantially the same results. Direct cost items of minor amount may be distributed as indirect costs as provided in 15–203.

* * * * *

15–203 Indirect Costs. (a) An indirect cost is one which, because of its incurrence for common or joint objectives, is not readily subject to treatment as a direct cost. Minor direct cost items may be considered to be indirect costs for reasons of practicality. After direct costs have been determined and charged directly to the contract or other work as appropriate, indirect costs are those remaining to be allocated to the several classes of work.

* * * * *

15–205.6 Compensation for Personal Services. Compensation for personal services includes all remuneration paid currently or accrued, in whatever form and whether paid immediately or deferred, for services rendered by employees to the contractor during the period of contract performance. It includes, but is not limited to, salaries, wages, directors' and executive committee members' fees, bonuses (including stock bonuses), incentive awards, employee stock options, employee insurance, fringe benefits, and contributions to pension, annuity, and management employee incentive compensation plans.

The treasurer of the Dixon Company thought that further discussion of this topic would be desirable. Consequently, he prepared, with the assistance of his chief accountant, a list of the types of labor payments likely to be incurred during the life of the contract. Recognizing that the magnitude of the expense would enter into the discussion, he included a rough estimate of the monthly anticipated cost to the Dixon Company for each type of labor. This list, which was to be used as a basis for discussion, follows:

1. Earnings of piece-rate workers (approximately $25,000).
2. Earnings of day-rate workers who worked on productive work (approximately $3,000).
3. Overtime payments (impossible to estimate; depends on delivery requirements of Mayer Company).
4. Payments to workers who for some reason or other were idle (approximately $1,250).
5. Payments for time spent setting up machines (very roughly $2,000).
6. Payments to workers for regular work time used in attending union meetings (approximately $200).
7. Payments to foremen and assistants (approximately $1,800).
8. Payments to inspectors (approximately $600).
9. Payments to office workers (approximately $2,600).
10. Payments to sweepers (approximately $450).
11. Payments to maintenance men (approximately $600).
12. Payments to man employed in the raw material stock room ($275).

13. Allowance for vacation pay (all the above employees had one week's vacation with pay each year).
14. The company's contribution to old-age benefit taxes (approximately 3 percent of all wages paid).
15. The company's unemployment insurance tax (approximately 2 percent of all wages paid).

Questions

1. Should the treasurer of the Dixon Company be concerned about this matter? Why?
2. In your opinion, which types of payments on the above list should be classified as direct labor and which should be classified as indirect labor and, therefore, included in overhead?
3. Comment on the usefulness of the definition of direct costs quoted in the case. Should it be made more precise?

CASE 21–11.   CONSOLIDATED METAL WORKS, LTD.

In January, 1959, the management of Consolidated Metal Works, Ltd., met to discuss a suggested formula for the allocation of overhead costs among the various manufacturing departments of the enterprise.

Consolidated Metal Works, Ltd., consisted of a number of metal-working manufacturing departments. Until recently these departments had been small, independent enterprises, each one handling some specific branch of metal work. In 1957 these establishments were merged under the name of Consolidated Metal Works, Ltd. The new company drew its central administrative staff mainly from the existing staff of the individual enterprises with the addition of a few new employees.

The manufacturing departments of the new enterprise were as follows:

		Employees
Department A:	Construction of bridges and cranes	180
Department B:	Manufacture of steel benches	80
Department C:	Manufacture of nails	50
Department D:	Manufacture of gas bottles	40
Department E:	Manufacture of locks	30
Total		380

In addition, there were the following selling and service departments:

Production Service, with sections for maintenance, production design, and production engineering.

Supplies and Sales, responsible for selling and also for the management of inventory of products, material, and stores.

All department heads reported to Mr. Pattish, the general manager.

A frequent subject of discussion in the new enterprise was the problem of calculating the profitability of the several manufacturing departments and their products. There had been no cost accounting problems before the consolidation, since each enterprise had charged its overhead expenses to its own production. After the consolidation, a number of joint costs and services had to be allocated to the producing departments. Each department manager complained about the various proposed formulas on the ground that he was being discriminated against.

The controller had decided finally to make things easy for himself and had stopped discussing this subject with the department managers. Instead, at the end of the year, he totaled all overhead items and allocated them roughly to the departments, and in this fashion he compiled the profit and loss accounts of each. It was alleged that he also took advantage of this opportunity to settle some of his personal grudges with the department managers by means of generous allocations of overhead costs.

This approach on the part of the controller provoked the resentment of most of the department managers. Things came to the point where the latter refused to acknowledge the calculations of the controller, not only as to the overhead costs of the enterprise, but also as to other cost calculations. Each department thereupon set up a small costing section which calculated the costs per unit produced on the basis of readily available data concerning material, labor, and other production costs. To these each department manager added what he considered a fair estimate of overhead to be borne by him. The controller and each department head consequently had his own way of computing costs and analyzing the profitability of the operations.

Matters reached a point which greatly perplexed the general manager. He had not ascribed much importance to the affair when it had started; moreover, he was not well versed in its technical aspects. He had hoped that the people concerned would somehow reach a solution, but this had not happened. One thing was clear to him: the practice of having different sets of overhead cost calculations had to stop, and the numerical data and the formulas for their allocation had to be made known and acknowledged by all concerned.

Accordingly, the general manager instructed the controller to prepare an annual budget of the overhead costs of the enterprise and to suggest formulas for the allocation of the various expense items to the departments and to bring up this matter for discussion before a committee composed of the members of management and of heads of departments. In this way he hoped to reach a general agreement.

On January 10, 1959, the first meeting of this committee took place. The following are minutes of this meeting:

Mr. Pattish (general manager) opens the meeting and announces that the controller has prepared a suggested allocation of the overhead expenses of the enterprise for 1959. The project is submitted to the members of the committee for perusal and remarks. He requests the members to refrain from personal remarks and to concentrate on the matter in hand, in order to achieve a fruitful discussion and an agreement on a method of overhead allocation.

MR. SADAN (controller) distributes copies of the above-mentioned allocation (Exhibit 1) among the members of the committee and explains it. Mr.

Exhibit 1

CONSOLIDATED METAL WORKS, LTD.

Suggested Allocation of Overhead Costs for 1959 Budget

Item	Amount	Formula for Allocation to Departments
Administration Costs	$200,000	Direct production cost of the department.
Production Engineering Office	50,000	a) Half the amount on basis of estimate of work performed for departments.
		b) Half the amount on basis of number of men employed working under standardized conditions.*
Technical Office (Engineering)	35,000	Estimate of the work done by the office for the departments. The estimate to be prepared by the Chief Engineer.
Storekeeping Costs	180,000	In proportion to the cost of the materials used by the departments.
Depreciation of Equipment	150,000	According to historic cost of the equipment of the departments.
Depreciation of Buildings	50,000	In proportion to the built-up area of the departments.
Consumption of Power	40,000	As indicated by meters (to be installed in the departments).
Maintenance of Buildings	35,000	In proportion to the built-up area of the departments.
Municipal Taxes	25,000	In proportion to the built-up area of the departments.
Payroll Department	25,000	According to the number of men employed by the departments.
Total	$790,000	

* About one half of the work force worked under standardized conditions based on motion and time studies.

Sadan asks the members of the committee to realize that there is an inherent difficulty in allocating the overhead expenses to the departments and that any formula is bound to be arbitrary to some extent. He therefore requests the members of the committee to approve the above suggested allocations.

MR. PELLED (bridge construction department): I cannot agree to the formula suggested by the controller for the allocation of administrative costs. My department is the largest in the enterprise, and its production costs amount to about half those of the whole enterprise. I would, therefore, have to carry a charge of $100,000, which is absurd; it might even put in question the profitableness of the department. I have no training in cost accounting and preparation of budgets, and I do not know which formula should be applied in this case. I would ask the controller, therefore, to find another more accurate formula.

MR. MAROM (bench manufacturing department): I definitely agree with the controller that the formula for the allocation of administrative costs should be based on the amount of the production costs of the department. I only disagree with the interpretation of the term "amount of production costs." According to the controller's explanation, he has not included in this term the value of customers' materials (i.e., materials supplied by customers which do not pass through the stores department); nor has he included in this term the costs of processing by subcontractors. Since the Bridge Construction Department is the only one to use customers' materials for its work and to require the services of subcontractors—and this to the tune of half a million dollars per year—it means that in this way the controller has reduced the share of overhead expenses which should be allocated to this department and has charged it to the other departments.

MR. SADAN: But the handling of customers' materials and of independent contractors places next to no extra work on the administrative staff of the enterprise, and therefore there would be no justification whatever in taking these factors into account in the formula.

MR. MAROM: You are quite mistaken. Administrative costs consist mainly of management, secretarial work, accounting, bookkeeping, office supplies, etc. What connection is there between these and customers' materials or subcontractors? Your opinion on this subject may bring us to an absurdity: If in a certain year most of the materials used in the Bridges and Cranes Department were to be customers' materials, I am sure that the administrative costs item, which amounts to $200,000, would not grow bigger or smaller by one single dollar, and the share of this expense to be charged to the Bridge Department, with its turnover of two million dollars (including customers' materials), would be equal to the amount charged to the Bench Department, with its turnover of three fourths of a million dollars. To sum up, I agree with the controller that the formula for the allocation of the administrative expenses of the enterprise should remain as suggested, but I insist on his including the financial value of the customers' material and of the services of independent contractors as well.

MR. LEVI (nails department): I would like to speak about the storekeeping costs item. As you know, this item amounts to the enormous sum of $180,000 per year. Since some 65 percent of the costs of my department consists of the cost of materials, it would be discriminatory in my case to use the factor of consumption of materials as an index for determining the allocation of storekeeping costs. It is true that such a formula is mentioned in books on cost accounting, but we should check whether it suits us. It is true that the consumption of materials in my department is expensive, but it dones not need much storekeeping work; so why should I suffer because the controller happened to choose this formula? I have investigated this matter, and I have found that this amount of $180,000 consists of the following:

Salaries of stores' employees	$ 70,000
Vehicles for interworks transportation	30,000
Transportation (internal)	65,000
Miscellaneous expenses	15,000
	$180,000

It will be seen from this that the lion's share of the storekeeping costs consists of salaries and haulage; now this is manpower which I don't use much, as my raw materials (wire in bundles) do not need much recording and very little hauling. I suggest therefore that the formula for the allocation of storekeeping costs should not be uniform for all of the $180,000, and that a special formula be set for each subitem instead.

MR. COHEN (gas bottles department): I have seen the estimates prepared by the chief engineer in connection with the allocation of the costs of the technical office, and I do not like them. With all due respect to the chief engineer, I cannot agree that he should make up and allocate wholly fictitious figures— 10 percent of the costs of the technical office to this one, 25 percent to that, etc. In this way we shall never be able to achieve accurate cost accounting, nor control of the cost of the technical office. I suggest, therefore, that any department of the enterprise which avails itself of the services of this office should be charged directly, in accordance with records (to be kept by the chief engineer) of the number of man-hours spent by his engineers and draftsmen. In this way any department manager who may want to invite the technical office to do some work will think twice about it before doing so. As a matter of fact, this concerns the Production Engineering Department as well, and I suggest that the possibility be examined of introducing here, too, exact recording and direct charging of costs to the departments concerned.

MR. EGOZI (supplies and sales): I have not taken part in the discussion until now, because I do not feel affected by this or that mode of allocation, not being the manager of a producing department. I should like to suggest something completely different. I notice that it is now a year since we have started carrying on the discussion about formulas, and each time we get more and more involved without ever reaching an agreement. I should like to suggest that we not allocate overhead to the departments at all. After all, what does it matter? The costs do remain within the consolidated enterprise. In my opinion the accounts of these cost items should be closed at the end of the year and charged to the profit and loss account of the enterprise. The production cost of the articles produced in the various departments should be calculated only on the basis of direct costs. I believe this to be the only possibility of getting out of this muddle.

MR. SADAN: I am very grateful to you, Mr. Egozi, for wishing to get me out of the muddle, but your suggestion can only make things more difficult instead of making them easy. What do we wish to achieve by the allocation of overhead to the departments? We want to get a complete and accurate idea of our own production costs for every single article made by the enterprise, in order to determine the profit or loss made from each and to formulate a pricing policy for the market.

Ours is not like an enterprise in which every department handles one stage of an overall manufacturing process; in such a case the allocation of overhead to the departments may not be so important. Here, each department makes a complete product, without having anything to do with the other departments, and is in fact a separate enterprise by itself. This being so, the overhead must be allocated to the departments, since otherwise we would be left completely in the dark concerning the profitableness of each department and product. If we were to adopt your suggestion, Mr. Egozi, all we should be able to compute at the end of the year would be the total profit or loss of the enterprise, which I find quite unsatisfactory.

MR. MAROM: I agree with the controller that we should not be satisfied with calculating the total profit or loss of the enterprise and that we should arrive at an accurate computation of the profitableness of each department or product. However, even my suggestion of dumping on the manufacturing departments the enormous overhead which accumulates at the end of every year will not give us the correct solution of the problem, as the profitableness of the manufacturing departments and their products depends too on the rate of efficiency and economy of the services. What would it avail me, for instance, to make every effort in order to make the work of my department more efficient, if the controller on his part were to engage more employees in the accounting department, if Mr. Egozi were to engage more porters in the stores and add more vehicles which would not be fully utilized, and so on and so on? The final result would be that my department would not pay its way and my products could not be sold in the market! If this is the kind of allocation of overhead meant by the controller, then, gentlemen, I ask—is this the way? Is this the right thing to do?

In my opinion this will cause confusion and misrepresentation. Before the consolidation, today's department managers were all managers of independent enterprises who had control of all expenses, including overhead. Now the situation has changed; it is the management which has this control, and the efficiency of those functions for which it is responsible should be measured as well.

I suggest therefore that we make a thorough investigation of the joint services of the enterprise, in order to ascertain the extent to which each service is required by every department—the standards of services, so to say. For this purpose we should appoint a committee, to be headed by the chief production engineer. Since he is neither the head of a manufacturing department nor a member of the management, he will be able to remain objective. This committee will make a thorough investigation and present its findings. I cannot guarantee that the findings of this committee will achieve a maximum of accuracy, but they will certainly be much more accurate than the formulas which the controller has suggested that we should adopt. This system will enable us to evaluate with much more certainty the profitableness of the manufacturing departments and their products, as well as the degree of efficiency of the joint services in the enterprise.

MR. SADAN: I feel that Mr. Marom's suggestions are very clever, but they are theoretical and, in my opinion, impractical. We shall never be able to set such standards in respect of our services; at any rate, we shall be unable to do so in respect of the majority of the items of which these services consist. I suggest therefore that my original suggestion be approved.

MR. PATTISH: I have heard here some remarks and arguments from various points of view. I am pleased to say that in the course of this meeting I have learned many things to which until now I had not attributed their proper importance. I suggest therefore that we pass no resolutions on this subject today; we shall postpone the conclusion of this meeting for a fortnight, and in the meantime we shall receive the minutes of the meeting and devote some time to individual thought.

Questions

1. Is the basis for the division of administrative expenses logical? Is there a better one? Should the material supplied by the customer and the work executed by the subcontractor be included under "total production costs"? Should the administrative expenditure be divided according to departments, at all?
2. Does the price of materials provide a proper basis to the stores' expenditures? What alternative bases are there? In which case, or cases, would you chose each one? Should there be more than one basis for the division of the stores' expenditures?
3. It is desirable that the design and production engineering departments keep track of the time of the engineers, technicians, and the time-study operators? If so, how would you calculate the rate of an hour's labor in these departments? How would you deal with hours which cannot be charged to an individual department, or hours of idleness? Should expenditure incurred by the production engineering department be regarded as expenses or as a long-run investment?
4. What do you think of Mr. Egozi's suggestion not to divide indirect expenditure among the departments? If you agree with him, which items listed in the budget would you not divide among the departments?
5. What do you think of Mr. Marom's suggestion to establish standards for the various administrative and service departments? Is this suggestion practicable? Does it help the costing?

CASE 21-12. CAMEO DEPARTMENT STORE

The Cameo Department Store consists of four selling departments. Departments I, II, and III are located in the main store, whereas department IV is located in a smaller building next to the main store. Until three years ago (January 1, 1958) the building occupied by department IV had been used as a warehouse. At that time alternative warehouse space was rented at a total annual rental of $11,000 and the warehouse was converted into a selling area at a cost of $12,000 excluding furnishings, which cost $9,000. Department IV has been used to display and sell seasonal merchandise, such as toys at Christmas, lawn and garden products in the spring and early summer, etc.

Financial data for the past three years consist of the following:

Selling Departments

1958	I	II	III	IV
Sales	$335,000	$398,000	$257,000	$156,000
Cost of goods sold	181,000	205,000	173,000	121,000
Purchases	185,000	210,000	165,000	90,000
Salaries	10,000	13,000	8,500	8,200
Supplies	2,500	2,650	2,300	1,900
1959	**I**	**II**	**III**	**IV**
Sales	343,000	405,000	265,000	158,000
Cost of goods sold	185,000	208,000	177,000	123,500
Purchases	190,000	206,000	168,000	116,000
Salaries	10,000	130,000	8,500	8,200
Supplies	2,450	2,700	2,100	1,950
1960	**I**	**II**	**III**	**IV**
Sales	351,000	408,000	268,000	153,000
Cost of goods sold	186,000	208,000	178,000	119,000
Purchases	180,000	205,000	182,000	113,000
Salaries	10,000	13,000	8,500	8,200
Supplies	2,600	2,700	2,250	

Sales commissions are 1 percent of sales in each department, and estimated uncollectible accounts average one half of 1 percent of sales.

Nonselling activities of the Cameo Department Store are divided into purchasing, sales promotion, and general administration. These costs for the past three years were as follows:

Purchasing

	1958	1959	1960
Salaries	$10,500	$10,500	$10,500
Supplies	1,325	1,300	1,370

Sales Promotion

	1958	1959	1960
Salaries	$14,000	$14,000	$14,000
Newspaper ads	9,800	10,400	12,100
Handbills	525	485	540
Price reductions on sales promotion	4,800	5,300	5,800
Other sales promotion costs	400	380	405
Supplies	1,480	1,535	1,600
	$31,005	$32,100	$34,445

General Administration

	1958	1959	1960
Salaries	$29,000	$29,000	$29,000
Supplies	2,900	2,870	2,920

Other Costs for the Three Years

	1958	1959	1960
Delivery costs	$11,780	$12,125	$12,320
Heat	8,575	8,225	8,380
Light and power	10,580	11,120	10,975

The main store building had a book value of $300,000 on January 1, 1958. Esimated useful life of the building as of that date was 20 years. The building occupied by department IV had a book value of $80,000, excluding renovation costs, and an estimated useful life of 20 years as of January 1, 1958. No extensive renovations are planned for department IV for at least 20 years.

Furnishings in each of the selling and nonselling departments remained constant during the past three years. The cost of furnishings in each department is as follows:

Selling Departments

I	$15,000
II	15,000
III	12,000
IV	9,000

Nonselling Departments

Purchasing	$2,500
Sales Promotion	4,000
General Administration	8,400

Estimated useful life for all furnishings is five years.

Three fourths of the floor space in the main building is shared equally by the selling departments, whereas the other one fourth is divided equally among the nonselling departments. The smaller store building contains one half the floor space of department I. Electrical equipment in the selling departments is of the same variety and amount, whereas the nonselling departments each had approximately one half as much electrical equipment as department I.

On the average, departments I and II use about an equal amount of space in handbills and newspaper advertising, and about twice that of departments III and IV. Warehousing costs include the annual rental of $11,000, a foreman's salary of $6,000 a year, and a helper's wage of $300 a month. The warehousing function includes receiving of all purchased merchandise, storage, and transferring of stored merchandise to the selling departments when needed.

Questions

1. Prepare departmental income statements for department IV for 1958, 1959, and 1960. Use whatever reasonable assumptions are necessary to distribute expenses to departments.
2. Prepare a list of the cost and revenue items that would be included in a statement that attempts to measure the contribution of department IV to the profit of the firm (dollar amounts not necessary). It is possible that some of the individual expense items included in the departmental income statement will be only partially includable in the contribution statement? Explain.

3. Prepare a list (dollars amounts not necessary) of the cost and revenue items that would be included in a statement that attempts to measure the financial performance of the manager of department IV. With what type of data might we compare the present performance of department IV in order to judge more adequately the financial performance of the manager? What other data might be useful in attempting to measure the financial performance of department IV's manager? Generally speaking, what has to be added to financial performance in order to build up to total performance?

4. A member of the board of directors has asked this question: In view of the losses shown in department IV, would it possibly be wise to discontinue the department? Alternative uses of the building occupied by department IV are as follows:

   a) Convert the building back into warehouse space at a cost of $10,000. Sell the furnishings for $8,000 and dispose of the warehouse space costing $11,000 a year.

   b) Sublease the building, including, furnishings, at an annual rental of $12,000, all utilities to be provided.

   c) Sell the building, including all fixtures and equipment, for $200,000.

   Prepare a schedule of cost and revenue data that will facilitate making a decision. Cite the limitations of these data (if any) as well as other factors that should be considered before the board of directors makes its decision. Make any assumptions you feel are necessary.

CASE 21–13. BELTON WOOLEN MILLS, INC.

In January 1958, executives of Belton Woolen Mills, Inc.—a firm that had held its own in the New England textile race for more than 50 years —found itself facing the typical question: How do we adjust to competitive pressures?

Word from the sales personnel in New York City had been received the afternoon before to the effect that Pattern 7031, priced by the company at $3 a yard, had aroused much interest on the part of buyers as they examined samples; in fact, this reception at the showing indicated that such a style would probably become a best seller in the current cloth season for eventual display at retail in the autumn of 1958 in women's coats.

The fly in the ointment was that a competitor was showing, at a price less by 20 cents a yard, or at $2.80, a fabric that seemed to be almost the same, having virtually the same distinctive pattern. In the judgment of sales personnel, who had sent a sample of the cloth from New York, the fabrics were so nearly alike that Belton Mills would have to match the $2.80 price if it expected to reap much benefit from the pattern's appeal to buyers.

At this time operations were on what was essentially a three-shift basis. Approximately 525 people were employed by the concern, about 485 in production. Seventeen shifts were worked during each week, only two reporting on Saturday. This was the level at which the firm preferred to work when orders permitted. In some parts of the plant, however, a third daily shift was not employed because of the great importance of supervision, which was both costly and difficult to obtain. Dyeing and finishing operations were in this category. Careful planning and an adequate amount of machinery in these processes kept them from becoming bottlenecks, however.

Cost Estimating

The firm's management of costs was built around a cost estimate sheet set up for each style or pattern in the process of planning its production. Essentially, the estimates were developed from actual historical costs of producing similar cloth; however, they reflected departures from historical data which were known or could be anticipated. For example, material estimates were stated at current or expected market price. Labor and operating cost estimates were regularly based on prior cost experience for similar operations, with allowance for expected rates in different operations. Burden cost estimates generally were not based entirely on either expectations or recent experience, but rather on rates developed in the relationship between production and estimated burden cost if activity should be at the 15-shift level (five-day week) for the year, on the average. This allocation procedure gave a burden estimate on cloth that was lower than expected-actual in cases in which the operating level was expected to average less than 15 shifts during the year, as was generally the case.

Burden was applied in cost estimates on the basis of the number of spinning units, for example, at $5 per spinning unit of 100,000 yards of yarn. For each pattern the number of ends (the individual threads of yarn running lengthwise and making up the full width of the cloth) and the number of picks (the number of individual threads of yarn running crosswise in a yard of finished cloth) were specified on the cost estimate sheet. To determine the number of yards of yarn in a yard of the fabric, the number of picks was multiplied by the number of yards of yarn in the pick, or width of the fabric; to this product was added the number of ends in the fabric. This sum then was multiplied by $5 (the assumed burden rate) and divided by 100,000, the spinning unit, to secure the burden cost of a yard of the cloth. Thus, for yarn of the same size and weight, the burden cost was actually estimated on the basis of cloth weight; and generally a weight basis would give substantially the same result. The burden item included both factory overhead and general and administrative expenses.

In decisions involving idle-capacity cost (as in changes in the number of shifts), it was generally assumed that burden costs, including general and administrative expense, were 55 percent variable and 45 percent fixed. The controller expressed the opinion, however, that the proportion was more nearly 50–50 for reductions in activity below 12 shifts a week. Also, certain variable-burden inefficiencies tended to develop at levels below 12 shifts.

The sum of material, labor, and burden called "total mill cost." Normal percentages were added in sequence for selling expense, returns and allowances, and cash discounts. Each of these was computed as a percentage of selling price. The addition of estimated net profit before income taxes gave the accumulated total, or the planned selling price. In general, the planned percentage for net profit, based on sales, was approximately the same for all styles.

Selling expense was considered a fixed cost for the year, no decline being expected when volume of production or sales decreased. This fixed cost was expressed as a percentage of expected annual sales volume to determine the percentage figure to be used for selling expense on the cost estimate sheet. The figure for returns and allowances were based on the past relationship between total sales and these deductions from sales. The allowance element was important in the woolen industry. Contracts generally provided for arbitration procedures in case the buyer considered the cloth delivered not up to specifications. Although the Belton management agreed that it could predict roughly the risk of allowances for a certain pattern and that this risk was much greater for some items than others, it did not consider it worthwhile to attempt to allow for this variation in originally estimating the cost of a certain pattern; therefore, the same average rate was used for all estimates in the season's planning. Since sales were made on terms of 1/10, n/60 from date of billing, the discount was estimated at 1 percent of selling price.

Pricing

As was customary in the woolen industry, numerous patterns of Belton Woolen Mills were grouped together and assigned the same "range number" and sales price. A range included cloth styles that were similar in fabric, pattern, production operations, and estimated cost. Ordinarily the estimates of cost for the specific items in a range varied not more than 10 percent from the average cost of the range.

Situation 1

With respect to the problem of Pattern 7031, Mr. Lincoln, general manager of the mill, made the decision at once that it would not be possible merely to meet the $2.80 price: "If we can't figure some way to

cut the fabric's cost, the sales office will just have to push something else."
He was convinced, however, that in view of the urgent appeal from New
York, this settlement of the issue would create some real danger of
Belton's securing a significantly smaller share of the total market for the
year.

"Of course, nobody can be certain of the ultimate effect," commented
another executive sympathetically, "for New York has weathered such
storms before."

But Mr. Lincoln knew immediately that he wanted some cost estimating work done before he and his group tried to reach a decision: "We've
got to decide whether we can get into the market on this popular style or
stay out. Let's find a way to do it if we can, boys."

This instruction meant that George Buchanan, a technical assistant,
who actually compiled the firm's cost estimates, had a job to do. He found
that Pattern 7031 was in Range 253 and that Range 253, priced at $3 a
yard, showed an average estimated total mill cost of $2.58 for a margin of
42 cents, or 14 percent, based on sales price, and an average net profit of
12 cents, or 4 percent. He found the highest total mill cost in the range to
be $2.68, and the lowest to be $2.52. He pulled the cost estimates sheet for
Pattern 7031 and found the following summary of the cost elements:

Raw materials	$1.40
Dyes	0.12
Emulsions and chemicals	0.05
Labor	0.54
Burden*	0.44
Subtotal	$2.55
5⅔% selling expense	0.17
3⅓% returns	0.10
1% discount	0.03
Net profit	0.15
Selling Price	$3.00

* Burden in this summary includes general and administrative expense.

Mr. Buchanan worked for hours on the problem, gathering information to present to the executives, in the form of a new cost estimate sheet,
for the decision as to whether "to get into the market." He compiled the
following notes on his findings, including reactions he received from key
personnel:

1. The competing fabric weighs 19½ ounces as compared with our 20-ounce
   cloth. Both are all wool.
2. The price of raw wool is now approximately 1½ percent lower than it
   was when preseason estimates were made.
3. I know that the yarn yield would be slightly higher than average on this
   particular fabric if its current popularity should increase the average lot
   size materially—maybe a saving of 2 or 3 cents a yard.
4. Our cloth has a brighter color, which is obvious when the samples are

compared closely. We can save at least a penny on dyes, for brightness is costly.

5. The competing fabric is not as well finished as ours is. If we match the finishing of the other fabric, our labor saving will be negligible, but the saving in machine time (largely in napping) will justify a 3 to 4 percent saving of the variable burden.

6. Neither Harris (vice president, dyeing and finishing) nor Lynn (vice president, other manufacturing) thinks we should try to further cheapen the fabric by blending with nylon.

7. This fabric is not the sort on which we will have much trouble with returns and allowances. Mr. Harris says this loss can probably be cut to 2 percent of sales.

8. We already have a plain color blend in a range priced at $2.75; we have nothing priced between that amount and $3.

9. Mr. Lynn says these fabric adjustments should put us in as good position as the competitor to get the business if we quote the same price. Generally we consider our line more popular than the competitor's.

10. Mr. Winthrop (controller) wonders if we can actually get larger production lots than average in this fabric if we have to share the market with the competitor.

11. Mr. Lynn and the production people think these changes are simple enough so that they can be made quickly.

Situation 2

Six months after the executives of Belton Woolen Mills made the decision called for above on Pattern 7031, Mr. Lincoln returned from a trip to the New York sales office and greeted Mr. Winthrop, the controller, with a request for more cost information. A firm known to buy exceptionally large quantities of cloth for manufacture in large lots for a chain of stores had offered to negotiate with the New York office, just the day before, with regard to Belton's best price on 12 samples, with billing to be made as of July 1, 1959, regardless of actual delivery time, and deliveries to be made between January 1 and July 31, 1959.

The controller knew that the president was fearful of a repetition of the experience of some previous fall quarters when the operating level had fallen below eight shifts a week on the average. He knew that Mr. Lincoln wanted to take some action to avoid this decline during the slow season and that many competing firms also would be trying to get volume business during the slow season, a fact also well known to large-lot buyers.

It was clear to Mr. Winthrop that he should set up the lowest possible costs for the specific patterns, cost figures which the president could use as a basis for discount negotiation, knowing that at these figures his firm could at least cover extra costs of production. In other words, he wanted to estimate those costs that would not be present at the eight-shift level, which was considered attainable without these special orders.

Belton Mills normally gave discounts for larger orders, but if the orders for the chain of stores were received, they would be much larger than the orders the firm usually received for regular season work.

Mr. Winthrop and Mr. Buchanan, with others, spent many hours discussing their cost-volume relationships and other problems raised by the assignment. Buchanan made the following notes concerning cost figures to be submitted to the president with respect to Pattern 7031:

1. If we get orders of the size indicated on the 12 patterns, we can operate at about a 12-shift level all fall except for the two-week closing for vacations.
2. Let's assume that we get enough extra business out of this negotiation to hold at the 10-shift level. At lower levels of operation we are not quite so efficient on variable burden costs as at the 15-shift level. Mr. Winthrop says that on ordinary lots our costs per unit should run 8 percent above the comparable 15-shift variable burden cost, as an approximation.
3. Raw wool prices will be figured 4.3 percent above the original estimates on 7031, prices having risen.
4. Labor cost can be cut by 5 percent.
5. Because of the larger lot sizes, yarn wastage should decrease and savings of 6 percent should be realized.
6. A given amount of cloth can move through machine operations at a faster rate per unit in a large lot than in a small lot. Because of this, we should be able to make savings of 5 percent in total burden over the amount indicated on the most estimate sheet.
7. If the buyer changes no specifications, returns and allowances can probably be held to 2 percent.
8. As we plan to schedule the production, we will have to carry the receivable about seven months before billing. Money is worth 5 percent per annum to us.
9. Mr. Lincoln wants a report showing all costs applicable to the expected order and relevant to this pricing decision. He will decide later how much more than this minimum amount he should try to secure.

Questions

1. What action do you think should be taken on Situation 1?
2. Prepare the estimate called for in Situation 2.

CASE 21–14.   GENERAL ELECTRIC COMPANY[5]

General Electric Company is a large, multilocation corporation engaged in the manufacture and marketing of a wide variety of electrical

---

[5] With the exception of the statistical information and publicly known facts presented in the introduction of this case, the sources for the facts making up the body of this case are *Executive Control—The Catalyst*, by William T. Jerone III

and allied products. In 1961, there were almost 400 separate product lines and over three million catalog items. Sales volume in that year totaled $4,457 million, and net income was $242 million. Total employment was about 250,000.

Early in the 1950's, General Electric initiated an extensive decentralization of authority and responsibility for the operations of the company. The basic unit of organization became the product department. As of 1961, there were over 100 of these departments.

The company recognized that if this decentralization was to be fully effective, it would need an improved system of management control. It also recognized that any improved system of control would require better measures of performance. To meet this need, the company established a Measurements Project and created a special organizational unit to carry out this project. This case summarizes the main features of this project, with particular emphasis on the measuring of performance of the operating (i.e., product) departments.

The Measurements Project

The Measurements Project was established in 1952. Responsibility for the project was assigned to accounting services, one of the corporate functional services divisions. A permanent organizational unit, initially called "measurements service," was set up to carry out this project.

An early step in the Measurements Project was the development of a set of principles by which the project was to be governed. Five such principles were formulated:

1. Measurements were to be designed to measure the performance of *organizational components*, rather than that of *managers*.
2. Measurements were to involve common *indexes* of performance, but not common *standards* of performance. (For example, rate of return on investment might be the index of performance common to all product departments, but the standard in terms of this index might be 12 percent for one department and 25 percent for another.)
3. Measurements were to be designed as aids to judgment in appraisal of performance, and not to supplant judgment.
4. Measurements were to give proper weight to future performance as well as current performance, in order to facilitate the maintenance of a balance between the long run and the near term.

(New York: John Wiley & Sons, Inc., 1961) pp. 217–37; and Robert W. Lewis, "Measuring, Reporting and Appraising Results of Operations with Reference to Goals, Plans and Budgets" in *Planning, Managing and Measuring the Business*, A Case Study of Management Planning and Control at General Electric Company (New York: Controllership Foundation, Inc., 1955).

5. Measurements were to be selected so as to facilitate constructive action, not to restrict such action.

The overall Measurements Project was divided into three major sub-projects:

1. Operational measurements of the results of a product department.
2. Functional measurements of the work of engineering, manufacturing, marketing finance, employee and plant community relations, and legal components of the organization.
3. Measurements of the work of managing as such—planning, organizing, integrating, and measuring itself.

The first step in the subproject on operational measurements was to develop an answer to the following question:

What are the specific areas for which measurements should be designed, bearing in mind that sound measurements of overall performance require a proper balance among the various functions and among the aspects (planning, organizing, for example) of managing?[6]

In seeking an answer to this question, the organization made a careful analysis of the nature and purposes of the basic kinds of work performed by each functional unit with the purpose of singling out those functional objectives that were of sufficient importance to the welfare of the business[7] as a whole, to be termed "key result areas."

The Key Result Areas

In order to determine whether an area tentatively identified according to the preceding analytical framework was sufficiently basic to qualify as a key result area, the organization established a criterion in the form of the following test question:

Will continued failure in this area prevent the attainment of management's responsibility for advancing General Electric as a leader in a strong, competitive economy, even though results in all other key areas are good?[8]

As an outcome of analysis and application of this test, eight key result areas were decided on. These were as follows:

1. Profitability.
2. Market position.
3. Productivity.

---

[6] Lewis, *op. cit.,* p. 30.
[7] The word "business" is used here to refer to a product department, not to the whole company.
[8] *Ibid.,* p. 30.

4. Product leadership.
5. Personnel development.
6. Employee attitudes.
7. Public responsibility.
8. Balance between short-range and long-range goals.

Each of these key result areas is described below.

1. PROFITABILITY. The key index used by General Electric to measure profitability was "dollars of residual income." Residual income was defined as net profit after taxes, less a capital charge. The capital charge was a certain percentage (say, 6 percent) of the net assets assigned to the department; it corresponded to an imputed interest charge. The criteria formulated to guide the development of a satisfactroy measure of profitability were expressed as follows:

a) An index that recognized the contribution of capital investment to profits.
b) An index that recognized what human work and effort contribute to profits.
c) An index that recognized the "corporate facts of life" (e.g., one consistent with General Electric's needs and organizational objectives).
d) An index that served to make the operating decisions of individual managers in the company's best interests.

In the process of selecting and developing a measure of profitability, the measurements organization considered several more conventional indices, including rate of return on investment, ratio of profit to sales, and ratio of profit to value added. A weakness of these ratios or indices was stated in this way:

. . . the acid test of an index should be its effectiveness in guiding decentralized management to make decisions in the best interest of the company overall, since operating managers' efforts naturally will be to improve the performance of their businesses in terms of the index used for evaluation. This test points up the particular weakness of rate of return and of other ratio indexes, such as per cent profit to sales. This weakness is the tendency to encourage concentration on improvement of the *ratios* rather than on improvement in *dollar* profits. Specifically, the business with the better results in terms of the ratios will tend to make decisions based on the effect the decisions will have on the particular business's current *ratios* without consideration of the *dollar* profits involved. This tends to retard incentive to growth and expansion because it dampens the incentive of the more profitable businesses to grow.[9]

2. MARKER POSITION. Performance is this key result area was measured in terms of the share of the market obtained during a given measurement period. The measurement was expressed as a percentage of available

---

[9] *Ibid.*, p. 32.

business in the market. "Market," as used in this sense, was expressed in dollars, units, kilowatt-amperes, or other meaningful terms.

The first major consideration in designing market position measurements is a determination of what constitutes a product line and what constitutes the market for each product line of a business. A product line may be defined as a grouping of products in accordance with the purposes they serve or the essential wants they satisfy. The definition is somewhat misleading in that a product line may be a broad classification, such as alarm clocks, kitchen clocks, or mantle clocks. In addition, product lines may overlap so that a particular product could be included in several product lines. Hence, the actual grouping of products by product lines must be accurately identified.

There may be wide variations in the interpretation of what constitutes the market for a given product line. Therefore, it is important that for each of their lines, our product departments identify such things as:

1. Whether the market includes not only directly competing products but also indirectly competing products (electric ranges vs. electric ranges; electric ranges vs. all types of ranges—electric, gas, oil, and others).
2. Whether the market includes sales by all domestic competitors or only those reporting to trade associations.
3. Whether the market includes imports, if foreign sellers are competing in the domestic market.
4. Whether the market includes export sales.
5. Whether the market includes captive sales.
6. Whether the market is considered to be represented by sales to distributors, or to retailers, to ultimate users.

In other words, in establishing measurements of market position there should be a clear understanding of precisely what comprises the product line and what comprises the market. The purpose of having sharp definitions of these two items is, of course, to avoid being misled into thinking we are doing better than we actually are simply because of failure to identify the nature and extent of our competition.[10]

3. PRODUCTIVITY. Although the concept of productivity is a relatively simple one—a relationship of output of goods and services to the resources consumed in their production—this concept proved a difficult one to make operational as a measure of performance. For the national economy as a whole, it has been the practice to look at productivity simply in terms of the amount of output per unit of labor input. In any given firm, however, labor is only one of the factors contributing to output. Therefore, the company sought to develop an index that would accomplish two things: (1) broaden the input base so as to recognize that capital as well as labor contributed to improvements in productivity, and (2) eliminate from the measure those improvements contributed by suppliers of materials.

On the output side of the productivity ratio, the company considered

---

[10] *Ibid.*, p. 33.

several refinements of "sales billed." One such refinement was the use of "value added" (e.g., sales billed less the cost of goods or services acquired outside the company). On the input side, the company considered payroll dollars plus depreciation dollars. Payroll dollars were employed as the variable, rather than labor hours, so as to give effect to differences in the labor skills employed. The inclusion of depreciation charges constituted an attempt to include the consumption to capital resources. All factors were to be adjusted for changes in the price level, so that changes in the resulting ratio would more nearly reflect real changes in productivity.

4. PRODUCT LEADERSHIP. Product leadership was defined as "the ability of a business to lead its industry in originating or applying the most advanced scientific and technical knowledge in the engineering, manufacturing and marketing fields to the development of new products and to improvements in the quality or value of existing products."[11] To make this definition operational, procedures were established for appraising periodically the products of each department. These appraisals were directed at providing answers to the following questions:

a) How did each product compare with competition and with company standards?
b) Where within the company was the research conducted upon which the product was based?
c) Who first introduced the basic product and subsequent improvements, General Electric or a competitor?

The appraisal procedures were based largely on qualitative rather than quantitative considerations. Appraisals were made by appropriate experts from the areas of engineering, marketing, accounting, and manufacturing. In general, these experts were located within the product department for which the appraisal was to be made. Standard forms were employed so as to facilitate as high a degree of consistency as possible.

The trends revealed by these appraisals over a period of time were considered to be as significant as the specific information revealed by an appraisal for a particular period.

5. PERSONNEL DEVELOPMENT. For the purposes of measurement, personnel development was defined as "the systematic training of managers and specialists to fill present and future needs of the company, to provide for further individual growth and retirements, and to facilitate corporate growth and expansion."[12] Management of General Electric defined personnel development as including "programs in each field of functional endeavor, such as engineering, manufacturing, marketing and finance, and broad programs aimed at developing an understanding of the principles of

---

[11] *Ibid.*, pp. 35–36.
[12] *Ibid.*, p. 37.

managing. Such programs must be designed to provide a continuous flow of potentially promotable employees in sufficient numbers to permit proper selection and development of individuals for each position. And, at the same time, these programs must encourage competition and initiative for further individual growth."[13]

Three steps were involved in the measurement of performance in this key result area: (1) the basic soundness of the various programs or techniques being sponsored by a product department for the development of its employees was appraised; (2) an inventory was taken of the available supply of trained men, as well as their qualifications, for the key positions that must eventually be filled within the department; (3) the effectiveness with which the department executed its personnel development programs was evaluated.

The first step consisted of judgments regarding the adequacy of the elements in the development process.

The second step was accomplished with the aid of manning tables and related inventorying procedures. These procedures were directed primarily at determining the training background of each man in the inventory; i.e., graduates of company-sponsored programs, those hired from outside the company, and those who attained their positions without the benefit of a company-sponsored program.

The investigating group used two statistical measures in carrying out the third step. The first of these was the ratio of the number of men promoted (both within department and through transfer to another department) in a given period (usually a year) to the total number of men regarded as "promotable" during the same period. The second measure was tied in with the personnel rating procedure that was employed throughout the company. At the conclusion of each performance review cycle, the rating forms for a particular department were analyzed to determine the proportions of employees whose performance was considered to be (*a*) improving, (*b*) unchanged, and (*c*) deteriorating.

6. EMPLOYEE ATTITUDES. For purposes of developing measures of performance in this key area, the group defined an attitude as "a generalized point of view towards objects, events or persons which might serve to influence future behavior." It used two basic approaches to the measurement of attitudes. The first involved the use of statistical indicators, such as turnover rate, absenteeism, number of grievances, lateness, accident experience, etc. The second approach involved a periodic survey of employees through questionnaires.

Several shortcomings were recognized in the first approach: (1) The statistical indicators provided little or no information about underlying causes. (2) In general, the indicators told of trouble only after the harm

---

[13] *Ibid.*

had been done. (3) Because these indicators were traditionally associated with the personnel functions, managers tended to minimize their importance or else place responsibility for improvement on the personnel function. (4) Unfavorable trends in certain of these indicators might be due to external factors (e.g., short labor supply) rather than to some shortcoming of management.

The attitude survey made use of a standardized questionnaire designed to reveal the attitudes of employees in a number of broad areas. The survey was administered at intervals of about 18 months. Results for each attitude area were tabulated in terms of proportion of responses that were favorable. Tabulations were made by work groups and not by individual employees; this practice helped protect the anonymity of responses, and thus the validity of the surveys.

7. PUBLIC RESPONSIBILITY. This key result area evolved from General Electric's recognition of its obligation to conduct itself as a good citizen within society, complying faithfully with the laws and ethics governing business conduct. The company believed its progress required not only an active recognition of the broad public interest, but also a responsiveness to certain special "publics" who had a stake in the success of the business; namely, shareowners, customers, employees, vendors, dealers and distributors, the plant community, educational institutions, and government.

While the responsibility to certain "publics," such as shareowners, educational institutions, and the federal govrenment, could best be measured from an overall company viewpoint rather than departmentally, nevertheless, the actions taken by a product department (including the individual acts of employees of that department) could have an important impact on the whole company's reputation as a good corporate citizen. Accordingly, the company attempted to assure wholehearted observance of the legal and ethical standards of business by insisting that all managerial and professional employees conduct periodic surveys (at least once a year) of the activities of those who reported to them with respect to antitrust compliance, conflict of interest, and other areas of business practice. These matters were discussed with each individual, who then signed a statement affirming his understanding and compliance.

Other measurements related to the effectiveness of department action in strengthening the company's reputation and business relationships. With respect to fulfilling obligations to customers, it was determined that the previously mentioned product leadership and market position areas were the best indicators. For the remaining "publics" the following measures were recommended:

Shareowners. The total shares of General Electric Company stock were to be "allocated" to the various operating components that were assigned responsibility for preserving and enhancing "their portion" of the shareowners' investment in the company.

Vendors, Dealers, and Distributors. Suppliers of raw materials and parts were to be surveyed periodically to determine their appraisal of the department's practices in conducting its business as compared with the practices of others who bought from them. Dealers and distributors were likewise to be interviewed from time to time, to measure whether these important relationships were being responsibly maintained.

Plant Community. Again, comprehensive reaction surveys were to be used, aimed at identifying the impact of the actions of a product department on the individuals who made up the community. These reactions disclosed by the opinion surveys were to be supplemented by use of trends developed from various types of data, such as community wage rates, number of employment applications received, volume of purchases made locally, contributions to local charities, and participation in civic, church, and business organizations.

8. Balance between Short-Range and Long-Range Goals. This factor was set out separately as a key result area in order to emphasize the importance of the long-term survival and growth of the company. Short-range goals and performance had to be balanced against the need for satisfactory performance 5, 10, 15 years in the future, since undue pressure for current profits could, in effect, borrow from the future.

Various means were employed to experiment with suggested measures in this key result area. However, it is important to note that when the eight key result areas were established, each of the first seven had both short-range and long-range dimensions. The eighth area, balance between short-range and long-range goals, had been specifically identified to make sure the long-range health of the company would not be sacrificed for short-term gains. The plans, goals, and actions in each of the other areas were, therefore, to be appraised in terms of both their short-term and their long-term implications.

Evaluation of the Project

During the period after the Measurements Project was established in 1952, deep research work was carried on to establish the specific measurements in each of the eight key result areas. Before communicating these measures to the product departments, the investigators reviewed the recommendations in each area with operating personnel and with officers, for their comments, suggestions, and final approval.

The company's business planning, budgeting, and forecasting program incorporated the use of selected key result areas in (1) reviewing the recent history and current status, (2) setting standards for each department, (3) planning to achieve the standards, and (4) periodic reporting and measurement of accomplishment. Since the first four key result areas lent themselves readily to numerical evaluations, they were a part of the planning, budgeting, forecasting, reporting, and measuring system. Building on this experience in using the key result areas to plan and measure performance, management at the General Electric Company made the search for effective business measurements a continuing, evolutionary process.

Questions

1. For the purpose described, how should profitability be defined? The definition should be specific enough so that a quantitative measure can be constructed from it.
2. What, if anything, do the factors other than profitability add to the proposed measurement system? Isn't the impact of the other factors reflected in the profitability measure if it is properly constructed?

Appendix Tables

Table A

PRESENT VALUE OF $1

Years Hence	1%	2%	4%	6%	8%	10%	12%	14%	15%	16%	18%	20%	22%	24%	25%	26%	28%	30%	35%	40%	45%	50%
1	0.990	0.980	0.962	0.943	0.926	0.909	0.893	0.877	0.870	0.862	0.847	0.833	0.820	0.806	0.800	0.794	0.781	0.769	0.741	0.714	0.690	0.667
2	0.980	0.961	0.925	0.890	0.857	0.826	0.797	0.769	0.756	0.743	0.718	0.694	0.672	0.650	0.640	0.630	0.610	0.592	0.549	0.510	0.476	0.444
3	0.971	0.942	0.889	0.840	0.794	0.751	0.712	0.675	0.658	0.641	0.609	0.579	0.551	0.524	0.512	0.500	0.477	0.455	0.406	0.364	0.328	0.296
4	0.961	0.924	0.855	0.792	0.735	0.683	0.636	0.592	0.572	0.552	0.516	0.482	0.451	0.423	0.410	0.397	0.373	0.350	0.301	0.260	0.226	0.198
5	0.951	0.906	0.822	0.747	0.681	0.621	0.567	0.519	0.497	0.476	0.437	0.402	0.370	0.341	0.328	0.315	0.291	0.269	0.223	0.186	0.156	0.132
6	0.942	0.888	0.790	0.705	0.630	0.564	0.507	0.456	0.432	0.410	0.370	0.335	0.303	0.275	0.262	0.250	0.227	0.207	0.165	0.133	0.108	0.088
7	0.933	0.871	0.760	0.665	0.583	0.513	0.452	0.400	0.376	0.354	0.314	0.279	0.249	0.222	0.210	0.198	0.178	0.159	0.122	0.095	0.074	0.059
8	0.923	0.853	0.731	0.627	0.540	0.467	0.404	0.351	0.327	0.305	0.266	0.233	0.204	0.179	0.168	0.157	0.139	0.123	0.091	0.068	0.051	0.039
9	0.914	0.837	0.703	0.592	0.500	0.424	0.361	0.308	0.284	0.263	0.225	0.194	0.167	0.144	0.134	0.125	0.108	0.094	0.067	0.048	0.035	0.026
10	0.905	0.820	0.676	0.558	0.463	0.386	0.322	0.270	0.247	0.227	0.191	0.162	0.137	0.116	0.107	0.099	0.085	0.073	0.050	0.035	0.024	0.017
11	0.896	0.804	0.650	0.527	0.429	0.350	0.287	0.237	0.215	0.195	0.162	0.135	0.112	0.094	0.086	0.079	0.066	0.056	0.037	0.025	0.017	0.012
12	0.887	0.788	0.625	0.497	0.397	0.319	0.257	0.208	0.187	0.168	0.137	0.112	0.092	0.076	0.069	0.062	0.052	0.043	0.027	0.018	0.012	0.008
13	0.879	0.773	0.601	0.469	0.368	0.290	0.229	0.182	0.163	0.145	0.116	0.093	0.075	0.061	0.055	0.050	0.040	0.033	0.020	0.013	0.008	0.005
14	0.870	0.758	0.577	0.442	0.340	0.263	0.205	0.160	0.141	0.125	0.099	0.078	0.062	0.049	0.044	0.039	0.032	0.025	0.015	0.009	0.006	0.003
15	0.861	0.743	0.555	0.417	0.315	0.239	0.183	0.140	0.123	0.108	0.084	0.065	0.051	0.040	0.035	0.031	0.025	0.020	0.011	0.006	0.004	0.002
16	0.853	0.728	0.534	0.394	0.292	0.218	0.163	0.123	0.107	0.093	0.071	0.054	0.042	0.032	0.028	0.025	0.019	0.015	0.008	0.005	0.003	0.002
17	0.844	0.714	0.513	0.371	0.270	0.198	0.146	0.108	0.093	0.080	0.060	0.045	0.034	0.026	0.023	0.020	0.015	0.012	0.006	0.003	0.002	0.001
18	0.836	0.700	0.494	0.350	0.250	0.180	0.130	0.095	0.081	0.069	0.051	0.038	0.028	0.021	0.018	0.016	0.012	0.009	0.005	0.002	0.002	0.001
19	0.828	0.686	0.475	0.331	0.232	0.164	0.116	0.083	0.070	0.060	0.043	0.031	0.023	0.017	0.014	0.012	0.009	0.007	0.003	0.002	0.001	
20	0.820	0.673	0.456	0.312	0.215	0.149	0.104	0.073	0.061	0.051	0.037	0.026	0.019	0.014	0.012	0.010	0.007	0.005	0.002	0.001	0.001	
21	0.811	0.660	0.439	0.294	0.199	0.135	0.093	0.064	0.053	0.044	0.031	0.022	0.015	0.011	0.009	0.008	0.006	0.004	0.002	0.001		
22	0.803	0.647	0.422	0.278	0.184	0.123	0.083	0.056	0.046	0.038	0.026	0.018	0.013	0.009	0.007	0.006	0.004	0.003	0.001	0.001		
23	0.795	0.634	0.406	0.262	0.170	0.112	0.074	0.049	0.040	0.033	0.022	0.015	0.010	0.007	0.006	0.005	0.003	0.002	0.001			
24	0.788	0.622	0.390	0.247	0.158	0.102	0.066	0.043	0.035	0.028	0.019	0.013	0.008	0.006	0.005	0.004	0.003	0.002	0.001			
25	0.780	0.610	0.375	0.233	0.146	0.092	0.059	0.038	0.030	0.024	0.016	0.010	0.007	0.005	0.004	0.003	0.002	0.001	0.001			
26	0.772	0.598	0.361	0.220	0.135	0.084	0.053	0.033	0.026	0.021	0.014	0.009	0.006	0.004	0.003	0.002	0.002	0.001				
27	0.764	0.586	0.347	0.207	0.125	0.076	0.047	0.029	0.023	0.018	0.011	0.007	0.005	0.003	0.002	0.002	0.001	0.001				
28	0.757	0.574	0.333	0.196	0.116	0.069	0.042	0.026	0.020	0.016	0.010	0.006	0.004	0.002	0.002	0.002	0.001	0.001				
29	0.749	0.563	0.321	0.185	0.107	0.063	0.037	0.022	0.017	0.014	0.008	0.005	0.003	0.002	0.002	0.001	0.001	0.001				
30	0.742	0.552	0.308	0.174	0.099	0.057	0.033	0.020	0.015	0.012	0.007	0.004	0.003	0.002	0.001	0.001	0.001					
40	0.672	0.453	0.208	0.097	0.046	0.022	0.011	0.005	0.004	0.003	0.001	0.001										
50	0.608	0.372	0.141	0.054	0.021	0.009	0.003	0.001	0.001	0.001												

Table B

PRESENT VALUE OF $1 RECEIVED ANNUALLY FOR N YEARS

Years (N)	1%	2%	4%	6%	8%	10%	12%	14%	15%	16%	18%	20%	22%	24%	25%	26%	28%	30%	35%	40%	45%	50%
1	0.990	0.980	0.962	0.943	0.926	0.909	0.893	0.877	0.870	0.862	0.847	0.833	0.820	0.806	0.800	0.794	0.781	0.769	0.741	0.714	0.690	0.667
2	1.970	1.942	1.886	1.833	1.783	1.736	1.690	1.647	1.626	1.605	1.566	1.528	1.492	1.457	1.440	1.424	1.392	1.361	1.289	1.224	1.165	1.111
3	2.941	2.884	2.775	2.673	2.577	2.487	2.402	2.322	2.283	2.246	2.174	2.106	2.042	1.981	1.952	1.923	1.868	1.816	1.696	1.589	1.493	1.407
4	3.902	3.808	3.630	3.465	3.312	3.170	3.037	2.914	2.855	2.798	2.690	2.589	2.494	2.404	2.362	2.320	2.241	2.166	1.997	1.849	1.720	1.605
5	4.853	4.713	4.452	4.212	3.993	3.791	3.605	3.433	3.352	3.274	3.127	2.991	2.864	2.745	2.689	2.635	2.532	2.436	2.220	2.035	1.876	1.737
6	5.795	5.601	5.242	4.917	4.623	4.355	4.111	3.889	3.784	3.685	3.498	3.326	3.167	3.020	2.951	2.885	2.759	2.643	2.385	2.168	1.983	1.824
7	6.728	6.472	6.002	5.582	5.206	4.868	4.564	4.288	4.160	4.039	3.812	3.605	3.416	3.242	3.161	3.083	2.937	2.802	2.508	2.263	2.057	1.883
8	7.652	7.325	6.733	6.210	5.747	5.335	4.968	4.639	4.487	4.344	4.078	3.837	3.619	3.421	3.329	3.241	3.076	2.925	2.598	2.331	2.108	1.922
9	8.566	8.162	7.435	6.802	6.247	5.759	5.328	4.946	4.772	4.607	4.303	4.031	3.786	3.566	3.463	3.366	3.184	3.019	2.665	2.379	2.144	1.948
10	9.471	8.983	8.111	7.360	6.710	6.145	5.650	5.216	5.019	4.833	4.494	4.192	3.923	3.682	3.571	3.465	3.269	3.092	2.715	2.414	2.168	1.965
11	10.368	9.787	8.760	7.887	7.139	6.495	5.937	5.453	5.234	5.029	4.656	4.327	4.035	3.776	3.656	3.544	3.335	3.147	2.752	2.438	2.185	1.977
12	11.255	10.575	9.385	8.384	7.536	6.814	6.194	5.660	5.421	5.197	4.793	4.439	4.127	3.851	3.725	3.606	3.387	3.190	2.779	2.456	2.196	1.985
13	12.134	11.343	9.986	8.853	7.904	7.103	6.424	5.842	5.583	5.342	4.910	4.533	4.203	3.912	3.780	3.656	3.427	3.223	2.799	2.468	2.204	1.990
14	13.004	12.106	10.563	9.295	8.244	7.367	6.628	6.002	5.724	5.468	5.008	4.611	4.265	3.962	3.824	3.695	3.459	3.249	2.814	2.477	2.210	1.993
15	13.865	12.849	11.118	9.712	8.559	7.606	6.811	6.142	5.847	5.575	5.092	4.675	4.315	4.001	3.859	3.726	3.483	3.268	2.825	2.484	2.214	1.995
16	14.718	13.578	11.652	10.106	8.851	7.824	6.974	6.265	5.954	5.669	5.162	4.730	4.357	4.033	3.887	3.751	3.503	3.283	2.834	2.489	2.216	1.997
17	15.562	14.292	12.166	10.477	9.122	8.022	7.120	6.373	6.047	5.749	5.222	4.775	4.391	4.059	3.910	3.771	3.518	3.295	2.840	2.492	2.218	1.998
18	16.398	14.992	12.659	10.828	9.372	8.201	7.250	6.467	6.128	5.818	5.273	4.812	4.419	4.080	3.928	3.786	3.529	3.304	2.844	2.494	2.219	1.999
19	17.226	15.678	13.134	11.158	9.604	8.365	7.366	6.550	6.198	5.877	5.316	4.844	4.442	4.097	3.942	3.799	3.539	3.311	2.848	2.496	2.220	1.999
20	18.046	16.351	13.590	11.470	9.818	8.514	7.469	6.623	6.259	5.929	5.353	4.870	4.460	4.110	3.954	3.808	3.546	3.316	2.850	2.497	2.221	1.999
21	18.857	17.011	14.029	11.764	10.017	8.649	7.562	6.687	6.312	5.973	5.384	4.891	4.476	4.121	3.963	3.816	3.551	3.320	2.852	2.498	2.221	2.000
22	19.660	17.658	14.451	12.042	10.201	8.772	7.645	6.743	6.359	6.011	5.410	4.909	4.488	4.130	3.970	3.822	3.556	3.323	2.853	2.498	2.222	2.000
23	20.456	18.292	14.857	12.303	10.371	8.883	7.718	6.792	6.399	6.044	5.432	4.925	4.499	4.137	3.976	3.827	3.559	3.325	2.854	2.499	2.222	2.000
24	21.243	18.914	15.247	12.550	10.529	8.985	7.784	6.835	6.434	6.073	5.451	4.937	4.507	4.143	3.981	3.831	3.562	3.327	2.855	2.499	2.222	2.000
25	22.023	19.523	15.622	12.783	10.675	9.077	7.843	6.873	6.464	6.097	5.467	4.948	4.514	4.147	3.985	3.834	3.564	3.329	2.856	2.499	2.222	2.000
26	22.795	20.121	15.983	13.003	10.810	9.161	7.896	6.906	6.491	6.118	5.480	4.956	4.520	4.151	3.988	3.837	3.566	3.330	2.856	2.500	2.222	2.000
27	23.560	20.707	16.330	13.211	10.935	9.237	7.943	6.935	6.514	6.136	5.492	4.964	4.524	4.154	3.990	3.839	3.567	3.331	2.856	2.500	2.222	2.000
28	24.316	21.281	16.663	13.406	11.051	9.307	7.984	6.961	6.534	6.152	5.502	4.970	4.528	4.157	3.992	3.840	3.568	3.331	2.857	2.500	2.222	2.000
29	25.066	21.844	16.984	13.591	11.158	9.370	8.022	6.983	6.551	6.166	5.510	4.975	4.531	4.159	3.994	3.841	3.569	3.332	2.857	2.500	2.222	2.000
30	25.808	22.396	17.292	13.765	11.258	9.427	8.055	7.003	6.566	6.177	5.517	4.979	4.534	4.160	3.995	3.842	3.569	3.332	2.857	2.500	2.222	2.000
40	32.835	27.355	19.793	15.046	11.925	9.779	8.244	7.105	6.642	6.234	5.548	4.997	4.544	4.166	3.999	3.846	3.571	3.333	2.857	2.500	2.222	2.000
50	39.196	31.424	21.482	15.762	12.234	9.915	8.304	7.133	6.661	6.246	5.554	4.999	4.545	4.167	4.000	3.846	3.571	3.333	2.857	2.500	2.222	2.000

Table C

PRESENT VALUE OF SUM-OF-YEARS' DIGIT DEPRECIATION

Years of Useful Life	2%	4%	6%	8%	10%	12%	14%	15%	16%	18%	20%	22%	24%	26%	28%	30%	35%	40%	45%	50%
3	0.968	0.937	0.908	0.881	0.855	0.831	0.808	0.796	0.786	0.764	0.745	0.726	0.707	0.690	0.674	0.658	0.621	0.588	0.558	0.531
4	0.961	0.925	0.891	0.860	0.830	0.802	0.776	0.763	0.751	0.728	0.706	0.685	0.665	0.646	0.628	0.611	0.572	0.538	0.507	0.479
5	0.955	0.914	0.875	0.839	0.806	0.775	0.746	0.732	0.719	0.694	0.670	0.647	0.626	0.606	0.588	0.570	0.530	0.494	0.463	0.435
6	0.949	0.902	0.859	0.820	0.783	0.749	0.718	0.703	0.689	0.662	0.637	0.613	0.591	0.570	0.551	0.533	0.492	0.456	0.425	0.398
7	0.943	0.891	0.844	0.801	0.761	0.725	0.692	0.676	0.661	0.633	0.606	0.582	0.559	0.538	0.518	0.500	0.458	0.423	0.392	0.366
8	0.937	0.880	0.829	0.782	0.740	0.702	0.667	0.650	0.635	0.605	0.578	0.553	0.530	0.508	0.488	0.470	0.429	0.394	0.364	0.338
9	0.931	0.869	0.814	0.765	0.720	0.680	0.643	0.626	0.610	0.580	0.552	0.527	0.503	0.482	0.462	0.443	0.402	0.368	0.338	0.313
10	0.925	0.859	0.800	0.748	0.701	0.659	0.621	0.604	0.587	0.556	0.528	0.502	0.479	0.457	0.437	0.419	0.378	0.345	0.316	0.292
11	0.919	0.848	0.786	0.731	0.682	0.639	0.600	0.582	0.565	0.534	0.506	0.480	0.456	0.434	0.415	0.397	0.357	0.324	0.297	0.273
12	0.913	0.838	0.773	0.715	0.665	0.620	0.580	0.562	0.545	0.513	0.485	0.459	0.435	0.414	0.394	0.376	0.338	0.306	0.279	0.257
13	0.907	0.828	0.760	0.700	0.648	0.602	0.562	0.543	0.526	0.494	0.465	0.439	0.416	0.395	0.376	0.358	0.320	0.289	0.264	0.242
14	0.902	0.818	0.747	0.685	0.632	0.585	0.544	0.525	0.508	0.476	0.447	0.421	0.398	0.377	0.358	0.341	0.304	0.274	0.250	0.229
15	0.896	0.809	0.734	0.671	0.616	0.569	0.527	0.508	0.491	0.459	0.430	0.405	0.382	0.361	0.343	0.326	0.290	0.261	0.237	0.217
16	0.890	0.799	0.722	0.657	0.601	0.553	0.511	0.492	0.475	0.443	0.414	0.389	0.367	0.346	0.328	0.312	0.277	0.248	0.225	0.206
17	0.885	0.790	0.710	0.644	0.587	0.538	0.496	0.477	0.460	0.428	0.400	0.375	0.352	0.332	0.315	0.298	0.264	0.237	0.215	0.196
18	0.880	0.781	0.699	0.631	0.573	0.524	0.482	0.463	0.445	0.413	0.386	0.361	0.339	0.320	0.302	0.286	0.253	0.227	0.205	0.187
19	0.874	0.772	0.688	0.618	0.560	0.510	0.468	0.449	0.432	0.400	0.372	0.348	0.327	0.308	0.291	0.275	0.243	0.217	0.196	0.179
20	0.869	0.763	0.677	0.606	0.547	0.497	0.455	0.436	0.419	0.387	0.360	0.336	0.315	0.296	0.280	0.265	0.233	0.208	0.188	0.171
21	0.863	0.754	0.666	0.594	0.535	0.485	0.442	0.424	0.406	0.376	0.349	0.325	0.304	0.286	0.270	0.255	0.224	0.200	0.181	0.164
22	0.858	0.746	0.656	0.583	0.523	0.473	0.431	0.412	0.395	0.364	0.338	0.315	0.294	0.276	0.260	0.246	0.216	0.193	0.174	0.158
23	0.853	0.738	0.646	0.572	0.511	0.461	0.419	0.401	0.384	0.354	0.327	0.305	0.285	0.267	0.252	0.238	0.208	0.186	0.167	0.152
24	0.848	0.729	0.636	0.561	0.500	0.450	0.409	0.390	0.373	0.344	0.318	0.295	0.276	0.258	0.243	0.230	0.201	0.179	0.161	0.147
25	0.842	0.721	0.626	0.551	0.490	0.440	0.398	0.380	0.364	0.334	0.308	0.286	0.267	0.250	0.236	0.222	0.195	0.173	0.156	0.142
30	0.818	0.683	0.582	0.504	0.442	0.393	0.353	0.336	0.320	0.292	0.269	0.249	0.232	0.216	0.203	0.191	0.167	0.148	0.133	0.120
35	0.794	0.648	0.542	0.463	0.402	0.355	0.317	0.300	0.286	0.260	0.238	0.220	0.204	0.190	0.178	0.168	0.146	0.129	0.116	0.105
40	0.771	0.616	0.507	0.428	0.368	0.323	0.286	0.271	0.257	0.233	0.213	0.196	0.182	0.170	0.159	0.149	0.129	0.114	0.102	0.093
45	0.749	0.586	0.476	0.397	0.339	0.296	0.261	0.247	0.234	0.212	0.193	0.178	0.164	0.153	0.143	0.134	0.116	0.103	0.092	0.083
50	0.728	0.559	0.448	0.370	0.314	0.272	0.240	0.227	0.214	0.194	0.176	0.162	0.150	0.139	0.130	0.122	0.106	0.093	0.083	

Source: From tables computed by Jerome Bracken and Charles J. Christenson. Copyright © 1961 by the President and Fellows of Harvard College. Used by permission. See page 638 for explanation of use of this table.

Index

INDEX

*This book has been set in 10 point Janson
with 10 point Caledonia Bold, leaded 2 points,
and 9 point Janson, leaded 2 points. Part numbers
are in 42 point Helvetica Medium Roman
and part titles are in 24 point Helvetica
Regular. Chapter numbers are in 14 and 24
point Helvetica Regular and chapter titles are
in 18 point Helvetica Medium. The size of
the type page is 27 x 45½ picas.*